The Routledge Handbook of Second Language Acquisition and Corpora

The Routledge Handbook of Second Language Acquisition and Corpora is a state-of-the-art collection of cutting-edge scholarship at the intersection of second language acquisition (SLA) and learner corpus research. It draws on data-driven, statistical analysis to outline the background, methods, and outcomes of language learning, with a range of global experts providing detailed guidelines and findings.

The volume is organized into five sections:

- Methodological and theoretical contributions to the study of learner language using corpora – setting the scene
- Key aspects in corpus design, annotation, and analysis for SLA
- Corpora in SLA theory and practice
- SLA constructs and corpora
- Future directions

This is a ground-breaking collection of essays offering incisive and essential reading for anyone with an interest in second language acquisition, learner corpus research, and applied linguistics.

Nicole Tracy-Ventura is Assistant Professor of Applied Linguistics at West Virginia University. Her research focuses on second language acquisition, study abroad, task-based language teaching, longitudinal research methods, and corpus linguistics. She is a founding member of the Languages and Social Networks Abroad Project (LANGSNAP).

Magali Paquot is FNRS Research Associate at the Centre for English Corpus Linguistics, UCLouvain. She specializes in the use of learner corpora to study key topics in second language acquisition and is particularly interested in methodological issues. She is co-editor in chief of the *International Journal of Learner Corpus Research* and one of the founding members of the Learner Corpus Research Association.

ROUTLEDGE HANDBOOKS IN SECOND LANGUAGE ACQUISITION

Susan M. Gass and Alison Mackey, Series Editors
Kimberly L. Geeslin, Associate Editor

The Routledge Handbooks in Second Language Acquisition are a comprehensive, must-have survey of this core sub-discipline of applied linguistics. With a truly global reach and featuring diverse contributing voices, each handbook provides an overview of both the fundamentals and new directions for each topic.

The Routledge Handbook of Second Language Acquisition and Pragmatics
Edited by Naoko Taguchi

The Routledge Handbook of Second Language Acquisition and Corpora
Edited by Nicole Tracy-Ventura and Magali Paquot

The Routledge Handbook of Second Language Acquisition and Language Testing
Edited by Paula Winke and Tineke Brunfaut

For more information about this series, please visit:
https://www.routledge.com/Second-Language-Acquisition-Research-Series/book-series/RHSLA

The Routledge Handbook of Second Language Acquisition and Corpora

Edited by Nicole Tracy-Ventura
and Magali Paquot

NEW YORK AND LONDON

First published 2021
by Routledge
52 Vanderbilt Avenue, New York, NY 10017

and by Routledge
2 Park Square, Milton Park, Abingdon, Oxon, OX14 4RN

Routledge is an imprint of the Taylor & Francis Group, an informa business

Library of Congress Cataloging-in-Publication Data
Names: Paquot, Magali, editor. | Tracy-Ventura, Nicole, editor.
Title: The Routledge handbook of second language acquisition and corpora /
edited by Magali Paquot and Nicole Tracy-Ventura.
Description: London; New York: Routledge, 2020. |
Series: Handbooks in SLA | Includes bibliographical references and index. |
Summary: "This is a ground-breaking collection of essays offering incisive
and essential reading for anyone with an interest in second language
acquisition, learner corpus research, and applied linguistics"– Provided by
publisher.
Identifiers: LCCN 2020028948 | ISBN 9780815352877 (hardback) |
ISBN 9781351137904 (ebook)
Subjects: LCSH: Second language acquisition. | Corpora (Linguistics)
Classification: LCC P118.2 .R683 2020 | DDC 418.0071–dc23
LC record available at https://lccn.loc.gov/2020028948

ISBN: 978-0-8153-5287-7 (hbk)
ISBN: 978-1-351-13790-4 (ebk)

Typeset in Times New Roman
by Deanta Global Publishing Services, Chennai, India

To Sylviane Granger, Rosamond Mitchell, and Florence Myles:

Pioneers and early advocates of learner corpora for SLA research, and mentors to whom we will always be grateful.

Contents

List of figures   x
List of tables   xii
List of contributors   xiii
Acknowledgements   xviii

1 Second Language Acquisition and Corpora: An Overview   1
   Nicole Tracy-Ventura and Magali Paquot

PART I
SETTING THE SCENE   9

2 Introduction to Corpus Linguistics   11
   Vaclav Brezina and Tony McEnery

3 Introduction to Learner Corpus Research   23
   Fanny Meunier

4 Introduction to SLA   37
   Jennifer Behney and Emma Marsden

PART II
KEY ASPECTS IN CORPUS DESIGN AND CORPUS USE FOR SLA   51

5 Designing Learner Corpora: Collection, Transcription, and Annotation   53
   Philippa Bell and Caroline Payant

6 Analyzing a Learner Corpus with a Concordancer   68
   Sandra Götz

7 Error Analysis   90
   María Belén Díez-Bedmar

8 Comparing Learner Corpora   105
   Sandra C. Deshors and Stefan Th. Gries

Contents

9   Statistical Analyses of Learner Corpus Data   119
    Stefan Th. Gries and Sandra C. Deshors

10 Combining Learner Corpora and Experimental Methods   133
    Gaëtanelle Gilquin

11 Overview of Available Learner Corpora   145
    Julieta Fernández and Tracy S. Davis

12 TalkBank for SLA   158
    Brian MacWhinney

PART III
THE ROLE OF CORPORA IN SLA THEORY AND PRACTICE   **173**

13 Usage-based Approaches   175
    Stefanie Wulff

14 Complex Dynamic Systems Theory (CDST)   189
    Marjolijn Verspoor and Wander Lowie

15 Processability Theory and Corpora   201
    Carrie Bonilla

16 Generative Approaches   213
    Cristóbal Lozano

17 Variationist Approaches   228
    Aarnes Gudmestad

18 Pragmatic Approaches   240
    Julieta Fernández and Shelley Staples

19 Corpora and Instructed Second Language Acquisition   252
    Rosamond Mitchell

PART IV
SLA CONSTRUCTS AND CORPORA   **265**

20 Input   267
    Anita Thomas and Annelie Ädel

21 Interaction   280
    Nicole Ziegler and Alison Mackey

22 Fluency   293
    Amanda Huensch

23 Accuracy   305
    Jennifer Thewissen

24 Complexity   318
    Nina Vyatkina and Alex Housen

25 Lexis   332
    Kristopher Kyle

26 Crosslinguistic Influence   345
    Ann-Kristin Helland Gujord

27 Variability   358
    Dana Gablasova

28 Formulaicity   370
    Fanny Forsberg Lundell

29 Context of Learning   382
    Joseph Collentine

30 Individual Differences   394
    Elma Kerz and Daniel Wiechmann

PART V
FUTURE DIRECTIONS   **407**

31 The Future of Corpora in SLA   409
    Nicole Tracy-Ventura, Magali Paquot, and Florence Myles

Index   *425*

Figures

3.1	Contrastive Interlanguage Analysis (Granger 1996)	27
3.2	CIA² (Granger 2015, p. 17)	27
6.1	Concordance of Adjectives in the Bulgarian Component of ICLE in AntConc (First 18 Hits)	71
6.2	(a) Opening "Concord" in WordSmith	72
6.2	(b) Selecting "Settings" to Choose Texts for Analysis in Wordsmith. (c) Uploading Texts to the Concordancer in Wordsmith.	73
6.3	(a) Conducting an Advanced Search to Filter Out Progressives in WordSmith: Typing in the Search Word (i.e. a Form of BE). (b) Performing an Advanced Search Extracting All Co-occurrences with Another Word Ending in –*ing* up to Four Words to the Right	74
6.4	First 24 Concordance Lines of Concordance Output of All Instances of BE + –*ing*, Excluding *Interesting, Boring, Amazing* in LINDSEI-GE in WordSmith	75
6.5	Deleting Unwanted Concordance Hits in WordSmith	75
6.6	Possible Annotation Layers That Can Be Added to a Concordance After It Is Downloaded from WordSmith or AntConc in a Spreadsheet Software	77
6.7	(a) Top 24 Wordlist Items of Written Chinese Learner Data Compiled from ICLE-CN Using the Wordlist Function in AntConc. (b) Top 24 Wordlist Items of Written German Learner Data, Compiled from ICLE-GE Using the Wordlist Function in AntConc	79
6.8	(a), (b) How to Compile a Word List in AntConc	80
6.9	(a), (b) Cluster Analysis Step 1: Making an Index	82
6.10	(a), (b) Cluster Analysis Step 2: How to Compute Clusters in WordSmith	83
6.11	Top 25 Hits of 3 and 4 grams in LINDSEI (a) vs. LOCNEC (b) Compiled with WordSmith	84
6.12	Collocational Strength of Collocates to the Left of *Good* in ICLE-SP (a) vs. LOCNESS (b) Conducted with AntConc	85
7.1	Main Stages and Steps in a CEA	92
7.2	(a)–(c) An Example of Multi-layered Standoff Annotation in the KANDEL Corpus Using EXMARaLDA	98
8.1	Integrated Contrastive Model (Borrowed from Gilquin, 2000/2001)	107
9.1	Simplistic Comparison of Observational and Experimental Data in LCR and SLA/FLA Research, Respectively	121

9.2	One Possible Regression Model for the Genitive Scenario	125
9.3	Possible Regression Results for the Genitive Scenario	126
9.4	Effects Plots for Two Hypothetical Main Effects	127
13.1	DEVIATION-values of Ten Speakers (Taken from Wulff & Gries, to Appear)	183
13.2	First (Bottom Row) and Second (Top Row) Language Pairings in the ESF Database	184
14.1	Holistic Scores of Learner 2 Over the Course of One Academic Year with a Moving Window (3 Data Points) of Minimum and Maximum Scores and a Linear Trend Line	193
14.2	Syntactic Development in Terms of Mean Length of T-unit (MLTU-left axis), Normalized Nominal Dependents Within Noun Phrases (NomDepNorm-left axis) and Dependent Clauses per T-unit (DC/T-right axis)	194
14.3	Syntactic Development in Terms of Mean Length of T-unit (MLTU-left axis) and Lexical Development in Terms of Type Token Ratio (Guiraud)	195
14.4	A GAM Analysis of the Amount of Variability Among the Participants at Subsequent Datapoints	195
16.1	A Fine-grained, Linguistically-motivated Tagset (Lozano 2016, p. 247)	218
20.1	Correlation between the Analyzed Input Sources and Learner Output in an Imitation Test (Based on Thomas 2009, 2010)	270
20.2	Sample Coding from Michel and Cappellini (2019, p. 198)	275
26.1	Integrated Contrastive Model (From Gilquin, 2000/2001, p. 100, Based on Granger, 1996, p. 47)	350

Tables

2.1	Corpus Tools (Adapted from Brezina & Gablasova, 2017b)	17
10.1	Summary of the Strengths and Limitations of Learner Corpora and Experimental Data	135
12.1	TalkBank Usage	160
15.1	Syntactic and Morphological Procedures Predicted by PT with Examples for Syntactic and Morphological Phenomena for Spanish	202
16.1	Different Research Methods Used in LCR vs GenSLA	216
16.2	Feature Configuration of Perfective/Imperfective Aspect in Native English, Native Spanish, and L1 English-L2 Spanish	221
19.1	Sample Searches from Chen & Flowerdew (2018, p. 103)	259
23.1	Weighted Clause Ratio Operationalisation (Foster & Wigglesworth, 2016, p. 106)	311
24.1	List of Automated Tools for Text Complexity Analysis in Chronological Order of Publication	325
25.1	Counterbalanced Collection Scheme for Three Collection Points and Topics	337

Contributors

Annelie Ädel is Professor of English linguistics at Dalarna University, Sweden. Her main research interests are in discourse analysis, corpus linguistics, learner language, and English for Specific Purposes.

Jennifer Behney is Associate Professor of Italian, Applied Linguistics, and World Language Education at Youngstown State University, USA. Her research interests include grammatical gender acquisition, spoken word recognition, eye-tracking, and foreign language teacher training. She is co-author of *Second Language Acquisition: An Introductory Course* 5th edition (with Susan Gass and Luke Plonsky) and co-editor of a volume on salience in SLA.

Philippa Bell is Associate Professor at the Université du Québec à Montréal. Her research focuses on the learning of grammar in different instructional contexts and literacy development in Quebec classrooms. Her work can be found in journals such as *Applied Linguistics* and the *Canadian Modern Language Review*.

Carrie Bonilla is Assistant Professor of Hispanic Linguistics at George Mason University. Her current research focuses on second and third language acquisition, particularly pedagogical practices as related to individual differences in the acquisition of morphosyntax in various learning contexts.

Vaclav Brezina is a Senior Lecturer in the Department of English Language and Linguistics at Lancaster University. He specializes in corpus methodology and is the author of *Statistics in Corpus Linguistics: A Practical Guide* (Cambridge University Press, 2018).

Joseph Collentine is Professor of Spanish at Northern Arizona University (NAU). His research interests involve corpus linguistics, Spanish as a second language, study abroad, and computer-assisted language learning.

Tracy S. Davis is Associate Professor of Educational Linguistics at Central Michigan University, USA, where she teaches courses in TESOL methods, second language acquisition, corpus linguistics, written analysis, and pedagogic grammar.

Sandra C. Deshors is Assistant Professor in the Second Language Studies Ph.D. program at Michigan State University. Her research, which specializes in quantitative corpus-based approaches to learner language, contrasts English as a Foreign Language (EFL), English as a Second Language (ESL), and World Englishes at large. Theoretically, her work is anchored in the usage-based theoretical framework and recognizes a correlation between speakers' mental knowledge of linguistic items and their uses in grammatical contexts.

María Belén Díez-Bedmar is Associate Professor at the University of Jaén (Spain). Her research interests include the compilation, analysis and exploitation of learner corpora, second language acquisition, and language testing and assessment.

Julieta Fernández is Assistant Professor of Applied Linguistics in the Department of Spanish and Portuguese and affiliated faculty in Second Language Acquisition and Teaching at the University of Arizona. Her research focuses on pragmatic dimensions of language use, language learning and technology, and second language learning and pedagogy.

Dana Gablasova is Senior Lecturer in the Department of Linguistics and English Language and a member of the ESRC Corpus-based Approaches to Social Science (CASS) research centre, Lancaster University. Her research focuses on building corpora representing L2 English and on corpus-based approaches to language learning, teaching, and testing.

Gaëtanelle Gilquin is Professor of English Language and Linguistics at the University of Louvain, Belgium. She is one of the editors of the *Cambridge Handbook of Learner Corpus Research* and the coordinator of the *Louvain International Database of Spoken English Interlanguage*.

Sandra Götz is Professor of English Didactics and Linguistics at Philipps University Marburg. She obtained a cotutelle-PhD on fluency in advanced German learner language from Justus Liebig University Giessen and Macquarie University Sydney in 2011.

Stefan Th. Gries is a Professor in the Department of Linguistics of the University of California, Santa Barbara and Chair of English Linguistics (Corpus Linguistics with a focus on quantitative methods) in the Department of English, Justus-Liebig-Universität Giessen. He is a quantitative corpus linguist with an interest in cognitive/usage-based as well as psycholinguistic applications.

Aarnes Gudmestad is Associate Professor in the Department of Modern and Classical Languages and Literatures at Virginia Polytechnic Institute and State University. Her research centers on the intersection of second language acquisition and sociolinguistics. She examines the language variation and change of morphosyntactic structures in Spanish and French.

Ann-Kristin Helland Gujord is Associate Professor in Second Language Acquisition in the Department of Linguistics, Literary and Aesthetic Studies at the University of Bergen. Her research concentrates on crosslinguistic influence and grammatical development in adult and child second language acquisition.

Alex Housen is a Professor of English and Applied Linguistics and Dean of the Faculty of Letters & Arts at the Vrije Universiteit Brussel, Belgium. His research interests include second language acquisition and education, multilingualism, psycholinguistics, and general linguistics.

Amanda Huensch is Assistant Professor in the Department of Linguistics at the University of Pittsburgh. Her research examines the development of second language fluency, the acquisition of second language phonology, and the pronunciation pedagogy practices of foreign language instructors.

Elma Kerz is a Post-Doctoral Researcher at RWTH Aachen University. She is interested in mechanisms used by humans in learning L1 and L2 languages and in the role of numerous individual differences factors in language development. Her research draws on diverse methodologies informed by an integrated transdisciplinary approach to language.

Kristopher Kyle is Assistant Professor in the Linguistics Department at the University of Oregon. He also holds a joint appointment as Assistant Professor in the English Department at Yonsei University. His research interests include second language acquisition, second language writing, corpus linguistics, computational linguistics, and second language assessment.

Wander Lowie is Chair of Applied Linguistics at the University of Groningen and is associate editor of *The Modern Language Journal*. His main research interest lies in the application of Dynamic Systems Theory to second language development (learning and teaching).

Cristóbal Lozano is Associate Professor of English Applied Linguistics at the Universidad de Granada (Spain). His main research interests are L2 acquisition, learner corpora, and L2 psycholinguistics. He is the designer and director of the CEDEL2 corpus (http://cedel2.learner-corpora.com). For more information, please visit his academic webpage: http://wpd.ugr.es/~cristoballozano

Fanny Forsberg Lundell is Professor of French at Stockholm University. Besides publishing extensively on formulaic language in L2 French, her work includes Second Language Pragmatics. She is currently involved in research on psychological and social factors in high-level L2 attainment.

Alison Mackey is Professor of Linguistics at Georgetown University in Washington, DC and Professor of Applied Linguistics at Lancaster University in the UK (Summers). She is also Editor-in-Chief of the *Annual Review of Applied Linguistics* (Cambridge University Press). Her interests include Second Language Acquisition and Research Methodology in Applied Linguistics.

Brian MacWhinney, Teresa Heinz Professor of Psychology, Computational Linguistics, and Modern Languages at Carnegie Mellon University, has developed a model of first and second language acquisition, processing, and disorders called the Competition Model. He is also the organizer of the TalkBank system for spoken language data-sharing (http://talkbank.org).

Emma Marsden is Professor of Applied Linguistics at the University of York, UK. Her research interests include morphosyntactic processing and development, classroom pedagogy, research methods, and open science. She is co-author of *Second Language Learning Theories* 3rd and 4th editions (with Rosamond Mitchell and Florence Myles), journal editor of *Language Learning*, and director of IRIS (iris-database.org) and OASIS (oasis-database.org). She founded and directs the National Centre for Excellence for Language Pedagogy (ncelp.org) in the UK.

Tony McEnery is Distinguished Professor in the Department of English Language and Linguistics at Lancaster University. He has published widely on corpus linguistics and is the author of *Corpus Linguistics: Method, Theory and Practice* (with Andrew Hardie, Cambridge University Press, 2011).

Fanny Meunier is Professor of English Language, Linguistics and Didactics at UCLouvain (Belgium). Her main research interest is the SLA/language pedagogy nexus. She is leading and taking part in several national and international research projects on multilingualism, multi- and digital literacies.

Rosamond Mitchell is Professor Emeritus of Applied Linguistics at the University of Southampton, UK. She trained originally as a teacher of languages and obtained her PhD in Education from the University of Stirling. She has longstanding research interests in instructed SLA and has created learner corpora in French and Spanish from beginner to advanced level.

Florence Myles is Professor of Second Language Acquisition at the University of Essex and Founding Director of its Centre for Research in Language Development throughout the Lifespan. She has co-constructed a range of freely available oral learner corpora of French and Spanish (www.flloc.soton.ac.uk; www.splloc.ac.uk).

Magali Paquot is FNRS Research Associate at the Centre for English Corpus Linguistics, UCLouvain. She specializes in the use of learner corpora to study key topics in SLA and is particularly interested in methodological issues. She is co-editor in chief of the *International Journal of Learner Corpus Research* and one of the founding members of the Learner Corpus Research Association.

Caroline Payant is Associate Professor at the Université du Québec à Montréal. Her research examines L2/L3 development through task-based interaction and literacy development with learners of English. Her work can be found in the *Canadian Modern Language Review, Foreign Language Annals*, and *Studies in Second Language Acquisition*.

Shelley Staples is Associate Professor of English Applied Linguistics/Second Language Acquisition and Teaching at University of Arizona. Her research focuses on the use of corpus-based discourse analysis to investigate (second) language use across spoken and written contexts, including pragmatic and functional dimensions.

Jennifer Thewissen is Lecturer in English Language and Linguistics at the University of Antwerp and Saint-Louis University, Belgium. She works on the concept of accuracy, which she looks at developmentally on the basis of learner corpus data.

Anita Thomas is Professor of French as a Foreign language at the University of Fribourg in Switzerland. Her main research interests are in second language acquisition, the influence of input and the use of corpora for second language teaching.

Nicole Tracy-Ventura is Assistant Professor of Applied Linguistics at West Virginia University. Her research focuses on second language acquisition, study abroad, task-based language teaching, longitudinal research methods, and corpus linguistics. She is a founding member of the Languages and Social Networks Abroad Project (LANGSNAP).

Marjolijn Verspoor is Professor of English Linguistics at the University of Groningen and Applied Linguistics at the University of Pannonia in Hungary. Her research focuses on the study of usage-based dynamics in second language learning and teaching.

Nina Vyatkina is Professor of German and Applied Linguistics and Chair of the Department of German Studies at the University of Kansas, USA. Her research interests include instructed second language acquisition, corpus-based language learning and teaching, and learner corpus research.

Daniel Wiechmann is Assistant Professor of English Linguistics and Senior Researcher at the Institute for Logic, Language and Computation at the University of Amsterdam. His main research interest is in the use of statistical learning and machine learning methodologies in the development of probabilistic models of (second) language knowledge, learning, and processing.

Stefanie Wulff is Associate Professor in the Linguistics Department at the University of Florida. Her research interests include corpus linguistics, second language acquisition, and student writing development. She is editor-in-chief of *Corpus Linguistics and Linguistic Theory* (de Gruyter Mouton).

Nicole Ziegler is Associate Professor of Second Language Studies at the University of Hawai'i at Mānoa. Her research agenda focuses on instructed second language acquisition, task-based language teaching (TBLT), computer-assisted language learning (CALL), and task-based approaches for Maritime English.

Acknowledgements

Compiling a handbook is a large undertaking, and it would not have been possible without the work and support of a number of people to whom we are most grateful. First, we would like to thank Sue Gass and Alison Mackey, the series editors, for trusting us with this topic and for their extremely helpful advice and feedback whenever needed. Next, we sincerely appreciate the work of the forty authors who contributed their time and expertise to writing (and reviewing) chapters. Their commitment to SLA and corpora is evident from the high-quality chapters they authored. Additionally, our gratitude goes to a number of colleagues who reviewed chapters and provided very helpful feedback for the authors and us as editors, in addition to Jhon Cuesta Medina and Tiffany Scohy who assisted us with detailed checking of formatting issues. Rosamond Mitchell was also extremely generous with her time, reviewing a number of chapters for us. We greatly benefited from her experience and knowledge of the field. Our Routledge editor, Ze'ev Sudry, was very patient and supportive, especially when COVID-19 started and we needed some extra time due to our roles as working mothers balancing homeschooling, teaching, and trying to complete all the final pieces. We very much appreciate his kind approach to editing. We also acknowledge the support of the Fonds de la Recherche Scientifique – FNRS and West Virginia University. And finally, we are grateful to our closest friends and families for their support, and especially to our children, who did not always have mom's full attention but we promise will now.

Nicole Tracy-Ventura and Magali Paquot
Morgantown, WV, USA and Louvain-la-Neuve, Belgium
May 28, 2020

Second Language Acquisition and Corpora

An Overview

Nicole Tracy-Ventura and Magali Paquot

Introduction

Ever since the 1970s when the field of second language acquisition (SLA) was developing, researchers have been analyzing 'corpora', collections of production data that range in size from very small (e.g., a case-study of one learner in one interview) to much larger samples (e.g., *the European Science Foundation Second Language Database*; see Klein & Perdue 1992; Perdue 1993). A major goal of SLA research is to understand the second language (L2) knowledge system that underlies learner language, its development and retention, and those factors which impact both. In addition to samples of learner language, SLA research utilizes data other than linguistic performance, including grammaticality judgment tasks where participants make decisions as to whether examples of language are grammatical or not (Jiang & Nekrasova, 2007). More recently, SLA research has also been incorporating psycholinguistic data such as working memory tests and eye-tracking data to examine language processing (Indrarathne & Kormos, 2018). It is also possible to find examples of SLA research that examine neurocognition of L2s using the event-related potential (ERP) technique (Morgan-Short et al. 2010). Thus, while SLA research has valued the contribution of corpus data, corpora have played a more marginal role in examining L2 language knowledge and use. This is in stark contrast to first language acquisition (L1) research, where naturalistic corpora of child speech have been central to the study of L1 acquisition, as perhaps best exemplified by the success of the Child Language Data Exchange System (CHILDES: MacWhinney, 2000), established over 30 years ago.

The field of corpus linguistics emerged around the same time as SLA when computers became more accessible (see Chapter 2, this volume). Researchers in this field began developing automatic and interactive computer-based methods for analyzing large collections of electronic texts, which they also referred to as 'corpora'. Important to this definition of a corpus is that corpus data are authentic and representative of explicitly stated kinds of language, or registers (e.g., conversation, academic writing). In contrast to the corpora collected in SLA, these corpora were not elicited by researchers but rather were examples of natural language in use. Additionally, they were formatted in a way that they could be analyzed with the use of computers. The fact that such corpora were machine-readable meant that very large samples of language could be analyzed at once, allowing for the identification of patterns that would be otherwise impossible to retrieve. Corpus linguists also began to realize that they could expand the range of possible analyses if they could annotate corpora in ways that reflected our theoretical understanding of language. As a result, tools such as part-of-speech taggers which assign a grammatical 'tag' to each word were developed, allowing for analyses that go beyond searches for individual words or word families, to investigations of grammatical categories and grammatical structures (Voutilainen, 2005). Such work led to important studies that demonstrated, for example, how certain parts of speech tended to co-occur in specific registers (Biber, 1988).

Inspired by what was happening in corpus linguistics, a small group of researchers led by Sylviane Granger at the Université catholique de Louvain in Belgium began to adopt similar methods in the 1990s to study second language learners' language use, and the field of learner corpus research (LCR) was born. In comparison to early SLA datasets, typically small and analyzed by hand, early studies in LCR focused primarily on written data due to the fact that it was much easier to gather at scale, compared to oral data which required the additional and time-consuming step of transcription. Another important difference between SLA and LCR was that from the beginning, LCR researchers prioritized building learner corpora that would be accessible to the research community. The *International Corpus of Learner English* (ICLE, Granger et al. 2002) was the first major learner corpus developed by a team of researchers that could later be purchased by other researchers for their own use. The team at Louvain, quickly joined by a growing and dynamic international LCR community, also began developing methods and creating programs that could be used to query and annotate learner corpora.

Over the last few decades, the tools that have been developed by corpus linguists and natural language processing researchers have become quite sophisticated and are now able to analyze corpora containing billions of words (e.g., Mark Davies' *News on the Web* corpus). Learner corpora are traditionally much smaller, but recent examples of learner corpora that contain several million words can be found (e.g., *The International Corpus of Learner English 3rd edition*, Granger et al., in press, and *The Trinity-Lancaster Corpus*, Gablasova et al., 2019). Methods for analyzing learner corpora often mirror those used in corpus linguistics, and as such, tend to involve frequency counts of different types (e.g. keywords in context, word lists and co-occurrence analysis) and the use of (semi-)automatic processing. SLA research, on the other hand, has been rather slow to incorporate computer-based analysis tools, with many researchers still undertaking their analyses by hand. For some analyses, this is the preferred method; however, much SLA research could benefit from transcribing data in formats that are suitable for more automatic and interactive corpus-based analyses.

Although SLA and LCR share the common goal of understanding L2 learning and development, the two fields have only just recently begun to consider a coming together of sorts. For example, most LCR research has been descriptive in nature, but studies which are hypothesis-testing have been on the rise (e.g., Murakami & Alexopoulou, 2015; see also most chapters in Le Bruyn & Paquot, in press). In SLA, some researchers have started using corpus tools to analyze larger datasets of learner language (e.g, Marsden & David, 2008; Tracy-Ventura & Myles, 2015). Some SLA researchers are also making use of L1 corpus data, for example, to investigate the role of frequency effects in language learning (Wulff, Ellis, Römer, Bardovi–Harlig, & Leblanc, 2009). Others are also taking a multimethod approach, including both experimental and corpus data in their design (Ellis et al., 2016; Meunier & Littre, 2013). Therefore, it is an opportune time to take stock of how corpora, both L1 and L2, have been used in SLA research to tackle questions such as:

1) What is the nature of the input that naturalistic and classroom learners are exposed to?;
2) How does frequency impact second language learning?;
3) What linguistic features are typical of learner language at different levels of proficiency?; and
4) How does formulaic language develop over time?

Furthermore, as corpus-based analysis tools become more readily available – to analyze oral, written, and visual data – it is important to provide researchers not yet familiar with such tools a place where they can gain the necessary background knowledge to begin using corpora and corpus-based methods. *The Routledge Handbook of SLA and Corpora* aims to accomplish these goals by surveying literature that focuses on methodological and theoretical contributions to the study of learner language using corpora.

In this introductory chapter, our goal is to explain the history of corpora in SLA research and by doing so, focus on the relationship that has developed between SLA and LCR over the past few decades. It is our hope that through this handbook and other recent publications (Le Bruyn & Paquot, in press; McEnery et al., 2019), collaboration between SLA and LCR will become the norm. This introduction also provides an overview of the handbook structure so that readers can gain an understanding of the major topics addressed and then delve directly into the chapters most relevant to their research needs.

SLA and LCR: A Brief History

In the early 1990s, Granger initiated the ICLE project to complement the *International Corpus of English* (Greenbaum, 1996), thus adding foreign/second language learner varieties to the large number of varieties of English that had already been sampled and stored in electronic corpora (Granger, 1996). As an offshoot of corpus linguistics, the field of LCR has always privileged "the least constrained types of data emanating from (near-)natural situations where learners can use their own wording rather than being prompted to produce a specific linguistic feature" (Granger, in press). Thus, learner corpora have typically been described as electronic collections of natural to near-natural data produced by foreign or second language learners and assembled according to explicit design criteria (e.g. Granger et al., 2015, Callies & Paquot, 2015). As explained by Granger (2017, p.338) quoting Ellis and Barkhuizen (2005), the term 'near-natural' is used to highlight the

> need for data that reflects as closely as possible 'natural' language use (i.e. language that is situationally and interactionally authentic) while recognizing that the limitations facing the collection of such data often obligate researchers to resort to clinically elicited data (for example, by using pedagogic tasks).
>
> *(Ellis & Barkhuizen, 2005, p. 7)*

As a matter of fact, a large majority of learner corpora today are best characterized as clinically elicited samples of learner language, although they result from "the use of tasks where learners are primarily concerned with message conveyance, need to utilize their own linguistic resources to construct utterances, and are focused on achieving some non-linguistic outcome" (Ellis & Barkhuizen, 2005, p. 23). The more open-ended types of contextualized production tasks used to elicit language samples from L2 learners are designed to approximate as closely as possible "what naturally occurring data are understood to be in the case of [foreign language] learners" (Díaz-Negrillo & Thompson, 2013, p. 19). Such tasks also do not aim to elicit samples that would seek to answer specific research questions; the idea behind a learner corpus compilation project is that the learner language samples can be used and re-used to answer a variety of research questions.

These characteristics make learner corpora a very different data type from the experimentally elicited samples of learner language that are more typically used in SLA and involve "the use of some kind of exercise, where learners attend primarily to form, are guided in the form to be produced and thus are focused on displaying usage of a specific linguistic form" (Ellis &

Barkhuizen, 2005, p. 23). The first learner corpora were also very different from the preferred data types in SLA as they were (1) primarily written (when many SLA specialists believe that oral productions are better suited to tap the productive system of the learner), (2) at best cross-sectional (when SLA is interested in language development and SLA researchers would like to see more longitudinal datasets available), and (3) targeted advanced learner language (see Myles, 2008, 2015, in press).

Early learner corpus studies were met with skepticism by many SLA researchers for other reasons than divergences in opinion about what can be considered as 'good data'. First, they were usually not informed by SLA theory and were essentially descriptive, "documenting differences between learner and native language rather than attempting to explain them" (Myles, 2005, p. 380). Indeed, most early learner studies reported on frequency counts, focusing on lexical items (single words and word combinations) that were overused, underused, or misused in learner language when compared to native language norms. Despite the fact that the first generation of learner corpora already came with a range of learner and task variables, a large majority of the early studies only considered L1 background as a control or independent variable. The reliance on a native speaker norm, especially as in the method of Contrastive Interlanguage Analysis (CIA; Granger, 1996), has also been subjected to criticism. For example, Barbieri (2010) criticized the field on the grounds that, "although growing steadily, [it] appears to have remained trapped in the comparative fallacy" (p. 149). This type of criticism was perceived as grossly unfair and triggered strong reactions in LCR:

> a look at the non-corpus-based SLA literature shows that the comparative fallacy is in fact pervasive but in a hidden undercover way, to the point that the term 'comparative hypocrisy' comes to mind.

> *(Granger, 2009, p. 18)*

LCR, and the method of CIA most particularly, were the target of fierce criticisms at a time when there were heated internal debates about the comparative fallacy and the native speaker norm in the field of SLA (see Cook, 1999; Davies, 2003). In both fields, there have been consistent proponents of the use of native speaker controls, with Myles (in press), for example, arguing that they are "essential in the case of many [SLA] research agendas". Today, then, it is clear that the use of a reference corpus in LCR should not be seen as a criterion that sets the two fields apart. See Granger (2009) for a more detailed rebuttal of the comparative fallacy in LCR, and Granger (2015) for how she addressed these criticisms in a revised version of CIA (see also Chapter 3, this volume).

Admittedly, LCR suffered from various teething problems, but the field has evolved tremendously since its beginning, and it is important for the field of SLA to recognize these recent developments. As testified by the list of learner corpora available on the "Learner corpora around the world" webpage (https://uclouvain.be/en/research-institutes/ilc/cecl/learner-corpora-around-the-world.html), more oral learner corpora and longitudinal learner corpora (for more languages) have been compiled (or are being compiled); new types of learner corpora are also being collected. Although still an exception, more data are being collected at the learner corpus compilation stage, including new types of metadata that are potentially of interest to the SLA community (e.g. data on motivation, and on cognitive and affective factors) as well as experimental data from the same learners (e.g. Möller, 2017) (see Chapter 10, this volume). Last but not least, the field has also matured in how it analyzes learner corpora: more attention is devoted to individual differences and individual contributions by different learners, with more studies focusing on a wider range of explanatory variables than only the learners' first language and adopting multifactorial designs (see Chapters 8, 9, and 30, this volume).

The aim of this volume is to take stock of these recent developments and further contribute to the recognition that corpora and corpus linguistic techniques should be part of the toolbox of every SLA specialist interested in analyzing second/foreign language development. There are at least two main reasons why this is the case, as explained by Myles (2005, p. 376). First, many of the current SLA hypotheses were formulated based on detailed case studies and studies involving just a small number of learners. The field now needs to test these hypotheses on larger and better constructed datasets. More generally, SLA research needs to explore whether findings of previous research are generalizable. Second, making use of electronic learner corpora and corpus linguistic techniques should ultimately ease the research process, by allowing SLA specialists to manipulate data in a number of useful ways. For example, by using a concordancer, it is possible to retrieve at once all instances of verbs used in the past tense or verbs used in the progressive from a morphosyntactically annotated learner corpus, which should be of great help to any researcher interested in tense and aspect. Similarly, the use of regular expressions (i.e. sequences of symbols and characters that define a search pattern) will allow for the extraction of linguistic patterns such as '[tag= "VB*"] []{0,1} [tag= "VVN"]', which will retrieve all instances of verbs in the passive form (operationalized as 'a form of the verb *be* + an optional word + a past participle form of a lexical verb', e.g. *given, worked*). Corpus tools can also be used to retrieve lexical bundles and collocations, which serve as a basis to explore formulaic language in learner language. Text analysis tools provide measures of syntactic complexity, lexical diversity and sophistication, global and local cohesion, etc., which can be applied to a large set of learner texts in batch processing. Additionally, spoken learner corpora are an invaluable resource for researchers interested in the development of oral language: transcriptions can be searched so as to quickly locate linguistic items of interest (from a specific phoneme to a word sequence), which can then be listened to in aligned sound files. These are just a few examples, and the handbook will provide many more. It will be shown that both L1 and learner corpora have already played an important role in SLA, and in the future will arguably play an even more important role as the open science movement becomes more mainstream (Marsden & Plonsky, 2018).

Structure and Features of This Handbook

This handbook is intended for advanced students and researchers interested in the design and use of corpora for investigating questions relevant to second language learning. As a result, the handbook presents an overview of the ways in which SLA research has been utilizing corpora and corpus-based analyses, providing recommendations and practical advice for how SLA can take advantage of new and developing methods from corpus linguistics and learner corpus research. For those with a limited background in SLA, this handbook also provides an introduction to SLA theories that are most directly aligned with corpus data.

The volume includes four main sections: 1) Setting the scene; 2) Key aspects in corpus design and corpus use for SLA; 3) The role of corpora in SLA theory and practice; and 4) SLA constructs and corpora. We conclude the handbook with a chapter on the future of corpora in SLA.

Chapters in Section 1 are foundational chapters to help novice researchers gain a better understanding of the different fields that influence this handbook: corpus linguistics, learner corpus research, and SLA. We chose to include such chapters to help researchers from other fields gain introductory knowledge that would assist them when reading other chapters in the handbook. For example, a corpus linguist who is starting a collaboration with SLA colleagues may find it useful to start with Chapter 4 to get an overview of the field of SLA. Likewise, an SLA researcher who wants to gain a better understanding of developments in LCR and corpus linguistics over the past few decades would benefit from reading Chapters 2 and 3, where methods and computerized tools that have been at the heart of corpus-based research are discussed.

Chapters in Section 2 focus on key aspects of corpus design and corpus use for SLA research. This practical section details important methodological considerations when designing a study using corpus data, including when building a corpus or when choosing to use a corpus that is already available. Topics such as methods of transcription, annotation, and statistical analysis are discussed, and different analysis tools are detailed as well. Additionally, chapters in this section describe learner corpora that have already been collected and analyzed for SLA and LCR research including those focusing on different L2s, proficiency levels, oral and written language, longitudinal corpora, specialized corpora, etc.

Chapters in Section 3 center on the role of corpora in SLA theory and practice. Six chapters are dedicated to major theories and approaches in SLA that utilize corpus data. Because LCR has often been criticized for being overly descriptive, we felt it was important to include chapters focusing on a range of SLA theories and approaches that could inspire future hypothesis-testing LCR. A final chapter in this section addresses instructed SLA, an area of research with potential for important corpus-based and corpus-informed studies but where there has been little collaboration between SLA and LCR researchers.

The last major section is section 4, which includes chapters examining how corpora have been used to examine a wide range of SLA constructs such as input, interaction, fluency, accuracy, complexity, lexis, crosslinguistic influence, variability, formulaicity, context, and individual differences.

The closing handbook chapter looks toward the future. The purpose of this concluding chapter is to take stock of what all the authors in this handbook have highlighted as areas of future research and to provide suggestions for the way forward. For example, we emphasize additional corpora that are needed and the kinds of new tools and analyses that could be developed for SLA research, as well as echoing MacWhinney (2017) in the call for a shared platform for second language research.

A major goal of the handbook was to bring together SLA and LCR researchers who have been utilizing corpora in their research and to demonstrate what has been achieved over the last three decades. SLA researchers have much to learn from LCR researchers and vice versa. Both fields aim to understand second language learning, and therefore, we believe that we should be incorporating aspects of both fields in our future investigations. We are already on this path, but there is much room for improvement. We hope that this handbook will inspire future researchers from both sides to make the leap and utilize the strengths that each contributes to our quest to better understand the process of second language learning and development.

References

Barbieri, F. (2010). Review of the book *Linking up contrastive and learner corpus research* by Gaëtenelle Gilquin, Szilivia Papp, and María Belén Díez-Bedmar (Eds.). *Studies in Second Language Acquisition*, *32*(1), 148–150.

Biber, D. (1988). *Variation across speech and writing*. Cambridge: Cambridge University Press.

Callies, M., & Paquot, M. (2015). Learner corpus research: An interdisciplinary field on the move. *International Journal of Learner Corpus Research*, *1*(1), 1–6.

Cook, V. (1999). Going beyond the native speaker in language teaching. *TESOL Quarterly*, *33*(2), 185–209.

Davies, A. (2003). *The native speaker: Myth and reality*. Clevedon: Multilingual Matters.

Díaz-Negrillo, A., & Thompson, P. (2013). Learner corpora: Looking towards the future. In A. Díaz-Negrillo, N. Ballier, & P. Thompson (Eds.), *Automatic treatment and analysis of learner corpus data* (pp. 9–29). Amsterdam: Benjamins.

Ellis, N. C., Römer, U., & O'Donnell, M. B. (2016). Constructions and usage-based approaches to language acquisition. *Language Learning*, *66*(S1), 23–44.

Ellis, R., & Barkhuizen, G. (2005). *Analyzing learner language*. Oxford: Oxford University Press.

Gablasova, D., Brezina, V., & McEnery, T. (2019). The trinity lancaster corpus: Development, description and application. *International Journal of Learner Corpus Research*, *5*(2), 126–158.

Granger, S. (1996). From CA to CIA and back: An integrated approach to computerized bilingual and learner corpora. In K. Aijmer, B. Altenberg, & M. Johansson (Eds.), *Languages in contrast: Text-based cross-linguistic studies* (pp. 37–51). Lund: Lund University Press.

Granger, S. (2009). The contribution of learner corpora to second language acquisition and foreign language teaching: A critical evaluation. In K. Aijmer (Éd.), *Corpora and language teaching* (pp. 13–32). Amsterdam: John Benjamins.

Granger, S. (2015). Contrastive interlanguage analysis : A reappraisal. *International Journal of Learner Corpus Research*, *1*(1), 7–24. https://doi.org/10.1075/ijlcr.1.1.01gra

Granger, S. (2017). Learner corpora in foreign language education. In S. Thorne & S. May (Eds.), *Language and technology: Encyclopedia of language and education* (vol. 9). Springer International Publishing. https://doi.org/10.1007/978-3-319-02237-6_33.

Granger, S. (in press). Commentary: Have learner corpus research and second language acquisition finally met? In B. Le Bruyn & M. Paquot (Eds.), *Learner corpus research meets second language acquisition*. Cambridge: Cambridge University Press.

Granger, S., Dagneaux, E., & Meunier, F. (2002). *The international corpus of learner English* (5th ed.). Louvain-la-Neuve: Presses Universitaires de Louvain.

Granger, S., Dupont, M., Meunier, F., Naets, H., & Paquot, M. (in press). *The international corpus of learner English* (5th ed.). Louvain-la-Neuve: Presses Universitaires de Louvain.

Greenbaum, S. (Eds.) (1996). *Comparing English worldwide: The international corpus of English*. Oxford: Clarendon Press.

Indrarathne, B., & Kormos, J. (2018). The role of working memory in processing L2 input: Insights from eye-tracking. *Bilingualism: Language and Cognition*, *21*(2), 355–374. https://doi.org/10.1017/S1366728917000098

Jiang, N., & Nekrasova, T. M. (2007). The processing of formulaic sequences by second language speakers. *The Modern Language Journal*, *91*(3), 433–445. https://doi.org/10.1111/j.1540-4781.2007.00589.x

Klein, W., & Perdue, C. (1992). *Utterance structure: Developing grammars again*. Amsterdam: John Benjamins.

Le Bruyn, B. S. W., & Paquot, M. (in press). *Learner corpora and second language acquisition*. Cambridge: Cambridge University Press.

MacWhinney, B. (2000). *The CHILDES project: Tools for analyzing talk* (3rd ed.). Mahwah: Lawrence Erlbaum.

MacWhinney, B. (2017). A shared platform for studying second language acquisition. *Language Learning*, *67*(S1), 254–275. https://doi.org/10.1111/lang.12220

Marsden, E., & David, A. (2008). Vocabulary use during conversation: A cross-sectional study of development from year 9 to year 13 among learners of Spanish and French. *The Language Learning Journal*, *36*(2), 181–198. https://doi.org/10.1080/09571730802390031

Marsden, E., & Plonsky, L. (2018). Data, open science, and methodological reform in second language acquisition research. In A. Gudmestad & A. Edmonds (Eds.), *Critical reflections on data in second language acquisition* (vol. 51, pp. 219–228). https://doi.org/10.1075/lllt.51.07tra

McEnery, T., Brezina, V., Gablasova, D., & Banerjee, J. (2019). Corpus linguistics, learner corpora, and SLA: Employing technology to analyze language use. *Annual Review of Applied Linguistics*, *39*, 74–92. https://doi.org/10.1017/S0267190519000096

Meunier, F., & Littre, D. (2013). Tracking learners' progress: Adopting a dual 'corpus cum experimental data' approach. *The Modern Language Journal*, *97*(S1), 61–76. https://doi.org/10.1111/j.1540-4781.2012.01424.x

Möller, V. (2017). *Language acquisition in CLIL and non-CLIL settings: Learner corpus and experimental evidence on passive constructions*. Amsterdam: Benjamins.

Morgan-Short, K., Sanz, C., Steinhauer, K., & Ullman, M. T. (2010). Second language acquisition of gender agreement in explicit and implicit training conditions: An event-related potential study. *Language Learning*, *60*(1), 154–193. https://doi.org/10.1111/j.1467-9922.2009.00554.x

Murakami, A., & Alexopoulou, T. (2015). L1 influence on the acquisition order of English grammatical morphemes. *Studies in Second Language Acquisition, FirstView*, 1–37. https://doi.org/10.1017/S0272263115000352

Myles, F. (2005). Interlanguage corpora and second language acquisition research. *Second Language Research*, *21*(4), 373–391. https://doi.org/10.1191/0267658305sr252oa

Myles, F. (2008). Investigating learner language development with electronic longitudinal corpora: Theoretical and methodological issues. In L. Ortega & H. Byrnes, *The longitudinal study of advanced L2 capacities* (pp. 58–72). New York: Routledge.

Myles, F. (2015). Second language acquisition theory and learner corpus research. In S. Granger, G. Gilquin, & F. Meunier (Eds.), *Cambridge handbook of learner corpus research* (pp. 309–331). Cambridge: Cambridge University Press.

Myles, F. (in press). Commentary: An SLA perspective on learner corpus research. In B. Le Bruyn & M. Paquot (Eds.), *Learner corpus research meets second language acquisition*. Cambridge: Cambridge University Press.

Perdue, C. (Ed.) (1993). *Adult language acquisition: Field methods* (vol. 1). Cambridge: Cambridge University Press.

Tracy-Ventura, N., & Myles, F. (2015). The importance of task variability in the design of learner corpora for SLA research. *International Journal of Learner Corpus Research*, *1*(1), 58–95. https://doi.org/10.1075/ijlcr.1.1.03tra

Voutilainen, A. (2005). Part-of-speech tagging. In R. Mitkov (Ed.), *The Oxford handbook of computational linguistics*. Oxford: Oxford University Press. Retrieved from https://www.oxfordhandbooks.com/view/10.1093/oxfordhb/9780199276349.001.0001/oxfordhb-9780199276349-e-11,

Wulff, S., Ellis, N. C., Römer, U., Bardovi–Harlig, K., & Leblanc, C. J. (2009). The acquisition of tense–aspect: Converging evidence from corpora and telicity ratings. *The Modern Language Journal*, *93*(3), 354–369. https://doi.org/10.1111/j.1540-4781.2009.00895.x

PART I
SETTING THE SCENE

2

Introduction to Corpus Linguistics

Vaclav Brezina and Tony McEnery

Introduction

Corpus linguistics is an approach to the study of language that uses computers to analyze large amounts of language data, both written and spoken, which we call corpora (sg. corpus). This simple definition situates corpus linguistics in the tradition of linguistically grounded analysis that makes use of the development of computational technology to draw on evidence about language use that would not be accessible otherwise. Corpus linguistics started to develop as a separate discipline in the 1960s, although early examples of corpus analysis were available before, and has flourished since the 1990s – hand in hand with the development of computational technology. Corpora allow us to search through and analyze millions or even billions of words, a task that would hardly be possible without the existence of adequate computational technology (both hardware and software). Corpus linguistics thus puts language use into perspective: drawing on the robust evidence that is available in corpora, we can answer questions about frequencies of different linguistic features and their distribution in different types of language use (see *Representative Corpora and Research*). Corpus linguistics can answer questions such as:

- Is this linguistic feature rare or typical in language use?
- Which words occur frequently across different genres?
- What are the typical collocations of a word of interest?
- What are typical contexts in which a word of interest occurs?

In essence, corpus linguistics analyses the information about the frequencies of occurrence of linguistic features and the contexts of their use in language sampled in corpora, a perspective that is unique to corpus analysis. As Leech (2011) pointed out, "[i]f asked what is the one benefit that corpora can provide and that cannot be provided by other means, I would reply 'information about frequency'" (p. 7). This does not mean that corpora do not provide qualitative information about language use in specific contexts. In fact, corpora provide both quantitative and qualitative information, which represents one of the strengths of this approach. This is because when interpreting an individual example such as (1) taken from the Spoken BNC2014 (Love et al., 2017), we need to know both how typical or unusual it is in language as sampled by the corpus (quantitative aspect) but also what the broader context is in which it occurs and, if available, what the situation and the background of the speaker is (qualitative aspect). In corpus linguistics, the quantitative and the qualitative aspects are inherently linked: qualitative findings are often the spur for quantitative investigations, whereas to make sense of quantitative data derived from a corpus, we often need to return to the texts it was derived from and engage in qualitative analysis.

(1) and he *ain't* got a television

Example (1) includes a non-standard form 'ain't', which in current spoken British English competes with standard forms of 'hasn't/haven't' and 'isn't/aren't etc.'. In this case, 'ain't' means 'hasn't', as can be also seen from the broader context (2), in which it alternates with 'hasn't' in the speech of the same speaker. Based on the Spoken BNC2014 data, we know that on average, 'ain't' occurs 113.81 per million words in informal spoken British English, whereas its standard competitor in this context ('hasn't/haven't') is much more frequent with 921.77 instances per million words, respectively.

(2)
S1 (male, 60+, South of England): he hasn't got a television
S2 (male, 60+, South of England): yeah?
S3 (female, 60+, South of England): never had one has he?
S1 (male, 60+, South of England): erm no he hasn't
S3 (female, 60+, South of England): not for years and years
S1 (male, 60+, South of England): and they want to know where his television is and *he ain't got a television*

The Spoken BNC2014 also provides information about the speakers in the conversation in (2), all of whom are older speakers (60+) from the South of England. The non-standard form is uttered apparently for emphatic purposes by a male speaker, a gender-based tendency, which is well documented in sociolinguistic literature (e.g. Cheshire, 1991).

So, as we can see, corpora have much to offer. At this stage, it is important to look at a more formal definition of this key term in corpus linguistics. A corpus is a dataset used in corpus linguistics. Following McEnery et al.'s (2006) definition, we can characterize a corpus as "a collection of (1) *machine-readable* (2) *authentic* texts (including transcripts of spoken data) which is (3) *sampled* to be (4) *representative* of a particular language or language variety" (p. 5). These four characteristics of a corpus define the nature of a corpus as a carefully sampled dataset and distinguish it from an arbitrary amount of text data that is collected without a sampling frame or clear principles of compilation. Let us expand on each of these characteristics. First, the requirement for machine-readability of the data as text (rather than an image of a text) allows us to process and search the corpus using specialized software (see *Main Research Methods*). Second, data compiled as tools corpora are typically not produced specifically for the corpus[1] through elicitation, but are authentic examples of language use; this allows us to observe a variety of contexts in which language is normally used, providing 'naturalistic data' that 'is contextualized' (Culpeper et al., 2018). Third, in most cases, a corpus is a sample of language. We usually take a (small) subset of all texts and speech events that were produced for a given variety. This sample is, however, carefully chosen to reflect the particular language or language variety we are interested in. This is what is called the representativeness of a corpus, the fourth characteristic from the definition above. Based on a corpus, we can, among other things, draw statistical inferences about a language or a specific variety that the corpus was designed to represent (Brezina, 2018; Gries, 2013).

To provide some background to corpus linguistic analyses, we need to briefly outline the history of the field. As with all histories, the history of corpus linguistics is subject to the dynamics of memory – the version given depends on perspective and the particular path through the events relevant to the topic that any one perspective suggests one takes. What is without doubt is that prior to the invention of the computer, a number of scholars, over a long stretch of time, appealed to attested language use in making claims about language. Sometimes this was very detailed and was akin to some of the methods of modern corpus linguistics, with concordances being produced for key cultural texts, e.g. the Bible, frequency wordlists being produced for language teaching, and even early conceptualization of the notion of collocation being produced. However, until the creation of computing machinery that allowed rapid and reliable storage, manipulation, and searching of large volumes of language data, these attempts to operationalize corpus linguistics were few and of a small scale. It is of note that very shortly after the creation of the digital computer in the 1940s, the potential for such equipment to be used to study language was realized in a range of places and by a range of people. Roberto Bussa started to use digitized texts, in the form of punch cards, to produce concordances in the late nineteen forties. Alphonse Juilland, at Stanford University, began his exploration in mechanolinguistics in the 1960s, producing a very fine set of frequency dictionaries for French, Italian, Romanian and Spanish. In Eastern Europe, researchers in Soviet Russia and East Germany in particular used corpus data, with Russian researchers, for example, using corpora to work in the paradigm of mathematical linguistics and East German researchers producing a corpus-informed grammar of English. In France, Textometry, an approach to the study of language based on corpus analysis, developed in the 1980s.

The authors of this chapter, while recognizing these many and varied roots of corpus linguistics, identify with the approach to the subject which developed out of approaches to corpus construction and exploitation that developed principally in northern and western Europe from the 1960s onwards, as discussed by McEnery and Hardie (2011, Chapter 4). This approach, which has within it a number of different schools, with slightly different methods and preconceptions, has proved the most influential, in part because of its links to large scale publishing, especially of state-of-the-art dictionaries and grammars and key academic outputs (e.g. Quirk et al., 1985; Biber et al., 1999), but also because that approach to the subject came into contact, early on, with a shift in computational linguistics towards using corpus data in the late 1970s. The work of pioneers in computational linguistics, such as Fred Jelinek at IBM, was influenced in part by contacts with corpus linguists, such as Geoffrey Leech, who also worked with other computer scientists, notably Roger Garside, to produce some of the earliest viable natural language processing products, notably, the CLAWS part-of-speech tagger (Garside, Sampson and Leech, 1988). Consequently, the impact of the work of corpus linguists working in this broad tradition was profound both in linguistics and beyond.

As the approaches to the use of corpus data developed, so too did the types of data used to study language – monolingual corpora for a wider range of languages across a greater span of time have become available; comparable corpora which allow different languages to be compared and contrasted have been produced; parallel corpora, which allow translations from one language to another to be explored have proved to have great utility (see Baker et al., 2004, for an example of a large and complex corpus covering both English and South Asian languages which incorporates comparable and parallel data) and, importantly for this volume, learner corpora, containing the written or spoken data produced by the learners of a specific language as a second or foreign language, have been developed that have facilitated new insights into the process of language learning (see Gilquin et al., 2010 for an example of such a corpus). Similarly, the tools of corpus linguistics, and especially the mathematics used to manipulate corpus data, has developed apace also (see Brezina, 2018).

Core Issues and Topics

Corpus Linguistics As a Methodological Approach

Corpus linguistics, as explained above, is a particular methodological approach to language analysis. Because corpora, which are the data in corpus analysis, are often very large (up to billions of running words), corpus linguistics relies on computing technology to process this data and help the human analyst to identify the most important patterns, typically relating to some feature that they are interested in, in the data. Corpora are thus analyzed using various computational techniques, which are often quantitative in nature, although some, such as concordancing (see Chapter 6 this volume), are designed to aid close reading.

Quantitative techniques in corpus linguistics involve the counting of linguistically meaningful items, e.g. words, phrases and grammatical structures. Where a corpus has been linguistically annotated (see Garside, Leech and McEnery, 1997 for examples of linguistic annotations), it may be the annotation of the text, e.g. parts of speech, or a combination of text and annotation that is counted, e.g. only the word *dog* marked as being a singular common noun, as opposed to the much rarer verb. As noted already, however, this does not mean that corpus linguistics cannot be used for the qualitative exploration of language. Corpora provide examples of language use with extended contexts, which always need to be analyzed qualitatively. Similarly, while quantitative information about a corpus is valuable, it is often the qualitative investigation of such data that adds nuance and depth to such findings. For example, one may find, through exploring part-of-speech annotations, that two corpora have a similar proportion of singular common nouns in them, yet close reading of the text may lead one to hypothesize that corpus one has a greater dependency on animate nouns. After adding further annotation to explore this point, the analysis may return to being quantitative, meaning that we may cycle between quantitative and qualitative analyses in our exploration of corpus data. A corpus can be likened to a lens through which one may observe language use in different contexts. We can zoom in to observe an individual example or zoom out to see the larger picture. An important feature of this approach, however, is that no matter how detailed or specific our analysis is, the larger picture is and should always be in the background guiding and controlling our analysis. Individual examples are thus not selected arbitrarily but systematically.

For example, if we are interested in the passive construction (e.g. *this has been done*) and its use in British English, we can look in the *British National Corpus* (BNC, Aston & Burnard, 1998), a 100-million-word sample of British English. There, we can find the information about its overall frequency (1,023,434 in the whole corpus) and its distribution in different genres and registers – uses of language in particular situational contexts – (it is most frequent in academic prose, and least frequent in conversation), as well as obtain a random sample of e.g. 100 examples, which we can analyze qualitatively in detail. Only if we have this type of information at our disposal can we draw conclusions that are meaningful and reasonably robust. This approach to data is often referred to as the "principle of total accountability" (Leech, 1992, p. 112): we need to account for all the data, and not subjectively curate pieces of evidence that we like and that fit neatly into our narrative. This is a crucial distinguishing feature helping us differentiate between scientific and other (non-scientific) approaches to language. Scientific approaches are based on careful research design and accounting for the totality of the data. They are also transparent to the extent that they are repeatable, and their design is well reported so that they can be repeated on other datasets. Also, importantly, they permit falsification – the conclusions arising from an investigation are susceptible to being tested and, if the evidence dictates, falsified.

Corpus Linguistics and Language Variation

Corpora bring evidence about linguistic variation (e.g. Biber, 1988). This evidence shows that language use is not monolithic but differs considerably depending on the situation of use and the speaker's background. For instance, examples (3) and (4) demonstrate the use of language in formal legal writing and in informal conversation, respectively.

(3) The general lines of reform must be to permit increases on prewar standard rents which will cover maintenance costs with a certain allowance for arrears; but these costs should be certified by the relevant local authority and only collectable upon that authority's certificate that the appropriate standard of maintenance has been attained. As soon as possible afterwards, the existing legal obligations on landlords in regard to repair and maintenance should be put into full force again.

(BNC)

(4)
S1: hold it and go. Did you beat Ryan?
S2: He's a fucker, I can't stick him he's the most snobbish little cunt I 've ever known I 'd like to see what stuff he had if he had to pay for it himself hard luck, no I 'd like to see what he 'd do with his stuff if he had to pay with it, pay for it himself. Cos he's well out of order, when you, were you there when he was were you there when he was like slamming his nine iron into one of those brick posts, that's sad.

(BNC)

The two examples differ considerably both in the vocabulary used as well as the grammatical structures. Example (3) consists of long, carefully edited, sentences with abundance of technical (legal) vocabulary such as *arrears*, *attained* and *permit*. On the other hand, the dialogue in (4) contains relatively short loosely connected structures (utterances) with many personal pronouns and swearwords (*fucker, cunt*). Corpus linguistics allows systematic analysis of these and similar patterns observable in the data (corpora) using techniques such as multi-dimensional analysis developed by Biber (1988) which allows one to explore such patterns acting in concert, rather than singly. To read more about a wide range of applications of this technique, see Berber Sardinha and Pinto (2014).

Corpus Linguistics and Statistics

To be able to systematically evaluate quantitative evidence, corpus linguistics relies on statistical procedures to collect and analyze the data. Statistical rigor in corpus linguistics is crucial (e.g. Gries, 2006). However, this should not create a stumbling block for a wide variety of uses of the corpus method in an ever-increasing range of fields including SLA (Brezina, 2018). Only if it remains accessible can corpus linguistics fulfil the potential to interact with other disciplines and contribute to linguistic, social, and educational theory.

Yet, it is important to note that corpus statistics has some specific characteristics. It deals with modelling language use, which shows inter-connectedness at multiple levels, and hence is not always easily analyzed using traditional statistical methods (e.g. Kilgarriff, 2005), most of which have been taken over from social statistics. This has led to the broadening, over time, from a near-exclusive reliance on mono-factorial analyses in corpus linguistics to a combination of multi- as well as mono-factorial analyses. At the same time, some of the assumptions behind some common statistics used, such as an assumption of normal distribution, have become carefully scrutinized as analysts have striven to avoid invalid generalizations arising from such assumptions (see, for example, Kilgarriff, 2001).

Statistical modelling of language should also strive to account for the size of observed effect, the magnitude of what is observed, that should be systematically reported in research reports (Brezina, 2018. Chapter 8, Plonsky & Oswald, 2014). Critical consideration of the linguistic and social effect of the results reported in corpus studies that go beyond simple noting of p-values is also important for the possibility of statistical synthesis of results from multiple studies (meta-analysis) and for the development of the field as a whole (see *Future Directions* and Mizumoto, Plonsky and Egbert, forthcoming).

Main Research Methods

This section offers an overview of main corpus methods and software tools available. While corpora present empirical evidence about language production, this evidence can be presented in different forms, and with different types of focus depending on the aim of the study and the research question(s). Traditionally, four basic corpus techniques have been recognized. (1) the study of *concordances*, (2) the creation of *frequency lists*, (3) the analysis of *collocations* and (4) *keywords*.

Frequency lists of items (word types, lemmas, part-of-speech categories, etc.) provide the most general insight into a corpus by showing items in descending order according to their frequencies in the corpus, with the highest-frequency items at the top. Frequency lists play an important role in language pedagogy and SLA (Brezina & Gablasova, 2017a; 2015) but are also useful for characterizing a corpus as a dataset more generally. Keyword analysis (Scott, 1997) compares two corpora, a corpus of interest and a reference corpus, to highlight items on frequency lists of these corpora that are relatively more or less frequent in one corpus when compared to the other. Collocational analysis investigates the co-occurrence of words in a corpus. Words that frequently, and/or exclusively, co-occur with a word of interest, the *node*, are identified statistically as its collocates. Finally, concordances provide a list of examples of occurrence of the word, phrase or grammatical structure of interest in its immediate context – several words to the left and several words to the right. These examples can be sorted and further analyzed for patterns of language use (e.g. Sinclair, 1991).

Appropriate software is necessary for corpus analysis. Table 2.1 displays an overview of the most common software tools used in corpus linguistics together with a brief description of their functionality and accessibility.

In addition to corpus-analytical tools, statistical tools may also be used for further analysis of corpus data. These include the statistical package R (Core team) or Lancaster stats tools online (Brezina, 2018).

Representative Corpora and Research

There are different types of corpora. The main distinction to be made is between general and specialized corpora. General corpora such as the BNC (Aston & Burnard, 1998) and *The Corpus of Contemporary American English* (COCA, Davies, 2009) represent general language use across different genres/registers. These corpora are typically very large (a hundred million words plus) and allow researchers to explore a wide range of uses of linguistic features across genres/registers. We can, for instance, say that the BNC (100M) broadly speaking represents British English in the 1990s, whereas COCA (more than 1 billion words) represents current American English. Other prominent general corpora include the web corpora EnTenTen corpora (different languages, Jakubíček et al., 2013) and WaC corpora (different languages, Baroni, et al., 2009). The scale of these corpora makes them useful if we want to describe a particular language for lexicographic, grammatical and other broad research purposes. General corpora can also be used as reference corpora in L2 research representing the target use of linguistic features.

Specialized corpora, on the other hand, focus on a specific context or a set of contexts in which language is used. They are typically much smaller (thousands or millions of words) than general corpora. For example, The *British Academic Written English* (BAWE) corpus (Alsop & Nesi,

Table 2.1 Corpus Tools (Adapted from Brezina & Gablasova, 2017b)

Tool	Analysis of own data	Provides corpora	Brief description
Desktop (offline) tools			
#LancsBox	YES	YES	This flexible tool, which runs on all major operating systems, represents a new generation of corpus analysis software. It provides a simple interface yet powerful analytical and visualization capabilities for corpus data. It allows multiple corpora to be easily compared and contrasted. The tool is freely available from http://corpora.lancs.ac.uk/lancsbox
AntConc	YES	NO	This tool is available in versions for different operating systems. AntConc is a toolbox which searches corpora and provides all core corpus analytical functionalities with easy linking between individual tools. The tool is freely available from http://www.laurenceanthony.net
MonoConc Pro	YES	NO	This Windows tool has a powerful search functionality and allows simple and advanced searches with easy navigation. It calculates and displays the distribution of linguistic features in individual text files. Paid license as well as a free simple version (MonoconcEsy) are available at http://www.monoconc.com
WordSmith	YES	NO	This Windows tool has a large number of analytical and data manipulation functionalities, with new features regularly added. The tool is recommended for more advanced users. Pay for a license for the latest version or access a free older version (v. 4) from http://www.lexically.net/wordsmith
Web-based (online) tools			
BYU corpora	NO	YES	This website offers large corpora of American and other varieties of English. It also contains NOW, a large monitor corpus of web-based newspapers and magazines updated daily. Non-English corpora include a corpus of Spanish and a corpus of Portuguese. The tool is freely available at http://corpus.byu.edu/. Its usability is somewhat limited by frequent requests for donations (after every 10-12 searches).
CQPweb	NO	YES	This tool offers a range of pre-loaded corpora for English (current and historical) and other languages including Arabic, Italian, Hindi, and Chinese. It has a number of powerful analytical functions. The tool is freely available at https://cqpweb.lancs.ac.uk/
SketchEngine	YES	YES	This tool can be used for processing users' own data, collecting data from the web, and exploring a very large number of pre-loaded corpora for all major languages. SketchEngine includes the TenTenTen family of web-based corpora, each of which consists of billions of words. Paid access as well as a free trial are available at https://www.sketchengine.co.uk/
Wmatrix	YES	NO	This tool allows users to process their own data and add part-of-speech and semantic annotation. Corpora can also be searched and compared with reference wordlists. Paid access as well as a free trial are available at http://ucrel.lancs.ac.uk/wmatrix/

2009) and the *Michigan Corpus of Upper Level Student Papers* (MICUSP, Römer & O'Donnell, 2011) are both specialized corpora representing student academic writing. Overall, there are a large number of specialized corpora, far too many to be listed, many of which were collected for a specific research study.

This section will provide examples of general and specialized corpora and studies based on these. While it makes no claim to exhaustiveness or impartiality in the selection (every selection is to some extent subjective), this overview highlights some prominent corpora and tools that might be of interest to readers.

The BNC (Aston & Burnard, 1998) is one of the most widely used corpora (Love et al., 2017). It represents British English – both speech and writing – across a wide range of genres/registers. While the BNC, with its 100 million running words is not the largest corpus of its kind, its representativeness, covering a broad spectrum of British English genres/registers including informal conversation (4.2 million words), makes it a unique source of information about British English. The BNC is often used as a reference corpus for the target variety with which L2 production can be compared. Because the BNC is now over 20 years old and thus no longer accurately reflects current English usage, a team of researchers at Lancaster University are working on a new version of the BNC – BNC2014. Currently, the spoken part has already been compiled and released (Love et al., 2017), while the written part will be made available during 2020[2]. As an example of how the BNC has been used, Leech (2000) presents a unique overview of spoken language corpora and research based on them, including the spoken part of the BNC. This review paper uses robust corpus evidence in published work to evaluate the unique properties of spoken grammars (as opposed to written ones) as well as their commonalities with writing systems. Leech (2000) provides multiple examples from real language use to argue that "spoken and written language utilize the same basic grammatical repertoire, however different their implementations of it may be" (p. 675). Implications for language learning are drawn at the end of the article.

COCA (Davies, 2009) is a general monitor corpus representing different registers in both written and spoken (film and TV scripts) American English. As of September 2020, the corpus consists of over 1 billion running words; it is being updated on a regular basis to monitor the developments in current American English (hence the term monitor corpus). Corpora of different varieties of a language raise the prospect of comparing and contrasting those varieties. Liu (2011) is an example of such a comparative study using both the BNC and COCA to investigate the frequency and distribution of phrasal verbs in British and American English. The study employs multiple searches and manual checking of the results to identify phrasal verbs in the datasets. Using cross-tabulation, it also traces the distributions of phrasal verbs in different registers of written and spoken English. It provides frequency and distribution information about 152 phrasal verbs listed in the Appendix, information that is useful for further research but also for pedagogical purposes.

The BAWE corpus (Alsop & Nesi, 2009) and MICUSP (Römer & O'Donnell, 2011) can be used to investigate academic writing by university students. While BAWE represents the British variety of English, MICUSP is a corpus of student essays produced at an American university. The BAWE corpus contains over 6.5 million words from thirty main disciplines ranging from Arts and Humanities to Social Sciences, Life Sciences, and Physical Sciences. MICUSP contains approximately 2.6 million words across a similar range of disciplines.

Larsson (2017) uses BAWE and MICUSP as reference L1 corpora and contrasts them with a corpus of L2 writing. The focus of the study is on the introductory *it* pattern in academic writing (e.g. *It is important to remember the differences*) that had been found challenging for learners of English. The study uses a combination of automated corpus searches with manual coding of examples for functional features such as a hedge (+/-H), affective attitude (+/-A) and/or an emphatic (+/-E). A statistical regression model is used to identify factors that play a role in the use of introductory *it* patterns in academic writing.

Future Directions

When looking at the field of corpus linguistics, two trends are clearly observable. These are 1) a convergence in the methodology and standardization of procedures and methods, and 2) a divergence in corpus applications. Both of these, we would argue, are to the benefit of the field. Corpus linguistics has the aspiration to be a scientific discipline hence it strives for the standardization of its procedures (e.g. Gries, 2013; Brezina, 2018) and calls for more methodological rigor (Gries, 2006) and replication (e.g. McEnery & Hardie, 2011; Granger & Bestgen, 2017). The following examples demonstrate this trend.

There has been a recent attempt to re-think basic categories within corpora such as token and text. Token, i.e. a running word, is a basic unit of counting in corpus linguistics. It plays a role in the normalization of frequency results (providing so-called relative frequencies) and also in the calculation of different statistical measures. However, as Brezina and Timperley (2017) show, the answer to the question of how many tokens a dataset such as the BNC has differs considerably depending on the analytical tool used. For example, whether the tool recognizes *wouldn't* and other clitic forms as one or two words may dramatically affect the word count of a corpus. Brezina and Timperley argue for adopting a traditional, surface-level definition of a token as "a string of contiguous alphanumeric characters with space on either side" (Kučera and Francis 1967, p. 3) and standard reporting on any deviation from this definition in different analytical procedures. Similarly, Egbert and Schnur (2018) consider the role of text as the basic unit of corpus sampling and organization in corpus studies. In contrast to "bag-of-words" approaches to corpus data, which assume that language is composed of sequences of words which can occur in any order, free of syntactic and other constraints, the authors argue for the text to figure as the central point in corpus studies as the unit of observation, allowing researchers to "account for the full range of variability in the use of a particular feature or set of features" (p. 168).

The bag-of-words approach to corpus data has also been criticized from the statistical point of view (Kilgarriff, 2005; Brezina & Meyerhoff, 2014) for severely underestimating Type I errors (false positives) in the results of corpus analyses. Instead, more robust procedures have been proposed for dealing with variability in corpora and taking into account individual variation and multi-variability of corpus data (e.g. Gries, 2003). Collaboration with other fields and triangulation of corpus-based and other methods has recently been demonstrated in volumes such as Baker and Egbert (2016). It is important to realize that triangulation is only possible if corpus linguistics clearly identifies and standardizes its core methods, realizes their limitations, and participates in shared co-construction of goals with other disciplines (McEnery, Brezina, Gablasova, & Banerjee, 2019). The fact that corpus linguistics as a method offers a wide range of applications not only in (applied) linguistics but also in a whole range of subjects in social science is apparent from the pioneering work of the ESRC Centre for Corpus Approaches to Social Science (CASS) at Lancaster University[3] and the uptake of the corpus method in disciplines such as political science (Germond, McEnery and Marchi, 2016) and sociology (Zinn, 2019).

While there is still a long way to go, we believe that corpora and corpus methods will play an ever important role in an ever wider range of disciplines. So, the future of corpus linguistics with relation to its potential applications is both complex and ripe with opportunity. Corpus linguistics will present researchers beyond the field with the opportunity to explore naturalistic data using linguistically-informed techniques. Yet in doing so, it will find that its methods, data gathering practices, and even epistemological frameworks may change as it adapts to work with other disciplines. This represents both an opportunity to corpus linguistics and an opportunity to all of the disciplines engaged in this fruitful dialogue.

Further Reading

Biber, D., & Conrad, S. (2019). *Register, genre, and style*. Cambridge: Cambridge University Press.

Biber & Conrad (2019) is dedicated to the investigation of language variation, one of the crucial components of corpus research, with the focus on register analysis. It covers spoken and written registers as well as new registers and genres in interpersonal electronic communication (text messages, forum posts, tweets). The book also offers an accessible introduction to the multi-dimensional analysis, a statistical procedure that provides a comprehensive description of register variation. The volume is an essential read for anyone interested in this important tradition of corpus studies.

Brezina, V. (2018). *Statistics in corpus linguistics: A practical guide*. Cambridge: Cambridge University Press.

Brezina (2018) offers an accessible overview of statistical techniques used in corpus linguistics. The book is organized according to areas of linguistic and social research covering a wide range of topics ranging from grammar and vocabulary to discourse and historical analyses. Each technique is explained and demonstrated with multiple examples; at the end of each chapter, a small case study is presented allowing the reader to see the application of statistics to real corpus data.

McEnery, T., & Hardie, A. (2011). *Corpus linguistics: Method, theory and practice*. Cambridge: Cambridge University Press.

McEnery & Hardie (2011) provides a comprehensive introduction to corpus linguistics including the history of the field as well as the most important approaches and conceptual issues. The book provides an overview of different schools of thought of corpus linguistics as well as of an interaction between corpus linguistics and other areas of linguistics such as studies of language variation, functional linguistics, and psycholinguistics. This is an essential reading to understand the core tenets of the field.

Related Topics

Chapters 3, 9, 27, and 31.

Notes

1 An exception would include some learner corpus data, where the data was elicited from language learners for no other purpose than inclusion in a corpus of learner language. The LINDSEI (Gilquin et al. 2010) and ISLE (Menzel et al. 2000) corpora are both composed of such elicited material (see Chapter 3).
2 For more information see http://cass.lancs.ac.uk/bnc2014/ (last accessed 8 November 2019).
3 See the CASS website for a description of current and past projects http://cass.lancs.ac.uk/(last accessed 8 November 19).

References

Alsop, S., & Nesi, H. (2009). Issues in the development of the British Academic Written English (BAWE) corpus. *Corpora*, *4*(1), 71–83.

Aston, G., & Burnard, L. (1998). *The BNC handbook: Exploring the British national corpus with SARA*. Edinburgh: Edinburgh University Press.

Baker, P., & Egbert, J. (2016). *Triangulating methodological approaches in corpus linguistic research*. New York: Routledge.

Baker, P., Hardie, A., McEnery, T., Xiao, R., Bontcheva, K., Cunningham, H., … Leisher, M. (2004). Corpus linguistics and South Asian languages: Corpus creation and tool development. *Literary and Linguistic Computing*, *19*(4), 509–524.

Baroni, M., Bernardini, S., Ferraresi, A., & Zanchetta, E. (2009). The WaCky wide web: A collection of very large linguistically processed web-crawled corpora. *Language Resources and Evaluation*, *43*(3), 209–226.

Berber Sardinha, T., & Pinto, M. V. (2014). *Multidimensional analysis, 25 years on*. Amsterdam: John Benjamins.

Biber, D. (1988). *Variation across speech and writing*. Cambridge: Cambridge University Press.

Biber, D., & Conrad, S. (2019). *Register, genre, and style*. Cambridge: Cambridge University Press.

Biber, D., Johansson, S., Leech, G., Conrad, S., Finegan, E., & Quirk, R. (1999). *Longman grammar of spoken and written English*. London: Longman.

Brezina, V. (2018). *Statistics in corpus linguistics: A practical guide*. Cambridge: Cambridge University Press.

Brezina, V., & Gablasova, D. (2015). Is there a core general vocabulary? Introducing the new general service list. *Applied Linguistics*, *36*(1), 1–22.

Brezina, V., & Gablasova, D. (2017a). How to produce vocabulary lists? Issues of definition, selection and pedagogical aims. A response to Gabriele stein. *Applied Linguistics*, *38*(5), 764–767.

Brezina, V., & Gablasova, D. (2017b). The corpus method. In J. Culpeper, P. Kerswill, R. Wodak, A. McEnery, & F. Katamba (Eds.), *English language: Description, variation and context*. Basingstoke: Palgrave.

Brezina, V., & Meyerhoff, M. (2014). Significant or random: A critical review of sociolinguistic generalisations based on large corpora. *International Journal of Corpus Linguistics*, *19*(1), 1–28.

Brezina, V., & Timperley, M. (2017). How large is the BNC? A proposal for standardised tokenization and word counting. Paper presented at the *International Corpus Linguistics Conference*, University of Birmingham.

Cheshire, J. (1991). Variation in the use of ain't in an Urban British English dialect. In P. Trudgill & J. K. Chambers (Eds.), *Dialects of English* (pp. 54–73). London: Longman.

Culpeper, J., Mackey, A., & Taguchi, N. (2018). *Second language pragmatics*. London: Routledge.

Davies, M. (2009). The 385+ million word corpus of contemporary American English (1990–2008+): Design, architecture, and linguistic insights. *International Journal of Corpus Linguistics*, *14*(2), 159–190.

Egbert, J., & Schnur, E. (2018). The role of the text in corpus and discourse analysis. In C. Taylor & A. Marchi (Eds.), *Corpus Approaches to Discourse. A Critical Review* (pp. 158–170). London: Routledge.

Garside, R., Leech, G., & McEnery, T. (1997). *Corpus annotation*. London: Longman.

Garside, R., Sampson, G., & Leech, G. (1988). *The computational analysis of English*. London: Longman.

Germond, B., McEnery, T., & Marchi, A. (2016). The EU's comprehensive approach as the dominant discourse: A corpus linguistics analysis of the EU's counter-piracy narrative. *European Foreign Affairs Review*, *21*(1), 137–156.

Gilquin, G., De Cock, S., & Granger, S. (2010). *The louvain international database of spoken English interlanguage. Handbook and CD-ROM*. Louvain-la-Neuve: Presses universitaires de Louvain.

Granger, S., & Bestgen, Y. (2017). Using collgrams to assess L2 phraseological development: A replication study. In de Haan, P.J., de Vries, C.M., & Vuuren, S.V. (Eds.), *Language, learners and levels: Progression and variation* (pp. 385–408). Louvain-la-Neuve: Presses universitaires de Louvain.

Gries, S. Th. (2003). *Multifactorial analysis in corpus linguistics: A study of particle placement*. London: Continuum.

Gries, S. Th. (2006). Some proposals towards a more rigorous corpus linguistics. *Zeitschrift für Anglistik und Amerikanistik*, *54*(2), 191–202.

Gries, S. Th. (2013). *Statistics for linguistics with R: A practical introduction*. Berlin: Walter de Gruyter.

Jakubíček, M., Kilgarriff, A., Kovář, V., Rychlý, P., & Suchomel, V. (2013, July). The tenten corpus family. Paper presented at the 7th International Corpus Linguistics Conference, Lancaster, UK.

Kilgarriff, A. (2001). Comparing corpora. *International Journal of Corpus Linguistics*, *6*(1), 232–263.

Kilgarriff, A. (2005). Language is never, ever, ever, random. *Corpus Linguistics and Linguistic Theory*, *1*(2), 263–276.

Kučera, H., & Francis, W. N. (1967). *Computational analysis of present-day American English*. Providence, RI: Brown University Press.

Larsson, T. (2017). A functional classification of the introductory it pattern: Investigating academic writing by non-native-speaker and native-speaker students. *English for Specific Purposes*, *48*, 57–70.

Leech, G. (1992). Corpora and theories of linguistic performance. In J. Svartvik (Ed.), *Directions in corpus linguistics* (pp. 105–122). Berlin: Mouton.

Leech, G. (2000). Grammars of spoken English: New outcomes of corpus-oriented research. *Language Learning*, *50*(4), 675–724.

Leech, G. (2011). Frequency, corpora and language learning. In F. Meunier, S. Cock, & G. Gilquin (Eds.), *A taste for corpora: In honour of sylviane granger* (pp. 7–31). Amsterdam: John Benjamins.

Liu, D. (2011). The most frequently used English phrasal verbs in American and British English: A multicorpus examination. *TESOL Quarterly*, *45*(4), 661–688.

Love, R., Dembry, C., Hardie, A., Brezina, V., & McEnery, T. (2017). The spoken BNC2014: Designing and building a spoken corpus of everyday conversations. *International Journal of Corpus Linguistics*, *22*(3), 319–344.

McEnery, T., Brezina, V., Gablasova, D., & Banerjee, J. (2019). Corpus linguistics, learner corpora, and SLA: Employing technology to analyze language use. *Annual Review of Applied Linguistics*, *39*, 74–92.

McEnery, T., & Hardie, A. (2011). *Corpus linguistics: Method, theory and practice*. Cambridge: Cambridge University Press.

McEnery, T., Xiao, R., & Tono, Y. (2006). *Corpus-based language studies: An advanced resource book*. New York: Routledge.

Menzel, W., Atwell, E., Bonaventura, P., Herron, D., Howarth, P., Morton, R., & Souter, C. (2000). The ISLE corpus of non-native spoken English. In M. Gavrilidou (Ed.), *Proceedings of LREC 2000: Language resources and evaluation conference, vol. 2. LREC 2000: Language resources and evaluation conference, May 31–June 02* (pp. 957–964). Athens: European Language Resources Association.

Mizumoto, A., Plonsky, L., & Egbert, J. (in press). Meta-analyzing corpus linguistic research. In M. Paquot & S. Gries (Eds.), *The practical handbook of corpus linguistics*. Berlin: Springer.

Plonsky, L., & Oswald, F. L. (2014). How big is "big"? Interpreting effect sizes in L2 research. *Language Learning*, *64*(4), 878–912.

Quirk, R., Greenbaum, S., Leech, G., & Svartvik, J. (1985). *A comprehensive grammar of the English language*. London: Longman.

Römer, U., & O'Donnell, M. B. (2011). From student hard drive to web corpus (Part 1): The design, compilation and genre classification of the Michigan Corpus of Upper-level Student Papers (MICUSP). *Corpora*, *6*(2), 159–177.

Scott, M. (1997). PC analysis of key words—And key key words. *System*, *25*(2), 233–245.

Sinclair, J. (1991). *Corpus, concordance, collocation*. Oxford: Oxford University Press.

Zinn, J. (2019). *Understandign risk taking*. London: Palgrave.

3

Introduction to Learner Corpus Research

Fanny Meunier

Introduction

Work in Learner Corpus Research (LCR) started around the 1980s as "an offshoot of corpus linguistics" (Granger et al., 2015, p. 1). Corpus linguistics and LCR share a set of common features, among which is the use of corpora and corpus tools to analyze language. A corpus is defined by McEnery et al. (2006, p. 5) as a "collection of machine-readable authentic texts (including transcripts of spoken data) which is sampled to be representative of a particular language or language variety". A learner corpus is thus a specific type of corpus which, to follow up on McEnery et al.'s definition, can broadly be defined as a collection of machine-readable texts consisting in representative samples of the language written and/or spoken by learners of an additional language (viz. not their mother tongue, but a foreign/second/nth target language). LCR uses learner corpus data as its main data source. As for the results of learner corpus studies, they typically serve two main purposes:

- inform SLA research,
- provide useful input for applied projects (including the creation or improvement of teaching materials/approaches, or the training/development of Natural Language Processing tools).

A comparison of the oft-cited definitions of LCR (see Gilquin, 2015 for more details) reveals that one of the key features of learner corpora is that the language they contain is meant to be as authentic as possible and is often defined as (near-) natural. As explained by Granger (2008, p. 337), "the term near-natural is used to highlight the 'need for data that reflects as closely as possible 'natural' language use (i.e. language that is situationally and interactionally authentic) while recognizing that the limitations facing the collection of such data often obligate researchers to resort to clinically elicited data (for example, by using pedagogic tasks (Ellis & Barkhuizen, 2005, p. 7))". As cases of purely spontaneous oral or written learners' productions are rare[1] – or, when they take place, cannot easily be 'spontaneously collected' – pedagogic tasks serve as the main prompts to (near)-natural learner language productions.

Another key feature is that the texts[2] included in learner corpora have been selected on the basis of a number of criteria or variables related to, among others:

- the learners themselves (e.g. target language, mother tongue, proficiency level),
- the type of communicative task (e.g. written/oral communication, descriptive/persuasive/narrative/expository writing/narrative, informal/formal level),

- the contextual conditions of language production or task setting (e.g. interactive tasks, computer–mediated communication, use of reference tools or not).

The criteria/variables listed above are typically used as metadata to organize the electronic storage of the data in large databases that can later be queried. Researchers can, for instance, select sub-sections of the data collected (e.g. only texts spoken by female learners of German as a foreign language/from a lower beginner level/collected during an informal discussion). The variables can later serve as dependent/independent/predictive variables in the linguistic analyses carried out (see section *Main Research Methods* for more details).

The learners' initial productions (often called 'raw' texts) are often further annotated to enable researchers to access richly annotated data. The texts can be annotated automatically with the help of natural language processing tools, edited with the help of semi-automated tools, or annotated fully manually. Some examples of typical linguistic annotations include:

- automatic part-of-speech tagging: each word in the corpus is attributed a part-of-speech (noun, verb, adjective, etc.) thanks to the help of fully automatic part-of-speech tagging software (see Chapters 5 and 6, this volume, for more information);
- computer-aided error annotation (CEA): as learner corpora are produced by learners, some researchers may be interested in spotting areas of difficulty that learners have in producing an L2. Annotating these aspects makes it possible to subsequently focus on them to help foster learners' proficiency. Errors/infelicities in the corpus are first spotted by researchers who then use an editor to insert codes in the corpus (e.g. a plural determiner followed by a singular common noun can receive a 'noun number' error code). More details on CEA can be found in Chapter 7.

As the two examples provided above show, annotations may include fully automatic tools (such as part-of-speech taggers, semantic taggers, or syntactic parsers), but also semi-automatic annotation tools requiring human intervention before the analysis can be done. Some annotations can also be done fully manually by researchers (by inserting codes in the text using text processing tools, for example) when the analysis cannot be automated, as would be the case for the inclusion of non-verbal comments in transcripts of videoed interactions ([laughs], [unfilled pauses], [gestures], [contextual comments], etc.). This type of tagging is often referred to as problem-oriented annotation/tagging, viz. the manual annotation by the researcher of any feature of interest.

A last key feature is that learner corpora, like any other type of corpus, can be queried using corpus tools such as concordancers (see Chapter 6, this volume), which can be used to:

- extract word lists, word combinations, tags, keywords or annotations,
- display occurrences of words/phrases/tags in the selected corpus,
- compare different subcorpora in terms of keywords, frequency distribution of items, etc.

Given the space limitations of an introductory chapter, it is not really possible to describe in detail all the tools that can be used to annotate or query learner corpora. I thus warmly recommend the Tools for Corpus Linguistics webpage to readers (see https://corpus-analysis.com/) as it offers an impressive list of 228 corpus tools, each described in terms of the following aspects: name, description, categories, platform, and pricing, plus a link to the tool. I also refer readers to the software index of the *Handbook of Learner Corpus Research* (Granger et al., 2015) as it contains a list of over 80 tools (annotation tools, DDL tools, statistical packages, text retrieval tools, iCALL and CALL packages, etc.) whose concrete use, description and illustration can be found in the handbook.

As can be seen from the list of key features above, technology is clearly part and parcel of LCR. Thanks to giant strides in computer technology in the last quarter of the 20th century, it became possible to collect data from much larger cohorts of learners and to use computer software to assist researchers in the annotation and analysis of the data. The affordances of technology also made it possible to perform data analyses that were either previously not conceivable or, at least, not feasible in a reasonable timeframe and at a reasonable cost. As the *Core Issues and Topics* section will show, LCR has evolved remarkably through its three decades of existence. Just as learners typically go through stages of development in their learning of an additional language, LCR also evolved from a novice field (filled with the excitement that usually goes with novelty) towards more competent and reflective practices. This evolution has impacted most of the core features and issues in LCR, as will be shown in the next section.

Core Issues and Topics

Size, Collection, Variables, and Analysis: Limits and Strengths

Access to large (for the time) electronic learner corpora in the 1990s led to a revolution in the way learner language was analyzed and described. The first learner corpora that exceeded one million word tokens in size were collected, and the new options offered by automatic corpus analysis tools (word lists ordered in decreasing order of frequency, retrieval of words in contexts through concordancers, automatic part-of-speech tagging, etc.) offered unprecedented insights into learner language. The urge to get access to previously inaccessible frequency information led to a 'descriptive fever' (analysis of productions by numerous learners; lists of the top *n* words in a corpus; frequency of errors; most frequently used verbs; overused and/ or underused linguistic items, often in relation to an L1 corpus etc.). The term 'fever' is not used here in any derogatory way but simply points to the focus of interest at the time, even if cautionary tales were already given. Granger (1994, p. 27) warned readers that "quantitative data should not be regarded as an end in itself" but rather "as a springboard for a qualitative investigation of the data" and of its patterns of use. Such cautionary tales notwithstanding, it must be acknowledged that numerous publications back then were essentially descriptive with frequency lists being provided and compared, with – in many cases – no clear reference to SLA theories, except for the sometimes simplistic reference to transfer. This led some researchers to consider learner corpus linguistics as synonymous to distributional number crunching, which – despite the limitations mentioned above – also constituted an unfair shortcut. Granger (2009) responded to criticism levelled against LCR and the lack of collaboration between LCR and SLA by pointing that one of the main assets of the former is that it brings to the SLA field a much wider empirical basis than previously available. She also explained that learner corpora which have been collected on the basis of strict, well-described criteria and which have been stored in easily queryable databases contain data from hundreds and sometimes thousands of learners, which greatly enhance representativeness of data. It also makes controlling the many variables that affect learner production possible.

Over the years, practices in LCR have also evolved significantly, moving from a focus on one main variable (mother tongue background) to studies analyzing the effects of and/or relationships between a much wider range of variables. Examples include planning time (Ädel, 2008), time of exposure/learning (Meunier & Littré, 2013), genre (Gentil & Meunier, 2018), or a combination of variables such as learning context and emotional aspects (De Smet et al., 2018).

Overall, the initial criticism levelled against LCR – be it fair or not – proved very fruitful as it prompted learner corpus researchers to explicitly verbalize the numerous advantages of LCR and move the field further. Gries (2009, p. 2), for instance, argued that corpus linguistic methods are "a method just as acceptability judgments, experimental data, etc." are and that "linguists of every theoretical persuasion can use corpus data". He also explained that usage-based cognitive-linguistic theories are particularly compatible with corpus linguistics methods, thereby throwing the spotlight on some of the specific strengths of LCR. The constant questioning and reassessment of LCR led to a more reflective and competent practice in LCR, also prompting the collection of a much larger variety of learner corpus types, which subsequently opened up new avenues for analysis. Whilst the first learner corpora were mainly targeting written L2 English by relatively advanced learners, typically university students, a much larger range of target languages and text types has since been collected. The 'Learner corpora around the world' webpage[3] maintained by the Centre for English Corpus Linguistics at the Université catholique de Louvain pays tribute to this variety of target languages (Arabic, French, German, Korean, Spanish, etc.), text types and production conditions (exam essays, argumentative and literary essays, letters, diaries, picture descriptions, book reviews, monologues, dialogues, computer-mediated communication, mails, translations, etc.). Other welcome advances have been made in terms of:

- proficiency levels (covering the whole range of proficiency levels, from beginners to advanced) and types of learners (children, teenagers, adults, non-native 'learners' but also non-native 'users' including teachers, heritage speakers, translators, etc.);
- variety of research designs (cross-sectional, quasi-longitudinal, longitudinal).

The publication of the first handbook of Learner Corpus Research (Granger et al., 2015) and the launch of the first journal entirely devoted to LCR, the *International Journal of Learner Corpus Research* (IJLCR) pay tribute to the variety of current LCR studies addressing areas as diverse as interdisciplinarity (Callies & Paquot, 2015), linguistic innovations and creativity in non-native Englishes (Deshors et al., 2018), and study quality (Paquot & Plonsky, 2017).

Other developments include the use of more complex statistical techniques to interpret quantitative data (see e.g. Gries, 2013) and the popularization of mixed-methods designs to complement LCR methods and studies (see Gilquin & Gries, 2009; Meunier & Littré, 2013). One of the limitations of LCR is that some of the language features studied by researchers may not naturally occur frequently enough in unconstrained, open-ended (semi-) authentic production. The collection and analysis of other data types to triangulate research results and offer converging or diverging evidence is then particularly useful. Such data types may include experimental data, questionnaires, semi-guided interviews, think-aloud protocols or ethnographic approaches (also see Chapter 10, this volume).

The (Native Speaker) Norm/Myth?

Native corpus studies have demonstrated their added value in making it possible to compare different varieties of the same language, both synchronically and diachronically, and in providing a more balanced/refined description of languages. For instance, books like *Brief Grammar for English* (attributed to William Bullokar in 1586 and which aimed to show that English was as rule-bound as Latin) were replaced by thick and detailed accounts like the Longman Grammar of Spoken and Written English (Biber et al., 1999) where the grammatical specificities of various text types/registers were minutely described.

The power of corpus data for comparing different language varieties is also a central asset of LCR. As Granger (2015, p. 8) explains, two types of comparison appeared to be particularly worthwhile in LCR:

- a comparison with native language (NL), seen as the ultimate attainment of learning a foreign/second language;

- a comparison of one sample of learner language (IL, for interlanguage) with other samples of learner language, particularly from learners with different mother tongue backgrounds, for example, E2F (the English produced by learners with French as an L1) vs E2G (the English produced by learners with German as an L1) in Figure 3.1.

This double entry approach to LCR, conceptualized by Granger in 1996, was labelled Contrastive Interlanguage Analysis, or CIA.

Whilst the IL vs IL approach has always been promoted and accepted, "CIA has been subjected to a range of criticism, most targeted at the L1/L2 branch" (Granger, 2015, p. 13), which prompted a new version of the methodology, abbreviated as CIA² (see Figure 3.2 for a visual representation). Put briefly, the reference to native speaker language was interpreted as the recognition of one idealized native speaker norm and even labelled as "imperialistic assumptions about the ownership of English" (Tan, 2005, p.: 128). This was an unfair criticism, according to Granger (2015, p. 15), as plenty of L1 standards (such as British, American, Australian, Canadian, Hong Kong, India, Singapore, Sri Lanka, etc.) have been used as reference corpora for CIA studies.

In CIA², new terms have been proposed to avoid misunderstandings: RLV (for Reference Language Varieties) and ILV (for Interlanguage Varieties). The use of RLV points to the large number of different reference points against which learner data can be set (inner circle varieties such as British or American English, outer circle varieties such as Indian or Singapore English), as well as corpora of competent L2 user data, English as a Lingua Franca. As for ILVs, they refer to learner language varieties, given the "highly variable nature of interlanguage" (Granger 2015, p. 18). Comparing an ILV with an RLV makes it possible to better understand the processes at

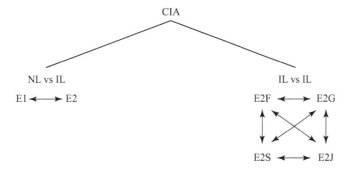

Figure 3.1   Contrastive Interlanguage Analysis (Granger 1996).

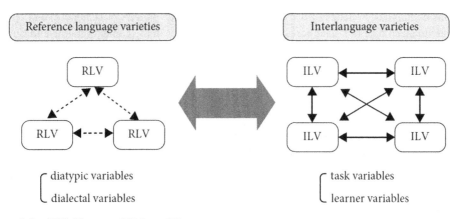

Figure 3.2   CIA² (Granger 2015, p. 17).

play in the acquisition of that specific ILV. A comparison of various ILVs (e.g. learners of L2 English whose mother tongues are French, Dutch, Italian, Greek, or Finnish) can help detect potential universal paths of acquisition versus L1 induced phenomena. A comparison of the language produced in various modes, genres or registers produced by the same learners (e.g. written and oral productions by the same learners) can help researchers discover mode/genre/register specific features (also see Chapter 8, this volume, for more details on comparing learner corpora).

Applied Perspectives in LCR: The Continuous/Contextualized Text Paradox in LCR

As explained in the introductory section, the applied perspectives of LCR are numerous. Mukherjee (2009, p. 212) states that '[l]earner corpus analyses always, at least implicitly, raise the question of what the language-pedagogical implications and applications might be" and numerous publications have addressed the links between (learner) corpora and pedagogy (see for instance Burnard & McEnery, 2000; Granger et al., 2002b; Granger, 2008; Aijmer, 2009; Meunier, 2010). Learner corpora have been used to inform lexicography, syllabus design, materials design, computer-aided language learning and pedagogical approaches such as data-driven learning. Some learners' dictionaries (e.g. the *Longman Dictionary of Contemporary English* (2009) or the *Cambridge Advanced Learner's Dictionary* (2008)) contain error notes intended to help learners avoid common mistakes. Learner corpora have also been used by textbook writers to inform the design of tasks addressing typical problems that learners face (see the error correction/rewriting exercises in the *Grammar and Beyond* textbook series[4]). Some large-scale initiatives like the English Profile Project (see http://www.englishprofile.org/ for more details and related publications) rely on learner corpus data to help teachers and educators understand what aspects of English are typically learned/acquired at each level of the Common European Framework of Reference for Languages (Council of Europe, 2001). Learner corpora can also be used to create data-driven learning activities, i.e. the use of corpora and concordances (typically keywords presented in their context of production) so that learners can work as language researchers in awareness-raising activities. Learners can check specific patterns of the use of keywords in native speaker texts and then compare that use to learners' productions.

Despite numerous publications on the pedagogical value of learner corpora, a lack of uptake of corpus-informed pedagogy has been noted (Granger, 2009; McCarthy, 2008; Shirato & Stapleton, 2007; Römer, 2009; Wilson, 2013; Meunier, 2018). Besides the technical problems that are often put forward, another reason that may explain the lack of uptake of corpus-informed pedagogy can be found in – what I would label – the contextual/continuous text paradox in LCR. Proponents of (learner) corpus studies lay strong emphasis on the fact that corpus data is unique in that it contains continuous stretches of discourse (not single words, phrases or sentences) and consist in contextualized data (i.e. data not produced in isolation but in the context of a meaningful, set task). And yet, when it comes to pedagogical applications, the use of learner corpus data rarely goes beyond the sentence level. This paradox would surely need to be addressed in the future to pay better tribute to the uniqueness of corpus data and maybe also ensure a clearer understanding on the part of learners and/or teachers of the usefulness of corpus-informed pedagogy (see the section *Future Directions* for some suggestions).

Main Research Methods

As some aspects related to research methods also constitute core issues in LCR, they have been addressed in the previous section (this includes contrastive interlanguage analysis (and its evolution over time) as well as a number of issues related to annotation and corpus analysis tools. This section will thus focus on only two aspects: the basic types of corpus approaches and the three main study designs typically used in LCR.

Corpus-based and Corpus-driven Approaches

Two basic approaches can be used to analyze a (learner) corpus. The corpus-based approach uses corpora as a source of information to explore a theory or hypothesis, aiming to validate it, refute it, or refine it. One concrete example would be the study of grammatical variation in terms of dative alternation, as speakers have a choice between the prepositional dative construction (e.g. give something to someone) and the double object construction (e.g. give someone something). SLA studies put forward different hypotheses when it comes to the dative alternation in L2 English (result of lexicalized verbal preferences, order of acquisition of the two constructions, etc.). As explained by Jäschke (2016, p. 19) "very few studies explored whether the learners' use and judgments of the two variants are governed by the same linguistic factors which have been found to be predictive for English native speakers". A corpus-based approach can be used in such cases to explore learners' actual use of dative constructions (as was done by Deshors, 2014).

In corpus-driven approaches, the corpus is viewed as a source of inspiration to formulate hypotheses about language (Tognini-Bonelli, 2001, p. 84–5). "The role of the researcher is to formulate questions and to draw conclusions derived from what corpus data reveal when subjected to statistical analysis rather than using the data to test a research hypothesis by approaching a corpus with a number of preconceived ideas" (Callies, 2015, p. 36). One concrete example of such an approach can be found in Belz and Vyatkina (2008) who investigated the pedagogical application of a learner corpus study in language teaching and in the developmental analysis of language learning in an instructed setting. The authors used L1 German data as a baseline against which learner German data was compared. Using a corpus-driven approach (thanks to a careful qualitative – usage in context – follow-up analysis of frequency lists), they spotted learners' emerging use of some focal features. These included the use of fixed and creative constructions of the German modal particles ja, denn, doch, and mal. Such studies contribute to second language acquisition research via dense documentation of micro-changes in learners' language use over time and to the formation of new hypotheses for future research.

Cross-sectional, Quasi-longitudinal, and Longitudinal Research Designs

Earlier studies in LCR were mostly cross-sectional, which means that they examined the language behavior of a group or groups of language learners at a single point in their development. Those studies usually compared one ILV with one or more other ILVs or with an RLV.

With a view to addressing developmental paths in SLA, researchers decided to carry out a comparison of cross-sectional studies of different groups of learners at different developmental stages, thereby adopting what Huat (2012, p. 197) calls a pseudo-longitudinal approach. The learners' productions are not from the same learners, hence the use of the 'pseudo' prefix, and the 'time' variable is somehow measured by proxies such as age or proficiency level. In such pseudo-longitudinal designs, researchers compare several groups of learners at different levels of proficiency.

Cross-sectional and pseudo-longitudinal designs do not allow for the analysis of individual development. Individual variation within each group or sub-group can however be analyzed – as can group development in pseudo-longitudinal designs.

Longitudinal study designs, in contrast to the two previous types, follow the same individual(s) over time. Longitudinal research is defined as 'emphasizing the study of change and containing at minimum three repeated observations on at least one of the substantive constructs of interest'

(Ployhart & Vandenberg, 2010, p. 97). As explained in Meunier (2015), the collection of longitudinal learner corpus data is time- and cost-consuming, and the analysis can only start when the entire data collection is over. Other issues include attrition (i.e. the sometimes significant number of participants dropping out before data-collection points). Such obstacles probably account for the scarcity of longitudinal studies in the early days of LCR.

In longitudinal study designs, group progress, individual variation within groups and individual trajectories can be analyzed. This requires the use of, for instance, multi-level modelling – also referred to as hierarchical linear modelling or mixed-effects models (see Raudenbush & Bryk, 2002; Baayen et al., 2008; Cunnings, 2012; Gries, 2015). "Multi-level modelling allows a variety of predictors to be analyzed, with 'time' being a key predictor in longitudinal studies: do participants become more proficient as time goes by and, if so, how strong is the effect of time? Such statistical modelling can be applied to individuals within groups as well as to individuals as individuals, by analyzing both endpoints and trajectories" (Meunier, 2015, p. 382).

With the benefit of hindsight, it can be argued that there has been a true qualitative evolution over time in the research methods used in LCR. The field broadly evolved from the descriptive analysis of aggregate data in cross-sectional designs to the use of inferential statistics and a focus on intra- and inter-learner variability in more complex types of designs (including longitudinal studies and mixed-methods approaches).

Representative Corpora and Research

The *International Corpus of Learner English* (ICLE) is probably the exemplar of first-generation learner corpora. It has been and is still being used massively by learner corpus researchers. Its first edition (Granger et al., 2002a) – resulting from ten years of international collaboration between numerous universities – contained 2.5 million words of English (mostly argumentative essays by university students of English) written by learners from eleven different mother tongue backgrounds and was released in CD-ROM format including an interface to compile tailor-made subcorpora on the basis of a set of predefined learner or task variables. The second version (Granger et al., 2009) differed from the first one in scope (larger amount and greater diversity of the learner data included) and in functionalities. It included a built-in concordancer and direct links between learner profile information and search results. A third extended and web-based version of ICLE (Granger et al., 2020) will soon be available. Ädel's (2008) study, presented below, is based on ICLE v1.

Ädel (2008) examines variables related to task effects on language use. The research question addresses how the variable of 'task setting' (time and reference sources available) affects the learners' writing styles on the written/spoken continuum. She uses the concepts of 'involvement' and 'detachment' typically used in variationist corpus-based approaches to language, with informal speech typically characterized as involved (first-person reference, emphatic particles, etc.) and formal writing as detached (passive constructions, inanimate subjects, etc.). The learners were university students of English with L1 Swedish who wrote argumentative and expository essays for the Swedish subcorpus of the *International Corpus of Learner English* (SWICLE: Granger et al., 2009) and the *Uppsala Student English Corpus* (USE; Axelsson, 2000). The overall results of the study show that learners exhibit more involvement features in timed than in untimed essays but less if they have access to source texts. In addition to a possible lack of register awareness, the study reveals that the extreme rate of involvement found in SWICLE is rather linked to both the lack of time that writers have to make the text more written-like and the lack of model texts to rely on.

The *Longitudinal Database of Learner English* (LONGDALE) (Meunier, 2016) is one representative example of truly longitudinal learner corpora. It currently contains data collected by five teams (Radboud University Nijmegen (the Netherlands), University of Hannover (Germany), University of Louvain (Belgium), University of Padua (Italy), and University Paris-Diderot (France). The same students are followed over a period of at least three years and data collections are organized at least once per year, with some teams organizing several data collections per year. The term 'database' (rather than 'corpus') has been used from the onset of the project as LONGDALE includes a wide range of data types including argumentative essays, narratives, and informal interviews, but also more guided types of productions (such as picture descriptions). Experimental data is also included for some of the subcorpora. The database also includes comprehensive learner profile information which is gathered during each data collection. The study presented below focuses on the acquisition of phonology/pronunciation.

Méli (2013) analyzes the segmental realizations of French learners of English with a view of checking whether 'perceived dissimilarity' is a hindrance or an advantage for the L2 acquisition of sounds that do not exist in the learner's L1. He focusses on the realizations of the interdental fricative, as well as some of the phonemic vowel length asymmetries for vowels, {/i/ in French, /i-/i:/ in English} and {/u/ in French, /u/-/u:/ in English}. Eighteen students were recorded longitudinally over three years (the date of year two and four are used in the present study). The acoustic characteristics of some features of native speech were compared – using the PRAAT software (Broesma, 2001) – to learners' realizations of the same sounds using the Bark Difference Metric method[5]. The analysis of the interdental fricatives stresses the importance of phonotactics (i.e. the syntax of phonemes) and of lexical frequency. It also mentions possible 'islands of reliability' (for expressions such as *I think*) which might help oral production in that learners may use these as 'buying time' devices or structuring features. The analysis also indicates different learning patterns for some sets of phonemes (with /u/~/u:/ being acquired later than /i/~/i:/). An analysis of the perception and the categorization of the phonemic realizations by learners themselves was also carried out. The paper tests how accurately the data found is predicted by known Second Language Acquisition (SLA) theoretical frameworks such as Flege's Speech Learning Model (1995). The results of the study show that the assumptions fail to predict differences in learning patterns.

The last corpus presented in this section is rather innovative. The *Multilingual, Traditional, Immersion, and Native Corpus* (MulTINCo: Meunier, Hendrikx, Bulon, Van Goethem, & Naets, 2020) includes both learner and native data types. It contains:

- learner data for two target languages: Dutch and English;
- learners' spoken and written, longitudinal data collected in two different educational settings: Content and Language Integrated Learning – CLIL – and traditional foreign language classes;
- data produced by the same learners in their L1 (on similar task types);
- comparable native data from native speakers of the learners' L2 of about the same age;
- a variety of background variables (age, gender, home language, amount of L2 curricular and extracurricular input, etc.).

Van Mensel et al. (2020) explores the impact of formal and informal input on learners' variability in writing. It compares two target language conditions (Dutch and English) in two different instructed settings, namely Content and Language Integrated Language Learning (CLIL) and traditional foreign language learning classes (non-CLIL) in French-speaking Belgium. The study is part of a large project whose main objective is to investigate the influence of CLIL – and other educational, motivational, and cognitive factors – on the acquisition of a foreign language. Over 900 French-speaking primary and secondary school pupils learning English or Dutch in CLIL and NON-CLIL settings were followed longitudinally for two consecutive school years

(2015–2016 and 2016–2017) and various data types were collected. Using regression models to check whether the type and amount of input that learners are exposed to[6] correlate with proficiency levels, the study shows that CLIL is a significant predictor of L2 outcomes for both target languages, but that the relative impact of formal and informal input differs depending on the target language. The results also highlight the importance of the L2 status in research on CLIL, because different L2s can yield different results.

Future Directions

As illustrated in the *Core Issues and Topics* section, LCR has constantly questioned its role, methods, and goals, and has, as a result, evolved remarkably over the last 30 years. It is almost impossible to accurately predict what will lay ahead of us, say, in the next 30 years to come, but I have identified two promising areas.

The first one is related to the very status of LCR, which has always been considered as a product-oriented approach and which actually has the potential to combine both process and product orientations in the future. Mäntylä et al. (2018), for instance, show how the use of keystroke logging software (Strömqvist et al., 2006) cannot only help researchers better understand the writing process but also – and perhaps even more importantly here – lead to a reconsideration of what is actually perceived or stored in the learner's mind as a formulaic sequence (Wray, 2002). Previous LCR research on formulaic language focused on 'learner-external' sequences (viz. the linguistic patterns produced). The recording of keyboard activities during the writing process on computers gives researchers unprecedented access to 'learner-internal' patterns (Myles & Cordier, 2017). A careful analysis of the pauses between words, for instance, can reveal difficulties in accessing a formulaic sequence but also the fact that the suite of words considered as a formulaic sequence on the basis of learner-external patterns may not have psycholinguistic reality in the learner's internally stored holistic lexicon (Durrant, 2013). Studies like this one are only the first steps towards studies that integrate both product- and process-oriented approaches. New technologies and digital tools make it possible to record processing 'moves' which will, hopefully, be integrated in LCR in the future and hence help researchers revisit some of the LCR findings in a new perspective.

The second promising area is the interest in – and need for – collecting more interactive data types. Whilst some learner corpora already include samples of language in interaction (such as the Telekorp: Belz & Vyatkina, 2008), they still constitute a minority of the data types collected. The interactive nature of communication is being increasingly stressed in SLA circles, with a focus on ecological approaches (Kramsch & Vork Steffensen, 2008; Thorne, 2013) and multilingualism (May, 2013; Ortega, 2013). As explained by Van Lier (2010, p. 2) "Ecological approaches focus primarily on the quality of learning opportunities, of classroom interaction and of educational experience in general. Important pedagogical principles in an ecological approach are the creation of ecologically valid contexts, relationships, agency, motivation and identity". Such an approach calls for more attention to be paid to the ecological value of tasks given to learners. As for the multilingual turn, it puts multilingualism at the forefront, thereby opening up new avenues for intrinsically multilingual corpora where, for instance, learners from different mother tongues can interact and translanguage. Instead of the rather homogeneous corpora of L2'x' with only one 'x', one could collect learner corpora of L2'xs'. This focus on interaction is also found in pedagogical circles where official curricular documents clearly distinguish the features of spoken and written competences with or without interaction and also insist on the non-verbal strategies that are key to interactive competence. Learner corpora like the *Giessen-Long Beach Chaplin Corpus* (GLBCC: Jucker, Müller, & Smith, 2006) or the *Multimedia Adult ESL Learner Corpus*

(MAELC: Reder, Harris, & Setzer, 2003) should inspire future learner corpus collections. The GLBCC consists of transcribed interactions between native English, ESL, and EFL speakers. As for MAELC, it contains videotaped classroom interactions associated with written materials (copies of classroom written materials, student work, teacher logs, and teacher reflections). The corpus includes materials from four years of adult ESL classes ranging from beginning to upper-intermediate proficiency with over 3600 hours of classroom interaction recorded by six cameras and multiple microphones. The corpus has been partly coded for participation pattern and activity, and portions of these classes have been transcribed, targeting student language during pair work. As explained on the MAELC website "examinations of dyadic interaction can focus on interactions between students from different first language backgrounds as well as on developmental studies of individual students who are recorded throughout several terms of study". It is also of primary importance to reach out and collect data from less favored groups of learners (such as migrants) in order for LCR to be representative of all types of learners both in formal (instructed) and informal (non-instructed) contexts.

Further Reading

Fuchs, R., & Werner, V. (Eds.) (2018). Tense and aspect in second language acquisition and learner corpus research [Special Issue]. *International Journal of Learner Corpus Research*, *4*(2), 143–163.

This edited volume presents five studies addressing a topic that has received much attention in SLA, viz. tense and aspect. It provides a fresh LCR perspective on tense and aspect issues.

Granger, S., Gilquin, G., & Meunier, F. (Eds.) (2015). *The Cambridge handbook of learner corpus research*. Cambridge: Cambridge University Press.

This volume is the first handbook entirely devoted to LCR. It offers a detailed overview of the field and of the affordances of learner corpora.

Paquot, M., & Granger, S. (2012). Formulaic language in learner corpora. *Annual Review of Applied Linguistics*, *32*, 130–149.

This article focuses on the formulaic/phraseological nature of language, one of the key aspects of language that corpus-linguistic methodology has helped reveal.

Related Topics

Chapters 2, 6, 7, 8, 9, and 11.

Notes

1 Whilst instances of informal interactions may be more likely, few learners spontaneously decide to write an argumentative or literary essay.
2 Corpus data are ideally continuous (i.e. consisting of longer stretches of discourse, not single words, phrases or sentences) and contextualized (i.e. not produced in isolation but in the context of a meaningful, set task).
3 Centre for English Corpus Linguistics (date of access 24th September 2018): Learner Corpora around the World. Louvain-la-Neuve: Université catholique de Louvain. https://uclouvain.be/en/research-institutes/ilc/cecl/learner-corpora-around-the-world.html
4 See https://www.cambridge.org/us/cambridgeenglish/catalog/english-academic-purposes/grammar-and-beyond/
5 Put simply, the Bark Difference Metric Method improves acoustic measurements by making it possible to filter out physiological differences in pronunciation while retaining sociolinguistic differences.
6 Computed thanks to a proxy gathering various types of information collected through questionnaires on input type and frequency.

References

Ädel, A. (2008). Involvement features in writing: Do time and interaction trump register awareness? In G. Gilquin, S. Papp, & M. B. Díez-Bedmar (Eds.), *Linking up contrastive and learner corpus research* (pp. 35–53). Amsterdam: Rodopi.

Aijmer, K. (2009). *Corpora and language teaching*. Amsterdam: John Benjamins.

Axelsson, M. W. (2000). USE – The Uppsala student English corpus: An instrument for needs analysis. *ICAME Journal, 24*, 155–157.

Baayen, H., Davidson, D., & Bates, D. (2008). Mixed-effects modeling with crossed random effects for subjects and items. *Journal of Memory and Language, 59*(4), 390–412.

Belz, J., & Vyatkina, N. (2008). The pedagogical mediation of a developmental learner corpus for classroom-based language instruction. *Language Learning and Technology, 12*(3), 33–52.

Biber, D., Johansson, S., Leech, G., Conrad, S., & Finegan, E. (1999). *Longman grammar of spoken and written English*. Harlow: Pearson Education Limited.

Boersma, P. (2001). Praat, a system for doing phonetics by computer. *Glot International, 5*(9/10), 341–345.

Burnard, L., & McEnery, T. (Eds.) (2000). *Rethinking language pedagogy from a corpus perspective: Papers from the third international conference on teaching and language corpora*. Frankfurt: Peter Lang Publishing.

Callies, M. (2015). Learner corpus methodology. In S. Granger, G. Gilquin, & F. Meunier (Eds.), *The Cambridge handbook of learner corpus research* (pp. 35–56). Cambridge: Cambridge University Press. doi:10.1017/CBO9781139649414.003.

Callies, M., & Paquot, M. (2015). Learner corpus research: An interdisciplinary field on the move. *International Journal of Learner Corpus Research, 1*(1), 1–6. doi: 10.1075/ijlcr.1.1.00edi

Council of Europe. (2001). *Common European framework of reference for languages: Learning, teaching, assessment*. Cambridge: Cambridge University Press.

Cunnings, I. (2012). An overview of mixed-effects statistical models for second language researchers. *Second Language Research, 28*(3), 369–382.

Deshors, S. C. (2014). A case for a unified treatment of EFL and ESL: A multifactorial approach. *English World-Wide, 35*(3), 277–305.

Deshors, S. C., Götz, S., & Laporte, S. (Eds.) (2018). *Rethinking linguistic creativity in non-native Englishes* (Volume 98). John Benjamins Publishing Company.

De Smet, A., Mettewie, L., Galand, B., Hiligsmann, P., & Van Mensel, L. (2018). Classroom anxiety and enjoyment in CLIL and non-CLIL: Does the target language matter? *Studies in Second Language Learning and Teaching, 8*(1), 47–71. doi:10.14746/ssllt.2018.8.1.3

Durrant, P. (2013). Formulaicity in an agglutinating language: The case of Turkish. *Corpus Linguistics and Linguistic Theory, 9*(1), 1–38.

Ellis, R., & Barkhuizen, G. (2005). *Analysing learner language*. Oxford: Oxford University Press.

Flege, J. E. (1995). Second-language speech learning: Theory, findings and problems. In W. Strange (Ed.), *Speech perception and linguistic experience: Theoretical and methodological issues* (pp. 229–273). Timonium: York Press.

Fuchs, R., & Werner, V. (Eds.) (2018). Tense and aspect in second language acquisition and learner corpus research [Special Issue]. *International Journal of Learner Corpus Research, 4*(2), 143–163

Gentil, G., & Meunier, F. (2018). A systemic functional linguistic approach to usage-based research and instruction: The case of nominalization in L2 academic writing. In A. E. Tyler, L. Ortega, M. Uno, & H. I. Park (Eds.), *Usage-inspired L2 instruction. Researched pedagogy* (pp. 267–289). Amsterdam: John Benjamins.

Gilquin, G. (2015). From design to collection of learner corpora. In S. Granger, G. Gilquin, & F. Meunier (Eds.), *The Cambridge handbook of learner corpus research* (pp. 9–34). Cambridge: Cambridge University Press.

Gilquin, G., & Gries, S. (2009). Corpora and experimental methods: A state-of-the-art review. In G. Gilquin (Ed.), Corpora and experimental methods [Special Issue]. *Corpus Linguistics and Linguistic Theory, 5*(1), 1–26.

Granger, S. (1994). The learner corpus: A revolution in applied linguistics. *English Today, 10*(3), 25–33. doi:10.1017/S0266078400007665

Granger, S. (1996). From CA to CIA and back: An integrated approach to computerized bilingual and learner corpora. In K. Aijmer, B. Altenberg, & M. Johansson (Eds.), *Languages in contrast: Text-based cross-linguistic studies*. Lund studies in English (vol. 88, pp. 37–51). Lund: Lund University Press.

Granger, S. (2008). Learner corpora in foreign language education. In N. Van Deusen-Scholl & N. H. Hornberger (Eds.), *Encyclopedia of language and education* (vol. 4, pp. 337–351). Boston: Springer.

Granger, S. (2009). The contribution of learner corpora to second language acquisition and foreign language teaching: A critical evaluation. In K. Aijmer (Ed.), *Corpora and language teaching* (pp. 13–32). Amsterdam: John Benjamins.

Granger, S. (2015). Contrastive interlanguage analysis: A reappraisal. *International Journal of Learner Corpus Research, 1*(1), 7–24. doi: 10.1075/ijlcr.1.1.01gra.

Granger, S., Dagneaux, E., & Meunier, F. (2002a). *International corpus of learner English. Handbook and CD-ROM.* Louvain-la-Neuve: Presses universitaires de Louvain.

Granger, S., Dagneaux, E., Meunier, F., & Paquot, M. (2009). *International corpus of learner English. Version 2 (Handbook + CD-ROM).* Louvain-la-Neuve: Presses universitaires de Louvain.

Granger, S., Dupont, M., Meunier, F., Naets, H., & Paquot, M. (2020). International corpus of learner English. *Version 3* (Handbook + web interface). Louvain-la-Neuve: Presses Universitaires de Louvain.

Granger, S., Gilquin, G., & Meunier, F. (Eds.) (2015). *The Cambridge handbook of learner corpus research.* Cambridge: Cambridge University Press.

Granger, S., Hung, J., & Petch-Tyson, S. (Eds.) (2002b). *Computer learner corpora, second language acquisition and foreign language teaching.* Amsterdam: John Benjamins.

Gries, S. (2009). What is corpus linguistics? *Language and Linguistics Compass, 3*(5), 1225–1241. doi:10.1111/j.1749-818X.2009.00149.x

Gries, S. (2013). Statistical tests for the analysis of learner corpus data. In A. Diaz-Negrillo, N. Ballier, & P. Thompson (Eds.), *Automatic treatment and analysis of learner corpus data* (pp. 287–310). Amsterdam: John Benjamins.

Gries, S. (2015). Statistics for learner corpus research. In S. Granger, G. Gilquin, & F. Meunier (Eds.), *The Cambridge handbook of learner corpus research* (pp. 159–182). Cambridge: Cambridge University Press. doi:10.1017/CBO9781139649414.008

Huat, C. M. (2012). Learner corpora and second language acquisition. In K. Hyland, C. M. Huat, & M. Handford (Eds.), *Corpus applications in applied linguistics* (pp. 191–207). London: Continuum.

Jäschke, K. (2016). *The dative alternation in English as a second language.* PhD dissertation. Düsseldorf: Heinrich-Heine-Universität. Retrieved from https://d-nb.info/1135382433/34

Jucker, A., Müller, S., & Smith, S. (2006). *GLBCC (Giessen - Long Beach Chaplin Corpus).* Oxford text archive. Retrieved from http://hdl.handle.net/20.500.12024/2506. See also http://ota.ox.ac.uk/desc/2506.

Kramsch, C., & Vork Steffensen, S. (2008). Ecological perspectives on second language acquisition and socialization. In N. H. Hornberger (Ed.), *Encyclopedia of language and education* (pp. 2595–2606). Boston: Springer.

Longman Dictionary of Contemporary English (Fifth edition). (2009). Harlow: Pearson Education Limited.

Mäntylä, K., Lahtinen, S., Vaakanainen, V., & Mäkilä, M. (2018). Using keystroke logging to analyse the writing process – tools for teaching writing. *EuroCALL 2018* (book of abstracts, p. 27), Jyväskylä, August 22.

May, S. (Ed.) (2013). *The multilingual turn: Implications for SLA, TESOL, and bilingual education.* London: Routledge.

McCarthy, M. (2008). Accessing and interpreting corpus information in the teacher education context. *Language Teaching, 41*(4), 563–574.

McEnery, T., Xiao, R., & Tono, Y. (2006). *Corpus-based language studies: An advanced resource book.* London: Routledge.

McIntosh, C. Cambridge Advanced Learner's Dictionary. (2008). Cambridge: Cambridge University Press.

Méli, A. (2013). Phonological acquisition in the French–English interlanguage: Rising above the phoneme. In A. Díaz-Negrillo, N. Ballier, & P. Thompson (Eds.), *Automatic treatment and analysis of learner corpus data* (pp. 207–226). Amsterdam: Benjamins.

Meunier, F. (2010). Learner corpora and English language teaching: Checkup time. *Anglistik: International Journal of English Studies, 21*(1), 209–220.

Meunier, F. (2015). Developmental patterns in learner corpora. In S. Granger, G. Gilquin, & F. Meunier (Eds.), *The Cambridge handbook of learner corpus research* (pp. 379–400). Cambridge: Cambridge University Press.

Meunier, F. (2016). Introduction to the LONGDALE project. In E. Castello K. Ackerley, & F. Coccetta (Eds.), *Studies in learner corpus linguistics: Research and applications for foreign language teaching and assessment* (pp. 123–126). Berlin: Peter Lang Publishing. Retrieved from https://uclouvain.be/en/research-institutes/ilc/cecl/longdale.html

Meunier, F. (2018). Promoting TPACK and professional learning communities: Focus on teaching and learning multiword units. *EuroCALL*, Jyväskylä, August 23. doi:10.13140/RG.2.2.26823.14244. Retrieved from https://www.researchgate.net/publication/327237628_Promoting_TPACK_and_professional_learning_communities_focus_on_teaching_and_learning_multiword_units_EuroCALL_conference_paper_Jyvaskyla_Finland_2X_August_2018

Meunier, F., Hendrikx, I., Bulon, A., Van Goethem, K., & Naets, H. (2020). MulTINCo: Multilingual traditional immersion and native corpus. Better-documented multi-literacy practices for more refined SLA studies. *International Journal of Bilingual Education and Bilingualism*. DOI: 10.1080/13670050.2020.1786494

Meunier, F., & Littré, D. (2013). Tracking learners' progress: Adopting a dual 'corpus cum experimental data' approach. *The Modern Language Journal*, *97*(1), 61–76.

Mukherjee, J. (2009). The grammar of conversation in advanced spoken learner English: Learner corpus data and language-pedagogical implications. In K. Aijmer (Ed.), *Corpora and language teaching* (pp. 203–230). Amsterdam: John Benjamins.

Myles, F., & Cordier, C. (2017). Formulaic sequences (FS) cannot be an umbrella term in SLA: Focusing on psycholinguistic FSs and their identification. *Studies in Second Language Acquisition*, *39*(1), 3–28. doi:10.1017/S027226311600036X

Ortega, L. (2013). SLA for the 21st century: Disciplinary progress, transdisciplinary relevance, and the bi/multilingual turn. *Language Learning*, *63*(1), 1–24.

Paquot, M., & Granger, S. (2012). Formulaic language in learner corpora. *Annual Review of Applied Linguistics*, *32*, 130–149.

Paquot, M., & Plonsky, L. (2017). Quantitative research methods and study quality in learner corpus research. *International Journal of Learner Corpus Research*, *3*(1), 61–94.

Ployhart, R. E., & Vandenberg, R. J. (2010). Longitudinal research: The theory, design, and analysis of change. *Journal of Management*, *36*(1), 94–120.

Raudenbush, S. W., & Bryk, A. S. (2002). *Hierarchical linear models: Applications and data analysis methods* (2nd ed.). Thousand Oaks: Sage Publications, Inc.

Reder, S., Harris, K., & Setzler, K. (2003). A multimedia adult learner corpus. *TESOL Quarterly*, *37*(3), 65–78. Retrieved from http://www.labschool.pdx.edu/maelc_access.html.

Römer, U. (2009). Corpus research and practice: What help do teachers need and what can we offer? In K. Aijmer (Ed.), *Corpora and language teaching* (pp. 83–98). Amsterdam: John Benjamins.

Shirato, J., & Stapleton, P. (2007). Comparing English vocabulary in a spoken learner corpus with a native speaker corpus: Pedagogical implications arising from an empirical study in Japan. *Language Teaching Research*, *1*(4), 393–412.

Strömqvist, S., Holmqvist, K., Johansson, V., Karlsson, H., & Wengelin, Å. (2006). What keystroke logging can reveal about writing. In K. P. H. Sullivan & E. Lindgren (Eds.), *Computer keystroke logging and writing: Methods and applications* (pp. 45–71). Amsterdam: Elsevier.

Tan, M. (2005). Authentic language or language errors? Lessons from a learner corpus. *ELT Journal*, *59*(2), 126–134.

Thorne, S. (2013). Language learning, ecological validity, and innovation under conditions of superdiversity. *Bellaterra Journal of Teaching and Learning Language and Literature*, *6*(2), 1–27.

Tognini-Bonelli, E. (2001). *Corpus linguistics at work*. Amsterdam: John Benjamins.

Van Lier, T. (2010). The ecology of language learning: Practice to theory, theory to practice. *Social and Behavioral Sciences*, *3*, 2–6.

Van Mensel, L., Bulon, A., Hendrikx, I., Meunier, F., & Van Goethem, K. (2020). Effects of input on L2 writing skills in English and Dutch: CLIL and non-CLIL learners in French-speaking Belgium. *Journal of Immersion and Content-Based Language Education*. DOI: 10.1075/jicb.18034.van

Wilson, J. (2013). *Technology, pedagogy and promotion. How can we make the most of corpora and data-driven learning (DDL) in language learning and teaching?* The Higher Education Academy. Retrieved from https://www.heacademy.ac.uk/system/files/corpus_technology_pedagogy_promotion2.pdf

Wray, A. (2002). *Formulaic language and the lexicon*. Cambridge: Cambridge University Press.

4

Introduction to SLA

Jennifer Behney and Emma Marsden

Introduction

The field of second language acquisition (SLA), a relatively new field of academic study, traces its roots only to the second half of the last century. Yet, in these few decades, as technological advances have increased the means by which processes of SLA can be investigated, research has flourished around the basic question of how one acquires another language after having acquired the first. SLA has an overarching goal of understanding the nature of second language (L2) knowledge, and the processes through which it is developed and used. Another goal of SLA is to gain an understanding of how learners store L2 knowledge and how this is similar to and different from other speakers of the same language, such as monolinguals from birth, bilinguals, and heritage speakers. SLA also attempts to explain the role that social context plays in constructing an L2 and how interaction, input (the language that learners hear and read), and output (learners' productions in speech and writing) affect acquisition of the L2. As the field has developed, different approaches to understanding SLA have arisen reflecting the various epistemological assumptions and methodologies of the traditions that have given rise to these approaches (Kasper & Ross, 2018). Thus, there is not one unified theory of SLA, but rather various theories that differ in how they account for, and the data they use to measure, acquisition. SLA researchers have been gathering and analyzing learner 'output' since the beginning of the field. Although some researchers have referred to such data as a corpus, it is only recently, as electronic corpora have become more available to researchers, that corpus linguistics, learner corpus research, and SLA have begun to intersect. These developments have also included the creation and use of corpora of the language that learners are (likely to be) exposed to (their 'input'), whether in naturalistic contexts or classrooms.

In order to have a better understanding of SLA, it is necessary to first define the common terminology used in the discipline. We will use the term *second language acquisition* (SLA) to refer both to the field of study and the process of learners acquiring a new language. The term *L2* refers not necessarily only to a second language learned after the first in terms of chronology, but is often used as an umbrella term for any language used after the first has been acquired. The term *L2* is also used here to cover a wide range of contexts of use and learning. For example, it is used both for languages acquired as a foreign language (where the language being learnt is largely only experienced in the classroom or formal learning environments) and in a more naturalistic context where the language is spoken in the community where the learner is located (i.e., a 'second language' context). The term *native speakers* refers to those who have been exposed to and spoken a given language as their first or dominant language since infancy. *Learners* refers to those who are learning the language as an L2. In SLA research, there has been a tendency to compare learner performance on some task to that of, generally monolingual, native speakers of the language. This practice is increasingly criticized by some SLA researchers as unfair, deficit-based, unhelpful, and invalid (Ortega, 2013; cf. Granger, 2009). The terms *learning* and *acquisition* are used synonymously in this chapter, and by many SLA researchers, with the most notable exception being that of early work by Krashen (1985) that differentiated between the two terms.

The field of SLA has roots in various disciplines and areas of study, including the fields of child first language (L1) acquisition, linguistics, psychology, and language pedagogy. In the mid-20th century, behaviorist psychological theories greatly influenced thinking about how children learn their L1 and, by extension, how learners learn foreign languages. Language learning was seen by some as an environmentally-dependent process of stimulus and response, of positive reinforcement and conditioning, of repetition and habit formation. In the 1960s, Chomsky (1959, 1968) claimed that language acquisition was not simply a matter of imitating what is heard in the environment, but rather the result of a biologically preprogrammed module in the mind, the language acquisition device, innate to the human species, which provides a blueprint for human grammars. In addition, findings emerged that influenced the way linguists thought about acquisition, such as instances of children overgeneralizing regular forms to irregular verbs (e.g., *goed* for *went*) and supplying correct morphology on invented words (Berko Gleason, 1958). This indicated that learners were applying the rules of the language they were learning in novel ways. The focus of SLA theories shifted to defining the nature of and access to an inborn, biological endowment for creating language.

A central question driving much early SLA research was how to explain the incomplete and 'errorful' nature of learning an L2. Strongly behaviorist-informed theories would posit that language learning, like all learning, was a question of habit formation, whereby L2 acquisition could be argued to be a process of substituting one set of habits, the L1, with a new set of habits, the L2. The Contrastive Analysis Hypothesis claimed errors that L2 learners made could be largely predicted by L1-L2 differences. However, it became clear that learners do not, in fact, always make the errors that were predicted by L1-L2 differences; instead, they make some errors that were not predicted by the nature of their L1, and importantly, learners from different L1s make some broadly similar errors that are not clearly or consistently determined by the nature of L1-L2 differences alone. These findings led researchers such as Corder (1967) to propose that learners' errors were not indicative of a set of L1 conditioned habits to be eradicated, but rather important evidence of the learner's developing system, or interlanguage. Interlanguage is defined as the learner's language system which can be distinct from both the L1 and the L2 systems, a system "which results from a learner's attempted production of a target language norm," (Selinker, 1972, p. 214). This idea took on great importance in SLA in the 1970s and continues to do so today. This perspective was, in part, informed by a series of studies showing that learners moved through a developmental sequence of acquisition of grammatical morphemes in English, both in the case of L1 acquisition (Brown, 1973) and in the case of L2 acquisition (e.g., Dulay & Burt, 1974). These studies drew on early corpora of learner production data that were analyzed for shifts over time from non-target-like to more target-like forms.

But the field was still lacking explanations for the kinds of L2 development that were being observed. Krashen's Monitor Model (1985) was an early attempt to apply Chomsky's innatist theories to the field of SLA. Krashen's Monitor Model has been credited with three important contributions to the field. First, the Input Hypothesis, which called for the provision of comprehensible input to learners, placed a focus on the significance of input, and this focus continues to the present in SLA theory-building. Second, the Affective Filter Hypothesis increased awareness of the importance of affect in learning and continues to play an important role in research on some individual differences in SLA (differences that exist between learners). Third, Krashen re-oriented researchers' attention to distinctions between different types of knowledge that are gained and used in language learning. Again, questions around this issue, and in particular around the contribution of awareness and explicit knowledge about L2 to L2 learning, still reverberate today in SLA research.

A central question emerging from this thinking about language acquisition was whether language knowledge is acquired by and held in a language-specific 'module' of the brain (as suggested by Chomsky), and/or whether more general learning and memory mechanisms are involved. An important tenet of Chomskyan linguistic models is that an innate language faculty is a biologically preprogrammed endowment and that the child must be exposed to input from the language during a critical period of development during which language acquisition must take place and after which it cannot occur to the same degree or in the same way. Because of cases of feral and neglected children who were not exposed to L1 input before puberty and who never developed native-speaker-like L1 grammars, linguistic innatist researchers argued that language learning (L1 or L2) after the critical period had closed would lead to a lack of native-speaker-like language ability. This proposal was partly what drove much SLA research of the 1970s and 1980s to focus on age effects on L2 learning, with studies investigating how the age of acquisition of the L2 affected the learners' ultimate attainment and native-like proficiency.

This interest in explaining differences between L1 and L2 learning by appealing to the different ages at which L1s and L2s are learnt clearly continues in much current research. However, the type of explanations offered have broadened over the last couple of decades to include accounts of learning that do not necessarily assume a biologically determined linguistic innate module. Many researchers, as will be described in the next section, became concerned with other explanations of differences between L1 and L2 acquisition and accounts of learning that draw on general cognitive (rather than language-specific) mechanisms. Such general learning mechanisms include 'statistical learning', 'priming', language processing, attention, and memory systems, such as working, declarative, and procedural memory (see Mitchell, Myles, & Marsden, 2019). Researchers have argued that such mechanisms, also 'innate', may change through the life-span, with individuals drawing on them differently as they age, thus potentially accounting for age effects in language learning. SLA researchers have also focused on how the 'outside world' (e.g., the nature and amount of input, social interaction, and practice opportunities) and individuals' varying needs and motivations to communicate meaning can influence learning processes. Thus, SLA has moved well beyond a one-sided focus on learner internal mechanisms, be they linguistic or cognitive.

This theoretical diversity is reflected in current empirical SLA research, including in corpus-based approaches. We now move on to introducing some of the key concerns that have emerged from these basic viewpoints and come to preoccupy the field, as well as particular SLA perspectives discussed more fully in Section 3 of the Handbook.

Core Issues and Topics

A central question in SLA has grown out of the observation that whereas L1 acquisition is marked by successful outcomes that are thought to represent a common 'core' among all native speakers (e.g., grammatical, lexical, and sound systems that are reliably successful and stable by the time children reach puberty), L2 acquisition is marked by notable differences in ultimate attainment of learners (i.e., some learners become near-native speakers of the L2 whereas others achieve no functional proficiency in the L2). Why is L2 acquisition unlike L1 acquisition in terms of ultimate attainment? Revolving around this central question, and perhaps linked to effects of age mentioned above, other concerns relate to what learners know about their L2 and the kinds of representations they hold, how they store the L2 in their minds, and the processes that they undergo as they interpret and produce it. Another question is how the L1 influences the acquisition and use of the L2. Equally important is the question of how interaction, input, and output affect learners' acquisition of the L2 and how the use and acquisition of the L2 is dependent on social context and individual differences between learners. These questions form the basis of the core issues in the field, and to illustrate the central role such questions continue to have, a new cluster of studies and state-of-the-art discussions on these topics have recently been published (Andringa & Dabrowska, 2019).

Differences between L1 and L2 Ultimate Attainment

A great deal of SLA research has concentrated on differences between L1 and L2 acquisition in terms of ultimate attainment. Much of this research, particularly in the first two or three decades of SLA, focused on the nature of the proposed innate language learning faculty and the logical problem of language learning described by Chomsky. The logical problem of language learning stated that there is a 'poverty of the stimulus' in that L1 input that children receive is low in quantity, particularly for certain grammatical constructions, is often of poor quality, and is relatively free of negative evidence (i.e., the stating of what cannot be said in the language), and therefore could not possibly be responsible for all that children intuitively know about their L1 (Slabakova, 2016). According to this view, the child is born with access to a Universal Grammar (UG), or principles that constrain all natural languages, and upon the provision of language input, the child's innate language faculty will set the parameters (rules and constraints) of the particular language that he/she is acquiring (Chomsky, 1968).

In this tradition, generativist SLA researchers have investigated whether L2 learners have access to UG, whether there is a Critical Period, or periods, for language acquisition, and whether learners who were no longer in the Critical Period of development for language acquisition could still acquire the L2 in a native-speaker-like way, or more specifically, which aspects of language could be acquired to a native-speaker-like degree of proficiency after the closing of the Critical Period. Theories such as the Fundamental Difference Hypothesis (Bley-Vroman, 2009), the Failed Functional Features Hypothesis (Hawkins & Chan, 1997), and the Representational Deficit Hypothesis (Hawkins & Casillas, 2008; Hawkins & Liszka, 2003) held that L2 learners lacked complete access to UG and were therefore unable to acquire syntactic features or morphological forms that were present in the L2 but lacking in the L1, like verbal tense marking or grammatical gender agreement marking. Other theories of L2 acquisition are based on the argument that L2 learners do still have access to UG even after the Critical Period and that nonnative-like levels of ultimate attainment are due to other issues (e.g., the Full Transfer Full Access theory [Prévost & White, 2000] and the Missing Surface Inflection hypothesis [Prévost & White, 2000]). All of these theories were generativist attempts to answer the question of why L2 acquisition is not marked by the same relatively uniform outcomes as L1 acquisition. (See Chapter 16, this volume, for more about formal/generative approaches, and see Hulstijn, 2019 for alternative views about the notion of uniform outcomes for L1 acquisition.)

Cognitive Theories of Learner L2 Knowledge

Another question that has guided much SLA research is how far can the nature of L2 knowledge and L2 learning be explained by general learning mechanisms? Unlike the theories mentioned above, which assumed there is a language-specific faculty in the mind, many cognitive-based researchers argue that language learning is much like any other learning that human beings do. This learning is not thought to be dependent on one grammar-specific blueprint in the brain, but it is thought to draw on mechanisms and systems that humans are endowed with at birth (just as with generativist perspectives). In this section, we outline key subgroups of SLA research that draw on, to varying extents, general learning mechanisms: Emergentism and Usage-Based approaches (proposing a largely implicit and statistical learning process, with a wide range of views on the 'units' or grain-size of representations of knowledge), Skill Acquisition approaches (proposing memory-based information processing model of how knowledge becomes automatized), and processing-based accounts (proposing limits in attentional and processing capacities, e.g., Processability Theory).

Some SLA researchers argue that learning is based on experience of language usage. Emergentist (Constructivist, or Usage-Based) SLA theories are grounded on the idea that learning takes place through processing of the L2 input, so that through the exposure to particular items and combinations in the input, connections form in the mind that, through frequency of usage and salience, become stronger over time. The learner tallies the frequency of occurrence of particular items and their combinations and calculates (without awareness) the probability of a particular construction being connected with a particular function or meaning (Ellis, 2007; Ellis, Römer, & McDonnell, 2016).

Other theories of SLA are based on the assumption that the mind has limited capacity systems. Cognitive resources that can be dedicated to attending to, processing, and storing linguistic (and other) material are limited. Through repeated exposure to linguistic input and practice, cognitive resources can be freed up and dedicated to other material. In Information Processing models of SLA (widely referred to as Skill Acquisition), there is a distinction between the processing of automatized knowledge, which does not require a great deal of cognitive resources and can take place whilst doing other tasks, and controlled processing of a different kind of knowledge, which requires more cognitive resources. Knowledge, according to Skill Acquisition Theory (DeKeyser, 2007), is of two types: declarative, or "knowledge that", and procedural, or "knowledge how" (p. 98). Whereas declarative knowledge is effortful and requires greater cognitive resources to access and use, procedural knowledge 're-packages' that knowledge into a different type of representation. This procedural knowledge can, if given sufficient practice, be retrieved with decreasing cognitive effort, increasing accuracy and speed (more fluency). With practice, this procedural knowledge results in highly skilled behavior which draws on automatized knowledge. Critically, it is different in nature and held in a different memory system to declarative knowledge. Once automatized knowledge has been established in the procedural memory system, the declarative knowledge that was originally held may no longer be accessible, or it might draw on cognitive resources to access it, thus perhaps rendering the task at hand less fluid or effective.

In sum, the cognitive perspectives presented in this section present strong inter-linking arguments about (a) what drives language development (due to progression being driven by learners freeing up cognitive resources, through automatization of knowledge and then being able to pay attention to other areas of language that require controlled processing), (b) why certain language features might be more difficult to learn than others (due to their frequency, saliency, communicative usefulness), (c) why certain combinations of L1 and L2 may cause particular, predictable learning problems (due to L1–L2 differences and similarities), and (d) why some learners may have more difficulty than others in learning second languages (due to differences in their cognitive systems involved in learning, such as memory, attention, and statistical learning capacity, particularly when learning happens after a certain age and/or in instructed contexts). For more about usage-based approaches specifically, and their application in corpus-based research, see Chapter 13, this volume.

L2 Storage, Retrieval, and Processing

A core issue of SLA is an understanding of how learners access the L2 as it is represented in their minds along with the associated lexical, grammatical, and conceptual information. Thus, researchers have made hypotheses about how L2 learners process input and access their existing representations of the L2. For example, Anderson's One to One Principle (1984) described a simplification procedure through which lower proficiency L2 learners associate one form with one meaning. Bates and MacWhinney's early Competition Model proposed how learners rely on (sometimes conflicting) syntactic (such as word order) and lexical (such as animacy) cues to interpret sentences in the L2 (1981). More recently, MacWhinney's Unified Competition Model (2008) proposed in more detail how these cues can be re-weighted over time and are in flux with experience (including that of other languages, such as the L1). Processability Theory (PT) also assumes a limited capacity linguistic processor and claims that L2 learners follow developmental sequences of acquisition for producing grammatical features such as English questions. The order of these sequences is thought to be determined by the ease or difficulty with which certain elements of sentences can be processed, or their *processability* (Pienemann, 1999). See Chapter 15, this volume, for more about Processability Theory.

Much recent SLA research into learner processes reflects a greater emphasis on L2 'online' processing (i.e., moment-to-moment comprehension while listening and/or reading the L2). Such researchers investigate, for example, the extent to which learners are sensitive to L2 grammar online (see section "The Relationship between Linguistic Knowledge and Language Processing," pp. 108–109, Mitchell, Myles, & Marsden, 2019). As described above, many of these researchers are also interested in the nature of L2 knowledge and ultimate attainment, and the effects of age, exposure, and L1 influence, but in contexts where learners do not have time to reflect on the language as it is experienced in real time. The findings from this line of research can usefully complement those from corpus-based research, which of course focuses on written or spoken 'offline' production. Researchers often use both online and offline measures in order to gather a more complete picture; for example, see research conducted on the SPLLOC and CEDEL2 learner corpora (e.g., Dominguez, Tracy-Ventura, Arche, Mitchell, & Myles, 2013; Lozano & Mendikoetxea, 2013; Mitchell, Dominguez, Arche, Myles, & Marsden, 2008).

Role of Interaction, Input, and Output in Learning

A great deal of research in SLA since the early 1980s has investigated the role that L2 interaction has in acquisition. One of the core issues addressed by interactionist research is whether interaction between learners and more proficient learners or native-speakers that contains modified input (which is marked by slower, more enunciated, repetitive speech and more questions) is facilitative of acquisition (Gass & Mackey, 2007). For example, research on L2 interaction has investigated the usefulness of interaction including clarification requests (e.g., *Sorry?*), confirmation checks (e.g., *Do you mean X?*), comprehension checks (e.g., *Do you know what I mean?*), and recasts (e.g., learner uses *goed* and the interlocutor might provide *went*). Interactive negotiation such as this has been referred to as negative evidence and its role, mainly in the classroom but also in more natural learning environments, has been widely investigated (Gass & Mackey, 2007). Long (1996) claimed in the Interaction Hypothesis that this negotiation of meaning in L2 interaction "facilitates acquisition because it connects input, internal learner capacities, particularly selective attention, and output in productive ways" (p. 452). The Output Hypothesis focused on this last part of the equation, proposing that input is necessary for acquisition, but it is not sufficient (Swain, 1985). Learners must be pushed to produce the language because this forces them to process the L2 syntactically, as they have to produce the language that expresses their needs most precisely and efficiently (rather than a so-called 'semantic' type of processing which is minimally required for comprehension and can be done by a cognitively mature listener by using a range of linguistic, discourse and situational cues). Schmidt's Noticing Hypothesis (Schmidt, 2001) stated that it was necessary (or, later, that it was at least helpful) for learners to notice (with consciousness) a linguistic feature in the input. Other researchers have proposed the idea that in order for learning to occur, it is important for learners to notice a 'gap' between the form that they hear or read in the input and what they currently have stored in their minds.

In their totality, these ideas led to a great deal of interactionist-oriented SLA research on the role of attention and awareness in L2 acquisition, as well as on the contribution of interlocutor feedback to L2 development. Certainly, native-speaker corpora, including data from interactions, provide a rich source of target-like forms for comparison with learner corpora, and for the design of pedagogically relevant materials (Granger, 2009). Interactionist research has been particularly concerned with classroom L2 learners and has made important contributions to the understanding of "instructed SLA", with some corpora specifically of classroom interaction being created and analyzed. See Chapters 19 and 21, this volume, for more about this research tradition.

Role of Social Context in SLA

Another important question for SLA researchers is how the social context in which language is learned affects acquisition. Sociocultural SLA researchers argue that language learning does not take place in a vacuum, so focusing only on what occurs in the minds of individual learners presents an incomplete picture of SLA. Sociocultural researchers point out that language takes place in social situations and that communication is created between participants. Sociocultural approaches to SLA are usually based on Vygotskian theory which asserts that language is a cultural artifact that differentiates humans from other animals (just like literacy, numeration, and intentionality) and foregrounds the notion that language can be used to mediate one's environment. Higher-order mental functions like language are organized in cultural activities. Imitation and internalization lead to language development, which like all learning, occurs in a zone of proximal development, a metaphorical space where a novice (i.e., the language learner) and an expert (i.e., a native speaker or a more experienced learner) co-construct language, and the novice is able to do more with the language than he/she is able to do on his/her own. Language is seen as closely intertwined with thought, and learners' thoughts are closely related to internalized private speech that develops from the social speech that learners co-construct in social interaction (Lantolf & Thorne, 2007).

Other research has shown concern for the wider context in which language acquisition takes place and less focus on individual learners' cognition. Some have adopted frameworks such as Conversation Analysis, which takes a very detailed approach to describing L2 interaction and longitudinal L2 change (Lee & Hellermann, 2014; Pekarek Doehler & Fasel Lauzon, 2015). Systemic Functional Linguistics and Language Socialization Theory (Duff, 2011; Williams, 2017) have all given a decidedly more social turn to the previously heavily individual-focused study of SLA. Functional approaches to explaining SLA emphasize how the learner's need to convey meaning (rather than specific linguistic or cognitive constraints) can determine L2 development and explain L2 interlanguage phenomena, such as learners' use of topic-comment patterns, pragmatic principles of presenting old then new information, and narration following chronological event order (see Dimroth, 2018 for a recent example). The study of L2 pragmatics (Eskildsen & Kasper, 2019) and learning in the wild, that is outside of the classroom or the laboratory (Kasper & Burch, 2016), has also contributed to a more socially-oriented SLA agenda. See Chapter 18, this volume, for more about pragmatic and functional approaches.

Many of the topics and perspectives we have covered here so far lend themselves to corpus-based research, and so are relevant to this book. However, they have (also) been investigated using a very wide range of research designs and methods, to which we now turn.

Main Research Methods

The types of research design, methods and tools used in SLA are closely related, although certainly not confined, to particular theoretical perspectives.

Design types of SLA studies include experimental, descriptive, cross-sectional, and longitudinal designs. Many types of linguistic data are gathered, such as samples of learner and native speaker elicited and spontaneous production, from laboratory, classroom, study abroad, and naturalistic settings. Of obvious relevance to the current book is that these learner productions can be gathered together into collections, or corpora, of language data. And indeed, SLA researchers have been collecting L2 learner production data since the beginning of the field, even if they were collected on a relatively small scale and often manually coded without the support of computer programs and the generalizability of large-scale corpora. Other linguistic data include judgment data, that is, learner intuitions about language. Researchers also increasingly collect processing data (e.g., reaction times, eye-tracking) and neurolinguistic data (e.g., event-related potentials and functional magnetic resonance imaging). Non-linguistic information is also used in SLA research, such as data from tests of working memory capacity, data about motivation and attitudes from questionnaires and interviews, or think-aloud data from learners' introspections about their own learning, attention, or awareness (Bowles, 2010). See Mackey and Gass (2016) for a general introduction to a range of research methods.

Some researchers, for example from interactionist approaches, consider that spontaneous production, particularly spoken and, more recently, written during online computer-based communication, provides one of the most valid windows into learners' language systems, as learners are attempting to communicate meaning, often under time pressure. This kind of elicitation technique underpins much of corpus-based research in SLA. For example, researchers administer elicitation measures where learners are encouraged to tell the plot of a story or movie, to converse or exchange information with a partner, or to write a composition. In this way, the researcher has data about learner productions that are similar to spontaneously or naturally produced output. (Whether or not such specially-elicited data can be considered as an authentic learner corpus is still a matter for discussion: Granger, 2002; Lozano & Mendikoetxea, 2013; Tono, 2016).

Episodes of L2 interaction, between a native speaker and a learner or between two learners, containing instances of negotiation of meaning, modified input, and negative evidence such as corrective feedback, are also paramount research evidence within the interactionist framework. Such studies have been conducted in the laboratory (e.g., Mackey, Gass, & McDonough, 2000) and classroom (e.g., Swain & Lapkin, 1998). Tasks are used that encourage interaction such as picture description tasks (where one participant describes to another a picture that he/she cannot see but must recreate) and spot the difference tasks (where the participants have slightly different pictures and must discuss them to find the differences between them). Examples of learner corpora that used such tasks include Marsden, Myles, Rule and Mitchell (2002) and Mitchell et al. (2008). See Chapter 21, this volume, for more about the use of corpora in interactionist approaches.

Some research conducted on L2 interaction has reflected a much more sociocultural approach and is typically more qualitative in nature. Conversation Analysis studies have analyzed L2 interaction for evidence of factors such as alignment (e.g., Atkinson, Churchill, Nishino, & Okada, 2007), turn-taking, and repair. Other Conversational Analysis studies have provided longitudinal investigations into L2 interaction and development (Eskildsen & Theodórsdóttir, 2015; Pekarek Doehler & Fasel Lauzon, 2015). Corpora of L2 interaction data examined using Conversational Analysis provide meticulous detail of verbal and non-verbal communication, albeit limited to few research participants.

More recent SLA research conducted within a cognitivist approach has been designed to provide online measures of processing and interpretation of the L2 and has thus shifted somewhat away from the analysis of naturalistic corpora. This includes measuring the speed of learners' reactions to linguistic stimuli, as learners read or listen to target language input, both grammatical and ungrammatical, with data presentation techniques such as self-paced reading (or moving windows) (see Avery & Marsden, 2019 for a synthesis and meta-analysis). The use of eye-tracking in SLA has become more prevalent in the past 10 years, and the number of studies conducted with this methodology has been steadily increasing (see Godfroid & Winke, 2018).

In addition, some recent neurolinguistic studies have used electroencephalography (EEG) to measure event-related potentials whilst exposing learners to the L2; others have used functional magnetic resonance imaging. However, some cognitivist researchers continue to test their ideas on learner corpora (e.g. the work of Ellis, Romer, & O'Donnell, 2016 on the learning of construction grammar).

SLA researchers have also relied on non-linguistic measures of learner characteristics to address important questions about how L2 acquisition is affected by differences between individual learners. Researchers have utilized measures of working memory (e.g., digit span and reading span tasks), language proficiency tests, language aptitude tests, and questionnaires about motivation, attitudes and identity. Such data can be combined with data from corpora to provide rich insights into how a range of factors affect language development (e.g., Siyanova-Chanturia & Spina, 2020; see also Chapter 9, this volume).

As noted above, production data are often viewed as a highly valid window into L2 learner systems (interlanguage), whether these data are transcripts of speech, the actual speech itself, or written language. Having learner productions available via electronic corpora has provided the field with a highly efficient research resource. Researchers can increasingly use existing corpora of L2 learner production to ask new questions, thereby decreasing the time, expense, and effort involved in such studies. The large numbers of tokens of items of interest, with some corpora containing millions of words, mean that researchers have a much greater data pool than that obtained via many other methods.

In addition to the benefits of the *amount* of data, corpora also bring other benefits, especially when they are accompanied by additional meta-data (i.e. information *about* the data themselves), and searchable tags or codes that are linked to the language. The various kinds of corpora, of different genres of production (e.g., written or oral, monologic or dialogic) with different learner characteristics (e.g., L1-L2 combinations, proficiencies, backgrounds, ages) enable the SLA researcher to investigate a wide range of phenomena, covering many of the questions and topics introduced in the first sections of this chapter. Corpora can be 'tagged' or coded for particular features of interest (e.g., about phonology, turn-taking, morphosyntax, or the lexicon – see Chapter 6, this volume), which can then be searched easily. This means that the data can be used for investigating, essentially, any theoretical perspective, from generative theory (e.g., Rule & Marsden, 2006) to usage-based theories (Ellis, Römer, & O'Donnell, 2016), and variationist perspectives (Gudmestad, Edmonds, & Metzger, 2019). As evidenced by the growing interest in the use of corpora in SLA, special issues on this topic have been published by journals such as *Language Learning* (2017) and *The Modern Language Journal* (2013). Corpora are particularly central to usage-based theories of language acquisition, as they can provide data about both the input that learners are exposed to and learners' productions, enabling detailed calculations about relationships between frequency in the input and output.

Representative Corpora and Research

One important corpus in the history of SLA is the European Science Foundation (ESF) Corpus, consisting of immigrant speech representing six different L1s and five different target languages, following uninstructed (i.e., naturalistic) adult learners in the 1980s (Perdue, 1993). Research on this corpus led Klein and Perdue to propose the existence of a Basic Variety in the learner's interlanguage before the learner develops a more complex version of the L2 with finite verbs (1997) (see Dimroth, 2018 for a recent extension of this research drawing on a classroom corpus of input data).

Other key L2 corpora include those found on the SLABank of Talkbank (MacWhinney, 2017 – see Chapter 13, this volume), a collection of corpora of learners of various L2s, including English, Spanish, Mandarin, French, German, Czech, and Hungarian and made up of over

4 million words. MacWhinney calls for the inclusion of more learner corpora in the SLABank and for researchers to make use of the existing data in the collection in his "vision for a shared infrastructure that can harvest and store data of this type for the advancement of SLA theory and practice" (2017, p. 254).

The *French and Spanish Learner Language Oral Corpora* (Marsden, Myles, Rule & Mitchell, 2002; Mitchell et al., 2008) are both freely available on SLA Bank. FLLOC contains oral production data from school-age classroom learners of French of various ages and SPLLOC contains spontaneous and elicited oral productions from L2 Spanish learners of different proficiency levels. Both corpora use CHILDES software and have facilitated a great deal of research. For example, Rule and Marsden (2006) investigated the development of negation in finite and non-finite verbs using FLLOC data, whereas Dominguez, Tracy-Ventura, Arche, Mitchell, and Myles (2013) used both SPLLOC and experimental data to investigate the Lexical Aspect Hypothesis in L2 Spanish.

Future Directions

Future research in SLA is likely to continue to make increasing use of existing L2 corpora, and as suggested by MacWhinney (2017) and other proponents of open science (e.g. Marsden, Mackey, & Plonsky, 2016; Marsden, 2020), SLA researchers should make corpora openly available. Corpus researchers were, in fact, at the forefront of the open science movement, often making their datasets freely and openly available, thus enhancing the transparency of researchers' work and SLA theory building. The gathering of vast collections of learner production in open repositories can only serve to help researchers develop and test their explanations of how individuals acquire languages after they have acquired their first. However, to allow others to use these datasets effectively, it is imperative that researchers describe their corpora in terms of how they were collected and the learners' characteristics. (See Bell, Collins, & Marsden, in press, for discussion about some of the challenges and decisions required when building a corpus of young learner language, for example.) Ideally, in addition to such basic metadata, corpora should also be tagged with codes that allow a range of features of the language to be searched and examined, an endeavor that the research community can contribute to collectively.

The field of SLA would benefit from the compilation and analysis of corpora consisting of not just L2 learner and monolingual native speaker data for comparison purposes, but also of data from bilingual and multilingual speakers and heritage language users. Similarly, corpora can provide us with a clearer view of learner development through the compilation of more longitudinal corpora (Ellis, 2017). In order to advance SLA theory and our understanding of some of the core issues of ultimate attainment, learner knowledge and mental representations, and the role of interaction in L2 development discussed earlier in the chapter, a wide variety of L1s, L2s, LXs, and proficiency levels must be represented in future corpora.

Finally, as with other types of SLA research, future directions in L2 corpora research should focus on methodology and the question of study quality and reporting (e.g., of effect sizes, precise p values, assumptions required for particular statistical tests) (Paquot & Plonsky, 2017).

Further Reading

Gass, S., Behney, J., & Plonsky, L. (2020). *Second language acquisition: An introductory course* (5th ed.). New York: Routledge.

This book provides a comprehensive introduction to the field of SLA and the history of the discipline.

Mitchell, R., Myles, F., & Marsden, E. (2019). *Second language learning theories* (4th ed.). Abingdon: Routledge.

This book examines, synthesizes, and evaluates a wide range of families of theories that are related.

Related Topics

All of the chapters in Sections 3 and 4 (Chapters 13–30).

References

Andersen, R. (1984). The one-to-one principle of interlanguage construction. *Language Learning, 34*(4), 77–95.

Andringa, S., & Dąbrowska, E. (2019). Individual differences in first and second language ultimate attainment and their causes. *Language Learning, 69*, 5–12.

Atkinson, D., Churchill, E., Nishino, T., & Okada, H. (2007). Alignment and interaction in a sociocognitive approach to second language acquisition. *The Modern Language Journal, 91*(2), 169–188.

Avery, N., & Marsden, E. J. (2019). A meta-analysis of sensitivity to grammatical information during self-paced reading: Towards a framework of reference for reading time effect sizes. *Studies in Second Language Acquisition, 41*(5), 1055–1087.

Bates, E., & MacWhinney, B. (1981). Second language acquisition from a functionalist perspective: Pragmatic, semantic and perceptual strategies. In H. Winitz (Ed.), *Annals of the New York academy of sciences conference on native and foreign language acquisition* (pp. 190–214). New York: New York Academy of Sciences.

Bell, P., Collins, L., & Marsden, E. J. (in press). Building a leaner corpus to address the instructional needs of L2 language learners in compulsory school programmes. In M. Paquot & B. Le Bruyn (Eds.), *Learner corpus research meets second language acquisition*. Cambridge: Cambridge University Press.

Berko Gleason, J. (1958). The child's learning of English morphology. *Word, 14*, 150–177.

Bley-Vroman, R. (2009). The evolving context of the fundamental difference hypothesis. *Studies in Second Language Acquisition, 31*(2), 175–198.

Bowles, M. (2010). *The think-aloud controversy in language acquisition research*. New York: Routledge.

Brown, R. (1973). *A first language: The early stages*. Cambridge: Harvard University Press.

Chomsky, N. (1968). *Language and mind*. New York: Harcourt Brace Jovanovich.

Chomsky, N., & Skinner, B. F. (1959). Review of B. F. Skinner. *Verbal Behavior Language, 35*(1), 26–58.

Corder, S. P. (1967). The significance of learners' errors. *International Review of Applied Linguistics, 5*, 161–170.

DeKeyser, R. (2007). Skill acquisition theory. In B. VanPatten & J. Williams (Eds.), *Theories in second language acquisition: An introduction* (pp. 97–113). London: Routledge.

Dimroth, C. (2018). Beyond statistical learning: Communication principles and language internal factors shape grammar in child and adult beginners learning Polish through controlled exposure. *Language Learning, 68*(4), 863–905.

Domínguez, L., Tracy-Ventura, N., Arche, M., Mitchell, R., & Myles, F. (2013). The role of dynamic contrasts in the L2 acquisition of Spanish past tense morphology. *Bilingualism: Language and Cognition, 16*(3), 558–577.

Duff, P. A. (2011). Second language socialization. In A. Duranti, E. Ochs, & B. Schieffelin (Eds.), *Handbook of language socialization* (pp. 564–586). Chichester: Wiley Blackwell.

Dulay, H. C., & Burt, M. K. (1974). Natural sequences in child second language acquisition. *Language Learning, 24*(1), 37–53.

Ellis, N. C. (2007). The associative-cognitive creed. In B. VanPatten & J. Williams (Eds.), *Theories in second language acquisition: An introduction* (pp. 77–95). London: Routledge.

Ellis, N. C. (2017). Cognition, corpora, and computing: Triangulating research in usage-based language learning. *Language Learning, 67*(S1), 40–65.

Ellis, N. C., Römer, U., & O'Donnell, M. B. (2016). Usage-based approaches to language acquisition and processing: Cognitive and corpus investigations of construction grammar. *Language Learning, 66*(S1), 1–358.

Eskildsen, S. W., & Kasper, G. (2019). Interactional usage-based L2 pragmatics. In N. Taguchi (Ed.), *The Routledge handbook of second language acquisition and pragmatics* (pp. 176–191). Abingdon: Routledge.

Eskildsen, S. W., & Theodórsdóttir, G. (2015). Constructing L2 learning spaces: Ways to achieve learning inside and outside the classroom. *Applied Linguistics, 38*(2), 143–164.

Gass, S., Behney, J., & Plonsky, L. (2020). *Second language acquisition: An introductory course* (5th ed.). New York: Routledge.

Gass, S., & Mackey, A. (2007). Input, interaction, and output in second language acquisition. In B. VanPatten & J. Williams (Eds.), *Theories in second language acquisition: An introduction* (pp. 175–199). London: Routledge.

Godfroid, A., & Winke, P. (2018, March 25). *One tool, many applications: Robust eye-tracking research across SLA disciplines*. Colloquium presented at the American Association of Applied Linguistics (AAAL) conference. Chicago.

Granger, S. (2002). A bird's-eye view of learner corpus research. In S. Granger, J. Hung, & S. Petch-Tyson (Eds.), *Computer learner corpora, second language acquisition and foreign language teaching* (pp. 3–33). Amsterdam: John Benjamin.

Granger, S. (2009). The contribution of learner corpora to second language acquisition and foreign language teaching. A critical evaluation. In K. Aijmer (Ed.), *Corpora and language teaching* (pp. 13–32). Amsterdam: John Benjamins Publishing Company.

Gudmestad, A., Edmonds, A., & Metzger, T. (2019). Using variationism and learner corpus research to investigate grammatical gender marking in additional language Spanish. *Language Learning, 69*(4), 911–942.

Hawkins, R., & Casillas, G. (2008). Explaining frequency of verb morphology in early L2 speech. *Lingua, 118*(4), 595–612.

Hawkins, R., & Chan, C. (1997). The partial availability of Universal Grammar in second language acquisition: The 'failed functional features hypothesis'. *Second Language Research, 13*(3), 187–226.

Hawkins, R., & Liszka, S. (2003). Locating the source of defective past tense marking in advanced L2 English speakers. In R. van Hout, A. Hulk, F. Kuiken, & R. Towell (Eds.), *The interface between syntax and lexicon in second language acquisition* (pp. 21–34). Amsterdam: John Benjamins.

Hulstijn, J. H. (2019). An individual-differences framework for comparing nonnative with native speakers: Perspectives from BLC theory. *Language Learning, 69*, 157–183.

Kasper, G., & Burch, A. R. (2016). Focus on form in the wild. In R. A. van Compernolle & J. McGregor (Eds.), *Authenticity, language, and interaction in second language contexts* (pp. 198–232). Bristol: Multilingual Matters.

Kasper, G., & Ross, S. J. (2018). The social life of methods: Introducing the special issue. *Applied Linguistics Review, 9*(4), 475–486.

Klein, W., & Perdue, C. (1997). The Basic Variety (or: Couldn't natural languages be much simpler?). *Second Language Research, 13*(4), 301–347.

Krashen, S. D. (1985). *The Input Hypothesis: Issues and implications*. Reading: Addison-Wesley Longman Ltd.

Lantolf, J., & Thorne, S. (2007). Sociocultural theory and second language learning. In B. VanPatten & J. Williams (Eds.), *Theories in second language acquisition: An introduction* (pp. 77–95). London: Routledge.

Lee, Y. A., & Hellermann, J. (2014). Tracing developmental changes through conversation analysis: Cross-sectional and longitudinal analysis. *TESOL Quarterly, 48*(4), 763–788.

Long, M. H. (1996). The role of the linguistic environment in second language acquisition. In W. Ritchie & T. Bhatia (Eds.), *Handbook of second language acquisition* (pp. 413–468). San Diego: Academic Press.

Lozano, C., & Mendikoetxea, A. (2013). Learner corpora and second language acquisition: The design and collection of CEDEL2. In A. Díaz-Negrillo, N. Ballier, & P. Thompson (Eds.), *Automatic treatment and analysis of learner corpus data* (pp. 65–100). Amsterdam: John Benjamins.

Mackey, A., & Gass, S. (2016). *Second language research: Methodology and design* (2nd ed.). New York: Routledge.

Mackey, A., Gass, S., & McDonough, K. (2000). Learners' perceptions about feedback. *Studies in Second Language Acquisition, 22*(4), 471–497.

MacWhinney, B. (2008). A unified model. In P. Robinson & N. Ellis (Eds.), *Handbook of cognitive linguistics and second language acquisition* (pp. 341–371). Mahwah: Lawrence Erlbaum Associates.

MacWhinney, B. (2017). A shared platform for studying second language acquisition. *Language Learning, 67*(S1), 254–275.

Marsden, E. (2020). Methodological transparency and its consequences for the quality and scope of research. In J. McKinley & H. Rose (Eds.), *The Routledge handbook of research methods in applied linguistics* (pp. 15–28). New York: Routledge.

Marsden, E., Mackey, A., & Plonsky, L. (2016). The IRIS repository: Advancing research practice and methodology. In A. Mackey & E. Marsden (Eds.), *Advancing methodology and practice: The IRIS repository of instruments for research into second languages* (pp. 1–21). New York: Routledge.

Marsden, E., Myles, F., Rule, S., & Mitchell, R. (2002). Using CHILDES tools for researching second language acquisition. In S. Sarangi & T. van Leeuwen (Eds.), *Applied linguistics & communities of practice British studies in applied linguistics* (pp. 98–113). London: Continuum.

Mitchell, R., Dominguez, L., Arche, M., Myles, F., & Marsden, E. (2008). SPLLOC a new database for Spanish second language acquisition research. *EUROSLA Yearbook, 8*(1), 287–304.

Mitchell, R., Myles, F., & Marsden, E. (2019). *Second language learning theories* (4th ed.). Abingdon: Routledge.

Ortega, L. (2013). SLA for the 21st century: Disciplinary progress, transdisciplinary relevance, and the bi/multilingual turn. *Language Learning, 63*, 1–24.

Paquot, M., & Plonsky, L. (2017). Quantitative research methods and study quality in learner corpus research. *International Journal of Learner Corpus Research, 3*(1), 61–94.

Pekarek Doehler, S., & Fasel Lauzon, V. (2015). Documenting change across time: Longitudinal and cross-sectional CA studies of classroom interaction. In N. Markee (Ed.), *The handbook of classroom discourse and interaction* (pp. 409–424). Chichester: Wiley Blackwell.

Perdue, C. (Ed.) (1993). *Adult language acquisition: Field Methods* (vol. 1). Cambridge: Cambridge University Press.

Pienemann, M. (1999). *Language processing and second language development: Processability theory.* Amsterdam: John Benjamins.

Prévost, P., & White, L. (2000). Missing surface inflection or impairment in second language acquisition? Evidence from tense and agreement. *Second Language Research, 16*(2), 103–133.

Rule, S., & Marsden, E. (2006). The acquisition of functional categories in early French second language grammars: The use of finite and non-finite verbs in negative contexts. *Second Language Research, 22*(2), 188–218.

Schmidt, R. (2001). Attention. In P. Robinson (Ed.), *Cognition and second language instruction* (pp. 3–32). Cambridge: Cambridge University Press.

Selinker, L. (1972). Interlanguage. *International Review of Applied Linguistics, 10*(1–4), 209–231.

Siyanova-Chanturia, A., & Spina, S. (2020). Multi-word expressions in second language writing: A large-scale longitudinal learner corpus study. *Language Learning, 70*(2), 420–463.

Slabakova, R. (2016). *Second language acquisition.* Oxford: Oxford University Press.

Swain, M. (1985). Communicative competence: Some roles of comprehensible input and comprehensible output in its development. In S. Gass & C. Madden (Eds.), *Input in second language acquisition* (pp. 235–253). Rowley: Newbury House.

Swain, M., & Lapkin, S. (1998). Interaction and second language learning: Two adolescent French immersion students working together. *The Modern Language Journal, 82*(3), 320–337.

Tono, Y. (2016). What is missing in learner corpus design? In M. Alonso-Ramos (Ed.), *Spanish learner corpus research: Current trends and future perspectives* (pp. 33–52). Amsterdam: John Benjamins.

Williams, G. (2017). Language socialization: A systemic functional perspective. In P. A. Duff & S. May (Eds.), *Encyclopedia of language and education: Language socialization* (3rd ed., pp. 33–47). Cham: Springer International Publishing.

PART II
KEY ASPECTS IN CORPUS DESIGN AND CORPUS USE FOR SLA

Designing Learner Corpora

Collection, Transcription, and Annotation

Philippa Bell and Caroline Payant[1]

Introduction

Researchers from the field of Second Language Acquisition (SLA) address a range of empirical questions to understand the nature of language and to uncover the processes underlying its development after first language (L1) acquisition. At the beginning of SLA theorizing, usually situated in the 1960s with seminal work by Selinker (1972) and Corder (1967), among others, researchers focused primarily on predicting learner errors. Today, SLA researchers have moved towards the investigation of the nature of language at various stages in terms of interlanguage development. To achieve a wide variety of SLA research objectives, it is necessary to elicit representative learner data that exemplify underlying systems of knowledge over time from learners of diverse L1 backgrounds acquiring various second languages (L2). SLA researchers have often drawn on limited language samples to test hypotheses in controlled experiments. However, certain SLA objectives may be better addressed with larger datasets that can also generate hypotheses for future testing. The field of Learner Corpus Research (LCR) has a rich tradition in doing just this, and the possibilities for collaboration have been pointed out over the past fifteen years (Myles, 2005, 2008) and are gaining ground based on collaborative work (Le Bruyn & Paquot, in press; Chapter 1, this volume).

This increased interest in combining the expertise of SLA and corpus linguistic researchers has led to questions concerning methodologies at all stages of corpora building and use (Paquot & Plonsky, 2017). Publications addressing general corpora design exist (e.g., Gilquin, 2015; Granger, 2008), and publications formalizing methodological decisions relating to design, collection, and transcription of specific learner corpora are on the rise (Bell, Collins & Marsden, in press; Lozano & Mendikoetxea, 2013; Tono, 2003, 2016). To add to this knowledge base, the objective of the present paper is to discuss variables of importance for designing, collecting, and transcribing corpora by drawing on LCR and SLA expertise in order to facilitate the sharing and use of large sets of learner language.

Core Issues and Topics

Defining Learner Corpora

Learner corpora can be defined as "electronic collections of natural or near-natural data produced by foreign or second language (L2) learners and assembled according to explicit design criteria"

(Granger, Gilquin, & Meunier, 2015, p. 1). This widely-used definition raises a number of que-ries when applied to the field of SLA[2]. The notion of *(near-)naturalness* has been scrutinized, as its boundaries are difficult to define. Some researchers consider only real-life tasks to constitute natural language use (Long, 2014); some corpora are classified as corpora by the researchers but include extremely controlled tasks such as reading a text aloud (Atwell et al., 2003). The term *learner* may also be problematic given that researchers can be interested in language users, and extant corpora have included (some) data from contexts more akin to language use than to language learning (e.g., *The European Science Foundation Second Language Database*, Perdue, 1993). L2 speakers may also identify themselves as a learner or user depending on what they are doing with the language at any given moment and their perceived target language profi-ciency. Additionally, the term *second* language is likely erroneous for a majority of individuals contributing to learner corpora as many are learners/users of multiple languages. The umbrella term *second language* has raised concerns within third/additional language (L3/Lx) circles, and researchers are advocating for more transparency in this regard (De Angelis, 2007). This should be of equal concern to LCR endeavors. Finally, a corpus ought to be representative of the target language variety (a specific learner population, Paquot & Plonsky, 2017), which links to its size (200,000 is the requirement for different language data sets in ICLE, for example). However, if design criteria are published and good metadata are available for each corpus, size becomes less important, as researchers have sufficient information to understand its representativeness and its possibilities for examining various dimensions of interlanguage development (see for example, the Markee corpus, Markee, 2000). Furthermore, size in itself is not a clear marker of representa-tiveness, as the number of participants needs to be considered, as does any information pertaining to possible instructions requiring participants to produce texts of a certain length (sample size), because this information undermines the principle of representativeness (Sinclair, 2005).

These observations motivate the need to be critical in how we define learner corpora for SLA research, which necessitates the expansion of existing boundaries. A learner corpus for SLA purposes is an electronic collection of learner produced data formatted for automatic analyses, elicited from L2 or L3/Lx learners or users that provides essential metadata, details critical infor-mation on elicitation tasks, and is built around explicit and published design criteria.

Documentation of Metadata

Metadata (background information) refers to all data aside from language samples (the corpus) collected from participants (e.g., learners' age, gender, proficiency level, language background). To increase the rigor, transparency, and usability of learner corpora, collecting and publishing substantial metadata (including how the metadata were collected) is essential (Gilquin, 2015; Tono, 2003). Its availability determines the suitability of a corpus for addressing its initial and any subsequent research objectives, which creates opportunities to advance knowledge through international collaborations. Creating a fixed list of essential metadata is difficult, as many types of data require separate questionnaires/tests, which when not required for the initial research objectives, may seem onerous in terms of time and budget. However, certain data should always be collected to ensure correct analysis and for interpreting any counter-intuitive results (Sinclair, 2005). Researchers typically report basic information, such as age and gender. However, several additional variables must also be reported.

A proficiency measure should always be included regardless of its requiring time to administer. In the past, proficiency has been classified as the number of years of exposure, age, institutional status, or by the data contained in the corpus (e.g., ICLE), which are all problematic (Hasko, 2013; Meunier & Littre, 2013), and researchers now encourage the use of external proficiency measures (Tono, 2003; Tono & Díez-Bedmar, 2014). For the English language, the Oxford Quick Placement Test, available for different age groups, is quick and easy to administer. For other languages, there are more limited options, but as demonstrated by Lozano and Mendikoetxea with Spanish learners (2013) through their use of self-proficiency ratings alongside a standardized placement test readily available online from the University of Wisconsin, this is changing. Furthermore, the database for Second Language Research Instruments (IRIS) also contains many measures that have been widely-employed with different populations (Marsden, Mackey, & Plonsky, 2016).

Advances in L3/Lx theorizing show that previous language learning experiences influence interlanguage development and metalinguistic knowledge (Jessner, Megens, & Graus, 2016). Therefore, researchers should also gather data concerning knowledge of all other languages used or studied by the learner, namely, mother tongue(s), home language(s), instructed additional language(s), extensive living-abroad experiences. Whereas proficiency tests must be included for the target language and should ideally be used for other language experience, uncovering details of the target population through self-report is a practical means of gathering metadata on previous language learning experiences that could help to explain certain interlanguage phenomena in a corpus (Marian, Blumenfeld, & Kaushanskaya, 2007).

An in-depth description of the environment and available resources in which the data were produced is key. At a minimum, we should know the type of institution(s) where the data were produced. Furthermore, detailing whether learners conducted prior research to inform their text's content, received training on the target genre, produced the text at home or at school, and/or utilized physical writing tools that may have mediated the contents (e.g., dictionaries, spellcheckers) is necessary. It is also essential to divulge information pertaining to the process in terms of feedback opportunities from peers and/or teachers and the amount of time dedicated to the process, as these are key for understanding the naturalness of the task and the likelihood that the participants were focused on making meaning and/or focusing on form.

Obtaining Consent

Differences with regard to consent exist across contexts, but erring on the side of caution by obtaining informed consent from each participant is good practice as it permits a corpus to be exploited for initial and future research objectives by researchers internationally. Dividing consent on the form (consent 1 = specific objectives; consent 2 = later endeavors including international collaborations) is useful as it augments the likelihood that participants understand to what they are consenting. The consent form should also outline the anonymous and confidential nature of all sharing to augment the probability of recruiting participants, and to ensure its usability in international contexts.

Piloting the Data Collection Process

Lacking a clear plan can lead to data that are of limited use to L2 researchers (Granger, 2012), thus the importance of piloting the data collection process. Aside from ensuring tasks are appropriate in terms of interest and difficulty, it can also uncover potential issues. For example, piloting by Bell et al. (in press) demonstrated that the prompts used to elicit a written narrative included a gender bias, which led to reduced opportunities for production of gendered determiners and pronouns to arise naturally in their written texts. Although these features were not specifically addressed in their objectives (the corpus followed Sinclair's principle of content selection, as the content was driven by its communicative function rather than linguistic choices), adapting the prompts permitted many more potential opportunities for well-known challenges to be included.

Piloting is also useful for demonstrating that the planned design and data collection protocol are understood by those involved and carried out accordingly. For example, during oral interviews, some research associates provide more language support than others (which is problematic for later analyses as priming may have occurred), which can be flagged before actual data collection begins. The decided means of organizing participants for oral interviews may not work if, for example, they need to move from room to room. This could lead to the decision to hire an extra research associate to organize the participants.

Lastly, the effects of piloting on the final design and composition of a corpus should form part of its published (accessible) documentation for the following reasons. Firstly, it makes certain design choices comprehensible. For example, Bell et al. (in press) allowed the use of L1 words to fill L2 lexical gaps (as they could not use dictionaries) during piloting, but learners were asked to put these words in quotation marks. However, students inconsistently adopted this practice, which added a layer of subjectivity to transcription (see discussion below) and thus the protocol was revised before data collection. Secondly, it helps researchers understand the number and type of decisions needed for corpus building. Finally, this information allows researchers to better understand the utility of this corpus for other research objectives, thus potentially reducing the workload for other researchers.

Designing a Learner Corpus

Designing a valid learner corpus requires consideration of design principles, which have been discussed in LCR and corpus linguistics (Sinclair, 2005, Tono, 2016). Discussing these principles is outside the scope of the present paper, and thus, the following information pertains to corpus issues specific to SLA/LCR research with reference, when relevant, to principles of import. In designing a corpus, careful selection, documentation, and justification of all criteria will increase the likelihood that the resulting corpus is methodologically-sound.

Text Selection Criteria

When building a corpus, one could focus on external criteria that permit contents selected only based on communicative function ("the sorts of documents that people are writing and reading, and the sorts of conversations they are having", Sinclair, 2005, p. 1), or internal criteria that allow a priori decisions relating to language (type of language) to shape the corpus's contents. From a corpus linguistic perspective, building a corpus by focusing on internal criteria decreases its authenticity, and therefore, using external criteria is a recommended practice. Specifically, texts are selected for their communicative functions (e.g., argumentative, expository) rather than linguistic features. Extending this notion to learner corpora, the aim is to include natural or near-natural data produced by learners in various language learning situations (Granger, Gilquin, & Meunier, 2015).

In SLA, researchers rely heavily on introspective methods and experimental data elicitation techniques (Myles, 2015). These practices are desirable because, compared to eliciting natural language, they increase the probability for the production of a target linguistic construction and highlight what learners know (or do not know) about said structure (Mackey & Gass, 2005). Furthermore, many open-ended elicitation tasks selected to highlight certain features (e.g., question formations in an interview task; past tense in a narration task; subjunctive mood in an advice column) also have the potential to elicit natural language.

For SLA/LCR endeavors, it is acknowledged that following external criteria can minimize potential biases in a corpus; however, the issue of underrepresentation arises, because not all texts elicit the same language, and other variables such as text length and text-topic can inadvertently lead to the underrepresentation, and surely overrepresentation, of particular forms (Caines & Buttery, 2017). As such, increasingly, a combination of elicitation techniques (see Chapter 10, this volume) is being used and researchers are making principled decisions regarding task variability and text types in the design of learner corpora (Tracy-Ventura & Myles, 2015) with the goal being to emphasize the importance of external criteria whilst accepting that some internal criteria can be useful for achieving research objectives. The example cited above (Bell et al., in press) concerning the elicitation task prompt that reduced the likelihood of eliciting kin-different possessive determiners is a good example of how internal criteria can be beneficial without reducing the corpus's representativeness.

Medium: Oral, Written, and Multimodal Corpora

The description of target language development rests largely on collections of oral and written language. The inclusion of both of these mediums, also referred to as mode or modality, is believed to be a valuable approach for capturing a global picture of language and its development given the unique cognitive demands each medium places on the learner (Kormos, 2014; Myles, 2015). Under time pressure, typically representative of oral tasks, learners may exhibit performance errors that may not be representative of their complete knowledge about the language. In the written medium, with additional time to process ideas and reflect on the language, fewer performance errors may occur. Although both oral and written texts provide a window into learners' interlanguages, unplanned oral data may be more representative of internalized rules compared to planned written data which provides evidence of a learner's system and ability to apply learned rules (when given enough time to plan and revise).

To date, existing corpora are largely written collections. The initial lack of oral corpora is likely due to the relative difficulty of collecting oral data (e.g., individual interviews, audio equipment, quiet spaces). Responding to the need for a more global picture of learners' interlanguage, we have witnessed a rise in the number of projects that are written representations of oral texts through transcription of audio files (see, e.g., Campillos Llanos, 2014; Tracy-Ventura, Mitchell, & McManus, 2016). These transcriptions are sometimes shared with their corresponding audio file and allow for phonetic studies. It is more common, however, to find unaccompanied transcripts, namely, mute spoken corpora (Ballier & Martin, 2015). These tend to lack fine-grained levels of annotation and given that the audio is frequently unavailable, only allow for lexical and syntactic feature analyses.

Newer types of corpora include signed language (Kotani, Yoshimi, Kotani, & Isahara, 2012) and multi-modal corpora, which are accompanied by video input permitting the analysis of gestures and gazes (Hashimoto & Takeuchi, 2012). SLA researchers, primarily from a Sociocultural Theory perspective, have demonstrated that native and native-like speakers will use gesture to co-express notions encoded in the language (e.g., manner and path of motion in verb constructions) (Lantolf, 2011). Learners, on the other hand, draw on gestures prior to producing oral output. The analysis of gestures in oral production tasks could thus contribute to our understanding of L2 development in unique ways.

Varied Genre in Learner Corpora

Genres are categories of texts that share similarities at rhetorical, organizational, and linguistic levels (Hyland, 2004). To date, the inclusion of diverse genres in LCR is limited with the argumentative essay being the most frequently documented genre (Callies, 2015). To ensure a balanced representation of learner interlanguage as genre dictates usage (e.g., historical present in narration), learner corpora should also include texts across genres to represent writing/speaking requirements across the fields of study (e.g. science, humanities).

SLA researchers draw on a range of genres to elicit learner language, including recounts, procedures, and descriptions. For instance, learners may be asked to discuss orally their first experience at the bank (recount) or detail the process of opening a new bank account (procedure). These different genres elicit unique linguistic constructions. SLA writing researchers also typically include production tasks ranging across genres, as this creates opportunities for the production of a target structure in a variety of communicative contexts. In trying to bridge SLA and LCR, researchers have attempted to include a variety of genres (i.e., task types) (Campillos Llanos, 2014; Tracy-Ventura & Myles, 2015). In his creation of an oral Spanish corpus, for example, Campillos Llanos (2014) collected oral output produced during three unique types of tasks, namely, a description task, story retelling task (using pictures), and opinion speech task with learners from nine different L1s. Each task targeted the production of morphology of the present and the past. In conducting this study, the researcher was interested in computer-aided error analysis and did not focus on the effects of genre type on interlanguage development. Nevertheless, these types of corpora open the door for subsequent analyses.

Text Elicitation Variables

The provision of information regarding the manner in which texts are elicited is critical for corpus building. One important variable is planning time, which has been demonstrated to impact various dimensions of written and oral texts in SLA research (Ellis & Yuan, 2004, 2005; Kormos, 2014). Another variable is the amount of time on task, as this provides information regarding learners' written or oral fluency. Learner corpora must also indicate whether the data reflect first or final drafts of written texts. Those texts which have gone through revisions will provide different information regarding learners' writing abilities compared to texts produced in-situ. The *Learner Corpus of Portuguese as Second/Foreign Language* (COPLE2) provides the students' original versions along with the teacher's edits (Mendes, Antunes, Janssen, & Gonçalves, 2016). Another dimension related to elicitation is whether learners have access to external sources to inform the content and language of their response: Dictionaries, grammar books, language processors, and source texts are all likely to impact textuality.

Learner Variables

Learner variables refer to all design criteria based on the learners who contribute to the corpus. Frequently, intrinsic criterion relates to the learners' age, socioeconomic status, and first/second/target languages. Aside from these, one may consider the construct of gender, as one would hope to have a fairly balanced contribution from male and female learners. Internal-affective measures may also play an important role. In contexts where a corpus is collected within an educational setting and forms a required task, a range in the level of motivation and attitude would be expected. In situations where individuals contribute on a voluntary basis, the corpus may not be representative of a learner population as those contributing may be more motivated or more confident in their L2 abilities (Gilquin, 2015). These trade-offs should be considered in the early stages of the corpus's design and all decisions should be reported, not necessarily controlled for.

Timeframe

The study of interlanguage development requires data from the same participant(s) (intra-individual) over an extended period of time. Longitudinal designs are ideal in that they are truly representative of an individual's development and can respond to diachronic research objectives. Yuldashev, Fernandez, and Thorne (2013), for example, examined the production of multi-word units from weekly blogs and instant messages written by learners of Spanish during 38 weeks of instruction. Academic constraints (e.g., long-term funding opportunities, necessity for timely publications) and associated risks of longitudinal data collection (e.g., attrition, context changes), however, may serve to explain why researchers collect cross-sectional or pseudo-longitudinal corpora. In fact, true longitudinal studies, such as Yuldashev et al., (2013) are the exception.

In LCR and SLA, learner corpora tend to capture interlanguage at a single point in time. To capture the evolution of language use, cross-sectional designs are encouraged such that data is collected from two or more groups that differ in terms of proficiency, at different times. These pseudo-longitudinal (or quasi-longitudinal) corpora can be used to capture development of interlanguage as data are collected from learners at different developmental stages as classified by an external variable such as a proficiency test or grade level. This can be problematic, as proficiency is not always measured in the same fashion and grade level within a school system does not reflect differences between students' proficiency which can vary greatly depending on external variables such as access to the target language outside the classroom (e.g., vacations, family members, neighborhood). Learners with additional intensive or naturalistic exposure to the target language are likely to further develop target language knowledge but will remain in their assigned grade level. Furthermore, despite certain inter-individual similarities, between-subject variation has been well-documented in SLA research (Lowie & Verspoor, 2015). Such pseudo-longitudinal data tend to treat language development as uniform, which creates the illusion that interlanguage development across learners is a stable and linear process (Ortega & Iberri-Shea, 2005).

Environment

Environment refers to the linguistic context in which a corpus is collected. In a second language context, language learners/users have access to and are exposed to the target language in mundane activities (e.g., grocery store, movie theatre). In foreign language contexts, opportunities are more restricted because the common context of target language use is the classroom (although note that in many FL settings, learners now have more access to certain target languages through cable TV and the internet, thus blurring the boundaries somewhat). Exposure and access to authentic target language may impact subsequent language production.

Main Research Methods

Learner Corpus Collection

In this section, practical information pertaining specifically to data collection will be discussed based on the design decisions presented above. The majority of points assume external help in terms of accessing data collection sites (e.g., teachers).

Data Collection Sites

In LCR, texts are often collected in classroom contexts given their accessibility. Classrooms, however, differ significantly across environments, and it is of utmost importance that classroom types and related activities be detailed. In addition to classrooms, some corpora have been built from essays on standardized tests or from on-line platforms. The choice of data collection site is often inherent to a corpus.

Recruitment

Researchers compile texts in a variety of ways – classrooms/schools, standardized test scores, on-line platforms. Each has different regulations with regard to access that must be understood beforehand to increase participation. For example, access to pupils may need to occur initially via a school board before teachers can be contacted, or access to university students may only be permitted outside of class time. Furthermore, it is at this point that the principle of representativeness whereby the corpus should represent the targeted language variety (Sinclair, 2005) needs to be considered, as this will affect recruitment.

Order of Data Collection Materials

Data collection always involves participants completing multiple documents. The order in which they are given is important for practical and research reasons. Consent forms should always come first, as it is unethical to collect data from those who do not consent. Furthermore, when collecting data from minors, parental consent is needed, and thus, consent forms need to be provided before data collection. After consent, any metadata that can affect the inclusion/exclusion of a participant should be collected. For example, a corpus of L1 English speakers should only include mother-tongue English speakers. An initial sociodemographic questionnaire can help ensure that data are not collected that cannot be analyzed. This point is most important if data collection requires one-on-one interviews.

If a number of tasks are being used to create the corpus, ideally, they should be completed in a counter-balanced design, a practice that is well established in experimental SLA designs. For example, if written argumentative and descriptive texts are being collected, asking half of the participants to provide the argumentative text first, and the other half the descriptive text first can help ensure the data collected from each genre is not affected overall by order.

Space and Equipment Needs

It is vital to understand the space requirements for the corpus's needs in order to ensure the proposed data collection sites will lead to successful data collection. Written data collection often unfolds in intact classrooms or laboratories, and it is important to ensure availability of computer labs or laptop computers if typed texts are wanted (this reduces transcription costs substantially). For oral data, a specific space may be needed. *The Learning Prosody in a Foreign Language* (LeaP) corpus (Gut, 2012) sought to capture prosodic features of L2 learners of German and English, so recordings had to be performed in a sound-treated chamber. This was necessary for the corpus to be valid, but is highly difficult to organize. The dearth of oral corpora when compared to written corpora justifies the collection of oral data in less ideal conditions if the research objectives are not linked to pronunciation. Nevertheless, researchers will still need access to extra rooms and reliable recording devices for oral data collection.

Equipment such as audio recording devices, lapel microphones, laptop computers, and speakers needs to be purchased and tested before collection, and all people collecting data need proper training. Equipment that is incorrectly used can have a large impact on data collection especially as the problem may not be picked up until data from many people have been collected (e.g., research associates allowing participants to touch the recording devices can mean all data from that/those day/s are unusable).

Other

When collecting data with the help of a third party, it is important that he/she has been informed of any design decision that he/she could inadvertently overturn. This is particularly important in classrooms when teachers may wish to explain instructions or help learners who raise their hands.

It is also important to bear in mind that participants are providing language samples in a language in which they may not feel comfortable. Discussing strategies for ensuring that participants feel comfortable throughout data collection with all research associates can help.

Learner Corpus Transcription

The collection of handwritten texts or oral texts involves the labor-intensive task of transcription. In recent learner corpus compilation projects, LCR researchers typically follow corpus linguistic guidelines on the importance of keeping the raw text produced by the learner (text format) separate from all annotation (information related to the text and its contained language; Sinclair, 2005). In SLA research, the Codes for the Human Analysis of Transcripts (CHAT) (MacWhinney, 2000) that integrate the texts and tags have frequently been used and recommended (MacWhinney, 2017; Myles, 2005). At this juncture, we invite researchers to work together to understand the advantages and disadvantages of the two different systems, which must consider the different programs that are currently available using these systems for automatic analyses. Unsurprisingly, the specific approach to data transcription should be in line with the research goals and for any medium, researchers will face transcription conundrums. In the case of handwritten texts, researchers will begin by transcribing the written production into digital formats. Transcriptions should be faithful to the original texts in the reproduction of errors, crossed out information, and in the formatting of texts. Perhaps one of the biggest challenges lies in the deciphering of poor penmanship. In trying to decipher what was written, there will be some subjective interpretation on the part of the transcriber, which can be reduced through verification and inter-coder reliability reporting (Mackey & Gass, 2005).

In the case of oral data, transcription is inevitable. There is a wealth of transcribing tools for researchers to select from, many of which are available at no cost online, and the appropriate one will be determined in light of the research objectives. For researchers interested in lexical analysis alone, using word processing tools may suffice; however, for close phonetic transcriptions and alignment, one may turn to specialized software (e.g., Praat, CLAN). For the most part, corpora rely on orthographic transcripts; however, there are some exceptions, such as the *Languages and Social Networks Abroad Project* (LANGSNAP) (Tracy-Ventura et al., 2016) and the aforementioned LeaP project (Gut, 2012). The LeaP project, which examined the acquisition of prosodic features by L2 learners of German and English, entailed a narrow transcription of several dimensions, namely stress, intonation, and speech rhythm. The transcribers participated in a three-month training process (approximately 8 hours per week). The allocated resources for this type are noteworthy. With oral texts, important decisions and subjective interpretations will also be made. Oral output is marked by reformulations, hesitations, repetitions, and false starts. Reformulations may in fact lead to target like constructions. Researchers will need to decide and report whether transcripts are true or whether they include reformulations only (elimination of original errors from the data). Drawing on SLA notions, identical transcripts would more closely reflect the learners' performance whereas transcripts that only include the reformulated construction would reflect their competence. In addition, researchers will have to make decisions regarding what they think they are hearing because learners' oral production is sometimes unclear, increasing ambiguities. For example, in the building of LANGSNAP and FLLOC, transcribers reported difficulties differentiating between the infinitive and the *imparfait* in some cases due to pronunciation being identical, and research demonstrating that infinitives are used as a default at the beginning of language development (Tracy-Ventura, personal communication). These decisions can influence the real and perceived errors. Transparency of these procedures is paramount for discussing language as a process or product.

Finally, researchers will want to become familiar with transcription conventions. One notable published handbook is the CHILDES project that offers detailed information about the CHAT transcription format (MacWhinney, 2000). Standardized conventions ensure consistency in the transcription of data and these transcripts can easily be converted into other formats (e.g., Praat, ANNIS, transcriber) increasing the potential for different types of analyses and possibilities for collaboration and corpora sharing.

Linguistic Annotation

It is often desirable to add linguistic annotation to a learner corpus. As mentioned by Granger (2004), "[w]hile a raw learner corpus is in itself a highly useful resource, it does not take long for the SLA/FLT researcher to realise that it would be even more useful if it contained an extra layer of information, which could also be counted, sorted and compared" (p. 128). Linguistic annotation makes it possible to retrieve linguistic items and patterns from the learner data that would otherwise be impossible to retrieve in large datasets, e.g. errors, grammatical categories such as prepositions or verbs, and grammatical patterns such as passive structures. Linguistic annotation can be done manually, automatically, or interactively.

Corpus tools such as UAM Corpus Tool (O'Donnell, 2012) or TEITOK (Janssen, 2016) often allow users to annotate corpora manually. One type of manual annotation that has enjoyed popularity in learner corpus research is error annotation (see Chapter 7, this volume), but there are potentially many other types of linguistic annotation that could usefully be added to a learner corpus (e.g. pragmatic and discourse annotation; see Chapter 18, this volume).

The most frequent type of automatic linguistic annotation in learner corpus research is Part-of-speech (POS) tagging. POS tagging involves assigning a label to each word that minimally identifies its word class (e.g. verb, noun, and adjective). POS tags also usually include some grammatical category information to distinguish more specific subclasses of words (e.g. different inflectional classes of verbs). Thus, sentence (1) is POS-tagged by CLAWS (http://ucrel-api.lan caster.ac.uk/claws/free.html) as represented in (2-3), where *issued*, for example, is identified as a lexical verb in past tense (VVD) and *condemning* is recognized as the *-ing* participle of a lexical verb (VVG).

1. *Several universities issued statements condemning the bill.*
2. C7 tagset, horizontal output:
   Several_DA2 universities_NN2 issued_VVD statements_NN2 condemning_VVG the_AT bill_NN1 ._.
3. C7 tagset, pseudo-xml output:
   <w id="2.1" pos="DA2">Several</w> <w id="2.2" pos="NN2">universities</w> <w id="2.3" pos="VVD">issued</w> <w id="2.4" pos="NN2">statements</w> <w id="2.5" pos="VVG">condemning</w> <w id="2.6" pos="AT">the</w> <w id="2.7" pos="NN1">bill</w> <w id="2.8" pos=".">.</w>

Automatic annotation tools can output annotated text in various formats. Sentences (2) and (3) are examples of inline or embedded annotation. A third type of format is multi-layer annotation, where the learner text and the annotations are represented in separate lines or layers (see Chapter 12, this volume, for examples using the CHAT system and Chapter 23 for a discussion of annotation format for error tagging; see also Gries & Berez, 2017, and Zeldes, in press for more detail about corpus architecture). The selection of format will typically depend on the range of annotations to be inserted in a corpus, the type of analyses to be conducted, and the tools that will be used to do so. For example, xml compliant corpora or multi-layered corpora will typically not be queried with the same tools.

The primary benefit of linguistically annotated learner corpora is that relevant annotations can support the identification of learner language use (e.g. articles, verbs in the past tense and verbs in the present tense, passive structures) and reduce the time required to analyze learner data. Fuchs and Werner (2018), for example, relied on a POS-tagged learner corpus to analyze the use of stative – progressives by school-aged learners of English (see Chapter 6, this volume, for more details).

However, studies based on an annotated learner corpus will only be as reliable as the annotations are accurate. For example, an accuracy rate of more than 90% is typical for POS tagging of general English, the most studied language, but this percentage will tend to decrease as the number of morpho-syntactic and orthographic errors increases (Nagata et al., 2011). There are two main approaches for dealing with learner errors when automatically annotating learner corpora.

The first one is to identify errors and formulate target hypotheses, i.e. minimal form changes that are required to turn the learner sentences into sentences which are well-formed in terms of the target language grammar, so that a corrected version of the learner data is subjected to further linguistic annotation (Meurers, 2015; Meurers & Dickinson, 2017; see also Chapter 7, this volume). However, as illustrated in Reznicek et al. (2013), the difficulty in identifying target hypotheses should not be underestimated. The second approach, i.e. not to correct learner data beforehand, has been used more in LCR for obvious practical time-related reasons. In some rare learner corpus compilation projects, POS tags are then checked and corrected, sometimes in an interactive way (e.g. Ragheb & Dickinson, 2013). Most of the time, however, they are not. In that case, it is extremely important to evaluate and report the accuracy of the automatic tools used, typically by means of a general accuracy score or precision and recall measures for specific word categories or syntactic structures (see Newman & Cox, in press).

For more details about POS-tagging and other forms of automatic linguistic annotation such as parsing, semantic, pragmatic, and discourse annotation, see Lu (2014). Also see Ballier and Martin (2015) for more information about the annotation of spoken learner corpora. For a comprehensive list of tools for corpus linguistics, including corpus annotation, see https://corpus-analysis.com/ and check keywords such as 'annotation', 'morphological tagger', 'POS tagger', 'parser', 'semantic parser', 'dependency parsing', etc.

Representative Corpora and Research

The majority of learner corpora focus on English, but to demonstrate the possibilities, existence, and importance of corpora building for other languages, two corpora for languages other than English are highlighted below.

A corpus targeting learners of Spanish is the *Spanish Learner Oral Corpus* (Campillos Llanos, 2014) which includes samples produced by learners from nine different linguistic backgrounds. The SLOC provides us with metadata including the participants' age and language background. While the learners' proficiency levels are reported, they are not the outcome of an independent placement test. The author explains that participant availability and time constraints precluded them from obtaining these scores. Another perceived limitation concerns the participants' language learning background. Information about additional language learning experiences are not reported. Despite these limitations, the author did provide information about the context (Erasmus students in Madrid). Information regarding consent and piloting were not provided. One of the major strengths of this project lies in the inclusion of diverse tasks covering multiple genres, albeit in the oral medium: learners participated in semi-spontaneous interviews, narrative and descriptive tasks. This small corpus includes 55,000 tokens; however, a perhaps more serious issue lies in the sample size because it included nine different L1s: each language is represented by a maximum of only four learners. Although the authors acknowledge this limitation, they argue that their corpus may be useful for pedagogical purposes.

The *Learner Corpus of Portuguese as Second/Foreign Language* (COPLE2) includes written and oral texts produced by 424 students of Portuguese (learning in Portugal) (Mendes, Antunes, Janssen, & Gonçalves, 2016). Their sample includes data produced in instructed and assessment contexts. The corpus includes various types of metadata: age, gender, L1, nationality, education level, knowledge of other languages, and proficiency, context of Portuguese program, length of stay in Portugal, and time studying Portuguese. These are important for sharing and subsequent research initiatives; however, the procedures for collecting learner proficiency data are unclear. In addition to the metadata, information specific to the written and the oral corpora is published. For the written corpus, information regarding the genre, the prompt/topic, the type of task (diagnostic test, formal test, homework), and text elicitation variables (with or without planning time or access to resources) was published. One of this corpus's strengths is that it covers not only the argumentative genre but includes informative texts, narrative texts, personal texts, letters, emails, and dialogues. The oral corpus is comparatively smaller with only 28 recordings from 54 participants. Recorded in the context of the proficiency of Portuguese as a foreign language test, these oral conversations typically included 2–3 learners. The researchers included information specific to this type of medium: duration of recording, location of the recording, quality of the recording, location of the recorder, degree of interaction, planning time, participation (role of researcher in elicited interaction), and the physical presence of the interlocutors (face-to-face, telephone, radio). Noteworthy aspects of this corpus include the provision of the original sound files and original handwritten texts for some of the data on the website: http://beta.clul.ul.pt/teitok/learn ercorpus/index.php?action=home. These are further encoded for student and teacher modifications. Annotations for part of speech, lemma, and learner errors are provided.

Future Directions

Interdisciplinary collaborations create multiple opportunities that advance our knowledge base. With each initiative, however, it is important that we reflect on its strengths and limitations. Our review of previous and current practices leads to the following recommendations for future research.

Firstly, recent interest in the development of oral corpora is encouraging for gaining a more fine-grained picture of interlanguage development of English and a number of additional languages. We encourage researchers to continue in this direction, but we also believe it is necessary for more attention to be paid to the tasks being used to build oral and written corpora in terms of genre and type of interaction (monologic and dialogic) if a complete picture of an individual's language system is to be collected.

Secondly, extant corpora focus on instructed learners, but understanding naturalistic learning is also vital for understanding L2 acquisition. Lozano and Mendikoetxea (2013) demonstrated the possibilities of collecting data through an on-line platform. This presents certain issues, but it is also exciting for conceptualizing new avenues for data collection that could reach L2 users, rather than learners, that have largely been ignored.

Thirdly, collecting corpora is a time- and budget-consuming endeavor. Ensuring a corpus meets the research objectives can be augmented when design, collection and transcription is conducted in an informed fashion. However, moving forward, it seems that sharing corpora internationally is a key means of developing knowledge whilst reducing budget and time constraints across the fields. Many points included in this chapter are directly relevant for corpus building from the perspective of future sharing. To add to this, we encourage the inclusion of audio files for oral corpora as this permits use by researchers interested in areas that cannot be captured by written transcripts of speech.

Finally, each corpus needs to be accompanied by a published (and accessible to all through normal scientific channels) document detailing its design, collection and transcription. This information permits researchers to fully understand each step in a corpus's development, which allows a proper understanding of published research using this corpus and provides informed possibilities for future research with the corpus.

Further Reading

Bell, P., Collins, L., & Marsden, E. (in press). Building an oral and written learner corpus of a school programme: Methodological issues. In B. Le Bruyn & M. Paquot (Eds.), *Learner corpus research meets second language acquisition*. Cambridge: Cambridge University Press.

Bell, Collins, & Marsden (in press) demonstrate the importance of piloting the design of a learner corpora prior to its collection by examining the suitability of their elicitation tasks, and the effects of language of directions on language produced. They also highlight transcription and coding issues that need to be borne in mind with suggestions for more collaboration to work towards some standardization.

Lozano, C., & Mendikoetxea, A. (2013). Learner corpora and second language acquisition: The design and collection of CEDEL2. In A. Díaz-Negrillo, N. Ballier, & P. Thompson (Eds.), *Automatic treatment and analysis of learner corpus data* (pp. 65–100). Amsterdam: John Benjamins Publishing Company.

Lozano and Mendikoetxea (2013) present the creation of the CEDEL2 by discussing each of the 10 principles proposed by Sinclair (2005) and the recommendations made by Tono (2003). After establishing the rigor of this project, they share details of their data collection process and, importantly, make the metadata forms available for individuals who are designing a corpus.

Related Topics

Chapters 3, 4, 8, 10, 11, and 12.

Notes

1 The author order is alphabetical; both authors contributed equally to this chapter.
2 This is a standard definition in LCR, but there is no consensus. See Gilquin (2015) for examples of corpora that blur this definition's boundaries.

References

Atwell, E., Howarth, P., & Souter, C. (2003). The ISLE corpus: Italian and German spoken learners' English. *ICAME Journal, 27,* 5–18.

Ballier, N., & Martin, P. (2015). Speech annotation of learner corpora. In S. Granger, G. Gilquin, & F. Meunier (Eds.), *The Cambridge handbook of English corpus linguistics* (pp. 107–134). Cambridge: Cambridge University Press.

Bell, P., Collins, L., & Marsden, E. (in press). Building an oral and written learner corpus of a school programme: Methodological issues. In B. Le Bruyn & M. Paquot (Eds.), *Learner corpus research meets second language acquisition.* Cambridge: Cambridge University Press.

Caines, A., & Buttery, P. (2017). The effect of task type and topic on opportunity of use in learner corpora. In V. Brezina & L. Flowerdew (Eds.), *Learner corpus research: New perspectives and applications* (pp. 5–27). London: Bloomsbury Publishing.

Callies, M. (2015). Learner corpus methodology. In F. Meunier, G. Gilquin, & S. Granger (Eds.). *The Cambridge handbook of learner corpus research* (pp. 35–56). Cambridge: Cambridge University Press. https://doi.org/10.1017/CBO9781139649414.003

Campillos Llanos, L. (2014). A Spanish learner oral corpus for computer-aided error analysis. *Corpora, 9*(2), 207–238. https://doi.org/10.3366/cor.2014.0058

Corder, S. P. (1967). The significance of learner's errors. *IRAL-International Review of Applied Linguistics in Language Teaching, 5*(1–4), 161–170.

De Angelis, G. (2007). *Third or additional language acquisition.* Clevedon: Multilingual Matters.

Dickinson, M., & Ragheb, M. (2013). *Annotation for learner English guidelines.* v. 0.1. Technical report, Indiana University, Bloomington, IN, June.

Ellis, R., & Yuan, F. (2004). The effects of planning on fluency, complexity, and accuracy in second language narrative writing. *Studies in Second Language Acquisition, 26*(1), 59–84.

Ellis, R., & Yuan, F. (2005). The effects of careful within-task planning on oral and written task performance. In R. Ellis (Ed.), *Planning and task performance in a second language* (vol. 11, pp. 167–192). Amsterdam: John Benjamins Publishing Company.

Gilquin, G. (2015). From design to collection of learner corpora. In S. Granger, G. Gilquin, & F. Meunier (Eds.), *The Cambridge handbook of learner corpus research* (pp. 9–34). Cambridge. https://doi.org/10.1017/CBO9781139649414.002

Granger, S. (2004). Computer learner corpus research: Current status and future prospects. In U. Connor & T. Upton (Eds.), *Applied corpus linguistics: A multidimensional perspective* (pp. 123–145). Amsterdam: Rodopi.

Granger, S. (2008). Learner corpora in foreign language education. In N. Van Deusen-Scholl & N. H. Hornberger (Eds.), *Encyclopedia of language and education* (vol. 4, pp. 337–351). Boston: Springer.

Granger, S. (2012). Learner corpora. In *The encyclopedia of applied linguistics* (pp. 3235–3242). Oxford: Wiley Blackwell. https://doi.org/10.1002/9781405198431.wbeal0669.

Granger, S., Gilquin, G., & Meunier, F. (2015). Introduction: Learner corpus research – past, present and future. In F. Meunier, G. Gilquin, & S. Granger (Eds.), *The Cambridge handbook of learner corpus research* (pp. 1–6). Cambridge: Cambridge University Press. Retrieved from https://doi.org/10.1017/CBO9781139649414.001.

Gries, S. Th., & Berez, A. (2017). Linguistic annotation in/for corpus linguistics. In N. Ide & J. Pustejovsky (Eds.), *Handbook of linguistic annotation* (pp. 379–409). New York: Springer.

Gut, U. (2012). The LeaP corpus: A multilingual corpus of spoken learner German and learner English. In T. Schmidt & K. Wörmer (Eds.), *Multilingual corpora and multilingual corpus analysis* (pp. 3–24). Amsterdam: John Benjamins Publishing Company.

Fuchs, R., & Werner, V. (Eds.) (2018). Tense and aspect in second language acquisition and learner corpus research [Special Issue]. *International Journal of Learner Corpus Research, 4*(2), 143–163

Hashimoto, K., & Takeuchi, K. (2012). Prototypical design of learner support materials based on the analysis of non-verbal elements in presentation. In T. Watanabe, J. Watada, N. Takahashi, R. J. Howlett, & L. C. Jain (Eds.), *Intelligent interactive multimedia: Systems and services* (pp. 531–540). Heidelberg: Springer.

Hasko, V. (2013). Capturing the dynamics of second language development via learner corpus research: A very long engagement. *Modern Language Journal, 97*(S1), 1–10. https://doi.org/10.1111/j.1540-4781.2012.01425.x

Hyland, K. (2004). *Genre and second language writing.* Ann Arbor, MI: University of Michigan Press.

Janssen, M. (2016). TEITOK: Text-faithful annotated corpora. *Proceedings of the tenth international conference on language resources and evaluation (LREC 2016), Portorož, Slovenia.* Retrieved from https://www.aclweb.org/anthology/L16-1637.pdf

Jessner, U., Megens, M., & Graus, S. (2016). Crosslinguistic influence in third language acquisition. In R. A. Alonso (Ed.), *Crosslinguistic influence in second language acquisition* (pp. 193–214). Bristol: Multilingual Matters Clevedon.

Kormos, J. (2014). Differences across modalities of performance: An investigation of linguistic and discourse complexity in narrative tasks. In H. Byrnes & R. Manchón (Eds.), *Task-based language learning - insights from and for L2-writing* (pp. 193–216). https://doi.org/10.1075/tblt.7.08kor

Kotani, K., Yoshimi, T., Kotani, S., & Isahara, H. (2012). Development of integrated learner corpus of Japanese sign language. *Japanese Journal of Sign Language Studies, 21,* 25–43. https://doi.org/10.7877/jasl.21.25

Lantolf, J. P. (2011). The sociocultural approach to second language acquisition: Sociocultural theory, second language acquisition, and artificial L2 development. In D. Atkinson (Ed.), *Alternative approaches to second language acquisition* (pp. 24–47). New York: Routledge.

Le Bruyn, B. S. W., & Paquot, M. (in press). *Learner corpus research meets second language acquisition.* Cambridge: Cambridge University Press.

Long, M. (2014). *Second language acquisition and task-based language teaching.* Wiley Blackwell.

Lowie, W., & Verspoor, M. (2015). Variability and variation in second language acquisition orders: A dynamic reevaluation. *Language Learning, 65*(1), 63–88.

Lozano, C., & Mendikoetxea, A. (2013). Learner corpora and second language acquisition: The design and collection of CEDEL2. In A. Díaz-Negrillo, N. Ballier, & P. Thompson (Eds.), *Automatic treatment and analysis of learner corpus data* (pp. 65–100). Amsterdam: John Benjamins Publishing Company.

Lu, X. (2014). *Computational methods for corpus annotation and analysis.* London: Springer.

Mackey, A., & Gass, S. M. (2005). *Second language research.* New York: Routledge.

MacWhinney, B. (2000). *The CHILDES project: Tools for analyzing talk* (3rd ed.). Mahwah: Lawrence Erlbaum Associates.

MacWhinney, B. (2017). A shared platform for studying second language acquisition. *Language Learning, 67*(S1), 254–275.

Marian, V., Blumenfeld, H. K., & Kaushanskaya, M. (2007). The Language Experience and Proficiency Questionnaire (LEAP-Q): Assessing language profiles in bilinguals and multilinguals. *Journal of Speech, Language, and Hearing Research, 50*(4), 940–967.

Markee, N. (2000). *Conversation analysis.* Mahwah: Lawrence Erlbaum.

Marsden, E., Mackey, A., & Plonsky, L. (2016). The IRIS repository: Advancing research practice and methodology. In A. Mackey & E. Marsden (Eds.), *Advancing methodology and practice: The IRIS repository of instruments for research into second languages* (pp. 1–21). New York: Routledge.

Mendes, A., Antunes, S., Janssen, M., & Gonçalves, A. (2016). The COPLE2 corpus: A learner corpus for Portuguese. In *Proceedings of the 10th international conference on language resources and evaluation* (pp. 3207–3214). Portoroz: LREC. Retrieved from http://www.lrec-conf.org/proceedings/lrec2016/pdf/439_Paper.pdf.

Meunier, F., & Littre, D. (2013). Tracking learners' progress: Adopting a dual 'corpus cum experimental data' approach. *The Modern Language Journal*, *97*(S1), 61–76.

Meurers, D. (2015). Learner corpora and natural language processing. In S. Granger, G. Gilquin & F. Meunier (Eds.), *The Cambridge handbook of learner corpus research* (pp. 537–566). Cambridge: Cambridge University Press.

Meurers, D., & Dickinson, M. (2017). Evidence and interpretation in language learning research: Opportunities for collaboration with computational linguistics. *Language Learning*, *61*(S1), 66–95.

Myles, F. (2005). Review article: Interlanguage corpora and second language acquisition research. *Second Language Research*, *21*(4), 373–391.

Myles, F. (2008). Investigating learner language development with electronic longitudinal corpora. In L. Ortega & H. Byrnes (Eds.), *The longitudinal study of advanced L2 capacities* (pp. 58–72). New York: Routledge.

Myles, F. (2015). Second language acquisition theory and learner corpus research. In *The Cambridge handbook of learner corpus research* (pp. 309–332). Cambridge: Cambridge University Press. https://doi.org/10.1017/CBO9781139649414.014

Nagata, R., Whittaker, E., & Sheinman, V. (2011). Creating a manually error-tagged and shallow-parsed learner corpus. In *Proceedings of the 49th annual meeting of the Association for Computational Linguistics: human language technologies* (vol. 1, pp. 1210–1219). Retrieved from http://aclweb.org/anthology//P11/P11-1121.pdf

Newman, J., & Cox, C. (in press). Corpus annotation. In M. Paquot & S. Th. Gries (Eds.), *The practical handbook of corpus linguistics*. Berlin: Springer.

O'Donnell, M. (2012). UAM corpus tool version 2.8 user manual. Retrieved from http://www.corpustool.com/Documentation/UAMCorpusToolManualv28.pdf

Ortega, L., & Iberri-Shea, G. (2005). Longitudinal research in second language acquisition: Recent trends and future directions. *Annual Review of Applied Linguistic*, *25*, 26–45.

Paquot, M., & Plonsky, L. (2017). Quantitative research methods and study quality in learner corpus research. *International Journal of Learner Corpus Research*, *3*(1), 61–94. https://doi.org/10.1075/ijlcr.3.1.03paq

Perdue, C. (Ed.) (1993), *Adult language acquisition: Cross-linguistic perspectives* (vol. 1)*: Field methods*. Cambridge: Cambridge University Press.

Reznicek, M., Lüdeling, A., & Hirschmann, H. (2013). Competing target hypotheses in the Falko corpus: A flexible multi-layer corpus architecture. In N. Ballier, A. Diaz-Negrillo, & P. Thompson (Eds.), *Automatic treatment and analysis of learner corpus data* (pp. 101–124). Amsterdam: John Benjamins.

Selinker, L. (1972). Interlanguage. *IRAL-International Review of Applied Linguistics in Language Teaching*, *10*(1–4), 209–232.

Sinclair, J. (2005). Corpus and text – basic principles. In M. Wynne (Ed.), *Developing linguisitc corpora: A guide to good practice* (pp. 1–16). Oxford: Oxbow Book Company.

Tono, Y. (2003). Learner corpora: Design, development and applications. *Proceedings of the corpus linguistics 2003 conference* (pp. 800–809).

Tono, Y. (2016). What is missing in learner corpus design? In M. Alonso-Ramos (Ed.), *Spanish learner corpus research: Current trends and future perspectives* (Vol. 78, pp. 33–52). Amsterdam: John Benjamins Publishing Company.

Tono, Y., & Díez-Bedmar, M. B. (2014). Focus on learner writing at the beginning and intermediate stages: The ICCI corpus. *International Journal of Corpus Linguistics*, *19*(2), 163–177.

Tracy-Ventura, N., Mitchell, R., & McManus, K. (2016). The LANGSNAP longitudinal learner corpus. In M. A. Ramos (Ed.), *Spanish learner corpus research: Current trends and future perspectives* (pp. 117–141). Amsterdam: John Benjamins Publishing Company.

Tracy-Ventura, N., & Myles, F. (2015). The importance of task variability in the design of learner corpora for SLA research. *International Journal of Learner Corpus Research*, *1*(1), 58–95.

Yuldashev, A., Fernandez, J., & Thorne, S. L. (2013). Second language learners' contiguous and discontiguous multi-word unit use over time. *The Modern Language Journal*, *97*(S1), 31–45.

Zeldes, A. (in press). Corpus architecture. In M. Paquot & S. Th. Gries (Eds.), *The practical handbook of corpus linguistics*. Berlin: Springer.

6

Analyzing a Learner Corpus with a Concordancer

Sandra Götz

Introduction[1]

One of the benefits of using (learner) corpora and applying corpus-linguistic techniques is the possibility of analyzing large amounts of learner data automatically. This enables a researcher to find and describe certain characteristics many learners have in common, instead of relying on a small number of learners. In order to conduct such analyses, researchers have developed concordancing programs (or concordancers) whose interfaces simplify such automatic analysis of (learner) corpora considerably. Concordancing programs can thus be seen as tools that make data extraction far less laborious than manual extraction. For example, concordancing programs typically include tools that automatically compile all occurrences of a certain key word in its naturally occurring context (i.e., concordances), a comprehensive word count of each word in a corpus (i.e., word lists), frequently occurring two- or more word combinations (i.e., clusters and collocations), all of which will be described in detail in this chapter. Such tools can be extremely helpful to answer research questions that are theoretically rooted within an SLA framework and need empirical testing on large amounts of learner data. For example, an SLA researcher might want to test the predictions of the Aspect Hypothesis regarding the use of the English progressive by learners from various L1 backgrounds (see sample study below). Here, instead of counting all occurrences of the progressive in a database of millions of words by hand, one can extract these occurrences automatically and within seconds by using a concordancer.

Data extraction as such, however, can only be considered to be one step in an ongoing analysis that should not be applied until a research question has been formed within a solid theoretical SLA-framework. After generating hypotheses of the most likely outcome of one's study, a suitable learner corpus can be selected (or built) whose analysis will allow the research question(s) at hand to be investigated. After data extraction, the data typically need to be manually post-edited or coded before they can be subjected to a statistical analysis (see Chapters 8 and 9, this volume). Only then can the data be interpreted in the light of one's research question(s) and hypothesis/-es. Applying such corpus-linguistic techniques also helps to make a study exhaustive (as a computer does not 'overlook' anything), intersubjectively verifiable, and repeatable (i.e., every researcher who uses the same database and the same programs will get the same results) (see Mukherjee, 2009); such factors can enhance the overall quality and transparency of a research study. There are a variety of tools, methods, and techniques available that can be relevant to SLA-based research projects, some of which will be introduced in the context of the present chapter.

Core Issues and Topics

Selecting a Concordancer

While some learner corpora have built-in concordancers that can be used online with that specific corpus, e.g. the latest edition of the *International Corpus of Learner English* (ICLE; Granger et al., 2020), others consist of the learner data alone. For analyzing the latter, there are several concordancing programs available that can be downloaded to a computer, allowing researchers to work with the corpus at hand. The two major concordance programs that have been used in (learner) corpus research in the past two decades are *AntConc* (Anthony, 2018a) and *WordSmith* (Scott, 2017). Both of these programs are regularly debugged, updated and maintained by linguists (i.e. Laurence Anthony and Mike Scott). At the time of writing, *AntConc* is available in version 3.5.8 and *WordSmith* in version 7.0. The main features of both of these programs will be described in the *Main Research Methods* section of this chapter, namely concordances, word lists, cluster analyses and collocations. There are many very handy tutorials on *YouTube* that explain the main features of both of these programs in detail. While I am not going to promote the use of one of these concordancers as superior to the other, I will try to balance all sample analyses between these two programs and mainly focus on their advantageous characteristics. What might be relevant to private users, however, is the fact that *AntConc* is offered as freeware (http://www.laurenceanthony.net/software.html), whereas *WordSmith* is only freely available as a demo-version that typically restricts the number of hits in the analysis at hand (http://www.lexically.net/WordSmith/downloads/); for its full version, a license can be purchased from the website.

Saving Learner Texts to Upload Them to a Concordancer

In order to upload learner data to a concordancer, they need to be available in a certain format. For example, neither *AntConc* nor *WordSmith* can 'read' .doc or .docx files. When compiling one's own learner corpus, it is therefore advisable to save data files as .txt-files or as .xml files to avoid any incompatibilities. A simple text-editor may be used to do that, such as *Notepad*, which is pre-installed on most computers or can be downloaded as freeware. It is also advisable to save each learner text into one separate file with a unique name, instead of creating only one large file. For example, each component of the *Louvain International Database of Spoken English Interlanguage* (LINDSEI; Gilquin et al., 2010) includes 50 interviews by learners of English from different L1s, and each of the interviews is saved as a unique file allowing for the identification of each learner text (e.g. GE001.txt-GE050.txt for the 50 German learner files in the corpus). This allows for the extraction of values for each individual learner file (instead of one value for the whole corpus). Having separate files/values is very important, as one can conduct more thorough analyses and, for example, take individual variation into account (i.e., learner language is typically very heterogeneous, so that one value per learner group often yields misleading findings; see Chapters 8, 9, and 30, this volume). Also, analyzing each learner separately allows for complementing findings with extra-linguistic information from learner profiles, such as their age, gender, etc. (see *Concordances* section).

Enriching the Learner Corpus with Annotations

The most 'basic' format of learner texts is 'raw' text, where each learner file contains nothing but the learner's actual output (which may be written or spoken transcriptions) in the file. This format is sufficient for many research purposes, and it is possible to conduct extremely fine-grained analyses on the basis of raw-text learner corpora alone. However, there are various ways in which learner corpus files can be annotated, as explained in several chapters of this Handbook, most particularly Chapters 5 and 7. I will therefore not go into details about annotation procedures, but only briefly mention the different options and exemplify how differently annotated files can be used with concordancers.

The first way to enrich learner corpora is by adding markup, typically in the form of pseudo-XML tags. Here, certain text passages are annotated with extra-information (such as speaker information) that might be relevant for an analysis at a later stage (see Chapter 5, this volume). Such tags are simply inserted into the raw texts and are put between angle brackets. Typically, they contain a beginning and an end tag, e.g. <example> this is the example </example>. For instance, in the example given below for interview data, concordancers are able to analyze only individual tasks or individual speakers separately. In the example below, it is possible to analyze everything that was said in the <Story Retell Task> or only what <B> said.

<LEARNER001>

<Story Retell Task>

<A> So, can you tell me what you see in these pictures </A>

 <B> Okay, in the first picture, there is a woman who wants her <foreign> Bild </foreign> erm I mean portrait painted […] </B>

</Story Retell Task>

</LEARNER001>

In a standard search on lexical items, the concordance program 'ignores' everything that is put between angle brackets, so that the tags themselves will not be counted as words. Thus, they will not appear in the concordance output. It is also possible to conduct a concordance search on tags instead of words. In the above example, the <foreign> tag could be used to search for all the foreign words the learners used in an interview (see De Cock, 2019).

Another way to annotate learner data is Part of Speech tagging, or POS-tagging. A POS-tagger automatically adds word-class information to each word in a corpus, i.e. whether a word is an adjective (*green*_ADJ) or a verb (e.g. *sunbathe*_VERB), etc. This can be done automatically by various taggers that are free of charge, some examples being the CLAWS tagger <http://ucrel-api.lancaster.ac.uk/claws/free.html>, the Stanford tagger <https://nlp.stanford.edu/software/tagger.shtml>, or the newly developed *TagAnt* interface, that conveniently allows users to tag a corpus using the Tree tagger <https://www.laurenceanthony.net/software/tagant/> (see Chapter 5, this volume, for more detail). The applications of POS-tagged corpora are versatile; for instance, one can test which adjectives or adjective intensifiers a learner uses, and one can test if the number of adjectives increases with increasing proficiency, etc. Concordancing a POS-tagged corpus also allows for searching variable frames, such as "*it is* ADJ *to*" or the like.

Another valuable way of annotating learner data is error-tagging. Formally, it works similarly to POS-tagging (i.e. each error in the corpus is tagged); however, the process – so far – only works manually (with satisfying accuracy) and is very laborious. Even deciding on whether something counts as a genuine error (as compared to a slip of the tongue) can sometimes be challenging. However, once a corpus is error-tagged, it opens up many possible research avenues, e.g. filtering out which errors are L1-specific and which ones are universal (see Dagneaux et al., 1998; Granger, 2003). Also, certain error types can be queried with a concordancer, allowing for sophisticated error-analyses of large amounts of data. For more detailed information on (computer-aided) error-analysis, see Chapter 7 of this volume.

Main Research Methods and Tools

Concordancers offer a selection of tools that may be used to extract data from learner corpora. In the following sections, I will introduce four functions that both *AntConc* and *WordSmith* include: concordances, wordlists, clusters and collocations.

Concordances

A concordance gives users information about the linguistic context in which a word occurs in the corpus, as it "displays all examples of a particular linguistic feature retrieved from the corpus [...], usually presented as one example per line, with a short section of surrounding text to the left and to the right" (Rayson, 2015, p. 40). Concordances are the most versatile tool in (learner) corpus research, because analyzing concordance lines can answer the most diverse research questions. As the context of a word is in focus here, concordances are often called "**Keyword** in Context"-Concordances, in short KWIC-Concordances. Probably due to the versatility of analytical possibilities, they are some of the most widely used and most valuable tools to retrieve information from a (learner) corpus. A KWIC-concordance created with *AntConc* on the POS-tagged version of the Bulgarian component of ICLE to illustrate all adjectives (tagged as 'JJ') is depicted in Figure 6.1.

Both *AntConc* and *WordSmith* allow for adaptations in the search- and display settings. For example, the number of words to the left and to the right can be changed, and the concordance can be sorted alphabetically, either seen from the right or the left of the key word, or chronologically following their occurrences in the corpus from file to file, in the reverse order, and so on.[2] It is also possible to use wildcards in a search by using so-called regular expressions instead of

Figure 6.1 Concordance of Adjectives in the Bulgarian Component of ICLE in AntConc (First 18 Hits).

concrete word forms (e.g. Weisser, 2016). For example, it is possible to search for all adjectives ending in -*ing* using *ing.

Apart from searches on single words, it is also possible to search for co-occurring word forms. For example, to search for the progressive aspect in learner English, it would probably be quite tedious to analyze all instances with an -*ing* ending. One helpful way to extract all instances of progressive forms would be a concordance analysis of all possible word forms of the verb *to be* (i.e. to perform a so-called lemmatized word search) followed by any word that ends with an -*ing* form, allowing, for example, for up to four words to the right (see example below). This is illustrated by using *WordSmith* 6.0. After opening the program and selecting "Concord" (see Figure 6.2a), the learner corpus files need to be uploaded to the program by clicking on "Settings" → "Choose texts" (see Figure 6.2b). The corpus files need to be uploaded from the hard drive by selecting the folder from the drop-down menu. The files then need to be highlighted by clicking on them and uploaded to the program by clicking on the arrow and then clicking on "OK" (see Figure 6.2c). The corpus files are now ready for the concordance search.

The first step in the search for the progressive on an untagged corpus would be to type in all forms of BE (*am/ 'm/are/ 're/is/ 's/was/were/have been/ 've been//has been/ 's been/had been/ 'd been*)[3]

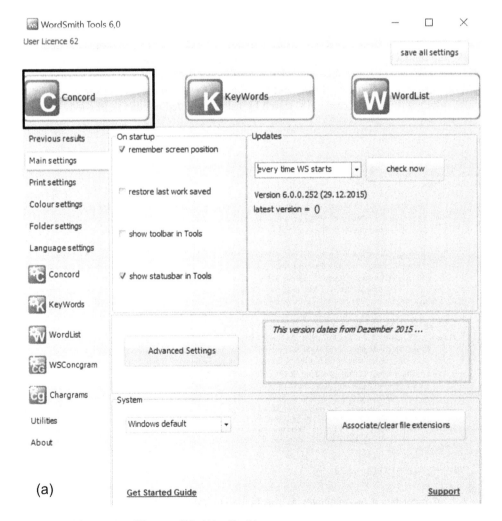

(a)

Figure 6.2   (a) Opening "Concord" in WordSmith.

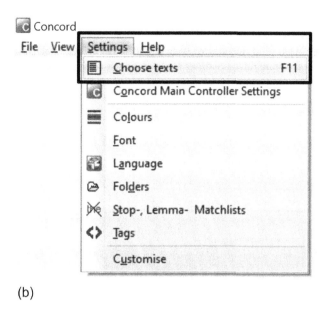

(b)

(c)

Figure 6.2 (b) Selecting "Settings" to Choose Texts for Analysis in Wordsmith. (c) Uploading Texts to the Concordancer in Wordsmith.

Sandra Götz

separated by forward slashes into the **Search Word** field (see screenshot in Figure 6.3a). Then, clicking the **Advanced** button will open an option to search for co-occurring context words, i.e. all words that follow a form of BE and end with an -*ing* form (i.e. using **ing*), as in *is laughing*. As this search would also generate false positives (such as *that is interesting*, *it was so boring*, *that's simply amazing*, etc.), one can exclude some obviously unwanted co-occurring words by entering them in the respective window under "exclude if search is or context contains" (see Figure 6.3b). Finally, clicking the "OK" button generates the concordance illustrated in Figure 6.4.

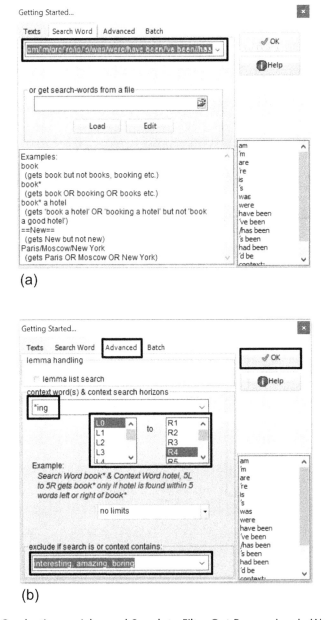

(a)

(b)

Figure 6.3   (a) Conducting an Advanced Search to Filter Out Progressives in WordSmith: Typing in the Search Word (i.e. a Form of BE). (b) Performing an Advanced Search Extracting All Co-occurrences with Another Word Ending in –*ing* up to Four Words to the Right.

As Figure 6.4 illustrates, this query retrieved all instances of BE followed by a word ending in *-ing* (besides BE + *interesting*, BE + *boring* and BE + *amazing*) from the corpus, including many progressives. However, it still includes some unwanted hits and false positives that need to be manually disambiguated and discarded from the query (see highlighted lines in Figure 6.4), before the data can be analyzed. In order to do so, one could either extend the list of unwanted hits and start a new search, or go through each line of the concordance (by clicking on it) and pressing the "delete" button on the keyboard in order to delete all unwanted hits (e.g. lines 5, 9, 10, 18-21) from the concordance. Then, selecting **Edit → zap** from the menu deletes all these unwanted hits and updates the concordance (see Figure 6.5).

Figure 6.4   First 24 Concordance Lines of Concordance Output of All Instances of BE + *–ing*, Excluding *Interesting, Boring, Amazing* in LINDSEI-GE in WordSmith.

Figure 6.5   Deleting Unwanted Concordance Hits in WordSmith.

As the rectangle at the bottom of Figure 6.5 highlights, *Concord* offers a set of additional tools, each of which can give insights into how words are used. These are collocates, plot, patterns, and clusters. The reader is referred to the manual for further details (see *Further Reading* section).

WordSmith also allows the researcher to download the complete concordance, either as a spreadsheet file or as a .txt-file. This can be done by selecting "File" → "Save as Excel Spreadsheet" or → "Save as text file" from the menu. Downloading the concordance allows the user to open the concordance with a spreadsheet program (such as *Excel* or *Calc*) and add information to the concordance. This can be used as an alternative to the "zapping-option" illustrated above to delete unwanted hits from a concordance (e.g. a first annotation layer TRUE/FALSE can be added to exclude false positives from the analysis and later only analyze the "TRUE" concordance items). This is the preferred option, because no information is deleted and one can still have access to the original raw concordance, in case the data should be used at a later stage and be annotated according to different criteria. Another advantage of downloading the concordance to a spreadsheet program is the possibility of being able to add additional information/coding to the concordance entries. The downloaded file will include the concordance itself and additional rows showing the keyword (in the present example, the form of BE; see Figure 6.6) and the filename (in Figure 6.6 called LEARNER). Additional information that would be relevant for the research question at hand can be added to the concordance, thus preparing it for a statistical analysis that goes beyond documenting over- or underuses of the progressive (as documented, for example, in Dose-Heidelmayer & Götz, 2016). This would allow for measuring the effect of a certain variable on the outcome such as whether or not the quality of the verb triggers a target-like or non-target like use by the learner. For instance, certain variables can be added to the occurrence, e.g., on the verb (see STATIVITY; TENSE in Figure 6.6), whether or not this was a target-like or non-target-like use of the progressive (se TARGET-LIKE in Figure 6.6), or information about the learners who uttered this progressive form (see GENDER, AGE in Figure 6.6). Other non-linguistic learning context variables may also be added, such as whether or not the learner had completed a stay abroad in the target-language community (see Mukherjee & Götz, 2015; Chapter 30, this volume). Also, other variables can be added that might have an effect on the learners (mis-)use of the progressive, such as the topic they were talking about during the interview, the mode the learner was using (esp. if you compare speech vs. writing or other task-effects), etc. One example of how concordance output can be post-edited and further annotated in the case of the progressive is illustrated in Figure 6.6.

	A	B	C	D	E	F	G	H	I	J
1	Concordance	BE FORM	TRUE/FALSE	LEMMA	TARGET-LIKE	TENSE	STATIVITY	LEARNER	GENDER	AGE
2	fine how are you doing well well too earl	are	TRUE	DO	TARGET-LIKE	PRES	NON-STATIVE	GE001.txt	FEMALE	22
3	actually took out a map and was looking where I was trying	was	TRUE	LOOK	TARGET-LIKE	SP	NON-STATIVE	GE001.txt	FEMALE	22
4	map and was looking where I was trying to get and I found o	was	TRUE	TRY	TARGET-LIKE	SP	NON-STATIVE	GE001.txt	FEMALE	22
5	rrible has happened and so I was sitting there in the in the	was	TRUE	SIT	TARGET-LIKE	SP	NON-STATIVE	GE001.txt	FEMALE	22
6	even looks as if he w he she was shouting at him or somethin	was	TRUE	SHOUT	TARGET-LIKE	SP	NON-STATIVE	GE001.txt	FEMALE	22
7	four weeks down there and I was in sitting in the airplane	was	TRUE	SIT	TARGET-LIKE	SP	NON-STATIVE	GE002.txt	MALE	22
8	y just can't be because they are living first of all everybo	are	TRUE	LIVE	NON-TLIKE	PRES	STATIVE	GE002.txt	MALE	22
9	ble in in the aircraft and I was reading and didn't think ab	was	TRUE	READ	TARGET-LIKE	SP	NON-STATIVE	GE003.txt	MALE	29
10	n title was and pff ja they were living somewhere in Iceland	were	TRUE	LIVE	NON-TLIKE	SP	STATIVE	GE003.txt	MALE	29
11	the landscape I I while I was watching television so I th	was	TRUE	WATCH	TARGET-LIKE	SP	NON-STATIVE	GE003.txt	MALE	29
12	shirts looked old and they were wearing and most of them ha	were	TRUE	WEAR	NON-TLIKE	SP	NON-STATIVE	GE003.txt	MALE	29
13	was is called Subways which is coming to Germany more and	is	TRUE	COME	TARGET-LIKE	PRES	NON-STATIVE	GE004.txt	MALE	22
14	n the first picture somebody is painting a woman who is sitt	is	TRUE	PAINT	TARGET-LIKE	PRES	NON-STATIVE	GE004.txt	MALE	22
15	body is painting a woman who is sitting in a chair and yeah	is	TRUE	SIT	TARGET-LIKE	PRES	NON-STATIVE	GE004.txt	MALE	22
16	he family I lived with they were they were working at the un	were	TRUE	WORK	NON-TLIKE	SP	STATIVE	GE006.txt	FEMALE	21
17	I lived with they were they were working at the university a	were	TRUE	WORK	NON-TLIKE	SP	STATIVE	GE006.txt	FEMALE	21
18	they didn't have a T V they were just reading books or or si	were	TRUE	READ	TARGET-LIKE	SP	NON-STATIVE	GE006.txt	FEMALE	21
19	tand the French because they are speaking so fast I I didn't	are	TRUE	SPEAK	NON-TLIKE	PRES	NON-STATIVE	GE006.txt	FEMALE	21
20	k it's different how who is looking and you at you or wh	is	TRUE	LOOK	TARGET-LIKE	PRES	NON-STATIVE	GE006.txt	FEMALE	21
21	ooking and you at you or who is thinking something about you	is	TRUE	THINK	NON-TLIKE	PRES	STATIVE	GE006.txt	FEMALE	21
22	but it depends on on who you are interacting with and how th	are	TRUE	NTERACT	NON-TLIKE	PRES	NON-STATIVE	GE006.txt	FEMALE	21
23	orkers and one street worker was working and all of the othe	was	TRUE	WORK	TARGET-LIKE	SP	NON-STATIVE	GE007.txt	FEMALE	23
24	rking and all of the others were standing around and looking	were	TRUE	STAND	TARGET-LIKE	SP	NON-STATIVE	GE007.txt	FEMALE	23
25	r to do the things and they were all having a smoke but not	were	TRUE	HAVE	TARGET-LIKE	SP	NON-STATIVE	GE007.txt	FEMALE	23

Figure 6.6 Possible Annotation Layers That Can Be Added to a Concordance After It Is Downloaded from WordSmith or AntConc in a Spreadsheet Software.

Word Lists

A word list can give a researcher an initial idea of what kinds of words are used *in* a corpus, how it is shaped, as it were, thus making it a "quick guide to the way words are distributed in a text" (Sinclair, 1990, p. 30). The word list tool simply counts all different word-forms (i.e. including all different orthographic appearances of all words) that occur in a corpus and makes a list that sorts them according to different purposes, either by frequency (in descending or ascending order), or alphabetically (or in reverse alphabetical order), or in a combination of both. Word lists can be used to either get an overview of the vocabulary used (frequently) in the corpus, to compare different (sorts of) corpora by analyzing keyword lists (e.g. Rayson & Potts, 2020), or simply to find all spelling variants that occur in a corpus quickly, e.g. learners might vary between British and American English spelling variants or make spelling errors. Also, a wordlist gives statistics about the total number of words in a corpus (i.e. tokens) as well as the total number of different words (i.e. types) used in a corpus, which is valuable information that is necessary in order to 'normalize' the findings. Normalizing means not only counting the total number of occurrences in a corpus, but setting them in relation to their occurrence per hundred/thousand/million words (phw, ptw, pmw), either per speaker or per corpus. This is particularly important for comparative purposes (e.g. when comparing a learner corpus and a native corpus), because corpora often do not have the same size, so that only comparing the total number of occurrences can sometimes be misleading. This becomes relevant in the following example, which illustrates two descending wordlists of the top 24 hits from Chinese and German learner writing (both taken from ICLE), where ICLE-CN consists of 498,755 tokens and ICLE-GE of only 234,568. If the frequencies of individual words in Chinese vs. German learner writing are analyzed,[4] it is necessary to normalize them by dividing the total number of hits by the corpus size and multiplying the result by 100, 1,000, or even one million, depending on the value you wish to normalize it to.[5] The two wordlists are shown in Figure 6.7a (on ICLE-CN) and 6.7b (on ICLE-GE).

As Figure 6.7 illustrates, the first c. 30 hits in a word list are typically function words and are often not particularly interesting for analysis. In this case, however, there is a noticeable difference between the Chinese and the German learners: While the Germans seem to make frequent use of personal pronouns (see, e.g. *I* on rank 8 and *you* on rank 17), these pronouns do not figure among the first 24 hits in the Chinese corpus. Chinese speakers seem to prefer constructions using the more general term *people* or *Hong Kong people* (see, e.g. *people* on rank 14 and *hong kong* on 18/19, respectively). At first sight, this might reflect a stylistic difference in writing styles between the two learner groups; however, this initial hypothesis would need to be verified by a thorough concordance analysis of the lexemes *people* and *Hong Kong*, *I* and *you* (see *Concordances* section).

In the case of the definite article *the*, we find it occurs with a frequency of 31,244 in total in ICLE-CN and only 12,230 times in ICLE-GE. As mentioned above, it is also important to examine the normalized frequencies, as well as the average number of occurrence per file: 63 times per thousand words (ptw) and at a mean value of 32 times per file (SD=13.21) in the Chinese data and 52 times ptw in the German data with a mean value of 28 times per file in the German subcorpus (SD=17.52). When this is subjected to a two-tailed t-test, this, it turns out to be a highly significant difference between the two learner groups (t= 25.77; p<0.0001). Such "contrastive interlanguage analyses" (see Granger, 1996, 2015) by way of measuring significant differences in frequencies either between different learner populations or between learners and native speakers can be conducted to quantify overuses (i.e. a significantly higher number of occurrences compared to another dataset) or underuses (i.e. a significantly lower number of occurrences compared to another dataset). These terms, however, are to be understood as strictly methodological terms (see Chapter 8, this volume).

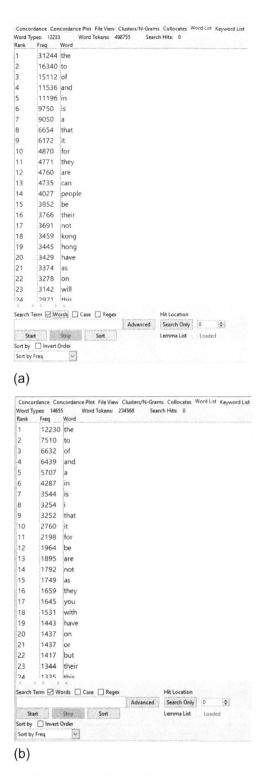

Figure 6.7 (a) Top 24 Wordlist Items of Written Chinese Learner Data Compiled from ICLE-CN Using the Wordlist Function in AntConc. (b) Top 24 Wordlist Items of Written German Learner Data, Compiled from ICLE-GE Using the Wordlist Function in AntConc

In order to compile a wordlist with *AntConc*, after opening the program by a double click, it is first of all necessary to upload the corpus files from one's hard drive by selecting **file → open files** in the menu at the top (see Figure 6.8a). The program will then analyze all files that are uploaded to this section. Figure 6.8b illustrates the individual files that were chosen in the left window and shows the number of files that were uploaded at the bottom of that window (here 982). From the

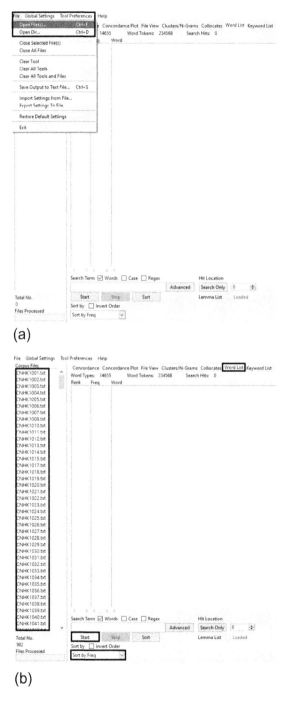

(a)

(b)

Figure 6.8 (a), (b) How to Compile a Word List in AntConc.

menu on the top right hand, **Word List** needs to be selected, as highlighted in the square on the top right side of Figure 6.8b. Clicking on the **Start** button at the bottom will generate a word list that looks like the ones in Figure 6.7a and 6.7b.

Apart from the default option of sorting a word list **by Frequency** (illustrated at the bottom in Figure 6.8b: "Sort by Freq"), i.e. in descending order, it is also possible to change the selection via the drop-down menu and sort the word list **by Word**, i.e., alphabetically, or **by Word End**, i.e., in a reverse alphabetical order, to study suffixation, for example. In the same way as described for concordances in the previous section, word lists can also be downloaded in *AntConc* and *WordSmith* to be edited or annotated further in programs like *Excel, Calc, R* or the like by clicking on **File → Save output to text file** (in *AntConc*). From here, all kinds of additional information can be added to the wordlist, or it can be further annotated/analyzed the manner described for concordances (see the *Concordances* section above).

Cluster Analysis

Over the last three decades or so, there has been increasing interest in describing prefabricated multiword units (e.g. *The point is that, you know what I mean*), both in native (e.g. Biber et al., 1999; Gray & Biber, 2015) as well as in nonnative language (e.g. De Cock, 2000; Götz & Schilk, 2011; Paquot & Granger, 2012; Paquot, 2013). Paquot and Granger (2012) find learner corpora to be an ideal resource to study the phrasicon of a learner group, because learner corpora are typically compiled of larger stretches of learner output, coming from tasks where the learners are allowed to use their own language (i.e. essays or interviews) (see also Chapter 28, this volume). I will thus introduce one of the most frequently researched types of formulaic sequences in corpus linguistics, namely multi-word clusters. This section describes how these can be extracted from learner corpora automatically to become ready for analysis.

It takes two steps to perform such a cluster analysis on a learner corpus. In the following section, I will demonstrate the procedure using *WordSmith* tools. After opening the program and opening the *WordList* tool, the learner corpus files need to be uploaded from the hard drive in the usual manner (exactly in the same way as was described for the compilation of *Concordances*; see section above). Only instead of clicking on "Make a word list now", one would first need to click on "Make/Add to index"[6] (see screenshot in Figure 6.9a). When the program asks where to save the index, an appropriate folder needs to be selected by clicking on the folder icon (see Figure 6.9b). The index needs to be given a meaningful name that can be easily recognized in the future (i.e., NOT Index1), after which the selection should be set to "delete existing index and start a new one" and confirmed by "OK" (see Figure 6.9b). After the index has been compiled, it is necessary to answer "yes" when the program asks if the index should be opened now.

When the index is open, the second step is to follow the menu to Compute → Clusters (see Figure 6.10a), after which choices can be made about the target cluster size (from 2 to 5) and the minimum total frequency of the cluster (5 is commonly used, but this is a completely random setup) (see Figure 6.10b).

Clicking "OK" will generate an output according to the pre-selections that lists all clusters that were found in the uploaded learner corpus files. The screenshots in Figure 6.11 show 3- to 4-gram lists compiled from LINDSEI (Figure 6.11a) compared to LOCNEC (Figure 6.11b), i.e. spoken learner data vs. spoken native speaker data by university students. By default, they are sorted in descending order, but, again, as illustrated in the bottom of the screenshot, they can also be sorted alphabetically. The other options in the menu give some more statistics on the cluster lists (such as the individual file size, the type-token ratio of the individual files, etc.).

At first glance, one can see some parallels and some first differences in the learners' and the native speakers' use of 3 and 4 grams. As for concordances and word lists, cluster lists can

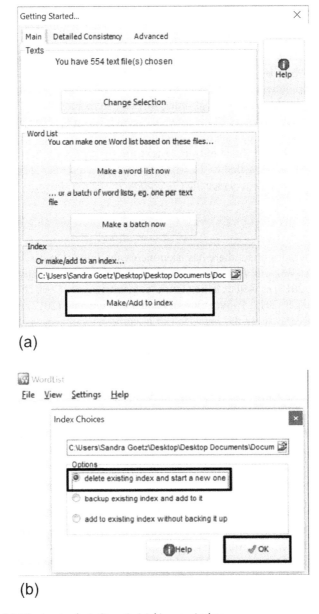

Figure 6.9   (a), (b) Cluster Analysis Step 1: Making an Index.

also be downloaded as .txt or .xls files in order to be analyzed further according to the research question(s) and hypotheses. For example, previous corpus-based research on clusters has revealed that learners typically overuse a limited set of frequent clusters, especially at lower proficiency levels (e.g. Crossley & Salsbury, 2011). Also, it is possible to compare learners with different L1 backgrounds (e.g. Leńko-Szymańska, 2014) and/or compare the different functions in which clusters are used (e.g. Götz & Schilk, 2011). Clusters can be extracted quite comfortably from (learner) corpora, and such extraction opens up a wide range of analytical possibilities (see, e.g. Paquot & Granger, 2012; Ebeling & Hasselgård, 2015).

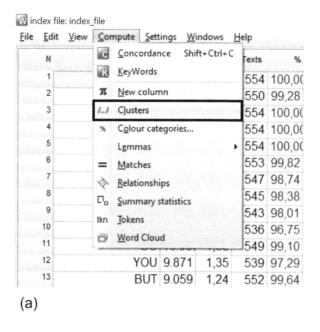

(a)

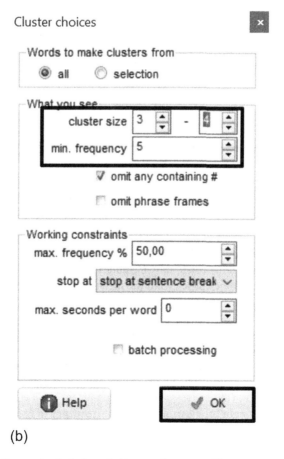

(b)

Figure 6.10   (a), (b) Cluster Analysis Step 2: How to Compute Clusters in WordSmith

index file: index_file

File Edit View Compute Settings Windows Help

N	Word	Freq.	%	Texts	%
1	I DON'T KNOW	2.158	0,29	440	79,42
2	A LOT OF	765	0,10	291	52,53
3	AND IT WAS	586	0,08	264	47,65
4	I THINK THAT	539	0,07	197	35,56
5	IT WAS A	452	0,06	233	42,06
6	AND I THINK	424	0,06	243	43,86
7	I THINK IT'S	410	0,06	227	40,97
8	YOU HAVE TO	400	0,05	192	34,66
9	I WANT TO	399	0,05	186	33,57
10	I WENT TO	396	0,05	205	37,00
11	IT WAS VERY	357	0,05	175	31,59
12	I THINK I	354	0,05	216	38,99
13	I DON'T THINK	325	0,04	185	33,39
14	TO GO TO	316	0,04	196	35,38
15	WOULD LIKE TO	315	0,04	174	31,41
16	YEAH YEAH YEAH	309	0,04	120	21,66
17	AND I I	302	0,04	193	34,84
18	I I I	300	0,04	164	29,60
19	I WOULD LIKE	299	0,04	160	28,88
20	I HAVE TO	290	0,04	170	30,69
21	I THINK IT	289	0,04	184	33,21
22	WHEN I WAS	289	0,04	190	34,30
23	BUT I THINK	287	0,04	201	36,28
24	THE THE THE	287	0,04	138	24,91
25	I WOULD LIKE TO	269	0,04	151	27,26

frequency alphabetical statistics filenames notes

21.912 entries Row 1 frequency: ou... T S

(a)

index file: index_file

File Edit View Compute Settings Windows Help

N	Word	Freq.	%	Texts	%
1	I DON'T KNOW	209	0,18	48	96,00
2	A LOT OF	129	0,11	42	84,00
3	YEAH YEAH YEAH	111	0,09	32	64,00
4	AND IT WAS	94	0,08	34	68,00
5	I MEAN I	86	0,07	31	62,00
6	THE I END	85	0,07	34	68,00
7	IT WAS A	80	0,07	34	68,00
8	IT WAS JUST	66	0,06	28	56,00
9	I'D LIKE TO	62	0,05	28	56,00
10	DON'T KNOW I	60	0,05	30	60,00
11	I DON'T KNOW I	59	0,05	30	60,00
12	IN THE I	59	0,05	35	70,00
13	YEAH YEAH I	59	0,05	30	60,00
14	I WENT TO	57	0,05	30	60,00
15	THINGS LIKE THAT	57	0,05	25	50,00
16	AND I WAS	56	0,05	28	56,00
17	AT THE I	56	0,05	25	50,00
18	YEAH IT WAS	56	0,05	32	64,00
19	YOU HAVE TO	56	0,05	29	58,00
20	I THINK I	53	0,04	25	50,00
21	IT WAS REALLY	53	0,04	26	52,00
22	OF THE I	53	0,04	23	46,00
23	I THINK IT'S	52	0,04	31	62,00
24	A BIT OF	50	0,04	29	58,00
25	AT THE MOMENT	50	0,04	26	52,00

frequency alphabetical statistics filenames notes

2.088 entries Row 1 T S

(b)

Figure 6.11 Top 25 Hits of 3 and 4 grams in LINDSEI (a) vs. LOCNEC (b) Compiled with WordSmith.

Collocations

Very often, the researcher is not only interested in the number of occurrences of a certain word, but also in its collocations, i.e. the significantly co-occurring words in which a certain lexeme is being used. For example, inspired by previous research on a lack of variability in adjective intensification even in advanced learners of English (see, e.g. Granger, 1998; Lorenz, 1999; Nesselhauf, 2005), it might be interesting to test the variability of adjective intensifiers in advanced Spanish learners' writing concerning the adjective *good*. In order to do so in *AntConc*, the option **Collocates** needs to be chosen from the menu at the top. Depending on the research question, in the **Search Term** window, the word whose collocates one would like to ascertain can be typed in, and via the **Window Span**, the researcher may select the search term's collocates to the left or to the right, as well as the span that is allowed. Additionally, the **Minimal Collocational Frequency**, which was (randomly) set to 1 in the present example, can be selected. The corpora chosen for comparison in this illustration are the Spanish component of ICLE and the *Louvain Corpus of Native English Essays* (LOCNESS). The output is illustrated in Figure 6.12a (the Spanish learners) and 6.12b. (the native speakers). This output can be sorted according to the so-called "collocational strength" of the example, by the frequency of its occurrence (left or right collocate) or alphabetically. Note, however, that the scores of the collocational strength (that is calculated on the basis of the MI score or the t-score;[7] following Stubbs, 1995) are **not** directly comparable in corpora that differ in size,[8]

(a)

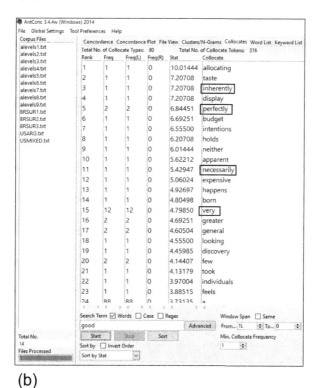

(b)

Figure 6.12 Collocational Strength of Collocates to the Left of *Good* in ICLE-SP (a) vs. LOCNESS (b) Conducted with AntConc.

An observation resulting from a comparison of the different ranks of the collocations with *good* in the Spanish learners and the native speakers, is that both groups manifest collocations with <u>*very*</u> *good* in the top 20 collocates (rank 17 vs. rank 15). However, the Spanish learners prefer modifying *good* with *excessively* [*sic!*] (rank 2), *totally* (rank 12), and *extremely* (rank 13), whereas the native speakers prefer the modifiers *inherently* (rank 3), *perfectly* (rank 5), and *necessarily* (rank 11). Although these rank lists need to be subjected to further qualitative analyses in order to arrive at conclusive results, they might still serve as a starting point. For example, learners' collocational preferences can be tested for L1-transfer effects. Another option for further analysis would be to compute concordances of these instances and subject them to further qualitative (for example, semantic) analyses. Of course, it is also possible to compute collocations using the POS-tagged version of a corpus and investigate adjective intensification for *all* adjectives in a corpus, instead of taking a purely lexeme-based approach.

A Critical Note on Concordancing Programs and Other Tools

Please note that concordance programs are convenient tools that can help extract relevant results from a learner corpus more quickly than would be possible manually. However, applying either of the corpus analytical techniques described in this section can only be considered as a tool – and hence only as a methodological interim step to take – during a research project. The quality of research will therefore not depend on which concordancing program is used. After data extraction, the quality of research will depend much more on how the data is post-edited and annotated, how the dataset is statistically analyzed, and – most importantly – how the findings are meaningfully interpreted in light of the theoretical framework and the research question(s) at hand.

Representative Corpora and Research

Fuchs and Werner (2018) investigated the use of stative progressives by school-aged learners of English in the *International Corpus of Crosslinguistic Interlanguage* (ICCI; Tono & Díez-Bedmar, 2014). The study is perfectly in line with the research layout promoted in this chapter, because it 1) is theoretically rooted within an SLA framework, 2) analyzes a learner corpus, 3) uses concordancing techniques for data extraction, 4) applies statistically sophisticated analyses in order to test the hypotheses, and 5) discusses the findings in light of their implications for SLA theory. Additionally, the authors describe each of the individual steps of their investigation in detail and supply additional material in an online-appendix.

The study focuses on a potential extension of the progressive aspect to stative verbs by beginning and lower intermediate school pupils of English. The study tests a major prediction of the Aspect Hypothesis (Andersen, 1991), which is that the progressive will be used with dynamic verbs (e.g., *walk*, *sleep*) and not overextended to stative verbs (e.g., *be*, *have*). The researchers included learner groups with and without progressive markers in their L1 (viz. Mandarin, Cantonese, Japanese, Spanish, German, Hebrew, and Polish). As mentioned above, this study relies on the ICCI corpus, which contains short essays written by beginners and intermediate school-aged learners of English at different school years (3–13, representing approximately the ages 8–19), comprising 9,001 learners and 729,408 words. After POS-tagging their corpus, the researchers used a regular expression in *AntConc* to extract all verb forms (i.e. progressive and non-progressive forms) of 42 moderate- to high-frequency stative verbs (e.g. by using the query "*(k|K)(now|nows|new|nowing)_V*" in order to extract all verb forms of the verb *to know*). The data were then manually post-edited in order to delete all unwanted hits (e.g. gerund constructions, incomplete verb phrases, etc.), before each hit was manually annotated for a variety of variables (e.g. the learners' L1, whether or not it was a target-like use, etc.). The progressive uses of each stative verb were then normalized, before they were subjected to a sophisticated statistical analysis using logistic mixed effects regression models (see Chapter 9, this volume). Overall, the results show that stative progressives, especially erroneous (i.e. non-target-like ones) uses, are – in line with the Aspect Hypothesis – generally used comparatively rarely, contrary to claims based on previous learner-corpus-based research. These findings are irrespective of the learners' L1s. The authors discuss these findings – among other things – to be in line with the predictions of the Aspect Hypothesis.

Future Directions

This chapter has aimed to illustrate some of the most widely used concordancing techniques and offered a small introduction to how these can be compatible with SLA-related research questions. Of course, in the context of this chapter, it was only possible to show – at most – the tip of the iceberg in terms of possible techniques. Many roads lie ahead in the area of concordancing, some of which will be mentioned in this section.

As useful as ready-made concordancers may be, they restrict a researcher to a certain extent in the freedom of his or her analysis, as there is a clear dependency on the features which are offered by the programs and the decisions the programmers of these concordancers made in choosing the algorithms behind the respective tools. While software developers certainly try to keep track of new methodological developments, it is not always possible to implement these immediately to their programs. It is therefore always advisable to check for methodological updates before deciding on a type of data analysis (see, for example, some concrete suggestions how to improve concordance analyses by Anthony, 2018b). Alternatively, other researchers (e.g. Gries, 2016) recommend extracting data from corpora by using programming languages such R (R Development Core Team, 2018) or *Python* in order to be able to conduct tailor-made analyses. This, however, requires prior knowledge of programming. Taking this step is therefore mainly recommendable for researchers with previous experience in the area of programming.

Another road ahead in concordancing concerns the layout of current corpora as well as the types of analyses conducted by way of using concordancers. The field is still in need of corpora that include more annotation, because at the moment, most studies are still purely lexically-based (see Granger, 2015). Once more annotation is added to the corpora (especially POS-tagging, error tagging, or even parsing), more in-depth studies could be conducted that include more fine-grained research questions that are even more relevant for research in the field of SLA.

Another desideratum for future analyses concerns data compatibility between corpus data and available corpus tools, as corpora are often only available in formats that cannot be analyzed with *WordSmith*, *AntConc*, or *R/Python*. As this often restricts possible searches to the functions that are offered by the corpus developers, it would be highly desirable to promote *one* (and only one) simple corpus format in which corpora are being compiled, so that the researcher has more flexible options to extract data from the corpus under scrutiny.

Further Reading

<https://www.laurenceanthony.net/software/AntConc/releases/AntConc358/help.pdf>
  Latest manual for *AntConc* including explanations on all features available.

<http://lexically.net/downloads/version6/HTML/index.html?getting_started.htm>
  Full online help system including all features available in *WordSmith*.

Paquot, M., & Gries, S. Th. (Eds.) (in press). *The practical handbook of corpus linguistics*. New York: Springer.

Sandra Götz

This handbook gives readers a very easily accessible and hands-on overview of corpus types, annotation, and methods after explaining in detail how to load, describe, and analyze data (including some advanced statistical techniques) and how to finally write them up comprehensively in a paper.

Weisser, M. (2016). *Practical corpus linguistics: An introduction to corpus-based language analysis*. Oxford: Wiley-Blackwell.

A very comprehensive introduction to corpus linguistics, its underlying theories, assumptions, and methods including explanations of how to do searches using online corpora and their built-in concordancers. Throughout the book, all analyses are conducted using *AntConc*.

Related Topics

Chapters 2 and 3.

Notes

1 I would like to thank two anonymous reviewers, the editors and Laurence Anthony for valuable input on previous versions of this chapter. All remaining errors are my responsibility alone.
2 For more detailed information on sorting options, please consult the two handbooks of the concordancers (see the section on further reading).
3 Note that in an actual search, it is sufficient to insert been only once (i.e. am/'m/are/'re/is/'s/was/were/ been). An alternative way of extracting progressives is shown in the sample study below.
4 However, comparing frequencies is not the most state-of-the-art approach towards analyzing learner data. For more sophisticated approaches, please see Chapters 8 and 9.
5 For more information on normalizing and choosing the accurate baseline for one's purposes, the reader is referred to Biber et al. (1998).
6 An index creates two files from the data that were uploaded: (1) a large file containing information about the position of every word token in the text files (token file), and (2) a file that stores the individual word types (types file).
7 For detailed Information on the MI and the t-score, please see https://wordbanks.harpercollins.co.uk/ other_doc/statistics.html). Note, however, that neither of these two measures remains entirely unchallenged (see, for example, Gries, 2013).
8 However, AntConc provides a way to restrict the list to only collocates that are statistically significant (using Log Likelihood, which is comparable across corpora of different sizes), and then rank the collocates by their MI value (Laurence Anthony, p.c., 6 February 2020).

References

Andersen, R. (1991). Developmental sequences: The emergence of aspect marking in second language acquisition. In T. Huebner & C. A. Ferguson (Eds.), *Crosscurrents in second language acquisition and linguistic theories* (pp. 305–324). Amsterdam: John Benjamins.
Anthony, L. (2018a). *AntConc (3.5.6 version) [Computer Programs]*. Tokyo: Waseda University. Retrieved from http://www.laurenceanthony.net/programs.
Anthony, L. (2018b). Visualization in corpus-based discourse studies. In C. Taylor & A. Marchi (Eds.), *Corpus approaches to discourse: A critical review* (pp. 197–224). Abingdon: Routledge.
Biber, D., Conrad, S., & Reppen, R. (1998). *Corpus linguistics: Investigating language structure and use*. Cambridge: Cambridge University Press.
Biber, D., Johannson, S., Leech, G., Conrad, S., & Finigan, E. (1999). *Longman grammar of spoken and written English*. Harlow: Pearson.
Crossley, S. A., & Salsbury, T. (2011). The development of lexical bundle accuracy and production in English second language speakers. *International Review of Applied Linguistics in Language Teaching*, *49*(1), 1–26.
Dagneaux, E., Denness, S., & Granger, S. (1998). Computer-aided error analysis. *System*, *26*(2), 163–174.
De Cock, S. (2000). Repetitive phrasal chunkiness and advanced EFL speech and writing. In C. Mair & M. Hundt (Eds.), *Corpus linguistics and linguistic theory* (pp. 51–68). Amsterdam: Rodopi.
De Cock, S. (2019). Foreign words in EFL learner interviewee speech: Lending learners a productive fluency helping hand? In L. Degand, G. Gilquin, L. Meurant, & A. C. Simon (Eds.), *Fluency and disfluency across languages and language varieties* (pp. 283–299). Louvain-la-Neuve: Presses universitaires de louvain.

Dose-Heidelmayer, S., & Götz, S. (2016). The progressive in advanced spoken learner language: A corpus-based analysis of use and misuse. *International Review of Applied Linguistics, 54*(3), 229–256.

Ebeling, S. O., & Hasselgård, H. (2015). Learner corpora and phraseology. In S. Granger, G. Gilquin, & F. Meunier (Eds.), *Cambridge handbook of learner corpus research* (pp. 207–229). Cambridge: Cambridge University Press.

Fuchs, R., & Werner, V. (2018). The use of stative progressives by school-age learners of English and the importance of the variable context: Myth vs. (corpus) reality. *International Journal of Learner Corpus Research, 4*(2), 195–224.

Gilquin, G., De Cock, S., & Granger, S. (2010). *The louvain international database of spoken English interlanguage.* Louvain-la-Neuve: Presses universitaires de louvain.

Götz, S., & Schilk, M. (2011). Formulaic sequences in spoken ENL, ESL and EFL. In M. Hundt & J. Mukherjee (Eds.), *Exploring second-language varieties of English and learner Englishes: Bridging a paradigm gap* (pp. 79–100). Amsterdam: John Benjamins.

Granger, S. (1996). From CA to CIA and back: An integrated approach to computerized bilingual and learner corpora. In K. Aijmer, B. Altenberg, & M. Johansson (Eds.), *Languages in contrast: Text-based cross-linguistic studies* (pp. 37–51). Lund: Lund University Press.

Granger, S. (1998). Prefabricated patterns in advanced EFL writing: Collocations and formulae. In A. P. Cowie (Ed.), *Phraseology: Theory, analysis and applications* (pp. 145–160). Oxford: Oxford University Press.

Granger, S. (2003). Error-tagged learner corpora and CALL: A promising synergy. *CALICO Journal, 20*(3), 465–480.

Granger, S. (2015). Contrastive interlanguage analysis: A reappraisal. *International Journal of Learner Corpus Research, 1*(1), 7–24.

Granger, S., Dagneaux, E., Meunier, F., & Paquot, M. (2020). *The international corpus of learner English: Version 3.* Louvain-la-Neuve: Presses Universitaires de Louvain.

Gray, B., & Biber, D. (2015). Phraseology. In D. Biber & R. Reppen (Eds.), *The Cambridge handbook of English corpus linguistics* (pp. 125–145). Cambridge: Cambridge University Press.

Gries, S. Th. (2013). 50-something years of work on collocations: What is or should be next … *International Journal of Corpus Linguistics, 18*(1), 137–165.

Gries, S. Th. (2016). *Quantitative corpus linguistics with R: A practical introduction* (2nd ed.). London: Routledge, Taylor & Francis Group.

Leńko-Szymańska, A. (2014). The acquisition of formulaic language by EFL learners. A cross-sectional and cross-linguistic perspective. *International Journal of Corpus Linguistics, 19*(2), 225–251.

Lorenz, G. (1999). *Adjective intensification. Learners versus native speakers: A corpus study of argumentative writing.* Amsterdam: Rodopi.

Mukherjee, J. (2009). *Anglistische korpuslinguistik: Eine Einführung.* Berlin: Erich Schmidt.

Mukherjee, J., & Götz, S. (2015). Learner corpora and learning context. In S. Granger, G. Gilquin, & F. Meunier (Eds.), *Cambridge handbook of learner corpus research* (pp. 423–442). Cambridge: Cambridge University Press.

Nesselhauf, N. (2005). *Collocations in a learner corpus.* Amsterdam: John Benjamins.

Paquot, M. (2013). Lexical bundles and transfer effects. *International Journal of Corpus Linguistics, 18*(3), 391–417.

Paquot, M., & Granger, S. (2012). Formulaic language in learner corpora. *Annual Review of Applied Linguistics, 32*, 130–149.

Paquot, M., & Gries, S. Th. (Eds.) (2020). *The practical handbook of corpus linguistics.* New York: Springer.

R Development Core Team (2018). *R: A language and environment for statistical computing.* Vienna: R Foundation for Statistical Computing. Retrieved from www.r-project.org

Rayson, P. (2015). Computational tools and methods from corpus compilation and analysis. In D. Biber & R. Reppen (Eds.), *The Cambridge handbook of English corpus linguistics* (pp. 32–49). Cambridge: Cambridge University Press.

Rayson, P., & Potts, A. (2020). Analyzing keyword lists. In M. Paquot & S. Th. Gries (Eds.), *Practical handbook of corpus linguistics* (pp. 119–139). New York: Springer.

Scott, M. (2017). *WordSmith tools version 7.* Stroud: Lexical Analysis Programs.

Sinclair, J. (1990). *Corpus, concordance, collocation.* Oxford: Oxford University Press.

Stubbs, M. (1995). Collocations and semantic profiles: On the cause of the trouble with quantitative studies. *Functions of Language, 2*(1), 23–55.

Tono, Y., & Díez-Bedmar, M. B. (2014). Focus on learner writing at the beginning and intermediate stages: The ICCI corpus. *International Journal of Corpus Linguistics, 19*(2), 163–177.

Weisser, M. (2016). *Practical corpus linguistics: An introduction to corpus-based language analysis.* Oxford: Wiley-Blackwell.

7

Error Analysis

María Belén Díez-Bedmar

Introduction

Error Analysis (EA) was a fruitful methodology in the 1970s to study the errors made by learners when acquiring a second language (L2) (Corder, 1967). While it went out of fashion in the 1980s, in part because of weaknesses in its methodological procedures (see Dulay et al., 1982), EA was revitalized in the 1990s through Computer-aided Error Analysis (CEA). CEA is a new version of the methodology which tries to overcome the main limitations observed in traditional EA by undertaking the reliable and systematic identification, classification, and annotation of errors or non-target uses of the language in learner corpora (Dagneaux et al., 1998). Nowadays, CEA is one of the main methodologies employed to analyze learner corpora (see Chapter 8, this volume, for more information about other methodologies used in the field) and attracts researchers' attention worldwide (e.g. Lüdeling & Hirschmann, 2015; Díez-Bedmar, 2015; Hinkel, 2018; Muñoz-Basols & Bailini, 2018).

Using a learner corpus to analyze errors in learner language has two main advantages. The first one is the possibility to use a large learner corpus in which learner productions in electronic format can be selected (regarding learners' L1, proficiency level, etc.) and (semi)automatically error-tagged following an error-tagging system. The electronic format of the corpus allows the researchers to annotate larger amounts of learner language. Second, corpus linguistics tools can be used to annotate the errors, check the annotation reliability for each error tag, observe error patterns (general trends, individual trajectories, etc.), obtain frequency counts for each error-tag, retrieve the occurrences of the errors in each error tag, calculate accuracy measures, and reuse or share the error-tagged learner corpus for further analyses. The results obtained from error-tagged learner corpora may inform the fields of Foreign Language Teaching (FLT), Language Testing and Assessment (LTA), Natural Language Processing (NLP), and Second Language Acquisition (SLA) (see Díez-Bedmar 2015 for an overview).

In SLA and LCR, errors are analyzed when focusing on accuracy, i.e., 'the ability to be free from errors while using language' (Wolfe-Quintero, Inagaki, & Kim, 1998, p.33; Chapter 23). LCR studies have frequently adopted traditional SLA accuracy measures to analyze accuracy in learner corpora and considered errors in three ways, namely in terms of frequencies (e.g., total number of errors), ratios (e.g. verb lexical errors per verb), and indices (e.g., error index) (Wolfe-Quintero et al., 1998). When ratios are employed, the measures may consider the relation between the incorrect use of the linguistic category under study and its correct use, as is the case in Pica's (1983) Target-like Utterance and Master's (1987) Used in Obligatory Contexts. Another option is to analyze the relation between a syntactic unit and the occurrences of an error type in the unit, as can be seen in the syntactic error per clause ratio (Wolfe-Quintero et al., 1998). Other measures to analyze accuracy, such as Díez-Bedmar & Pérez-Paredes's (2012) Effective Use and Effective Selection, and Thewissen's (2013, 2015) Potential Occasion Analysis (POA), have also been put forward in LCR.

There are three main differences in the analysis of errors in SLA and LCR. First, SLA studies have traditionally analyzed errors in learner language elicited in experimental language conditions and/or has made use of a limited number of students' productions. The type of language (and errors) elicited in these publications is controlled so that learners produce the linguistic item under study (e.g., article use) and their competence regarding such item can be analyzed. However, LCR studies have analyzed errors in large learner corpora composed of the production of learners in the most naturalistic contexts possible. As a consequence, the language (and errors) produced by the learners is less controlled, which sheds light on the learners' performance. Second, unlike LCR studies, SLA studies rarely use corpus linguistics tools to annotate errors, which may limit the size of the error-tagged learner corpus and may make the error-tagging process and the quantification and retrieval of results troublesome. Third, SLA studies have interpreted learner language in light of SLA theories, while LCR studies have mainly described learner language (Granger, 2012; Myles, 2015; Tracy-Ventura & Myles, 2015). Nowadays, efforts are being made to conduct "corpus-based SLA studies" (Gablasova et al., 2017, p. 130) so that a more comprehensive study of learner language is conducted. Since this type of study is recent, publications in which error annotation is used in learner corpora to test SLA theories are still scarce (e.g., Fuchs & Werner, 2018; Ionin & Díez-Bedmar, in press; Mitkovska & Bužarovska, 2018; Murakami & Alexopoulou, 2016).

Core Issues and Topics

A CEA may be divided into three main stages, as can be seen in Figure 7.1 (see Díez-Bedmar 2015 for a detailed account). In the first stage, the error-tagging system and the error annotation type are selected. The second stage consists in three main steps:

1. Errors are identified (this includes detecting an error and locating the stretch of language that is incorrect, e.g. a morpheme, a word, a phrase) and corrected.
2. The error-tagging process is piloted. As a result of this piloting, the error-tagging system may be fine-tuned.
3. The learner corpus is then error-tagged, and further amendments to the error-tagging system can be made, if necessary.

The three steps described above involve checking inter- and intra-rater agreement (on error identification) and inter- and intra-annotator agreement (on error annotation). In the last stage, the corpus is prepared for posterior data retrieval and statistical analyses. The most important aspects of each stage are discussed in detail here and in the next section.

The Error-tagging System

One of the first decisions to make is what error-tagging system to use to error-tag a learner corpus. Important aspects to consider include how errors are classified, the granularity of the tagset, the availability of the error-tagging manual, and whether the focus is on written or spoken learner data. In an error-tagging system, errors can be classified according to one or more error

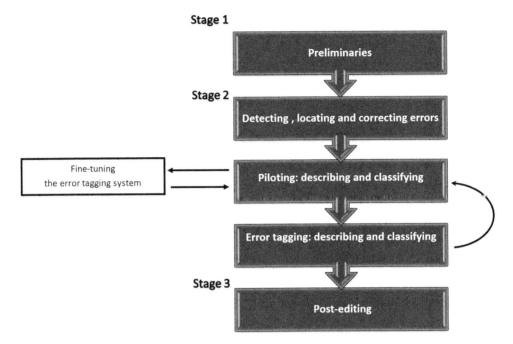

Figure 7.1   Main Stages and Steps in a CEA.

classification criteria. Dulay et al. (1982) presented a four-way classification of errors, which is still used today:

1. The linguistic category describes errors according to the language component and/or linguistic constituent the errors affect.
2. The surface strategy taxonomy is also descriptive and focuses on how the target language has been altered (considering the omission, addition, miss- formation, miss-ordering of language, and the presence of blends).
3. The comparative taxonomy analyzes the errors considering their causes.
4. The communicative effect taxonomy analyzes errors by considering their gravity.

With the exception of the classification for error gravity, which is not considered in CEAs, the different error classifications have often been combined in LCR, as they are considered complementary (Dagneaux et al., 1998; Granger, 2003; James, 1998). The Louvain error-tagging system (Dagneaux et al., 1996; Granger et al., in press) is an example of an error-tagging system that combines three different types of taxonomy: it uses error tags from a linguistic category (e.g., GNN for the expression of number in a noun), error tags from a surface taxonomy (e.g., GADVO, in which adverb word order is classified), and error tags related to the source of error (as in the case of the error tag for False Friends [LSF]).

Error-tagging systems are also characterized by 'the granularity of the tagsets, […] and the possibility of introducing one or more levels of analysis' (Granger et al., 2007, p. 256). Hierarchical and flexible error-tagging systems are recommended, as they allow for the inclusion of new error-tags for a more comprehensive analysis of learner language. This being said, although a higher number of error tags in an error-tagging system would seem to be the best option, as it would provide a more detailed analysis of learner language, a manageable number of error tags should be preferred instead (Granger, 2003). Overly detailed error taxonomies can be cognitively taxing for the annotators, since a high number of error tags can slow down the annotation process; they can also affect inter-annotator agreement (Leacock et al., 2014). Care should be taken to strike a balance between the effort involved in the error-tagging process and research interests (Dickinson & Ledbetter, 2012).

The recommended error-tagging system is the one that comes with an error-tagging manual. Such a document helps systematize error annotation, as it includes the error-tags, their descriptions, and examples of use (Granger, 2003). It also warns about issues that may arise when applying the error-tagging system to learner language (e.g., how to error-tag instances in which a learner attaches a plural morpheme to a determiner, as in the use of *'thats', instead of 'those'). Error-tagging manuals often have different versions, as more specific information on the error tagging system can be provided when fine-tuning the error-tagging system (see Figure 7.1).

The mode of the language in the learner corpus is another aspect to consider when selecting an error-tagging system. Although most taxonomies have been designed for written learner language, some of them have been adapted to the characteristics of oral learner language, such as the distinction between errors and disfluencies (cf. Gilquin & De Cock, 2011). This is the case with the Louvain error-tagging system (Gillová, 2014; Kämmerer, 2009) and the *Cambridge Learner Corpus* (CLC) error-tagging system (Nicholls, 2003; Caines et al., 2017).

Error Identification and Correction

The definition of what an error or non-target use of the language is has always been a subject of debate (James, 1998; Lennon, 1991), although most researchers would agree that an error is an 'unsuccessful bit of language' (James, 1998, p. 1). To identify errors and correct them, native speaker judgments have traditionally been used, sometimes with the help of reference tools. This approach to error identification and correction is, however, controversial. For example, taking the native speaker's judgement or production as the target in the language acquisition process has been criticized as a 'comparative fallacy' (Bley-Vroman, 1983), i.e., learner language should be analyzed on its own and without comparison to a target language. The native speaker model, however, remains a matter of debate in the fields of SLA and LCR (e.g., Granger, 2009, 2015; see also Chapter 8, this volume). Second, decisions must be made regarding the people who will identify errors in the learner corpus, as they represent the reference variety (Granger, 2015), and their error identification judgments may determine the results obtained (Rao & Li, 2017). If native speakers are selected, their profiles need to be explicitly described, as there is no single homogenous native-speaker community (Larsen-Freeman, 2014). Another possibility may be to select speakers of other varieties, such as English as a Lingua Franca and World Englishes speakers (Jenkins, 2009; Mauranen, 2012). In some cases, bilingual speakers (referred to in some publications as near-native speakers) undertake identification and correction tasks. Practically, in many projects, two variables will determine who will be in charge of the identification and correction of errors: the reference variety selected and funding limitations.

Ensuring validity and reliability in the identification and correction of errors is another core issue in error analysis. The ideal scenario would be to have a team of two or more people in charge of that step so that inter-rater reliability could be calculated. Checking inter-rater reliability (as well as intra-rater reliability) is necessary due to issues related to the degree of strictness in error correction (Andreu-Andrés et al., 2010; Díez-Bedmar, 2010; Tetreault & Chodorow, 2008), as well as the difficulty in agreeing on the identification of certain lexical, discursive, and stylistic errors (Andreu-Andrés et al., 2010; Lüdeling & Hirschmann, 2015). One option is to have a bilingual team comprising a representative of the target variety familiar with the students' L1 and a representative of the learners' L1 variety (Andreu-Andrés et al., 2010; Díez-Bedmar, 2015; Granger, 1998). Another option is to ask two or more representatives of the target variety to identify and correct the errors in the learner corpus, thus removing potential bias from the L1 speaker. However, having a representative of the L1 in the team is a plus due to their ability to identify transfer issues or code-switching between languages, especially at lower levels. Again, funding limitations will often determine the number and characteristics of the people in charge of error identification and correction. For this reason, it is necessary that the profiles of the people in charge of error identification and correction are specified in an error annotation project.

Other key aspects in error identification and correction are related to training in error identification and correction and familiarity with the learner data. First, different error identification criteria can be employed, namely correctness, acceptability, or adequacy (or felicity) of learner language (Corder, 1981; James, 1998). Therefore, the criterion selected should be made explicit to the people in charge of error identification. Training sessions should be run with them, ensuring that they keep the student's original wording as much as possible in in-text annotation (and there is no temptation to rewrite the whole text) and that all possible corrections and target hypotheses of each error are listed in the case of multi-layered standoff annotation (see below). Second, the people in charge of the identification and correction of the errors should be familiar with the topics covered in the learner corpus to help them identify certain error types. For instance, in texts written about the film *Twilight* in the ICCI corpus (Tono & Díez-Bedmar, 2014), knowing which male and female characters were wolves or vampires proved decisive when identifying and correcting errors, as the learners indistinctly used any pronoun to refer to them.

Advances have been made to automatize error identification and correction in learner language (Harvey-Scholes, 2018; Kempfert & Köhn, 2018, Leacock et al., 2014; Rosen, 2017). However, the NLP techniques developed to date are most effective for specific error types (e.g., morphological errors). Grammar- and spell-checkers or NLP techniques may represent a first step towards identifying some error types, but human expertise will still be required to make informed decisions about the identification, classification and correction of errors.

Error-tagging the Learner Corpus

The terms 'error-tagging' and 'error annotation' mainly refer to the process of assigning a tag or code which identifies, describes, and, in some cases, explains, the errors made by language learners when acquiring a second language. This is done by classifying the errors that students make when producing the L2 following an error-tagging system (also called an error annotation system or error taxonomy). Other error types, such as the ones which stem from learning disorders, are not considered in error-tagging (see Díez-Bedmar, 2011b).

The annotator, that is, the person who error-tags or annotates the learner corpus following an error-tagging system, may have been involved in the identification and correction of errors (e.g., Vyatkina, 2016) or may be a different person, responsible only for the annotation of errors previously identified (Díez-Bedmar, 2018; Thewissen, 2013). This is so because the people in charge of identifying and correcting errors may not be familiar with the error-taxonomy being employed or may not have enough experience with the error-tagging process. In these cases, an experienced annotator who is familiar with the error-tagging system and the stages needed to error-tag a learner corpus is necessary. Again, however, funding limitations or methodological decisions may determine the number and profile of people involved in the process.

Ideally, people responsible for error-tagging or annotating errors in the learner corpus would meet four requirements:

1. Have experience in error-tagging.
2. Have a good command of the target variety and the learners' L1 variety, which ensures understanding of how error identification and correction were conducted by the people in charge of such tasks.
3. Be part of a bilingual team in which there are people who share the learners' L1 variety and people who represent the target variety.

4. Be familiar with applied linguistics, corpus linguistics, and the linguistics of the L2 to select the appropriate error-tag. This person may need to resort to their knowledge in applied linguistics, especially second language acquisition, manage corpora, and use the necessary metalanguage to classify errors and explain the possible adjustments in the error-tagging ship's log when fine-tuning the error-tagging system.

Although it has been suggested that two annotators are needed to assign an error tag to each error (Granger, 2009), funding limitations will again determine whether a second annotator can indeed participate in the process to ensure consistency by means of inter-annotator agreement tests. If it is not possible to have a second annotator error-tag the whole learner corpus, another option would involve having a second annotator error-tag some sections of the learner corpus (preferably the part used for the piloting of the error-tagging system). This would make it possible to conduct inter-annotator agreement tests on those sections analyzed (Dahlmeier et al., 2013) and apply resolution techniques if necessary.

Fine-tuning the Error-tagging System

With every new CEA project, the error-tagging system employed is put to the test. A new learner corpus may pose different challenges to the error-tagging system, as occurrences of error types that were not included in the original taxonomy may be found. Similarly, the learners' production may call for further specification of the errors to be error-tagged with a specific tag. For example, how should *'musts' be error-tagged? As a morphological error or as a modal verb error? Informed decisions on how to consistently error-tag such cases are to be made and detailed in a recursive and cyclical process (see 'Fine-tuning the error taxonomy', Figure 7.1; see also Díez-Bedmar, 2015). These decisions are reported in an error-tagging ship's log. The ship's log is different from the error-tagging manual in that it is an internal document used by the annotators to add comments and annotations detailing the decisions made when the error-tagging system does not address a specific error type found in a learner corpus or does not specify in detail the errors to be annotated with an error-tag. Whenever new decisions are included in the ship's log, it is necessary to check the learner corpus sample which has already been error-tagged to ensure consistency in the error-tagging of the error types affected by such decisions.

The information contained in the error-tagging ship's log is validated throughout the error-tagging process. When the learner corpus has been error-tagged, the information included in the error-tagging ship's log during the fine-tuning process is included in a new version of the error-tagging manual or included in the current version of the error-tagging manual as an appendix or addendum, always describing the characteristics of the learner corpus (e.g., the learners' L1 and their proficiency level[s]) from which the ship's log is derived. Thus, other researchers interested in using the same error-tagging system to analyze similar learner language will benefit from the experience already gained in previous projects.

Reliability in Error Annotation

The subjectivity involved in identifying, correcting and classifying errors, which makes the process a time-consuming, effort-driven, and challenging task (Andersen, 2011; Díez-Bedmar, 2015; Granger, 2003, 2004), is a characteristic of the error-tagging process. For this reason, it is advisable to a) use an error-tagging system which has been documented in detail thanks to the fine-tuning process described above; and b) to check intra-annotator and inter-annotator agreement. The usefulness of an error-tagged learner corpus depends on the validity and reliability of its annotation. Special attention is to be paid to errors at the lexical, phraseological and discursive levels, as these give rise to a lower inter-annotator agreement, as opposed to errors related to grammatical correctness (Andreu-Andrés et al., 2010; Díez-Bedmar, 2010; Vyatkina, 2016). This fact can also be seen in automatic error identification (Rosen, Hana, Štindlova, & Feldman, 2014).

A first step to improve the annotation is to check intra-annotator reliability, i.e., annotation consistency of one annotator at different stages of the annotation process. For example, this can be done by annotating some sections of the corpus again after some time to check if the annotation is the same, or by extracting concordance lines for all occurrences of a specific error tag and double-checking that the errors to which that error tag has been assigned were coded in agreement with the error-tagging system. A second step is to check inter-annotator agreement, i.e., consistency in the annotation by two or more different annotators. To do so, Cohen's Kappa (Cohen, 1960) is the most frequently employed statistic in papers which report inter-annotator reliability, with values above 0.8 considered high levels of agreement (see, for instance, Dahlmeier et al., 2013; Lee, et al., 2012; Stindlová et al., 2011; Valverde Ibáñez & Ohtani, 2014). Although Cohen's Kappa is still frequently used, issues have also been raised about using this measure for linguistic classification tasks (Artstein & Poesio, 2008). Other statistics, such as the Intraclass Correlation Coefficient (Bartko, 1966) have also been reported (e.g. Crosthwaite et al., 2016). When there is low or no agreement, it is necessary to use resolution techniques. These entail, among others, having other independent annotators check the data and/or discuss the errors on which there is disagreement with a view to reaching a consensus in annotation sessions (see, for instance, Vincze et al., 2016).

Main Research Methods

This section discusses two methodological decisions that are to be made before starting the error-tagging process. It also reviews error editors and annotation tools.

Full Error-tagging vs. Problem-oriented Error Tagging

Research interests (or funding limitations) will determine if all the errors in a learner corpus are to be error-tagged or if the focus will be placed on one specific error type. In the first case, a general error-tagging system such as the Louvain error-tagging system or the CLC error-tagging system is employed, as it covers language use at different linguistic levels (e.g., morphology, lexis). The outcome is a fully error-tagged learner corpus which provides information on the error types and their occurrences in the learner corpus, thus revealing the problematic areas of the learners' L2 use (see, for example, Díez-Bedmar, 2011a; MacDonald et al., 2013). This bird's-eye view of the errors in learner production can be used to then decide on the linguistic feature (e.g., tense and aspect, morphology, collocation) to be analyzed in a follow-up study in which the correct and incorrect (or non-target) uses in learner language can be considered for a better understanding of the language acquisition process.

By contrast, problem-oriented error-tagging typically focuses on just one error type (e.g., learners' use of articles). Researchers who adopt this second approach often develop a more detailed error-tagging system, as in Díez-Bedmar and Papp's (2008) study on article use in Chinese and Spanish learner writing. To annotate correct and incorrect article uses in both learner corpora, they developed a taxonomy which included the features [± specific reference] and [± hearer knowledge], following Bickerton's (1981) semantic wheel. As a result, a more comprehensive analysis of article use in both learner groups was conducted.

Error Annotation Types and Corresponding Tools

There are two types of annotation, flat-level, or in-text annotation, and multi-layered standoff annotation. Both of them allow the annotation of correct and incorrect uses of the language.

When error-tagging using flat-level or in-text annotation, the error-tags are inserted into the text. Example (1), from Díez-Bedmar (2011a), illustrates the use of the Louvain error-tagging system. As can be seen, the first error is the use of the definite article, error-tagged with (GA), which is an error tag for article errors in the error-tagging system employed. In in-text annotation, the correction of the errors can also be annotated so that the language which the learner attempted to produce, but failed to, thus making an error, can be automatically retrieved and analyzed together with the error made. In Example (1) the correct version is placed between dollar signs at the end of the error scope, that is, when the erroneous stretch of language analyzed finishes. In this case, it includes '0' to mean that no article should have been used. The second error found is the use of 'ireland' instead of 'Irish'. For this reason, there are two error-tags. The first one, (FS), indicates that there is a spelling error as Ireland should be capitalized. The correction of this error is inserted between dollar signs, $Ireland$. The second error in this word is the word class employed by the learner, a noun instead of an adjective. This is error-tagged with (GWC), following the error-tagging system, and corrected with the information between the second set of dollar signs $Irish$.

(1) to taste (GA) the 0 (FS) (GWC) ireland $Ireland$ $Irish$ food (et_34582)

Examples of error editors for in-text annotation include the first version of the UCL Error Editor (Hutchinson, 1996), as well as the second, which is XML-compliant (Granger, forthcoming), the TagEditor (Izumi et al., 2003), and the error editor used by Lee et al. (2014). Well-known learner corpora which have been error-tagged with in-text annotation include the CLC (Nicholls, 2003), the ICLE (Dagneaux et al., 1998; Thewissen, 2013), the FRIDA corpus (Granger, 2003), and the NICT JLE Corpus (Izumi et al., 2003).

Multi-layered standoff annotation allows the annotation of different aspects of learner language in layers, rather than in the learner text itself. As illustrated in Figure 7.2a,[1] where the 'tok' line features the learner's sentence, each layer represents a different level of annotation. For example, the layers at the top include a linguistic analysis, with tokens ('ctok'), lemmas ('ctok-lemma'), POS analysis with two different taggers ('ctokpos' and 'ctokrfPos') and morphological analysis ('ctokrfMorph'). This practice is in line with the 'clean-text policy' (Sinclair, 1991, p. 21) by means of which learner texts are kept 'clean' or raw so that they are ready for further analyses.

Irrespective of the error-tagging system employed or the type of annotation conducted, it is necessary to bear the target form or target hypothesis in mind when error-tagging the learner corpus (Dagneaux et al., 1998; Lüdeling & Hirschmann, 2015). Although it is impossible to be completely sure what the learner was trying to produce and the processes they went through resulting in (incorrect or non-target like) language, the experienced researcher may predict what the student was aiming at. In multi-layered annotation, it is possible to suggest different target hypotheses. In Figure 7.2a, for example, the learner sentence 'Also have I eat for my guest.' in the 'tok' line has been morphosyntactically annotated. The 'ZH1' lines in Figure 7.2b present the output of error annotation based on the Minimal Target Hypothesis, which considers the minimal number of changes in learner language to make the sentence a grammatically correct one in the target language. This annotation is often used as input for further automatic analyses (cf. the 'ctok' lines) as automatic tools often provide better analyses for language samples that approximate as closely as possible the language models on which they have been trained (see Chapter 5, this volume). In this case, the change in ZH1 is a grammatical change: the verb 'essen' ('to eat', lower case) has been changed (ZH1Diff = CHA) to the noun 'Essen' ('food', upper case). In Figure 7.2c, the 'ZH2' lines are used to represent error analyses based on the Extended Target Hypothesis, which goes beyond the form and annotates the errors for meaning,

(a)

ctok	Auch	habe	ich	essen	für	meinen	Gast	.
ctoklemma	auch	haben	ich	essen	für	mein	Gast	.
ctokpos	ADV	VAFIN	PPER	VVINF	APPR	PPOSAT	NN	$.
ctokrfMorph		Aux.1.Sg.Pres.Ind	Pers.Subst.1.Nom.Sg.*6	Full2	Other.XY	Poss.Attr3.Acc.Sg.Masc	Reg.Acc.Sg.Masc	Pun.Sent
ctokrfPos	ADV	VAFIN	PPER	VVINF	XY	PPOSAT	NN	$.
tok	Auch	habe	ich	essen	für	meinen	Gast	.

(b)

ZH1	Auch	habe	ich	Essen	für	meinen	Gast	.
ZH1DepID	102,000000	103,000000	104,000000	105,000000	106,000000	107,000000	108,000000	109,000000
ZH1Diff			CHA					
ZH1S	s10							
ZH1lemma	auch	haben	ich	Essen	für	mein	Gast	
ZH1lemmaDiff			CHA					
ZH1pos	ADV	VAFIN	PPER	NN	APPR	PPOSAT	NN	$.
ZH1posDiff			CHA					
ZH1rfMorph		Aux.1.Sg.Pres.Ind	Pers.Subst.1.Nom.Sg.*6	Reg.Acc.Sg.Neut	Reg.Nom.Sg.Masc	Poss.Attr3.Acc.Sg.Masc	Reg.Acc.Sg.Masc	Pun.Sent
ZH1rfPos	ADV	VAFIN	PPER	NN	NN	PPOSAT	NN	$.
tok	Auch	habe	ich	essen	für	meinen	Gast	

(c)

ZH2	Ich		habe	auch		Essen	für	meine	Gäste	.
ZH2Diff	MOVT	MOVS		MOVT	MOVS	CHA		CHA	CHA	
ZH2lemma	ich		haben	auch		Essen	für	mein	Gast	.
ZH2lemmaDiff	MOVT	MOVS		MOVT	MOVS	CHA				
ZH2pos	PPER		VAFIN	ADV		NN	APPR	PPOSAT	NN	$.
ZH2posDiff	MOVT	MOVS		MOVT	MOVS	CHA				
tok		Auch	habe	ich		essen	für	meinen	Gast	.

Figure 7.2   (a)–(c) An Example of Multi-layered Standoff Annotation in the KANDEL Corpus Using EXMARaLDA.

communicative function, and style of learner language (Rezniceck et al., 2012). The ZH2 is 'I have also food for my guests', which shows additional stylistic changes to the learner's original sentence. First, the adverb 'auch' ('also') has been moved (ZH2Diff = MOVT, MOVS) since it is stylistically better not to start the sentence with it. After moving 'auch' away from the initial position, the subject 'ich' ('I') had to be moved to the beginning of the sentence because it cannot start with a verb ('habe'). Another change is seen in 'meinen Gast' (sg) which is changed (ZH2Diff = CHA, CHA) to 'meine Gäste' (pl) because the learner describes a party with several guests (in the plural).

Another advantage of multi-layered standoff annotation is that different layers can be used to include competing error corrections, i.e., error corrections that may be possible when trying to envisage the language the learner was attempting (Lüdeling et al., 2005; Lüdeling & Hirschmann, 2015). Although this practice may be useful to study how errors can be approached from different perspectives, listing competing error corrections in a learner corpus may often be difficult because of funding or time limitations.

Examples of annotation tools that can be used to undertake multi-layered or multi-tier standoff error annotation are the UAM Corpus Tool (http://www.corpustool.com/), EXMARaLDA (http://exmaralda.org/en/), ANNIS (http://corpus-tools.org/annis/), and TEITOK (http://beta.clu l.ul.pt/teitok/site/index.php?action=home); all of them are freely available online. This type of annotation is found, for instance, in the FALKO corpus (Lüdeling et al., 2005), the CzeSL corpus (Rosen et al., 2014), and the KANDEL corpus (Vyatkina, 2016).

Representative Corpora and Research

Fuchs and Werner (2018) examined whether EFL students at beginning and lower-intermediate levels from different L1 backgrounds extend the progressive to stative verbs, thus testing part of the Aspect Hypothesis (AH). To do so, the written production of learners whose L1s have a grammaticalized progressive or continuous construction (Cantonese, Japanese, Mandarin, and Spanish) and those whose L1s do not (German, Hebrew, and Polish) were analyzed in the *International Corpus of Crosslinguistic Interlanguage* (ICCI) (Tono & Díez-Bedmar, 2014). This corpus was used because it is a cross-sectional written learner corpus composed of productions in a variety of topics by learners at all levels in the secondary education system in eight different regions/countries around the world.

After retrieving the progressive and non-progressive verb forms of forty-two stative and two dynamic verbs, the authors opted for problem-oriented (error-)tagging, as they manually annotated both the target-like and non-target like (or erroneous) stative progressives. The results showed that learners at these levels rarely used stative progressives regardless of their L1. The data obtained in the study also suggest that the existence of the progressive construction in the learners' L1 is not a facilitating factor. The learners whose L1s do not have a progressive construction produced more target-like patterns than the learners who have the progressive construction in their L1s.

Ionin and Díez-Bedmar (in press) analyzed the role played by L1 (Spanish, a language with an article system and Russian, a language without an article system) and proficiency (B1 and B2 levels in the CEFR) in article use in learner language and tested the degree to which the factor of 'specificity as speaker intent to refer' governs the overrepresentation of 'the', as found for elicited data (Ionin et al., 2004). To do so, 200 texts were retrieved from the CLC. This corpus is composed of the Cambridge ESOL English exams that students take all over the world. These exams are aligned to the CEFR levels and include different text types (e.g., argumentative, descriptive, informative, etc.).

A taxonomy was designed for the manual problem-oriented (error-)tagging of correct and incorrect article use. The following five variables were considered in the taxonomy: 1) correct vs. incorrect use, 2) category, 3) article used by the learner vs. target article, 4) type and plurality, and, 5) linguistic context in which the article is employed (e.g., *there*-construction, predicative, wide-scope). The findings showed that the learners' L1 affected article use, as Spanish learners produced fewer errors than their Russian counterparts, and they were the only learner group who showed a decrease in the number of errors made as proficiency increased. The definite article was not overrepresented in the Spanish learner corpus, as there were only a few cases. However, this overrepresentation was found in Russian B2 learners. The analysis of such cases revealed that when *the* was overrepresented with specific indefinites, 'specificity as speaker intent to refer' played an important role. However, this was not so when *the* was overrepresented with non-specific indefinites, a finding which had not been found in elicited data.

Future Directions

The number of error-tagged learner corpora is increasing nowadays (see Thewissen's 2015 overview), with more attention being paid to oral learner language and target languages other than English. However, most error-tagged learner corpora are not normally shared, being kept by research teams or individual researchers. If more error-tagged learner corpora were made available, the role played by non-target uses of the language could be further explored in the light of SLA theories, enriching them and obtaining a better understanding of second or foreign language acquisition.

Efforts should also be made to improve the methodology. First, studies on the difficulties posed by both identifying and classifying errors are needed. Given that lower inter-rater agreement rates are found in lexical, phraseological and discursive aspects of the language, it is necessary to improve inter-annotator agreements in the identification and classification of these errors.

This can be done by fine-tuning the error-taxonomies, reporting intra-annotator agreement, working in teams so that inter-rater and inter-annotator agreements can be obtained, and documenting the resolution techniques employed to minimize the subjectivity involved in the process.

Second, the description of error-tagging systems should include information on the learner corpora in which they have been used. Those error-tagging systems which have been fine-tuned for different L1s, proficiency levels or topics should clearly indicate so, including the result of such fine-tuning process as an appendix. If this is done, researchers interested in using that error-tagging system for a similar corpus can benefit from the effort previously made, thus saving time and resources. Likewise, it would be ideal that error-tagging manuals, and especially those which have been fine-tuned after having been used with actual learner corpora, are made available to help researchers decide on the suitability of an error-tagging system for their own research purposes. Although there are some manuals available online (see, for instance, the ones for Falko[2] and the TREACLE project[3]) many others are not.

Finally, the NLP techniques developed to date to automatically detect and classify errors may be of help in the error annotation process, mostly to identify and annotate some grammatical aspects of learner language. Advances such as the ones in Crossley et al. (2019) are promising. However, further joint research between LCR and NLP is needed. To achieve this two-way collaboration, reliably error-tagged learner corpora are required so that gold standards are provided to NLP practitioners. With the information provided, NLP colleagues can advance on solid ground in developing new tools to ensure that the use of NLP techniques to identify and correct errors results in high-quality error-tagged learner corpora.

Further Reading

Andreu-Andrés, M., Astor-Guardiola, A., Boquera-Matarredona, A., Macdonald, M., Montero-Fleta, P. B., & Pérez-Sabater, C. (2010). Analysing EFL learner output in the MiLC project: An error it's*, but which tag? In M. C. Campoy-Cubillo, B. Bellés-Fortuño, & M. L. Gea-Valor (Eds.), *Corpus-based approaches to English language teaching* (pp. 167–188). London: Continuum.

This chapter describes some of the difficulties encountered when using an error-tagging system for the first time.

Dagneaux, E., Denness, S., & Granger, S. (1998). Computer-aided error analysis. *System, 26*(2), 163–174.

This paper can be considered the bridge between EA and CEA. After presenting the limitations of EA, CEA and its advantages are introduced.

Lüdeling, A., & Hirschmann, H. (2015). Error annotation systems. In S. Granger, F. Meunier, & G. Gilquin (Eds.), *The Cambridge handbook of learner corpus research* (pp. 135–157). Cambridge: Cambridge University Press.

This chapter reviews the main aspects related to error annotation. It is especially recommended for researchers interested in multi-layered standoff annotation.

Related Topics

Chapters 6 and 23.

Notes

1 My gratitude to Nina Vyatkina for this screenshot.
2 https://www.linguistik.hu-berlin.de/de/institut/professuren/korpuslinguistik/forschung/falko/Falko-Handbuchv2.0.pdf/view
3 http://www.treacle.es/error.html

References

Andersen, Ø. E. (2011). Semi-automatic ESOL error annotation. *English Profile Journal*, 2, e1.

Andreu-Andrés, M., Astor-Guardiola, A., Boquera-Matarredona, A., Macdonald, M., Montero-Fleta, P. B., & Pérez-Sabater, C. (2010). Analysing EFL learner output in the MiLC project: An error it's*, but which tag? In M. C. Campoy-Cubillo, B. Bellés-Fortuño, & M. L. Gea-Valor (Eds.), *Corpus-based approaches to English language teaching* (pp. 167–188). London: Continuum.

Artstein, R., & Poesio, M. (2008). Inter-coder agreement for computational linguistics. *Computational Linguistics*, *34*(4), 555–596.

Bartko, J. J. (1966). The intraclass correlation coefficient as a measure of reliability. *Psychological Reports*, *19*(1), 3–11.

Bickerton, D. (1981). *Roots of language*. Ann Arbor: Karoma Press.

Bley-Vroman, R. (1983). The comparative fallacy in interlanguage studies: The case of systematicity. *Language Learning*, *33*(1), 1–17.

Caines, A., Nicholls, D., & Buttery, P. (2017). *Annotating errors and disfluencies in transcriptions of speech*. Technical report no. 915. Cambridge: University of Cambridge.

Cohen, J. (1960). A coefficient of agreement for nominal scales. *Educational and Psychological Measurement*, *20*(1), 37–46.

Corder, P. (1967). The significance of learners' errors. *International Review of Applied Linguistics*, *5*(4), 161–170.

Corder, P. (1981). *Error analysis and interlanguage*. Oxford: Oxford University Press.

Crossley, S. A., Bradfield, F., & Bustamante, A. (2019). Using human judgments to examine the validity of automated grammar, syntax, and mechanical errors in writing. *Journal of Writing Research*, *11*(2), 251–270.

Crosthwaite, P., Choy, L., & Bae, Y. (2016). "Almost people": A learner corpus account of L2 use and misuse of non-numerical quantification. *Open Linguistics*, *2*(1), 317–336.

Dagneaux, E., Denness, S., & Granger, S. (1998). Computer-aided error analysis. *System*, *26*(2), 163–174.

Dagneaux, E., Denness, S., Granger, S., & Meunier, F. (1996). *Error tagging manual version 1.1*. Louvain-la-Neuve: Centre for English Corpus Linguistics, Université catholique de Louvain.

Dahlmeier, D., Ng, H. T., & Wu, S. M. (2013). Building a large annotated corpus of learner English: The NUS corpus of learner English. *Proceedings of the 8th workshop on innovative use of NLP for building educational applications (BEA)*. Retrieved from http://www.aclweb.org/anthology/W13-1703

Dickinson, M., & Ledbetter, S. (2012). Annotating errors in a Hungarian learner corpus. In N. Calzolari et al. (Eds.), *Proceedings of the international conference on language resources and evaluation*. LREC. Retrieved from http://www.lrec-conf.org/proceedings/lrec2012/pdf/758_Paper.pdf

Díez-Bedmar, M. B. (2010). *Analysis of the written expression in English in the university entrance examination at the university of Jaén*. PhD dissertation. Jaén: University of Jaén.

Díez-Bedmar, M. B. (2011a). Spanish pre-university students' use of English: CEA results from the university entrance exam. *International Journal of English Studies*, *11*(2), 141–158.

Díez-Bedmar, M. B. (2011b). Detecting learning disorders in students' written production in the foreign language: Are learner corpora of any help? *Porta Linguarum*, *15*, 35–54.

Díez-Bedmar, M. B. (2015). Dealing with errors in learner corpora to describe, teach and assess EFL writing: Focus on article use. In E. Castello, K. Ackerley, & F. Coccetta (Eds.), *Studies in learner corpus linguistics: Research and applications for foreign language teaching and assessment* (pp. 37–69). Bern: Peter Lang Publishing.

Díez-Bedmar, M. B. (2018). Fine-tuning descriptors for CEFR B1 level: Insights from learner corpora. *ELT Journal*, *72*(2), 199–209.

Díez-Bedmar, M. B., & Papp, S. (2008). The use of the English article system by Chinese and Spanish learners. In G. Gilquin, S. Papp, & M. B. Díez-Bedmar (Eds.), *Linking up contrastive and learner corpus research* (pp. 147–175). Amsterdam: Rodopi.

Díez-Bedmar, M. B., & Pérez Paredes, P. (2012). A cross-sectional analysis of the use of the English articles in Spanish learner writing. In Y. Tono, Y. Kawaguchi, & M. Minegishi (Eds.), *Developmental and crosslinguistic perspectives in learner corpus research* (pp. 139–157). Amsterdam: John Benjamins.

Dulay, H., Burt, M., & Krashen, S. (1982). *Language two*. Oxford: Oxford University Press.

Fuchs, R., & Werner, V. (2018). The use of stative progressives by school-age learners of English and the importance of the variable context. Myth vs. (corpus) reality. *International Journal of Learner Corpus Research*, *42*(2), 195–224.

Gablasova, D., Brezina, V., & McEnery, T. (2017). Exploring learner language through corpora: Comparing and interpreting corpus frequency information. *Language Learning*, *67*(s1), 130–154.

Gillová, L. (2014). *Tagging a spoken learner corpus*. MA dissertation. Prague: Univerzita Karlova v Praze.

Gilquin, G., & De Cock, S. (2011). Errors and disfluencies in spoken corpora: Setting the scene. *International Journal of Corpus Linguistics*, *16*(2), 141–172.

Granger, S. (1998). The computerized learner corpus: A versatile new source of data for SLA research. In S. Granger (Ed.), *Learner English on computer* (pp. 3–18). London: Addison Wesley Longman.

Granger, S. (2003). Error-tagged learner corpora and CALL: A promising synergy. *CALICO Journal*, *20*(3), 465–480.

Granger, S. (2004). Practical applications of learner corpora. In B. Lewandowska-Tomaszczyk (Ed.), *Practical applications in language and computers* (pp. 291–301). Frankfurt: Peter Lang Publishing.

Granger, S. (2009). The contribution of learner corpora to second language acquisition and foreign language teaching: A critical evaluation. In K. Aijmer (Ed.), *Corpora and language teaching* (pp. 13–32). Amsterdam: John Benjamins.

Granger, S. (2012). How to use foreign and second language learner corpora. In A. Mackey & S. Gass (Eds.), *Research methods in second language acquisition: A practical guide* (pp. 7–29). Malden: Blackwell Publishing.

Granger, S. (2015). Contrastive interlanguage analysis: A reappraisal. *International Journal of Learner Corpus Research*, *1*(1), 7–24.

Granger, S. (in press). *Université catholique de Louvain error editor. Version 2 (UCLEEv2)*. Louvain-la-Neuve: Centre for English Corpus Linguistics. Université catholique de Louvain.

Granger, S., Kraif, O., Ponton, C., Antoniadis, G., & Zampa, V. (2007). Integrating learner corpora and natural language processing: A crucial step towards reconciling technological sophistication and pedagogical effectiveness. *ReCALL*, *19*(3), 252–268.

Granger, S., Meunier, F., Neff, J., Swallow, H., & Thewissen, J. (in press). *The Louvain error tagging manual. Version 2.0*. Louvain-la-Neuve: Centre for English Corpus Linguistics. Université catholique de Louvain.

Harvey-Scholes, C. (2018). Computer-assisted detection of 90% of EFL student errors. *Computer Assisted Language Learning*, *31*(1–2), 144–156.

Hinkel, E. (2018). Error analysis. In J. Liontas (Ed.), *The TESOL encyclopedia of English language teaching, V, teaching grammar & teaching vocabulary* (pp. 2729–2733). Oxford: Wiley-Blackwell.

Hutchinson, J. (1996). *UCL error editor*. Louvain-la-Neuve: CECL, Université catholique de Louvain.

Ionin, T., & Díez-Bedmar, M. B. (in press). Article use in Russian and Spanish learner writing at CEFR B1 and B2 levels: Effects of proficiency, native language, and specificity. In B. Le Bruyn & M. Paquot (Eds.), *Learner corpus research meets second language acquisition*. Cambridge: Cambridge University Press.

Ionin, T., Ko, H., & Wexler, K. (2004). Article semantics in L2 acquisition: The role of specificity. *Language Acquisition*, *12*(1), 3–69.

Izumi, E., Uchimoto, K., Saiga, T., Supnithi, T., Uchimoto, K., & Isahara, H. (2003). The development of the spoken corpus of Japanese learner English and the applications in collaboration with NLP techniques. In D. Archer, P. Rayson, A. Wilson, & T. McEnery (Eds.), *Proceedings of the corpus linguistics* (pp. 359–566). Lancaster: Lancaster University.

James, C. (1998). *Errors in language learning and use. Exploring error analysis*. London: Longman.

Jenkins, J. (2009). English as a lingua franca: Interpretations and attitudes. *World Englishes*, *28*(2), 200–207.

Kämmerer, S. (2009). Error-tagging spoken features of (learner) language: The UCL error editor revisited [conference session]. *30th conference of the international computer archive of modern and medieval English (ICAME 30)*. Lancaster.

Kempfert, I., & Köhn, C. (2018). An automatic error tagger for German. In *Proceedings of the 7th workshop on NLP for computer assisted language learning at SLTC 2018 (NLP4CALL 2018)*. Stockholm: LiU Electronic Press.

Larsen-Freeman, D. (2014). Another step to be taken: Rethinking the end point of the interlanguage continuum. In Z. -H. Han & E. Tarone (Eds.), *Interlanguage: Forty years later* (pp.203–220). Amsterdam: John Benjamins.

Leacock, C., Chodorow, M., Gamon, M., & Tetreault, J. (2014). *Automated grammatical error detection for language learners* (2nd ed.). San Rafael: Morgan and Claypool Publishers Publishers.

Lee, L.-H., Lee, K.-C., Chang, L.-P., Tseng, Y.-H., Yu, L-C., & Chen, H.-H. (2014). A tagging editor for learner corpora annotation and error analysis. In C.-C. Liu et al. (Eds.), *Proceedings of the 22nd international conference on computers in education* (pp. 806–808). Japan: Asia Publishing-Pacific Society for Computers in Education.

Lee, S.-H., Dickinson, M., & Israel, R. (2012, July 12-13). Developing learner corpus annotation for Korean particle errors. In *Proceedings of the 6th linguistic annotation workshop* (pp. 129–133). Jeju, Korea: The Association of Computational Linguistics (ACL)

Lennon, P. (1991). Error: Some problems of definition, identification, and distinction. *Applied Linguistics*, *12*(2), 180–195.

Lüdeling, A., & Hirschmann, H. (2015). Error annotation systems. In S. Granger, F. Meunier, & G. Gilquin (Eds.), *The Cambridge handbook of learner corpus research* (pp. 135–157). Cambridge: Cambridge University Press.

Lüdeling, A., Walter, M., Kroymann, E., & Adolphs, P. (2005). Multi-level error annotation in learner corpora. In P. Danielsson & M. Wagenmakers (Eds.), *Proceedings of the corpus linguistics 2005 conference*. Retrieved from http://www.corpus.bham.ac.uk/PCLC/Falko-CL2006.doc

MacDonald, P., García-Carbonell, A., & Carot-Sierra, J. M. (2013). Computer learner corpora: Analysing interlanguage errors in synchronous and asynchronous communication. *Language Learning and Technology*, *17*(2), 36–56.

Master, P. (1987). *A cross-linguistic interlanguage analysis of the acquisition of the English article system*. Doctoral dissertation. University of California.

Mauranen, A. (2012). *Exploring ELF: Academic English shaped by non-native speakers*. Cambridge: Cambridge University Press

Mitkovska, L., & Bužarovska, E. (2018). Subject pronoun (non)-realization in the English learner language of Macedonian speakers. *Second Language Research*, *34*(4), 463–485.

Muñoz-Basols, J., & Bailini, S. (2018). Análisis y corrección de errores / error analysis and error correction. In J. Muñoz-Basols, E. Gironzetti, & M. Lacorte (Eds.), *The Routledge handbook of Spanish language teaching: Metodologías, contextos y recursos para la enseñanza del español L2* (pp. 94–108). London: Routledge.

Murakami, A., & Alexopoulou, T. (2016). L1 influence on the acquisition order of English grammatical morphemes: A learner corpus study. *Studies in Second Language Acquisition*, *38*(3), 365–401.

Myles, F. (2015). Second language acquisition theory and learner corpus research. In S. Granger, G. Gilquin, & F. Meunier (Eds.), *The Cambridge handbook of learner corpus research* (pp. 309–331). Cambridge: Cambridge University Press.

Nicholls, D. (2003). The Cambridge learner corpus: Error coding and analysis for lexicography and ELT. In D. Archer, P. Rayson, A. Wilson, & T. McEnery (Eds.), *Proceedings of the corpus linguistics 2003 conference* (pp. 572–581). UCREL: Lancaster University. Retrieved from http://ucrel.lancs.ac.uk/publications/CL2003/papers/nicholls.pdf

Pica, T. (1983). Methods of morpheme quantification: Their effect on the interpretation of second language data. *Studies in Second Language Acquisition*, *6*(1), 49–78.

Rao, A., & Li, X. (2017). Native and non-native teachers' perceptions of error gravity: The effects of cultural and educational factors. *The Asia-Pacific Education Researcher*, *26*(1–2), 51–59.

Reznicek, M., Lüdeling, A., Krummes, C., & Schwantuschke, F. (2012). *Das Falko-Handbuch. Korpusaufbau und Annotationen Version 2.0*. Retrieved from https://www.linguistik.hu-berlin.de/de/institut/professuren/korpuslinguistik/forschung/falko/Falko-Handbuchv2.0.pdf/view

Rosen, A. (2017). Introducing a corpus of non-native Czech with automatic annotation. In P. Pęzik, J. Waliński, & K. Kosecki (Eds.), *Language, corpora and cognition* (pp. 163–180). Frankfurt am Main: Peter Lang Publishing.

Rosen, A., Hana, J., Štindlova, B., & Feldman, A. (2014). Evaluating and automating the annotation of a learner corpus. *Language Resources and Evaluation*, *48*(1), 65–92.

Sinclair, J. (1991). *Corpus, concordance, collocation*. Oxford: Oxford University Press.

Štindlová, B., Rosen, A., Hana, J., & Škodová, S. (2012). CzeSL – An error tagged corpus of Czech as a second language. In P. Pęzik (Ed.), *Corpus data across languages and disciplines* (pp. 21–32). Frankfurt am Main: Peter Lang Publishing.

Tetreault, J. R., & Chodorow, M. (2008). Native judgments of non-native usage: Experiments in preposition error detection. In COLING workshop on human judgement in computational linguistics. Retrieved from http://www.aclweb.org/anthology/W08-1205.pdf

Thewissen, J. (2013). Capturing L2 accuracy developmental patterns: Insights from an error-tagged EFL learner corpus. *The Modern Language Journal*, *97*(S1), 77–101.

Thewissen, J. (2015). *Accuracy across proficiency levels: A learner corpus approach*. Louvain-la-Neuve: Presses universitaires de Louvain.

Tono, Y., & Díez-Bedmar, M. B. (2014). Focus on learner writing at the beginning and intermediate stages: The ICCI corpus. *International Journal of Corpus Linguistics*, *19*(2), 163–177.

Tracy-Ventura, N., & Myles, F. (2015). The importance of task variability in the design of learner corpora for SLA research. *International Journal of Learner Corpus Research*, *1*(1), 58–95.

Valverde Ibáñez, M. P., & Ohtani, A. (2014). Annotating article errors in Spanish learner texts: Design and evaluation of an annotation scheme. In W. Aroonmmanakun, T. Supnithi, & P. Boonkwan (Eds.),

Proceedings of the 28th Pacific Asia conference on language, information and computation (PACLIC) (pp. 234–243). Phuket: Thailand.

Vincze, O., García-Salido, M., Orol, A., & Alonso-Ramos, M. (2016). A corpus study of Spanish as a foreign language learners' collocation production. In M. Alonso-Ramos (Ed.), *Spanish learner corpus research. Current trends and future perspectives* (pp. 299–331). Amsterdam: John Benjamins.

Vyatkina, N. (2016). The Kansas developmental learner corpus (KANDEL). *International Journal of Learner Corpus Research, 2*(1), 102–120.

Wolfe-Quintero, K., Inagaki, S., & Kim, H.-Y. (1998). *Second language development in writing: Measures of fluency, accuracy, and complexity*. Honolulu: University of Hawaii Press.

8

Comparing Learner Corpora

Sandra C. Deshors and Stefan Th. Gries

Introduction

The comparison of learner data is a fundamental notion in the fields of Learner Corpus Research (LCR) and Second Language Acquisition (SLA). Indeed, comparing learner data is important for two main reasons. First, by comparing how the use of a given second/foreign language (e.g. English) by a particular learner population (e.g. French learners of English) differs from how native speakers use that language, researchers can explore how the learner variety (or *interlanguage*) differs from the native variety and to what extent observed differences in the learners' output can tell us something about learners' systematic knowledge of their interlanguage. Second, by comparing how different learner populations (e.g. learners with different native language backgrounds) use a common second language, researchers can explore to what extent learners' native language influences their respective interlanguage. Put differently, researchers can capture and understand the forces that drive cross-linguistic transfer during second language production.[1] Importantly, however, although the notion of comparing learner data is central to both LCR and SLA, the two fields have approached the notion differently. In LCR, comparability has been at the core of the methodological framework(s) upon which the entire research field has developed over the past twenty years. Further, the notion has also been at the forefront of the design and compilation of major learner corpora and the development of gradually more and more sophisticated statistical approaches. Back in the late 1990s when the first large-scale learner corpus, the *International Corpus of Learner English* (ICLE; ICLEv1: Granger et al., 2002; ICLEv2: Granger et al., 2009) was developed, comparability across learner Englishes was a central part of the corpus design as scholars recognized that "the main innovative aspect of ICLE is the systematic approach to corpus design and the compilation of *comparable* sub-corpora produced by learners with a wide range of mother-tongue backgrounds" (Hasselgård & Johansson, 2011, p. 37; our emphasis). However, maximizing the comparability of learner corpora is a complex task that calls for scholars' attention at all stages of corpus research. In this context, and to increase the reliability of learner corpora comparisons, theoretical frameworks such as the Contrastive Interlanguage Analysis (CIA; i.e. comparisons of native vs. non-native language and/or comparisons of non-native varieties) and the Integrated Contrastive Model (ICM; i.e. combination of a contrastive analysis that compares original data in different native languages and CIA), which we discuss below, were developed and widely applied within the learner corpus research community, mainly for the description of learner language. However, amongst SLA scholars, those two frameworks have not been at the center of attention (see for example, Ellis et al., 2016 and Ellis & Ferreira-Junior, 2009, scholars who do not represent 'mainstream' LCR in the sense that although they still use corpus comparison as a main research method, they have done so without necessarily referring to CIA/ICM). Further, in the SLA community, the two frameworks have met some resistance, particularly with regard to comparability and the notion of normative standard. For instance, Hunston (2002) and Larsen-Freeman (2014) have questioned the validity of comparing interlanguage varieties (ILs) with a target language (TL; i.e. a native norm) on the grounds that such comparisons suffer from a 'comparative fallacy': Comparisons with the TL can seriously hinder the description of the IL (Bley-Vroman, 1983, p. 2) because ILs have been argued to be linguistic systems that should be described "in their own terms" (Selinker, 2014, p. 230). However, as noted in Paquot (2007), a large proportion of SLA research has nonetheless succumbed to the 'comparative fallacy' (see Lakshmanan & Selinker, 2001 and Firth & Wagner, 1998). In addition, Larsen-Freeman (2014) objects to how TL vs. IL comparisons imply that learners are deficient speakers; and Hunston (2002) criticizes LCR for assuming a native-speaker norm that learners would target with their IL, which does not quite align with Selinker's notion of describing IL systems in their own terms. That being said, much of SLA research compares learners of different proficiency levels and is small scale. Compared to existing LCR work though, fewer SLA studies include learners of different native language backgrounds learning the same target language (Granger, 2009; however, see McManus, 2015, for an example of an SLA study that does distinguish between L1 groups).

In this context, this chapter explores theoretical and methodological issues related to comparing learner data with a view to first highlight how corpora allow us to analyze larger data sets and second how, in this regard, SLA can learn from LCR.[2] We begin the chapter by presenting the Integrated Contrastive Model (ICM) and the Contrastive Interlanguage Analysis (CIA) methodological frameworks upon which the field of Learner Corpus Research has developed. Then, we present the main research methods and tools scholars have used within the ICM and CIA traditions. We continue by discussing representative research approaches trends in LCR including the description and clustering of learner language varieties as well as the prediction of learners' linguistic choices. Finally, we end with guidelines for future directions on how to ensure greater, more reliable comparisons of learner corpora.

Core Issues and Topics

Theoretical Frameworks at the Core of Learner Corpus Research: The Integrated Contrastive Model (ICM) and Contrastive Interlanguage Analysis (CIA)

For the past two decades, LCR has developed around two main and related methodological frameworks that have shaped the field by establishing principled approaches to comparing learner corpora, Granger's (1996) ICM and CIA approaches. As for the CIA, Hasselgård and Johansson (2011) argue that the approach "has turned out to be a fruitful paradigm" (p. 57); and as for the ICM, Gilquin (2000/2001) notes that the framework "has undoubtedly much to offer to anyone interested in SLA" (p. 123). The success of both the CIA and ICM lies in their ability to help scholars characterize individual interlanguage (IL) varieties through the use of automatic and semi-automatic computerized tools. More specifically, with the CIA and ICM, the field has witnessed the emergence of studies highlighting general lexical or morpho-syntactic behavioral tendencies within interlanguage varieties. Based on those tendencies, scholars have been able to identify (dis)similarities between different learner populations (see Hasselgård & Johansson, 2011 for a recent review of the field).

In essence, together, the frameworks capture linguistic patterns that allow researchers to better distinguish the linguistic systems of learner language from those of native language as well as those of different learner language varieties. The frameworks are related in that the CIA is a part of the ICM framework, as illustrated in Figure 8.1, but they are also different. First, they serve different purposes: whereas the ICM mainly captures cases of cross-linguistic transfer, the CIA serves to explore (individual) learner varieties. Second and consequently, they differ with regard to the type of (learner) language comparisons they involve.

As shown in Figure 8.1, the ICM combines Contrastive Analysis (CA; i.e. the comparison of source and translated data on the basis of translation corpora) in the upper part of the figure and CIA in the lower part of the figure. In Granger's (1996) words, "[t]he [ICM] model involves constant to-ing and fro-ing between CA and CIA. CA data helps analysts to formulate predictions about interlanguage which can be checked against CIA data [...] Conversely, CIA results can only be reliably interpreted as being evidence of transfer if supported by clear CA descriptions" (p. 46). As such, the ICM framework targets the notion of transfer as similarities between the learner's behavior in interlanguage and his/her native language help scholars identify cases of transfer (Gilquin, 2008). The CIA, by contrast, involves two major types of comparisons: (i) NL vs. IL, i.e. comparison of native language and interlanguage and (ii) IL vs. IL, i.e. comparison of different interlanguages (Granger, 1998, p. 12).

With regard to (i), Granger (2015) explains that, with this more popular branch of CIA, comparisons of a TL with IL can help reveal overuse that may indicate misuses: "For example, the overuse of *on the contrary* by French learners of English results from a faulty one-to-one equivalence with the French connector *au contraire*" (p. 5; more on over- and underuses below).

With regard to (ii), IL vs. IL comparisons, Granger (1993) argues

> [i]n order to be able to distinguish those features of L2 English [or any other natural language] that were L1-dependent, i.e. the result of transfer from the mother tongue, from those which were common to all learners, irrespective of mother tongue, i.e. the cross-linguistic invariants, it [is] essential to enlarge the corpus and include learners from different language backgrounds.

(p. 60)

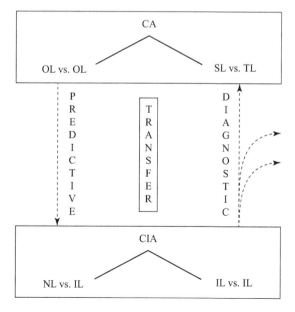

Figure 8.1 Integrated Contrastive Model (Borrowed from Gilquin, 2000/2001)[3]

The CIA introduced a type of comparison that served as "a particularly apt basis for a *quantifica-tional* contrastive typology of a number of English ILs [or any other natural language]" (Granger, 1998, p. 12; our emphasis), something that since then has gradually become characteristic (if not a trademark) of LCR: Both the ICM and CIA frameworks assume that distributional patterns of formal elements in an IL help us describe and distinguish individual types of IL and better understand why learners shape it the way they do. This view is based on the general assumption within the LCR community that, much like general usage-based theory in linguistics (see Chapter 13, this volume), L2 learning is probabilistic in nature: Acquiring a second/foreign language involves increasing knowledge of the frequency of (co-)occurrence of linguistic items in the TL, and distributional differences of formal elements in native and learner language allow researchers to capture traces of non-nativeness (Granger, 2004), which is why over-/underuses of linguistic items in IL are central in the field. More specifically, for Granger (2002), identifying over-/under-uses helps "bring out the words, phrases, grammatical items or syntactic structures that are either over- or under-used by learners" (p. 132), which is relevant because over- or underuses of formal elements in interlanguage contribute to the "foreign-soundingness [...] even in the absence of downright errors" (Granger, 2004, p. 132). Despite their prominence in LCR, criticisms of these notions will be brought up later.

Undeniably, the over-/underuse methodological approach has resulted in numerous descriptive accounts of ILs as well as criticism from some SLA researchers (for instance, the over-/underuses of linguistic items in a learner corpus may not be enough to explain how learner language changes over time, which is a central issue in SLA). However, it has arguably contributed to the development of LCR as a scientific discipline. At the same time, a growing number of LCR scholars have begun to gradually move away from a mere form-based study of over-/underuse towards more context-sensitive (broadly defined, see below) ways of studying quantitatively the complexity of NL vs. IL comparisons (especially when coming from a usage-based theoretical perspective). This analytical shift has led scholars to adopt more sophisticated statistical approaches such as cluster analysis, correspondence analysis, and logistic regression modeling (see our discussion on *Main Research Methods* below). This recent development reflects an important effort within the LCR community to harness – rather than move away from – the full potential of the ICM and CIA frameworks and their benefits as theoretical concepts by adopting state-of-the-art methodological approaches and statistical techniques. Indeed, the ICM and CIA can include quantitative techniques that not only allow scholars to compare learner corpora descriptively but also predictively and in an explanatory fashion, which helps respond to criticism from SLA researchers (see Chapter 9, this volume).

Comparison Configurations in CIA: Some Limitations and a Second-generation Framework

The CIA framework does not require that scholars use a specific native variety as the norm and, fittingly, the notion that any *single* English variety can serve as *the one* native norm has become questionable. This development was recently shown by Gilquin (2018) in a study of whether American English is a more important source of influence than British English for the other varieties of English (including English as an institutionalized second language and English as a foreign language). Overall, the results point towards a global influence of American English, but also show that varieties are not necessarily homogeneous in this respect and that more local contextual factors may affect the degree of American and/or British influence.

In an attempt to address the above points of criticism, the original CIA framework (CIA[1]) was recently revised (CIA[2]) by introducing a larger number of reference points against which learner data can be set/compared and broadening its scope to include not just English as a Foreign

Language (EFL) varieties, but also English as a Second Language (ESL) varieties and English as a Lingua Franca (see Granger, 2015 for a detailed description of CIA[2] and see Crosthwaite et al., 2016 for an example of a study based on the revised CIA framework).[4] With regard to over- and underuses, the CIA[1] underwent a change in terminology as over- and underuses have become over- and underrepresentations (Granger, 2015). Despite these changes, though, to a large extent, the framework remains similar.

Applying the ICM and CIA Frameworks: Corpus Comparison, Comparisons across Learner Varieties, and Comparisons across Language-production Modes

In this section, we consider the application of ICM and CIA in various contexts of L2 uses. Generally, applying these methodological frameworks is not as straightforward as one may think. In order to ensure comparability of native and learner language, various corpus-external and speaker-related factors need to be considered; these include (i) the comparability of corpora in terms of their architecture and their types of data, (ii) the comparability of language production characteristics such as modes (i.e. speech vs. writing) but also contextual characteristics such as genre, formality, and purpose of the communication and topic, and (iii) interspeaker variation triggered by factors such as gender, age, regional affiliation, socioeconomic background, cultural background, as well as factors involving aptitude, motivation, proficiency, and others (see, e.g., Gablasova, Brezina and McEnery 2017). Within the ICM and CIA, it would be crucial that contrasted corpora are similar in enough of the above aspects that observed differences across native speakers and learners can confidently be attributed to the language varieties investigated.

With regard to (i), comparability of corpora, the design and architecture of the ICLE provides a relatively good example of a corpus set up for sound comparisons of IL varieties.[5] As a corpus of IL varieties, ICLE (v2) includes 16 IL varieties. To enhance comparability, all ICLE data were collected all over the world according to the same criteria related to age (young adults of approximately 20 years of age), learning context (studying English in a non-English speaking environment), proficiency level (*advanced* as defined by their seniority in an undergraduate degree in English), medium of communication (writing) and (argumentative/literary) essay writing. In addition, variables such as sex of the participant, mother tongue, region, other foreign languages, practical experience (i.e. number of years of English teaching), topic of discussion, and task setting (Granger, 1998) were included, too. While those features, which are part of ICLE's metadata, are also accounted for in corpora of spoken EFL such as the *Louvain Corpus of Spoken English Interlanguage* (LINDSEI; Gilquin et al., 2010), making EFL comparisons across IL varieties and language-production modes relatively straightforward, comparing EFL and ESL quickly becomes complex when one needs to contrast corpora whose respective architecture and design vary widely; comparisons become especially tricky given that corpora often differ considerably in the amount, resolution, and precision of their metadata (see Chapter 5, this volume). Further, more recent learner corpora have adopted different designs and have strived to include more characteristics in their annotation; see the relevant chapter(s) on corpus design and annotation in this volume.

To date, the only corpus of learner English (i.e. EFL) that allows for full comparison with ESL varieties is the *Corpus of Dutch English* (Edwards, 2016), modeled on the design of the *International Corpus of English* (ICE; Greenbaum & Nelson, 1996), a corpus collected to contrast varieties of English worldwide. This, in turn, raises the important issue of text-type comparability, which explains why studies such as Deshors (2016), which contrast the two types of learners (i.e. EFL vs. ESL learners), are limited to using a small portion of the ICE data, namely, the student writing sub-part most comparable to ICLE's argumentative texts. Given its importance, this aspect of learner corpora comparisons was integrated into the revised version of the

CIA framework in terms of *diatypic* variables (Granger, 2015). While the operationalization of such variables remains to be made clear, in essence, they are recognized to be "essential to ensure text-type comparability" (Granger, 2015, p. 17).

Moving on to (ii), language production characteristics (e.g. language production modes (speech vs. writing), and contextual characteristics) are essential to sound comparisons of learner corpora. As Gablasova, Brezina and McEnery (2017) note, "[w]hen deciding whether two corpora can be meaningfully compared, the likelihood of occurrence of the target linguistic features also has to be considered with respect to the nature of the linguistic data in the corpus" (p. 137). With regard to language production modes specifically, Biber's (1988, *passim*) multidimensional analysis has shown that the two language modes attract different lexico-grammatical features (see also McCarthy & Carter, 2001). In the case of learner language, however, this distinction between language modes is not always as clear-cut as it is in native language: Gilquin and Paquot (2008) have shown that EFL learners experience difficulties distinguishing between the two modes. In writing, for instance, their uses of linguistic features tend to be more typical of speech than of academic prose, suggesting that they are largely unaware of, or unfamiliar with, register differences. Further, Deshors and Gries (2015) note "without a mode distinction, one cannot be sure that observed pattern differences across corpora are due to variation across varieties rather than registers" (p. 132), which means that comparing language production modes in L2 requires ensuring that, linguistically, the features selected for analysis can be compared meaningfully across modes and that remaining potential differences of modes and genres are accounted for statistically.

Genre variation is not an aspect that can be said to have *really* been explored within the bounds of LCR or SLA, mainly due to the fact that most learner corpora tend to consist of argumentative essays (in written corpora) and academic (in the sense of 'being conducted in university contexts') interviews (in spoken data) as opposed to representing a variety of different genres. Therefore, existing learner corpora are much less representative of the wide range of written and spoken genres found in large-scale corpora of native English such as the ICE. This means that it is hard to assess whether or to what extent linguistic patterns in IL are (also) influenced by genre, as pointed out by Paquot and Biber (2015), and the lack of alignment regarding genres, tasks, etc. in the design of EFL, ESL, and English as a Native Language (ENL) corpora has led scholars to restrict their data to the 'student writing' or 'academic writing' subsections of large-scale corpora such as ICE when contrasting EFL with ESL and ENL data.

As for the final point, (iii) inter-speaker variation, this is an extremely important, yet largely understudied, aspect of LCR and SLA. In a nutshell, accounting for inter-speaker variation means including or controlling for speaker-specific characteristics that may affect speakers' uses of language such as personality, language aptitude, motivation, proficiency, and others (see Gries, 2018 for a programmatic discussion). The importance of examining inter-learner variation lies in the fact that it provides a way to "determine to what extent the quantitative summary (e.g., a measure of central tendency such as the mean) can be used to represent the language produced by individual users in the corpus" (Gablasova, Brezina & McEnery, 2017, p. 138). Take, for example, the case of learners' proficiency levels, an aspect of learner corpus comparisons that is currently gaining much attention because of how it provides an important statistical control variable. As such, it is often used as a main predictor and/or a dependent variable. Although the notion of learner proficiency has never been completely absent from conversations on comparing learner corpora (e.g. the ICLE was designed with a focus on advanced proficiency levels in mind), it has not always been rigorously and comparably operationalized. For instance, Callies, Díez-Bedmar and Zaytseva (2014) note that the ways in which 'advancedness' has been operationalized in published research differ considerably and, even now, the effects of varying levels of proficiency among subjects remain relatively unknown, thereby to some degree weakening learner corpus comparisons. Thus, developing and operationalizing corpus-based indicators of non-native language proficiency has become a fast-growing branch of LCR (Gablasova, Brezina & McEnery, 2017; also see Callies & Götz, 2015; Callies, Díez-Bedmar & Zaytseva, 2014; and, in the context of regression-based methodological approaches, see Gries & Deshors, 2015, and Chapter 9, this volume). Finally, it should be noted that the development of corpora such as the MERLIN corpus (https://www.merlin-platform.eu/) and the Trinity Lancaster Corpus, which include metadata on speakers' proficiency levels based on the Common European Framework of Reference for Languages, could allow scholars to account for speakers' proficiency systematically and in a fine-grained fashion (see McEnery et al., 2019, for a special issue of the *International Journal of Learner Corpus Research* on 'Corpus-based Approaches to Spoken L2 Production: Evidence from the Trinity Lancaster Corpus').

Main Research Methods

Methodologically, learner language research both in LCR and SLA has involved the development and application of various approaches that we discuss below including frequency counts, association measures, hierarchical cluster analysis, and regression-based statistical modeling techniques. However, in LCR, perhaps more than in SLA, methodological developments tend to be closely related to how learner corpus linguists have recently shifted their analytical approach from form-based to context-based analyses to explore how and to what extent usage-based theoretical frameworks can help us better understand learner language as a linguistic system (see recent research conducted by Gries and colleagues as well as N. Ellis and colleagues which has had significant methodological implications for LCR). Since the early days of LCR, three main approaches have emerged in the type of linguistic patterns that scholars have investigated: (i) early form-based approaches to learner language focused on isolated linguistic items and their over- or underuse in IL compared to a TL; (ii) influence from research in dialectology led to typological approaches towards comparing learner corpora involving comparisons of IL and SL varieties based on catalogs of linguistic items (e.g. Szmrecsanyi & Kortmann, 2011); and (iii) multifactorial methodologies anchored in constructionist/usage-based theoretical frameworks led to studies contrasting IL and native varieties by focusing on the co-occurrence patterns of linguistic features within grammatical constructions and across learner corpora. Over time, those analytical approaches to learner language have required analysts to use increasingly sophisticated methods for both the extraction of complex linguistic patterns and the subsequent statistical analysis of richly annotated data.

Focusing on the former process, corpus tools such as user-friendly concordance software (e.g. Wordsmith Tools: Scott, 2017; AntConc: Anthony, 2010) have played an important role in LCR by allowing fast data-extraction and computation of relatively simple statistics such as frequency counts and type-token ratios (see Chapter 6, this volume). Granger (2015) even argued that "[p]atterns of over- and underuse of linguistic features can readily be identified with the appropriate software tools and methods and provide impetus for further analysis" (p. 5) (see also Gilquin, 2015, for discussion of over- and underuse and observed (dis)similarities between institutionalized second-language varieties of English and foreign varieties of English in the areas of syntax, lexis, phraseology and pragmatics). However, as the linguistic phenomena being studied became more complex, the limitations of such approaches became apparent and began to require other, more sophisticated approaches. Therefore, while some research goals are attainable with current corpus tools in terms of extraction (e.g. regular expressions), many more complex studies now involve fine-grained annotation schemes and programming languages such as R or Python to extract (and then statistically analyze) complex linguistic patterns. Such fine-grained annotation schemes have important repercussions on how (complex) comparisons of learner varieties are computed.

Focusing on the statistical side of things, LCR, just like other corpus research, relies on the distributional hypothesis, i.e. the notion that the distribution of words and constructions on their own and with other linguistic elements reveals something about their functions and/or processing characteristics as well as, potentially, the minds of the speakers whose language production is studied – in LCR, obviously L2 learners' knowledge of a target language: "The frequency with which speakers use linguistic features can provide us with an insight into the state of their interlanguage and is a first step in the study of what motivates the use (or avoidance) of these features in their language" (Gablasova, Brezina, & McEnery, 2017, p. 135).

One can identify different ways of approaching distributional information for the ultimate purpose of comparing learner corpora: for instance, amongst others, (i) frequency counts for automatic profiling of learner varieties (e.g. Granger & Rayson, 1998); (ii) association measures to pinpoint linguistic features most strongly associated with grammatical constructions in L2 (e.g. Martinez-Garcia & Wulff, 2012); (iii) hierarchical cluster analysis to group together non-native varieties that are typologically similar (Szmrecsanyi & Kortmann, 2011); and (iv) regression-based statistical models to predict learner language (such as MuPDAR; Gries & Deshors, 2015).[6] Crucially, although these different statistical approaches all fit within the methodological frameworks of the ICM and CIA, they do not abide by the over-/underuse characteristic of the frameworks: the ICM/CIA have undergone a shift in the type of quantitative techniques that are used to contrast learner varieties. While the ICM/CIA were designed with largely descriptive objectives, today, they provide the background for much more advanced quantitative analysis of learners' linguistic choices that allow for testing specific hypotheses about learner language (see Gries and colleagues, *passim*; see Chapter 9, this volume, for in-depth illustration and discussion on statistical analyses of learner corpora). This development should not be underestimated as, paradoxically, it speaks to both the potential and the limitation of the ICM and CIA frameworks today. Finally, the above notwithstanding, it is important to keep in mind that even though quantitative approaches have dominated LCR overall, qualitative corpus-based comparisons of learner data should not be underestimated regarding the key notions of over- and underuse; for instance, the relevant literature stresses that frequency alone is not sufficient, but that usage needs to be considered as well (e.g. Rosen, 2018).

Representative Corpora and Research

Much representative research comparing corpora is based on corpora such as the *International Corpus of Learner English* (ICLE), *the Louvain Corpus of Native English Conversations* (LOCNEC), *Louvain Corpus of Native English Essays* (LOCNESS) and *Louvain International Database of Spoken English Interlanguage* (LINDSEI), all compiled at the Center for English Linguistics at the Université catholique de Louvain (UCL) in collaboration with a network of research centers worldwide. Generally, all corpora present data produced by university students at an upper-intermediate to advanced proficiency level in English as a foreign language or by students approaching university entrance, in the case of the native data.

Using these and other corpora, several different research trends in learner corpus research have emerged, including (i) describing and profiling interlanguage varieties, (ii) clustering learner varieties, and (iii) predicting learners' linguistic choices. With regard to (i), the work of Granger and Rayson (1998) is an example of how frequency counts can help CIA researchers identify salient lexical behavior in L2 through automated profiling to "form a quick picture" of individual learner populations (Granger & Rayson, 1998, p. 131) and then compare the lexical profiles of those populations. This can, for instance, help identify traces of cross-linguistic transfer. Contrasting French-English IL and native English using ICLE and LOCNESS, Granger and Rayson (1998) first selected a number of word categories (e.g. nouns, adjectives, prepositions, conjunctions) and then computed frequency counts within each word category to draw a usage profile for individual word categories within a particular learner variety and for each investigated word category, which helps identify linguistic usage patterns characteristic of (individual) learner varieties; in addition, one can assess which members of that category learners over-/underuse compared to a native norm. Despite its statistical simplicity, this type of contrastive approach accounts for the permeable nature of interlanguage systems while offering a coarse-grained, holistic picture of how learner corpora compare.

With regard to (ii), clustering learner varieties, this approach helps explore degrees of cross-varietal (dis)similarities in the uses of particular linguistic items by speakers of different language populations and based on a (large) number of contextual clues. More advanced than Granger and Rayson's (1998) automated profiling technique, this approach involves computing behavioral profiles (comprehensive inventories of elements that co-occur with a word within the confines of a single clause or sentence in actual speech or writing [see Divjak & Gries 2006]) of investigated linguistic items within language varieties and comparing variety-specific profiles across those language varieties. Behavioral profiles therefore provide form- or sense-specific summaries of the semantic and morpho-syntactic behavior of the linguistic items studied. Based on those profiles, techniques such as hierarchical cluster analysis organize investigated linguistic items by finding (dis)similarities between their profiles across English varieties and by grouping similar varieties together.

The benefits of this type of contrastive technique have been shown in a number of studies such as Szmrecsanyi and Kortmann (2011), which involved 25 varieties/languages (11 EFLs, 5 ESLs, 3 standard British English benchmark registers, and 6 European mother-tongue languages) based on part-of-speech classes, Edwards and Laporte (2015) on the use of prepositions in British, American, Singapore, Indian, Hong Kong, and Dutch Englishes, Rautionaho et al. (2018) on progressive marking in EFL and ESL, and Deshors (2016) on the *may* vs. *can* lexical alternation in French-English interlanguage. From a language-learning perspective, this powerful approach can help (i) assess to what extent learners with different native backgrounds can develop L2 varieties that are similar typologically and (ii) capture how different learner populations make use of complex linguistic co-occurrence patterns and ultimately develop abstract (mental) representations of linguistic patterns characteristic of their L2.

Finally, research trend (iii) involves comparing NL and IL for the purpose of predicting and explaining (rather than describing and grouping) learners' linguistic choices. This type of multifactorial regression approach involves capturing systematic co-occurrence patterns of semantic and morpho-syntactic features with linguistic choices in IL. Such approaches help understand when and why English learners make nativelike and non-nativelike linguistic choices, offering a whole new perspective on what it means to compare learner corpora. A landmark within this research trend is the recent development of the MuPDAR protocol (Gries & Deshors, 2014, Gries & Adelman, 2014) which, still within the confines of the ICM/CIA frameworks, introduces a new procedure to compare learner corpora: Instead of contrasting observed linguistic patterns in NL and IL, data from the native variety are used to predict what a native speaker would have produced in a specific situation, which can then be compared to what a learner actually did say, given each specific linguistic context using a two-set regression approach (described in Chapter 9, this volume). As such, MuPDAR is the first real implementation of what Péry-Woodley (1990, p. 143) wished for nearly 30 years ago: "Comparing/contrasting what non-native and native speakers of a language do in a comparable situation", where the "comparable situation" is defined by linguistic and contextual features captured in the multivariate annotation, from which a statistical method predicts what the native speaker would have produced. Such approaches offer the important benefit of being compatible with cognitive-linguistic / usage-based theory, thus informing explorations of the psycholinguistic relevance of corpus findings. Combining technical sophistication and theoretical relevance, multifactorial approaches to the comparison of learner corpora have started to show how studies primarily based on the over-/underuse of isolated linguistic items do not always tend to do justice to the complexity of interlanguage systems (e.g. see Gries & Wulff, 2013 for an application of the approach to the genitive alternation in Chinese- and German-English IL; and Gries & Adelman, 2014 for an application to subject realization in Japanese conversation by native speakers and learners). Next, we briefly consider the case of Deshors and Gries (2015), a study that brings together a number of the comparison-related issues we have raised so far throughout the present paper.

Deshors and Gries' (2015) study uses the alternation between ditransitive and prepositional dative constructions in native and non-native Englishes as a case in point to illustrate the central (and too often underestimated) issue of comparability of corpus data in LCR. Specifically, the authors examine 1265 occurrences of both constructions across written and spoken corpora: two EFL corpora (French- and German-English IL), three ESL corpora (Hong Kong, Indian, Singapore Englishes), and British English. Their analysis focused on the question of how ESL and EFL speakers' constructional choices differ from those of native speakers of BrE and how those differences are best explored statistically. Nine linguistic predictors of the dative alternation were included in the analysis (including recipient and patient accessibility, semantics, animacy, pronominality, length difference) as was the hierarchical structure of the corpus (with files/speakers nested into variety and into corpus type), something most corpus studies fail to account for. Consequently, the authors are able to show how appropriate mixed-effects modeling techniques can identify fine differences between NS and NNS speakers' behavior while simultaneously controlling for the differences within and between corpora, idiosyncratic effects of speakers and lexical items, and the general complexity of IL within a usage-based approach to SLA. Given the complexity of corpora as datasets along with the complexity of linguistic usage patterns in IL in particular, the adoption of such techniques has become almost inevitable in order to compare learner data rigorously.

Future Directions

As this chapter shows, the notion of comparability when dealing with learner data is a thorny notion that requires much attention on the part of LCR and SLA analysts to ensure reliable comparisons across varieties, registers, modes, or any other corpus parts. A first main take-home message from our discussion is that ensuring comparability of learner corpora requires much meta- and linguistic data information – particularly speaker-specific information – that is not yet routinely included in corpus compilation and analysis. Much existing corpus work underutilizes the available data, which can lead to distorted views of linguistic patterns characteristic of interlanguage varieties.

A second take-home message is more theoretical in nature and involves the cross-linguistic part of the ICM. Indeed, since the late 1990s, ICM-based studies contrasting interlanguage, target language, and learners' native language in single analyses have remained underrepresented compared to CIA-based studies contrasting NL vs. IL and IL vs. IL. In the future, this research gap should be addressed, especially given its potential to explore transfer-related questions in L2 (see Gilquin, 2000/2001). While addressing this gap will ensure a more frequent exploitation of the ICM theoretical framework (see Gilquin, 2017 for a recent study that begins to address this gap or Paquot, 2014, theoretically based on Jarvis's, 2000, model, which has gained ground for transfer studies both in LCR and SLA), the resulting more balanced representation of theoretical frameworks will undoubtedly help us connect the fields of LCR and SLA more than before.

Another take-home message involves a seemingly growing disconnect between the methodological framework of ICM/CIA, upon which LCR as a field was created, and the practical implementations that have been developed within the confines of ICM/CIA. As mentioned above, ICM/CIA is set up to contrast language varieties against other language varieties. However, while scholars have slowly begun to make a strong case for the need to account for speaker-specific characteristics, currently, these frameworks do not provide a well-developed theoretical apparatus that can account for these characteristics and that is psycholinguistically and SLA-informed. Therefore, there is a gap between current theoretical frameworks, their practical implementations, and what empirical studies are showing is needed. While awareness of this disconnect is growing (see Le Bruyn & Paquot, in press), much work remains to be done in order to (i) assess, quantify, and explore how much between-speaker variability actually diminishes the role of between-variety variability (see Gries, 2018) and (ii) make sure learner corpora contain enough metadata for each individual speaker (other than speaker proficiency) to do anything with speakers' individual variation.

Further Reading

Gablasova, D., Brezina, V., & McEnery, T. (2017). Exploring learner language through corpora: Comparing and interpreting corpus frequency information. *Language Learning*, *67*(S1), 130–154.

This paper revisits the comparative corpus-based method to explore the notions of interspeaker variation in native and non-native language use, the representativeness and comparability of corpus data, and how to interpret observed differences across corpora.

Gries, S. Th. (2006). Exploring variability within and between corpora: some methodological considerations. *Corpora 1*(2), 109–151.

In this paper, Gries explores corpus variability by showing (i) how degrees of variation should be quantified, (ii) how to capture and investigate the source of variation, and (iii) how to assess corpus homogeneity based on individual linguistic features. Overall, Gries makes a case for resampling methods and exploratory data analysis accounting for the fact that superficially different results may reflect similar underlying tendencies, the communicative dimensions that surround the use of a given linguistic phenomenon, and actual linguistic phenomena to assess corpus homogeneity rather than relying on word frequencies.

Gries, S. Th. (2018). On over- and underuse in learner corpus research and multifactoriality in corpus linguistics more generally. *Journal of Second Language Studies*, *2*(1), 276–308.

This paper demonstrates the urgent need to reassess existing quantitative methodological standards in LCR. Specifically, it makes a case for a complete revision of monofactorial over-/underuse approaches to learner corpora by discussing and showcasing the benefits of multifactorial regression-based statistical techniques to research observational (learner) data.

Related Topics

Chapters 6, 13, and 26.

Notes

1 Please note that although the present chapter focuses exclusively on English-language research, the core issues, topics, and general principles we discuss also apply to other languages.
2 See the now relatively large number of studies that have used Jarvis's (2000) framework to investigate transfer.
3 In the context of the ICM (Figure 8.1), CA: Contrastive analysis (in the traditional sense of the term); OL: Original Language; SL: Source Language; TL; Translated Language; NL: Native Language; IL: interlanguage. Outside of Figure 8.1, however, SL stands for second language, TL stands for target language.
4 EFL and ESL differ in that with EFL, English is learnt in the environment of one's native language (L1) whereas ESL is learnt in the environment in which it is spoken.
5 Specific information about ICLE and other widely used UCL corpora can be found here: https://uclouvain.be/en/research-institutes/ilc/cecl/corpora.html
6 Other possible approaches could include Native Language Identification (NLI) studies, Granger's collgrams, or studies looking into frequency but not for automatic profiling. Due to space constraints, however, we only focus on the four approaches we list in this paper

References

Anthony, L. (2010). *AntConc (3.2.1 version) [computer software]*. Tokyo: Waseda University.

Biber, D. (1988). *Variation across speech and writing*. New York: Cambridge University Press.

Bley-Vroman, R. (1983). The comparative fallacy in interlanguage studies: The case of systematicity. *Language Learning*, *33*(1), 1–17.

Callies, M., Díez-Bedmar, M. B., & Zaytseva, E. (2014). Using learner corpora for testing and assessing L2 proficiency. In P. Leclercq, H. Hilton, & A. Edmonds (Eds.), *Measuring L2 proficiency: Perspectives from SLA (second language acquisition series)* (pp. 71–90). Clevedon: Multilingual Matters.

Callies, M., & Götz, S. (2015). *Learner corpora in language testing and assessment (studies in corpus linguistics, band 70)*. Amsterdam: John Benjamins.

Crosthwaite, P., Lavigne, L. Y. C., & Yeonsuk, B. (2016). "Almost People": A learner corpus account of L2 use and misuse of non-numerical quantification. *Open Linguistics*, *2*(1), 317–336.

Deshors, S. C. (2016). *Multidimensional perspectives on interlanguage: Exploring may and can across learner corpora*. Corpora and Language in Use. Louvain: Presses Universitaires de Louvain.

Deshors, S. C., & Gries, S. Th. (2015). EFL and/vs. ESL? A multi-level regression modeling perspective on bridging the paradigm gap. *International Journal of Learner Corpus Research*, *1*(1), 130–159.

Divjak, D. S., & Gries, S. Th. (2006). Ways of trying in Russian: Clustering behavioral profiles. *Corpus Linguistics and Linguistic Theory*, *2*(1), 23–60.

Edwards, A. (2016). *English in the Netherlands: Functions, forms and attitudes (varieties of English around the world, vol. G56)*. Amsterdam: John Benjamins.

Edwards, A., & Laporte, S. (2015). Outer and expanding circle Englishes: The competing roles of norm orientation and proficiency levels. *English World-Wide*, *36*(2), 135–169.

Ellis, N. C., & Ferreira-Junior, F. (2009). Constructions and their acquisition: Islands and the distinctiveness of their occupancy. *Annual Review of Cognitive Linguistics*, *7*, 188–221.

Ellis, N. C., Römer, U., & O'Donnell, M. B. (2016). *Usage-based approaches to language acquisition and processing: Cognitive and corpus investigations of construction grammar*. Language Learning Monograph Series. Wiley-Blackwell.

Firth, A., & Wagner, J. (1998). SLA property: No trespassing! *Modern Language Journal*, *82*(1), 91–94.

Gablasova, D., Brezina, V., & McEnery, T. (2017). Exploring learner language through corpora: Comparing and interpreting corpus frequency information. *Language Learning*, *67*(S1), 130–154.

Gilquin, G. (2000/2001). The integrated contrastive model: Spicing up your data. *Languages in Contrast*, *3*(1), 95–123.

Gilquin, G. (2008). Combining contrastive and interlanguage analysis to apprehend transfer: Detection, explanation, evaluation. In G. Gilquin, S. Papp, & M. B. Díez-Bedmar, *Linking up contrastive and learner corpus research* (pp. 3–33). Amsterdam: Rodopi.

Gilquin, G. (2015). At the interface of contact linguistics and second language acquisition research: New Englishes and learner Englishes compared. *English World-Wide*, *36*(1), 91–124.

Gilquin, G. (2017). A collostruction-based approach to the integrated contrastive model: The idiomaticity of causative constructions in English, French and French learner English. Paper presented at the Idiomaticity workshop. Oslo: University of Oslo. Retrieved from https://www.hf.uio.no/ilos/english/research/projects/idiomaticity/events/gilquin-oslo2017-handout.pdf

Gilquin, G. (2018). American and/or British influence on L2 Englishes - does context tip the scale(s)? In S. C. Deshors (Ed.), *Modeling world Englishes in the 21st century: Assessing the interplay of emancipation and globalization of ESL varieties* (pp. 187–216). Amsterdam: John Benjamins.

Gilquin, G., De Cock, S., & Granger, S. (2010). *Louvain international database of spoken English interlanguage. Handbook and CD-ROM*. Louvain-la-Neuve: Presses universitaires de louvain.

Gilquin, G., & Paquot, M. (2008). Too chatty: Learner academic writing and register variation. *English Text Construction*, *1*(1), 41–61.

Granger, S. (1993). The international corpus of learner English. In J. Aarts, P.de Haan, & N. Oostdijk (Eds.), *English language corpora: Design, analysis and exploitation* (pp. 57–71). Amsterdam: Rodopi.

Granger, S. (1996). From CA to CIA and back: An integrated approach to computerized bilingual and learner corpora. In K. Aijmer, B. Altenberg, & M. Johansson (Eds.), *Languages in contrast. Text-based cross-linguistic studies* (pp. 37–51). Lund: Lund University Press.

Granger, S. (1998). The computer learner corpus: A versatile new source of data for SLA research. In S. Granger (Ed.), *Learner English on computer* (pp. 3–18). London: Longman.

Granger, S. (2002). A bird's eye view of learner corpus research. In S. Granger, J. Hung, & S. Petch-Tyson (Eds.), *Computer learner corpora, second language acquisition and foreign language teaching* (pp. 3–33). Amsterdam: John Benjamins.

Granger, S. (2004). Computer learner corpus research: Current status and future prospects. In C. Ulla & U. Thomas (Eds.), *Applied corpus linguistics: A multidimensional perspective* (pp. 123–145). Amsterdam: Rodopi.

Granger, S. (2009). The contribution of learner corpora to second language acquisition and foreign language teaching: A critical evaluation. In K. Aijmer (Ed.), *Corpora and language teaching* (pp. 13–32). Amsterdam: John Benjamins.

Granger, S. (2015). Contrastive interlanguage analysis: A reappraisal. *International Journal of Learner Corpus Research, 1*(1), 7–24.

Granger, S., Dagneaux, E., Meunier, F., & Paquot, M. (2002). *The international corpus of learner English. Version 1. Handbook and CD-Rom.* Louvain-la-Neuve: Presses Universitaires de Louvain.

Granger, S., Dagneaux, E., Meunier, F., & Paquot, M. (2009). *The international corpus of learner English. Version 2.* Handbook and CD-Rom. Louvain-la-Neuve: Presses Universitaires de Louvain.

Granger, S., & Rayson, P. (1998). Automatic lexical profiling of learner texts. In S. Granger (Ed.), *Learner English on computer* (pp. 119–131). London: Longman.

Greenbaum, S., & Nelson, G. (1996). The international corpus of English (ICE) project. *World Englishes, 15*(1), 3–15.

Gries, S. Th. (2018). On over- and underuse in learner corpus research and multifactoriality in corpus linguistics more generally. *Journal of Second Language Studies, 2*(1), 276–308.

Gries, S. Th., & Adelman, A. (2014). Subject realization in Japanese conversation by native and non-native speakers: Exemplifying a new paradigm for learner corpus research. In J. Romero-Trillo (Ed.), *Yearbook of corpus linguistics and pragmatics 2014: New empirical and theoretical paradigms* (pp. 35–54). Cham: Springer.

Gries, S. Th., & Deshors, S. C. (2014). Using regressions to explore deviations between interlanguage and native language: Two suggestions. *Corpora, 9*(1), 109–136.

Gries, S. Th., & Deshors, S. C. (2015). EFL and/vs. ESL? A multi-level regression modeling perspective on bridging the paradigm gap. *International Journal of Learner Corpus Research, 1*(1), 130–159.

Gries, S. Th., & Wulff, S. (2013). The genitive alternation in Chinese and German ESL learners: Towards a multifactorial notion of context in learner corpus research. *International Journal of Corpus Linguistics, 18*(3), 327–356.

Hasselgård, H., & Johansson, S. (2011). Learner corpora and contrastive interlanguage analysis. In F. Meunier, S. De Cock, G. Gilquin, & M. Paquot (Eds.), *A taste for corpora, honour of Sylviane Granger* (pp. 33–61). Amsterdam: John Benjamins.

Hunston, S. (2002). *Corpora in applied linguistics.* Cambridge: Cambridge University Press.

Jarvis, S. (2000). Methodological rigor in the study of transfer: Identifying L1 influence in the interlanguage lexicon. *Language Learning, 50*(2), 245–309.

Lakshmanan, U., & Selinker, L. (2001). Analysing interlanguage: How do we know what learners know? *Second Language Research, 17*(4), 393–420.

Larsen-Freeman, D. (2014). Another step to be taken: Rethinking the end point of the interlanguage continuum. In Z. Han & E. Tarone (Eds.), *Interlanguage. Forty years later* (pp. 203–220). Amsterdam: John Benjamins.

Le Bruyn, B., & Paquot, M. (in press). *Learner corpus research meets second language acquisition.* Cambridge: Cambridge University Press.

Martinez-Garcia, M. T., & Wulff, S. (2012). Not wrong, yet not quite right: Spanish ESL students' use of gerundial and infinitival complementation. *International Journal of Applied Linguistics, 22*(2), 225–244.

McCarthy, M., & Carter, R. (2001). Ten criteria for a spoken grammar. In E. Hinkle & S. Fotos (Eds.), *New perspectives on grammar teaching in second language classrooms* (pp. 51–75). Mahwah: Lawrence Erlbaum Associates.

McEnery, T., Brezina, V., & Gablasova, D. (Ed.) (2019). Corpus-based approaches to spoken L2 production: Evidence from the trinity lancaster corpus. *International Journal of Learner Corpus Research, 5*(2), 119–125.

McManus, K. (2015). L1-L2 differences in the acquisition of form-meaning pairings in a second language. *Canadian Modern Language Review, 71*(2), 51–77.

Paquot, M. (2007). *EAP vocabulary in EFL learner writing: From extraction to analysis: A phraseology-oriented approach.* PhD thesis. Université catholique de Louvain, Centre for English Corpus Linguistics.

Paquot, M. (2014). Cross-linguistic influence and formulaic language: Recurrent word sequences in French learner writing. In L. Roberts, I. Vedder, & J. Hulstijn (Eds.), *EUROSLA yearbook* (pp. 216–237). Amsterdam: John Benjamins.

Paquot, M., & Biber, D. (2015, May 27–31). The impact of genre on EFL learner writing: A MDA perspective. Paper presented at 36th annual conference of the international computer archive for modern and medieval english (ICAME 36), Words, words, words - corpora and lexis. Trier University.

Péry-Woodley, M. P. (1990). Contrasting discourses: Contrastive analysis and a discourse approach to writing. *Language Teaching, 24*(3), 205–214.

Rautionaho, P., Deshors, S. C., & Meriläinen, L. (2018). Revisiting the ENL-ESL-EFL continuum: A multifactorial approach to grammatical aspect in spoken Englishes. *ICAME Journal, 42*(1), 41–78.

Rosen, A. (2018). The fate of linguistic innovations: Jersey English and French learner English compared. In S. C. Deshors (Ed.), *Modeling world Englishes: Assessing the interplay of emancipation and globalization of ESL varieties* (pp. 171–191). Amsterdam: John Benjamins.

Scott, M. (2017). *WordSmith tools version 7.* Stroud: Lexical Analysis Software.

Selinker, L. (2014). Interlanguage 40 years on. Three themes from here. In Z. Han & E. Tarone (Eds.), *Interlanguage. Forty years later* (pp. 221–246). Amsterdam: John Benjamins.

Szmrecsanyi, B., & Kortmann, B. (2011). Typological profiling: Learner Englishes versus L2 varieties of English. In J. Mukherjee & M. Hundt (Eds.), *Second-language varieties of English and learner Englishes: Bridging the paradigm gap* (pp. 167–207). Amsterdam: John Benjamins.

9

Statistical Analyses of Learner Corpus Data

Stefan Th. Gries and Sandra C. Deshors

Introduction

Learner corpus research (LCR), i.e. the field studying learner/non-native speaker performance using corpora, has established itself as a vibrant sub-field of general corpus linguistics. LCR inherits from corpus linguistics the notion that virtually everything a (learner) corpus researcher studies must be operationalized on the basis of frequencies of (co-)occurrence in corpora; thus, the analysis of such data requires statistical analysis (because statistics is the science teaching us how to 'make sense of' frequency data). However, LCR adds to corpus linguistics the connection to research on second/foreign language acquisition (SLA/FLA) with all the complexities that these entail for the kinds of statistical analyses that are ultimately required. While we will not exemplify in detail the wide range of issues that much statistical work in LCR exhibits, it is instructive to consider the state of the field as discussed in Paquot and Plonsky (2017). Their survey of 378 published LCR studies shows that the field's statistical sophistication is only slowly increasing and much remains to be done for LCR to become relevant to SLA/FLA research. For instance, currently, about 90% of all statistical analyses in LCR are one of the following: chi-squared tests (23%), the log-likelihood ratio G^2 (10%), t-tests (20%), simple correlation (17%), analysis of variance (14%), and regression (6%). Even this alone indicates that much of LCR is still monofactorial in nature, which is highly problematic given how that (i) guarantees that the real complexity of the phenomena studied will be underestimated and (ii) increases the probability of false positives in LCR research, i.e. findings that appear important and/or significant in a monofactorial analysis of aggregate data but would not in a more appropriate multifactorial analysis (see Gries, 2018 for discussion). In the next section, we discuss some of the central issues that affect and complicate the statistical analysis of learner corpus data.

Core Issues and Topics

For a long time, much corpus-linguistic work has underanalyzed the complexity the statistical analysis of corpus data requires. Unfortunately, the analysis of learner corpus data is often even more complex. The following is a brief overview of the many interrelated challenges that scholars using learner corpus data need to confront; for didactic purposes, we present these in two groups, but this implies no particular theoretical commitment or ranking.

The first kind of challenges result from learner corpus data being observational data rather than data from the carefully controlled experiments typical of SLA research, in which many potential sources of noise/variability are controlled and where, often, the balanced number of responses per experimental condition is known by design in advance:

- there is considerable *variability between corpora* and *variability within corpora*. Regarding the former (between-corpus variability), different corpora differ from each other in many ways: (i) corpora even from within the same compilation project can differ in terms of how the data are collected, from whom the data are collected, how exactly the collected data were generated, how much annotation/metadata is available for them, etc., and ideally all of this information would be controlled for at least statistically (if one cannot afford controlling it by, say, including only corpora whose metadata suggest a high degree of comparability). Regarding the latter (within-corpus variability), corpora have an internal structure one needs to consider. In simple cases, this can just arise from the fact that a researcher compiles their own corpus from existing corpora, e.g., by studying learner data from the combination of both spoken and written data such as the *International Corpus of Learner English* (ICLE, Granger et al., 2009) and the *Louvain International Database of Spoken English Interlanguage* (LINDSEI, Gilquin, De Cock, & Granger, 2010); in such a case, each file/ speaker would be nested into a mode and into an L1 (but the L1s in turn could be crossed with, i.e. observed in, both the written and the spoken corpus data).
- corpus data often pose problems with regard to what is called *dispersion*, the degree to which an expression/structure is evenly distributed throughout a corpus (see Gries, to appear). This is important because, if an expression is distributed clumpily/unevenly in a corpus, then most of the data points for that expression are only provided by a potentially small minority of the speakers whereas most speakers provide only few data points, which leads to problems with the generalizability of the results. A second and more extreme case is that extreme clumpiness can of course even result in the fact that most files/speakers do not contain the element in question even once: For instance, Hasselgård and Johansson (2011) study the use of the word *quite* in native and non-native writing and in their data; more than 80% of the files do actually not contain *quite* at all. This is important because it raises the question of what to do with speakers/files not exhibiting a particular expression. Shall one assume that not using *quite* was a conscious choice (because the speakers preferred *rather*, *very*, … each time) or shall one consider the possibility that (some) speakers did not even know the word *quite*? Obviously, whichever one chooses will affect the interpretation of the results.
- corpus data are notorious for their *Zipfian distributions* (Ellis et al., 2016) and, often, high degrees of *multicollinearity* (Tomaschek et al., 2018). The former (Zipfian distributions) means that, for most expressions/structures, many or even most frequencies of (co-)occurrence will be quite low, whereas (very) few frequencies of (co-)occurrence will be quite high; that is, very few types may account for many, if not most, tokens, whereas many types will each only be instantiated with very few tokens. This kind of distribution can make statistical analysis difficult, because it means that for many word types, data will be problematically sparse. The latter (multicollinearity) means that, often, predictors in corpus data – causes – will be correlated with each other in ways that complicate the analysis of unbalanced data sets.

The second kind of challenges is related to the *multivariate and multilevel structure of the data*:

- for many phenomena, there will be a *repeated-measurements structure* just as in experiments, but much less balanced/regular: Some, but not all, speakers may contribute 2+ data points to the corpus, but different speakers contribute a different amount (and many none), similarly, there may be multiple data points for each lexical item one studies. That also means there are often temporal effects in corpus data due to priming/persistence effects (speakers' preferences to re-use expressions/structures). Speakers will be nested into corpora and L1s, but might be crossed with tasks or might be observed multiple times over time (in longitudinal learner corpus data), etc. In some studies, some of the above might be predictors of interest (e.g., we may be interested in how different tasks affect an outcome), in others they may be statistical controls (e.g., we may be interested in temporal development, but must partial the effect of different tasks out of the temporal changes).

- all linguistic phenomena are *multifactorial* in nature, i.e. every statistical analysis needs to be multifactorial to account for multiple potential causes of an effect at the same time *and* to control for already known causes of an effect so that a suggested new cause can be shown to add to our understanding. To this, we must add the fact that ...

- LCR studies often have an implicit *multilevel design*: many variables – predictors and controls – operate on different levels. For instance, many variables are observation-level variables (i.e., they describe an individual usage event involving specific words and/or constructions) and may require difficult-to-operationalize constructs involving concreteness ratings, meaningfulness ratings, age-of-acquisition data, phonological or orthographic neighborhood densities, etc. The same is true of variables located at the speaker-level (capturing speaker-specific variability), which, too, are often hard to operationalize (e.g., when it comes to constructs such as aptitude, intelligence, motivation, proficiency, etc.). Other variables operate at the level of the corpus (e.g., annotation preferences adopted in one compilation project), and yet others are located at the level of tasks (e.g., task-specific and mode-specific effects). Variability can be observed at each of these levels and must be carefully separated from the predictors of interest to avoid anti-conservative results (i.e. results that lead researchers to reject a null hypothesis that should not be rejected).

In sum, observational LCR data and the typically more experimental data in SLA/FLA research can be located on a 'multidimensional continuum' as indicated in Figure 9.1.

Arguably, the observational data of LCR come with a higher degree of ecological validity compared to the more controlled data in SLA/FLA experiments, but because of the characteristics of these data, they also require quite sophisticated statistical analyses, certainly more complex than those currently practiced in most LCR work (recall Paquot & Plonsky, 2017 from above).

Next, we discuss practical implications and guidelines for statistical analyses of LCR data; in keeping with the fact that the vast majority of LCR statistical applications is hypothesis-testing in nature, we concentrate on such applications.

observational/corpus	dimension	experimental
low	artificiality/control	high
collinear & Zipfian	distribution	controlled & equal/balanced
harder	statistical analysis	simpler

Figure 9.1 Simplistic Comparison of Observational and Experimental Data in LCR and SLA/FLA Research, Respectively.

Main Research Methods

Regression As a Multi-purpose Tool: The Set-up of the Data

Given the above data/research situation, the one central research method/tool that would benefit LCR most is proper mixed-effects/multilevel regression modeling. While that claim may seem simplistic, much of the statistics in LCR are already instances of regression modeling even if practitioners might not be very aware of that fact:

- t-tests, simple ANOVAs, linear regression, and Pearson's r are all cases of linear regression models; they all involve a numeric dependent/response variable and, while they differ in terms of whether the independent/predictor variable is binary (t-test), categorical (simple ANOVA) or numeric (linear regression/r), their results are identical;
- chi-squared tests are closely related to log-likelihood/G^2-values, which – either as significance tests or as association measures computed from 2×2 co-occurrence tables – correspond to results from generalized linear regression or multinomial models, as do association measures such as MI, t-scores, z-scores, or ΔP-values.

However, the vast majority of statistical applications in LCR, no matter whether they are conceived of as traditional tests or as regression models, are too simplistic: Usually, they are monofactorial (i.e. excluding both other relevant predictors and required controls) and often also fraught with other problems (such as multiple testing without corrections etc.). In what follows, we describe the ways in which appropriate regression modeling would boost the discipline's analytical power, and as an example to motivate our discussion, we will use a scenario in which a researcher is interested in how learners of English use the two variants, or constructions, in (1):

> (1) a. the owl's beak s-genitive: possessor's possessum
>   b. the beak of the owl of-genitive: possessum of possessor

In our scenario, the researcher has corpus data from learners of two L1s, say German and Mandarin Chinese, which cover both spoken and written data (say, from LINDSEI and ICLE), which means each speaker is represented with only one file in only one mode/corpus. Our hypothetical researcher is interested in the following two potential causes of genitive choices (and, for the sake of simplicity, we ignore the fact that even a study focusing only on these two linguistic predictors would have to include more linguistic predictors to ensure that these predictors have an impact even when everything else is controlled for, see Gries, 2018):

- the animacy of the possessor (because animate possessors prefer s-genitives);
- the length difference between possessors and possessums (because of a general short-before-long preference).

First, a proper statistical analysis in this scenario requires the data to be in the case-by-variable format, where every genitive – each of and each s – is represented by its own row in, most likely, a spreadsheet software and where every column represents one variable – predictor, control, or a 'data organization' variable (such as the files/speaker, corpus, or L1 a data point belongs to/is from, see below). This means one must not use data aggregated over many speakers, but for each genitive, we need columns for

- the dependent variable: which genitive was observed (of or s);

- the animacy of the possessor (e.g., the simplest possible case of just *animate* vs. *inanimate* or any more complex hierarchy; in (1), *the owl* could be classed as *nun-human/animate*);
- the length difference between possessor and possessum (e.g., measured in characters or syllables; in (1), one character).

However, to address (i) variability between corpora, (ii) variability within corpora, (iii) the genitives' dispersion throughout the corpora, and (iv) speaker-specific effects (e.g., speakers who behave very differently from the overall average), we also need columns for

- the corpus the example is from (ICLE vs. LINDSEI);
- the L1 of the speaker of the current example (German or Mandarin Chinese and if native speakers were included, then of course also English);
- the file in which corpus the example is from (as a proxy for the speaker the genitive is from).

This allows us to do what LCR knows it needs but does not always do, namely "keep the group perspective […], while at the same time taking individual variability into account" (Granger et al., 2015, p. 2). Then, to address lexically specific effects (e.g., possessors that invariably take only one genitive or possessors that learners use in a fairly consistently non-nativelike way), we need columns for

- the lexical item that is the possessor (perhaps in lemma form, *owl* in (1));
- the lexical item that is the possessum (perhaps in lemma form, *beak* in (1)).

In addition, we need to control for temporal effects such as speakers' tendency to re-use previously used structures, which, by the way, are the reason why one should not randomly sample on the level of the individual genitives (if one does not want to study all data points found in a corpus). Instead, one needs to randomly sample on the level of files, conversations, or speakers so that all genitives from one conversation are included and allow the study of temporal effects. Thus, we minimally need columns for

- the genitive choice that precedes the current one (*of* or *s*) to account for priming effects operating while the student wrote the essay/participated in the conversation, and maybe
- the line number in which each genitive was found (so we can determine how far apart in 'text time' the two constructional choices happened).

However, the above does not exhaust the range of possibilities. While the above annotation scheme provides for every single genitive the speaker who produced it, with the right corpus annotation, it is still possible and often necessary to include additional speaker-level information in the analysis to better accommodate individual differences (see Dörnyei, 2005). Individual differences relevant to much SLA research include, but are not limited to, personality, aptitude, cognitive predisposition and learning styles, motivation, etc., all of which are complex constructs. For instance, with regard to aptitude, we might distinguish grammatical sensitivity, phonological decoding ability, memory capacity, and inductive learning ability (Carroll & Sapon, 1959); obviously, in LCR, we will usually also be interested in including speakers' proficiency level (however operationalized). For instance, with regard to motivation, we might distinguish intrinsic and extrinsic motivation, and so forth, see Wulff and Gries (to appear) for more of an overview.

Unfortunately, most learner corpora do not provide much in terms of speaker-level information other than maybe age, sex, a global proficiency score (e.g. CEFR), or the length of exposure to English. Naturally, this absence of metadata is problematic for LCR practitioners wanting to benefit from recent work in SLA/FLA research. Some such information can be approximated, as when lacking proficiency scores are operationalized via lexical or formulaic diversity and/or syntactic complexity scores computed directly from the corpus files (see Gries & Wulff, to appear, for an example), but more fine-grained information would, of course, be better; for our scenario, let us consider that we have a column with proficiency scores for each speaker.

With such data, most morphosyntactic LCR analyses (e.g., of over-/underuse, of alternations) would boil down to formulating a regression model that codifies, with regard to the sources of the data, the structure of the corpus data (e.g., how speakers/files are nested into corpora) and, with regard to the predictors in question, the hypothesized causal or correlational structure of the data. One example – not the most comprehensive one possible or necessary – is the model defined in Figure 9.2 in a format that corresponds to how this could be formulated within the R statistical language and environment (R Core Team, 2018). We are using R because (i) it is more powerful than SPSS, (ii) it is freely available, (iii) it is the leading platform for the development of new statistical tools, and (iv) it is a full-fledged programming language, which means it can be used for more than just statistical analysis (e.g. corpus processing, Gries, 2016) and which means that exchange of code makes analyses perfectly replicable.

Next, we briefly discuss how the results from such a regression model can be interpreted.

Regression Results and Their Interpretation

The analysis of a regression model such as that in Figure 9.2 usually returns four parts of results. First, there will be some overall statistics describing the quality of the model (see 1. in Figure 9.3), where *quality* refers to the degree to which the model fits the data. For regression models, quality should be assessed by the following statistics:

- some form of an R^2-value (marginal and/or conditional) quantifying the model's quality (typically, $0 \leq R^2 \leq 1$, with higher values being better);
- a classification accuracy in percent stating how many of the studied cases the model classifies correctly; ideally, this would be complemented by corresponding accuracy values from cross-validation, i.e. a process where the regression model is computed from test data (often 90% of the original data) and then applied to training data (the remaining 10% of the original data);
- scores such as C ($0.5 \leq C \leq 1$), precision (e.g., how many of the genitives predicted to be *s*-genitives are really *s*-genitives?), and recall (how many of all the s-genitives were found?), and the baseline against which accuracies are compared.

Second, for the so-called *random effects*, i.e. the adjustments made for the corpora, files/speakers, and lexical items that are treated as if they were randomly sampled from a larger population, we would obtain estimates of their variability, with larger estimates indicating that the variables in question exhibit a large amount of variability (that needs to be accounted for). As exemplified in Figure 9.3, one might obtain a large estimate for FILE and a small one for CORPUS, which would mean that, once speaker-specific variability is taken into account (with FILE), differences between corpora are less relevant; thus, this integrates corpus comparisons into such analyses. In addition, any lexically specific effects could be reflected in the variances for POSSESSOR and POSSESSUM.

Finally, for the *fixed effects*, i.e. the variables whose values in the sample (the corpus data) we consider to exhaust the possible ranges of values in the population (the world), we obtain two kinds of results. First, one *p*-value for the overall significance of each predictor that could be dropped from the model (see 3a). Second, for each coefficient estimated, we get (see 3b)

GENITIVE ~	the dependent variable is modeled as a function of
1 +	an overall intercept
ANIMACY +	a main effect of the critical predictor ANIMACY
LENGTHDIFF +	a main effect of the critical predictor LENGTHDIFF
ANIMACY:LENGTHDIFF +	an interaction of the critical predictors
L1 +	a main effect of the speaker's L1
ANIMACY:L1 +	an interaction term allowing the effect of ANIMACY to
be	different in the two L1s
LENGTHDIFF:L1 +	an interaction term allowing the effect of LENGTHDIFF
to	be different in the two L1s
ANIMACY:LENGTHDIFF:L1 +	an interaction term allowing the effect of ANIMACY:
	LENGTHDIFF to be different in the two L1s
PROFICIENCY +	a main effect of the speaker's proficiency level
PROFICIENCY:L1 +	an interaction term allowing the effect of PROFICIENCY
	to be different in the two L1s
LASTGENITIVE +	a main effect of priming, i.e. which genitive was produced
produced	last time
(1|CORPUS/FILE) +	an adjustment for the fact that each file/speaker, which is
	nested into one corpus, may behave differently
from others	
(1|POSSESSOR) +	an adjustment for each possessor lemma
(1|POSSESSUM)	an adjustment for each possessum lemma

Figure 9.2 One Possible Regression Model for the Genitive Scenario.

- an estimate or coefficient indicating how much and in what direction a change in a variable affects the probability of the predicted genitive (in a certain statistical situation);
- an estimate of that coefficient's uncertainty (a standard error);
- a significance test for the coefficient: does it differ significantly from 0 or not?

To some degree, one can interpret such a model on the basis of its fixed-effects coefficients: The value of -1.89 for ANIMACY means that, in a certain condition, inanimate possessors make

1. Overall results			
$R^2_{marginal/conditional}$	0.672 / 0.698	LR-test=243.89, df=12, p<0.001	
classification accuracy	0.87	baseline	0.55
precision / recall	0.9 / 0.8	C	0.87

2. Random-effects variances	intercept
CORPUS	0.1
FILE	0.8
POSSESSOR	0.5
POSSESSUM	0.2

3a. Significance of fixed-effects predictors	LR-test	df	$p_{deletion}$
ANIMACY : LENGTHDIFF : L1	15.47	1	<0.0001
PROFICIENCY	5.2	3	0.158

[…]

3b. Coefficients (intercept=0.81, predicted: s-genitive)	coefficient	std. error	z	p
ANIMACY$_{animate \to inanimate}$	-1.89	0.12	-15.75	<0.0001
LENGTHDIFF	-0.06	0.021	-2.86	0.0042
ANIMACY$_{animate \to inanimate}$: LENGTHDIFF	0.1	0.23	0.43	0.6672
L1$_{Chinese \to German}$	0.2	0.06	3.33	0.0009
ANIMACY$_{animate \to inanimate}$: L1$_{Chinese \to German}$	0.17	0.07	2.43	0.0151
LENGTHDIFF:L1$_{Chinese \to German}$	0.1	0.2	0.5	0.6171
ANIMACY$_{animate \to inanimate}$: LENGTHDIFF L1$_{Chinese \to German}$	:0.4	0.057	7.02	<0.0001
PROFICIENCY$_{B1 \to B2}$	0.3	0.22	1.36	0.1738
PROFICIENCY$_{B1 \to C1}$	0.17	0.15	1.13	0.2585

[…]

Figure 9.3   Possible Regression Results for the Genitive Scenario.

s-genitives less likely (the negative sign) than animate possessors; similarly, the value of -0.06 for LENGTHDIFF means that, in a certain condition, an increase of length difference by 1 makes *s*-genitives less likely (the negative sign). However, this is much less straightforward once more complex models are interpreted; for instance, Figure 9.3 reveals a significant three-way interaction of ANIMACY: LENGTHDIFF: L1, i.e., the two learner varieties differ in how ANIMACY and LENGTHDIFF affect their genitive choices – such findings should be visualized by plotting

- for numeric predictors (such as LENGTHDIFF), a regression line whose location and slope reveal how LENGTHDIFF values are related to changes in the predicted probabilities of *s*-genitives;
- for categorical predictors (such as L1), points whose location reveal the predicted probabilities of *s*-genitives for the different levels of L1.

And of course, in the case of an interaction, one might have to plot several regression lines (e.g. one for every level of a categorical predictor that a numeric predictor interacts with) or several sets of points that cover all predicted values arising from the interaction of 2+ categorical predictors.

Within the R environment, we recommend using effects plots (see Fox, 2003; Fox & Hong, 2009), which show effects of predictors with all other predictors in the model controlled (by holding them constant at typical values). If the predictors ANIMACY and LENGTHDIFF were significant and did not participate in interactions, such plots might look like Figure 9.4.

The left panel shows that *s*-genitives are more likely with animate possessors (as expected) with the point sizes and error bars representing the frequencies of the animacy levels and the 95% confidence intervals respectively. The right panel shows that *s*-genitives are less likely the longer the possessor is relative to the possessed (also as expected) with rugs on the *x*-axis representing the observed length differences and the grey band representing the 95% confidence band.

While this example might appear specialized – a constructional alternation with no native speaker data included and no other speaker-level controls – and while we did not discuss all possible predictors and their effects, the above is a methodological blueprint of how, currently at least, the majority of LCR studies can be conducted (in better ways) to inform SLA/FLA research. The above regression-based logic extends to all kinds of alternation cases, be they morphosyntactic like here, lexical, pragmatic, or something else; it extends to cases where more than two competing expressions are studied, to cases where the dependent variables are accuracies of uses of expressions (e.g.,

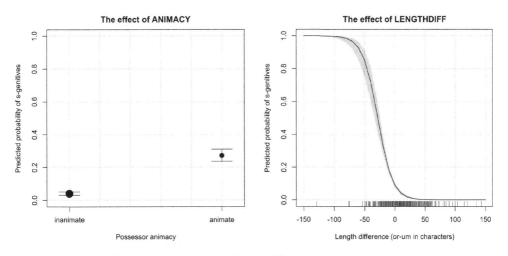

Figure 9.4 Effects Plots for Two Hypothetical Main Effects.

in percent) or ordinal proficiency levels, and even to cases of mere over-/underuse frequencies. In fact, most studies counted by Paquot and Plonsky (2017) as involving a regression-like procedure can not only be recast in the above framework, but actually improved because of how, now, many more 'quirks' of learner corpus data are accommodated: speaker-specific effects, lexically-specific effects, repeated measurements, corpus structure, multifactoriality, and more.

For instance, many classical over-/underuse studies such as Aijmer (2005), Hasselgård and Johansson (2011), or Laufer and Waldman (2011) could benefit from being reframed in this way, if only to address, e.g., the issue of within- and between-corpus variability, namely the repeated measurements of some speakers but no occurrences from others. As another instance, consider Durrant and Schmitt (2009), who compare native and non-native writers' use of collocations. They determine frequencies and compute association strengths – *MI* and *t* – of Adj-N and N-N pairs in comparable corpora of native and non-native English. They also (laudably!) compute text-based results as opposed to pooling all data, but even their analysis could benefit from a regression reframing. For example, their analysis of the association measures proceeds on the basis of grouping collocations into seven bins of association strengths, which loses much of the information contained in the originally numeric scores and would not have been required in a regression-based framework.

It is important to point out that there is a variety of reasons why regression modeling will not always be a viable option. Most of these reasons involve the size and the structure of the data one is trying to analyze. Obviously, regression modeling requires a certain sample size depending on the number of variables one wishes to study; simplistically speaking, the more predictors, the larger the sample size should be. In addition, even large samples can prove problematic for regression modeling when the data are unevenly distributed in a way that leaves few data points for many combinations of predictors, when the predictors are highly correlated with each other, when some predictor combinations are perfectly predictive of the response, and/or when the response variable is extremely skewed (see Gelman & Hill, 2008). However, there are few hard-and-fast rules, and it takes exploration and experience to determine when other methods are likely to be more useful; alternative methods used in linguistics are especially conditional inference trees and random forests (see Baayen et al., 2013).

Representative Corpora and Research

Lester (2019) is a study on the realization of the relativizer *that* in non-subject-extracted relative clauses (NSRCs) as in (2).

(2) a. This is the communicator that Lieutenant Reed forgot on the planet
     b. This is the communicator ____ Lieutenant Reed forgot on the planet

This paper embodies the approach of regression-based studies in LCR, in particular the MuPDAR (Multifactorial Predication and Deviation Analysis with Regressions, see Gries & Adelman, 2014; Gries & Deshors, 2014) approach discussed in Chapter 8, this volume. Lester extracted all NSRCs manually from the *Louvain Corpus of Native English Conversation* (LOCNEC) corpus and the German and Spanish components of the LINDSEI corpus. First, he documents over-/underuse patterns using generalized linear mixed-effects modeling of the type discussed above: The Spanish learners produced significantly fewer NSRCs and fewer tokens without *that* than the German learners but were closer to the native speaker performance; the German learners produced more NSRCs and more tokens without *that* than the native speakers.

He then did a MuPDAR analysis of these data: Both the native and non-native speaker data were annotated with regard to a dozen variables, many of which are familiar from the regression discussion above. They included whether *that* was absent or present, the L1 of the speaker, a code for each speaker, the task type in which the example was produced (monologic vs. dialogic), the length of the relative clause subject, self-priming from previous relative clauses, etc. He then fitted a generalized additive mixed model – a regression model good at handling curvature or non-linearity in how numeric predictors affect the response – to the native speaker data, trying to predict whether or not a *that*-relativizer would be used.

Next, he determined that the resulting regression model yielded good prediction accuracy using cross-validation and then applied the model to the non-native speaker data to generate for each non-native speaker NSRC (i) a prediction of whether a native speaker would have produced *that* or not and (ii) a score of how much the learner choices differed from what a native speaker would have produced.

Finally, he fit a second regression model to predict the deviation scores based on the same predictors as the first regression. To mention just a few of the results: he found that

- Spanish learners used *that*-relativizers in a more nativelike way than German learners;
- learners' choices became less nativelike as the relative clause subjects (*Lieutenant Reed* in (2) above) became longer;
- learners' choices became less nativelike in more disfluent speech (i.e. under higher processing load);
- learners from both L1s exhibited self-priming effects (Spanish learners more so than German learners).

Lester concluded that his study is the "first to reveal a tendency for learners to omit optional grammatical markers in complex environments", a finding that differs from other LCR findings, e.g., Wulff et al.'s (2018) on *that* as a complementizer and that suggests that "the costs of producing different types of constructions in L2 can lead to different, construction-specific communicative strategies."

Wulff et al. (2009) is concerned with the Aspect Hypothesis (Andersen & Shirai, 1994), the assumption that language learners of both L1 and SL/FL learners acquire tense and aspect morphology in ways that are influenced by the inherent semantic aspect of verbs and the events they describe: Using Vendler's aspectual categories, perfective past morphemes are used first with telic predicates (achievements and accomplishments) whereas progressive markings are used first with atelic predicates (activities).

First, Wulff et al. explored the frequencies and associations between verbs and tense-aspect marking in native speaker data (from the spoken component of the *British National Corpus* and in learner data (from the *Michigan Corpus of Academic Spoken English*, Simpson et al., 2002). Regarding the verbs' frequencies, they found Zipfian distributions such that, for each tense-aspect pattern studied, (i) a few highly frequent types account for very many tokens whereas (ii) very many types are extremely infrequent. Regarding the verbs' co-occurrence preferences, they used multiple distinctive collexeme analyses (Gries & Stefanowitsch, 2004), an extension of a measure of association for 2×2 co-occurrence tables (such as G^2) to more than two elements, to determine which verbs are significantly attracted to which tense-aspect morphemes. Here, too, they found Zipfian distributions such that each morpheme has only a few verbs strongly attracted to it, and the verbs attracted to each tense-aspect morpheme come in straightforward semantic groups. This case study of Wulff et al. therefore shows a strong confirmation of the Aspect Hypothesis for both native and non-native speakers.

As a validation, Wulff et al. then collected telicity ratings for 86 verbs from 20 subjects in a rating task. They computed average telicity ratings for all verbs (*be* and *love* scored lowest, *end* and *finish* scored highest in telicity) and then reported

- the results of independent *t*-tests to determine whether, in both native and non-native language, verbs associated with past tense in the corpus data (from case study 1) received significantly higher telicity ratings, which they did;

- the results of Pearson's *r* correlations for whether the five most frequent past and progressive verbs were significantly correlated with their mean telicity ratings; they found correlations in the expected direction, but only significantly so for progressive verbs.

This study clearly confirms the Aspect Hypothesis and points to why it might hold: The tense-aspect patterning is strong in the input in terms of both frequency and contingency, so learners pick up on it and use it themselves. At the same time, this supports our earlier point of the relevance of proper regression modeling. In particular, case study 2 could have benefited from a more comprehensive regression-based approach (rather than just simple *t*-tests). In a single unified regression model, one could have determined whether the telicity ratings of the subjects were predictable from all verbs' overall frequencies, their associations to all tense-aspect morphemes, and a predictor for L1 vs. L2. Nonetheless, Wulff et al. is a nice study at the interface of learner corpus research and (more experimental) SLA work.

Future Directions

The above overview leads to straightforward future directions. Regarding corpus compilation, we need more detailed metadata for our corpora. Put differently, while learner corpus compilers usually get told that researchers want bigger corpora and (more) longitudinal corpora – and of course we want all that, too – we also urge compilers towards including more and more detailed annotation regarding speaker and task characteristics so that LCR can begin to implement the above regression-based strategies and bridge the gap to much work happening in SLA/FLA.

Regarding statistical analysis of learner corpus data, the main desideratum is to have more studies that conform to the above blueprint. While the number of more advanced analyses has grown, as witnessed by publications and paper presentations at, say, the LCR conference, progress is too slow, given how much faster both general linguistics and corpus linguistics are evolving quantitatively; a more widespread adoption of the kinds of methods that are now routinely used in other linguistic sub-disciplines is simply a must, especially given how much of a quantum leap this would mean for the field. This would be especially true if this adoption was coupled with a concomitant increase in awareness of some additional tools, such as the relevance of exploring non-linear relationships (as in Lester, 2019), user-defined contrasts (see Fox & Weisberg, 2019, Section 4.7) to test specific hypotheses directly, and model diagnostics (to determine whether our models need to be tweaked or whether other statistical approaches are required, see Fox & Weisberg, 2019, Chapter 8). Such other approaches include *robust statistics* (useful for data that violate the assumptions of many parametric statistical methods, see Larson-Hall & Herrington, 2009; Wilcox, 2012), but also general *machine-learning kinds of methods* such as random forests or, on the exploratory side of things, *association rules* (see Hastie, Tibshirani, & Friedman, 2009 or James et al., 2013). We admit that this raises the desired level of complexity of the field of LCR to a whole new level and few linguists, including ourselves, have that kind of training, but given the kinds of data learner corpora offer and their complexity, the field as a whole will have to move things up a notch or two in order to address the challenges the data and our theories about the data pose to us.

Further Reading

Bestgen, Y. (2017). Beyond single-word measures: L2 writing assessment, lexical richness and formulaic competence. *System*, *69*(1), 65–78.

In this paper, Bestgen explores the degree to which association measures (specifically, *MI* and *t*) computed on learner bigrams using frequencies from native speaker use in the British National Corpus correlate with the quality of learner texts. Using simple and multiple regression models as well as cross-validation, he shows that formulaic richness measures, in particular *MI*, outperform lexical diversity scores in predicting measures of learner text quality.

Desagulier, G. (2017). *Corpus linguistics and statistics with R*. Berlin: Springer.

This textbook covers both the processing of data with R (corpora and tabular spreadsheet kinds of data) as well as various statistical analysis techniques. As for the former, Desagulier covers regular expressions and programming basics to generate concordances, frequency lists etc. from corpora (see Gries, 2016 for a book-length treatment); as for the latter, while he discusses some hypothesis-testing approaches (although not much in terms of regression modeling, for that see Baayen, 2008 or Gries, 2021), his book is particularly strong when it comes to exploratory methods.

Larson-Hall, J., & Herrington, R. (2009). Improving data analysis in second language acquisition by utilizing modern developments in applied statistics. *Applied Linguistics*, *31*(3), 368–390.

This article makes two suggestions about how to improve statistical analyses in SLA research. The first suggestion is seemingly modest but nonetheless vital and promotes more and more insightful visualization of SLA data, in particular preferring box plots over bar plots and regression lines involving curvature over straight ones (for the kinds of non-linear effects often found). The second suggestion involves, as alluded to above, a greater reliance on robust statistics, i.e., a family of methods that is geared towards handling data that violate the assumptions of many kinds of parametric tests (e.g., by exhibiting non-normality, outliers, etc.).

Related Topics

Chapters 2, 3, 6, 8, 10, and 13.

References

Aijmer, K. (2005). Modality in advanced Swedish learners' written interlanguage. In S. Granger, J. Hung, & S. Petch-Tyson (Eds.), *Computer learner corpora, second language acquisition, and foreign language teaching* (pp. 55–76). Amsterdam: John Benjamins.

Andersen, R. W., & Shirai, Y. (1994). Discourse motivations for some cognitive acquisition principles. *Studies in Second Language Acquisition*, *16*(2), 133–156.

Baayen, R. H. (2008). *Analyzing linguistic data: A practical introduction to statistics using R*. Cambridge: Cambridge University Press.

Baayen, R. H., Janda, L. A., Nesset, T., Endresen, A., & Makarova, A. (2013). Making choices in Russian: Pros and cons of statistical methods for rival forms. *Russian Linguistics*, *37*(3), 253–291.

The British national corpus, version 3 (BNC XML Edition). (2007). Distributed by Bodleian Libraries, University of Oxford, on behalf of the BNC Consortium.

Carroll, J. B., & Sapon, S. (1959). *Modern Language Aptitude Test (M.L.A.T.)*. New York: The Psychological Corporation.

Dörnyei, Z. (2005). *The psychology of the language learner: Individual differences in second language acquisition*. New York: Routledge.

Durrant, P., & Schmitt, N. (2009). To what extent do native and non-native writers make use of collocations. *International Review of Applied Linguistics*, *47*(2), 157–177.

Ellis, N. C., Römer, U., & Brook O'Donnell, M. (2016). *Usage-based approaches to language acquisition and processing: cognitive and corpus investigations of construction grammar. Language Learning* 66 (Suppl. 1, Language Learning Monograph Series). New York: John Wiley.

Fox, J. (2003). Effect displays in R for generalised linear models. *Journal of Statistical Software*, *8*, 1–27.

Fox, J., & Hong, J. (2009). Effect displays in R for multinomial and proportional-odds logit models: Extensions to the effects package. *Journal of Statistical Software*, *32*, 1–24.

Fox, J., & Weisberg, S. (2019). *An R companion to applied regression* (3rd ed.). Los Angeles: Sage.

Gelman, A., & Hill, J. (2008). *Data analysis using regression and multilevel/hierarchical models*. Cambridge: Cambridge University Press.

Gilquin, G., De Cock, S., & Granger, S. (2010). *Louvain International Database of Spoken English Interlanguage (CD-ROM + handbook)*. Louvain-la-Neuve: Presses universitaires de Louvain.

Granger, S., Dagneaux, E., Meunier, F., & Paquot, M. (2009). *International corpus of learner English v2 (Handbook + CD-Rom)*. Louvain-la-Neuve: Presses Universitaires de Louvain.

Granger, S., Gilquin, G., & Meunier, F. (2015). Introduction: Learner corpus research – past, present and future. In S. Granger, G. Gilquin, & F. Meunier (Eds.), *The Cambridge handbook of learner corpus research* (pp. 1–5). Cambridge: Cambridge University Press.

Gries, S. Th. (2016). Quantitative corpus linguistics with R (2nd rev. & ext. ed., pp. 274).

Gries, S. Th. (2018). On over- and underuse in learner corpus research and multifactoriality in corpus linguistics more generally. *Journal of Second Language Studies, 1*(2), 276–308.

Gries, S. Th. (2021). Statistics for linguistics with R (3rd rev. & ext. ed.). Berlin: De Gruyter Mouton.

Gries, S. Th. (in press). Analyzing dispersion. In M. Paquot & St. Th. Gries (Eds.), *Practical handbook of corpus linguistics*. Berlin: Springer.

Gries, S. Th., & Adelman, A. S. (2014). Subject realization in Japanese conversation by native and non-native speakers: Exemplifying a new paradigm for learner corpus research. In J. Romero-Trillo (Ed.), *Yearbook of corpus linguistics and pragmatics 2014: New empirical and theoretical paradigms* (pp. 35–54). Cham: Springer.

Gries, S. Th., & Deshors, S. C. (2014). Using regressions to explore deviations between corpus data and a standard/target: Two suggestions. *Corpora, 9*(1), 109–136.

Gries, S. Th., & Stefanowitsch, A. (2004). Extending collostructional analysis: A corpus-based perspective on "alternations". *International Journal of Corpus Linguistics, 9*(1), 97–129.

Gries, S. Th., & Wulff, S. (to appear). Examining individual variation in learner production data: A few programmatic pointers for corpus-based analyses using the example of adverbial clause ordering. *Applied Psycholinguistics*.

Hasselgård, H., & Johansson, S. (2011). Learner corpora and contrastive interlanguage analysis. In F. Meunier, S. De Cock, G. Gilquin, & M. Paquot (Eds.), *A taste for corpora: In honour of sylviane granger* (pp. 33–61). Amsterdam: John Benjamins.

Hastie, T., Tibshirani, R., & Friedman, J. (2009). *The elements of statistical learning: Data mining, inference, and prediction* (2nd ed.). Berlin: Springer.

James, G., Witten, D., Hastie, T., & Tibshirani, R. (2013). *An introduction to statistical learning with applications in R*. Berlin: Springer.

Larson-Hall, J., & Herrington, R. (2009). Improving data analysis in second language acquisition by utilizing modern developments in applied statistics. *Applied Linguistics, 31*(3), 368–390.

Laufer, B., & Waldman, T. (2011). Verb-noun collocations in second language writing: A corpus analysis of learners'. *English. Language Learning, 61*(2), 647–672.

Lester, N. A. (2019). That's hard: Relativizer use in spontaneous L2 speech. *International Journal of Learner Corpus Research, 5*(1), 1–32.

Paquot, M., & Plonsky, L. (2017). Quantitative research methods and study quality in learner corpus research. *International Journal of Learner Corpus Research, 3*(1), 61–94.

R Core Team. (2019). *R: A language and environment for statistical computing*. Vienna: R Foundation for Statistical Computing.

Simpson, R. C., Briggs, S. L., Ovens, J., & Swales, J. M. (2002). *The Michigan corpus of academic spoken English*. Ann Arbor: The regents of the University of Michigan.

Tomaschek, F., Hendrix, P., & Baayen, R. H. (2018). Strategies for addressing collinearity in multivariate linguistic data. *Journal of Phonetics, 71*, 249–267.

Wilcox, R. (2012). *Modern statistics for the social and Behavioral Sciences: A practical introduction*. Boca Raton: Chapman and Hall/CRC Press.

Wulff, S., Ellis, N. C., Römer, U., Bardovi-Harlig, K., & Leblanc, C. (2009). The acquisition of tense-aspect: Converging evidence from corpora and telicity ratings. *The Modern Language Journal, 93*(3), 354–369.

Wulff, S., & Gries, S. Th. (in press). Exploring individual variation in learner corpus research: Some methodological suggestions. In B. Le Bruyn & M. Paquot (Eds.), *Learner corpus research meets second language acquisition*. Cambridge: Cambridge University Press.

Wulff, S., Gries, S. Th., & Lester, N. A. (2018). Optional that in complementation by German and Spanish learners. In A. Tyler, L. Huan, & H. Jan (Eds.), *What is applied cognitive linguistics? Answers from current SLA research* (pp. 99–120). Berlin: De Gruyter Mouton.

10

Combining Learner Corpora and Experimental Methods

Gaëtanelle Gilquin

Introduction

In the foreword to a special issue of *Language Learning* on "experimental, computational, and corpus-based approaches to language learning", Ellis (2017) notes that "[t]he investigation of a complex phenomenon like language acquisition naturally requires insights, tools, and methods from many disciplines, yet it is still relatively rare to find studies that combine multiple approaches" (p. 5). This chapter deals with the combination of two such methods to investigate the acquisition of a second or foreign (L2) language, namely the use of learner corpora and experimentation. [1] Learner corpora represent a (more or less) naturalistic kind of data, collected with no (or very little) control over what learners say or write. Experimental data, on the other hand, represent a more constrained type of data, with some degree of imposition on what the subjects say, write, or, indeed, do. In the well-known threefold distinction between naturally occurring samples of learner language, clinically elicited samples, and experimentally elicited samples (Ellis, 2008, pp. 916–921), learner corpora can be said to correspond to the first two types (see Granger, 2012, p. 8): some learner corpora contain fully authentic and natural data ('naturally occurring samples'), whereas others are the result of a task, such as a picture description or a role play, requiring learners to use language for a certain communicative purpose (e.g. apologize to a customer) but letting them choose whatever linguistic resources they want – or are able – to use ('clinically elicited samples'). In 'experimentally elicited samples', on the other hand, it is the linguistic form itself that is constrained: through certain exercises such as gap fills or sentence translations, learners are guided to produce certain (types of) linguistic items (e.g. imperative forms). In this chapter, the term experimentation will cover the experimental elicitation of samples of learner language, as just described, but also experimental designs in which learners are asked to "do something with language they usually do not do" (Gilquin & Gries, 2009, p. 5), for example, judge the grammaticality of sentences or read a text while their eye movements are tracked (these correspond to 'non-production performance data' in Ellis, 2008). It should be emphasized that these different types of data represent a continuum, with some being nearer to the "no control" pole, others nearer to the "close control" pole, and yet others somewhere in the middle (Ellis, 2008, pp. 916–917). Consequently, there is no strict dichotomy between corpora and experimental data. Indeed, what certain scholars call a corpus might be considered experimental data by others and vice versa (Gilquin & Gries, 2009).

Traditionally, learner corpora and experimentation have been associated with different paradigms, namely learner corpus research (LCR) and second language acquisition research (SLA), respectively. This can be explained by referring to the traditional focus of each of these paradigms. While LCR has mainly focused on learners' performance (Granger, 1998a), SLA has often been more interested in their competence (Ellis & Barkhuizen, 2005). Performance, that is, how learners actually use the L2, is visible by examining their authentic production, as attested in learner corpora. By contrast, competence, i.e. learners' underlying knowledge of the L2, is more efficiently studied through experimentation, which typically seeks to bring to light mental and psychological processes. Experimentation also makes it possible to control and manipulate different variables, with a view to determining their possible effect. It is thus ideally suited to fulfill one of the purposes of SLA theory, namely "to better understand the nature of learner language, its development, and *what impacts upon both*" (Myles, 2015, p. 310; emphasis added). This does not mean that SLA has relied exclusively on experimental data. It has also frequently used observational data, reflecting learners' production. Some of these correspond to learner corpora like those used in LCR. Most of the time, however, these observational data are more constrained than learner corpora, being "elicited in one way or another" (Cook, 1993, p. 47). They also tend to be taken from a small number of learners, unlike learner corpora, which usually include data from many different learners and which can arguably be used to generalize about a whole learner population. In addition, the observational data used in SLA are not usually analyzed with the tools and techniques of corpus linguistics. In what follows, only the combination of *bona fide* learner corpora with experimental data will be considered.

Core Issues and Topics

Combining Learner Corpora and Experimentation in LCR and SLA

Although, as suggested in the previous section, LCR has primarily relied on naturalistic data while SLA has traditionally favored more constrained data, both paradigms have also occasionally combined these two types of data with each other. The fact that LCR and SLA have gradually opened up to each other on a theoretical level (see Chapter 1, this volume) also means that they have started to share methodologies. LCR has progressively moved beyond the description of L2 performance that characterized the field in its early stages, and it has become more rigorous in its attempts to understand and explain the phenomena observed. In this evolution, it has benefited from the insights of experimental data, which add a more cognitive dimension to the study of interlanguage. SLA, on the other hand, has recognized the importance of representativeness and generalizability, and learner corpora have provided it with the material necessary to consider larger groups of learners and to bring to light more general tendencies.

One of the first studies that combined learner corpora with experimental data dates back to the early days of LCR. In 1998, Granger investigated the use of amplifying adverbs in *-ly* by French-speaking learners of English (Granger, 1998b). Relying on corpus data from the *International Corpus of Learner English* (ICLE, as published a few years later in Granger, Meunier, & Dagneaux, 2002), she showed that learners underused collocations typical of native English (e.g. *readily available* or *vitally important*) and used atypical collocations (e.g. *dangerously threatened* or *irretrievably different*). She was able to explain this behavior by means of an elicitation test, which revealed "an underdeveloped sense of salience and of what constitutes a significant collocation" (Granger, 1998b, p. 152) among learners. She gave learners and native speakers a list of amplifier + adjective combinations (*readily significant/reliable/ill/different/essential*, etc.) and asked them to highlight any adjective that they felt collocated with the amplifier. The learners highlighted a larger range of combinations than the native speakers, and the combinations they highlighted only partially overlapped with those marked by the native speakers. This suggested that "the learners' sense of salience is not only weak, but also partly misguided" (Granger, 1998b, p. 152) and explained why, in their free production, they underused some highly idiomatic combinations and, conversely, used some atypical combinations. Since Granger (1998b), several studies have explored the possibility of combining learner corpora and experimental data to gain a better understanding of learner language (so-called 'interlanguage') and how it is acquired. The next section outlines some of the reasons why learner corpora and experimentation can be a winning combination.

Why Combine Learner Corpora and Experimentation?

The combined use of learner corpora and experimentation can be related to the growing appeal for methodological pluralism (also referred to as multimethod or mixed-methods approaches), which recommends triangulation, that is, the use of multiple methodologies to investigate the same phenomenon. If these methodologies point in the same direction, we have a case of 'converging evidence' (see Schönefeld, 2011), which makes a conclusion more reliable than if a single source of evidence had been consulted. Scholars who use both learner corpora and experimental data, however, do not necessarily expect their results to converge. They may simply combine them in the hope that each of them provides different insights into the phenomenon under study. As Ellis and Barkhuizen (2005) rightly point out, "no one method will provide an entirely valid picture of what a learner knows or thinks" (p. 49). The combined use of learner corpora and experimentation, in fact, makes it possible to marry the advantages of each type of data, while compensating for their respective weaknesses. The strengths and limitations of learner corpora and experimental data are summarized in Table 10.1.

Learner corpora have the advantage of being made up of (potentially) large amounts of (more or less) naturalistic learner language. Thanks to appropriate tools and techniques (see Chapter 6, this volume), it is possible to extract all the instances of a given linguistic item in the corpus and to see how they are used in authentic contexts. This free production corresponds to learners' performance, which learner corpora thus give direct access to. More generally, learner corpora give access to what could be described as 'textual phenomena', which include frequency of use (how often do learners use a certain linguistic item?) and patterns of use (how do learners typically use this linguistic item – in terms of register, collocations, colligations, etc.?). As a rule, learner corpus data provide more reliable information about learners' performance and other textual phenomena than experimental data, which are largely decontextualized (test items typically consist in single words or isolated sentences)[2] and which tend to be relatively artificial, representing guided or forced language production and being sometimes collected in environments (e.g. laboratory or soundproof room) and with techniques (e.g. eye-tracking technology) that learners are unlikely to be accustomed to.

Table 10.1 Summary of the Strengths and Limitations of Learner Corpora and Experimental Data

	Learner corpora	Experimental data
+	• Naturally occurring language • Potentially large amounts of data • Access to performance (production) and textual phenomena • Language in context	• Systematic control for variables • Possible focus on infrequent phenomena • Access to competence (productive and receptive knowledge) and mental phenomena
–	• Dependent on learners' linguistic choices • Finite sample of language	• Artificiality of the test situation • Largely decontextualized data

Learner corpora, on the other hand, can only provide very indirect information about learners' competence. Observing what learners get right or wrong in a corpus gives an indication of what they know or do not know, of course, but the unconstrained nature of corpus data means that learners are free to choose certain linguistic resources and avoid others. This phenomenon of avoidance (see, e.g., Kleinmann, 1977) explains why, in Cook's (1993) words, "[a]ny natural L2 data may under-represent the learner's problems and hence distort the description of competence" (p. 48). A learner's free production may not contain many errors, but this may be due to his/her avoidance of words or structures that s/he feels unsure about. This, Cook (1993) continues, "is partly prevented by putting the learners in situations where they cannot avoid particular forms" (p. 48) – although, as he notes, this comes at the price of a loss in the naturalness of the communication. It should also be underlined that, because a corpus is a finite sample of the whole language production and is thus never exhaustive, a word or structure which is not found in a corpus may still be perfectly familiar to the learner (productively and/or receptively). Again, using more guided data collection methods, it is possible to check whether the learner can actually produce a certain linguistic item when required to or, if receptive knowledge is tested, whether s/he can recognize and understand the item. This also works for items which are infrequent in learner language and may not appear in (even large) corpora. Besides competence, experimental data can give access to other mental phenomena, such as salience (cf. Granger's (1998b) study described earlier), association (between words within the L2 or between words in the L2 and their translations in the learner's native language, cf. Gilquin, 2009), and degree of certainty (see, e.g., Gilquin, 2007, described below; Littré, 2015).

Another advantage of experimentation is that, as already noted, it allows for the systematic control of variables. To a certain extent, this is the case with learner corpora too. Using the rich metadata that usually accompany learner corpora (see Gilquin, 2015; Chapter 5, this volume) as well as the linguistic context that surrounds the search item, one can assess the effect of, say, the learner's mother tongue, the time s/he spent in a target language country, the use of backchannels by the interlocutor, or the presence of an animate or inanimate subject in the sentence. However, in corpus analyses, the researcher is dependent on the variables and values that are present in the corpus. If no relative clauses with an animate antecedent and an object relative pronoun occur in the corpus data, for example, it will be impossible to study the impact of this linguistic environment on the choice of a relative pronoun. By contrast, given an appropriate experimental design, one can easily manipulate variables such as the antecedent of a relative clause (animate vs inanimate) and the function of the relative pronoun (subject vs object) and see what relative pronoun learners opt for in these different linguistic contexts.

Working with both learner corpora and experimentation thus gives researchers access to both textual/performance and mental/competence data and enables them to combine the advantages of large quantities of naturalistic language in context and of targeted data aimed at testing very specific hypotheses about even infrequent phenomena.

Challenges

The advantages of combining corpus and experimental data should not obscure the difficulties involved in such a combination. Here, I will not deal with the challenges associated with each of the two methodologies considered individually, but with the challenges arising from the combined use of learner corpora and experimental methods.

The first issue has to do with the fact that corpus data and experimental data are normally collected at different stages in the research process. Learner corpus data are typically part of a data-driven approach, in which the data themselves take center stage. Data collection tends to come first, with learner corpora often being conceived of as general-purpose resources which can serve to answer various research questions about the interlanguage of the population represented in the corpus. Experimental data, on the other hand, are more usually part of a theory-driven approach, in which theory is central. It is thus usually hypothesis forming that comes first, and experiments are designed with a specific research question in mind. Reconciling such approaches (data-driven and theory-driven) may not necessarily be easy and may require some adjustments in one's methodological routines. Even more fundamentally, special skills are necessary to deal with learner corpora or to design an experiment, and this may constitute another obstacle to some researchers, who may have to develop corpus literacy or learn how to set up a good linguistic experiment. Interdisciplinary research, involving the collaboration between researchers from different fields and with different types of expertise, is another way in which the two methods can successfully be combined.

Next to these considerations, another central issue is that of comparability. Learner corpus analysis and experimentation represent different methods, which tap into different aspects of learner language. In order for their combination to be legitimate, they should be sufficiently comparable (see also Arppe, Gilquin, Glynn, Hilpert, & Zeschel, 2010). In particular, the question of the subjects should be addressed. Sometimes, it is necessary for the subjects to be different, for example, if the aim is to see how learners process non-standard features in L2 written texts or whether they can understand certain mispronounced words in L2 spoken texts. If, on the other hand, the objective is to investigate the same linguistic phenomenon in the two types of data (e.g. the use of collocations in corpus and experimental data), then, ideally, the subjects who contribute data to the learner corpus should be the same as those who take part in the experiment. However, this is likely to reduce the number of subjects and hence to negate one of the key advantages of learner corpora, namely that they can give access to vast quantities of data produced by large samples of a learner population (see previous section). In addition, relying on the same subjects to collect corpus and experimental data may be difficult, among other reasons because of the order in which data collection and hypothesis forming typically take place (see above). By the time a learner corpus has been collected and researchers start exploiting it by devising research questions and putting forward hypotheses, it might already be too late to track down the learners who were involved in the corpus data collection and ask them to participate in an experiment – or too much time may have passed, and the subjects may have reached another stage of interlanguage development, thus being, in a way, different learners. If one uses an off-the-shelf learner corpus, contacting the contributors to the corpus is automatically ruled out, because their identity should be hidden from the users of the corpus for privacy reasons. Having access to corpus and experimental data from the same subjects at the same stage of development implies that the researchers know right from the start what their objective is and what data they will need, and that they collect all the data at the same time for this very specific purpose (for two such examples, see Domínguez, Tracy-Ventura, Arche, Mitchell, & Myles, 2013 and Möller, 2017, described below). If the contributors to the learner corpus and the participants in the experiment have to be different, which corresponds to the most common situation, the researcher should make sure that they are similar enough (in terms of mother tongue background, proficiency level, exposure to the L2, etc.), presenting only minor differences that are not expected to (fundamentally) affect the data.

Main Research Methods

Several chapters in this handbook are devoted to the tools and techniques used in LCR (see, in particular, Chapters 6 and 8). This section will therefore deal with experimental methods, focusing on those that have been combined with learner corpus methods. Following Ellis's (2008) typology, described in the introduction to this chapter, a distinction will be drawn between 'experimentally elicited samples' and 'non-production performance data', which will be referred to as L2 elicitation data and L2 non-production data, respectively. I will also discuss cases where multiple sources of corpus and experimental evidence are exploited.

L2 Elicitation Data

L2 elicitation data result from experiments which elicit learners' production of some linguistic items (word, phrase, construction, sentence, etc.). Elicitation relies on some kind of prompt, which can be linguistic (e.g. cloze test) or visual (picture, video). The use of linguistic prompts is very common to elicit L2 data. In Römer, Roberson, O'Donnell, and Ellis (2014), for example, verb argument constructions (VACs) are examined in spoken and written corpora of learner English and then compared against data collected in lexical production tasks which take the form of VAC frames to be completed by means of a verb (e.g. *She _____ against the...*). In De Knop (2015), subjects also have to fill in a verb, but the aim is to elicit posture verbs in German, and in particular the verb *sitzen* 'to sit' (e.g. *Er _____ in der Falle* 'He … in the trap'). Ozeki and Shirai (2007) study the use of relative clauses in L2 Japanese on the basis of a learner corpus analysis and a sentence-combining experiment, which requires the subjects to combine two sentences into one, using a relative clause (e.g. *Mr. Hayashi is waiting for a friend in the room* and *The friend is Japanese* can be combined into *The friend who Mr. Hayashi is waiting for in the room is Japanese*).[3] In some cases, another language (typically the learner's native language) may be used to elicit interlanguage. Thus, in Gilquin (2007), a French translation is used to elicit collocations with *make* among a group of French-speaking learners of English (see below for a more detailed description of the study and how this translation task is combined with other experimental data and with learner corpus data). The use of translation makes it possible to specify the expected meaning and hence further constrain the learner's production.

L2 data collected on the basis of a visual prompt can be described either as corpus data or as experimental data, depending on the extent to which the task simply aims to elicit a narrative (cf. the Giessen – Long Beach Chaplin Corpus; Jucker, Smith, & Lüdge, 2003) or targets specific linguistic items. In Tracy-Ventura and Myles (2015), a study which combines different types of data produced with varying degrees of control, the picture-based task is clearly more controlled, as it seeks to elicit past tense forms in L2 Spanish. It should be noted, however, that the pictures are accompanied by discourse prompts (such as *Gwen de niña ... cada fin de semana* 'When Gwen was a child … every weekend') and infinitival phrases describing the pictures (e.g. *(leer) un libro* '(read) a book'), and that these, probably more than the pictures themselves, contribute to the experimental nature of the data.

L2 Non-production Data

A literature review shows that when learner corpus data are combined with experimental data, the latter most often represent L2 non-production data, in which learners are not required to actually produce language, but to carry out a linguistic task. Most of the time, the task involves judging the acceptability of sentences (or phrases, as in Granger, 1998b), a very direct way of tapping into learners' (implicit) knowledge of what is correct and what is not (e.g. Domínguez et al., 2013; Meunier & Littré, 2013; Littré, 2015; Mendikoetxea & Lozano, 2018). More occasionally, learners are shown combinations of letters and have to decide whether these correspond to existing words or not (lexical decision task, see Tracy-Ventura, 2017). In Meunier and Littré (2013), learners' *explicit* knowledge of the L2 is also tapped into, as they are asked to provide metalinguistic justification for their acceptability judgments. Another experimental task used in combination with learner corpus analysis and found in Valenzuela Manzanares and Rojo López (2008) or in Kim and Rah (2016) consists of sorting sentences according to their overall meaning.

Such sentence-sorting tasks are typical of Construction Grammar studies and aim to determine whether learners sort sentences based on verbs (e.g. sorting together sentences such as *Mike kicked the dog* and *David kicked the wall down*, which both include the verb *kick*) or based on constructions (e.g. sorting together sentences such as *David kicked the wall down* and *John threw the box apart*, which both correspond to resultative constructions).[4] In the case of a (predominantly) construction-based sorting, it can be assumed that learners have developed abstract constructional knowledge (knowledge of the resultative construction in the above example). The types of experiments just described all involve a linguistic task whose outcome is recorded, thus providing offline measures.

Other types of experiments are more psycholinguistic in nature, measuring reaction time, eye movement, or electrical activity in the brain while learners are processing language (typically, reading words, word combinations, or sentences). These provide online measures, which seek to record an ongoing process. While such experiments, individually, are quite commonly used to investigate the acquisition of an L2, it is extremely rare to find them in combination with learner corpus analyses. One exception is Siyanova and Schmitt (2008), who combine corpus and experimental data to study the production and processing of adjective-noun collocations by learners of English. Like several of the studies mentioned above, this one compares the interlanguage production in a learner corpus with learners' judgments as elicited through a controlled task (here, it is not the acceptability of the word combinations that is judged, though, but their "commonness in the English language" (Siyanova & Schmitt, 2008, p. 441)). What is special about Siyanova and Schmitt's (2008) study, however, is that they also measure the speed with which judgments are made. These reaction times are taken as an indication of the "fluency of collocation knowledge" (Siyanova & Schmitt, 2008, p. 449), that is, the speed with which learners process certain (high-frequency and low-frequency) adjective-noun collocations.

Multiple Sources of Corpus and Experimental Evidence

The example of Siyanova and Schmitt (2008) in the previous section shows that it is possible to combine learner corpus data with evidence from different experimental tasks. Sometimes the tasks correspond to the same type of data. Thus, in Valenzuela Manzanares and Rojo López (2008), the sentence-sorting experiment is combined with an acceptability judgment task, both of which correspond to non-production offline data. In Siyanova and Schmitt (2008), on the other hand, non-production offline data (from the judgment task) are combined with non-production online data (from the reaction time test), while in Azazil (2020) elicitation data (from a sentence completion task with linguistic prompts) are combined with non-production data (from an acceptability judgment task). The combination of one experimental task with learner corpus data representing multiple text types is possible too. Tracy-Ventura and Myles (2015) consider four sources of L2 evidence: a semi-structured interview, a picture description, a picture-based narrative with discourse prompts, and a picture-based narrative with discourse prompts and verb phrases to be used in the narratives. Of these four, the first three are described as corpus data and the last one as experimental data.

This multiplicity of sources can make the process of data interpretation quite complex, especially in case of divergent results. As Cook (1993) points out with respect to experimentation, "[m]uch of the L2 research shows that different experimental tasks elicit different behaviour, relevant to second language acquisition methodology but saying little about the L2 learner's actual ability to adapt speech to circumstance let alone acquire an L2" (p. 91). Similarly, Gablasova, Brezina, and McEnery (2017) demonstrate that using different (but comparable) corpora or applying different corpus methods may bring to light apparent differences in language use (e.g. in terms of frequencies), but that these differences may in fact be "an artifact of the corpus design

Gaëtanelle Gilquin

or the analytical tool used" (Gablasova, Brezina, & McEnery, 2017, p. 149). Interestingly, when considering four sources of L2 evidence, Tracy-Ventura and Myles (2015) precisely want to make a methodological point, showing that past tense morphology varies across tasks and that researchers should therefore rely on a range of tasks when investigating the L2 acquisition of a linguistic phenomenon (see also *Future Directions*).

Representative Corpora and Research

Gilquin (2007) investigates the use of collocations with *make* among French-speaking learners of English, by relying on a combination of corpus and experimental methods. The corpus data come from the French component of the *International Corpus of Learner English* (Granger, Meunier, & Dagneaux, 2002), ICLE-FR, a general-purpose learner corpus made up of argumentative essays. The corpus study consisted of an error analysis, which revealed an error rate of 7% in *make*-collocations, and a comparison with native corpus data, which showed that French-speaking learners tend to underuse *make*-collocations. Two experimental tests were designed to elicit *make*-collocations among French-speaking learners whose profile was similar to that of the ICLE-FR contributors (same university, all English majors, same level). In the first test, the subjects were required to fill in the verb in sentences whose translation in French was provided (e.g. *She _____ the choice of never seeing her son again = Elle fit le choix de ne plus jamais revoir son fils*), while in the second test they had to judge the acceptability of *make*-collocations in the context of a sentence (e.g. *Countries now have a feeling that they make part of Europe*) and correct unacceptable collocations. For both tests, the subjects were also asked to indicate their degree of certainty. The experimental data yielded a much higher error rate than in the corpus data (51% for the fill-in exercise and 43% for the acceptability judgment task) and a generally poor assessment of the correctness (or otherwise) of the given answers. These results can explain the underuse of *make*-collocations in the corpus data (learners are not sure how to use them and prefer to avoid them) as well as the low error rate (learners mainly rely on collocations that they are sure of). They also show that only the combination of corpus and experimental data makes it possible to obtain a full picture of learners' acquisition of a linguistic item.

The study by Domínguez et al. (2013) relies on a combination of experimentation and spoken learner corpus data. It deals with the acquisition of Spanish past tense morphology and seeks to offer new evidence for the Lexical Aspect Hypothesis, according to which "certain form-meaning associations (i.e. telic-Preterit and atelic-imperfect) guide the emergence of past tense forms in L2 grammars" (Domínguez et al., 2013, p. 558). A corpus of L2 Spanish was specifically collected among English speakers for this research project, the *Spanish Learner Language Oral Corpora 2* (SPLLOC2), and consisted of three production tasks with varying degrees of control, carried out by the same learners. It should be pointed out that even the least controlled task, a personal narrative produced within a semi-structured interview, represents peripheral corpus data, because "*[e]xperimenters* were coached to use *specific* questions to *elicit* both the Imperfect (…) and Preterit" (Domínguez et al., 2013, p. 564; emphasis added). As for the most controlled task, in another publication (Tracy-Ventura & Myles, 2015), it is referred to as experimentation, which seems justified given that (i) the subjects had to use certain target verbs when describing pictures, and (ii) contexts were created so as to represent different pairings of lexical aspect class (state/activity/accomplishment/achievement) and discourse grounding (foreground/background). In addition to these production tasks, the same learners carried out an experimental comprehension task, rating the appropriateness of (Imperfect and Preterit) sentences to describe various situations, created by combining certain types of contexts (one-time event, habitual, progressive, or continuous) and certain types of predicates (eventive or stative). The results of the study challenge the validity of the Lexical Aspect Hypothesis for the acquisition of Spanish past tense morphology by demonstrating that it is dynamicity rather than telicity that influences learners' choices. The paper also shows that different tasks produce different results and that more controlled tasks are necessary to check learners' capacity to produce certain non-prototypical forms that are rare in naturally occurring language.

In Möller (2017), one of the only book-length studies to date that combines learner corpora and experimentation, the focus is on the English passive voice and how it is used or not used by German learners of English participating in a CLIL (Content and Language Integrated Learning) program. The *Secondary-Level Corpus of Learner English* (SCooLE), collected by the author, brought together argumentative essays written by these learners, from which all passive forms were extracted and analyzed. Those data were supplemented by experimental data from a task requiring the same learners to transform active sentences into passive sentences. In both sets of data, CLIL learners used the passive in a more native-like manner than non-CLIL learners, but the impact of CLIL was clearer and more significant in the experimental data. What is particularly interesting in Möller's study is that the rapprochement between LCR and SLA is not limited to the combination of learner corpus data and experimental data. It also materializes in two other ways. First, in addition to the metadata that typically accompany learner corpora, Möller collected information about cognitive and affective factors (e.g. regarding learners' motivation) through various psychometric tests. Second, besides the aggregate approach that is usually adopted in LCR, Möller took into account individual variation, as is often done in SLA, using multifactorial statistical analysis. Examining the possible influence of individual variables (including cognitive and affective variables) made it possible to distinguish between the actual impact of CLIL and its selectivity (i.e. the fact that students who enter CLIL programs tend to be more intelligent and motivated), and Möller was able to demonstrate that "the selectivity of the CLIL system impacts upon linguistic outcomes more than attendance of CLIL lessons does" (Möller, 2017, p. 361).

Future Directions

Despite the obvious advantages of combining learner corpus and experimental data, there are few studies so far that have adopted such a multimethod approach. With the growing popularity of triangulation and converging evidence, however, it is to be expected (and hoped) that such studies will become more common. We can also hope that the more such studies are carried out, the more diversified and sophisticated they will become. As shown in this chapter, most experimental data used in combination with learner corpora are either elicitation data, which require learners to produce certain linguistic items, or non-production offline data, which record the outcome of a linguistic task. Non-production online data, which seek to record an ongoing process while learners are carrying out a linguistic task, are extremely rare but should be used more often in combination with learner corpora, because they can be very useful measures of the way learners process language. It also appears from the studies mentioned in this chapter that most of the time they rely on written, rather than spoken, learner corpora. This can most certainly be related to the predominance of written learner corpora (see Gilquin, 2015) and the fact that written corpus data are easier to collect than spoken corpus data. However, it is very unfortunate that spoken learner corpora have not been combined more often with experimentation, especially because the results of experimental tasks seem to come closer to naturalistic speech than to naturalistic writing (see Baayen, Feldman, & Schreuder, 2006; Gilquin, 2008; Gilquin 2010).

As noted earlier, one of the major limitations of the current studies combining learner corpora and experimental methods is that the contributors to the corpus are usually different from the participants in the experiment. This is likely to change in the future. With LCR being increasingly inclined to adopt an individual approach (in addition to a global approach considering the corpus as an aggregate), it will soon become unthinkable for scholars to rely on a combination of corpus and experimental data that rules out the study of (the same) individuals across the two types of data. Approaching the combination of learner corpora and experimentation on an individual basis should be relatively easy if the learner corpora of the future are "multidimensional" databases that contain data produced by the same learners in different situations and across different tasks involving different degrees of control (Gilquin, 2015, p. 29; see also Tracy-Ventura & Myles, 2015). As learner corpus data and experimental data become more comparable to each other, however, it should be borne in mind that they each have their own specificities and that they will always remain distinct types of data. It is important that they should be recognized as such in any research design, at the risk of ending up comparing apples and oranges. Further research combining corpus analysis and experimentation should help us gain a better understanding of each method and of the relation between the two (see Gilquin & Gries, 2009, p. 17) and thus contribute to discriminating the effects of the method from those related to the acquisition of an L2.

Finally, as LCR and SLA move closer to each other, we may expect that more scholars will be able and willing to cross methodological boundaries and, eventually, create new synergies between the two fields of research. At the same time as the combination of learner corpora and experimentation is facilitated by the closer dialogue between LCR and SLA, this methodological rapprochement may in turn also contribute to a theoretical rapprochement between the two paradigms.

Further Reading

Durrant, P., & Siyanova-Chanturia, A. (2015). Learner corpora and psycholinguistics. In S. Granger, G. Gilquin, & F. Meunier (Eds.), *The Cambridge handbook of learner corpus research* (pp. 57–77). Cambridge: Cambridge University Press.

This paper gives an overview of the links between LCR and psycholinguistics. It offers a broad perspective on the topic, also covering cases where learner corpora are used as evidence for psycholinguistic hypotheses.

Gass, S. M., & Mackey, A. (2007). *Data elicitation for second and foreign language research.* New York: Routledge.

This book is a guide to the techniques that can be used to elicit data for the study of second and foreign language acquisition. It also includes a brief discussion of naturalistic data. The book is abundantly illustrated with examples from the literature and points to possible limitations of the different techniques.

Gilquin, G., & Gries, S. Th. (2009). Corpora and experimental methods: A state-of-the-art review. *Corpus Linguistics and Linguistic Theory*, 5(1), 1–26.

This article provides a review of studies combining corpus and experimental data and compares the linguistic and psycholinguistic approaches to such a combination. It is the introductory paper of a special issue on "Corpora and Experimental Methods".

Related Topics

See chapters 1, 3, 5, and 30.

Notes

1 Only combinations of L2 corpus data and L2 experimental data will be considered in this chapter. Studies that combine native corpus data with L2 experimental data (e.g. Gries & Wulff, 2009) or learner corpus data with native experimental data (e.g. Wulff, Ellis, Römer, Bardovi-Harlig, & Leblanc, 2009) will thus be excluded.
2 See Meunier and Littré (2013) and Littré (2015) for notable exceptions.
3 The example is taken from Ozeki and Shirai (2007, p. 181).
4 The examples are taken from Kim and Rah (2016, p. 722) and adapted from Bencini and Goldberg (2000).

References

Arppe, A., Gilquin, G., Glynn, D., Hilpert, M., & Zeschel, A. (2010). Cognitive corpus linguistics: Five points of debate on current theory and methodology. *Corpora, 5*(1), 1–27.

Azazil, L. (2020). Frequency effects in the L2 acquisition of the catenative verb construction – evidence from experimental and corpus data. *Cognitive Linguistics, 31*(3), 417–451.

Baayen, R. H., Feldman, L. B., & Schreuder, R. (2006). Morphological influences on the recognition of monosyllabic monomorphemic words. *Journal of Memory and Language, 55*(2), 290–313.

Bencini, G. M. L., & Goldberg, A. E. (2000). The contribution of argument structure constructions to sentence meaning. *Journal of Memory and Language, 43*(4), 640–651.

Cook, V. (1993). *Linguistics and second language acquisition*. London: Macmillan Education.

De Knop, S. (2015). Conceptual tools for the description and acquisition of the German posture verb *sitzen*. *Corpus Linguistics and Linguistic Theory, 11*(1), 127–160.

Domínguez, L., Tracy-Ventura, N., Arche, M. J., Mitchell, R., & Myles, F. (2013). The role of dynamic contrasts in the L2 acquisition of Spanish past tense morphology. *Bilingualism: Language and Cognition, 16*(3), 558–577.

Ellis, N. C. (2017). Foreword. *Language Learning, 67*(S1), 5.

Ellis, R. (2008). *The study of second language acquisition* (2nd ed.). Oxford: Oxford University Press.

Ellis, R., & Barkhuizen, G. (2005). *Analysing learner language*. Oxford: Oxford University Press.

Gablasova, D., Brezina, V., & McEnery, T. (2017). Exploring learner language through corpora: Comparing and interpreting corpus frequency information. *Language Learning, 67*(S1), 130–154.

Gilquin, G. (2007). To err is not all. What corpus and elicitation can reveal about the use of collocations by learners. *Zeitschrift für Anglistik und Amerikanistik, 55*(3), 273–291.

Gilquin, G. (2008). What you think ain't what you get: Highly polysemous verbs in mind and language. In J.-R. Lapaire, G. Desagulier, & J.-B. Guignard (Eds.), *Du fait grammatical au fait cognitif. From gram to mind: Grammar as cognition* (vol. 2, pp. 235–255). Pessac: Presses universitaires de Bordeaux.

Gilquin, G. (2009). Bringing the learner back into the picture: Corpora and elicitation in transfer studies. In C. M. Bretones Callejas et al. (Eds.), *Applied linguistics now: Understanding language and mind / La lingüística aplicada actual: Comprendiendo el lenguaje y la mente* (pp. 1399–1408). Almería: Universidad de Almería.

Gilquin, G. (2010). Language production: A window to the mind? In H. Götzsche (Ed.), *Memory, mind and language* (pp. 89–102). Newcastle: Cambridge Scholars Publishing.

Gilquin, G. (2015). From design to collection of learner corpora. In S. Granger, G. Gilquin, & F. Meunier (Eds.), *The Cambridge handbook of learner corpus research* (pp. 9–34). Cambridge: Cambridge University Press.

Gilquin, G., & Gries, S. Th. (2009). Corpora and experimental methods: A state-of-the-art review. *Corpus Linguistics and Linguistic Theory, 5*(1), 1–26.

Granger, S. (1998a). The computer learner corpus: A versatile new source of data for SLA research. In S. Granger (Ed.), *Learner English on computer* (pp. 3–18). London: Longman.

Granger, S. (1998b). Prefabricated patterns in advanced EFL writing: Collocations and formulae. In A. P. Cowie (Ed.), *Phraseology: Theory, analysis, and applications* (pp. 145–160). Oxford: Clarendon Press.

Granger, S. (2012). How to use foreign and second language learner corpora? In A. Mackey & S. M. Gass (Eds.), *Research methods in second language acquisition: A practical guide* (pp. 7–29). Chichester: Wiley-Blackwell.

Granger, S., Meunier, F., & Dagneaux, E. (2002). *The International Corpus of Learner English. Handbook and CD-ROM*. Louvain-la-Neuve: Presses universitaires de Louvain.

Gries, S. Th., & Wulff, S. (2009). Psycholinguistic and corpus-linguistic evidence for L2 constructions. *Annual Review of Cognitive Linguistics, 7*, 163–186.

Jucker, A. H., Smith, S. W., & Lüdge, T. (2003). Interactive aspects of vagueness in conversation. *Journal of Pragmatics, 35*(12), 1737–1769.

Kim, H., & Rah, Y. (2016). Effects of verb semantics and proficiency in second language use of constructional knowledge. *The Modern Language Journal, 100*(3), 716–731.

Kleinmann, H. H. (1977). Avoidance behavior in adult second language acquisition. *Language Learning, 27*(1), 93–107.

Littré, D. (2015). Combining experimental data and corpus data: Intermediate French-speaking learners and the English present. *Corpus Linguistics and Linguistic Theory, 11*(1), 89–126.

Mendikoetxea, A., & Lozano, C. (2018). From corpora to experiments: Methodological triangulation in the study of word order at the interfaces in adult late bilinguals (L2 learners). *Journal of Psycholinguistic Research, 47*(4), 871–898.

Meunier, F., & Littré, D. (2013). Tracking learners' progress: Adopting a dual 'corpus cum experimental data' approach. *The Modern Language Journal, 97*(S1), 61–76.

Möller, V. (2017). *Language acquisition in CLIL and non-CLIL settings: Learner corpus and experimental evidence on passive constructions.* Amsterdam: John Benjamins.

Myles, F. (2015). Second language acquisition theory and learner corpus research. In S. Granger, G. Gilquin, & F. Meunier (Eds.), *The Cambridge handbook of learner corpus research* (pp. 309–331). Cambridge: Cambridge University Press.

Ozeki, H., & Shirai, Y. (2007). Does the noun phrase accessibility hierarchy predict the difficulty order in the acquisition of Japanese relative clauses? *Studies in Second Language Acquisition, 29*(2), 169–196.

Römer, U., Roberson, A., O'Donnell, M. B., & Ellis, N. C. (2014). Linking learner corpus and experimental data in studying second language learners' knowledge of verb-argument constructions. *ICAME Journal, 38*(1), 115–135.

Schönefeld, D. (2011). *Converging evidence: Methodological and theoretical issues for linguistic research.* Amsterdam: John Benjamins.

Siyanova, A., & Schmitt, N. (2008). L2 learner production and processing of collocation: A multi-study perspective. *The Canadian Modern Language Review / La Revue canadienne des langues vivantes, 64*(3), 429–458.

Tracy-Ventura, N. (2017). Combining corpora and experimental data to investigate language learning during residence abroad: A study of lexical sophistication. *System, 71*, 35–45.

Tracy-Ventura, N., & Myles, F. (2015). The importance of task variability in the design of learner corpora for SLA research. *International Journal of Learner Corpus Research, 1*(1), 58–95.

Valenzuela Manzanares, J., & Rojo López, A. M. (2008). What can language learners tell us about constructions? In S. De Knop & T. De Rycker (Eds.), *Cognitive approaches to pedagogical grammar: A volume in honour of René Dirven* (pp. 197–230). Berlin: Mouton de Gruyter.

Wulff, S., Ellis, N. C., Römer, U., Bardovi-Harlig, K., & Leblanc, C. J. (2009). The acquisition of tense-aspect: Converging evidence from corpora and telicity ratings. *The Modern Language Journal, 93*(3), 354–369.

11

Overview of Available Learner Corpora

Julieta Fernández and Tracy S. Davis

Introduction

Although the field of Learner Corpus Research (LCR) has been among the more recent additions to the field of applied linguistics, it has had an increasing impact on Second Language Acquisition (SLA). Ever since its inception in the late 1980s and early 1990s, LCR has allowed SLA researchers to accomplish a gamut of tasks ranging from gaining a better understanding of learner errors (Granger, 2003) to developing in-house teaching materials (Granger, 2008). The use of learner corpora, definable as principled collections of "authentic, continuous and contextualized language use (spoken or written) by L2 learners stored in electronic format" (Callies & Paquot, 2015, p. 1), has increasingly attracted SLA researchers who see great value in having immediate access to large pools of learner data to add to the generalizability of their findings (Myles, 2005). As summarized by McEnery, Brezina, Gablasova, and Banerjee (2019), the benefits of using available corpora include the shareability of datasets, which enhances hypothesis testing and promotes replication; the suitability of corpus analysis to be combined with experimental SLA methods to look beyond observable language output; and the greater scale of analysis that affords confidence in drawing broader conclusions. These benefits, as well as the relative ease with which datasets can be navigated, can offer developmental opportunities for early career researchers to hone their questions without committing to lengthy data collection and transcription efforts. This chapter discusses issues around using existing learner corpora to conduct SLA research, and provides an overview of several corpora available to SLA researchers online or upon request from corresponding authors.

Core Issues and Topics

Choosing a Corpus

Accumulated knowledge and experience, coupled with advances in technology, mean there are now many learner corpora readily accessible either for a nominal fee or free of charge (for the general public, with an institutional account, or with the permission of the compiler[s]). When choosing a corpus, the researcher's intentions may necessitate a corpus comprising hundreds of learners and dozens of outside-the-classroom contexts that would afford a wider scale of analysis. On the other hand, a researcher's intentions may require a database following a small group of learners using language over an extended period in limited in-class contexts. When one considers whether to collect one's own data or use a learner corpus, data fit is key. One way to find a suitable corpus is to examine existing research within the area of interest. This could be done by exploring specialized journals such as the *International Journal of Learner Corpus Research*[1], by accessing online bibliographies such as the Learner Corpus Bibliography[2], or through a Google Scholar search. In addition, lists of available learner corpora can be found through current databases, such as the "Learner Corpora around the World" webpage maintained by the Centre for English Corpus Linguistics, UCLouvain[3]. This webpage is perhaps the most comprehensive list of learner corpora available at the moment. It includes the name of the corpus, target language(s), L1(s), medium, text and task type, proficiency level, size in words, project director, and availability, and is sortable by any one of these features. Another useful resource is the SLABank available on the TalkBank project website[4]. This page comprises a three-column list with links to corpora/ databases organized by language along with a brief description of the corpus and the name of the contributor(s) (see also Chapter 12, this volume, and MacWhinney, 2017 for a description of the SLABank and BilingBank corpora and tools available).

One of the central issues is deciding what constitutes a learner corpus. Within corpus linguistics, a corpus is often understood as consisting of continuous, open-ended, and spontaneous or authentic (in this context meaning non-experimentally elicited) data. As such, some corpus linguists would not consider certain databases that have been used for researching particular aspects of learner language use and development as 'corpora' in the narrow sense because these are often collected using "carefully designed data elicitation tasks where learners are asked to produce spoken and/or written language" (Tracy-Ventura & Myles, 2015, p. 59). The varying task types that learners are asked to perform can be found on a continuum of 'naturalness' (or authenticity), with, for example, reading aloud and fill-in-the-blank tasks at the lower end of naturalness, and free compositions ranking much higher (Granger, 2008, p. 260). Nevertheless, the texts in these corpora are representative of language produced for a communicative purpose, even if for an instrumental goal, and, particularly in the case of instructed learners, representative of language produced in the natural communicative context of the L2 (Tracy-Ventura & Myles, 2015), the text from elicitation tasks for the corpus often reflects the types of communicative tasks learners perform in the L2 classroom. Some learner corpus researchers, such as Granger (2008), however, caution that corpora arising from more controlled tasks (where learners cannot freely choose their own wording) should still be considered 'peripheral'. When the learner data come from both authentic and more controlled tasks, the term 'database' is sometimes used, as in the *Louvain International Database of Spoken English Interlanguage* (LINDSEI) (Gilquin, 2015). Whichever term is preferred, it is not uncommon to see the distinction between corpus and database addressed in a publication, so any search for the term "corpus" in the body of texts (as opposed to the title only) is likely to yield the most potentially relevant hits.

Corpora are often compiled following 'external criteria', that is, according to the communicative function of the texts included, rather than based on the language in the texts, or what is referred to as 'internal criteria' (Sinclair, 2005). As noted by Lozano and Mendikoetxea (2013), however, "some learner corpus designers have followed internal criteria when using semi-natural or even controlled tasks to elicit specific linguistic structures from their learners, which are the structures those researchers are interested in" (p. 75). This is an important consideration when working with an already existing corpus because, as Lozano and Mendikoetxea caution, these corpora are biased in that the frequency of the linguistic structures that were elicited obviously may not represent their frequency in (more) naturally occurring interactions (p. 76).

The Importance of Research Questions

While the process might be different for qualitative and quantitative researchers, often, the first step when conducting an SLA study is to identify one or more feasible research questions that address current issues in the field (Mackey & Gass, 2016) and then collect data that will allow exploration of those questions. Corpora, however, have traditionally been used either as "an exploratory tool to arrive at a hypothesis" (an inductive approach) and, to a much lesser extent, as a tool to test a hypothesis or address research questions about the nature of learner language (a deductive approach) (Lozano & Mendikoetxea, 2013, p. 69). As a result, so far, learner corpus research (LCR) has made a more substantial contribution to empirical learner language description than to an understanding of the L2 knowledge underlying language learner development (Myles, 2005) although this trend is changing.

It is also important to keep in mind that corpora tend to be created with a specific research purpose in mind. By way of illustration, the tasks used to compile the *Spanish Learner Language Oral Corpora 1* (SPLLOC 1; Mitchell, et al., 2008) were explicitly designed to elicit the production of morphosyntactic properties of Spanish, such as word order (task 7) and clitics (tasks 5 and 6). As a result, unless a general-purpose learner corpus is being used (that is, one that has been compiled without a particular research agenda) the purpose of the readily available corpus may or may not align well with the aims of an SLA study. Any answers to the research questions are necessarily affected by the decisions behind the creation of a corpus that is used to answer them. For example, Fernández (2013) underscores the fact that her analysis of student interviews in SPLLOC is exploratory because the corpus had a different research purpose (p. 319). As has been discussed in earlier chapters of this section and the corpus literature (e.g., Sinclair, 2005), the representativeness, balance, size, and design of a corpus will determine what sort of information can be gleaned from the data included therein. In the absence of a suitable corpus/database, one may collect their own data. If a suitable corpus can be found, however, drawing from a pre-existing learner corpus can economize time and effort.

SLA researchers are also cautioned to avoid construct underrepresentation, which occurs when the data does not provide enough empirical evidence (linguistic behavior) to draw an intended interpretation of the data (Norris & Ortega, 2003). It is essential to make sure that the learner corpus being used has enough instances of the learner language feature that the researcher intends to study. For example, if there are no instances of a particular linguistic behavior in a corpus, the researcher may have trouble elucidating whether this is the case because learners did not know it or because the task did not result in its use (Tracy-Ventura & Myles, 2015). SLA researchers should consider what empirical evidence is required to address the research question(s), and "then link these requirements to empirically, or at least logically, related elicitation tasks or situations, which are themselves understood in terms of the behavior(s) that they elicit" (Norris & Ortega, 2003, p. 729). In the same vein, Buttery and Caines (2012) argue that, when interpreting their results, SLA researchers need to account for learners' 'opportunity of use' of a particular linguistic feature (lexical or syntactic construction), which depends on the tasks, topics, and length of the documents used to collect learner language in the corpus being used (especially when the goal is to compare learners at different levels of proficiency) (see also Caines & Buttery, 2017 for recommendations about how to control for task and topic, especially when prompts are not available). Finally, it is important to consider whether instances of a particular feature can be extracted from several learners (and not just many from one) thereby addressing representativeness (Granger, 2012). Drawing from one learner (even if many instances are obtained) would be questionable (Myles, 2008) given the difficulty to assert the findings as applicable to other learners (Gass & Selinker, 2008).

Corpus Availability

Learner corpora are made available in different formats. Some can be accessed in a variety of ways. An example is *The Arabic Learner Corpus* (Alfaifi, Atwell & Hedaya, 2014), which is available online as the ALC search website (restricted by registration, but free for research purposes), on arabicorpus.byu.edu (restricted by registration), and on *Sketch Engine* (a text analysis tool with advanced search options available for a monthly fee; Kilgarriff, Rychly, Smrz & Tugwell, 2004). Particularly useful is the fact that researchers using this corpus have options for accessing the data; there is a web interface with a user guide as well as downloadable files. Using an interface is useful for many second language researchers who may wish to rely on the tool(s) built into the interface (as opposed to external stand-alone corpus tools) which often include basic search functionalities. Whether a built-in search interface is minimalistic or elaborate, it is prudent to examine all the options. *Sketch Engine,* for example, allows users to work with more than one corpus at the same time. Tools available to users through the website include concordancing, word lists, n-grams, diachronic analysis, bilingual term extraction, and a variety of word specific tools including the word sketch (a one-page summary of a word's collocations organized by grammatical relations).

Although built-in search engines clearly offer convenience, when the corpus files are made available for download, data handling options increase, for example with concordancing software such as *Wordsmith Tools* (Scott, 2016) and *Antconc* (Anthony, 2017) (see Chapter 6, this volume), or with scripts written using a programming language such as R or Python.

Learner corpora are also occasionally available in a CD-ROM with its own search interface, as is the case with *Louvain International Database of Spoken English Interlanguage* (LINDSEI). Other learner corpora, such as the *Longman Learners' Corpus*, have been collected by publishing houses for commercial purposes, such as textbook or dictionary development, and are typically not available (in full) to the researcher community at large. For example, the *Cambridge Learner Corpus* (CLC, part of the Cambridge International Corpus) can be accessed by authors and researchers working for Cambridge University Press and members of the University of Cambridge Local Examination Syndicate (Pravec, 2002). However, a subset of CLC (2.9 million words at the time of writing), the *Open Cambridge Learner Corpus* (Uncoded) is available through *SketchEngine*.

Forms of Annotation

Annotating a corpus involves adding "any information about the learner samples that the researcher wants to code" (Granger, 2017, p. 435). Therefore, available learner corpora differ in the kinds of annotation that are included, if available at all. Language features typically annotated in learner corpora include lexical, grammatical, syntactic, semantic, phonetic, stylistic, and discursive features that are annotated manually, semi-automatically, or automatically, with different levels of accuracy (Myles, 2007).

The two most common types of annotation in available learner corpora are morpho-syntactic (such as POS tagging and lemmatization; see also Chapter 5, this volume) and error annotation (Granger, 2017; see also Chapter 7, this volume). The benefits of annotations for the researcher are that they allow for various automatic analyses (e.g., statistical, descriptive) that would otherwise be very time-consuming. For example, if a researcher is interested in examining which tense is more prevalent in written assignments, having annotations for each verb tense would allow for the automatic retrieval of all the past tense verbs as opposed to, say, going verb-by-verb to note the tense individually (see Chapter 6, this volume).

The types of annotation available in learner corpora vary depending on the research purpose for which the corpora were compiled. For example, the *Learning Prosody in a Foreign Language* (LeaP) corpus (Gut, 2012) was compiled with a focus on the differences in the use of phonetic and prosodic features. To that end, it was phonetically annotated in 8 tiers (except for the nonsense word list reading task), two completed automatically (part-of-speech (POS) and lemmatization) and six carried out manually using ESPS/waves+ and PRAAT (Boersma & Weenink, 2019), yielding 359 annotated files from 131 speakers.

One type of annotation found in learner corpora relates to learner's language use that deviates from what "a native speaker would have produced in the identical context" (Gries & Berez, 2017, p. 391). Error annotation can vary, as do researchers' definitions of what constitutes an error (see Chapter 7, this volume). Based on their research agenda, corpus compilers can choose to annotate for mispronunciations, departures from expected usage for lexical items, and grammatical errors (such as gender, or subject-verb agreement), among others. Error annotation systems can also vary in terms of sophistication, from flat annotation to multi-level annotation systems (see Lüdeling et al., 2005 for details). As an illustration, the *Languages and Social Networks Abroad Project* (LANGSNAP; Tracy-Ventura, Mitchell, & McManus, 2016) is annotated for mispronunciations and lexical variations (Tracy-Ventura & Huensch, 2018), but grammatical errors are not annotated. Part-of-speech (POS) tags are also available in LANGSNAP and can be used to search for grammatical errors, such as errors in grammatical gender between nouns and adjectives. Researchers within particular fields of SLA might be interested in information about how learner errors were transcribed and tagged, if such annotations are made available. When the annotation and layers of coding necessary to carry out a study are not provided in a readily available corpus (e.g., whether audio recordings are provided in case phonetic transcription is necessary), SLA researchers may be able to add their own, data permitting.

Available Learner Corpora

Most corpora that can be found online include extensive information about design and compilation principles, such as how and when they were built, the size, the types of texts included (written, spoken, or multimodal), and the proficiency level of the learners. For example, the primary webpage for the *International Corpus Network of Asian Learners of English* (ICNALE; Ishikawa, 2013) contains all the relevant information about the structure of the corpus, participants, and tasks, as well as terms of use and how to cite various portions of the corpus. Metadata of interest to the SLA researcher, such as learner and task variables, can be found integrated into the texts directly, included in the header of each text or sometimes made available in a database that is linked to the text files (in this case, the researchers can search by variable(s) and select the part of the corpus that interests them). In this section, we provide an overview of available learner corpora organized by variables important for SLA researchers.

Languages

One of the key elements that identify learner corpora is the first (L1) and second/additional (L2) language(s) used by the participants. Some corpora include participants from multiple language backgrounds (such as *The European Science Foundation Second Language Data Bank*, see Chapter 18, this volume), while others have a more homogenous set (for example, the SPLLOC). Other learner corpora have multiple L2s, such as the corpus PAROLE (*PARallèle Oral en Langue Etrangère*; Hilton, 2009), which includes several different L1 participants learning English, French, or Italian.

The SLA researcher should note that the term 'learner corpus' has not always been applied homogeneously; some corpora are collections of texts produced by non-native speakers who are not L2 learners per se, but rather L2 users (see Mauranen, 2011). Corpora of speakers using English as a non-native language, for example, can include texts produced by EFL speakers (such as *The International Corpus of Learner English*, or ICLE; Granger et al., 2009), and by English as a Lingua Franca (ELF) speakers (such as *English as a Lingua Franca in Academic Settings*; ELFA, 2008). Although similarities have been found (e.g., in language processing) between L2 learners' and L2 users' language (Mauranen, 2011), researchers drawing on existing corpora should be mindful of this distinction.

Language Proficiency

Beyond the L1 and L2, participants will have different levels of language proficiency. An important consideration is how these levels were determined, if determined at all. Carlsen (2012) argues that proficiency assignments in learner corpora follow two main patterns; they are either assigned to texts based on learner characteristics, such as age or institutional status (learner-centered method) or determined based on the text's characteristics alone, such as scores on standardized tests (text-centered method). She identifies a preponderance of learner-centered methods to establish language proficiency, especially common criteria being year of instruction or institutional status (e.g., second-year students). For example, learners in SPLLOC were differentiated by the number of years of instruction (approximate number of hours of instruction, and educational level according to the British system). In a learner-centered method, the results of a test are interpreted in terms of "what learners can do at a particular level of language proficiency as specified, for example, in the *Common European Framework of Reference for Languages*" (Callies et al., 2014, p. 73). Whether assigned by local institutions or based on a scale like CEFR, language proficiency is an area that stands to benefit from LCR-SLA interaction, as researchers use proficiency to investigate corpora and use corpora to investigate proficiency.

Information About the Learners

Some types of learner metadata of interest when conducting an SLA study, such as the age of the learners, language learning biography, length of input, and stays abroad, are not consistently reported in the currently available learner corpora. One corpus which records all of these metadata, for example, is the *Norwegian Second Language Corpus* (ASK; Tenfjord, Meurer, & Hofland, 2006). ASK is a compilation of texts from learners of Norwegian from 10 different L1s and includes information about the learners' age, educational background, length of stay in Norway, years of formal instruction, and social contact with Norwegian speakers (Carlsen, 2012). Another example is the LeaP corpus (Gut, 2012) which, in addition to metadata about learners' age, gender, L1, L2, age at first contact with the L2, type of contact, information about stays abroad, duration, and type of formal lessons in prosody (if any), also includes information about motivation and attitudes. Whereas the metadata provided with a corpus is often immutable, it may be possible to contact the compiler(s) to ask for more information.

Medium (Spoken, Written)

Learner corpora can result from the collection of written texts, the transcriptions of spoken interaction, and/or audio-visual data (multimodal corpora). Although the number of spoken corpora continues to increase, written corpora still outnumber them (Gilquin, 2015). In their recent meta-analysis, Paquot and Plonsky (2017) found an oversampling of L2 written English produced in university settings. This imbalance is likely due to the difficulty and time involved in compiling a spoken learner corpus (which entails audio or video recording the L2 speakers and transcribing their speech with different levels of detail depending on the project) as compared to a written one. Multimodal learner corpora are fairly new. One example is the *Multimedia Adult ESL Learner Corpus* (MAELC; Reder, Harris, & Setzler, 2003), which is a compilation of over 3,600 hours of video and audio recorded classroom interactions and associated written materials. Another type of relatively new learner corpora are those which collect computer-mediated interactions among learners (such as the *Spanish AP learner corpus:* Yuldashev, Fernández, & Thorne, 2013).

Individual corpora can contain one or several of these media. For example, the *Multilingual Academic Corpus of Assignments – Writing and Speech* (MACAWS, Staples et al., 2019) is a corpus of assignments (texts, spoken discourse, and multimedia products) produced across language learning programs (including two Less Commonly Taught Languages (LCTL), Portuguese and

Russian). The learner language samples in the corpus are complemented by pedagogical artifacts (e.g., syllabi, assignment sheets, lesson plans) provided by the instructors, which can be used to further contextualize student production. These artifacts are particularly helpful given that, as mentioned before, the task and topic provided to the students can affect various linguistic features in their production (e.g., Caines & Buttery, 2017; Newton & Kennedy, 1996).

Within each medium, corpora can be of different types. Written corpora, for example, can include scanned typewritten as well as handwritten learner texts (especially earlier corpora, given that currently learners tend to produce most texts electronically). An example of a recent handwritten corpus is the *Marburg Corpus of Intermediate Learner English* (MILE), which is a longitudinal database of written texts from German learners of English grades 9–12. Scanning the learner texts introduces its own complications, such as the possibility of an inaccurate reproduction of the learner texts or the inability to reproduce the learner texts in publications for data-protection concerns. However, it has the benefit of providing 'important information on the foreign language competence of the writer' by showing alterations in the texts (e.g., words crossed out or inserted) (Kreyer, 2015, p. 22).

Spoken corpora can consist of only the written transcriptions (referred to as 'mute spoken corpus', Ballier & Martin, 2015), or be accompanied by the audio files (referred to as a 'speech corpus', Wichmann, 2008). Importantly, audio-visual corpora follow a wide variety of data transcription conventions. While most of these learner corpora are orthographically transcribed, the level of precision in text transcriptions varies according to the compiler(s)' available resources and aim(s) (Gilquin, 2015). Corpora with audio files are particularly useful for SLA researchers interested in language processing or phonology who might find downloadable digitized sound files that can be analyzed with dedicated speech analysis software particularly useful (Myles, 2005).

Tasks/Genre

Another variable to consider when surveying existing learner corpora is text type, which can vary considerably. For instance, a corpus may include academic papers (e.g., *Corpus Escrito del Español L2 (CEDEL2);* Lozano & Mendikoetxea, 2013), interviews (e.g., *Corpus Parlato di Italiano L2;* Spina et al., 2006), individual tasks using a photo stimulus or role-plays between two learners (e.g., the *Linguistics Development Project*), monologues (*MACAWS*), or a combination of text types. All of these tasks have the potential to elicit different types of grammatical structures, vocabulary, and other linguistic features and, depending on the research question, could have an effect on research results (Tracy-Ventura & Myles, 2015).

The corpus may also offer different levels of detail about the tasks themselves and the context of their production (for example, whether it was timed or whether the learners were allowed to use outside resources). For example, the texts in the CLC, which is a collection of Cambridge English exams taken by learners from over 100 different L1s, includes task-related metadata about task style (e.g., argument, descriptive), format (e.g., email, essay), and task register (e.g., neutral, formal, informal).

Design: Cross-sectional, Pseudo-/Quasi-longitudinal, and Longitudinal

A final consideration is how the texts were collected. Cross-sectional corpora provide "a snapshot of learners' knowledge of the target language at a particular moment" (Gilquin, 2015, p. 14). In this type of corpus, texts from first-year students might be collected as well as texts from third-year students, but the two sets of participants would not be the same students. The *French Learner Language Oral Corpora* (FLLOC; Rule, et al., 2003), for example, is a cross-sectional collection of L2 French corpora that includes digital sound files and their transcripts of L2 French speakers from eight different projects, thus including a wide range of tasks, learners, and data types. Some cross-sectional corpora have been described as "pseudo-/quasi-longitudinal" (Gilquin, 2015, p. 14) in that they have been used to investigate second language development because they include learners of the same L2 at different levels of proficiency (Carlsen, 2012). For example, Pravec (2002) argues that the *Japanese English as a Foreign Language Learner* (JEFLL) corpus can be used to study language development (at the lexical, grammatical, and semantic level) because it includes student essays from learners at the junior high, high school, and university levels.

Longitudinal corpora, on the other hand, include texts from the same participants over time, so the same participants produce several different texts over the duration of the collection period. Some examples of longitudinal corpora are the Falko Georgetown longitudinal corpus (Reznicek et al., 2010; *Fehlerannotiertes Lernerkorpus* 'error-annotated learner corpus'), and the *Progression Project* (Mitchell & Dickson, 1997). The Falko Georgetown longitudinal corpus collected several semesters of data from German learners at Georgetown University in the US and is included with several other corpora of L2 German under the ANNIS Falko system. This corpus contains students work from levels 2 and 3 in the beginning sequence of German classes at the university. The *Progression Project* is a longitudinal corpus of 60 L1 English speakers beginning to learn French in UK public schools starting at the age of 11 or 12. The oral data were collected in six rounds over the span of two years and included a variety of task types. From an SLA perspective, longitudinal corpora are particularly valuable, especially when large and diverse, because investigating the development of L2 capacities requires tracking the different stages learners go through over a lengthy period of time (Myles, 2008).

Representative Corpora and Research

The number of learner corpora accessible to researchers constantly increases, and overviewed here is a sample of the corpora available at the time of writing. To show the diversity of corpora, we describe a longitudinal corpus of L2 English, a cross-sectional corpus of L2 French, and a multimodal corpus of L2 Spanish.

The InterFra corpus (*Interlangue française – développement, interaction et variation;* cf. Bartning & Schlyter, 2004) was collected over several years (starting with a group of first- and second-year students in 1988/89). The 'core' corpus consists of longitudinal and cross-sectional data from instructed and semi-instructed French as a foreign language secondary and university students (referred to as FFL groups). A second group of data from French as a second language learners and users (referred to as the FSL group) was added at a later stage. InterFra also includes data from different control groups of native speakers of French. Audio digital files, together with the XML transcripts and background information about the participants, are available at KORP, Språkbanken (University of Göteborg). The core corpus (except the data from doctoral students) is tagged for grammatical categories. InterFra has been used to examine different areas of second language acquisition and use, such as cross-linguistic influence (Lindqvist, 2009) and L2 vocabulary (formulaic sequences and lexical richness) and pragmatic marker use (i.e., *déjà, encore, toujours, alors, après*, and *maintenant* ['already', 'still', 'always', 'so', 'then', and 'now')] (Forsberg & Lindqvist, 2012; Hancock, 2014).

The *Barcelona English Language Corpus* (BELC) is available on TalkBank. BELC was collected as part of the Barcelona Age Factor (BAF) research project, which was designed to investigate the acquisition of English as a foreign language of students at four different ages (i.e., 8, 11, 14 and 18+) in Catalonia, Spain. BAF collected data from 2063 participants who had different hours of instruction. The participants had Spanish and Catalan as their L1s. BELC includes longitudinal data collected from participants at two, three or four points over a period of seven years. Participants completed four different types of tasks. The first task was a timed written composition about a familiar topic. The second was an oral narrative using a set of pictures as a stimulus. The third task took the form of a semi-structured interview that allowed for participant-initiated topics in order to create the conditions for an interaction as naturally as possible. The fourth task was a role-play between two participants who took on the roles of parent and child. The corpus was updated in 2014, when data for a subsample of 21 participants was added.

Muñoz (2006) is an edited collection of chapters making use of BELC to investigate the effects of age on the rate of foreign language learning in classroom settings. The chapters examine a wide range of areas of second language learning including pronunciation, morphology, oral fluency, vocabulary, and language learning strategies, among others. For example, Mora (2006) used data from the picture-elicited narratives from two groups of learners matched for L2 exposure but of different ages of onset to compare oral fluency measures. She found that late starters outperformed early starters on the majority of fluency measures she used.

The *Corpus Español Multimodal de Actos de Habla* (Spanish Multimodal Corpus of Speech Acts, or COR.E.M.A.H.; Vacas Matos, 2017) was collected in the US and Spain and resulted from the transcription of role-plays performed by a group of 24 intermediate (three semesters of Spanish study) and a group of 24 advanced (MA level) learners of Spanish, as well as a control group of 24 Spanish native speakers. The web interface gives researchers access to the video recordings (in .mp4/.mv4 format) and transcriptions (following the Computerized Language Analysis, or CHAT, transcription system), together with annotations about nonverbal language use and tags for different strategies used to perform three types of speech acts: apologies, compliments, and refusals. Vacas Matos (2017) used COR.E.M.A.H. to compare the speech act production of these three groups and found that they differed in their interpretation of speech acts, but more importantly in the verbal and non-verbal strategies that they used to produce them. Vacas Matos argues that some of these differences are the result of L1 negative transfer. COR.E.M.A.H. is a recent corpus, and while it has a lot of potential, it has yet to be used extensively in L2 research.

Future Directions

As more language researchers discover the benefits of corpus approaches, there are more learner corpora being constructed and made available, with increases in number and variation in type. This is a mutually propitious symmetry, but several areas remain in need of further progress. One of them, according to MacWhinney (2017), is the lack of publicly available "densely collected [...] longitudinal SLA data" (p. 7), although such corpora as the LANGSNAP have begun to address this gap. While time-consuming, cumbersome, and expensive, it is the densely collected longitudinal databases that played a significant role in developing usage-based understanding of language development (Tomasello, 2009). Developing similar databases comprising samples of additional language use could lead to similar breakthroughs in the future.

As applied linguistics experiences the tension between the calls for further diversity of theoretical approaches and pleas for consolidating what appears to be an increasingly fragmented field, it shapes the context for similar hopes and directions for research using learner corpora. It is our hope that more corpora of heretofore-undersampled data and learner populations will continue to be created and distributed. These include spoken corpora, longitudinal corpora, corpora of languages other than L2 English, corpora of beginner and intermediate learners, multimodal, and local learner corpora[5] (Gilquin, 2015). If more information about participants is provided as metadata to offer richer context for research across the board, more inter-corpus parallels could be established (e.g. similar tasks for learners of certain proficiency levels) to allow for far-reaching comparisons. In terms of accessibility and distribution of the data, there already are software platforms designed to host corpora (e.g. *SketchEngine* and *TalkBank* for various languages or the *ANNIS3* used with the Falko corpora of L2 German), with more platforms being developed. Tools for working with corpus data are increasingly user-friendly, and even error-annotation and part-of-speech tagging are becoming more accurate with learner language. The escalating sophistication and diversity in LCR are reflective of the state of applied linguistics as a field and should be considered a fecund direction toward a more nuanced understanding of language use and development.

Further Reading

Paquot, M., & Plonsky, L. (2017). Quantitative research methods and study quality in learner corpus research. *International Journal of Learner Corpus Research*, *3*(1), 61–94.

This study applies a synthetic approach to primary learner corpus research (LCR) studies included in the Learner Corpus Bibliography (LCB). It uncovers several limitations of LCR, such as oversampling of academic essays written by young adult learners of English as a foreign language; a strong focus on written learner language; a lack of consistency in proficiency assessment; a heavy reliance on null hypothesis significance testing; and high-levels of underreported or missing data. Some positive trends identified include a move toward more theoretically minded studies and relatedly, an increase in the inclusion of research questions. The authors conclude with important recommendations for future LCR research.

Tracy-Ventura, N., & Huensch, A. (2018). The potential of publicly shared longitudinal learner corpora in SLA research. In A. Gudmestad & A. Edmonds (Eds.), *Critical reflections on data in second language acquisition* (pp. 149–169). Amsterdam: John Benjamins.

This chapter addresses the issue of the scarcity of openly available longitudinal learner corpora and gives a detailed description of both the LANGSNAP and LANGSNAP 3.0, an addition to the original project that collected follow-up data 3 years later from 33 of the original 56 participants to create a 5-year longitudinal corpus. Crucially, the chapter discusses issues in longitudinal data collection and public access. Among the topics included are ways to reduce participant attrition, considerations for study design, and flexibility with data collection.

Related Topics

Chapters 5, 6, 7, 10, and 12.

Notes

1 Available at: https://benjamins.com/catalog/ijlcr (last accessed 6 December 2019).
2 Available at: https://www.learnercorpusassociation.org/resources/lcb/ (last accessed 6 December 2019).
3 Available at: https://uclouvain.be/en/research-institutes/ilc/cecl/learner-corpora-around-the-world.html (last accessed 6 December 2019).
4 Available at: https://sla.talkbank.org/ (last accessed 6 December 2019).
5 Local learner corpora often result from the efforts of instructors, who collect language samples from their own students, who also have access to the corpus. As a result, local learner corpora tend to be small, but they are "directly useful to" and benefit the students "for whom, ultimately, they have been compiled" (Gilquin, 2015, p. 17) and thus increase their motivation (Granger, 2012).

Websites for Learner Corpora Discussed in This Chapter

Arabic Learner Corpus: http://www.alcsearch.com/alcsearch/ (last accessed 6 December 2019).
   Barcelona English Language Corpus: https://slabank.talkbank.org/access/English/BELC.html (last accessed 6 December 2019).
Cambridge Learner Corpus: https://www.sketchengine.eu/cambridge-learner-corpus/ (last accessed 6 December 2019).
Corpus Escrito del Español L2: http://cedel2.learnercorpora.com/.
Corpus Español Multimodal de Actos de Habla: http://www.lllf.uam.es/coremah/ (last accessed 6 December 2019).

Corpus Parlato di Italiano L2: http://elearning.unistrapg.it/osservatorio/Corpora.html (last accessed 6 December 2019).

English as a Lingua Franca in Academic Settings corpus: http://www.helsinki.fi/englanti/elfa/elfacorpus (last accessed 6 December 2019).

French Learner Language Oral Corpora: http://www.flloc.soton.ac.uk/ (last accessed 6 December 2019).

Longman Learners' Corpus: http://www.pearsonlongman.com/dictionaries/corpus/learners.html (last accessed 6 December 2019).

Merlin Corpus: https://merlin-platform.eu/C_data.php (last accessed 6 December 2019).

Multilingual Academic Corpus of Assignments - Writing and Speech (MACAWS): https://sites.google.com/email.arizona.edu/macawswebinar/home (last accessed 6 December 2019).

Multimedia Adult English Learner Corpus: http://www.labschool.pdx.edu/maelc_access.html (last accessed 6 December 2019).

Spanish Corpus Proficiency Level Training: http://www.laits.utexas.edu/spt/ (last accessed 6 December 2019).

Spanish Learner Language Oral Corpora: http://www.splloc.soton.ac.uk/ (last accessed 6 December 2019).

The Norwegian Second Language Corpus: http://clarino.uib.no/korpuskel/clarino-metadata?identifier=ask (last accessed 6 December 2019).

References

Alfaifi, A., Atwell, E., & Hedaya, I. (2014). Arabic learner corpus (ALC) v2: A new written and spoken corpus of Arabic learners. In *Proceedings of the learner corpus studies in Asia and the world (LCSAW)*, May 31. Kobe.

Anthony, L. (2017). *AntConc (3.5.0 version) [computer software]*. Tokyo: Waseda University. Retrieved from www.laurenceanthony.net/software/antconc/

Ballier, N., & Martin, P. (2015). Speech annotation of learner corpora. In S. Granger, G. Gilquin, & F. Meunier (Eds.), *The Cambridge handbook of learner corpus research* (pp. 107–134). Cambridge: Cambridge University Press.

Bartning, I., & Schlyter, S. (2004). Itinéraires acquisitionnels et stades de développement en français L2. *Journal of French Language Studies, 14*(3), 281–299.

Boersma, P., & Weenink, D. (2019). *Praat: doing phonetics by computer [computer program]*. Version 6.1.01. Retrieved August 16, 2019, from http://www.praat.org/

Buttery, P., & Caines, A. (2012). Normalizing frequency counts to account for 'opportunity of use' in learner corpora. In Y. Tono, Y. Kawaguchi, & M. Minegishi (Eds.), *Developmental and crosslinguistic perspectives in learner corpus research* (pp. 187–204). Amsterdam: John Benjamins.

Caines, A., & Buttery, P. (2017). The effect of task and topic on opportunity of use in learner corpora. In L. Flowerdew & V. Brezina (Eds.), *Learner corpus research: New perspectives and applications* (pp. 5–27). London: Bloomsbury Publishing Academic.

Callies, M., Díez-Bedmar, M. B., & Zaytseva, E. (2014). Using learner corpora for testing and assessing L2 proficiency. In P. Leclercq, A. Edmonds, & H. Hilton (Eds.), *Measuring L2 proficiency: Perspectives from SLA* (pp. 71–90). Clevedon: Multilingual Matters.

Callies, M., & Paquot, M. (2015). Learner corpus research. An interdisciplinary field on the move. *International Journal of Learner Corpus Research, 1*(1), 1–6.

Carlsen, C. (2012). Proficiency level – A fuzzy variable in computer learner corpora. *Applied Linguistics, 33*(2), 161–183.

ELFA (2008). *The corpus of English as a Lingua Franca in academic settings*. Director: Anna Mauranen. Retrieved from http://www.helsinki.fi/elfa/elfacorpus

Fernández, J. (2013). A corpus-based study of vague language use by learners of Spanish in a study abroad context. In C. Kinginger (Ed.), *Social and cultural aspects of language learning in study abroad* (pp. 229–331). Amsterdam: John Benjamins.

Forsberg, F., & Lindqvist, C. (2012). Vocabulary aspects of advanced L2 French. Do lexical formulaic sequences and lexical richness develop at the same rate? *Language, Interaction and Acquisition, 3*(1), 73–92.

Gass, S., & Selinker, L. (2008). *Second language acquisition. An introductory course* (3rd ed.). New York: Routledge.

Gilquin, G. (2015). From design to collection of learner corpora. In S. Granger, G. Gilquin, & F. Meunier (Eds.), *The Cambridge handbook of learner corpus research* (pp. 9–34). Cambridge: Cambridge University Press.

Granger, S. (2003). Error-tagged learner corpora and CALL: A promising synergy. *CALICO Journal*, *20*(3), 465–480.

Granger, S. (2008). Learner corpora. In A. Lüdeling & M. Kytö (Eds.), *Corpus linguistics: An international handbook* (pp. 259–275). Berlin: Mouton de Gruyter.

Granger, S. (2012). How to use foreign and second language learner corpora. In A. Mackey & S. Gass (Eds.), *Research methods in second language acquisition. A practical guide* (pp. 7–29). Oxford: Wiley-Backwell.

Granger, S. (2017). Learner corpora in foreign language education. In S. Thorne & S. May (Eds.), *Language, education and technology. Encyclopedia of language and education* (3rd ed., pp. 427–440). New York: Springer.

Granger, S., Dagneaux, E., Meunier, F., & Paquot, M. (Eds.) (2009). *The international corpus of learner English. Handbook and CD-ROM*. Louvain-la-Neuve: Presses universitaires de Louvain.

Gries, S. Th., & Berez, A. L. (2017). Linguistic annotation in/for corpus linguistics. In N. Ide & J. Pustejovsky (Eds.), *Handbook of linguistic annotation* (pp. 379–409). Berlin: Springer.

Gut, U. (2012). The LeaP corpus: A multilingual corpus of spoken learner German and learner English. In T. Schmidt & K. Wörner (Eds.), *Multilingual corpora and multilingual corpus analysis* (pp. 3–23). Amsterdam: John Benjamins.

Hancock, V. (2014). Pragmatic use of temporal adverbs in L1 and L2 French: Functions and syntactic positions of textual markers in a spoken corpus. In C. Lindqvist & C. Bardel (Eds.), *The acquisition of French as a second language. New developmental perspectives* (pp. 29–52). Amsterdam: John Benjamins.

Hilton, H. (2009). Annotation and analyses of temporal aspects of spoken fluency. *CALICO Journal*, *26*(3), 644–661.

Ishikawa, S. (2013). The ICNALE and sophisticated contrastive interlanguage analysis of Asian learners of English. In S. Ishikawa (Ed.), *Learner corpus studies in Asia and the world, 1* (pp. 91–118). Kobe: Kobe University.

Kilgarriff, A., Rychly, P., Smrz, P., & Tugwell, D. (2004). The sketch engine. *EURALEX. Proceedings, 1*, 105–115.

Kreyer, R. (2015). The Marburg corpus of intermediate learner English (MILE). In M. Callies & S. Gotz (Eds.), *Learner corpora in testing and assessment* (pp. 13–34). Amsterdam: John Benjamins.

Lindqvist, C. (2009). The use of the L1 and L2 in French L3: Examining cross-linguistic lexemes in multilingual learners' oral production. *International Journal of Multilingualism*, *6*(3), 281–297.

Lozano, C., & Mendikoetxea, A. (2013). Learner corpora and second language acquisition: The design and collection of CEDEL2. In A. Díaz-Negrillo, N. Ballier, & P. Thompson (Eds.), *Automatic treatment and analysis of learner corpus data* (pp. 65–100). Amsterdam: John Benjamins.

Lüdeling, A., Maik, W., Kroymann, E., & Adolphs, P. (2005). Multi-level error annotation in learner corpora. *Proceedings of the Corpus Linguistics Conference Series*, *1*(1), 105–115.

Mackey, A., & Gass, S. (2016). *Second language research: Methodology and design*. New York: Routledge.

MacWhinney, B. (2017). A shared platform for studying second language acquisition. *Language Learning*, *67*(S1), 254–275.

Mauranen, A. (2011). Learners and users - who do we want corpus data from? In F. Meunier, S. De Cock, G. Gilquin, & M. Paquot (Eds.), *A taste for corpora. In honour of Sylviane Granger* (pp. 159–175). Amsterdam: John Benjamins.

McEnery, T., Brezina, V., Gablasova, D., & Banerjee, J. (2019). Corpus linguistics, learner corpora, and SLA: Employing technology to analyze language use. *Annual Review of Applied Linguistics*, *39*, 74–92.

Mitchell, R., & Dickson, P. (1997). Progression in foreign language learning. *Report of a project funded by the economic and social research council, 1993–1996. Centre for language in education*. Occasional paper no. 45. University of Southampton, Southampton.

Mitchell, R., Dominguez, L., Arche, M., Myles, F., & Marsden, E. (2008). SPLLOC: A new database for Spanish second language acquisition research. *EUROSLA Yearbook*, *8*(1), 287–304.

Mora, J. (2006). Age effects on oral fluency development. In C. Muñoz (Ed.), *Age and the rate of foreign language learning*. Clevedon: Multilingual Matters.

Muñoz, C. (Ed.) (2006). *Age and the rate of foreign language learning*. Clevedon: Multilingual Matters.

Myles, F. (2005). Interlanguage corpora and second language acquisition research. *Second Language Research*, *21*(4), 373–391.

Myles, F. (2007). Using electronic corpora in SLA research. In D. Ayoun (Ed.), *French applied linguistics* (pp. 377–400). Amsterdam: John Benjamins.

Myles, F. (2008). Investigating learner language development with electronic longitudinal corpora: Theoretical and methodological issues. In L. Ortega & H. Byrnes (Eds.), *The longitudinal study of advanced L2 capacities* (pp. 58–72). Hillsdale: Lawrence Erlbaum Associates.

Newton, J., & Kennedy, G. (1996). Effects of communication tasks on the grammatical relations marked by second language learners. *System*, *24*(3), 309–322.

Norris, J. M., & Ortega, L. (2003). Defining and measuring SLA. In C. J. Doughty & M. H. Long (Eds.), *Handbook of second language acquisition* (pp. 717–761). Malden: Blackwell Publishing.

Paquot, M., & Plonsky, L. (2017). Quantitative research methods and study quality in learner corpus research. *International Journal of Learner Corpus Research*, *3*(1), 61–94.

Pravec, N. A. (2002). Survey of learner corpora. *ICAME Journal*, *26*, 81–114.

Reder, S., Harris, K., & Setzler, K. (2003). The multimedia adult ESL learner corpus. *TESOL Quarterly*, *37*(3), 546–557.

Reznicek, M., Walter, M., Schmidt, K., Lüdeling, A., Hirschmann, H., Krummes, C., & Andres, T. (2010). *Das Falko-Handbuch: Korpusaufbau und Annotationen*. Berlin: Institut für Deutsche Sprache und Linguistik, Humboldt-Universität zu Berlin.

Rule, S., Marsden, E., Myles, F., & Mitchell, R. (2003). Constructing a database of French interlanguage oral corpora. In D. Archer, P. Rayson, E. Wilson, & T. McEnery (Eds.), *Proceedings of the corpus linguistics 2003 conference*, UCREL. Technical Papers no. 16 (pp. 669–677). University of Lancaster.

Scott, M. (2016). *WordSmith tools version 7*. Stroud: Lexical Analysis Software.

Sinclair, J. (2005). How to build a corpus. In M. Wynne (Ed.), *Developing linguistic corpora: A guide to good practice* (pp. 79–83). Oxford: Oxbow books.

Spina, S., Pazzaglia, S., & Perini, M. (2006). *Corpus parlato di italiano L2*. Retrieved from http://elearning.unistrapg.it/osservatorio/Corpora.html

Staples, S., Novikov, A., Picoral, A., & Sommer-Farias, B. (2019). *Multilingual academic corpus of assignments—writing and speech (MACAWS)*.

Tenfjord, K., Meurer, P., & Hofland, K. (2006). The ASK corpus – A language learner corpus of Norwegian as a second language. In *Proceedings of the from 5th international conference on language resources and evaluation (LREC)*, Genova.

Tomasello, M. (2009). *Constructing a language*. Cambridge: Harvard university press.

Tracy-Ventura, N., & Huensch, A. (2018). The potential of publicly shared longitudinal learner corpora in SLA research. In A. Gudmestad & A. Edmonds (Eds.), *Critical reflections on data in second language acquisition* (pp. 149–169). Amsterdam: John Benjamins.

Tracy-Ventura, N., Mitchell, R., & McManus, K. (2016). The LANGSNAP longitudinal learner corpus. In M. Alonso-Ramos (Ed.), *Spanish learner corpus research: Current trends and future perspectives* (pp. 117–142). Amsterdam: John Benjamins.

Tracy-Ventura, N., & Myles, F. (2015). The importance of task variability in the design of learner corpora for SLA research. *International Journal of Learner Corpus Research*, *1*(1), 58–95.

Vacas Matos, M. (2017). *Diseño y compilación de un corpus multimodal de análisis pragmático para la aplicación a la enseñanza de español L2/LE*. Doctoral Dissertation. Madrid: Universidad Autónoma de Madrid.

Wichmann, A. (2008). Speech corpora and spoken corpora. In A. Lüdeling & M. Kytö (Eds.), *Corpus linguistics. An international handbook* (pp. 203–228). Berlin: Mouton de Gruyter.

Yuldashev, A., Fernández, J., & Thorne, S. (2013). Second language learners' contiguous and discontiguous multi-word unit use over time. *Modern Language Journal*, *97*(S1), 31–45.

12

TalkBank for SLA

Brian MacWhinney

Introduction

Written language learner corpora are fairly easy to obtain. In comparison, corpora providing data on learners' spoken language usage are much less available. A major exception is the TalkBank system, which provides online multimedia data for 14 types of spoken language data. Of these 14 data banks, the three that are most directly relevant to studies of second language learning are SLABank at https://slabank.talkbank.org, which includes data from second language learners, BilingBank at https://biling.talkbank.org, which includes data from bilinguals, and the BiLing segment of CHILDES at https://childes.talkbank.org which includes data from children learning two or more languages. In addition, the methods being developed within the context of the FluencyBank project (https://fluency.talkbank.org) are important for analysis of the tradeoffs and interactions between complexity, accuracy, lexis, and fluency (CALF) (Wen & Ahmadian, 2019) in L2 written and oral productions. The materials of greatest relevance to learner corpus research (LCR) and second language acquisition (SLA) are the tagged transcripts and recordings that are all freely downloadable from and immediately browsable at https://slabank.talkbank.org. This chapter reviews these resources and the framework they provide for standardization and integration in and between LCR and SLA. Although our focus here is on SLABank and BilingBank, it is important to understand the overall shape of TalkBank and how all 14 components work together to share web resources, programs, standards, and funding. Moreover, we can learn from the successes in the other banks how best to advance the growth and usage of SLABank and BilingBank.

Let us consider the relative advantages and disadvantages of written vs. spoken language data for the study of SLA. In comparison with spoken data, data from learners' written samples are much easier to collect in large quantities across languages and groups of learners. For example, the EFCamDat database (Geertzen, Alexopoulou, & Korhonen, 2013) contains over 83 million words from a million assignments written by 174,000 learners at various levels and speaking a wide variety of first languages (L1s). It is possible to apply automatic methods to tag this corpus for parts of speech and grammatical relations, although errors must be tagged by hand. This tagging then further facilitates a wide variety of methods for LCR analysis. Another advantage of written corpora is that it is easy to ensure full anonymization, as long as the writers do not insert identifying material in their essays.

In contrast, obtaining, transcribing, and analyzing spoken language data is much more difficult. Often, audio or video recordings must be made in person one at a time, and full consent must be obtained for use of either anonymized or non-anonymized data. Accurate transcription of spoken language data can take up to 20 hours for one hour of recording. To analyze fluency patterns, the transcripts must also be linked to the audio at least on the level of the utterance and preferably on the level of individual words. Together, these processes of elicitation, recording, transcription, and linkage involve a much greater investment of time and effort than for written data.

However, there are also important advantages to studying spoken language data. In many classrooms, learners and instructors view the attainment of oral fluency as the most important goal in L2 learning. From the viewpoint of SLA theory, oral production is "a better window into implicit knowledge" (Myles, 2015, p. 314). From the viewpoint of functional and cognitive linguistics, oral performance is understood as the central determinant of language structure and function (MacWhinney, 2014). From the viewpoint of psycholinguistics and neurolinguistics, spoken language usage provides the most direct measure of language processing and functioning (Kemmerer, 2015; Magnuson, Dixon, Tanenhaus, & Aslin, 2007). From the viewpoint of Conversation Analysis (Goodwin, 2003), spoken interactions are fundamental to understanding social interactions and practices.

Furthermore, spoken language data has access to a variety of communicative channels that are not present in written language. These include a wide variety of variations in speed, loudness, breathiness, and other vocal qualities that signal emotional and attitudinal dimensions in the spoken signal. Spoken utterances are often interlaced with "thetical" (Kaltenboeck & Heine, 2015) comments such as "you know" or "I would say" that provide metacommentary on the basic sentential content. Face-to-face interactions are also accompanied by a wide variety of gestures (Kendon, 1982), facial expressions (Ekman & Friesen, 1978), and proxemics (Hall, 1966) that encode emotional, relational, perspectival, and attitudinal information that is not expressed in written communication. Because of this greater complexity, some researchers working with learners' spoken language data find it best to focus their attention on small segments of production in which the interaction between all of these channels and constraints can be examined closely (Eskildsen, 2012). However, it is then necessary to examine the generality of such patterns, and this can only be done in the context of larger, openly available, spoken language corpora.

Components of TalkBank

TalkBank provides data collected during spoken language interactions. The TalkBank system (https://talkbank.org) is the world's largest open access integrated repository for spoken language data, providing language corpora and resources in 14 areas to support researchers in Psychology, Linguistics, Education, Computer Science, and Speech Pathology. The National Institutes of Health (NIH) and the National Science Foundation (NSF) have provided support for the construction of five central components of TalkBank:

1. AphasiaBank at https://aphasia.talkbank.org for the study of language in aphasia in six languages,
2. CHILDES at https://childes.talkbank.org for the study of child language development in 42 languages from infancy to age 6,
3. FluencyBank at https://fluency.talkbank.org for the study of language fluency and disfluency in stuttering, aphasia, second language learning, and normal processing,
4. HomeBank at https://homebank.talkbank.org for the study through automatic speech recognition of untranscribed daylong recordings in the home and elsewhere, and
5. PhonBank at https://phonbank.talkbank.org for the analysis of children's phonological development in 18 languages.

The construction of DilingBank and SLABank have not yet received grant support.

Table 12.1 TalkBank Usage

	CHILDES	SLABank	AphasiaBank	PhonBank	FluencyBank	HomeBank	TalkBank
Corpus Age	30	12	10	7	1	2	14
Words (millions)	59	4.7	1.8	0.8	0.5	audio	47
Linked Media (TB)	2.8	0.15	0.4	0.7	0.3	3.5	1.1
Languages	41	13	6	18	4	2	22
Publications	7000+	67	256	480	5	7	320
Users	2950	50	390	182	50	18	930
Web hits (millions)	5.0	0.1	0.5	0.1	0.1	0.4	1.7

Table 12.1 summarizes the size, usage, and age of these databases. In that table, the contents of the other nine areas in TalkBank (ASDBank, BilingBank, CABank, ClassBank, DementiaBank, RHDBank, SamtaleBank, SLABank, and TBIBank) are given in the column labelled "TalkBank". As this table shows, the CHILDES database has supported far more publications than the other databases, but this is largely a result of the fact that so much data has been available for so many years to such a large academic community. After CHILDES, the next oldest databases are AphasiaBank and PhonBank which are supporting more and more publications over time. In comparison, there are far fewer publications arising from BilingBank and SLABank.

Core Issues and Topics

The TalkBank system is grounded on six basic principles: maximally open data-sharing, a standardized transcription format, format-compatible software, interoperability, responsivity to research group needs, and compliance with international standards.

Principle 1: Maximally Open Data-sharing

In the physical sciences, the process of data-sharing is taken as a given. Lamentably, data-sharing for spoken language data has not yet been adopted as the norm. This failure to share research results – much of it supported by public funds – represents a huge loss to science. Researchers often cite privacy concerns as reasons for not sharing data on spoken interactions. However, as illustrated at https://talkbank.org/share/irb/options.html, there are many ways in which data can be made available to other researchers, while still preserving anonymity. It is important for researchers to consider these options and to have the correct IRB approvals and consent forms in place from the beginning of a new project. Fortunately, data that have already been collected can still be included in SLABank, as long as they are properly anonymized.

In many areas of biomedical and psychological science, evidence has accumulated regarding the non-reproducibility of widely-cited findings. SLA researchers have also become increasingly concerned with the need for methods to evaluate replicability (Marsden & Plonsky, 2018). To support this effort, scientists have encouraged the development of Open Science based on open data-sharing. In their *Manifesto for Reproducible Science* Munafò et al. (2017) note that "once it is accepted as the norm, we doubt that data-sharing will ever go out of fashion." TalkBank is grounded on this same basic principle. To achieve replicability in the area of LCR (Marsden, Morgan-Short, Thompson, & Abugaber, 2018), there must be not only full data-sharing, but also consistent and transparent methods for transcription and computational analysis. Ideally, it should be possible for any researcher to verify the accuracy of a published finding based on corpus analysis of openly available data by running a series of commands that are fully described in the relevant publication.

Until publications provide this level of consistency and transparency, it is difficult to replicate published findings. This is not to say that researchers would knowingly publish misleading results. However, replication of results by a second research team provides a way of checking for errors and for illuminating areas of substantive disagreement about codes and categories of analysis.

Open-access data-sharing means that researchers should be able to obtain the complete content of a given corpus. All TalkBank corpora are accessible in this way. In contrast, there are many other corpus sites that provide only a limited form of query interface to their corpus. For example, they may only support key word in context (KWIC) searches or searches through a single CQL command. Such sites do not allow downloading of the corpus or the related media. Without providing full access to corpora, it is difficult for researchers to examine all possible patterns in corpora. In some cases, these restrictions are said to be necessary to preserve anonymity. However, anonymity can easily be preserved through other methods, such as avoidance of personal identifiers in filenames, replacement of last names with *Lastname*, replacement of identifying place names with *Placename*, and silencing of segments of the audio that align with these replacements.

Principle 2: A Standardized Transcription Format

Individual research projects are typically designed to sample from specific language contexts. The hope is that, by comparing the results of projects from a wide variety of contexts, one can formulate general principles of language learning and usage. However, if each project develops and uses its own idiosyncratic methods for transcription and analysis, comparison across projects can become difficult. To address this problem, some subfields have developed transcription standards, but these are often not compatible with those used in nearby fields. In order to provide maximum harmonization across these formats, TalkBank has created an inclusive transcription standard, called CHAT, that recognizes all the features required by the many different disciplines studying spoken language, as well as written language. The features and codes available in this system are documented in the CHAT manual which can be downloaded from https://talkbank.org/manuals/chat.pdf. CHAT can also be automatically converted to XML format through use of the Chatter program (https://talkbank.org/software/chatter.html) in accord with the schema available at https://talkbank.org/software/xsddoc/index.html. Although the overall system is complex, most aspects of CHAT are only necessary for special purposes.

CHAT provides several facilities of specific importance for studies of L2 learning.

1. **Linkage to audio.** CHAT allows for tagging in milliseconds of the beginning and ending points of words, phrases, and utterances. To facilitate reading of the transcript, these time marks can be hidden or displayed through an option in the CLAN program.
2. **Support for Conversation Analysis (CA) analysis.** CA (Schegloff, 2007) uses a wide variety of markings for intonational and conversational patterns. Originally, these markings were entered using typewriter alignment supplemented with handwritten symbols. To represent these markings in computer format, CHAT uses Unicode characters as summarized at https://ca.talkbank.org/codes.html.
3. **Phonological encoding.** CHAT supports a system for phonological analysis with IPA characters. This system is encoded in CHAT XML which is also compatible with the Phon program (https://phon.ca) for complete analysis of phonological patterns and development. Because Phon incorporates the complete codebase for Praat, all Praat analyses can be conducted inside Phon, providing further compatibility with CHAT.
4. **Error marking.** CHAT also includes a well-developed system for marking semantic, syntactic, morphological, phonological, and pragmatic errors. This system has been used most extensively for analyzing aphasia speech, but it is also relevant for the analysis of second language productions.

Principle 3: Format-compatible Software

The program used for analysis of TalkBank data is called CLAN. Because all TalkBank data are in a single, consistent format, commands in CLAN are able to maximize the use of detailed features of this format. Moreover, because everything is in a consistent format which fully matches the requirements of the software, users only need to learn one program to analyze all of the data in TalkBank, rather than having to learn a different program for each corpus that they study. The use of the CLAN program will be discussed in the section on *Main Research Methods and Tools*.

Principle 4: Interoperability

Although CLAN has been designed to cover a wide range of analysis methods and research goals, there are other software packages that are better adapted to certain specific tasks. For example, although CLAN includes most of the facilities of the popular AntConc program, the interface for AntConc is more easily controlled. As a result, for work with written corpora, users may wish to export CHAT data to AntConc. To facilitate analysis of TalkBank data in AntConc, CLAN has a program called CHAT2TXT that can remove the various CHAT features unique to spoken language, such as retracing, pauses, etc. for export to AntConc.

To support this type of interoperability, TalkBank has developed a series of programs to convert from CHAT to other formats. These programs can automatically convert both to and from the formats required for Praat (http://praat.org), Phon (http://phon.ca), ELAN (tla.mpi.nl/tools/elan), CoNLL-U (universaldependencies.org/format.html), SRT (for video captions), LIPP, ANVIL (http://anvil-software.org), EXMARaLDA (http://exmaralda.org), SALT (http://saltsoftware. com), LENA (http://lenafoundation.org), and Transcriber (http://trans.sourceforge.net) formats. Users may wish to do further analysis or coding in some of these programs. In that case, in order to guarantee convertibility back to CHAT, they must be careful not to alter codes in CHAT format that mark aspects not recognized by the other programs. There are no cases in which information created in the other programs cannot be represented in CHAT, because CHAT is a superset of the information represented in these other programs.

Principle 5: Responsivity to Research Community Needs

TalkBank seeks to be maximally responsive to the needs of individual researchers and their research communities. We attempt to implement all features that are suggested by users in terms of software features, data coverage, documentation, and user support. We provide this support in six ways:

1. **Corpus Pages**: We have configured separate web servers for each of the 14 TalkBank communities, each within the talkbank.org domain. Each web site provides an index to the available corpora. For example, the index at https://slabank.talkbank.org lists the 37 available corpora from second language learners, organized by target language. Clicking on any one of these links, such as the one for "English-Qatar" brings up a page with a description of the corpus, photos, and contact information for the contributors, articles for citation along with their DOI numbers, a link for downloading the media, and a link for downloading the transcripts. The corpora vary widely in terms of the amount of description provided. For example, the English-Qatar corpus page only tells us that these are interviews with Qatari adult learners of English. Other corpora, such as the one described at https://slabank.talkbank.org/access/French/PAROLE.html provide more extensive documentation.

2. **TalkBank Browser**: Each corpus page also includes a link to a facility called the TalkBank browser that allows users to playback linked multimedia corpora and read the corresponding

segment of the transcript directly in their web browser. Users can choose to have continuous playback or playback of specific sections or utterances.

3. **Instructional Pages**: For AphasiaBank, TBIBank, and RHDBank there are segments of the websites that use linked video with professional commentary to teach students about the nature of these language disabilities. In the future, we hope to add such pages to SLABank.

4. **Tutorials:** We have created screencast tutorials for learning to use the database and programs at https://talkbank.org/screencasts/. These are hosted both at our own servers and through YouTube for better distribution in certain areas of the globe.

5. **Mailing lists:** For each TalkBank area, we maintain a user-oriented mailing list at https://groups.google.com. The BilingBank group is used for discussions of both SLA and bilingualism.

6. **Presentations and Workshops**: We also conduct several presentations and workshops each year at international conferences.

The guiding principle underlying all these user support methods is that we seek to be maximally responsive to the needs of researchers and research groups, as well as instructors and clinicians. We try to fulfill all requests for new corpora, new methods, new protocols, and new computational resources. In this way, we are able to maximize the participation of research groups in TalkBank.

Principle 6: Compliance with International Standards

The sixth basic TalkBank principle is a commitment to international standards for database and language technology. Toward this end, TalkBank has joined the European CLARIN (Common Language Resources and Technology Infrastructure) Federation (https://clarin.eu). CLARIN is an association of computational linguistic communities in 21 European countries, supported by the European Union and the governments of the individual countries. CMU (Carnegie Mellon University) TalkBank is currently the only member of CLARIN outside of Europe. Much like TalkBank, CLARIN seeks to provide uniform computational methods for accessing and processing language data. Toward this end, CLARIN centers have implemented standards for publishing corpus metadata using the CMDI (Component MetaData Infrastructure) format with the Handle server (https://handle.net) and OAI-PMH (Open Archives Initiative - Protocol for Metadata Harvesting) software. Based on these metadata, CLARIN has constructed a Virtual Linguistic Observatory (VLO) (https://vlo.clarin.eu) for locating linguistic resources, and nearly a third of the corpora in that system derive from TalkBank. CLARIN also promotes participation in the Core Trust Seal program for accreditation of data centers, and TalkBank has received this approval as noted in the extensive documentation at https://www.coretrustseal.org/wp-content/uploads/2017/10/TalkBank.pdf. The Core Trust Seal program emphasizes the adoption of international standards in areas such as ease of data access, protection of confidentiality, organizational infrastructure, data integrity, data storage, data curation, and data preservation. In accord with recent emphases on reproducibility of experimental (Munafò et al., 2017) and computational analyses (Donoho, 2010), TalkBank maintains incremental GIT repositories at https://git.talkbank.org for all of its datasets. Using this resource, researchers interested in replicating earlier analyses can obtain copies of segments of the database from any particular date.

Compliance with international standards represents an important step toward securing sustainability. Because the TalkBank programs and data are publicly available, open-sourced, and deployed to machines in the CMU Cloud Computing facility with systematic maintenance scripts, it is easy for other sites to mirror, archive, and extend the system. For this basic level of survivability, the Carnegie Mellon University Library has assured long-term maintenance support. NIH and NSF have provided financial support for the development of TalkBank since 1984. However, provision of this support is subject to ongoing progress in each database. To achieve this, we are working to pass on control of TalkBank to the next generation of researchers. We also are working to establish agreements for mutual support with two related database systems: the Linguistic Data Consortium (https://www.ldc.upenn.edu) and CLARIN (https://clarin.eu).

Main Research Methods

CLAN, written by Leonid Spektor, is a program specifically designed for the analysis of TalkBank data in CHAT. Since its beginning in 1987 as a series of DOS commands, CLAN has expanded to address the needs of researchers in an increasingly wide variety of fields, based on advances in Computational Linguistics (Le Franc et al., 2018; Lubetich & Sagae, 2014; Sagae, Davis, Lavie, MacWhinney, & Wintner, 2010) and the growing capabilities of computers and the web. The CLAN editor uses Unicode UTF-8 which supports data entry in all the world's languages. Because of this, CLAN commands work for all languages. However, part-of-speech taggers are only available for Cantonese, Chinese, Danish, Dutch, English, French, German, Hebrew, Italian, Japanese, and Spanish. Currently, CLAN includes 95 commands. We can divide these commands into 5 types.

1. analysis commands,
2. profiling commands
3. format conversion commands,
4. utility commands, and
5. morphosyntactic tagging commands.

The first four command groups are described in separate chapters in the CLAN manual which is freely downloadable from https://talkbank.org/manuals/clan.pdf. The fifth group of commands is described in the MOR manual, which is downloadable from https://talkbank.org/manuals/mor.pdf. In the next five sections, we discuss the commands in each of these 5 categories. All CLAN commands can be run recursively on a directory structure, potentially analyzing every file in the database. In addition, all of the commands can send output to files or the screen.

Analysis Commands

CLAN includes 23 commands for the basic corpus analysis functions of string searching and index tabulation. Of these, the most frequently used are FREQ, KWAL, and COMBO. FREQ produces tabulations of word, lemma, or word group frequencies. It is highly customizable with over 30 switches that allow for producing output with reverse concordance, exclusion of repetitions, output in context, spreadsheet output, etc. KWAL (key word in line) outputs each matched utterance along with its line number. As in many of the other commands, KWAL and FREQ output can be triple-clicked to go back to the exact place in the original file where a string has matched. KWAL can also output a certain number of lines of context before and after the utterance in which the desired match was located. COMBO extends the capacity of KWAL to include regular expression (RegEx) matching ability.

CLAN's tabulation commands compute indices such as MLU (mean length of utterance), MLT (mean length of turn), MAXWD (the N longest words in a file), and WDLEN (word lengths in histograms). COOCCUR computes n-grams (bigrams, trigrams, etc.); vocD computes lexical diversity (Malvern, Richards, Chipere, & Purán, 2004); and TIMEDUR computes total time and pause time. There are also four analysis programs (CHAINS, CHIP, DIST, and KEYMAP) that track speech acts, sequences, and overlaps between speakers across a discourse.

Format Conversion Commands

To maximize interoperability, CLAN includes 18 format conversion programs. Of these, 7 convert from CHAT format to other formats, including ANVIL, CA, CONLL, ELAN, Praat, SRT (for subtitles), and EXMaRALDA, and there are 11 programs that convert from other formats to CHAT, including ANVIL, CONLL, ELAN, LAB, LENA, LIPP, Praat, RTF, SALT, SRT, and Text.

Profile Computation

CLAN also includes 9 programs that compute profiles. These profiles output the results of a "canned" or "packaged" group of analysis commands such as FREQ, MLU, and vocD. Profiling commands can be run in two modes. In "summary" mode, they simply output the results for each of the analyses without making comparisons against a larger database. In summary mode, one can run the profiling command on any number of transcripts in a single pass. The results will then go to a large Excel spreadsheet in which each row represents the output for one of the many input files.

In the second or "comparison" mode, the focus is on comparing the current transcript with a larger database. In such cases, the question being asked is whether the language from the current participant can best be compared against some other reference group. For example, in the case of the KIDEVAL profiling command, the question is whether the current child is well matched to others in their age group or whether they may be ahead or behind that comparison group. To evaluate this, KIDEVAL provides output on 28 standardized language measures, along with the tabulation of the use of the 14 most common inflectional morphemes in English. For each of these measures and morpheme counts, KIDEVAL can compare the current transcript with age-matched transcripts from the CHILDES database, providing a standard deviation that indicates how closely the current participant matches the larger group. For example, a transcript from an English-speaking child aged 3;6 (three years and six months) would be compared with 350 transcripts from other English-speaking children of that age to evaluate whether the child's language was consistently within the range of the comparison group. If the child had scores that fell more than one standard deviation below those of the comparison group, then the child could be considered to be a candidate for speech therapy.

For people with aphasia, the EVAL program compares a person with groups such as controls, Broca's, Wernicke's, or conduction aphasics. Other packaged profiling commands compute C-NNLA (Thompson et al., 1995), C-QPA (Rochon, Saffran, Berndt, & Schwartz, 2000), DSS (Lee, 1974), IPSyn (Scarborough, 1990), FluCalc (Bernstein Ratner & MacWhinney, 2018), MORTABLE, and SUGAR (Pavelko & Owens, 2017). Of the 9 profiling commands, the one that seems most ideal for use with L2 data is FluCalc, because it focuses directly on the measure of language fluency, accuracy, and complexity, as discussed in the section on complexity, accuracy, lexis, and fluency (CALF) below.

For second language data, we can currently only run the profiling commands in corpus-internal summary mode. For example, within the BELC corpus of L2 English in Barcelona, we can compare the results for a given 12-year-old in the *interviews* folder with the mean and standard deviation of the other 44 12-year-olds who participated in this activity. We can even compare this adolescent with the mean and standard deviation of the 26 10-year-olds or the 9 14-year-olds who took this task. However, because we do not have data from other contexts or languages, our comparison cannot extend beyond this corpus. However, if corpus creators could make consistent use of a particular picture book or video retelling task (i.e. *Frog where are you? Loch Ness Monster, Modern Times,* etc.), then it would be possible to compare samples from a given age group in Barcelona to those from the same age group in a similar learning context with other L1s (i.e. German L1 in Hamburg or Mandarin L1 in Beijing).

Utility Commands

CLAN includes 33 commands that are used to improve file consistency and format. These are quite useful during corpus development. However, once a corpus is fully curated, tagged, and checked, there is seldom need to rely on these programs.

Morphosyntactic Tagging

CLAN provides part-of-speech taggers and grammatical dependency taggers for Cantonese, Chinese, Danish, Dutch, English, French, German, Hebrew, Italian, Japanese, and Spanish. These taggers rely on lexicons designed specifically to deal with spoken language. Morphological tagging is done through a set of rules determining patterns of allomorphy and affix sequencing. Once all possible taggings are generated, they are disambiguated automatically by a trainable program called POST (Parisse & Le Normand, 2000). After that, the MEGRASP program (Sagae, Davis, Lavie, MacWhinney, & Wintner, 2007) creates a syntactic analysis in terms of grammatical dependency relations. Here is an example of the output created by the running of these programs on a single utterance in written segment of the BELC corpus:

```
*TEX:    my name is David.
%mor:    det:poss|my n|name cop|be&3S n:prop|David.
%gra:    1|2|MOD 2|3|SUBJ 3|0|ROOT 4|3|PRED 5|3|PUNCT
*TEX:    my animal favorite is the dog.
%mor:    det:poss|my n|animal n|favorite cop|be&3S det:art|the n|dog.
%gra:    1|3|MOD 2|3|MOD 3|4|SUBJ 4|0|ROOT 5|6|DET 6|4|PRED 7|4|PUNCT
*TEX:    my eyes is browns.
%mor:    det:poss|my n|eye-PL cop|be&3S v|brown-3S.
%gra:    1|2|MOD 2|3|SUBJ 3|0|ROOT 4|3|PRED 5|3|PUNCT
*TEX:    my from is Barcelona Spain.
%mor:    det:poss|my prep|from cop|be&3S n:prop|Barcelona n:prop|Spain.
%gra:    1|0|INCROOT 2|1|JCT 3|2|POBJ 4|5|NAME 5|3|PRED 6|1|PUNCT
```

Although the automatic tagging is accurate, there are learner error patterns here which require further coding. In the second utterance, *favorite* is tagged as a noun, rather than an adjective. This error likely arises from the fact that Spanish places the adjective after the noun. So, there should be the error code [* wo] here to indicate the wrong word order. Also, in the third utterance, there is a violation of subject-verb agreement which should be coded as [* m:vsg:a] for a morphological agreement error using a singular verb. Although tagging is automatic, these error codes must be added by hand.

Once a corpus has been tagged for part-of-speech on the %mor line and grammatical relations on the %gra line, it is possible to conduct a wide variety of further automatic analyses, often using the KWAL and COMBO commands. The profiling commands described earlier make extensive use of the %mor and %gra tiers to track the use of morphological and syntactic forms by learners.

It is also possible to use combinations of monolingual taggers with bilingual corpora. To do this, transcribers need to place precode marks such as [- eng] on utterances that contain switches from one language to another. Here is an example from the hogan2.cha file in the Eppler German-English corpus in BilingBank:

```
*FRI:    [- eng] police (.) want to see someone upstairs.
*SOP:    [- eng] the drug factory.
*SOP:    wir haben eine drug@s factory@s oben.
```

Because the primary language of this transcript is German, utterances in German are unmarked, whereas utterances in English use the [-eng] code. However, when an English word is used within a largely German utterance, as in the case of the third utterance with *drug factory*, then the code-switched words are marked with @s. Once a transcript has been marked in this way, it is then possible to run the two sets of morphosyntactic taggers automatically to tag the complete corpus.

Database Searches

In order to promote fuller and more direct access to the entire database, including both CHILDES and the 13 other TalkBank components, we have recently developed a database search system called TalkBankDB at https://talkbank.org/DB. TalkBankDB relies on a POSTgreSQL database in JSON format. The front end web interface of TalkBankDB is written in standard HTML, CSS, and JavaScript to ensure cross-browser support. Care is taken so the JavaScript code is clearly commented and maintainable, following the popular "web component" design pattern common in many large-scale web apps. Searches are composed by successive additions of criteria. For L2 corpora, users first select SLABank and then can either choose a particular corpus or search by target language. Once the search criteria are configured, there is a button to conduct the search, and the browser will then return all files that match the criteria. At this point, it is possible to either run further analyses on the web or else download the matched set of files for further analysis in R, Python, or a statistical package, using the **Save** button. It is also possible to click on the matched items in the left-hand column to directly open up the relevant file(s).

CA Analysis

Both CHAT and CLAN provide full support for transcription and analysis in classic Jeffersonian format (Hepburn & Bolden, 2013; MacWhinney & Wagner, 2010) for Conversation Analysis (CA). Although this format is very different from the basic CHAT format used elsewhere in the databases, both formats can be expressed fully in the CHAT XML. Some important features of CLAN's support for CA analysis include the ability to mark beginnings and ends of overlaps in a way that allows CLAN's INDENT command to automatically re-align overlaps after editing has changed the spacing. Another feature is the introduction of a set of 26 special Unicode characters (see https://ca.talkbank.org/codes.html) for features of CA markup such as tone movement, final contour, speeding up and slowing down, creaky voice, and so on.

CA analysis can provide an interesting second window on corpora. Corpus linguistic analysis can reveal pervasive patterns across learners, genre, and development. CA analysis, on the other hand, is better designed to study the detailed ways in which learners interact with other conversational participants. By looking closely at small segments of interactions, sometimes involving as few as a dozen utterances, we can come to understand how learners deal in real time with conversational issues such as repair, sequencing, misunderstanding, word retrieval, face presentation, and topic continuation. A particular strength of TalkBank in general and SLABank in particular is the fact that many of the transcripts are directly linked on the utterance level to the corresponding segment of the audio or video. Based on methods like this, one can study the use of forms both in the general case and in specific interactional contexts.

Protocol Development

There is currently no standard set of methods for the elicitation of spoken second language corpus data. However, our experience with the construction of the AphasiaBank database indicates that SLA and LCR could benefit from the introduction of a common set of data elicitation methods in the shape of a recognized data collection protocol. The reason for this is that data collected using the same set of methods are much more comparable than data collected in diverse and often incomparable ways. Because the bulk of the data in AphasiaBank were collected using this protocol, researchers have been able to use the database in over 300 additional publications.

The details of the AphasiaBank protocol can be viewed at https://aphasia.talkbank.org/protocol/. The protocol includes a series of standardized tests, a conversation about the stroke that led to aphasia, descriptions of several cartoon picture series, a retelling of the Cinderella story, and description of the simple procedure of making a peanut butter and jelly sandwich. It takes about 60 minutes to administer this protocol, and the whole interaction is recorded through video for subsequent transcription in CHAT using CLAN. This protocol has now been used in English with 420 persons with aphasia and 286 control participants. A smaller number of protocols have been collected in other languages. Because of the consistency of data administration, transcription, and analysis of this corpus, researchers have been able to publish nearly 300 papers based on this dataset.

A similar approach could be used for the creation of a unified second language learning database. In fact, corpora such as FLLOC (http://flloc.soton.ac.uk), SPLLOC (http://splloc.soton.ac.uk), and LANGSNAP (http://langsnap.soton.ac.uk) that are included in SLABank have already taken this approach, by including recognized tasks such as interviews and story retelling. Other useful protocol segments include passage reading, word list reading, map tasks, translation tasks, error correction, and sentence combining. Each of these components can provide important and somewhat independent sources of information regarding learners' abilities and development.

1. **Passage reading** and **word list reading** can provide consistently comparable data across participants that can then be aligned against target forms using automatic speech recognition (ASR) technology. Diarization through automatic speech recognition (ASR) (Cristia, Ganesh, Casillas, & Ganapathy, 2018) can provide marks of the beginning and end of each word and segment. ASR analysis can also analyze deviations in learner pronunciations from the target forms. We have been using this methodology in the AphasiaBank project to study people with apraxia of speech (AoS).

2. **Interviews** provide a view of learners' abilities in a maximally natural conversation.

3. **Story retelling** has provided extremely rich data in fields such as child language and aphasia. The corpora in the European Science Foundation (ESF) database (which is included in SLABank) rely heavily on the retelling of the stories in short movie clips. In dozens of CHILDES corpora, children are asked to retell stories about a boy, his dog, and a frog. In the AphasiaBank protocol, both control participants and participants with aphasia retell the Cinderella story after being reminded of the plot by scanning through a wordless picture book. Data from these retellings can be used for the study of the control of fluency, grammatical correctness, morphosyntactic development, lexical diversity, and narrative structure.

4. **Map tasks** and similar procedural tasks can evaluate the use of language for conversational problem solving.

5. **Translation and error correction** tasks can assess the ability of learners to apply specific language patterns in areas such as syntax, lexicon, and morphology. They also provide consistent data on error patterns for specific targets.

6. **Sentence combining** tasks can evaluate learners' control of methods for constructing complex constructions.

The IRIS database (http://iris-database.org) includes a wide range of further task types. If SLA and LCR researchers could agree on a core set of these tasks that would constitute a shared protocol, then it would be possible to achieve the same level of database structure already achieved for AphasiaBank, FluencyBank, and TBIBank. The tasks in such a general protocol can also be applied in successive sessions across months or even years to study the overall course of second language learning.

Complexity, Accuracy, Lexis, and Fluency

Proposals regarding a tradeoff between fluency and accuracy (Skehan, 1998) have generated many interesting attempts to measure and characterize fluency and accuracy objectively (Wen & Ahmadian, 2019). This concept of a tradeoff between these dimensions has been further elaborated by many researchers, including several in this volume, to include the dimensions of syntactic and lexical complexity. As a result, the full set of dimensions now includes complexity, accuracy, lexis, and fluency (CALF). Each of these dimensions is the subject of a chapter in this handbook. The specific measures discussed in these chapters are very close to those being computed by CLAN's FLUCALC, VOCD, MATTR, and MEGRASP programs.

Fluency. As noted by Huensch (Chapter 22, this volume), CLAN has been used to evaluate fluency in terms of pause duration, retracing, filled pauses, and disfluencies. Once transcription is complete, CLAN's FLUCALC program calculates and tabulates each of these features automatically. In addition, CLAN's interoperability with additional programs such as Praat and Phon facilitates further fluency analyses.

Accuracy. CLAN can evaluate accuracy using the TalkBank system of error analysis (Chapter 23, this volume) that has been developed based on experience in coding errors in aphasia and child language learning. The description of the TalkBank error coding system can be found in Chapter 18 of the CLAN manual (http://talkbank.org/manuals). TalkBank's system for error coding and analysis is very similar in terms of both the level of coding and the mechanisms for analysis as the system developed in Louvain (Dagneaux, Denness, & Granger, 1998; Granger, 2003) for SLA texts.

Lexis. CLAN provides three methods for computing lexical diversity (Chapter 25, this volume). The FREQ program computes the traditional TTR (type-token ratio) measure, based either on the specific words being spoken or on an analysis of lemmas, as analyzed on the tagged and analyzed morphological analysis tier (%mor). The second method uses the vocD framework (Malvern et al., 2004) which is less sensitive to sample size than TTR, and the third uses the MATTR computation (Covington & McFall, 2010), which is even less sensitive to sample size than vocD. CLAN's RARITY program examines the extent to which a speaker uses words that are less frequent in the general spoken vocabulary.

Complexity. CLAN's analysis of complexity (Chapter 24, this volume) relies on the automatic computation of a full grammatical dependency tagging (%gra) for each utterance, as displayed in the previous section on morphosyntactic tagging. Once this tagging is available, there is a specific version of the FREQ command described in the CLAN manual that can send the required data to Excel to tabulate and add complex structures and compute the ratio of complex grammatical relations over all grammatical relations.

Representative Corpora and Research

SLABank currently includes 37 corpora from second language learners, and BilingBank includes 13 corpora from bilinguals. Nearly all of these corpora are accompanied by audio, although only a few have been linked to the audio at the utterance level. In addition to these corpora from adult learners and bilinguals, the CHILDES database has 32 corpora tracing the development of childhood bilingualism. For a detailed description of the research engendered by each corpus, please consult the corpus pages located from the index at https://slabank.talkbank.org/access/ for SLABank, https://biling.talkbank.org/access/ for BilingBank, and https://childes.talkbank.org/access/Biling/ for the bilingual corpora in CHILDES.

The corpora in languages for which we have MOR taggers have been annotated for morphological structure (%mor), and some have also been automatically annotated for grammatical relation structure (%gra). The languages for which taggers are available include Cantonese, Danish, Dutch, English, French, German, Hebrew, Italian, Japanese, Mandarin, and Spanish

(MacWhinney, 2008). This means that, for SLA Bank, we cannot currently tag the corpora dealing with the learning of Czech and Hungarian.

Studies based on the current SLABank corpora have largely been conducted by the groups who developed and contributed the corpora. For example, the Vercellotti corpus of L2 English has been carefully time-aligned at the phrasal level. As a result, it was amenable to a close analysis for CALF features (Vercellotti, 2017), such as pause duration, retracing, and lexical diversity. The large *Barcelona English Language Corpus* (BELC) was collected for the purpose of evaluating the effects of age on the acquisition of English as a second language (Muñoz, 2006). As a result, the use of CLAN programs for that corpus focused on comparison of lexicon and syntax across different age groups. The Eppler corpus of German-English code-switching includes thorough marking of the source language for each sentence and marking of sentence-internal switches. The fact that the corpus is fully tagged for both English and German has made it possible to examine the predictions from three alternative syntactic theories for mixed determiner-noun constructions (Eppler, Luescher, Deuchar, & Theory, 2017). The CLAN programs were also used in the analysis of the FLLOC corpus on the learning of French (Marsden & David, 2008) and the SPLLOC corpus on the learning of Spanish (Domínguez & Arche, 2014), among many others.

Future Directions

To be maximally effective, SLABank needs to address three major goals. The first is to encourage researchers to share the data they have collected. Researchers may avoid data-sharing because of concerns regarding prohibitions from Institutional Review Boards or regulations such as the General Data Protection Regulation (GDPR) and the California Data Privacy Protection Act (CDPPA). However, good methods exist for addressing all of these requirements. Moreover, funding agencies and universities expect that researchers will share their data as much as possible. Another possible barrier to data-sharing is that TalkBank data must be coded in CHAT format. However, many projects already use CHAT, and for those that are using other formats, there are 11 CLAN format conversion programs, and more can be created as needed. A third barrier to data-sharing is that many researchers are unfamiliar with the use of CLAN tools for data analysis. However, for those more comfortable with tools such as AntConc or ELAN, it is easy to output CHAT data for use by these other programs.

Increased data-sharing of SLA corpora will improve our current coverage of learner groups and target languages. Currently, the most heavily represented target languages are English, Spanish, and French. Adding data from other major target languages such as Arabic, German, Mandarin, and Russian is important. It is also important to have data on the L2 acquisition of less commonly studied languages, as well as data collected from alternative language-learning contexts, including online learning, instructed learning in the classroom, study abroad, learning in bilingual homes, learning in immigrant communities, and so on. The possibility of collecting data through online methods is particularly appealing, given the large potential coverage of these methods. Such data could include oral and/or written story retelling, oral passage reading, and spoken or written translation. These data could also be linked to data from online tutorial and online experimental methods (MacWhinney, 2017).

A second major goal for the LCR and SLA communities will be the creation of a shared protocol for data elicitation. Such a protocol would greatly improve our ability to characterize patterns in second language learning across L1s, L2s, learner types, contexts, and ages. To develop this protocol, the SLABank system will need to solicit input from all segments of the community and researchers will need to pilot the method in new projects.

Work on these goals will require extensive buy-in from the LCR and SLA communities, as well as major support from funding agencies. The good news is that it is clear what needs to be done and how to proceed.

Further Reading

MacWhinney, B. (2008). Enriching CHILDES for morphosyntactic analysis. In H. Behrens (Ed.), *Trends in corpus research: Finding structure in data* (pp. 165–198). Amsterdam: John Benjamins.

This paper explains morphosyntactic and grammatical dependency tagging in CLAN.

MacWhinney, B. (2017). A shared platform for studying second language acquisition. *Language Learning*, *67*(S1), 254–275.

This paper focuses on the collection of L2 learning data through web-based exercises, but also includes a discussion of how these methods can be linked to corpus development.

MacWhinney, B. (2019). Task-based analysis and the Competition Model. In Z. Wen & M. Ahmadian (Eds.), *Researching Second Language Task Performance and Pedagogy: Essays in Honor of Peter Skehan.* (pp. 305–315). New York: John Benjamins.

This paper explores links between the Competition Model and CALF trade-off analysis, using the CLAN programs.

MacWhinney, B. (2019). Understanding spoken language through TalkBank. *Behavior Research Methods*, *51*, 1919–1927.

This article explains how TalkBank methods have been used in various fields to explore psychological, clinical, and linguistic issues.

Related Topics

Chapters 22, 23, 24, and 25.

References

Bernstein Ratner, N., & MacWhinney, B. (2018). Fluency bank: A new resource for fluency research and practice. *Journal of Fluency Disorders*, *56*, 69–80. doi:10.1016/j.jfludis.2018.03.002

Covington, M. A., & McFall, J. D. (2010). Cutting the Gordian knot: The moving-average type–token ratio (MATTR). *Journal of Quantitative Linguistics*, *17*(2), 94–100. doi:10.1080/02687038.2012.693584

Cristia, A., Ganesh, S., Casillas, M., & Ganapathy, S. (2018). Talker diarization in the wild: The case of child-centered daylong audio-recordings. Paper presented at the Interspeech, Hyderabad.

Dagneaux, E., Denness, S., & Granger, S. (1998). Computer-aided error analysis. *System*, *26*(2), 163–174.

Domínguez, L., & Arche, M. J. J. L. (2014). Subject inversion in non-native Spanish. Lingua, *145*, 243–265.

Donoho, D. L. (2010). An invitation to reproducible computational research. *Biostatistics*, *11*(3), 385–388.

Ekman, P., & Friesen, W. (1978). *Facial action coding system: Investigator's guide*. Palo Alto: Consulting Psychologists Press.

Eppler, E. D., Luescher, A., Deuchar, M. J. C. L., & Theory, L. (2017). Evaluating the predictions of three syntactic frameworks for mixed determiner–noun constructions. *Corpus Linguistics and Linguistic Theory*, *13*(1), 27–63.

Eskildsen, S. W. (2012). L2 negation constructions at work. *Language Learning*, *62*(2), 335–372.

Geertzen, J., Alexopoulou, T., & Korhonen, A. (2013). *Automatic linguistic annotation of large scale L2 databases: The EF-Cambridge open language database (EFCAMDAT).* Paper presented at the proceedings of the 31st second language research forum. Cascadilla Proceedings Project, Somerville.

Goodwin, C. (2003). Conversational frameworks for the accomplishment of meaning in aphasia. In *Conversation and brain damage* (pp. 90–116). Oxford: Oxford University Press.

Granger, S. (2003). Error-tagged learner corpora and CALL: A promising synergy. *CALICO Journal*, *20*, 465–480.

Hall, E. (1966). *The hidden dimension*. New York: Random House.

Hepburn, A., & Bolden, G. B. (2013). The conversation analytic approach to transcription. In J. Sidnell & T. Stivers (Eds.), *The handbook of conversation analysis* (pp. 57–76). New York: Wiley.

Kaltenboeck, G., & Heine, B. (2015). Sentence grammar vs. thetical grammar: Two competing domains. In B. MacWhinney, A. Malchukov, & E. Moravcsik (Eds.), *Competing motivations in grammar and usage* (pp. 348–363). New York: Oxford University Press.

Kemmerer, D. (2015). *The cognitive neuroscience of language*. New York: Psychology Press.

Kendon, A. (1982). The study of gesture: Some observations on its history. *Recherches Sémiotiques/Semiotic Inquiry*, 2(1), 45–62.

Lee, L. (1974). *Developmental sentence analysis*. Evanston: Northwestern University Press.

Le Franc, A., Riebling, E., Karadayi, J., Yun, W., Scaff, C., Metze, F., & Cristia, A. (2018). The ACLEW DiViMe: An easy-to-use diarization tool. Paper presented at the Interspeech 2018, Mumbai.

Lubetich, S., & Sagae, K. (2014). Data-driven measurement of child language development with simple syntactic templates. Paper presented at the COLING 2014, Dublin, Ireland.

MacWhinney, B. (2008). Enriching CHILDES for morphosyntactic analysis. In H. Behrens (Ed.), *Trends in corpus research: Finding structure in data* (pp. 165–198). Amsterdam: John Benjamins.

MacWhinney, B. (2014). Presentation. In L. Scliar-Cabral (Ed.), *O português na plataforma CHILDES* (pp. 9–20). Florianopolis: Editora Insular.

MacWhinney, B. (2017). A shared platform for studying second language acquisition. *Language Learning*, 67(S1), 254–275.

MacWhinney, B., & Wagner, J. (2010). Transcribing, searching and data sharing: The CLAN software and the TalkBank data repository. *Gesprachsforschung*, 11, 154–173.

Magnuson, J., Dixon, J., Tanenhaus, M., & Aslin, R. (2007). The dynamics of lexical competition during spoken word recognition. *Cognitive Science*, 31(1), 133–156.

Malvern, D., Richards, B., Chipere, N., & Purán, P. (2004). *Lexical diversity and language development*. New York: Palgrave Macmillan.

Marsden, E., & David, A. (2008). Vocabulary use during conversation: A cross-sectional study of development from year 9 to year 13 among learners of Spanish and French. *Language Learning Journal*, 36(2), 181–198.

Marsden, E., Morgan-Short, K., Thompson, S., & Abugaber, D. (2018). Replication in second language research: Narrative and systematic reviews and recommendations for the field. *Language Learning*, 68(2), 321–391. doi:10.1111/lang.12286

Marsden, E., & Plonsky, L. (2018). Data, open science, and methodological reform in second language acquisition research. In A. Gudmestad & A. Edwonds (Eds.), *Critical reflections on data in second language acquisition* (pp. 219–228). Amsterdam: John Benjamins.

Munafò, M. R., Nosek, B. A., Bishop, D. V., Button, K. S., Chambers, C. D., du Sert, N. P., ... Ioannidis, J. P. (2017). A manifesto for reproducible science. *Nature Human Behaviour*, 1, 0021.

Muñoz, C. (2006). *Age and rate of foreign language learning*. Clevedon: Multilingual Matters.

Myles, F. (2015). Second language acquisition theory and learner corpus research. In S. Granger, G. Gilquin, & F. Meunier (Eds.), *Cambridge handbook of learner corpus research* (pp. 309–331). Cambridge: Cambridge University Press.

Parisse, C., & Le Normand, M.-T. (2000). Automatic disambiguation of the morphosyntax in spoken language corpora. *Behavior Research Methods, Instruments, and Computers*, 32(3), 468–481.

Pavelko, S., & Owens, R. (2017). Sampling utterances abd grammatical analysis revised (SUGAR): New normative values for language sample analsysi measures. *Language, Speech, and Hearing Services in Schools*, 48(3), 197–215.

Rochon, E., Saffran, E., Berndt, R., & Schwartz, M. (2000). Quantitative analysis of aphasic sentence production: Further development and new data. *Brain and Language*, 72(3), 193–218.

Sagae, K., Davis, E., Lavie, A., MacWhinney, B., & Wintner, S. (2007). High-accuracy annotation and parsing of CHILDES transcripts. In *Proceedings of the 45th meeting of the association for computational linguistics* (pp. 1044–1050). Prague: ACL.

Sagae, K., Davis, E., Lavie, A., MacWhinney, B., & Wintner, S. (2010). Morphosyntactic annotation of CHILDES transcripts. *Journal of Child Language*, 37(3), 705–729. doi:10.1017/S0305000909990407

Scarborough, H. S. (1990). Index of productive syntax. *Applied Psycholinguistics*, 11(1), 1–22. doi:10.1017/S0142716400008262

Schegloff, E. (2007). *Sequence organization in interaction: A primer in conversation analysis*. New York: Cambridge University Press.

Skehan, P. (1998). *A cognitive approach to language learning*. Oxford: Oxford University Press.

Thompson, C. K., Shapiro, L. P., Tait, M. E., Jacobs, B. J., Schneider, S. L., & Ballard, K. J. (1995). A system for the linguistic analysis of agrammatic language production. *Brain and Language*, 51, 124–129.

Vercellotti, M. L. (2017). The development of complexity, accuracy, and fluency in second language performance: A longitudinal study. *Applied Linguistics*, 38(1), 90–111.

Wen, Z., & Ahmadian, M. (Eds.) (2019). *Researching L2 task performance and pedagogy: In honor of Peter Skehan*. Amsterdam: John Benjamins.

PART III
THE ROLE OF CORPORA IN SLA THEORY AND PRACTICE

13
Usage-based Approaches

Stefanie Wulff

Introduction

The label "usage-based linguistics" (henceforth UBL) is a framework subsuming several theories including Construction Grammar (Goldberg, 2006), Cognitive-Functional Linguistics (Evans, Bergen, & Zinken, 2007), emergentism (MacWhinney, 1987), and Complex Dynamic Systems Theory (de Bot, Lowie, & Verspoor, 2007). What holds all usage-based accounts of language (learning) together is that they minimally share two fundamental assumptions (Ellis & Wulff, 2020):

(1) Language learning primarily depends on ambient language, that is, input learners receive and output they produce in a communicatively rich human environment.
(2) Language learning recruits cognitive mechanisms that are involved in learning of any kind, not just language learning. (p. 63)

Given (1), all usage-based frameworks agree that the examination of naturally occurring language data (performance data) is a worthwhile endeavor – in fact, looking at authentic language is argued to often be preferable to relying solely on other data like speaker intuitions or judgments (Schütze, 2016). That renders all usage-based frameworks inherently compatible with corpus linguistics as a method, because corpora provide, at least in the ideal scenario, dense and representative samples of authentic language use. Correspondingly, corpus data are featured in second language acquisition studies that adopt any of these usage-based frameworks (see the references above); unfortunately, a detailed and differential description of that entire body of work is beyond the scope of this chapter, so the following mainly focuses on a Construction Grammar perspective on SLA.

The object of acquisition in UBL is a structured inventory of form-meaning pairs or constructions (Goldberg, 2006). In this warehouse of constructions, called a *constructicon*, "abstract grammatical patterns and the lexical instantiations of those patterns are jointly included ..., and ... may consist of many different levels of schematic abstraction" (Tummers, Heylen & Geeraerts, 2005, pp. 228–229). That is, simple morphemes such as *-tastic* (meaning 'extremely') are constructions in the same way as simple words like *cookie* (meaning 'small wheat cake'), collocations like *cookie dough*, idiomatic noun phrases like *smart cookie* (meaning 'smart person'), and abstract syntactic frames like Subject-Verb-Object-Object (meaning that something is being transferred, as realized in sentences as diverse as *Max gave Maya a cookie*, *Max gave Maya a hug*, or *Max baked Maya a cake*, where cookies, hugs, and cakes are being transferred, respectively). Not all constructions carry meaning in the traditional sense; many constructions rather serve a more functional purpose, like the passive construction, which serves to shift the focus of attention in an utterance from the agent of the action to the patient undergoing the action (compare the passive *A cake was baked for Maya* with its active counterpart).

Because complex constructions comprise several smaller constructions, constructions have to be simultaneously stored in the mental lexicon in multiple forms. For example, the words *cookie* and the plural *-s* morpheme are simple constructions; both are stored also as constituent parts of the more complex construction *cookies* ('more than one cookie'). Different levels of constructional schematization are illustrated in the fully lexicalized formula *There you go* versus the partially schematized slot-and-frame greeting pattern [*Happy* + (occasion)], which can be realized as *Happy birthday* and *Happy anniversary*; and the completely schematic [Noun Phrase + Noun Phrase] construction, which could be realized as *raisin cookie*, *kitchen helper*, or *weather forecast*, to give but three examples.

Sentences are not the product of applying a rule to a number of words to arrange them in a grammatical sequence, but of combining constructions. *What did Max give Maya?*, for instance, is a combination of the following constructions: *Max*, *Maya*, *give*, *what*, and *do*; VP and NP constructions; the Subject–Verb–Object–Object construction; and the Subject–Auxiliary inversion construction. Language competence is thus defined as knowledge of the properties of constructions, which other constructions they combine with, and how they do so.

Usage-based approaches to language acquisition differ from formal approaches (Chapter 16, this volume; White, 2015) to language acquisition in a number of ways: firstly, formal approaches postulate that, in child first language acquisition, learners access a universal grammar, which is inborn knowledge of linguistic regularities that are subsequently modified to fit the specific language environment the child is in. For second language acquisition beyond the onset of puberty, formal approaches vary in their hypotheses regarding if and to what extent universal grammar is still accessed. UBL, in contrast, works on the assumption that while there is a cognitive blueprint – a set of mechanisms we employ for learning – that blueprint is not custom-tailored to the learning of language, but designed to adapt to learning anything. Similarly to those formal approaches that claim access to universal grammar in late-onset second language acquisition, UBL assumes that the blueprint is available to learners of any age, yet the way it is used changes as a function of the learner's age given (i) maturational changes in the brain and (ii) the fact that the learner has already acquired, or is in the process of acquiring, a first language.

A second difference between UBL and formal approaches falls out from the different position on nativism; the view that language rules are not inborn, but learnable from scratch promotes a theory of language in which the different elements comprising language differ not fundamentally, but continually from each other. While formal approaches uphold the existence of two separate modules, a grammar containing the rules and a lexicon containing the words, UBL postulates the afore-mentioned all-encompassing constructicon in their place.

In contemporary research, these differences are less divisive than previously assumed. A discussion of recent developments that speak to an increasing reconciliation of theories is beyond the scope of this chapter (see Rothman & Slabakova, 2018). However, it is important to point out the considerable impact these original differences have had on the respective theoretical foci: while formal approaches have devoted more attention to the characterization of the initial stages of acquisition and questions pertaining to ultimate attainment in different learner populations, UBL has focused more on understanding how language development unfolds over time. Likewise, while formal theory has focused on describing the nature of linguistic *competence*, defined as the unconscious knowledge one has of their language(s) and how it is modulated by other factors to often differ from performance, UBL has considered *performance* data a much more direct reflection of the learning process and the mechanisms underlying it.

As various scholars have pointed out (Gries, 2018; Schönefeld, 1999), the focus of UBL on performance and its inherent affinity with performance data are key to understanding why UBL turned to corpus linguistics earlier and more eagerly than advocates of less performance-driven theories. Two strands of research in corpus-based UBL on second language acquisition stand out: research that examines the nature of ambient language (input and output) and the role of the input in language learning and research that examines the nature of formulaic language, i.e. expressions comprising multiple words and its role in the second language acquisition process. The following section discusses each in turn.

Core Issues and topics

Input Properties and Their Role in Second Language Learning

One main question in usage-based approaches to language acquisition is what the properties of the input are that make it learnable. Evidence – much of it corpus-based – suggests that human language processing and acquisition responds to a variety of input properties, each of which will be discussed briefly in turn.

Token, Type, and Contingent Frequency

The frequency of a construction plays a crucial role in acquisition. Counter to common misunderstandings of the role of frequency in UBL, the assumption is not simply that the more frequent a construction is, the more easily and faster it will be acquired. Instead, we need to distinguish between different levels of granularity at which frequency operates. At the lowest level of granularity, token frequency is the frequency with which a particular construction occurs in the input. The English plural *-s* morpheme has a high token frequency, for example; it occurs frequently in any given context. At a higher level of granularity, we can consider the type frequency of the plural *-s* morpheme, which is defined as the number of distinct realizations of a given construction. Plural -s has a high type frequency because it occurs with thousands of different nouns. In contrast, irregular plurals as in *mice*, *geese*, or *teeth* may also have a high token frequency, but the type frequency is low; only a few nouns form an irregular plural. The higher the type frequency of a construction, the more, and more varied, opportunities a learner has to process the construction and build a schematic representation of its form and meaning/function (Bybee & Hopper, 2001); high token frequency instead leads to conservation of specific variants of a construction (Bybee, 2006).

Yet another kind of frequency that plays a significant role for language learning is the frequency with which constructions co-occur with each other (as opposed to de-contextualized counts). When the occurrence of one construction is strongly tied to that presence of another – i.e., when one is contingent on the other or associated with the other – then hearing one construction raises the listener's ability to predict what comes next. Thus, contingent or associated construction pairs or arrangements foster *chunking*, i.e. the development of associative connections in long-term memory; these chunks serve an important role in automatizing speech and thus increasing fluency (Divjak & Caldwell-Harris, 2015). Evidence from learner corpus research is presented by Ellis and Ferreira-Junior (2009b), who examined L2 learners' use of verbs in three argument structure constructions in the European Science Foundation (ESF) corpus. For each verb-argument construction pairing, they calculated the association between the verb and the construction using DeltaP, a measure that is based on conditional probabilities. The results suggest that the verbs that are first learned are those most distinctively associated with the three different constructions, so rather than frequency alone, it is contingency, or frequency in context, that kickstarts the acquisition of these constructions.

Counter to common misrepresentations of UBL, frequency is not a catch-all; the (token/type/ co-occurrence) frequency of a construction is neither a sufficient nor a necessary condition for a construction to be learnable. For example, formulaic expressions such as *pay through the nose*, *hang on*, or *make ends meet* are comparatively rare, yet acquired easily – they attract attention, and are thus learnable, not by virtue of being frequent, but by virtue of being rare and meaningful. Likewise, many formulaic sequences like *and of the* or *but it is* are quite frequent yet do not yield psychological salience or coherence (Schmitt, 2004), so clearly, other aspects of constructional frequency must also be at play.

Distribution of Constructions in the Input

One such property is the distribution of the occurrences of a construction in the input, especially in the early stages of learning a construction. Rather than being evenly dispersed, children's input and output reflect Zipf's Law (Zipf, 1935): the frequency of a word is inversely proportional to its rank in a frequency table. This means that the most frequent word occurs about twice as often as the second most frequent word, three times as often as the third most frequent word, etc. Goldberg, Casenhiser and Sethuraman (2004) showed that Zipf's Law holds when counting words in a given sample of authentic speech, and importantly, it also holds for verbs *within* a given construction. According to Goldberg et al., the Zipfian input distribution directs attention to specific typical verbs that are made salient by being extremely frequent in the input, which then can serve as the "path-breaking verbs" for category formation. Ellis and Ferreira-Junior (2009a, 2009b) examined data from naturalistic L2 acquisition and likewise confirmed that the type/token ratio of the verbs in argument structure constructions is Zipfian. Furthermore, they demonstrated that the most frequent and prototypical verbs seem to act as "verb islands" around which verb argument constructions gradually emerge, as suggested by Tomasello (2003) for L1 acquisition.

Recency of Constructions in the Input

Alongside frequency and context, research in cognitive psychology points to the central role that recency plays (Anderson & Schooler, 2000). Recency (variably also called priming or persistence) is an implicit memory effect such that exposure to a stimulus affects a response to a later stimulus. Recency has been shown to impact processing across linguistic levels from phonology to syntax (McDonough & Trofimovich, 2008).

Prototypicality of Function

In Prototype Theory (Rosch, Mervis, Gray, Johnson, & Boyes-Braem, 1976), the prototype of a category is defined as an idealized mental representation that unites the most representative features of that category. Other exemplars are judged as more or less central members of a category compared to the prototype. To use the by now classic example, sparrows are good examples of the category BIRD because they incorporate various representative attributes (they are average in size, beak size, color, etc.). For instance, people are fast to confirm that sparrows are birds (Posner & Keele, 1970) because sparrows have many attributes that we associate with birds as a category; conversely, people are slower to confirm that albatrosses are birds.

Prototypicality can be correlated with token frequency in that high token frequencies often form the prototypes of categories. Goldberg et al. (2004) provided corpus-based evidence that in L1 acquisition, children's first uses of verbs in verb-argument constructions tend to be highly frequent, semantically typical generic types that encapsulate the central meaning of the construction (*go* for verb-locative, *put* for verb-object-locative, and *give* for the ditransitive construction).

Ellis and Ferreira-Junior (2009a) found highly similar results for L2 learners (see also Divjak & Arppe, 2013).

At the same time, prototypicality and frequency should not be equated; instead, prototypicality arises from a variety of different factors, including frequency, none of which are sufficient in isolation (Taylor, 2015). Evidence comes from corpus studies by Deignan and Potter (2004) and Hilpert (2006), who show that while figurative uses of words for body parts (*eye*, *head*, and *heart*) are often at least as frequent as their literal uses, we cannot conclude that the figurative uses form the prototypes of these categories.

In summary, we know that all these input properties conspire in the second language acquisition process. However, we are only beginning to understand exactly when and how they affect and shape L2 development across learners with different L1 backgrounds, in different learning contexts, and at different stages of proficiency.

The Role of Formulaic Language in Second Language Learning

The definition of constructions outlined above enables us to view formulaic sequences as constructions as well; they are complex (i.e., multi-morphemic) constructions that vary on the schematization continuum from fully to partially lexically specified. In other words, formulaic sequences are right at the heart of the constructicon, which seems an adequate reflection of the fact that a significant portion of language is formulaic in nature; in spoken language, Biber, Johansson, Leech, Conrad, and Finegan (1999) estimate the share to be as high as 28%. Consequently, much of the corpus-based research in SLA has focused on formulaic language and its role in L2 development (on the crucial role of formulaic constructions in L1 acquisition, see Lieven, 2014).

Early research focused on if and to what extent children acquire larger chunks of language in initial stages of L2 learning that they subsequently decompose, in contrast to the traditional assumption that learning proceeds from simple morphemes to larger grammatical structures (see Krashen & Scarcella, 1978 for an overview). For early L2 learners, several studies presented evidence in favor of concurrent formula-based and bottom-up learning (Hatch, 1972; Hakuta, 1976; Wong-Fillmore, 1976).

As far as late learners are concerned, in contrast, research is much more divided as to how heavily formulaic language weighs into the acquisition process (see Wray, 2002, pp. 172–198 for a detailed overview). While adult L2 learners were shown to have knowledge of formulaic language at advanced stages of proficiency, grammatical development, especially at earlier stages, seems to hinge less on prefabricated language compared to child L2 learners (Schumann, 1978; Ellis, 1984). Krashen and Scarcella (1978) even questioned adult learners' ability to merely retain prefabricated routines and advised against teaching them: "The outside world for adults is nowhere near as predictable as the linguistic environment around Fillmore's children was" (Krashen & Scarcella, 1978, p. 298).

More recent research adds more nuance, suggesting that while formulaic language indeed appears to matter less in early stages of late L2 acquisition, it gains relevance in later stages of L2 development (Eskildsen & Cadierno, 2007; Myles, 2004).

A similar picture emerged in Mellow's (2008) longitudinal case study of a Spanish learner of English, who initially used complex constructions only with a limited number of verbs before expanding the repertoire of verbs to combine with these complex constructions.

The conservative behavior of L2 learners of restricting the use of complex constructions to a sub-set of verbs was also observed by Sugaya and Shirai (2009), who observed that lower proficiency learners of Japanese restricted the Japanese aspect markers to specific verbs before applying the aspect markers more productively across the full range of verbs. Sugaya and Shirai suggested that memory-based and rule-based processes co-exist at least for particular linguistic forms and that linguistic knowledge should thus be seen as a formulaic-creative continuum (see Bolinger, 1976).

Other research findings, however, point out that formulaic sequences do not necessarily pre-date productive applications of rules, even in verb-centered constructions. For example, Bardovi-Harlig (2002) examined the development of future expression involving *will* and *going to* in a longitudinal study of 16 adult L2 English learners. She found that 11 learners used *going to* productively with a range of verbs from the beginning; moreover, future *will* was not tied to any formulaic combinations in any learner's development. Eskildsen (2009) also cautions that formulaic sequences are highly task- and discourse-dependent.

Another strand of research that informs our understanding of the role of formulaic language in SLA involves computational simulation. McCauley and Christiansen (2017), for instance, applied a chunk-based learning model to L1 data from 7 children in the CHILDES corpus and L2 data from 7 learners the ESF corpus (matched by utterance lengths); their findings suggest that formulaic language plays a comparatively modest role in L2 learning because adults learn fewer useful chunks, rely on them less, and arrive at them through different means than children acquiring their first language do (see also Arnon, McCauley & Christiansen, 2017).

In summary, formulaic sequences that are frequent and semantically transparent can serve as points of departure at intermediate stages of language development, especially when they are useful in a particular discourse situation or task. In contrast, less frequent and idiomatic formulaic sequences constitute targets in ultimate attainment stages that even advanced learners may never fully reach (Erman, Forsberg Lundell & Lewis, 2016). To disentangle effects of age, proficiency level, and task demands (among other contributing factors) in the L1 and L2 acquisition of formulaic language, more, more varied, and more longitudinal corpora will be needed. The majority of available learner corpus data capture college-age learners at intermediate-advanced stages of L2 proficiency. In order to examine if and to what extent the age at which learners started learning their L2 plays any role, corpora would need to comprise data from learners with varying starting ages of acquisition. In order to examine the (potentially differential) role that formulaic language plays at earlier or later stages of acquisition (and to see to what extent there may be an interaction between such developmental stages and how they unfold as a function of the learners' age of acquisition), it would be necessary to have access to a longitudinal corpus that captures learners' development from initial stages of learning throughout their most proficient stages. Furthermore, most available corpora to date capture a limited set of genres and registers, typically academic speech and writing; more comprehensive coverage of different text types and discourse situations would be required to gain a more representative picture of how formulaic language develops in a learners' repertoire at large.

Main Research Methods

Strictly speaking, any corpus-linguistic method is applicable to the study of SLA from a usage-based perspective, yet some methods have been applied more prominently than others, including qualitative and quantitative analyses of concordances, frequency lists, and collocation displays of learner productions, qualitative error analyses, and quantitative analyses of over-and underuse, to give a few typical examples. At the same time, the number of studies in learner corpus research that employ methodologies directly inspired by usage-based theory is much smaller. In the next section, I will focus on two corpus-linguistic methods that have been or are being developed to implement usage-based assumptions about language learning, processing, and representation: collostructional analysis as a usage-based extension of collocation analysis and MuPDAR(F) (for multifactorial prediction and deviation analysis using regression/random forests), a usage-based extension of traditional analyses of over- and underuse.

Collostructional Analysis (CA)

Maybe the most widely used corpus-linguistic method inspired by usage-based assumptions in SLA research is collostructional analysis (CA), originally outlined by Stefanowitsch and Gries (Stefanowitsch & Gries, 2003). CA extends the well-established corpus-linguistic notion of collocations – two words that occur more often in the vicinity of each other than expected by chance – to constructions as defined above. That is, CA can be applied to identify significant associations not only between two words, but between any two constructions such as, say, a word and a morpheme ending, or a word and the larger syntactic frame it is embedded in. Since its inception, the CA family has been expanded to include multiple extensions such as distinctive collexeme analysis, which is specifically designed to identify the collocates in two or more competing constructions to identify subtle differences between them and co-varying collexeme analysis, which allows researchers to identify the co-dependency of two constructions in larger constructions (Gries & Stefanowitsch, 2004a, 2004b). As Wulff and Gries (2011) point out, CA can also be applied as a measure of L2 accuracy: "Collostructional analysis is a technical operationalization of accuracy when defined as native-like selection, asking: what is the likelihood of a construction X in the environment of another construction Y?" (p. 71). Correspondingly, researchers have applied CA to compare native and non-native speaker use of phenomena like causative constructions (Gilquin, 2012), complementation choice (Martinez-Garcia, Maria & Wulff, 2012), or intensifying constructions (Hendrikx, van Goethem & Wulff, 2019).

For one example, Gries and Wulff (2009) employed collostructional analysis to identify the most distinctive verbs in gerundial and infinitival complement constructions. To that end, four frequencies had to be determined:

- the frequency of the verb with gerundial complement constructions;
- the frequency of the verb with infinitival complement constructions;
- the frequency of the gerundial complement construction;
- the frequency of the infinitival complement construction.

On the basis of these four frequencies, one can calculate an association measure such as a Fisher Yates Exact test or a DeltaP association statistic to express the degree of association between a verb and either construction; a script like coll.analysis 3.2 (Gries, 2007) allows batch processing.

To give an example of an SLA research study employing collostructional analysis, Gries and Wulff (2009) determined the distinctive verbs for both complement constructions this way: *start*, *stop*, and *avoid* are examples of verbs distinctively associated with the gerundial complement construction; *try*, *manage*, and *attempt* are significantly biased towards the infinitival construction instead. Gries and Wulff selected a number of distinctive verbs as stimuli in a sentence completion and acceptability rating task administered to advanced German learners of English to see if they would be sensitive to verb-specific constructional preferences as previously shown for double object constructions (Gries & Wulff, 2005). Their results suggest that advanced learners are in fact aware of the differential, and differently strong, constructional biases that individual verbs display in native speaker production data. This lends further credence to the assumption in UBL that learners pick up on pattern distributions in the input.

MuPDAR(F)

One of the basic tenets of usage-based approaches is that language is a complex system (Beckner et al., 2009). Linguistic choices at every level, from syntax to phonology, typically involve a number of factors that jointly shape the final outcome. These factors can be internal to the language, but also depend upon language-external factors like perceptual and other cognitive mechanics and social motivations. Correspondingly, the methods required to adequately operationalize, describe, measure, and predict language must allow for complexity: if one has reason to assume, for example, that a speaker's choice of a particular structure is shaped by at least three different factors, then only an analysis that includes all three factors, as well as possible interactions between them, promises to yield meaningful results. Correspondingly, Gries (2015) writes that "the recognition that corpus-linguistic statistics has to go multifactorial is maybe the most important recommendation for the field's future development" (p. 64). The same rationale extends to corpus-based studies in SLA, irrespective of the particular theoretical lens adopted (Paquot & Plonsky, 2017).

Responding to his own call, Gries and colleagues proposed a multifactorial method that is tailored to research on learners and indigenized varieties called MuPDAR(F) (for multifactorial prediction and deviation analysis using regression/random forests) (Gries & Adelman, 2014; Gries & Deshors, 2014; see also Chapter 9, this volume). The method allows for a systematic and context-sensitive (that is, multifactorially described) comparison of choices made by a target group (such as language learners) and a reference level group (such as monolingual speakers of the second language, or any other speaker group deemed meaningful for comparison, such as bilingual speakers, advanced learners, etc.). MuPDAR(F) comprises three steps:

- fitting a regression/random forest $R(F)_1$ that predicts the choices that speakers of the reference level make with regard to the phenomenon in question;
- applying the results of $R(F)_1$ to the target speakers in the data to predict, for each attestation, what a reference group speaker would have done in their place (i.e., given the same contextual features of the attestation);
- fitting a regression/random forest $R(F)_2$ that explores how the target speakers' choices differ from those of the reference group speakers; predictors that turn out to be significant in this regression are the ones that help understand where, and to what extent, the choices made by target and reference group speaker differ from each other.

In SLA, MuPDAR(F) has been applied to various phenomena comparing non-native and native speakers, including subject drop in Japanese (Gries & Adelman, 2014), adjective order in English (Wulff & Gries, 2015), and verb complementation in English (Wulff, Gries & Lester, 2018). To give but a cursory impression of the kinds of results that MuPDAR(F) yields, let us take a look at a few results from a recent study that compared English native speakers' choices between *s*-genitives (*the squirrel's nest*) and *of*-genitives (*the nest of the squirrel*) with those of Chinese and German L2 learners of English (Wulff & Gries, in press). By including the L1 background of the speakers as well as a predictor, representing each speaker as a random effect, and allowing all predictors to interact with each other (see the above references for further description of, and rationale for, and technical details of the method), MuPDAR(F) enables us to look at differences between the native speakers and the learners at various levels of resolution. For example, we can consider differences between different learner groups, here the Chinese and German learners of English. One result showed that the complexity of the noun phrase denoting the possessor affects the two learner groups differently; when the possessor is complex, both learner groups make more native-like choices. However, when the possessor is simple, the Chinese learners make fewer nativelike choices than the German learners such that they tend to underuse the *s*-genitive. (3) and (4) are examples from the data.

(3) … the recycling industry is mainly driven by the awareness and the choice **of** consumers. [Chinese learner]
(4) They claim that public construction increases the expensing **of** the government [Chinese learner]

Acknowledging that individual variation is the default expectation across phenomena and should thus be carefully measured (see Wulff & Gries, to appear), MuPDAR(F) can also drill down to individual learners. For example, we looked at 10 speakers with the highest error rates in more detail. Figure 13.1 plots the learners' genitive choices (as dots) and means of choices (as ×) against what we refer to as Deviation values, which quantify the degree to which the learners' choices deviate from those of native speakers, with values falling below 0 indicating that they chose an *of*-genitive where a native speaker would have picked an *s*-genitive, and vice versa for values higher than 0. The larger the Deviation value in absolute terms, the stronger the deviation.

We can identify at a glance individual learners' overuse the *of*-genitive (a number of the German learners on top of the plot), whereas other learners (the Chinese learners at the bottom of the plot) overused the *s*-genitive. So, at the finest level of resolution, MuPDAR(F) can provide valuable pointers for subsequent qualitative follow-up analysis to better understand the underlying reasons why learners make fewer nativelike choices in specific contexts.

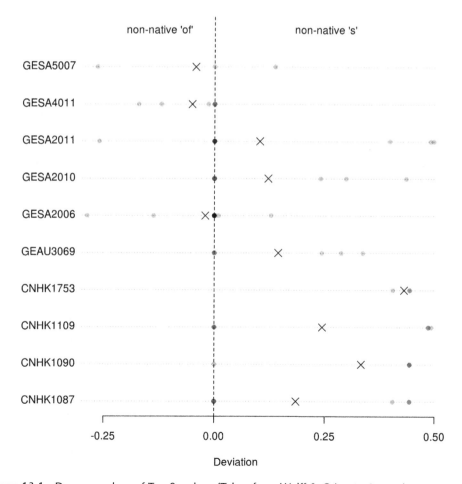

Figure 13.1 Deviation-values of Ten Speakers (Taken from Wulff & Gries, to Appear)

Representative Corpora and Research

Given limited space, I will briefly describe two learner corpora that have been, or promise to be, widely used in SLA research, alongside pointing to one study based on the corpus that adopted a usage-based approach specifically. For a wider list of learner corpora, visit the web page maintained by the Centre for English Corpus Linguistics at the Catholic University of Louvain: https://uclouvain.be/en/research-institutes/ilc/cecl/learner-corpora-around-the-world.html

The ESF (European Science Foundation Second Language) Database is a corpus compiled by research teams in France, Germany, Great Britain, The Netherlands, and Sweden (Feldweg, 1991; Perdue, 1993). The corpus contains data from forty adult immigrant workers (speaking Arabic, Finnish, Italian, Punjabi, Spanish, and Turkish as their L1) living in these countries in conversation with native speakers. Data was collected over 5½ years preceded by a one-year pilot study and included solicitation through different tasks like free conversation, interviews, retell tasks, role play, route descriptions, stage descriptions, and vocabulary elicitation. For each target language, speakers with two different L1 backgrounds were recorded to allow systematic comparison of L1 influences on second language acquisition; Figure 13.2 provides an overview of the language pairings.

Ellis and Ferreira-Junior (2009b) is an example of a study based on the ESF Database through a usage-based lens. Examining the type/token distributions in verb-argument constructions produced by the seven learners captured in 234 sessions in the ESF corpus with English as their L2, they demonstrate that naturalistic L2 learning of these constructions is affected by the frequency distribution of specific exemplars in each construction, as well as by their prototypicality and contingency.

A new addition to learner corpora is the *Trinity Lancaster Corpus*, which consists of transcribed recordings from the General Examinations of Spoken English (GESE) developed and delivered by Trinity College London, a major international examination board. The corpus includes transcribed interactions between candidates from China, India, Italy, Mexico, Russia, and Spain with examiners from B1 to C2 level of the Common European Framework of Reference (CEFR). Each candidate participated in two to four different speaking tasks (Gablasova, Brezina, McEnery & Boyd, 2017).

Römer and Garner (2019) investigated how verb-argument constructions (VACs) emerge in spoken language across the different proficiency levels in a 2-million-word subset of the corpus. Recruiting entropy measures, correlation analyses, and regression analysis, they show that, across L1 backgrounds, more proficient learners are more productive in their VAC use and closer to the L1 usage norm than less proficient learners.

Future Directions

Addressing current questions in usage-based approaches to SLA using corpus linguistics crucially hinges on the availability of the "right" kind of corpus data. For one, given that UBL is committed to providing an account of language acquisition, processing, and use that stands in accord with what we know about cognition in general (the *Cognitive Commitment*; see Evans, Bergen & Zinken, 2007), it is crucial that corpus data be complemented by as much information as possible about the overall cognitive profile of the speakers captured therein. Ideally, learner

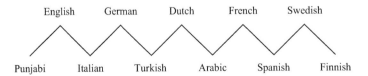

Figure 13.2 First (Bottom Row) and Second (Top Row) Language Pairings in the ESF Database.

corpora would include, for each learner, a rich battery of cognitive measures known to impact learning (working memory, executive control, aptitude, etc.) as well as information about the learner's affect (their attitudes towards learning, their level of desire to learn another language, etc.) and their socio-economic background.

An inevitable outcome of the complex network of language-internal and -external factors shaping language acquisition is that language use (comprehension, production, and acquisition alike) is a highly individualized endeavor, with lots of variation occurring between learners. Research in one usage-based framework in particular, namely Complex Dynamic Systems Theory (see Chapter 14, this volume), reveals that no learners behave identically, and learning trajectories are typically non-linear, with dips and spikes emerging before a learner reaches a more robust performance plateau. In order to track and model these individual learning curves more adequately, longitudinal corpora are needed, that is, corpora that capture the entire developmental curve of a set of learners from initial stages to ultimate attainment and not just intermediate-advanced levels like most publicly available corpora. A similar argument can be made for the development of corpora that do not only contain foreign language learners, but also learners who are acquiring a language immersively, as well as learners who speak their two or more languages with varying degrees of L1 or L2 dominance, as all these differences can be assumed to impact learning trajectories.

As these types of corpora hopefully become available, corpus linguists will have to expand their methodological tool box accordingly. As Plonsky and Gass (2011) point out, "progress in any of the [...] sciences depends on sound research methods, principled data analysis, and transparent reporting practices" (p. 325). The more complexity corpus data will offer, the more important it becomes to employ adequate statistical analyses to fully reap the benefits of the richness of the data and to present meaningful results. Paquot and Plonsky's (2017) meta-analysis of learner corpus research suggests that there is considerable room for improvement in the methodological expertise presented in learner corpus research.

To add a final desideratum for future research, just as much as researchers need to be competent in *how* to properly analyze data, they should be held accountable for *what* they claim to be testing in the first place. The richest data and most sophisticated statistics present but an offering to the theoretically informed researcher to interpret them in meaningful ways. This requires a deep understanding of a theoretical viewpoint, a succinct grasp of what predictions fall out from that theory, and a profound respect for how to operationalize concepts in ways that are true to their theoretical definitions. This is often not the case. I gave the example above of overly simplistic definitions of frequency effects in UBL and how they play out across different stages of language development, which can result in premature rejection of this concept. Another common misrepresentation of usage-based claims is that *everything* is assumed to be acquirable from the input without recruitment of cognitive machinery of any kind; this can result in overgeneralizations of what we can glean from corpus data alone. A third misunderstanding is that first and second learning are regarded as identical in terms of processes and attainment, which has led to the vast majority of studies in learner corpus research – and I am including my own research here – comparing learner data against monolingual speaker data, which wrongly implies that the end point of L2 acquisition is isomorphic to monolingualism. If and only if data and their analysis reflect theory adequately, empirical research can finesse and, at times even radically change, our theoretical understanding of language (acquisition). I am optimistic that usage-based corpus linguists are well on their way.

Further Reading

Ellis, N. C. (2017). Cognition, corpora, and computing: triangulating research in usage-based language learning. *Language Learning*, 76(1), 40–65.

This article surveys recent developments in psychology, acquisition research, psycholinguistics, corpus linguistics, and computational linguistics and discusses current issues such as the proper analysis of input distributions, longitudinal research, and computational approaches to complexity.

Gries, S. Th. (2018). Operationalizations of domain-general mechanisms cognitive linguists often rely on: A perspective from quantitative corpus linguistics. In S. Engelberg, H. Lobin, K. Steyer, & S. Wolfer (Eds.), *Wortschätze: Dynamik, Muster, Komplexität* (pp. 75–90). Berlin: De Gruyter.

Gries discusses corpus-linguistic operationalizations of four cognitive mechanisms (frequency, contingency, context, and recency) that are frequently used in usage-based studies of the constructicon.

Related Topics

Chapters 14 and 20.

References

Anderson, J. R., & Schooler, L. J. (2000). The adaptive nature of memory. In E. Tulving & F. I. M. Craik (Eds.), *The Oxford handbook of memory* (pp. 557–570). London: Oxford University Press.

Arnon, I., McCauley, S. M., & Christiansen, M. H. (2017). Digging up the building blocks of language: Age-of-acquisition effects for multi-word phrases. *Journal of Memory and Language, 92,* 265–280.

Bardovi-Harlig, K. (2002). A new starting point? *Studies in Second Language Acquisition, 24*(2), 189–198.

Beckner, C., Ellis, N. C., Blythe, R., Holland, J., Bybee, J., Ke, J., … Schoenemann, T. (2009). Language is a complex adaptive system: Position paper. *Language Learning, 59*(1), 1–26.

Biber, D., Johansson, S., Leech, G., Conrad, S., & Finegan, E. (1999). *Longman grammar of spoken and written English.* Harlow: Longman.

Bolinger, D. (1976). Memory and meaning. *Forum Linguisticum, 41*(1), 1–14.

Bybee, J. (2006). *Frequency of use and the organization of language.* Oxford: Oxford University Press.

Bybee, J., & Hopper, P. (Eds.) (2001). *Frequency and the emergence of linguistic structure.* Amsterdam: John Benjamins.

de Bot, K., Lowie, W., & Verspoor, M. (2007). A dynamic system theory approach to second language acquisition. *Bilingualism: Language and Cognition, 10*(1), 7–21.

Deignan, A., & Potter, L. (2004). A corpus study of metaphors and metonyms in English and Italian. *Journal of Pragmatics, 36*(7), 1231–1252.

Divjak, D., & Arppe, A. (2013). Extracting prototypes from exemplars: What can corpus data tell us about concept representation? *Cognitive Linguistics, 24*(2), 221–274.

Divjak, D., & Caldwell-Harris, C. L. (2015). Frequency and entrenchment. In E. Dabrowska & D. Divjak (Eds.), *Handbook of cognitive linguistics* (pp. 53–74). Berlin: De Gruyter mouton.

Ellis, N. C., & Ferreira-Junior, F. (2009a). Construction learning as a function of frequency, frequency distribution, and function. *Modern Language Journal, 93*(3), 370–386.

Ellis, N. C., & Ferreira-Junior, F. (2009b). Constructions and their acquisition: Islands and the distinctiveness of their occupancy. *Annual Review of Cognitive Linguistics, 7*(1), 188–221.

Ellis, N. C., & Wulff, S. (2020). Usage-based approaches in second language acquisition. In B. VanPatten, G. Keating, & S. Wulff (Eds.), *Theories in second language acquisition: An introduction* (pp. 63–82). London: Routledge.

Ellis, R. (1984). *Classroom second language development.* Oxford: Pergamon Press.

Erman, B., Forsberg Lundell, F., & Lewis, M. (2016). Formulaic language in advanced second language acquisition and use. In K. Hyltenstam (Ed.), *Advanced proficiency and exceptional ability in second languages* (pp. 111–148). Boston: Walter de Gruyter.

Eskildsen, S. W. (2009). Constructing another language – usage-based linguistics in second language acquisition. *Applied Linguistics, 30*(3), 335–357.

Eskildsen, S. W., & Cadierno, T. (2007). Are recurring multi-word expressions really syntactic freezes? Second language acquisition from the perspective of usage-based linguistics. In M. Nenonen & S. Niemi (Eds.), *Collocations and idioms 1: Papers from the first Nordic conference on syntactic freezes* (pp. 86–99). Joensuu: Joensuu University Press.

Evans, V., Bergen, B. K., & Zinken, J. (Eds.) (2007). *The cognitive linguistics reader.* London: Equinox Publishing.

Feldweg, H. (1991). *The European science foundation second language database.* Nijmegen: Max-planck-Institute for Psycholinguistics.

Gablasova, D., Brezina, V., McEnery, T., & Boyd, E. (2017). Epistemic stance in spoken L2 English: The effect of task and speaker style. *Applied Linguistics*, *38*(5), 613–637.

Gilquin, G. (2012). Lexical infelicity in English causative constructions: Comparing learner and native collostructions. In J. Leino & R. van der Waldenfels (Eds.), *Analytical causatives: From 'give' and 'come' to 'let' and 'make'* (pp. 41–63). Munich: Lincom Europa.

Goldberg, A. E. (2006). *Constructions at work: The nature of generalization in language*. Oxford: Oxford University Press.

Goldberg, A. E., Casenhiser, D. M., & Sethuraman, N. (2004). Learning argument structure constructions. *Cognitive Linguistics*, *15*(3), 289–316.

Gries, S. Th. (2007). *Coll.analysis 3.2a*. A program for *R* for Windows 2.x.

Gries, S. Th. (2015). Quantitative designs and statistical techniques. In D. Biber & R. Reppen (Eds.), *The Cambridge handbook of English corpus linguistics* (pp. 50–71). Cambridge: Cambridge University Press.

Gries, S. Th. (2018). Operationalizations of domain-general mechanisms cognitive linguists often rely on: A perspective from quantitative corpus linguistics. In S. Engelberg, H. Lobin, K. Steyer, & S. Wolfer (Eds.), *Wortschätze: Dynamik, Muster, Komplexität* (pp. 75–90). Berlin: De Gruyter.

Gries, S. Th., & Adelman, A. S. (2014). Subject realization in Japanese conversation by native and non-native speakers: Exemplifying a new paradigm for learner corpus research. In J. Romero-Trillo (Ed.), *Yearbook of corpus linguistics and pragmatics 2014: New empirical and theoretical paradigms* (pp. 35–54). Cham: Springer.

Gries, S. Th., & Deshors, S. C. (2014). Using regressions to explore deviations between corpus data and a standard/target: Two suggestions. *Corpora*, *9*(1), 109–136.

Gries, S. Th., & Stefanowitsch, A. (2004a). Extending collostructional analysis: A corpus-based perspectives on 'alternations'. *International Journal of Corpus Linguistics*, *9*(1), 97–129.

Gries, S. Th., & Stefanowitsch, A. (2004b). Co-varying collexemes in the into-causative. In M. Achard & S. Kemmer (Eds.), *Language, culture, and mind* (pp. 225–236). Stanford: CSLI.

Gries, S. Th., & Wulff, S. (2005). Do foreign language learners also have constructions? Evidence from priming, sorting, and corpora. *Annual Review of Cognitive Linguistics*, *3*(1), 182–200.

Gries, S. Th., & Wulff, S. (2009). Psycholinguistic and corpus linguistic evidence for L2 constructions. *Annual Review of Cognitive Linguistics*, *7*(1), 163–186.

Hakuta, K. (1976). A case study of a Japanese child learning. *English. Language Learning*, *26*(2), 321–351.

Hatch, E. (1972). Some studies in language learning. *UCLA Workpapers in Teaching English as a Second Language*, *6*, 29–36.

Hendrikx, I., van Goethem, K., & Wulff, S. (2019). Intensifying constructions in French-speaking L2 learners of English and Dutch: Cross-linguistic influence and exposure effects. *International Journal of Learner Corpus Research*, *5*(1), 63–103.

Hilpert, M. (2006). Keeping an eye on the data: Metonymies and their patterns. In A. Stefanowitsch & S. Th. Gries (Eds.), *Corpus-based approaches to metaphor and metonymy* (pp. 123–152). Berlin: Mouton de Gruyter.

Krashen, S., & Scarcella, R. C. (1978). On routines and patterns in language acquisition and performance. *Language Learning*, *28*(2), 283–300.

Lieven, E. (2014). First language development: A usage-based perspective on past and current research. *Journal of Child Language*, *41*(Suppl.1), 48–63.

MacWhinney, B. (1987). Applying the competition model to bilingualism. *Applied Psycholinguistics*, *8*(4), 315–327.

Martinez-Garcia, Maria T., & Wulff, S. (2012). Not wrong, yet not quite right: Spanish ESL students' use of gerundial and infinitival complementation. *International Journal of Applied Linguistics*, *22*(2), 225–244.

McCauley, S. M., & Christiansen, M. H. (2017). Computational investigations of multiword chunks in language learning. *Topics in Cognitive Science*, *9*(3), 637–652.

McDonough, K., & Trofimovich, P. (2008). *Using priming methods in second language research*. London: Routledge.

Mellow, J. D. (2008). The emergence of complex syntax: A longitudinal case study of the ESL development of dependency resolution. *Lingua*, *118*(4), 499–521.

Myles, F. (2004). From data to theory: The over-representation of linguistic knowledge in SLA. *Transactions of the Philological Society*, *102*(2), 139–168.

Paquot, M., & Plonsky, L. (2017). Quantitative research methods and study quality in learner corpus research. *International Journal of Learner Corpus Research*, *3*(1), 61–94.

Perdue, C. (Ed.) (1993). *Adult language acquisition: Crosslinguistic perspectives*. Cambridge: Cambridge University Press

Plonsky, L., & Gass, S. (2011). Quantitative research methods, study quality, and outcomes: The case of interaction research. *Language Learning*, *61*(2), 325–366.

Posner, M. I., & Keele, S. W. (1970). Retention of abstract ideas. *Journal of Experimental Psychology*, *83*(2 Pt.1), 304–308.

Römer, U., & Garner, J. R. (2019). The emergence of verb constructions in spoken learner English: Tracing effects of usage and proficiency. *International Journal of Learner Corpus Research*, *5*(2), 207–230.

Rosch, E., Mervis, C. B., Gray, W. D., Johnson, D. M., & Boyes-Braem, P. (1976). Basic objects in natural categories. *Cognitive Psychology*, *8*(3), 382–439.

Rothman, J., & Slabakova, R. (2018). The generative approach to SLA and its place in modern second language studies. *Studies in Second Language Acquisition*, *40*(2), 417–442.

Schmitt, N. (Ed.) (2004). *Formulaic sequences: Acquisition, processing, and use*. Amsterdam: John Benjamins.

Schönefeld, D. (1999). Corpus linguistics and cognitivism. *International Journal of Corpus Linguistics*, *4*(1), 137–171.

Schumann, J. H. (1978). Second language acquisition: The pidginization hypothesis. In E. M. Hatch (Ed.), *Second language acquisition: A book of readings* (pp. 256–271). Rowley: Newbury House.

Schütze, C. T. (2016/1996). *The empirical base of linguistics: Grammaticality judgments and linguistic methodology*. Berlin: Language Science Press.

Stefanowitsch, A., & Gries, S. Th. (2003). Collostructions: Investigating the interaction between words and constructions. *International Journal of Corpus Linguistics*, *8*(2), 209–243.

Sugaya, N., & Shirai, Y. (2009). Can L2 learners productively use Japanese tense-aspect markers? A usage-based approach. In R. Corrigan, E. A. Moravcsik, H. Ouali, & K. M. Wheatley (Eds.), *Formulaic language*, *2. Acquisition, loss, psychological reality, functional applications* (pp. 423–444). Amsterdam: John Benjamins.

Taylor, J. R. (2015). Prototype effects in grammar. In E. Dabrowksa & D. Divjak (Eds.), *Handbook of cognitive linguistics* (pp. 562–579). Berlin: Walter de Gruyter.

Tomasello, M. (2003). *Constructing a language*. Boston: Harvard University Press.

Tummers, J., Heylen, K., & Geeraerts, D. (2005). Usage-based approaches in cognitive linguistics: A technical state of the art. *Corpus Linguistics and Linguistic Theory*, *1*(2), 225–261.

White, L. (2015). Linguistic theory, universal grammar, and second language acquisition. In B. VanPatten & J. Williams (Eds.), *Theories in second language acquisition: An introduction* (2nd ed., pp. 34–53). New York: Routledge.

Wong-Fillmore, L. (1976). *The second time around: Cognitive and social strategies in second language acquisition*. Doctoral Dissertation. Stanford University.

Wray, A. (2002). *Formulaic language and the lexicon*. Cambridge: Cambridge University Press.

Wulff, S., & Gries, S. Th. (2011). Corpus-driven methods for assessing accuracy in learner production. In P. Robinson (Ed.), *Second language task complexity: Researching the Cognition Hypothesis of language learning and performance* (pp. 61–87). Amsterdam: John Benjamins.

Wulff, S., & Gries, S. Th. (2015). Prenominal adjective order preferences in Chinese and German English. *Linguistic Approaches to Bilingualism*, *5*(1), 122–150.

Wulff, S., & Gries, S. Th. (in press). Exploring individual variation in learner corpus research: Some methodological suggestions. In B. S. W. LeBruyn & M. Paquot (Eds.), *Learner corpus research meets second language acquisition*. Cambridge: Cambridge University Press.

Wulff, S., Gries, S. Th., & Lester, N. (2018). Optional *that* in complementation by German and Spanish learners. In A. Tyler & C. Moder (Eds.), *What is applied cognitive linguistics? Answers from current SLA research* (pp. 99–120). New York: de Gruyter Mouton.

Zipf, G. K. (1935). *The psycho-biology of language: An introduction to dynamic philology*. Cambridge: MIT Press.

14

Complex Dynamic Systems Theory (CDST)

Marjolijn Verspoor and Wander Lowie

Introduction

In the field of Applied Linguistics (AL), the application of Complex Systems was first introduced in a seminal paper by Larsen-Freeman (1997), but it did not really catch on in the AL community until about 10 years later when de Bot, Lowie, and Verspoor (2007) published a paper on DST in a special issue of *Bilingualism: Language and Cognition*. Their main conclusion was that it was time to acknowledge the limits of traditional statistical methods used in SLA studies thus far:

> Most importantly, though, we should look at our data with a more open mind. Traditional statistics is meant to reveal how a group performs as a whole and may be useful to see the grand sweep of things, but if we really want to know what happens in the actual process of language acquisition we should also look at the messy little details, the first attempts, the degree of variation at a developmental stage, and the possible attrition. It is very well possible that if we look closely enough, we find that the general developmental stages that individuals go through are much less similar than we have assumed thus far.
>
> *(p. 19)*

Within the field of AL, the two terms Complex Systems and Dynamic Systems Theory are both used. They are compatible in that they view language or language learning as a complex dynamic system that varies and self-adapts through the interaction of subsystems, components, or sub-elements. The term Complexity and Dynamic Systems Theory (CDST) was proposed by de Bot (2017). Today, CDST has provided a powerful framework to study the developmental processes in second language (L2) learners showing that development is an individually owned process, which is not predictable and always non-linear.

Core Issues and Topics

In most SLA studies, especially corpus studies, the goal is to find measures or developmental patterns that may apply to most L2 learners. To find these developmental patterns, usually, group studies are conducted. However, as Lowie and Verspoor (2018) show, there is a problem with such a view because groups of humans are not *ergodic ensembles*. Ergodic ensembles are groups of individual elements that have predictable behavior, and humans are not entirely predictable in their behavior. For example, if we do a statistical analysis on a group of L2 learners in a pre-post test and find out that over the course of one year the learners have shown a significant increase in sentence length, this usually does not apply to all learners. In other words, a statistical analysis over the entire ensemble of people at a certain moment in time cannot be generalized to all individuals. And vice versa, one statistical analysis for one person over a certain period of time cannot be generalized to the group. An ensemble is ergodic only if the two types of statistics give the same result.

This means that although group studies can give us a great deal of information on general trends in L2 development, they cannot predict exactly what an individual learner may do at any particular moment in time and in what order. Therefore, if we are interested in the actual process of development, we need to complement group studies with individual case studies in which we investigate the changing relations in L2 learners over time.

The goal of CDST research in L2 language is thus to discover the actual process of development. It sees language development as a dynamic process in which various subsystems interact over time. The terms subsystems, components or elements, which can be used interchangeably, are very vague and undetermined and can be filled in depending on what the researcher is interested in studying. For example, in L2 development, the subsystems could refer to purely linguistic ones such as the types of constructions (e.g. syntactic subsystems) used by the learner or the use of words and phrases (e.g. lexical subsystems). However, they could also be operationalized as individual factors such as degrees of motivation, willingness to communicate, or anxiety. The basic characteristics of dynamic systems will be explained briefly below with examples pertaining to the field of L2 development.

When a system starts to develop, *initial conditions*, the conditions that are already in place, are very important for further development. Relevant initial conditions in L2 research could be the learner's L1, age (maturity), proficiency in the L2, knowledge of additional languages, aptitude, or motivation.

Iteration – the basic process in a dynamic system – is related to *emergence*. Through iterations of simple procedures that are applied over and over again with the output of the preceding iteration as the input of the next, complexity in language emerges. Because the interaction of subsystems can be different for each iteration, development is not predetermined, and the system is said to 'emerge'.

Complete interconnectedness is another key aspect of a complex dynamic system. This means that change in one element affects all other elements in the system. For example, we could say that the L2 learner's linguistic subsystem consists of lexical, syntactic, and morphological subsystems, which are interdependent. In other words, if one element changes, all other elements may be affected to different degrees. Moreover, the linguistic subsystem is connected to other subsystems such as the L2 learner's cognitive and emotional subsystems, which in turn interact with various external variables such as the amount of meaningful interaction in the L2.

Self-organization refers to the process of changing relationships of the elements in a subsystem over time. In language development, a good example of self-organization can be heard in Deb Roy's Ted-Talk (2011). We hear how his son acquires the word "water". If we listen carefully, we can hear how the little boy seems to get various aspects of the word (vowels, consonants, stress patterns) right separately and rather randomly. He also frequently regresses to non-adult forms (which would be considered variability in a CDST approach). Then at the end, he pronounces the word as one whole unit, in which all the subsystems have now *coordinated* through self-organization.

Because of iteration, the interconnectedness of all subsystems of a learner's L2, the various interactions of these elements with the environment over time, and self-organization, development is not a neat step-by-step predictable process, but *non-linear*. Some subsystems may need to develop before others can occur, and some subsystems may compete with each other for a while before they settle. Non-linearity can be seen in U-shaped behavior often noted in developmental studies. Learners sometimes may overdo things before they are mastered. Additionally, a learner whose L2 system is not stable yet may find elements competing; for example, when s/he is focusing on learning words, the syntax may not develop very much, but once there are enough words in place, the (unintentional) focus may go to the syntax rather than the lexicon. These processes cause *variability*, which means doing things right for a while and then all of a sudden incorrectly for a while until the competing systems settle more and begin to coordinate.

Within a CDST perspective, variability (here defined as intra-individual alternate behaviors) is seen as a prerequisite of development, and therefore, it takes a central role in the analyses of single variables. The reason is that learners are not assumed to have a pre-determined developmental path, but simply try out new strategies or modes of behavior that are not always successful and may therefore alternate with old strategies or modes of behavior. According to Thelen and Smith (1994), such variability occurs especially during periods of rapid development. However, studies have shown that such variability can also occur in very advanced learners who are trying to master academic genres. For example, Penris and Verspoor (2017) saw such a transition in average word length (which stands for lexical sophistication) towards the end of the 13-year data collection time of one learner. It is assumed that some level of variability is intrinsic and functional in all development as it permits flexible and adaptive behavior.

In development, various behaviors may first develop rather independently, then perhaps compete, and then eventually coalesce to create a coordinated new behavior. Van Geert (1991) calls these *precursor*, *competitive*, and *supportive* relations. For instance, investigating the development of syntax and vocabulary in L1 acquisition, he showed that the lexicon could be seen as a precursor, because syntactic development can only start once a minimal vocabulary size has been attained. Over time, the interaction between lexicon and syntax may compete, as the rate at which words are learned decreases when the child starts to make longer utterances. Then the behaviors are no longer developing somewhat independently but coordinate in a supportive relationship.

In summary, the main goal of CDST inspired research is to explore individual learners' trajectories to discover to what extent variability and interacting variables play a role in the emergence of new forms and self-organization of the linguistic system.

Main Research Methods

The methods described in this chapter pertain mostly to written or transcribed texts, as there are few longitudinal spoken texts available. The methods can also be found in a book dedicated to this topic with actual how-to sections (Verspoor, de Bot & Lowie, 2011), which detail most of the methods.

Data Collection

The data needed for a longitudinal study from a CDST perspective are determined by the length of time over which a change will take place and the rate at which one expects this to happen. For example, Deb Roy's example of the birth of a word (water) was based on samples during one whole year, so he was able to trace almost every single sound the child uttered, and his corpus was therefore as dense as it could be. Such dense corpora would be ideal to have in any developmental study, but they are hardly possible in L2 development, especially for older learners. Still, as far as length of study is concerned, we need a time span that is long enough to discover the changes that we want to focus on. For example, if we want to see how absolute beginners develop their L2 to an intermediate level, we probably need at least one academic year of data. If we want to trace how a highly proficient learner may develop his/her academic writing ability (including such matters as achieving coherence and cohesion) we may even need three years.

In addition, the frequency of data collection (density) is important. If we want to see detailed changes, we need to have as many data points as possible, especially with beginners, as they are assumedly more variable and will change rapidly (cf. Verspoor, Schmid & Xu, 2012). From the studies published so far, we have learned that about 12 data points per academic year is the minimum needed to discover any dynamic pattern, but weekly or bi-weekly data points are preferred. To avoid variability due to task effects, it would be good to keep task assignments in the same genre and similar conditions. Schoonen (2005) points out that task effects are usually less noticeable in scoring variance if we look at language use rather than content. However, task effects can never be excluded and are accepted as one of the many factors contributing to variability. Because data collection and coding are very intensive (see next section) as each individual's variables are traced over time, it is not always practical to observe large groups. In our own work, we have often relied on students who had saved their writings over the course of their studies (Penris & Verspoor, 2017; Verspoor, Lowie, Chan, & Vahtrick, 2017), and we selected writings that met specific criteria (e.g. academic genre). We have also asked teachers to collect writings in high school (Verspoor et al., 2012; Lowie & Verspoor, 2018). Vyatkina (2012) collected the writings of her own students at college level and Murakami (2013) used a huge learner corpus including texts written by the same individuals over time.

Coding the Data

A text can be coded for whatever variables are of interest depending on the research question. For example, Cancino, Rosansky, Schumann, and Hatch (1978) explored how six L1 Spanish learners of different ages, residing in the US, developed in their L2 English negated verb phrases. They coded for four categories, in line with what L1 learners do: no constructions, don't constructions, constructions with auxiliaries, and constructions with the fully conjugated do (cf. Van Dijk, Verspoor, & Lowie, 2011). Many other studies thus far have traced the development of different complexity, accuracy, and fluency (CAF) measures. From studies like Bulté and Housen (2018) and Verspoor et al. (2012), we have also learned that broad measures that average out over many instances, like average sentence length, a type-token ratio such as the Guiraud, the total number of errors, and so on, usually correlate best with holistic scores as they occur frequently enough. Isolated items such as chunks (formulaic sequences) are more difficult to trace in detail as they tend to be idiosyncratic. However, as Gustafson-Smiskova and Verspoor (2018) and Hou, Loerts, and Verspoor (2016) have shown, a chunk coverage measure (total number of words found in chunks divided by the total number of words in the text) has also shown to be a useful overall measure that can be traced. Other variables that can be measured over time is how authorial voice (Zhao, 2013) or coherence and cohesion develop. These are very interesting measures to trace, but they develop rather slowly, so the data needs to span a relatively long time and is also very dependent on the type of task, as lack of knowledge of a given topic may compete with achieving coherence.

One developmental measure of general L2 proficiency that has proven to be quite robust in our studies has been holistic scores, obtained with trained raters (Schoonen, 2005). Using human judges, a text can be rated not only on linguistic sophistication in terms of complexity, accuracy, and fluency measures, but also on idiomaticity, coherence, and functional adequacy (Kuiken & Vedder, 2017). As in CDST studies we are trying to see small changes over time, general rubrics as in the CEFR are usually too broad. For holistic rating it is therefore better to use a ranking system, preferably starting with 10 randomly chosen writings and ranking them relative to each other. Another set of 10 should be done in a similar way until all raters agree on what constitutes a weaker and stronger writing sample. Depending on the range of proficiency levels, scores of 1 can be assigned to the weakest and 5 or higher to the strongest writings. The texts in these first samples then serve as benchmarks for the other texts, and general rubrics may be written to help rate the remainder of the texts (cf. Verspoor et al., 2012).

Many developmental measures can be counted automatically with various computer tools (see www.linguisticanalysistools.org). The advantage of automated counts is that they are fast, consistent, and objective, but at the same time, they are limited in what they can do, especially in terms of overall proficiency gains, formulaic sequences, or accuracy measures. As research in CDST often involves a limited number of participants and covers a relatively long period of time, the data can be annotated using a combination of automatic and manual coding, which is useful in that the researcher may observe interesting phenomena that an automated tool will not identify.

Analyzing the Data

To be able to explain how the analyses are usually done, we will discuss learners from our most recent study (Lowie & Verspoor, 2018). This study includes 22 young Dutch learners of English as an L2 who were traced in their first year of a bilingual (Dutch-English) program. Here we will take learner 2, who wrote 18 texts, as an individual example, and at the end we will discuss how we were able to discover dynamic patterns that may apply to other individuals in the group.

The first step to take in a CDST analysis is to observe the data by plotting them in a data base program sheet. Figure 14.1 gives various views of the same data. The thick solid line shows the holistic scores over time. As expected, the learner does improve over time, starting with scores around 2 and ending with scores around 4. However, the learner does not develop linearly, as indicated by the linear trend line. The two other lines show moving averages (the average score of 1, 2, and 3, then 2, 3, and 4, then 3, 4, and 5, etc.) of the minimum and the maximum scores. These min-max scores show the bandwidth of variability. We can see that between data points 1 and 4 and points 8 and 13 (in square brackets) the bandwidths are wider, suggesting that these are the times that the learner is exploring and less stable than at other times.

Figure 14.2 shows some aspects of the learner's syntactic development. The lines show that the learner does not fluctuate much in terms of NomDep, which stands for more complex noun phrases. However, the learner is making his or her sentences longer, and although the lines do not match perfectly, there is a strong correlation (r_{xy} = .89) between mean length of T-unit (MLTU)

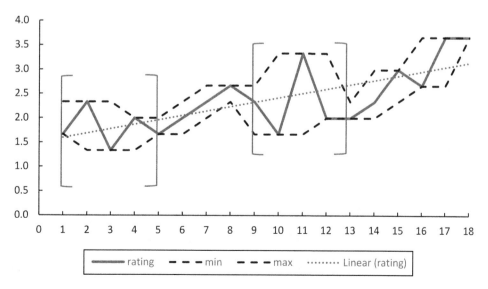

Figure 14.1   Holistic Scores of Learner 2 Over the Course of One Academic Year with a Moving Window (3 Data Points) of Minimum and Maximum Scores and a Linear Trend Line

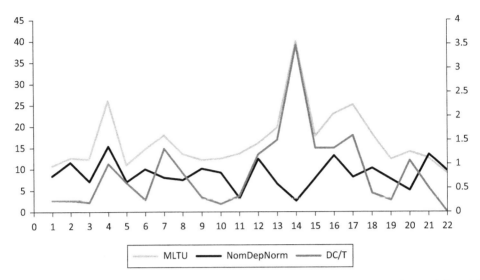

Figure 14.2 Syntactic Development in Terms of Mean Length of T-unit (MLTU-left axis), Normalized Nominal Dependents Within Noun Phrases (NomDepNorm-left axis) and Dependent Clauses per T-unit (DC/T-right axis).

and dependent clauses per T-unit (DC/T). In other words, at this level, the learner is making longer sentences by using dependent clauses. The most interesting aspect of this development is the peak at point 14, which is not isolated, as the values around it are also relatively high. To see if this is not just a random peak, a Monte Carlo analysis can be run. To run a Monte Carlo analysis, a model is set up first (see Verspoor et al., 2011) to measure the difference between the highest and the lowest number (data point 14 has the highest value with 40; data point 22 has the lowest value with 9). In this case, the difference is 31. This number becomes our testing criterion. Then the original data with numbers is copied, and in this model, the numbers in the time series are scrambled, replacing some numbers with other numbers from the same range. This can be done automatically for as many times as needed (1,000 times is usually sufficient) and the difference between the highest and lowest number is recalculated for each run. This analysis will tell us how often the difference was 31 or greater. If the chance is less than 5% that such a great difference is found again, we assume the peak is not coincidental and can be interpreted as evidence that the learner was exploring the possibilities. In the case of learner 2, the MLTU peak observed at week 14 was found to be significant.

Figure 14.3 shows that the learner's language increased in the lexical measure first with a small peak that was not significant (and could easily have been a random effect) but that the lexical measure increased steadily after that. The syntactic jump took place later. This leads to the assumption that this beginner first developed lexically and then syntactically. This assumption was tested with the help of complementary group statistics on the holistic scores. To find out which measure predicted holistic scores best, Lowie and Verspoor (2018) ran a regression analysis with the holistic scores of the 388 samples written by all the learners over the course of the academic year and syntactic and lexical measures. They found that only two lexical measures, mean length of words (MLW) and Guiraud, were significant predictors for the holistic scores.

To see if we could find similar patterns for all 22 learners, Verspoor, Lowie, and Wieling (in prep) used an analysis based on a General Additive Model (GAM), which is a dynamic model in that it includes iterative learning and variability in its algorithms. The model calculates the group mean and quantifies per data point how much variation there is among the group members

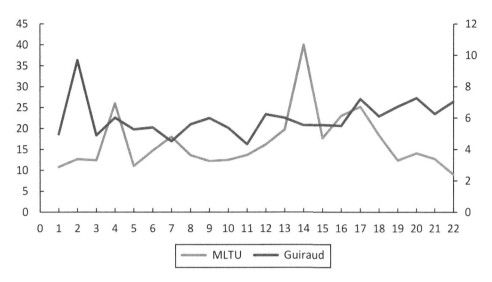

Figure 14.3 Syntactic Development in Terms of Mean Length of T-unit (MLTU-left axis) and Lexical Development in Terms of Type Token Ratio (Guiraud).

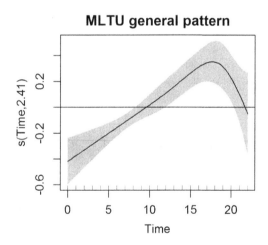

Figure 14.4 A GAM Analysis of the Amount of Variability Among the Participants at Subsequent Datapoints.

(shown in the gray bandwidth in Figure 14.4). By comparing lexical development with syntactic development, they were able to show that there was a significant difference in the way these developed, confirming the CDST assumption that different subsystems may develop differently.

Finally, Lowie and Verspoor (2018) explored whether the degree of variability which the same learner showed over time was an indicator of development. They calculated the coefficient of variance (CoV) – a standardized measure of dispersion (SD/Mean) – for each learner and ran a correlation analysis with the gains in proficiency. As the correlation was strong, they concluded that learners who showed the highest degree of variability were the ones that made the most gains in proficiency as measured by the holistic scores.

To summarize, the methods and analyses in CDST start from individual observations to trace degrees of variability in single measures and interactions among various measures. The analyses always start with visual observations, sometimes of the raw data, but if that is too detailed, with non-linearly smoothed data such as a LOESS function. Correlation analyses can be run to see if various measures develop simultaneously or not. To test for significance in a single time series, Monte Carlo analyses can be used. To discover common developmental patterns among learners, GAM analyses can be used. In some studies, (cf. Caspi, 2010, see below) a precursor model was tested by means of computer modeling. Other studies (cf. Chan, Verspoor, & Vahtrick, 2015, see below) have used Hidden Markov Models to discover phase shifts in the learner's data.

Representative Corpora and Research

Because a dynamic perspective is relatively new in corpus studies, there are few ready-made corpora available. The type of corpus needed is often difficult to assemble as teachers and participants have to be motivated to collect longitudinal data that contain many instances in a time series. Below, we will give a short summary of the main corpora studies that have been done from a CDST perspective and discuss the corpora used and the main findings.

The corpus used by Penris and Verspoor (2017) consisted of 49 texts in an academic genre written over the span of 13 years with an interval of five years, which is longer than any of the other studies we know of, and it gives good insight into the actual process of development at the more advanced stages of L2 development. After high school, the learner was quite advanced already (estimated low B2 level) and entered teaching training college, after which he did an MA in Applied Linguistics. By the time he finished his MA thesis, he was able to write an academic research paper with the proper academic register (estimated C2 level). Over the course of 13 years (with a gap of five years), he wrote many texts, but only 49 were selected, as they were clearly written for academic purposes in an academic genre. The analyses show that his writing development was a long, complex, dynamic process, in which different sub-components of the language changed in interaction with each other. During his teacher training program, his language developed substantially differently than it did during his university program, where more of an academic register is expected. As the language developed, longer noun phrases occurred, and more academic words appeared, as reflected in a longer average word length. The linguistic system became more accurate, as the process of acquisition continued, at one point quite abruptly, but even at the end of the participant's studies, his writing still contained some errors.

This study not only gives insight into the differences between characteristics of advanced formal writings and academic writing, but also has implications for the assessment and measurement of linguistic development. It turns out that not a single dependent variable develops linearly, and they all level off during development. However, at the end, the finite verb token ratio appeared to be the best overall complexity and sophistication developmental measure, as it correlated highly with all other linguistic variables. The studies by Spoelman and Verspoor (2010) and Verspoor, Lowie, Chan, and Vahtrick (2017) also explored the texts written and saved over the course of individual students' academic studies.

The corpus on which Chan et al. (2015) was based was collected by one of the researchers. It was unique in that it consisted of 100 oral and 100 written texts gathered over the course of eight months. Moreover, the Taiwanese learners of English as an L2 were identical twins with similar personalities and similar contextual factors, which would allow for very similar developmental paths. This particular study compared the development of sentence complexity in speaking versus writing. The findings suggested that the two learners initially developed syntactic complexity in their oral language, but over time, they showed inverse trends and developed more syntactic complexity in the written language. This study made use of a Hidden Markov Model to discover moments of self-organization, i.e. moments in which the interaction among various measures changes and takes on a new configuration. One of the most striking observations in these data is that in spite of the high similarity in virtually all respects, the twins showed clearly different developmental patterns, which is what is expected from a CDST perspective. There are several other studies conducted in a similar vein. Larsen-Freeman (2006) investigated the development of five adult Chinese learners of English over the course of several months and concluded that assumptions of variability and variation were met and that complexity, fluency, and accuracy emerged as the system adapted to the changing context. Bulté and Housen (2018) showed that their twelve L2 Dutch learners of English developed rather regularly at the group level, but that individual developmental paths were characterized by a high degree of variability and often deviated from the mean group trends. The corpus on which Tilma (2014) based her study consisted of approximately 35 writing samples written by eight different writers in L2 Finnish in two conditions (as a foreign language with a great deal of explicit instructions and as second language learners in Finland with a more communicative, implicit type of instruction). The learners were compared in a group study and as two individuals from the two groups with similar L1 backgrounds. The group study showed similarities in syntactic and morphological complexity (increase), but differences in favor of the explicit group in case use and some related complexity and accuracy measures. The two focal learners showed some striking differences early on, but were quite similar towards the end, suggesting that explicit instruction may speed up the use of some more or less frequent or complex constructions, but that given time, the implicit learner catches up. Caspi (2010) collected weekly data from four advanced learners who had just arrived at the University of Groningen for one academic year, assuming that these learners would progress rapidly in an immersion context. She traced both vocabulary and writing development. Caspi provided an excellent example of CDST methods and incorporated the type of modeling Van Geert advocates (Lowie, Caspi, Van Geert, & Steenbeek, 2011). Her most interesting findings were that there were indeed precursor relations between lexicon and syntax and that each had to develop before becoming accurate. This was found especially for the lexicon. Apparently, learners first try out new words that they have heard, but often not in a target-like manner.

Future Directions

The collection of CDST inspired studies thus far has shown that L2 development is dynamic with individual learners following their individual trajectories. Each study has shown that variability, sometimes with significant peaks, is the norm. Learners apparently need to explore new forms and meanings before they become accurate, and there is increasing evidence that the amount of variability coincides with the degree of learning. The other general observation is that learners at different levels of proficiency work on different subsystems (such as lexicon before syntax or alternating with each other) and that measures that may be meaningful at early levels of development (e.g. Guiraud) may not really show much change at a higher levels, when, for example, in academic writing, the number of finite dependent clauses decrease, and there are more non-finite constructions in terms of longer nominalizations and other non-finite constructions, and the finite verb ratio tends to be more meaningful.

In these studies, the instruments of analysis adopted to measure development of individual learners have mainly centered on CAF measures. And although this has given us valuable information, the use of other measures may allow us to answer questions beyond complexity, accuracy, and fluency. For instance, Lesonen et al. (2018) in a longitudinal study on learning Finnish as an L2 has explored how an absolute beginner developed in her ability to express the meaning she wished to express, in particular how she expressed positive or negative evaluation towards something. They found that the learner used mainly verbs that express liking or disliking in the first phase, and then she started using mainly adjectives. Towards the end, the learner had a better mix between verbs and adjectives. What was also interesting in terms of variability and competitive constructions is that when verbs were first used, there was a great variety of types of verbs, but when the adjectives were used, the number of types of verbs decreased and vice versa. Other analyses worthy of future research include qualitative differences such as the development of voice described in Larsen-Freeman (2006) which has not received the attention it deserves. Another example is the work of Kyle (2018) on automated extraction of Verb Argument Constructions, which may be very interesting to trace over the course of an individual learner's trajectory.

In addition to a time-focused attention to the development of individual learners, an abundance of virtually unexplored opportunities can be found in corpora of learner – teacher interactions over time, of which there are very few. A notable example is the promising study of Smit, de Bot, and Van de Grift (2016), who used space state grids to explore classroom interactions in terms of open and closed questions and the type of responses that were elicited over time, showing that after an intervention, teachers were able to move from one attractor state (asking predominantly closed questions) to another (asking open questions that resulted in more learner engagement and interaction).

Future directions may also be expected in statistical advancement. Currently, a necessary distinction has to be made between group studies that focus on linear interactions of variables at one moment in time (product-oriented studies) and case studies that focus on the dynamic and non-linear interaction of variables over time (process-oriented studies). Due to ergodicity constraints, the two types of studies cannot be conflated (Lowie & Verspoor, 2018). New developments that have been applied to studies in the area of sociolinguistics, which are always rife with variation and variability, have used methods and techniques such as GAM analyses that might be of use to study individuals or groups of individuals over time. The future will hopefully bring a healthy synergy between group and individual studies, where group findings will be traced in individuals and vice versa, each acknowledging their limitations and recognizing complementary contribution of the types of studies.

One of the most important future directions is making the existing longitudinal corpora discussed in this chapter available for further analysis. For example, the corpora with hand-coded formulaic sequences might be used to build automatic tools that can count them. Also, the holistic scores for all the texts could be used to test new or combined automated measures.

Finally and even more importantly, the findings from CDST studies need to be communicated to L2 teachers. The finding that second language development is a strongly individual and emerging process has relevant implications for language teaching. It may be a comforting thought for teachers to realize that second language learning is highly variable and non-linear. Language development follows a natural and non-linear pattern, and learner variability can be interpreted as an indication of learning. Learners' "errors" may signal their exploration of new forms. Teachers should therefore be aware of the dynamic process of L2 acquisition and be patient when their learners produce inconsistent L2 output. After all, variability is key. And finally, as any experienced teacher may confirm, what works for one learner may not work for another.

Further Reading

Hiver, P., & Al-Hoorie, A. H. (2016). A dynamic ensemble for second language research: Putting complexity theory into practice. *The Modern Language Journal*, *100*(4), 741–756.

The paper outlined outlines the basic tenets of Complex Dynamic Systems Theory and the conceptual tools needed for empirical studies.

Verspoor, M., de Bot, K., & Lowie, W. (Eds.) (2011). *A dynamic approach to second language development: Methods and techniques*. Amsterdam: John Benjamins.

Although this book is already a bit dated, it is useful in understanding CDST in relation to corpus analysis, as it outlines useful types of measures used, methods, and tools. It has detailed how-to sections for the various methodologies described in the current chapter.

Related Topics

Almost every chapter in this handbook is relevant for doing research from a CDST perspective, but especially Chapters 20–30, which all focus on separate constructs, might be very useful in determining variables to study over time. Moreover, CDST is a meta theory and not a specific linguistic theory, which is needed to do linguistic research. The linguistic theory that is most compatible with CDST is a usage-based perspective as discussed in Chapter 13.

References

Bulté, B., & Housen, A. (2018). Syntactic complexity in L2 writing: Individual pathways and emerging group trends. *International Journal of Applied Linguistics, 28*(1), 147–164.

Cancino, H., Rosansky, E., Schumann, J., & Hatch, E. (1978). The acquisition of English negatives and interrogatives by native Spanish speakers. In E. M. Hatch (Ed.), *Second language acquisition: A book of readings* (pp. 207–230). Rowley: Newbury House.

Caspi, T. (2010). *A dynamic perspective on second language development*. Doctoral Dissertation. University of Groningen, Groningen.

Chan, H., Verspoor, M., & Vahtrick, L. (2015). Dynamic development in speaking versus writing in identical twins. *Language Learning, 65*(2), 298–325.

de Bot, K. (2017). Complexity theory and dynamic systems theory. same or different? In L. Ortega & Z. Han (Eds.), *Complexity theory and language development* (pp. 51–58). Amsterdam: John Benjamins.

de Bot, K., Lowie, W. M., & Verspoor, M. H. (2007). A dynamic systems theory approach to second language acquisition. *Bilingualism: Language and Cognition, 10*(1), 7–21.

Gustafson-Smiskova, H., & Verspoor, M. (2018). Development of chunks in Dutch L2 learners of English. In J. Evers-Vermeul & E. Tribushinina (Eds.), *Usage-based approaches to language acquisition and language teaching* (pp. 235–263). Berlin: De Gruyter Mouton.

Hou, J., Loerts, H., & Verspoor, M. (2016). Chunk use and development in advanced Chinese L2 learners of English. *Language Teaching Research, 22*(2), 148–168.

Kuiken, F., & Vedder, I. (2017). Functional adequacy in L2 writing: Towards a new rating scale. *Language Testing, 34*(3), 321–336.

Kyle, K. (2018). Measuring verb-argument construction use: A comprehensive, automated approach. In *Presentation at the 3rd constructionist approaches to language pedagogy (CALP) conference*. Austin.

Larsen-Freeman, D. (1997). Chaos/complexity science and second language acquisition. *Applied Linguistics, 18*(2), 141–165.

Larsen-Freeman, D. (2006). The emergence of complexity, fluency, and accuracy in the oral and written production of five Chinese learners of English. *Applied Linguistics, 27*(4), 590–619.

Lesonen, S., Suni, M., Steinkrauss, R., & Verspoor, M. (2018). From conceptualization to constructions in Finnish as an L2. *Pragmatics and Cognition, 24*(2), 212–262.

Lowie, W. M., Caspi, T., Van Geert, P., & Steenbeek, H. (2011). Modeling development and change. In M. H. Verspoor, K. de Bot, & W. Lowie (Eds.), *A dynamic approach to second language development: Methods and techniques* (pp. 22–122). Amsterdam: John Benjamins.

Lowie, W. M., & Verspoor, M. H. (2018). Individual differences and the ergodicity problem. *Language Learning*. Online pre-publication. Retrieved from https://onlinelibrary.wiley.com/doi/abs/10.1111/lang.12324

Murakami, A. (2013). *Individual variation and the role of L1 in the L2 development of English grammatical morphemes: Insights from learner corpora*. Doctoral Dissertation. Cambridge University.

Penris, W., & Verspoor, M. (2017). Academic writing development: A complex, dynamic process. In S. Pfenniger & J. Navracsics (Eds.), *Future research directions for applied linguistics* (pp. 215–242). Bristol: Multilingual Matters Ltd.

Roy, D. (2011, March). *Deb Roy: The birth of a word* [Video file]. Retrieved from https://www.ted.com/talks/deb_roy_the_birth_of_a_word

Schoonen, R. (2005). Generalizability of writing scores: An application of structural equation modeling. *Language Testing*, *22*(1), 1–30.

Smit, N., de Bot, K., & Van de Grift, W. (2016). Using state space grids to analyze the dynamics of teacher-student interactions in foreign language classrooms. In *Presentation at the AAAL conference*, April 10. Portland Press.

Spoelman, M., & Verspoor, M. (2010). Dynamic patterns in development of accuracy and complexity: A longitudinal case study in the acquisition of Finnish. *Applied Linguistics*, *31*(4), 532–553.

Thelen, E. S. L. B., & Smith, L. B. (1994). *A dynamic systems approach to the development of cognition and action*. Cambridge: MIT Press.

Tilma, C. (2014). *The dynamics of foreign versus second language development in Finnish writing*. Groningen/Jÿvaskyla: University of Groningen/University of Jÿvaskyla dissertation.

Van Dijk, M., Verspoor, M., & Lowie, W. (2011). Variability and DST. In M. Verspoor, K. de Bot, & W. Lowie (Eds.), *A dynamic approach to second language development: Methods and techniques* (pp. 55–84). Amsterdam: John Benjamins.

Van Geert, P. (1991). A dynamic systems model of cognitive and language growth. *Psychological Review*, *98*(1), 3.

Verspoor, M., de Bot, K., & Lowie, W. (Eds.) (2011). *A dynamic approach to second language development: Methods and techniques*. Amsterdam: John Benjamins.

Verspoor, M., Lowie, W., Chan, H. P., & Vahtrick, L. (2017). Linguistic complexity in second language development: Variability and variation at advanced stages. *Recherches en didactique des langues et des cultures. cahiers de l'Acedle*, *14*(1), 14–11.

Verspoor, M., Lowie, W., & Wieling, M. (in press). L2 developmental measures from a dynamic perspective. In: B. LeBruyn & M. Paquot (Eds.) *Learner corpus research meets second language acquisition*. Cambridge: Cambridge University Press.

Verspoor, M., Schmid, M. S., & Xu, X. (2012). A dynamic usage based perspective on L2 writing. *Journal of Second Language Writing*, *21*(3), 239–263.

Vyatkina, N. (2012). The development of second language writing complexity in groups and individuals: A longitudinal learner corpus study. *The Modern Language Journal*, *96*(4), 576–598.

Zhao, C. G. (2013). Measuring authorial voice strength in L2 argumentative writing: The development and validation of an analytic rubric. *Language Testing*, *30*(2), 201–230.

15

Processability Theory and Corpora

Carrie Bonilla

Introduction

A common observation among researchers in second language acquisition (SLA) and language practitioners is that the sequence of instruction in instructed language learning often does not follow the sequence of language acquisition. For example, in a second language (L2) Spanish classroom, the concept of number agreement (i.e., an adjective must agree in number with the noun it modifies, e.g., *los cuadernos azules* 'the blue notebooks') typically appears in the first few chapters of a beginning Spanish language textbook. Yet, students may struggle into the intermediate and advanced levels to produce target-like inflections for nouns and adjectives in conversation. Even the most seemingly simple rules, such as matching nouns and adjectives for number, can be difficult to produce in conversation. This observation brings to light an important issue in SLA research: the consideration that language learners follow relatively consistent patterns of acquisition regardless of external factors such as instruction. Processability Theory (PT: Pienemann, 1998, 2005, 2015) addresses this issue by hypothesizing a set of stages through which language learners must pass while acquiring a second language.

Specifically, PT addresses why learners follow similar routes in learning to produce language spontaneously. PT draws from Levelt's (1989) model of speech production as the basis of how a speaker moves from generating a concept to producing a fully inflected and coherent utterance. To illustrate, consider that a speaker thinks of a concept or thought he or she wishes to express such as "The flower is red". According to Levelt's model (Levelt, 1989, p. 55), this message generation is considered to occur in the *Conceptualizer*. Once a speaker has formed this message, it is passed to the *Formulator*. The *Formulator* generates the grammatical and phonological encoding. For example, a speaker must decide on the appropriate syntax of the utterance, i.e. in which order to put the elements of the utterance, such as the subject and verb. The speaker must also decide whether any morphology is needed, e.g. verb endings to mark tense or noun markings to indicate number. A speaker must also know whether any phonological marking, i.e. systematic sound changes that may occur depending on the surrounding context, are needed. Once the utterance has been appropriately marked for grammatical and any phonological markings, the message is sent to the *Articulator* for physical production. The prediction of PT focuses on the speech processing procedures necessary for grammatical encoding in the *Formulator* as conceptualized by Levelt. While competent speakers can move through each speech processing procedure in real-time, Pienemann's main claim is that learners must acquire this ability to process grammatical encoding one procedure at a time.

Table 15.1 Syntactic and Morphological Procedures Predicted by PT with Examples for Syntactic and Morphological Phenomena for Spanish

Stage	Exchange of information	Procedures	Syntax	Morphology
5	Interclausal	Subordinate (S') clause procedure	Subordinate clause word order	Subjunctive Relative clause agreement
4	Interphrasal	Sentence (S) procedure	SV-inversion Clitic placement	Object agreement Predicative agreement
3	Phrasal	Phrasal procedure	XP-adjunction	NP (attributive) agreement
2	None	Category procedure	SVO	Plural –s marking
1	None	Lemma access	'words'	

Adapted from Testing Processability Theory in L2 Spanish: Can readiness or markedness predict development? (p. 34), by C. Bonilla, 2012, Pittsburgh: University of Pittsburgh. Copyright 2012 by Carrie L. Bonilla. Reprinted with permission.

In summary, the main claim of PT is an explanation of how the ability of grammatical encoding is acquired in spontaneous speech production for L2 learners. Table 15.1 summarizes the five fixed stages predicted by PT for each stage in L2 acquisition along with examples of corresponding syntactic and morphological phenomena.

The five processing procedures are shown in the first column. The theory predicts that each procedure is acquired from the bottom up, from Stage 1 to Stage 5. It follows that at Stage 1, a learner would just be able to produce words or formulaic chunks. At Stage 2, a learner would be able to produce both Stage 2 (Category procedure) and Stage 1 (Lemma access), and so on. A description of each procedure follows with examples of morphology and syntax from the learner corpus data analyzed in Bonilla (2014).

At Stage 1 (Lemma access), we would expect learners to produce bare lexical items with no agreement or syntax such as 'mucho' [a lot] or 'casa' [house]. Next, at Stage 2 (Category procedure), learners start to systematically use lexical morphemes to mark concepts such as plurality, as illustrated in (1):

1. *mi   hermanas

    My-singular(sing)   sisters-plural(pl)

    'My sisters.'

In (1), the -s morpheme on *sisters* expresses plurality, but the learner has not yet reached the stage of being able to match plural marking across the noun phrase which is required in Spanish (*mis hermanas*). For syntax, at Stage 2, learners are predicted to produce canonical word order. This order will vary by language, but the prediction is that learners will place the most prominent argument role (for example, the actor that is performing the action such as the subject) at the beginning of the utterance. An example of SV (subject then verb) word order is shown in (2).

2. un chico   pone   una camiseta

    a boy-Subject   puts on-Verb   a shirt-Object

    'A boy puts on a shirt.'

At Stage 3 (Phrasal procedure), a process called feature unification is hypothesized to be available to speakers. Feature unification is a process by which speakers identify feature information, for example, number, from a lexical entry, temporarily store that information, and share it with another lexical entry. At this stage, learners are predicted to produce number agreement within the noun phrase, as in (3).

3.　　cosas　　　　interesantes　　　por ejemplo　　　el　　　maquillaje

things-pl　　interesting-pl　　for example　　the　　makeup

'interesting things like makeup.'

In (3), the phrase *cosas interesantes* (interesting things) agrees in number. The process of matching number within a phrase is known as phrasal agreement. For syntax at Stage 3, phrasal procedure is available, the result of which is that learners begin to front adverbs, prepositional phrases or question words to canonical utterances. In (4), the prepositional phrase (PP) *en un foto* is fronted before a canonical subject-verb word order.

4.　　*En un foto　　　　los chicos　　　　son　　　　en la playa

In one picture-PP　　the kids-Subject　　are-Verb　　at the beach-PP

'In one picture, the kids are on the beach.'

In this example, although the determiner is assigned masculine gender rather than feminine gender for the feminine noun *foto* (picture), the structure of the utterance reflects the Stage 3 syntax predicted at this stage.

At Stage 4 (S-procedure), learners are predicted to match number, for example, across phrases. This process is known as interphrasal agreement. For example, at Stage 4, learners can produce plural -s agreement across phrases, such as (5). In this example, *the*, *cultures*, and *different* agree in number.

5.　　las　　　　culturas　　　　son　　　　diferentes

The-pl　　cultures-pl　　are　　different-pl

'The cultures are different.'

At Stage 4 (S-procedure), learners are predicted to be able to process target word order rules. For example, at this stage, learners can change the order of the subject and verb as needed in the target language, such as (6). In the example, the verb comes before the subject in a question.

6.　　Por qué　　están limpiando　　estos　　　　chicos

Why-Interr.　are cleaning-Verb　these-Dem.　boys-Subject

'Why are these boys cleaning?'

At Stage 5 (S'procedure), learners are predicted to produce agreement across clauses. Additionally, at Stage 5, subordinate clause word order is found as illustrated in (7). Example 7 shows an example of interclausal morphology with a verb *vengan* in the subjunctive mood as well as an example of subject/verb inversion in a subordinate clause with *mis padres* following *vengan*.

7.　　Espero　　　que　　vengan　　　　　　　　　mis padres

I hope-SV　　that　　are coming-Verb/Subjunctive　　my parents-Subject

'I hope my parents come.'

In his seminal work presenting PT as a formal theory of L2 learner oral production, Pienemann (1998, pp. 165–214) showed typological evidence for these predicted PT stages in syntax and morphology based on a review of multiple corpus-based studies in the L2 acquisition of German, English, Swedish, and Japanese. Pienemann (1998) discusses the type of data to be collected and the methods for determining a learner's stage and assessing any gaps in the implicational sequence. Regarding the type of data, PT is limited to an explanation of the acquisition of speech processing procedures in spontaneous, oral speech production. Furthermore, PT focuses on emergence – not mastery, accuracy, or any intermediate level of competence – of the speech processing procedures. Pienemann (1998) defined emergence as the following: "From a speech processing point of view, emergence can be understood as the point in time at which certain skills have, in principle, been attained or at which certain operations can, in principle, be carried out" (p. 138). In other words, assessing whether a stage has emerged for a learner involves analyzing whether a learner is using a structure systematically and productively regardless of the accuracy of the structure produced. Once learners' stages have been assessed according to the emergence criteria, the implicational nature and order of the stages can be tested via implicational scaling of the stages of a group of learners (or one or more learners over time in the case of a longitudinal study). Implicational scaling is a statistical approach to analyzing whether the stages are acquired in order over time (Hatch & Lazarton, 1991).

Throughout this chapter, I focus on the centrality of spontaneous, oral production in PT predictions with respect to the challenges and advantages for corpus research (for a comprehensive introduction to PT, see Dyson and Håkannson, 2017). I first discuss several core issues in PT research including applying PT to novel languages and describing learner variability. I continue by illustrating the research methods used in PT research. I conclude by offering suggestions and direction for future research taking advantage of learner corpora.

Core Issues and Topics

In this section, I discuss several core issues and topics in PT research germane to corpus-based SLA research. I first highlight several studies investigating the universal nature of the stages for some syntax and morphology phenomena for different L2s, which has been one of the main areas of PT research. I next look at studies questioning learner variability in research on PT acquisition. Throughout this section, I will focus especially on the emergence criteria for each study, the type of spontaneous oral data collected, and the congruency or incongruency with the PT predictions.

Typological Plausibility

A major thread of PT research since Pienemann (1998) has been analyzing the typological plausibility of the PT predictions, in other words, applying the PT hypothesis regarding the five fixed processing stages to novel L2s. As Dyson and Håkannson (2017) note, whereas there are approximately 6,000 languages spoken around the world, only 17 languages have been tested to date for the PT predictions. For instance, a selection of studies that have confirmed the acquisitional sequence for other languages predicted by PT are the following: Pienemann and Håkansson (1999) on Swedish syntax and morphology, Kawaguchi (2005) on Japanese topicalization and passives, Zhang (2005) on Chinese morphology, Mansouri (2005) on Arabic morphology, and Sakai (2008) on English word order. To address which syntactic and morphological phenomena are processable at each stage, the five processing procedures can be linked to specific grammatical structures across languages via a theory of how grammar is organized in language use called Lexical-functional grammar (LFG: Kaplan & Bresnan, 1982). In other words, when analyzing an L2 learners' use of grammar in a language previously unanalyzed for the PT predictions, an analysis of how information is exchanged in that language according to LFG would first need to be performed.

In this section, I highlight several studies that have tested the PT predictions for typologically distinct languages for a subset of syntactic or morphological phenomena. First, Glahn, Håkansson, Hammarberg, Holmen, Hvenekilde, and Lund (2001) applied the PT hierarchy to the L2 acquisition of Danish, Norwegian, and Swedish attributive and predicative adjectives and subordinate clause syntax. To test the PT predictions, Glahn et al. elicited the target structures through several types of communicative activities. For example, to elicit predicative adjectives, participants were asked questions about different objects in many color illustrations. Glahn et al. compared different metrics for emergence; a structure was considered emerged by counting just one occurrence, when supplied in 50% of possible contexts for the structure or when supplied in 80% of the possible contexts. While these results were generally supportive of the PT predictions regardless of the varying emergence criteria, the results also highlighted that learners did not show emergence of all structures at a given stage at the same time, as evidenced in this study by the emergence of number marking prior to gender agreement. Still, this result is consistent with PT theory, given that gender is a highly idiosyncratic feature across languages and generally must be acquired individually for each lexical item.

Another study tested typological plausibility of PT for Italian and Japanese. Di Biase and Kawaguchi (2002) analyzed cross-sectional data of formal learners of Italian and Japanese in Australia and found the sequence of morpheme acquisition predicted by PT. For the Italian learners, Di Biase and Kawaguchi interviewed six learners at three different levels of Italian proficiency (beginning, intermediate, and advanced). The interviews involved free conversation, picture description, a story-telling task, and a conversational task designed to elicit objects. For the Japanese learners, nine learners were interviewed longitudinally or cross-sectionally via free conversation and picture tasks. A morpheme was considered emerged if it was used more than once in a lexically and structurally varied environment. In order to assess whether an item met these criteria, Di Biase and Kawaguchi performed a distributional analysis for each morpheme for each language. This analysis, according to Pienemann (1998, p. 158), is a method of checking whether a learner's use of a morpheme correlates with contexts for the morpheme, as well as checking for non-use of the morpheme in contexts where it is not required.

A third study highlights a slightly different methodology for testing typological plausibility. Baten (2011) applied German case marking to the PT stages of morphology, and then measured Dutch native speakers' (ages 15–18 in grades 10, 11, and 12) use of case marking in a time-constrained fill-in-the-blanks task. Although this data is not spontaneous or naturally occurring, the advantage of this task is that it yields a great deal of data on case marking that would have otherwise been challenging to elicit via meaningful spontaneous tasks. The authors further note that one of the primary goals of the study was to develop a baseline to inform further research on German case morphology acquisition. Designing tasks that will elicit certain structures in a spontaneous and naturalistic way is a challenge for SLA studies using learner corpora (see Tracy-Ventura & Myles, 2015). According to the authors, the study yielded a corpus of 13,376 sentences (i.e., 19 sentences each from 704 participants). Given the nature of the data, Baten did not perform an analysis of emergence but rather analyzed the proportion of grammatical case marking in various contexts. In that way, Baten could analyze target and non-target like case use in order to get a sense of a learners' developing case system.

While most studies applying the PT stages to a novel language have analyzed the development of a selection of syntactic or morphological phenomena, Bonilla (2014) proposed and analyzed a syntactic and morphological structure for each of the five stages of L2 Spanish acquisition. To test whether learners progress through these five stages in the order predicted, Bonilla analyzed spontaneous oral data from the *Spanish Language Learner Oral Corpus* (SPLLOC: Mitchell,

Myles, Dominguez, Marsden, Arche, and Boardman, 2008). This corpus was chosen for the presence of spontaneous oral learner data from learners at varying levels of acquisition (e.g. beginner, intermediate, and advanced). A portion of a picture description and personal interview task in which a native Spanish speaker and learner discussed several pictures, then transitioned to a discussion of a learner's current interests, past activities, and plans for the future was isolated for analysis. This task was chosen for analysis due to the need to analyze spontaneous interactions and particularly because the researchers consistently asked similar questions in all interviews. This similarity in questions allows for a consistent analysis of application or non-application of the target syntax and morphological structures in question. For syntax, a structure was considered emerged if a minimum of four total contexts for the rule (non-rote-learned) were also present (following Pienemann, 1998, p. 145; Jansen, 2008). A non-rote-learned structure is considered to be a creative, productive example and not a rote learned or chunked phrase. For morphology, the item in question was considered to be emerged if it was used systematically and productively with lexically varied words in a minimum of four contexts (Pallotti, 2007; Pienemann, 1998, p. 13). Overall, Bonilla (2014) found that the order and cumulative nature of the stages were upheld in the analysis of the syntactic and morphological production. The only stage that could not be verified was Stage 5 morphology, as not enough contexts were evident in the data to show acquisition or non-acquisition of subjunctive morphology.

Learner Variability

For the most part, the studies reviewed thus far were oriented to demonstrating typological plausibility of the theory. Dyson (2009, 2016) has taken a more detailed look at inter-learner and intra-learner variation in stage acquisition. Dyson (2009) analyzed the acquisition of L2 English by two first language (L1) Chinese learners (Philomena and Daniel) in a longitudinal study conducted over a year. Dyson conducted six interviews with each learner over the course of the academic year consisting of communication tasks and interviews. Following Pienemann (1998) and Mansouri (2005), Dyson (2009) defined emergence as the "existence of two tokens with different lexical items and different structural/morphological forms" (p. 362). While the PT stages were generally found to emerge in the order predicted, Dyson noted variations in the emergence of syntax and morphology between the two learners. In particular, one learner, Daniel, seemed more disposed to mark morphology, while Philomena appeared to be more focused on syntax. Dyson (2016) further investigated learner patterns in syntactic and morphological development with a group of L2 learners of English with varied L1s (Arabic, Mandarin Chinese, and Bosnian). Dyson interviewed each learner six times between March and December through different kinds of communicative tasks designed to elicit the target structures such as story-telling, answering questions, asking questions, or describing pictures. Dyson (2016) defined emergence as "the use of at least two tokens with different lemmas and/or morphological variation in a single lemma" (p. 356). Furthermore, if a structure was shown to have emerged at one interview, but not at the next two successive interviews, the structure was not considered to have emerged. Dyson (2016) analyzed the patterns of emergence of syntax and morphology with respect to how learners avoided, omitted, or committed errors with the target structures. Interestingly, although the overall order largely followed the PT predictions, the results highlight how learners may vary in time needed to acquire processing structures as well as in the order for some structures. Dyson (2016) suggests that learners tend to be either syntactically-oriented, i.e. moving more quickly through the syntactic stages or more morphologically-oriented, i.e. moving more quickly through the morphological stages. Dyson suggests further research with learners of the same language background would offer more insight into this aspect of the developmental hierarchy.

Since the publication of Pienemann (1998) and the typological studies discussed in this section, several key methodological questions have surfaced in assessing the theory's predictions such as how to define emergence along with how to account for learner variation. In the next section, I discuss some of these challenges in PT research.

Main Research Methods

In this section, I discuss the main research methodology employed in PT corpus studies. I adhere to a broad definition of corpus as a collection of spontaneous oral production data that represents multiple linguistic phenomena.

Production Data

Any corpus with spontaneous, spoken learner data could potentially be utilized for further research on PT. In order to investigate stages of acquisition predicted by PT, a corpus from language learners at varying stages or levels of acquisition at one point in time (i.e., a cross-sectional corpus) or via following multiple language learners over a period of time (i.e., a longitudinal corpus) is necessary. Given the nature of the theory's predictions, spontaneous language production precludes any kind of task that allows a learner to reflect explicitly on his or her language production.

Most PT researchers have designed oral production tasks for participants, while few have analyzed oral production data from already existing corpora not collected specifically for PT analysis. As discussed in *Core issues and topics,* most researchers have chosen to collect their own oral data from participants via tasks like interviews, eliciting questions, picture description tasks, story-telling, and the like. Due to the very specific nature of the syntactic and morphological phenomena that most researchers have been looking for, it is beneficial for a researcher to design tasks certain to elicit the target structures. In addition, researchers may already have a population of learners they have access to, which is another advantage of researchers creating their own corpus. Bonilla (2014) is one of the few researchers who has analyzed a publicly available electronic corpus with language data that was not collected specifically for PT analysis. Bonilla (2014) could use the corpus because the type of tasks collected and the learner population in SPLLOC aligned with the goals of the study.

Data Coding

In this section, first I will discuss the overall procedures for coding corpora data for the PT structures. Next, I will point out three main areas of challenges for PT coding.

Once the corpus has been selected or oral data collected, transcripts of learners' utterances are manually coded for the key syntactic and morphological features. Tagged corpora could also be used to find examples of the morphological features in question. However, given that the analysis of learner productions is not based on accuracy but based on a careful analysis of whether a learner is producing a syntactic or morphological structure systematically and productively, a researcher generally must analyze each utterance individually. Clauses in L1 or exact repetitions of phrases or words from the learner should be excluded. Once the researcher has identified the syntactic and morphological features produced for each learner, the emergence criteria are applied for each learner for syntax and morphology separately. Once the emergence criteria have been applied, the learners are organized by stage acquired in an implicational table to allow for a visualization of learner progress through the stages. Once the table has been constructed, several statistics are calculated in order to test the adherence of the data to the hypothesized order and independent nature of each stage (see Hatch & Lazarton, 1991).

A key issue for PT analysis is defining the emergence criteria, i.e. standard ways of assessing that a learner has arrived at a certain stage as evidenced by an onset of systematic and productive use of the morphosyntax in question. Again, one of the central predictions of PT is that learners initially acquire the ability to produce grammatical structures in their L2 in a fixed order. A main challenge of this prediction is operationalizing the emergence criteria in order to assess acquisition or non-acquisition of stages. As illustrated in the section *Core issues and topics*, researchers have varied on how to interpret emergence. For example, Di Biase and Kawaguchi (2002) considered a morpheme emerged if it was used more than once in a lexically and structurally varied environment, while Baten (2011) analyzed proportions of grammatical case marking in various contexts. Dyson (2016) defined emergence similarly to Di Biase and Kawaguchi (2002), but with an important difference. Learners had to show emergence of a structure over three successive time points in order for the structure to be considered acquired. While many of these criteria have overlapped, it is difficult for researchers to duplicate PT research without a clear sense of which criteria to use. To combat these variances in interpretation in PT research, Pallotti (2007) offers an operationalization of the emergence criteria. Pallotti notes that the presence of a structure alone cannot be considered evidence that a structure is processable; rather, a structure must be shown to be used systematically and productively in order for emergence to be determined. For syntax, Pallotti suggests a minimum of four total contexts for the rule must be present (see Jansen, 2008; Pienemann, 1998, p. 145). The concept of including a minimum number of contexts ensures that enough evidence exists to test application or non-application of a rule. For morphology, the item in question must be shown to be used systematically and productively with lexically varied words in a minimum of four contexts (Pallotti, 2007; Pienemann, 1998, p. 13). The question of standardizing the emergence criteria is relevant to the question of researchers collecting spontaneous oral data or utilizing already existing corpora. If a minimum number of contexts must be met in order for emergence to occur, researchers generally have opted to design their own conversational tasks in order to ascertain that enough contexts exist for learners to produce the target structures.

Other challenges besides accounting for the emergence criteria include identifying formulaic chunks. Formulaic chunks are lexical phrases learners may produce as unanalyzed lexical examples of the target syntactic or morphological structures. For example, a learner production of *buenos días* 'good morning', while it demonstrates number agreement between *buenos* [good-pl] and *días* [days-pl], is a common lexical chunk that learners may produce early in language acquisition as an unanalyzed lexical phrase. However, the judgment of which phrases are lexical chunks is often made subjectively by researchers due to their knowledge of the learning context and intuitions. In addition, if researchers are relying on a corpus of spontaneous oral data collected with a small group only for purposes of the study, it is unlikely that there is sufficient data to find more examples of the target lexical items in the chunk to assess whether the learner is producing a rule productively or just producing a lexical chunk. Larger amounts of production data available in large corpora would be advantageous to provide evidence in these kinds of scenarios.

A related issue in PT data analysis is assessing acquisition or non-acquisition of a stage when no contexts for a particular structure exist in the data. Jansen (2008) noted this issue in a study of L2 German acquisition. While the results were supportive of the PT predictions, Jansen noted that there were many gaps in the data where non-acquisition could not be determined. Bonilla (2014) also could not demonstrate emergence of Stage 5 morphology due to gaps in the data. Furthermore, some structures targeted in PT research are optional, not obligatory. For example, the target word order structures in Spanish hypothesized for Stage 4 are not all obligatory word order rules. Rather, the use of variable target word order can depend on a speakers' intentions to emphasize the subject. For these reasons, as illustrated by the kinds of tasks used in PT studies, many researchers have tended to create a corpus of spoken data derived from conversational tasks designed to elicit the target structures in question, rather than use an existing corpus. Another possibility researchers could consider is using a mix of publicly available corpus data supplemented as needed by tasks designed to elicit certain grammatical structures in order to increase the possible contexts for target structures.

These methodological considerations raise important questions to move PT research forward. It is important to demonstrate that the stages exist for learners in any spontaneous oral language, regardless of the corpus type or task types. In fact, Pienemann (1998, 2005) proposed the *steadiness hypothesis,* which states the PT predictions should be met regardless of task type as long as the tasks are based on the same skills. The limitation of certain tasks for some grammatical structures raises a related issue, which is that many studies tend to focus on a subset of syntactic or morphological structures, but it is rare to see a single study focus on all morphosyntax produced by learners. Given the focus of most PT studies on the predicted syntax and morphology, it is a question for future research what other syntactic and morphological phenomena may be found in more natural conversations and how those structures fit into the theory predictions. These shortcomings of PT research are fruitful areas to explore in future PT research on spontaneous oral corpora.

Representative Corpora and Research

While the traditional method of designing spontaneous oral tasks for learners in order to elicit certain structures has advantages, one way forward for PT research is taking greater advantage of already existing corpora. In this section, I highlight three corpora – the *French Learner Language Oral Corpora* (FLLOC), SPLLOC, and the Housen *Corpus of Young Learner Interlanguage* (CYLIL) – for use in further PT research. These corpora are suggested for PT analysis due to their inclusion of various spontaneous oral production task types elicited by L2 learners of different proficiency levels.

Rule, Marsden, Myles, and Mitchell (2003) developed the FLLOC project. Multiple corpora are available from the FLLOC website. Rule et al. (2003) collected spontaneous oral data from different groups of instructed learners of L2 French with L1 English. The corpus has cross-sectional data from students between ages 13–14, 14–15, and 15–16 as well as longitudinal oral data collected from 30 students of ages 16–17. Task types for both corpora included tasks based on learner output, such as a learner narrating a story based on pictures or a photo description and personal interview task, as well as more interactive tasks with the researcher, including for example, an information gap task where learners must find out missing information from the researcher. Although no studies to date have used the FLLOC corpus to test the predictions of PT, given the types of tasks included in the corpus, the FLLOC corpus is an important potential resource for future PT research.

SPLLOC (Mitchell et al., 2008) consists of oral data from 60 instructed learners of L2 Spanish with L1 English. The SPLLOC corpora consists of two waves of data collection. SPLLOC 1, collected between April 2006 and March 2008 consists of personal narratives, interviews, and picture description tasks. Participants in SPLLOC 1 are students of ages 13–14 (beginners), 17–18 (intermediate), and 21–22 (advanced). SPLLOC 2, collected between August 2008 and January 2010, consists of oral data targeted specifically at acquisition of past-tense morphology. Participants were of similar ages as those in SPLLOC 1: students of ages 14–15 (low intermediate), 17–18 (intermediate), and 21–22 (advanced). Five different tasks designed to elicit past tense morphology were collected. The tasks included a guided interview, two narrative tasks, a picture task demonstrating simultaneous past actions, and a semantic interpretation task in which learners made judgments about sentences in Spanish. For an overview of a study using SPLLOC 1, see the description in *Core issues and topics* of Bonilla (2014).

Another corpus that has been used for developmental research is CYLIL (Housen, 2002). This corpus contains spontaneous oral data from English language learners of different L1s (Dutch, French, Greek, and Italian). The participants are students between ages of 9 and 17, as well as six students between the ages of 9 and 13 who were followed longitudinally over three years. The task types for the oral data consist of both free conversation as well as guided conversation in order to elicit the desired speech tasks such as story retells and picture description. Housen's (2002) cross-sectional study investigated learners' stages of development of English verbs. The participants were 23 L1 Dutch students and 23 L1 French students from five different age groups between 9 and 17. Housen analyzed learners' lexical diversity, verb types, and syntactic diversity in order to group learners into four proficiency groups representing four stages of interlanguage development. Next, Housen analyzed learners' systematic use of verb forms for patterns of use, including overuse, underuse, and accurate use. Overall, although Housen found some similarities in patterns of development in verb marking in this cross-sectional study as had been found in a similar longitudinal analysis of learner verb marking, he notes that individual variation in development routes and patterns of distribution are clearer in longitudinal data.

Other corpora that could be used in further PT research include the corpus from the Zweitspracherwerb Italienischer und Spanischer Arbeiter (ZISA) group on German L2 acquisition (see Meisel, Clahsen, and Pienemann, 1981). PT has its origins in research on L2 German word order acquisition from the ZISA research project in the late 1970s and early 1980s that found a similar pattern in word order development for L1 Italian and L1 Spanish speakers. There are also a number of SLA corpora with oral data available in the SLABank of the Child Language Data Exchange System (CHILDES: MacWhinney, 2000 – see also Chapter 12, this volume).

Future Directions

Results regarding the hierarchical nature of the PT stages for a variety of language types have been generally robust, but many questions remain for future research. To further PT research with learner corpora, I will discuss three key areas.

First, future PT studies would benefit from taking advantage of any available corpora for the language of interest, provided that the data consist of spontaneous, oral production data. Given that one of the central tenets of PT is the cross-linguistic nature of the stages, there is much work to be done regarding testing whether the predictions hold up for languages of varying typology. Likewise, replications of earlier studies could be performed using available corpora or through designing one's own corpus. A further consideration would be to focus on more studies of longitudinal data regarding PT predictions. As Housen (2002) notes, cross-sectional studies may not be fine-grained enough to illustrate individual patterns in linguistic development. Thus, future studies should consider comparing cross-sectional and longitudinal data.

Second, the notion of emergence has not only been challenging for PT theory given difficulties in interpreting the criteria, but it also leaves predictions unspecified for language development beyond any initial signs of implementation of the predicted speech processing procedures. Although PT studies have documented in detail the emergence of syntax and morphology, how learners progress beyond emergence in relation to the five processing procedures has been relatively underexplored in the theory. These are the kinds of questions Dyson (2009, 2016) has raised in work on variability. For instance, once a learner attains a stage, is it typical for the learner to attain target-like accuracy with all structures at that stage before advancing to the next stage? Or, do learners tend to progress more quickly through all stages then retroactively fill in any structures missing from already attained stages?

A third question for future PT research is the role of input (e.g. instruction or exposure to the target language receptively) on the development of productive abilities in PT. Beyond continuing research on typological plausibility of the PT stages for various combinations of L1s and L2s, other core issues that have arisen in current PT research include the effect of instruction on stage development (Bonilla, 2015; Pienemann, 1984, 1989; Zhang & Lantolf, 2015) and the acquisition and the applicability of PT to receptive language processing (Buyl & Housen, 2015; Spinner, 2013). Analyzing a corpus of recordings of oral speech used in language classrooms along with learner productive development could be a start to analyzing the relationship between exposure to the spoken or written language and development of productive abilities. All of these questions and others are vital to strengthen our understanding of the stages of acquiring second language morphosyntax.

Further Reading

Bonilla, C. (2014). From number agreement to the subjunctive: Evidence for processability theory in L2 Spanish. *Second Language Research*, *31*(1), 53–74.

Bonilla analyzed the PT predictions for L2 Spanish syntax and morphology through a corpus-based analysis of spontaneous learner data at three different levels of proficiency: beginner, intermediate, and advanced.

Housen, A. (2002). A corpus-based study of the L2 acquisition of the English verb system. In S. Granger, J. Hung, & S. Petch-Tyson (Eds.), *Computer learner corpora, second language acquisition and foreign language teaching* (pp. 77–116). Philadelphia: John Benjamins.

Housen investigated the developmental patterns of verb marking for L2 English learners with L1 Dutch and French in a cross-sectional corpus of spontaneous and guided conversations.

Pienemann, M. (2015). An outline of processability theory and its relationship to other approaches to SLA. *Language Learning*, *65*(1), 123–151.

In this special issue of *Language Learning* devoted to developmental sequences, Pienemann discusses the history and focus of PT in response to alternative theories regarding learner developmental patterns.

Related Topics

Chapter 19.

References

Baten, K. (2011). Processability theory and German case acquisition. *Language Learning*, *61*(2), 455–505.

Bonilla, C. (2012). *Testing processability theory in L2 Spanish. Can readiness or markedness predict development*. Doctoral Dissertation. University of Pittsburgh, Pittsburgh.

Bonilla, C. (2014). From number agreement to the subjunctive: Evidence for processability theory in L2 Spanish. *Second Language Research*, *31*(1), 53–74.

Bonilla, C. (2015). Instructing stages of processability theory in L2 Spanish: Next or next +1? In K. Baten, M. Herreweghe, A. Buyl, & K. Lochtman (Eds.), *Theory development in processability theory*. Amsterdam: John Benjamins.

Buyl, A., & Housen, A. (2015). Developmental stages in receptive grammar acquisition: A processability theory account. *Second Language Research*, *31*(4), 523–550.

Di Biase, B., & Kawaguchi, S. (2002). Exploring the typological plausibility of processability theory: Language development in Italian second language and Japanese second language. *Second Language Research*, *18*(3), 274–302.

Dyson, B. (2009). Processability Theory and the role of morphology in English as a second language development: A longitudinal study. *Second Language Research*, *25*(3), 355–376.

Dyson, B. (2016). Variation, individual differences and second language processing: A processability theory study. *Linguistic Approaches to Bilingualism*, *6*(4), 341–395.

Dyson, B., & Håkannson (2017). *Understanding second language processing: A focus on processability theory*. Amsterdam: John Benjamins.

Glahn, E., Håkannson, G., Hammarberg, B., Holmen, A., Hvenekilde, A., & Lund, K. (2001). Processability in Scandinavian second language acquisition. *Studies in Second Language Acquisition, 23*(3), 389–416.

Hatch, E., & Lazarton, A. (1991). *The research manual: Design and statistics for applied linguistics.* New York: Newbury House.

Housen, A. (2002). A corpus-based study of the L2 acquisition of the English verb system. In S. Granger, J. Hung, & S. Petch-Tyson (Eds.), *Computer learner corpora, second language acquisition and foreign language teaching* (pp. 77–116). Philadelphia: John Benjamins.

Jansen, L. (2008). Acquisition of German word order in tutored learners: A cross-sectional study in a wider theoretical context. *Language Learning, 58*(1), 185–231.

Kaplan, R., & Bresnan, J. (1982). Lexical-functional grammar: A formal system for grammatical representation. In J. Bresnan (Ed.), *The mental representation of grammatical relations* (pp. 173–281). Cambridge: The MIT Press.

Kawaguchi, S. (2005). Argument structure and syntactic development in Japanese as a second language. In M. Pienemann (Ed.), *Cross-linguistic aspects of processability theory* (pp. 253–298). Philadelphia: John Benjamins.

Levelt, W. J. M. (1989). *Speaking. From intention to articulation.* Cambridge: MIT Press.

MacWhinney, B. (2000). *The CHILDES project: Computational tools for analyzing talk.* Hillsdale: Lawrence Erlbaum.

Mansouri, F. (2005). Agreement morphology in Arabic as a second language: Typological features and their processing implications. In M. Pienemann (Ed.), *Cross-linguistic aspects of processability theory* (pp. 117–154). Philadelphia: John Benjamins.

Meisel, J. M., Clahsen, H., & Pienemann, M. (1981). On determining developmental stages in natural second language acquisition. *Studies in Second Language Acquisition, 3*(2), 109–135.

Mitchell, R., Myles, F., Dominguez, L., Marsden, E., Arche, M., & Boardman, T. (2008). *Spanish learner language oral corpora (SPLLOC).* Retrieved from http://www.splloc.soton.ac.uk/

Pallotti, G. (2007). An operational definition of the emergence criterion. *Applied Linguistics, 28*(3), 361–382.

Pienemann, M. (1984). Psychological constraints on the teachability of languages. *Studies in Second Language Acquisition, 62*(2), 186–214.

Pienemann, M. (1989). Is language teachable? Psycholinguistic experiments and hypotheses. *Applied Linguistics, 10*(1), 52–79.

Pienemann, M. (1998). *Language processing and second language development: Processability theory.* Amsterdam: John Benjamins.

Pienemann, M. (2005). An introduction to processability theory. In M. Pienemann (Ed.), *Cross- linguistic aspects of processability theory* (pp. 1–60). Philadelphia: John Benjamins.

Pienemann, M. (2015). An outline of processability theory and its relationship to other approaches to SLA. *Language Learning, 65*(1), 123–151.

Pienemann, M., & Håkansson, G. (1999). A unified approach toward the development of Swedish as L2: A processability account. *Studies in Second Language Acquisition, 21*(3), 383–420.

Rule, S., Marsden, E., Myles, F., & Mitchell, R. (2003). Constructing a database of French interlanguage oral corpora. In D. Archer, R. Rayson, E. Wilson, & T. McEnery (Eds.), *Proceedings of the corpus linguistics 2003 conference* (vol. 16, pp. 669–677). UCREL Technical Papers, University of Lancaster.

Sakai, H. (2008). An analysis of Japanese university students' oral performance in English using processability theory. *System, 36*(4), 534–549.

Spinner, P. (2013). Language production and reception: A processability theory study. *Language Learning, 63*(4), 704–739.

Tracy-Ventura, N., & Myles, F. (2015). The importance of task variability in learner corpora for SLA research. *International Journal of Learner Corpus Research, 1*(1), 58–95.

Zhang, X., & Lantolf, J. (2015). Natural or artificial: Is the route of L2 development teachable? *Language Learning, 65*(1), 152–180.

Zhang, Y. (2005). Processing and formal instruction in the L2 acquisition of five Chinese grammatical morphemes. In M. Pienemann (Ed.), *Cross-linguistic aspects of processability theory* (pp. 155–178). Amsterdam: John Benjamins.

16

Generative Approaches

Cristóbal Lozano

Introduction

Generative approaches to second language acquisition (GenSLA) is an explanatory, theory-driven approach that focuses on the acquisition of linguistic knowledge in an L2, leaving aside individual factors and social aspects. Following Chomsky's (1986) three major questions (*What constitutes knowledge of language? How is knowledge of language acquired? How is knowledge of language put to use?*), GenSLA has focused more on L2 competence (how the implicit or unconscious knowledge of the L2 is acquired and represented in the mind) than on performance (how such knowledge is put to use) and on how Universal Grammar (UG) shapes such knowledge (Hawkins, 2001, 2007; Rothman & Slabakova, 2018; White, 1989, 2003, 2012). L2 learners' developing grammatical knowledge, standardly known as interlanguage grammars (ILGs), are the result of multiple factors: (i) influence from learners' L1 (transfer), (ii) L2 input, (iii) universal and cognitive mechanisms common to all learners irrespective of their L1.

UG has been reconceptualised over the decades. Under the Principles and Parameters (P&P) theory (Chomsky, 1981), UG consists of innate universal principles common to all languages and language-specific parameters of variation that must be fixed by experience (input). For example, all languages have subjects, but the null-subject parameter stipulates that overt pronominal subjects must be realised in some languages (English: *He found a solution*) but null pronouns (Ø) are licensed in others (Spanish: *Él/Ø encontró una solución*). Parameters were originally envisaged as clusters of properties, e.g., null-subject languages additionally allow Subject-Verb inversion (*Existen los androides*) whereas non null-subject languages do not (**Exist androids*). In L1 acquisition, the input the child is exposed to (English or Spanish) is simply a trigger to set the parameter. In L2 acquisition, the learner must reset parameters when the L1–L2 parametric values do not coincide (White, 1989).

After UG, the Minimalist Program (MP) (Chomsky, 1995) became the general framework for the study of generative approaches to language acquisition. The minimalist approach capitalizes on the lexicon; variation between languages is located in the features of functional categories. UG consists of a computational system and a lexicon containing a universal inventory of features, a set of which are selected in the process of L1 acquisition. For example, the functional category Aspect, which may be realised in different morphological ways across languages, can host a variety of features ([perfective], [imperfective: continuous], [imperfective: habitual], [imperfective: progressive]). Differences between languages therefore lie in which features (out of the inventory of UG) are selected in each language and how these features are assembled onto functional categories. The GenSLA question is whether learners can acquire the L2 features that were not selected during L1 acquisition and, if they were selected, whether they can remap them onto new L2 forms. After the publication of the MP, GenSLA saw an upsurge of different feature-based theories trying to account for the (lack of) success in L2 acquisition, like the Failed Functional Features Hypothesis, the Feature Reassembly Hypothesis, the Missing Surface Inflection Hypothesis, the Interpretability Hypothesis, and others (for an overview of those theories see White, 2012). The notion of ultimate attainment is relevant in these models; whereas children eventually attain native-like competence in their L1, learners fail to do so in their L2 as a result of either deficits in knowledge (learners' inability to fully acquire new functional features in their L2) or processing limitations (their inability to (re)map the features onto their corresponding morphological exponents), sometimes as a result of a critical period after which new features are unacquirable (Liceras, Zobl & Goodluck, 2008 and articles therein for overviews). Such deficits typically result in learners' incomplete and divergent grammars when compared to native grammars (Sorace, 2000).

Recent developments (Chomsky, 2000, 2005, 2011) within the 'biolinguistic' approach focus on the properties which (external) interface conditions impose on the design of the language faculty (UG). In GenSLA, attention has shifted from UG access, parameter (re)setting, and feature reassembly to how the computational system of UG (i.e., the syntactic module) interfaces with other language-internal modules (lexicon) and language-external modules (phonology, semantics/pragmatics). Much of recent GenSLA research has been motivated by the syntax-discourse and syntax-semantics interfaces (Montrul, 2011; Rothman & Slabakova, 2011; White, 2011), which have been argued to be a locus of residual variability and optionality in ILGs (Sorace, 2000, 2011).

Core Issues and Topics

L1 Transfer and Learner Corpora

The role of L1 transfer in L2 acquisition, which is a key issue in SLA, has been reinterpreted over the years in GenSLA. The P&P model predicts that learners transfer their L1 parametric settings (and their associated cluster of properties) onto their L2. Feature-based models like the Feature Reassembly Hypothesis (FRH) (Lardiere, 2009) envisage SLA as a feature (re)assembly process. Learners must (i) acquire new L2 features if they are not present in their L1, and, (ii) if those features are present in both L1 and L2, abandon their L1 feature-form mapping and reassemble the features onto the corresponding L2 forms. Theoretically-informed approaches like the FRH allow researchers to finely discriminate between L1 transfer vs universal effects, so corpus data can be used to investigate such hypotheses in a more nuanced way as will be illustrated below in the subsection on *Representative Corpora and Research*. Many LCR studies have traditionally been more descriptive than explanatory (Myles, 2015) and have readily attributed learners' errors to L1 transfer (Callies, 2015, p. 49), when in fact many are developmental or universal in nature. A theoretically-informed approach to L2 corpus data, such as one that examines the predictions of the FRH, therefore provides a more nunanced understanding of L1 effects (if any).

Frequency, Input, and Access to UG

Frequency effects have been treated cautiously in GenSLA, because it is well known that highly frequent functional categories (e.g., third-person singular -*s*, past-tense -*ed*) and even the most frequent category in English (the definite article *the*) are not readily acquired in L2 English and typically pose persistent problems (Hawkins, 2001; Lardiere, 2007). GenSLA provides theoretically motivated accounts of why some properties and not others are persistently problematic despite their high frequency in the input. The input often underdetermines the complex and subtle linguistic knowledge the learner eventually attains. This is known as the poverty of the stimulus (PoS) and is a key issue in generative L1 acquisition; the child eventually knows linguistically more than what is obvious from the input thanks to UG (Chomsky, 1986). A classic question in GenSLA, known as the access-to-UG debate, is whether this innate device (UG) is still available to the adult learner in L2 acquisition. L2 knowledge of PoS phenomena is a crucial piece of evidence to argue for access to UG in SLA. For example, the Overt Pronoun Constraint (Montalbetti, 1986) is a universal stating that a null pronominal subject (Ø) in a subordinate clause can co-refer with a quantified subject antecedent in a main clause but an overt pronominal subject cannot as it must refer to someone else (*Nadie$_i$ dice que Ø$_i$/él$_{j/*i}$ ha aprobado el examen* 'Nobody$_i$ says that Ø$_i$/he$_{j/*i}$ has passed the exam'). Experimental data (Lozano, 2003) show that English learners of L2 Spanish have native-like knowledge of the OPC from early stages, although their knowledge cannot derive from (i) their L1 English (only overt pronominal subjects are allowed in English), (ii) language teaching or textooks (as the OPC is never explained), and (iii) the Spanish input, because the structural combination *[quantifier$_i$ ... [Ø$_i$]]* is very rare in the input, as proven by its absence in large Spanish native corpora. POS structures may therefore be eventually acquired, which may explain why corpora have not been traditionally favoured as a source of data in GenSLA.

The Role of the Interfaces

The interfaces have received much attention in recent GenSLA. The Interface Hypothesis, IH (Sorace, 2011, 2012) postulates that constructions that are constrained by narrow syntax (e.g., the licensing of null pronominal subjects in null-subject languages) are typically acquired early in development, whereas constructions constrained by language-external interfaces (e.g., the use of null pronouns when regulated by topic and focus at the syntax-discourse, see the subsection on pronouns and anaphora below) are persistently problematic and lead to optionality even in near-native levels of L2 competence. This results from the complexity of simultaneously integrating and processing syntactic knowledge with discursive knowledge (but see White [2011] for an argument that not all interface properties are equally problematic). Taking the IH and White's criticism as a departure point, Lozano (2016, 2018) proposed the Pragmatic Principles Violation Hypothesis (PPVH). Not all pronominal deficits at the syntax-discourse interface are equally problematic: (i) learners often violate the Pragmatic Principle of Economy because in topic-continuity contexts, they produce redundant overt pronouns, which happens to be more frequent with two than with one potential antecedent; (ii) they tend to avoid ambiguity (i.e., the use of null pronouns in topic-shift scenarios) as it would lead to a communicative breakdown therefore violating the Principle of Clarity. In short, there are pragmatic reasons why learners are more redundant and overexplicit than ambiguous, a phenomenon commonly reported in the L2 literature.

To summarise, the centrality of linguistic theory in GenSLA has two consequences for SLA: (i) a high level of prediction and explanatory power and (ii) a way to make sense of bodies of data (Rothman & Slabakova, 2018). Both consequences are relevant for LCR. First, a high level of prediction allows the researcher to search the corpus for a particular linguistic phenomenon amongst a mass of data (hypothesis-testing approach). Second, new meaningful factors may be uncovered in that mass of data in light of the theory (hypothesis-finding approach). GenSLA corpus-based approaches should therefore make use of a top-down approach (departing from a hypothesis to interrogate the corpus) but also the bottom-up approach that has been typical in LCR, i.e., exploring the corpus to find hypotheses (Callies, 2015; Mendikoetxea, 2014; Myles, 2007).

Main Research Methods

In SLA research, there is always a tension between the need for natural data vs the degree of control of the data (Table 16.1), with some researchers favoring corpus data whereas others favor experimental data. To test specific hypotheses, GenSLA researchers have traditionally used more controlled but less natural data (experiments) than corpus methods, which are less controlled but more natural (Lozano & Mendikoetxea, 2013; Myles, 2007). Experiments are typically divided into offline vs online. Offline methods measure the learner's competence/knowledge of the L2 after the linguistic stimulus has been presented, whereas online methods measure performance/processing in real time as the stimuli unfold. The most widely-used offline experiments in the GenSLA tradition are acceptability judgment tests (AJT) (Ionin, 2012; Sorace, 1996). Participants rate the acceptability of one (or two) target sentence(s) (usually on a 1–5 Likert scale, where 1 is unacceptable and 5 is acceptable), which may be often preceded by a context which biases towards one interpretation (e.g., imperfect tense in example (1b) over preterit tense in example (1a) below) (Domínguez, Arche, & Myles, 2017). The simultaneous presentation of two target sentences, each followed by a Likert scale, allows for testing of a key issue in GenSLA, optionality, as it is often the case that learners' ILGs tolerate both structures to varying degrees. The Self-Paced Reading Task (SPRT) (Roberts, 2012) is a typical online experiment that measures the milliseconds it takes readers to parse (i.e., syntactically analyze) a sentence as it unfolds in real time. For example, learners are presented with sentences like example (2) in a word-by-word fashion (marked by '/') on a computer screen. The learner presses the key to advance to the next word. Crucially, when the learner's parser (mental syntactic processor) reaches the pronoun *he*, an ambiguity is created because it could refer to either the subject *John* or the object *Peter*. The computer accurately measures the extra time it takes to process such ambiguities when compared to similar but non-ambiguous sentences. The combined use of offline vs online methods is important for the latest versions of the IH (Sorace, 2011, 2012), which stipulates that, although near-native learners may show native-like competence/knowledge in offline tasks, their performance/parsing may be non native-like because integrating syntactic with discursive knowledge uses additional cognitive resources.

(1) When Ana was a child she had a very close friend, Amy, and she like to spend a lot of time at her house after school.
    (a) Ana estuvo mucho en casa de Ana al salir del colegio. -2 -1 0 +1 +2
    (b) Ana estaba mucho en casa de Ana al salir del colegio. -2 -1 0 +1 +2
    'Ana was$_{pret/imperf}$ in Amy's house a lot after getting off school'

(2) John / greeted / Peter / as / he / opened / the / door.

Table 16.1 Different Research Methods Used in LCR vs GenSLA

LCR tradition		GenSLA tradition
− control		+ control
+ natural		− natural
Corpora	**Controlled production tasks**	**Experiments**
• *Single-task L2 corpora*	• Sentence completion tasks	*Offline experiments:*
• *Multi-task L2 corpora*	• Gap filling tasks	• AJT
		• Interpretation tasks
		Online experiments:
		• SPRT

Experimental methods have been favoured in GenSLA for several reasons. Researchers are often interested in linguistic phenomena that may have low frequency in an L2 corpus (known as *construct underrepresentation*). They often need to know what learners accept/produce as a possible ILG, but also, crucially, what they reject or rule out. Additionally, the production of a form in the corpus may not necessarily reflect the learner's competence, and the absence of a form does not entail lack of knowledge. Lack of production may be a sampling issue; the form may be absent due to the learner's use of avoidance strategies, or there may not be enough instances of the form in the corpus so as to assume competence. Experiments can tap competence more directly that corpora do.

The use of L2 corpora in GenSLA has been therefore rather limited to date (but see Lardiere, 2007; Myles, 2005, 2015; Rutherford & Thomas, 2001). A notable exception was Patty's corpus, which was used to test the Feature Reassembly Hypothesis (Lardiere, 2007) on an L1 Chinese-L2 English adult immigrant in the USA after 10 years of residence, but the data of this *ad-hoc* case-study corpus are rather limited (4 recordings and 25 emails in total) (Lardiere, 2008). Such case-study corpora lack extrapolability to the learner population. There is therefore a "need to test hypothesis on larger and better constructed databases" (Mendikoetxea, 2014, p. 12) for several reasons (Lozano & Mendikoetxea, 2013; Myles, 2005, 2007, 2015). First, L2 corpora can provide a wider empirical basis against which to test specific hypotheses than previous small-scale experimiental studies. Additionally, the process of tagging ILG data also serves as an exploratory process that allows the researcher to uncover new factors that might have gone unnoticed in experimental work, which in turn can help the researcher design a new and better-informed experiment whose results can be triangulated against corpus data. For example, Mendikoetxea and Lozano (2018) investigated the acquisition of L2 English Subject-Verb inversion as in example (3) (postverbal subjects shown in bold). The corpus data confirmed a classic hypothesis that has been tested in experiments, namely, the Unaccusative Hypothesis (UH). It basically states that subjects can appear postverbally with a set of instransitive verbs called unaccusatives, such as *exist, occur, appear*, but the corpus data also revealed new insights about the nature of the preverbal element (shown in italics), which could take the form of the grammatical expletive *there* (3a), but also ungrammatical *it* (3b) and null expletives (3c) or even a loco-temporal PP (3d). The corpus findings were, in turn, implemented in an experiment, which provided newer insights into the acquisition of the preverbal element.

(3)   a. *There* exist **about two hundred organizations such as Greenpeace, which have increased the number of its members laterly**.
       b. … *it* had occurred **many important events**.
       c. ... exist **the science technology and the industrialisation**.
       d. *In some places* still exist **popularly supported death penalty**.

L2 corpus data can additionally provide natural and rich discursive information that is essential to fully understand phenomena at the interfaces (e.g., information-structure fators like anaphora resolution at the syntax-discourse interface, as will be seen below). If well-designed, a corpus containing precise learner metadata can provide insights into GenSLA issues like near native-ness, age effects and so on, as will become clear in the following paragraphs.

Different L2 corpus software tools have been used in LCR including concordancers, taggers, and annotators (Chapter 6, this volume, on concordancers). Because GenSLA researchers test specific hypotheses, they need fine-grained, linguistically-informed tagsets that incorporate the multiple factors that previous research has shown to be relevant, as in the study of anaphora resolution in L2 acquisition (Lozano, 2009b, 2016) (Figure 16.1) (see the subsection on pronouns and anaphora below for details). In GenSLA, broad error tagging and even automatic POS tagging have not been used because they may overlook crucial ILG phenomena (e.g., the information

Cristóbal Lozano

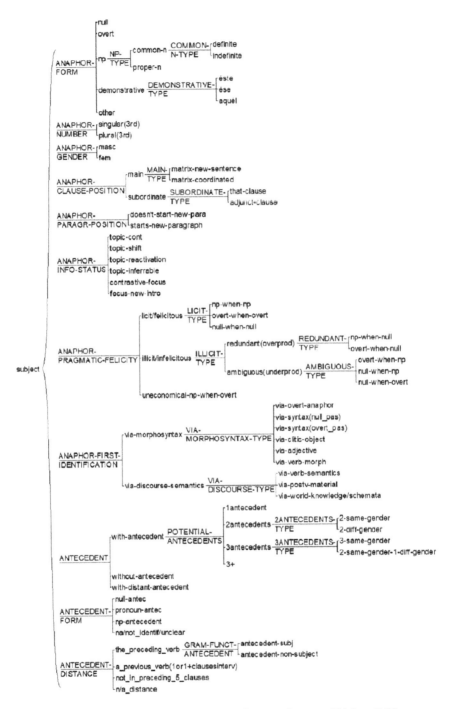

Figure 16.1   A Fine-grained, Linguistically-motivated Tagset (Lozano 2016, p. 247).

status of the anaphor, the number of potential antecedents of the anaphor, the distance between the anaphor and the antecedent, etc). The UAM Corpus Tool software[1] (O'Donnell, 2009) allows researchers to build complex tagsets for manual annotation and to later perform complex statistical contrasts amongst tags in ways which have not been previously possible in (Gen)SLA. For example, researchers can get statistics for all tags in the tagset in Figure 16.1, or statistically compare all/some/each of them amongst subcorpora or amongst individual texts, or get statistics for a combination of tags (e.g., null pronouns & topic continuity scenarios) and compare them amongst subcorpora (Lozano, in press for a practical illustration).

When designing a corpus (see Chapter 5, this volume, for an overview), (Gen)SLA researchers should follow general corpus design principles and collect (Gen)SLA-relevant variables (see Lozano & Mendikoetxea, 2013 for tips), e.g.:

i. Multi-L1 corpora: A variety of learner subcorpora sampling different L1s (ideally with some L1s differing in terms of parameters/features) will shed light on possible UG influence in case all learners behave similarly irrespective of their L1s.

ii. SLA-motivated learner variables: Recording certain types of learner metadata is crucial to understand some SLA phenomena, e.g.: *age of exposure to the L2* to investigate the Critical Period Hypothesis and age-related effects on learners' deficits with features, as explained above; *length of residence in the L2 target country* to check whether immersion and native input may help learners overcome certain residual deficits after prolonged exposure to the L2, as in the case of Patty explained above; the *languages used* by the learner in daily interactions to explore language dominance and attrition effects, as discussed above; and the *proficiency level* of the learners (as measured by a standardised placement test and not by ad-hoc measures like year/grade at school, as often done in LCR) to investigate language development. These variables help select and filter out learners in theoretically-motivated GenSLA studies of, e.g., ultimate attainment, where it is essential to discriminate near-natives from very advanced learners.

iii. Control corpus: It is essential to use a comparable native control corpus whose design is similar to the L2 corpus (i.e., same tasks, same linguistic variables). The L2 corpus can then be contrasted against the native corpus so as to determine (i) whether native-input frequency (as reflected in the native corpus) shapes the learners' ILGs, because GenSLA has shown that L2 acquisition is not always driven by input frequency alone; (ii) learners' overuse/underuse/misuse of linguistic items when compared to natives, which is central to LCR (Callies, 2015, p. 40) and which may shed light on a key issue in GenSLA: ultimate attainment in near natives; (iii) whether the observed L2 variability/optionality is either genuine learner variability triggered by the representational/processing deficits explained above or rather a natural reflection of the variability present in the native grammar (i.e., theoretical models may predict a certain phenomenon to be categorical in native grammars, but corpus production data may reveal it is variable). Finally, GenSLA researchers may need to use two native corpora as control corpora, i.e., a native corpus of the learners's L1 and a native corpus of the learners' L2 (see section on *Future Directions* below for a justification).

Importantly, corpus data may be complemented with experimental data, as they are not mutually exclusive but rather complementary (see Chapter 10, this volume). Triangulating methods to investigate the same phenomenon represents an advance in (Gen)SLA (see the section on *Future Directions* below).

Representative Corpora and Research

A couple of representative GenSLA studies will illustrate how corpus data can inform the acquisition of grammar in an L2. See Rankin (2015) and Myles (2015) for general reviews of corpus-based studies on L2 grammar and Lozano and Mendikoetxea (2008, 2010) and Rankin (2009) for specific GenSLA corpus-based studies on word order.

Domínguez et al., (2017) is a GenSLA study that shows how the combined use of corpus data and experimental data provide better insights into aspectual contrasts in L2 acquisition.

Corpus and method: Data were taken from the *Spanish Learner Language Oral Corpus* (version 2), SPLLOC2[2] http://www.splloc.soton.ac.uk/ (Domínguez, Tracy-Ventura, Arche, Mitchell, & Myles, 2013), a spoken corpus of L1 English-L2 Spanish learners at three proficiency levels (beginner/intermediate/advanced according to hours of instruction), plus a comparable Spanish native subcorpus. They compared results from two corpus tasks eliciting different past tense/ aspect contrasts (a guided interview about the participant's past and a more controlled narrative retell task with eliciting prompts) against a contextualised AJT, as in example (1) above.

Phenomenon: With past tense, perfective aspect encodes finished events but imperfective aspect encodes unfinished events that can be of three types: continuous (ocurring any number of occasions), habitual (ocurring more than once) and progressive (ocurring once) (Table 16.2). Spanish assembles this aspectual contrast straightforwardly: perfective features→preterit tense; imperfective features→imperfect tense. But English is not so straightforward: perfective & imperfective (continuous and habitual[3])→past-simple tense; imperfective (progressive)→periphrasis (*be*+verb-*ing*). The task of L1 English-L2 Spanish learners is (i) to acquire that there is straightforward meaning-form correspondence in Spanish (perfectivity-preterit, imperfectivity-imperfect), (ii) to remap/reassemble the imperfective features (continuous, habitual, progressive), which already exist in their L1 English, onto their new Spanish imperfect verbal morphology. More importantly, learners have to remap the aspectual meanings encoded by the English past simple onto the new Spanish forms (preterit, imperfect).

Predictions: According to the FRH (see section on *Core Issues* above), learners are expected to have problems when remapping or reassembling the perfective/imperfective aspectual distinction onto their corresponding forms in L2 Spanish because English and Spanish differ in the way this distinction is assembled in morphological forms. Learners will overextend the aspectual meanings associated with English past simple morphology (perfective, imperfective continuous/ habitual) to the Spanish preterit morphology.

Results: Imperfect verbal morphology is correctly produced/accepted from early stages, but the array of interpretations (continuous, habitual, progressive) is not completely acquired even at advanced levels (see Table 16.2, last column). Learners incorrectly overextend preterit forms (*estuvo, cantó*) to all three imperfective contexts, although the degree of overextension depends on the nature of the task (corpus production vs experimental interpretation task). Overextenstion was highly problematic in continuous contexts in the experiment (i.e., acceptance of ungrammatical *Marta *estuvo enferma cuando la visité*), but in habitual contexts in the corpus (i.e., production of *Marta *cantó en un coro cuando era pequeña*). These mapping problems are predicted by the FRH. Importantly, if only corpus data had been used, the researchers would have concluded that overextension happens only in habitual contexts. If only experimental data had been used, only continuous contexts would have been shown to be problematic. In short, the combined used of corpus and experimental data, coupled with theoretically motivated predictions, provides nuanced insights into aspectual distinctions in SLA.

Another representative study is Lozano (2016). Taking the IH as a starting point (see section on *Core Issues* above), he used L2 Spanish corpus data and proposed the PPVH to account for anaphora resolution (AR).

Phenomenon: AR refers to how referential expressions (REs) like overt pronouns (*ella* 'she'), null pronouns (*Ø*) and NPs (*el abogado* 'the lawyer'), shown in bold in examples (4) and (5), refer to previously mentioned antecedents (in italics) in the discourse. REs can syntactically alternate in subject position (*El abogado/él/Ø tiene problemas*), but such alternation is constrained at the syntax-discourse interface by information structure in native Spanish; in topic continuity, the

Table 16.2 Feature Configuration of Perfective/Imperfective Aspect in Native English, Native Spanish, and L1 English-L2 Spanish

	Features	English native forms		Spanish native forms		L1 English-L2 Spanish learner forms
PERFECTIVE	[finished] [1 occasion]	*Marta* **was** *ill last sunday*	**Preterit**	*Marta* **estuvo** *enferma el domingo*	**Preterit**	*Marta* **estuvo** *enferma el domingo*
IMPERFECTIVE	CONTINUOUS [unfinished] [any occasions]	*Marta* **was** *ill (when I visited her)*	**Past simple** — *Be+V-ing*	*Marta* **estaba** *enferma (cuando la visité)*	**Imperfect** — ***Preterit overextension*** — **Imperfect**	*Marta* **estaba/*estuvo** *enferma (cuando la visité)* FINDINGS:[c] ○ Exper: most problematic ○ Corpus: problematic
	HABITUAL [unfinished] [>1 occasion]	*Marta* **sang**[a] *in a choir when she was little*		*Marta* **cantaba**[a] *en un coro cuando era pequeña*		*Marta* **cantaba/*cantó** *en un coro cuando era pequeña.* FINDINGS:[c] ○ Exper: least problematic ○ Corpus: most problematic
	PROGRESSIVE [unfinished] [1 occasion]	*Marta* **was singing** *when we arrived*		*Marta* **cantaba**[b] *cuando llegamos*		*Marta* **cantaba/*cantó** *cuando llegamos.* FINDINGS:[c] ○ Exper: problematic ○ Corpus: least problematic

Notes: [a] Periphrastic forms are also used to express habitual imperfective aspect both in English (*Marta would sing/used to sing in a choir*) and in Spanish (*Marta solía cantar en un coro*). [b] Periphrastic forms are also possible in Spanish for progressive imperfective aspect (*Marta estaba cantando cuando llegamos*). [c] For simplicity reasons, findings refer only to the advanced learners.

sentential topic is maintained via a null pronoun (*el abogado*$_i$ ... $\emptyset_i$ in [5a] and *Ella*$_i$ ... $\emptyset_i$ in [4]), but an overt pronoun represents a topic shift (*el abogado*$_i$ ... *Ella*$_j$ in [5b]), although an NP could also mark a topic shift (*Ella*$_j$ ... $\emptyset_j$ ... *El abogado*$_i$ in [4]).

(4) *Este abogado*$_i$ tiene sus proprias problemas con *su hija*$_j$. **Ella**$_j$ es una adicta de heroína, y [**Ø**$_j$] le$_j$ llama casi cada día, pidiendo ayuda o dinero. **El abogado**$_i$ casi le$_j$ ha renunciado… [L1 Eng-L2 Spa advanced learner, CEDEL2 corpus]

'This lawyer$_i$ has his own problems with his daughter$_j$. She$_j$ is an addict to heroin, and [she$_j$] calls him$_j$ nearly every day, asking for help or money. The lawyer$_i$ has nearly renounced her$_j$ …

(5) a. El abogado$_i$ tiene problemas con su hija$_j$. [**Ø**$_i$] Buscará una solución.
      b. *El abogado*$_i$ tiene problemas con su *hija*$_j$. **Ella**$_j$ buscará una solución.
      'The lawyer has problems with his daughter. [He] / She will find a solution.'

Corpus and method: Lozano (2016) analysed the multi L1-L2 Spanish CEDEL2[4] (*Corpus Escrito del Español L2*) (Lozano, 2009a; Lozano & Mendikoetxea, 2013). He compared very advanced L1 English-L2 Spanish learners with an equally-designed native Spanish control corpus. Film-retell tasks were annotated with a linguistically informed fine-grained tagset (Figure 16.1 above) implemented in the UAM Corpus Tool software.

Predictions: The IH predicts that, at the syntax-discourse interface, L2 learners will produce overt (instead of null) pronominal subjects as the default form due to the difficulty of integrating syntactic information (licensing of null pronouns) and discursive information (topic continuity vs topic shift). Taking the IH as a starting point, Lozano used natural corpus production data to test the PPVH (see section on *Core Issues* above).

Results: In topic-continuity contexts, learners differed from natives, as they redundantly used overt pronouns, as predicted by the IH, but the corpus data uncovered a more complex picture that previous GenSLA experimental studies had overlooked: the number of potential antecedents in the previous discourse shapes the form of the RE in subtle ways, i.e., (i) in topic continuity such 'redundant' pronouns are produced when there are two competing antecedents but not when there is one; (ii) in topic shift, both natives and learners use an overt pronoun more often than an NP when there are two competing antecedents, but with three competing antecedents an NP is the norm. Learners' show native-like sensitivity to the number of competing antecedents, but they are more often redundant than ambiguous. The PPVH was proposed to account for these new corpus findings.[5] The GenSLA hypothesis-testing (coupled with a corpus-based hypothesis-finding model) can shed new light on factors that could have been overlooked in previous studies using experimental methods.

Future Directions

This section discusses key issues and recommendations for future GenSLA/LCR researchers. The first issue relates to triangulation, which is the standard scientific practice of using different research methods to investigate a phenomenon. Some researchers recently began advocating for the triangulation of corpus and experimental data in SLA research (Díaz-Negrillo & Thompson, 2013; Gilquin, this volume; Lozano & Mendikoetxea, 2013; Tracy-Ventura & Myles, 2015), particularly when the phenomenon under investigation is infrequent in the corpus (Callies, 2015). Recall that combining corpus and experimental data provides new insights into tense-aspect contrasts (Domínguez et al., 2017; Domínguez et al., 2013). Mendikoetxea and Lozano (2018) show how corpus and experimental methods can be used to investigate the very same linguistic phenomenon (postverbal subjects) in a cyclic fashion, whereby the new factors that were uncovered in the corpus and which went undetected in previous experimental studies, can be implemented in a new experiment, whose results may ultimately inform future corpus analyses.

A second issue concerns the use of two native control corpora. Apart from including an equally-designed native control corpus of the learners' target language (as done in CEDEL2 and SPLLOC), a further step is using an additional control corpus. For example, the L1 English-L2 Spanish data from CEDEL2 (version 2.0) can be compared against two control corpora: an L1 Spanish native control subcorpus from CEDEL2 itself and an equally designed L1 English native control subcorpus from COREFL[6] (*Corpus of English as a Foreign Language*) (Lozano, Díaz-Negrillo & Callies, 2020). GenSLA researchers can thus (i) use real native production data to understand how a given linguistic phenomenon works in natural contexts in both the learners' native language and in the language they are acquiring; (ii) better understand how the linguistic features of those two languages shape the makeup of the learners' ILGs; and (iii) explore other types of L1 influence as well as L2 input influence on the learners' ILG.

Another issue is the design of L1↔L2 bidirectional corpora. This design principle is important because it allows researchers to test the same linguistic phenomenon bidirectionally, e.g., L1 English-L2 Spanish (CEDEL2) vs L1 Spanish-L2 English (COREFL). This allows GenSLA researchers to determine which ILG properties are the result of L1-specific factors vs. those that are universal and therefore observable in both corpora.

An additional design issue is bimodal corpora. Whereas most L2 corpora are written (with some cases of spoken corpora like SPLLOC), a welcome addition to SLA would be the use of equally-designed bimodal corpora (written vs spoken) sampling the very same learners producing both tasks. This allows researchers to test the effect of modality, because it has been claimed that learners' competence is reflected better in spoken than written corpora (Myles, 2015, p. 313), but this is an empirical issue that needs further LCR-based corroboration. Additionally, spoken (dialogic) data are suitable to test interface effects when discourse information (new/old, topic/focus) constrains syntactic choices (syntax-discourse interface).

Another issue relates to the use of developmental L2 corpora. Some of the main aims of GenSLA is to understand (i) how ILGs develop over time (from initial states through transitional states up to end-states), (ii) how parametric/featural choices develop across stages, and (iii) whether native-like competence is eventually attainable (end-states). Longitudinal corpora are ideal to test this, but it is logistically complex to track the development of the same group of learners across the years as their proficiency increases. Cross-sectional L2 corpora are a logistically simpler solution, as in CEDEL2 and SPLLOC. Most traditional L2 English corpora, like ICLE, sample advanced learners only, but recent attempts, like the *Longitudinal Database of Learner English*, LONGDALE (Meunier, 2016), represent truly longitudinal corpora.

An important design issue concerns different types of exposure. There is a need for more L2 corpora sampling (ideally the same) learners under different conditions of exposure, as in LANGSNAP[7] (*Languages and Social Networks Abroad Project*) (Tracy-Ventura, Huensch & Mitchell, forthcoming), who tracked L1 English-L2 Spanish/French university learners before, during, and after a residence abroad programme. For advanced learners, genuine exposure to the L2 during residence abroad is expected to enhance discursive aspects, which may be beneficial for syntax-discourse interface phenomena.

An additional design issue relates to the variety of learners. Many L2 corpora sample homogeneous groups (i.e., university learners studying English degrees and performing similar tasks as part of their curriculum, as in ICLE). This can undermine the balance/representativeness of the corpus (Gilquin, 2015), as findings may not be extrapolable to the entire population of L2 learners. Such corpora may not be sufficient to address theoretical questions like ultimate attainment, which typically require the learner to have resided in the target country for several years to be considered as a near native. Current GenSLA research shows that L2 dominance, which is often the result of the learner's prolonged exposure to (and use of) the L2 in the target country, affects certain peripheral areas (interfaces) of the L1, although these effects appear not to be irreversible (Chamorro, Sorace, & Sturt, 2016; Domínguez, 2013; Sorace, 2004). This is known as L1 attrition, but to date, there is no publicly available corpus of L1 attriters. Therefore, corpora with varied types of bilinguals are ideal, as Gilquin (2015) argues:

> What is particularly interesting about this corpus [CEDEL2] is that, unlike most learner corpora which are collected in a small number of environments …, speakers of Spanish all over the world were invited to contribute. This results in a wide range of writer profiles, using different varieties of (learner and native) Spanish.

(p. 23)

A final corpus design issue is the variety of communicative tasks. Argumentative essays have been the mainstream task in many L2 corpora, but different communicative tasks provide learners with opportunities to make relevant linguistic contrasts in a variety of contexts (Callies, 2015; Myles, 2015). Tracy-Ventura and Myles (2015) used a variety of corpus tasks from the SPLLOC corpus and showed that if only a standard descriptive task had been used instead of other highly controlled narrative tasks, certain tense-aspect contrasts would not have shown up in the learner data. Multi-task corpora may therefore provide a better reflection of learners' competence. Unlike previous experimental studies, Lozano (2009b) found that, out of 12 tasks from CEDEL2 (descriptive, narrative, and argumentative), learners were shown to exhibit deficits only in those tasks eliciting anaphora resolution contexts in third person singular human contexts and not in tasks eliciting first or second person.

To summarise, hypothesis-testing studies that are backed up by properly designed and SLA-motivated L2 corpus data can provide new insights into key aspects in GenSLA.

Further Reading

Lozano, C., & Mendikoetxea, A. (2013). Learner corpora and second language acquisition: The design and collection of CEDEL2. In A. Díaz-Negrillo, N. Ballier, & P. Thompson (Eds.), *Automatic treatment and analysis of learner corpus data* (pp. 65–100). Amsterdam: John Benjamins. doi:10.1075/scl.59.06loz

Lozano & Mendikoetxea (2013) discuss L2 corpus design principles and variables. They highlight ten basic principles of learner corpus design (taking CEDEL2 as a case in point) as well as a proposal for the type of learner and task variables needed if the corpus intends to answer SLA-relevant questions (see also Gilquin's 2015 review of the design of CEDEL2, which also contains additional recommendations for L2 corpus design principles and how to collect the data).

Myles, F. (2015). Second language acquisition theory and learner corpus research. In S. Granger, G. Gilquin, & F. Meunier (Eds.), *The Cambridge handbook of learner corpus research* (pp. 309–332). Cambridge: Cambridge University Press.

Myles, F. (2007). Using electronic corpora in SLA research. In D. Ayoun (Ed.), *Handbook of French applied linguistics* (pp. 377–400). Amsterdam: John Benjamins.

Myles (2015) and her earlier version (Myles, 2007) focus on how LCR can best contribute to SLA theory. Myles also discusses what is needed in an L2 corpus for SLA research, which will provide insights for future (Gen)SLA L2 corpus designers.

Related Topics

Chapters 5, 6, and 10.

Notes

1 http://www.corpustool.com (last accessed 16 December 2019).
2 http://www.splloc.soton.ac.uk (last accessed 16 December 2019).
3 Note that habitual can be also realised periphrastically with *would/used to*.
4 http://cedel2.learnercorpora.com (last accessed 16 December 2019).
5 Recent corpus-informed experimental data confirm the PPVH (Lozano, 2018).
6 http://corefl.learnercorpora.com (last accessed 23 September 2020).
7 http://langsnap.soton.ac.uk/ (last accessed 16 December 2019).

References

Callies, M. (2015). Learner corpus methodology. In S. Granger, G. Gilquin, & F. Meunier (Eds.), *The Cambridge handbook of learner corpus research* (pp. 35–55). Cambridge: Cambridge University Press.
Chamorro, G., Sorace, A., & Sturt, P. (2016). What is the source of L1 attrition? The effect of recent L1 re-exposure on Spanish speakers under L1 attrition. *Bilingualism: Language and Cognition, 19*(3), 520–532. doi:10.1017/S1366728915000152

Chomsky, N. (1981). *Lectures on government and binding*. Dordrecht: Foris.

Chomsky, N. (1986). *Knowledge of language: Its nature, origin and use*. New York: Praeger.

Chomsky, N. (1995). *The minimalist program*. Cambridge: MIT Press.

Chomsky, N. (2000). *The architecture of language*. Oxford: Oxford University Press.

Chomsky, N. (2005). Three factors in language design. *Linguistic Inquiry*, *36*(1), 1–22.

Chomsky, N. (2011). Language and other cognitive systems. What is special about language? *Language Learning and Development*, *7*(4), 263–278.

Díaz-Negrillo, A., & Thompson, P. (2013). Learner corpora: Looking towards the future. In A. Díaz-Negrillo, N. Ballier, & P. Thompson (Eds.), *Automatic treatment and analysis of learner corpus data* (pp. 9–29). Amsterdam: John Benjamins.

Domínguez, L. (2013). *Understanding interfaces: Second language acquisition and first language attrition of Spanish subject realization and word order variation* (vol. 55). Amsterdam: John Benjamins. Retrieved from http://www.jbe-platform.com/content/books/9789027271990

Domínguez, L., Arche, M. J., & Myles, F. (2017). Spanish imperfect revisited: Exploring L1 influence in the reassembly of imperfective features onto new L2 forms. *Second Language Research*, *33*(4), 431–457. doi:10.1177/0267658317701991

Domínguez, L., Tracy-Ventura, N., Arche, M. J., Mitchell, R., & Myles, F. (2013). The role of dynamic contrasts in the L2 acquisition of Spanish past tense morphology. *Bilingualism: Language and Cognition*, *16*(3), 558–577. doi:10.1017/S1366728912000363

Gilquin, G. (2015). From design to collection of learner corpora. In S. Granger, G. Gilquin, & F. Meunier (Eds.), *The Cambridge handbook of learner corpus research* (pp. 9–34). Cambridge: Cambridge University Press.

Hawkins, R. (2001). *Second language syntax: A generative introduction*. Oxford: Wiley-Blackwell.

Hawkins, R. (2007). The nativist perspective on second language acquisition. *Lingua*, *118*(4), 465–477.

Ionin, T. (2012). Formal theory-based methodologies. In A. Mackey & S. M. Gass (Eds.), *Research methods in second language acquisition: A practical guide* (pp. 30–52). Oxford: Wiley-Blackwell.

Lardiere, D. (2007). *Ultimate attainment in second language acquisition: A case study*. Mahwah: Lawrence Erlbaum Associates.

Lardiere, D. (2008). Feature assembly in second language acquisition. In J. M. Liceras, H. Zobl, & H. Goodluck (Eds.), *The role of formal features in second language acquisition* (pp. 106–140). New York: Lawrence Erlbaum Associates.

Lardiere, D. (2009). Some thoughts on the contrastive analysis of features in second language acquisition. *Second Language Research*, *25*(2), 173–227. doi:10.1177/0267658308100283

Liceras, J. M., Zobl, H., & Goodluck, H. (Eds.) (2008). *The role of formal features in second language acquisition*. Mahwaw: Lawrence Erlbaum Associates.

Lozano, C. (2003). *Universal grammar and focus constraints: The acquisition of pronouns and word order in non-native Spanish*. PhD. University of Essex.

Lozano, C. (2009a). CEDEL2: Corpus Escrito del Español como L2. In C. M. Bretones et al. (Eds.), *Applied linguistics now: Understanding language and mind/La lingüística aplicada actual: Comprendiendo el lenguaje y la mente* (pp. 197–212). Almería: Universidad de Almería.

Lozano, C. (2009b). Selective deficits at the syntax-discourse interface: Evidence from the CEDEL2 corpus. In Y.-I. Leung, N. Snape, & M. Sharwood-Smith (Eds.), *Representational deficits in second language acquisition* (pp. 127–166). Amsterdam: John Benjamins. doi:10.1075/lald.47.09loz

Lozano, C. (2016). Pragmatic principles in anaphora resolution at the syntax-discourse interface: Advanced English learners of Spanish in the CEDEL2 corpus. In M. A. Ramos (Ed.), *Spanish learner corpus research: Current trends and future perspectives* (pp. 235–265). Amsterdam: John Benjamins. doi:10.1075/scl.78.09loz

Lozano, C. (2018). The development of anaphora resolution at the syntax-discourse interface: Pronominal subjects in Greek learners of Spanish. *Journal of Psycholinguistic Research*, *47*(2), 411–430. doi:10.1007/s10936-017-9541-8

Lozano, C. (in press). Corpus textuales de aprendices para investigar sobre la adquisición del español LE/L2. In M. C. Piñol (Ed.), *E-Research y español LE/L2: Investigar en la era de las tecnologías*. New York: Routledge.

Lozano, C., Díaz-Negrillo, A., & Callies, M. (2020). Designing and compiling a learner corpus of written and spoken narratives: COREFL. In C. Bongartz & J. Torregrossa (Eds.), *What's in a narrative? Variation in story-telling at the interface between language and literacy* (pp. 9–32). Frankfurt: Peter Lang Publishing.

Lozano, C., & Mendikoetxea, A. (2008). Postverbal subjects at the interfaces in Spanish and Italian learners of L2 English: A corpus analysis. In G. Gilquin, S. Papp, & M. B. Díez-Bedmar (Eds.), *Linking up contrastive and learner corpus research* (pp. 85–125). Amsterdam: Brill Rodopi. doi:10.1163/9789401206201_005

Lozano, C., & Mendikoetxea, A. (2010). Interface conditions on postverbal subjects: A corpus study of L2 English. *Bilingualism: Language and Cognition, 13*(4), 475–497. doi:10.1017/S1366728909990538

Lozano, C., & Mendikoetxea, A. (2013). Learner corpora and second language acquisition: The design and collection of CEDEL2. In A. Díaz-Negrillo, N. Ballier, & P. Thompson (Eds.), *Automatic treatment and analysis of learner corpus data* (pp. 65–100). Amsterdam: John Benjamins. doi:10.1075/scl.59.06loz

Mendikoetxea, A. (2014). Corpus-based research in second language Spanish. In K. L. Geeslin (Ed.), *The handbook of Spanish second language acquisition* (pp. 11–29). Oxford: Wiley-Blackwell.

Mendikoetxea, A., & Lozano, C. (2018). From corpora to experiments: Methodological triangulation in the study of word order at the interfaces in adult late bilinguals (L2 learners). *Journal of Psycholinguistic Research, 47*(4), 871–898. doi:10.1007/s10936-018-9560-0

Meunier, F. (2016). Introduction to the LONGDALE project. In E. Castello K. Ackerley, & F. Coccetta (Eds.), *Studies in learner corpus linguistics. Research and applications for foreign language teaching and assessment* (pp.123–126). Berlin: Peter Lang Publishing. Retrieved from https://uclouvain.be/en/research-institutes/ilc/cecl/longdale.html

Montalbetti, M. (1986). How pro is it? In *Studies in romance linguistics* (pp. 137–152). Dordrecht: Foris.

Montrul, S. (2011). Multiple interfaces and incomplete acquisition. *Lingua, 121*(4), 591–604. doi:10.1016/j.lingua.2010.05.006

Myles, F. (2005). Interlanguage corpora and second language acquisition research. *Second Language Research, 21*(4), 373–391.

Myles, F. (2007). Using electronic corpora in SLA research. In D. Ayoun (Ed.), *Handbook of French applied linguistics* (pp. 377–400). Amsterdam: John Benjamins.

Myles, F. (2015). Second language acquisition theory and learner corpus research. In S. Granger, G. Gilquin, & F. Meunier (Eds.), *The Cambridge handbook of learner corpus research* (pp. 309–332). Cambridge: Cambridge University Press.

O'Donnell, M. (2009). The UAM corpus tool: Software for corpus annotation and exploration. In C. M. Bretones et al. (Eds.), *Applied linguistics now: Understanding language and Mind/La Lingüística Aplicada actual: Comprendiendo el Lenguaje y la Mente* (pp. 1433–1447). Almería: Universidad de Almería.

Rankin, T. (2009). Verb second in advanced L2 English: A learner corpus study. In M. Bowles, T. Ionin, S. Montrul, & A. Tremblay (Eds.), *Proceedings of the 10th generative approaches to second language acquisition conference* (pp. 46–59). Somerville: Cascadilla Proceedings Project.

Rankin, T. (2015). Learner corpora and grammar. In S. Granger, G. Gilquin, & F. Meunier (Eds.), *The Cambridge handbook of learner corpus research* (pp. 231–254). Cambridge: Cambridge University Press.

Roberts, L. (2012). Psycholinguistic techniques and resources in second language acquisition research. *Second Language Research, 28*(1), 113–127. doi:10.1177/0267658311418416

Rollinson, P., & Mendikoetxea, A. (2010). Learner corpora and second language acquisition: Introducing WRICLE. In J. L. Bueno Alonso et al. (Eds.), *Analizar datos > Describir variación / Analysing data > Describing variation* (pp. 1–12). Vigo: Universidade de Vigo (Servizo de Publicacións).

Rothman, J., & Slabakova, R. (2011). The mind-context divide: On acquisition at the linguistic interfaces. *Lingua, 121*(4), 568–576.

Rothman, J., & Slabakova, R. (2018). The generative approach to SLA and its place in modern second language studies. *Studies in Second Language Acquisition, 40*(2), 417–442. doi:10.1017/S0272263117000134

Rutherford, W., & Thomas, M. (2001). The child language data exchange system in research on second language acquisition. *Second Language Research, 17*(2), 195–212.

Sorace, A. (1996). The use of acceptability judgments in second language acquisition research. In W. C. Ritchtie & T. K. Bhatia (Eds.), *Handbook of second language acquisition* (pp. 375–409). London: Academic Press.

Sorace, A. (2000). Syntactic optionality in non-native grammars. *Second Language Research, 16*(2), 93–102.

Sorace, A. (2004). Native language attrition and developmental instability at the syntax-discourse interface: Data, interpretations and methods. *Bilingualism: Language and Cognition, 7*(2), 143–145.

Sorace, A. (2011). Pinning down the concept of "interface" in bilingualism. *Linguistic Approaches to Bilingualism, 1*(1), 1–33.

Sorace, A. (2012). Pinning down the concept of "interface" in bilingualism: A reply to peer commentaries. *Linguistic Approaches to Bilingualism, 2*(2), 209–216.

Tracy-Ventura, N., Huensch, A., & Mitchell, R. (in press). Understanding the evolution of L2 lexical diversity over time: The contribution of a longitudinal learner corpus. In B. Le Bruyn & M. Paquot (Eds.), *Learner corpus research meets second language acquisition*. Cambridge: Cambridge University Press.

Tracy-Ventura, N., & Myles, F. (2015). The importance of task variability in the design of learner corpora for SLA research. *International Journal of Learner Corpus Research, 1*(1), 58–95. doi:10.1075/ijlcr.1.1.03tra

White, L. (1989). *Universal grammar and second language acquisition.* Amsterdam: John Benjamins.

White, L. (2003). *Second language acquisition and universal grammar.* Cambridge: Cambridge University Press.

White, L. (2011). Second language acquisition at the interfaces. *Lingua, 121*(4), 577–590. Retrieved from https://doi.org/16/j.lingua.2010.05.005

White, L. (2012). Universal grammar, crosslinguistic variation and second language acquisition. *Language Teaching, 45*(3), 309–328. doi:10.1017/S0261444812000146

17

Variationist Approaches

Aarnes Gudmestad

Introduction

Variationism is an area of sociolinguistics that examines the linguistic and social factors that condition language variation and change. It has shown that variability is both systematic and inherent in language. Variationist approaches began with William Labov's work on native speakers (NSs; Labov, 1966) and were later applied to the study of additional-language learners (see Bayley & Preston, 1996; Tarone, 2007).

Four constructs are central to this paradigm: linguistic variable, variant, variable context, and constraints. Phenomena that exhibit variation in language are called linguistic variables. Variationist approaches first examined phonological variables, with researchers later expanding the scope of inquiry to include morphosyntactic and lexical variables. One of the most well-studied examples is (ing), in forms like *running* and *studying* in English (Tagliamonte, 2012). Linguistic variables are realized by two or more forms that express the same function or meaning, termed variants. In the case of (ing), the variants are *running* ([ɪŋ]) and *runnin'* ([ɪn]), among others. The variable context, or envelope of variation, pertains to where variation of the linguistic variable occurs and excludes categorical use. For (ing), the variable context is "word-final unstressed *-ing*" (Walker, 2010, p. 12). In order to explain the patterning of the variants, variationists identify linguistic (internal) and social (external, extra-linguistic) constraints or factors that condition the use of a given variant. Grammatical category and speaker sex are examples of linguistic and social constraints, respectively, that influence (ing), with nouns, adjectives, and women favoring the use of [ɪŋ] (Tagliamonte, 2012).

In terms of research methods (see *Main Research Methods* for details), scholars have built different kinds of corpora geared toward analyses of language variation and change among NSs (Tagliamonte, 2012). For oral data, a sociolinguistic interview, which aims to elicit personal narratives from participants, has been a widely used tool for collecting vernacular speech samples. Sociolinguists have also created written corpora, with data coming from sources such as literary work or online newspapers and blogs. After collecting data (and transcribing, if necessary), researchers code data for a given linguistic variable and a range of linguistic and extra-linguistic constraints that are thought to impact the use of the variants. Finally, variationist researchers tend to analyze data quantitatively.

Despite its initial focus on NSs, the variationist paradigm has been extended to the field of second language acquisition (SLA), in part because it has been able to further knowledge about communicative competence. Variationist approaches enable researchers to consider grammatical and sociolinguistic competences simultaneously (see Canale & Swain, 1980) and, consequently, to make observations about how the linguistic and social components of an additional language develop. In this way, Preston's (2000) psycholinguistic model for interlanguage variation offers a theoretical account of additional-language variation. This model demonstrates that linguistic structures are mediated by social and linguistic contexts and time. Learners' (un)conscious selection among variants is not random but rather conditioned probabilistically by different factors, which are grouped into three levels in the model. Level 1 addresses extra-linguistic factors, such as learning context (e.g., Kanwit, Geeslin & Fafulas, 2015) and learner gender (e.g., Regan, Howard & Lemée, 2009). Level 2 refers to linguistic factors, which are generally specific to a given linguistic phenomenon. Examples of linguistic factors for future-time reference in Spanish include temporal distance of the event and person/number of the verb (e.g., Kanwit, 2017). Level 3 pertains to time and explains how the linguistic and extra-linguistic factors that influence variation evolve as acquisition progresses and consists of both cross-sectional (e.g., Geeslin, 2000; Gudmestad, 2012; Kanwit, 2017) and longitudinal investigations (e.g., Gudmestad, Edmonds & Metzger, 2019; Regan, 2004; Tarone & Liu, 1995).

Furthermore, variationist SLA differentiates between two types of variation (see Rehner, 2002). Type I variation pertains to that which occurs during acquisition and includes non-targetlike and targetlike forms. An example in French is the variability between the non-targetlike use of a masculine modifier with a feminine noun (*le cuisine* 'the kitchen') and the targetlike use of a feminine modifier and noun (*la cuisine*). Type II variation exists among targetlike forms only and is characteristic of NS use. Namely, Type II variation aligns with the aforementioned concept of a linguistic variable, which is often termed a variable structure in variationist SLA scholarship. Examples in Spanish are the verb forms used to express futurity (primarily, the periphrastic future, inflectional future, and present indicative). Both kinds of variation, however, can be investigated in tandem within a single linguistic phenomenon. Li (2010), for instance, investigated both types of variation with the Mandarin particle DE. Regardless of the type of variation, variationist SLA research has focused on morphosyntactic (e.g., copular verbs in Spanish, Geeslin, 2000; plural marking in English, Young, 1991) and phonological (e.g., (ing) in English, Adamson & Regan, 1991; intervocalic /d/ in Spanish, Solon, Linford & Geeslin, 2018) structures, although studies on pragmatic (e.g., address pronouns in French, Dewaele, 2004), and lexical (e.g., words for 'car' in French, Nadasdi, Mougeon, & Rehner, 2008) phenomena exist. As I discuss variationist approaches and SLA throughout this chapter, I offer more examples of Type II variation, as it has received greater attention in the literature among variationist researchers (see Geeslin, Gudmestad, Kanwit, Linford, Long, Schmidt, & Solon, 2018).

Core Issues and Topics

In this section, I address three of the overarching topics and issues that pertain to variationist SLA, all of which are germane to the field of SLA more generally: the developmental trajectory, targetlikeness, and individual variation.

The Developmental Trajectory

First, variationist approaches have sought to answer questions about the developmental trajectory. Acquisitional change tends to be observed in three primary ways within variationist approaches: the inventory of variants, the frequency of occurrence of these forms, and the linguistic and extra-linguistic contexts in which the variants occur. Kanwit (2017), who investigated variable future-time reference in Spanish among additional-language learners (at five instructional levels), illustrates each of these characterizations of interlanguage development. The data came from a task in which participants were presented with a series of prompts that served to elicit future-time contexts. Participants responded to the prompts orally and recorded their speech. Regarding the repertoire of variants and the frequency of their occurrence, Kanwit distinguished between commonly and less-commonly used forms. In terms of forms that were used infrequently in the dataset, differences were observed according to proficiency. The lower-level proficiency groups used infinitives, past-time forms (preterit and imperfect), verbless phrases, and invented forms, whereas the more proficient groups produced the future perfect and various subjunctive forms (imperfect, periphrastic, and present perfect). Focusing on the seven most frequent verb forms in the dataset (present indicative, periphrastic future, inflectional future, lexical future, present subjunctive, conditional, and progressive forms), Kanwit found that each learner group exhibited use of these forms, indicating that this type of multifunctionality is not restricted to very advanced learners. Regarding the frequency of use of the common forms, the data revealed clear changes as learners gained more instructional experience with the language. For example, use of the present indicative decreased steadily from Level 1 to Level 5, meanwhile the periphrastic future increased between Levels 2 and 5. Other forms, such as the inflectional future and lexical future, showed more vacillations cross-sectionally. In addition to documenting how the inventory of forms and their frequency of occurrence changed along the acquisitional path, variationist researchers investigate the contexts in which these forms occur. Kanwit analyzed one extra-linguistic and five linguistic factors (see the article for additional details) and found that, as learners' proficiency increased, future-time verb forms became linked to more contexts. For instance, whereas the tense-mood-aspect of the preceding verb, lexical type of the verb, and temporal distance influenced the variants used by Level 1, these factors, as well as person/number of the verb, adverb type, and study-abroad country, conditioned use for Level 5. Thus, variationist approaches have uncovered complex and nuanced changes along the developmental trajectory in the repertoire and frequency of forms and the contexts in which they occur, detailing both systematicity and dynamicity.

Targetlikeness

A second overarching issue that variationist SLA research has addressed is that of targetlikeness, or whether learners can converge with native speakers or bilinguals on variable structures. Donaldson (2017) investigated negation (the variable deletion of the pre-verbal negative particle *ne*) among near-native speakers and NSs of Hexagonal French (French in France) who participated in informal conversations. He found that the near-native speakers deleted *ne* as often as the NSs and that the linguistic and extra-linguistic factors that impacted their variable use of *ne* were quite similar, thus offering evidence that the near-native speakers had largely acquired this linguistic variable. Another example showing that adult additional-language users can approach a targetlike norm is Gudmestad (2012). This study analyzed data from three oral-elicitation tasks in order to investigate mood distinction (the subjunctive-indicative contrast) in Spanish and found results similar to those in Donaldson (2017). The graduate-level additional-language users produced the subjunctive and indicative moods at the same rate as a group of NSs (bilinguals whose first language [L1] was Spanish). While the same linguistic and extra-linguistic factors impacted use for both groups, subtle differences in the way they responded to certain factors were uncovered. For example, the NSs used the subjunctive most often in past-hypothetical contexts, and the additional-language users produced the subjunctive most frequently in nonhypothetical contexts. These studies have demonstrated that additional-language learners can approximate a NS norm, at least with some variable structures.

Individual Variation

Third, variationist scholars have explored the degree to which observations made from analyses of aggregate data reflect individual learners. Varying results on this issue have emerged. Bayley and Langman (2004) in a study of Type I variation and Regan (2004) in an investigation of Type II variation (see also Regan et al., 2009) both found that individual patterns largely correspond to group trends. For example, Bayley and Langman (2004) examined the additional-language acquisition of the use of the past tense in Hungarian and English by L1 speakers of Chinese who participated in sociolinguistic interviews and found that the results for individual learners were similar to those of their group. They concluded that "we are justified from an empirical and a theoretical viewpoint in reporting group results in studies of second language acquisition" (p. 315). Other investigations of Type II variation, nevertheless, have found evidence of individual variability. For instance, Hansen Edwards (2011) examined /t/ and /d/ deletion in word-final consonant clusters in additional-language English among NSs of Mandarin who participated in an interview. She found that, although the same factors impacted deletion for the group and the individuals, the effect that certain factors had on deletion differed between the aggregate data and several individuals. Moreover, Geeslin, Linford, Fafulas, Long, and Díaz-Campos (2013) in their investigation of subject expression in Spanish found evidence of individual variability in a written contextualized task, although differences between individuals and their group diminished as proficiency in the target language increased cross-sectionally. These investigations demonstrate that the extent to which individual learners' patterns of variation conform to that of their group is a complex issue that is in need of further research.

Main Research Methods

In this section, I describe the data elicitation, coding, and analyses that are common in this line of inquiry. I also identify challenges and opportunities that corpora offer variationist SLA research, and I make some brief connections between, one the one hand, variationist SLA research and, on the other, learner corpus research (LCR, e.g., Granger, Gilquin, & Meunier, 2015) and corpus linguistics (e.g., O'Keeffe & McCarthy, 2010; Szmrecsany, 2017), as the latter two are areas of research in linguistics where corpora take center stage.[1] As I discuss the main methods that researchers have employed to investigate additional-language variation, I work with the following definition of a corpus: a dataset that consists of (at least somewhat) spontaneous language production elicited through an open-ended task (e.g., interview, conversation) and that can be used to investigate a range of linguistic phenomena.

Data Elicitation

Scholars have collected various types of data in order to investigate additional-language variation. Variationist corpora in SLA have consisted of oral data: semi-guided interviews (e.g., Geeslin & Gudmestad, 2010; Hansen Edwards, 2011; Kennedy Terry, 2017; Mougeon, Nadasdi, & Rehner, 2010) and dyadic conversations (e.g., Donaldson, 2017). This feature of corpora differs from LCR, which has traditionally focused on written language, although oral corpora have become more common (Rankin, 2015). While some of these corpora were created for the purpose of examining variation, importantly, they were not designed to elicit just one particular variable structure. For example, Mougeon et al. (2010) investigated numerous instances of Type II variation in French, such as first-person-plural subject pronouns, negation, and /l/, among immersion learners in Canada. In addition to creating corpora for the purpose of investigating additional-language variation, researchers have begun to use publicly available corpora, which appear to be a promising area for continued research. Gudmestad et al. (2019) conducted an analysis of Type I variation with the LANGSNAP corpus (Mitchell et al., 2017: http://langsnap.soton.ac.uk/), comprised of oral and written production data collected multiple times during a 21-month period. This study examined the developmental trajectory of grammatical gender marking in additional-language Spanish before, during, and after residence abroad in a Spanish-speaking country.

Although corpora are an invaluable tool for furthering knowledge about additional-language variation, other types of data-elicitation measures are necessary (see Geeslin, 2010). For one, while open-ended, extended-language production has the potential advantage of reflecting naturally occurring language, it does not necessarily lend itself easily to the examination of all linguistic structures (see Tracy-Ventura & Myles, 2015). Infrequent linguistic phenomena may not occur often enough in a corpus for (quantitative) analysis. In other words, the feasibility of using a corpus to investigate any structure, whether it is variable or not, hinges on its frequency of occurrence. Some cases of Type II variation, such as subject expression in Spanish, are quite frequent, so a corpus is likely to be a rich source of data to investigate learner use or development of this phenomenon (e.g., Gudmestad, House, & Geeslin, 2013). For others, however, like mood distinction (the subjunctive-indicative contrast) in French, it is challenging to obtain a large data sample from an open-ended production task. Not only are many present-tense indicative and subjunctive forms in French homophonous, but forms that are overtly marked for the subjunctive mood have been found to be infrequent in NS speech and writing, occurring in two percent and one percent, respectively, of all dependent clauses (O'Connor DiVito, 1997, p. 47). Thus, a corpus-based, variationist analysis of an infrequent linguistic phenomenon may not be feasible. In these instances, experimental data or the combination of experimental and corpus data are essential (see Tracy-Ventura & Myles, 2015, for a discussion of underrepresented forms in corpora and Chapter 10, this volume). In the case of mood distinction in French, Gudmestad and Edmonds (2015) collected data using two written instruments: a contextualized-clause-elicitation task and a contextualized-verb-elicitation task. Each instrument consisted of 30 items that were potential contexts for the linguistic variable, allowing for a large enough dataset to analyze mood distinction quantitatively.

Another reason for eliciting other types of data pertains to the multifaceted nature of language and additional-language acquisition. While a semi-guided interview, for example, can provide important details about (somewhat) spontaneous production in an additional language, production data do not enable researchers to draw conclusions about every dimension of language. In this way, variationist researchers have designed instruments that allow for observations to be made about other language abilities. Two examples come from variationist work on Spanish. Kanwit and Geeslin (2014) designed a written instrument to explore the interpretation of the present indicative and present subjunctive in variable contexts with adverbial clauses. For this task, participants read sentences with either a subjunctive or indicative form in the subordinate clause and were asked to select if the event had yet to occur, was habitual, or whether both interpretations were possible. In another study, Schmidt (2018) investigated the perception of a dialect feature in Spanish (/s/-weakening) using an identification task in which participants listened to nonce words and then selected the written representation of the words that they heard. Thus, controlled tasks provide a necessary complement to corpora, as analyses of different types of data help SLA to "fully understand what a learner grammar looks like and how it develops" (Geeslin, 2010, p. 506).

Data Coding

Variationist research involving corpora typically entails extensive coding, as researchers must not only identify the variable context and all occurrences of the variants of a linguistic variable but also code for a host of independent variables.[2] For example, as previously mentioned, Hansen Edwards (2011) examined /t/ and /d/ deletion in additional-language English. She coded each instance of /t/ and /d/ in word-final codas containing two or three consonants for seven linguistic and two extra-linguistic factors. In another study, Gudmestad et al. (2013) investigated the role that eight linguistic and two extra-linguistic factors played in the use of variable third-person subject expression in interviews in Spanish among advanced additional-language speakers and NSs. Although corpus tools offer linguists the opportunity to code large amounts of data more quickly for information like parts of speech, error tagging (see *Data analysis* and Chapter 5, this volume), and syntactic parsing (van Rooy, 2015), variationist SLA researchers do not often report having used corpus tools. This could be in part because one challenge for variationist researchers is that they often code for factors that are not typically (or easily) annotated in corpora. In the case of phonological work like Hansen Edwards' study, for instance, the dependent variable cannot be coded by relying on transcripts alone, but rather, researchers need to listen to the audio files and/or perform acoustic analyses in order to identify the variant used in each word. Moreover, Gudmestad et al. (2013) coded for perseveration and switch reference,[3] two independent, linguistic variables that require understanding the discourse and tracking previous mentions of a referent. Common automated tools in corpus linguistics do not tag these aforementioned features, and they may be difficult to implement given the range of criteria that are used to operationalize them.

Despite this challenge, other corpus tools can be valuable for variationist SLA research. Just as techniques to measure frequency are commonly used by corpus linguists and learner corpus researchers (Cobb & Horst, 2015; Evison, 2010), scholars have begun to explore the relationship between lexical frequency and the additional-language variation of morphosyntactic and phonological structures. One example is Linford, Long, Solon, Whatley, and Geeslin (2016), who investigated the role that the frequency of the verb plays in variable subject expression in NS and additional-language Spanish. Focusing on third-person subjects and a measure of frequency that was internal to their corpus, they found that lexical frequency interacted with other independent factors and had a mediating effect, rather than an independent effect, on subject expression. Gudmestad et al. (2019) also investigated lexical frequency and found that a measure of noun frequency from the *Corpus del Español* (Davies, 2016) did not influence targetlike gender marking in Spanish but that the frequency with which individual participants used a given noun with a modifier overtly marked for gender did condition targetlike gender marking. These studies demonstrate that there are ways in which certain corpus tools can be useful to the study of additional-language variation.

Data Analysis

Similar to LCR and variationist and corpus linguistics research on NSs, variationist SLA research has relied increasingly on quantitative analyses (see Callies, 2015; Crawford & Csomay, 2015; Tagliamonte, 2012). A typical variationist analysis consists of not only documenting the frequency of occurrence of each variant but also performing a multivariate statistical test (e.g., a logistic regression) that enables researchers to investigate the impact that multiple linguistic and extra-linguistic factors have on the linguistic variable (see Chapter 9, this volume). For instance, Regan et al. (2009) investigated the variable deletion of /l/ in certain contexts in French among Irish learners after they had spent a year in France. Their analysis revealed that the learners deleted /l/ 33 percent of the time and that one extra-linguistic and four linguistic factors impacted use. Specifically, deletion was more likely to occur with the impersonal pronoun *il* 'he/it', when the following phonological segment was a consonant and the preceding phonological segment was a vowel or a pause, when the following grammatical category was not a verb, and with women. Strengths of this type of analysis are that it reveals intricacies of interlanguage systematicity, that it uncovers the multifaceted nature of developmental change, and that it allows for learner varieties to be described and explained in their own right (Gudmestad, 2012).

The ability for variationist approaches to examine interlanguage as an independent system, however, does not preclude assessments of targetlikeness. Many studies have included a group of bilinguals (L1 speakers of the target language) who have completed the same task (e.g., Gudmestad et al., 2013) or NSs who live in the same region where learners are living or studying (e.g., Donaldson, 2017).[4] NS data are measured in terms of the variants' frequency of occurrence and the factors influencing their use, in the same way that learner behavior is examined. Learners can then be compared to NSs, and similarities and differences between the two can be identified. Notably, these assessments of targetlikeness do not compare interlanguage to an idealized or prescriptive norm. In fact, variationist researchers have argued that error analyses are inappropriate for the investigation of Type II variation, because NS use is not categorical (Geeslin, 2000). While this feature of variationist analyses diverges from LCR that has relied heavily on error analyses in its examination of learner language (Callies, 2015), it shares traits with proposals for methodological revision in LCR (Gries & Deshors, 2014), and the multivariate analyses in general align with those in corpus linguistics (Szmrecsany, 2017).

Like LCR (see Granger et al., 2015) and as discussed in *Core Topics and Issues*, variationist analyses have traditionally examined aggregate data, but scholars are increasingly recognizing the presence of individual variability. This methodological change has been seen in two primary ways. For one, researchers have included a random effect for participants in regression models in order to account for individual variability in analyses of aggregate data (e.g., Gudmestad et al., 2013; Kennedy Terry, 2017). In other investigations, analyses of group trends have been coupled with those of individuals, which gives an indication of how much aggregate findings represent each participant and offers specific details on how individuals may diverge from patterns observed for their group (e.g., Donaldson, 2017; Hansen Edwards, 2011; Regan et al., 2009). Although variationist research has been dominated by quantitative analyses, qualitative examinations of individuals may be fruitful for better understanding individual variability.

Representative Corpora and Research

I highlight in this section two corpora that are informed by the variationist paradigm. The first focuses on immersion students of French and the second on advanced additional-language speakers of Spanish. To my knowledge, neither corpus is publicly available.

Beginning with the immersion students of French (see Mougeon et al., 2010, for a thorough overview), researchers first began creating this corpus by collecting questionnaire data (e.g., demographic information, language usage) from 322 students enrolled in French immersion programs in high schools in and around Toronto, Canada. They then selected 41 participants based on two criteria: They chose participants who were not raised in homes where French was used among family members and who corresponded to three levels of competence in French (low, mid, and high) (Mougeon et al., 2010, p. 47). The participants completed a semi-directed interview with a NS of French. This corpus of immersion learners has been used to study many linguistic variables in French: restrictive expressions meaning *only*, future-time reference, negation, first-person-plural subject pronouns, inter alia (Mougeon & Rehner, 2001; Nadasdi, Mougeon & Rehner, 2003; Rehner & Mougeon, 1999; Rehner, Mougeon & Nadasdi, 2003). Because NS data do not form part of this corpus, the researchers compare the immersion students to various datasets: sociolinguistic interviews of speakers of Quebec French, sociolinguistic interviews of Ontario French, the speech of French immersion teachers during class time, and written teaching materials used in French classes in the immersion programs.

An example study is Rehner et al.'s (2003) investigation of *nous* and *on* (first-person-plural subject pronouns), where the former is a formal variant, and the latter is mildly marked in Canadian French. The findings indicated that the learners produced *on* more often than *nous*. This trend was similar to that of the immersion teachers, although they used *on* more often than the learners did. Furthermore, learners' pronoun usage was in contrast to pedagogical materials that exhibited higher rates of *nous* compared to *on*. The researchers investigated one linguistic and several extra-linguistic factors in order to determine what constrained learners' use of *on*. The linguistic factor showed that referents that were both nonspecific and unrestricted significantly favored the use of *on*.[5] In general, the extra-linguistic constraints revealed that learners favored *on* when they had more exposure to French outside of the classroom, were male, and were from English-speaking upper-working-class families.

A second corpus that has been studied quite extensively is one that consists of highly proficient additional-language speakers and NSs of Spanish (e.g., Geeslin & Gudmestad, 2010). The 16 advanced additional-language speakers were L1 speakers of English who were enrolled in graduate programs in Spanish in the United States. The NSs were Spanish-English bilinguals, came from various Spanish-speaking regions, and were enrolled in graduate programs at the same university as the additional-language participants. All participants interacted socially and/or professionally. The corpus data came from semi-guided interviews (completed with two NSs of Spanish from different countries) and an oral film retell, although most studies to date have only examined the former. The participants also completed a grammar test in Spanish and a background questionnaire in which they provided details on their education and language experiences. Researchers have used this corpus to investigate Type II variation. Examples of variable structures include subject expression, future-time reference, present-time reference, and word-internal, intervocalic /d/ (e.g., Gudmestad et al., 2013; Gudmestad & Geeslin, 2011; Geeslin & Fafulas, 2012; Solon et al., 2018, respectively).

Regarding word-internal, intervocalic /d/, Solon et al. (2018) examined the interview data and a subset of the participants (13 of each group). Their acoustic analysis of aggregate data consisted of two phases, each with a different dependent variable. For the first part, they classified every instance of word-internal, intervocalic /d/ as a spirant, stop, deletion, or "other." For the second phase, they quantified the "degree of reduction [for] all /d/ realizations that were not deleted" (p. 16). The independent variables were lexical item, grammatical category of the word, the preceding vowel, the following vowel, stress of the syllable, number of syllables in the word, and frequency of the lexical item in the corpus. The results of the first analysis revealed that each participant group produced all four categories of /d/, but their rates of use of the stop, spirant, and deletion differed. For example, the most frequent realization for the NSs was deletion, whereas the additional-language speakers used the spirant most often. The findings for the second phase of the analysis revealed that the additional-language speakers showed a lower degree of reduction of /d/ than the NSs. Moreover, in both analyses, the additional-language speakers exhibited nativelike patterns of use with certain linguistic factors (e.g., preceding vowel) but not others (frequency of the lexical item). Finally, in addition to these group trends, the researchers assessed individual rates of deletion for both participant groups and found varying rates of /d/ deletion among NSs and the additional-language speakers.

Future Directions

While there now exists a substantive body of variationist investigations in SLA, future research on a number of questions is needed. I focus here on four issues that could be aided by corpora. For one, variationist approaches have concentrated on morphosyntactic and phonological phenomena, rather than lexical ones. Given that "corpora are ideally suited to the investigation of lexical acquisition" (Myles, 2015, p. 317), utilizing corpora to examine lexical variation in interlanguage is a clear avenue for future work. Variationist SLA, moreover, is limited in the languages it has investigated, centered primarily on English, French, and Spanish. The creation of new corpora that involve learners whose L1 and additional language(s) expand the languages investigated is crucial. Third, although Preston's (2000) psycholinguistic model for interlanguage variation includes levels for both social and linguistic variation (Levels 1 and 2, respectively), previous studies have overwhelmingly prioritized exploring linguistic factors. There is, therefore, clearly a need to build corpora that allow for greater exploration of the role that extra-linguistic factors play in the additional-language acquisition of variation. Corpora that allow for extra-linguistic factors to be investigated would need diversity with regard to characteristics such as ethnicity and socioeconomic class of the participants. Finally, because frequency of occurrence impacts the feasibility of investigating certain linguistic phenomena, and because understanding additional-language acquisition involves more than examinations of language use, corpora that are coupled with experimental tasks or data on other abilities, such as comprehension and perception, are invaluable, as they will enable variationist researchers to more fully explore the multifaceted nature of interlanguage variation. In these ways, variationist analyses of corpora are in a position to continue to contribute valuable insights into additional-language development.

Further Reading

Geeslin, K. L., & Long, A. Y. (2014). *Sociolinguistics and second language acquisition: Learning to use language in context*. New York: Routledge.

This book connects two fields – SLA and sociolinguistics – and examines the role of social context in additional-language acquisition. Although it also addresses both cognitive and social approaches to sociolinguistic competence, it offers a thorough introduction to variationist approaches and their application to SLA, and it provides a comprehensive discussion of topics such as study abroad and pedagogical implications.

Mougeon, R., Nadasdi, T., & Rehner, K. (2010). *The sociolinguistic competence of French immersion students*. Clevedon: Multilingual Matters.

This book is a culmination of numerous investigations of sociolinguistic competence, stemming from a corpus of interview data collected from high school students who were enrolled in a French immersion program in Canada. In addition to reporting on linguistic constraints and social factors such as social class, the researchers examine the stylistic status of the variants.

Regan, V., Howard, M., & Lemée, I. (2009). *The acquisition of sociolinguistic competence in a study abroad context*. Clevedon: Multilingual Matters.

This investigation explores the acquisition of sociolinguistic competence in additional-language French among Irish-speaking learners of French. It addresses four linguistic variables in French – negation, first-person-plural subject pronouns, future-time reference, and /l/ – and it examines how learners' use of these linguistic phenomena change after a year abroad.

Related Topics

Chapters 2, 3, 9, 10, 13, and 27.

Notes

1 For further discussion on connections between corpus linguistics and (variationist) sociolinguistics see, for example, Andersen (2010) and Szmrecsanyi (2017). Although there are similarities between the two areas of research, Szmrecsanyi identifies six key differences between variationism and corpus linguistics (pp. 688-689). One example is that variationist research has investigated phonetic variation extensively, but corpus linguistics has not.

2 With controlled instruments, researchers design their tasks in order to manipulate relevant linguistic factors (e.g., Geeslin, 2003).
3 Perseveration classifies the subject form of the previous mention of the referent. Switch reference determines whether the referent in the previous clause is the same or different from the subject form being analyzed.
4 While this is common, it does not apply to all additional-language variationist research. For instance, in Regan et al. (2009) learners are compared to previously published research on NSs by other scholars.
5 Rehner et al. (2003) offer the following example of a nonspecific and unrestricted context: "*Nous sommes vraiment en danger notre monde.* 'In this world of ours we are really in danger'" (p. 144).

References

Adamson, H. D., & Regan, V. M. (1991). The acquisition of community speech norms by Asian immigrants learning English as a second language. *Studies in Second Language Acquisition*, *13*(1), 1–22.

Andersen, G. (2010). How to use corpus linguistics in sociolinguistics. In A. O'Keefe & M. McCarthy (Eds.), *The Routledge handbook of corpus linguistics* (pp. 547–562). London: Routledge.

Bayley, R., & Langman, J. (2004). Variation in the group and the individual: Evidence from second language acquisition. *International Review of Applied Linguistics in Language Teaching*, *42*(4), 303–318.

Bayley, R., & Preston, D. R. (1996). *Second language acquisition and linguistic variation.* Amsterdam: John Benjamins.

Callies, M. (2015). Learner corpus methodology. In S. Granger, G. Gilquin, & F. Meunier (Eds.), *The Cambridge handbook of learner corpus research* (pp. 35–55). Cambridge: Cambridge University Press.

Canale, M., & Swain, M. (1980). Theoretical bases of communicative approaches to second language teaching and testing. *Applied Linguistics*, *1*(1), 1–47.

Cobb, T., & Horst, M. (2015). Learner corpora and lexis. In S. Granger, G. Gilquin, & F. Meunier (Eds.), *The Cambridge handbook of learner corpus research* (pp. 185–206). Cambridge: Cambridge University Press.

Crawford, W., & Csomay, E. (2015). *Doing corpus linguistics.* London: Routledge.

Davies, M. (2016–). *Corpus del Español: Two billion words, 21 countries.* Retrieved from http://www.corpusdelespanol.org/web-dial/

Dewaele, J.-M. (2004). *Vous* or *tu*? Native and non-native speakers of French on a sociolinguistic tightrope. *International Review of Applied Linguistics in Language Teaching*, *42*, 383–402.

Donaldson, B. (2017). Negation in near-native French: Variation and sociolinguistic competence. *Language Learning*, *67*(1), 141–170.

Evison, J. (2010). What are the basics of analysing a corpus? In A. O'Keefe & M. McCarthy (Eds.), *The Routledge handbook of corpus linguistics* (pp. 122–135). London: Routledge.

Geeslin, K. L. (2000). A new approach to the second language acquisition of copula choice in Spanish. In R. Leow & C. Sanz (Eds.), *Spanish applied linguistics at the turn of the millennium: Papers from the 1999 conference on the L1 and L2 acquisition of Spanish and Portuguese* (pp. 50–66). Somerville: Cascadilla Press.

Geeslin, K. L. (2003). A comparison of copula choice: Native Spanish speakers and advanced learners. *Language Learning*, *53*(4), 703–764.

Geeslin, K. L. (2010). Beyond "Naturalistic": On the role of task characteristics and the importance of multiple elicitation methods. *Studies in Hispanic and Lusophone Linguistics*, *3*(2), 501–520.

Geeslin, K. L., & Fafulas, S. (2012). Variation of the simple present and present progressive forms: A comparison of native and non-native speakers. In K. L. Geeslin & M. Díaz-Campos (Eds.), *Selected proceedings of the 14th hispanic linguistics symposium* (pp.179–196). Somerville: Cascadilla Proceedings Project.

Geeslin, K. L., & Gudmestad, A. (2010). An exploration of the range and frequency of occurrence of forms in potentially variable structures in second-language Spanish. *Studies in Second Language Acquisition*, *32*(3), 433–463.

Geeslin, K. L., Gudmestad, A., Kanwit, M., Linford, B., Long, A. Y., Schmidt, L., & Solon, M. (2018). Sociolinguistic competence and the acquisition of speaking. In R. A. Alonso (Ed.), *Speaking in a second language* (pp. 2–25). Amsterdam: John Benjamins.

Geeslin, K. L., & Long, A. Y. (2014). *Sociolinguistics and second language acquisition: Learning to use language in context.* New York: Routledge.

Geeslin, K., Linford, B., Fafulas, S., Long, A., & Díaz-Campos, M. (2013). The L2 development of subject form variation in Spanish: The individual vs. the group. In J. Cabrelli Amaro, G. Lord, A. de Prada Pérez,

& J. E. Aaron (Eds.), *Selected proceedings of the 16th hispanic linguistics symposium* (pp. 156–174). Somerville: Cascadilla Proceedings Project.

Granger, S., Gilquin, G., & Meunier, F. (2015). Introduction: Learner corpus research – past, present and future. In S. Granger, G. Gilquin, & F. Meunier (Eds.), *The Cambridge handbook of learner corpus research* (pp. 1–5). Cambridge: Cambridge University Press.

Gries, S. Th., & Deshors, S. C. (2014). Using regressions to explore deviations between corpus data and a standard/target: Two suggestions. *Corpora, 9*(1), 109–136.

Gudmestad, A. (2012). Acquiring a variable structure: An interlanguage analysis of second-language mood use in Spanish. *Language Learning, 62*(2), 373–402.

Gudmestad, A., & Edmonds, A. (2015). Categorical and variable mood distinction in hexagonal French: Factors characterising use for native and non-native speakers. *Canadian Journal of Applied Linguistics, 18*(1), 107–131.

Gudmestad, A., Edmonds, A., & Metzger, T. (2019). Using variationism and learner corpus research to investigate grammatical gender marking in additional-language Spanish. *Language Learning, 69*(4), 911–942.

Gudmestad, A., & Geeslin, K. L. (2011). Assessing the use of multiple forms in variable contexts: The relationship between linguistic factors and future-time reference in Spanish. *Studies in Hispanic and Lusophone Linguistics, 4*(1), 3–33.

Gudmestad, A., House, L., & Geeslin, K. L. (2013). What a Bayesian analysis can do for SLA: New tools for the sociolinguistic study of subject expression in L2 Spanish. *Language Learning, 63*(3), 371–399.

Hansen Edwards, J. G. (2011). Deletion of /t, d/ and the acquisition of linguistic variation by second language learners of English. *Language Learning, 61*(4), 1256–1301.

Kanwit, M. (2017). What we gain by combining variationist and concept-oriented approaches: The case of acquiring Spanish future-time expression. *Language Learning, 67*(2), 461–498.

Kanwit, M., & Geeslin, K. (2014). The interpretation of the Spanish subjunctive in adverbial clauses: A cross-sectional study. *Studies in Second Language Acquisition, 36*(3), 487–533.

Kanwit, M., Geeslin, K., & Fafulas, S. (2015). Study abroad and the SLA of variable structures: A look at the present perfect, the copula contrast, and the present progressive in Mexico and Spain. *Probus, 27*(2), 307–348.

Kennedy Terry, K. M. (2017). Contact, context, and collocation: The emergence of sociostylistic variation in L2 French learners during study abroad. *Studies in Second Language Acquisition, 39*(3), 553–578.

Labov, W. (1966). *The social stratification of English in New York City.* Washington: Center for Applied Linguistics.

Li, X. (2010). Sociolinguistic variation in the speech of learners of Chinese as a second language. *Language Learning, 60*(2), 366–408.

Linford, B., Long, A. Y., Solon, M., Whatley, M., & Geeslin, K. L. (2016). Lexical frequency and subject expression in native and non-native Spanish. In S. Sessarego & F. Tejedo (Eds.), *Issues in hispanic and lusophone linguistics* (pp. 197–215). Amsterdam: John Benjamins.

Mitchell, R., Tracy-Ventura, N., & McManus, K. (2017). *Anglophone students abroad: Identity, social relationships and language learning.* New York: Routledge.

Mougeon, R., Nadasdi, T., & Rehner, K. (2010). *The sociolinguistic competence of French immersion students.* Clevedon: Multilingual Matters.

Mougeon, R., & Rehner, K. (2001). Variation in the spoken French of Ontario French immersion students: The case of *juste* versus *seulement* versus *rien que. Modern Language Journal, 85*(3), 398–415.

Myles, F. (2015). Learner corpora and grammar. In S. Granger, G. Gilquin, & F. Meunier (Eds.), *The Cambridge handbook of learner corpus research* (pp. 309–331). Cambridge: Cambridge University Press.

Nadasdi, T., Mougeon, R., & Rehner, K. (2003). Emploi du future dans le français parlé des élèves d'immersion française. *Journal of French Language Studies, 13*(2), 195–219.

Nadasdi, T., Mougeon, R., & Rehner, K. (2008). Factors driving lexical variation in L2 French: A variationist study of automobile, auto, voiture, char and machine. *French Language Studies, 18*(3), 365–381.

O'Connor DiVito, N. (1997). *Patterns across spoken and written French: Empirical research on the interaction among forms, functions and genres.* Boston: Houghton Mifflin.

O'Keeffe, A., & McCarthy, M. (Eds.) (2010). *The Routledge handbook of corpus linguistics.* London: Routledge.

Preston, D. (2000). Three kinds of sociolinguistics and SLA: A psycholinguistic perspective. In B. Swierzbin, F. Morris, M. Anderson, C. Klee, & E. Tarone (Eds.), *Social and cognitive factors in second language acquisition: Selected proceedings of the 1999 second language research forum* (pp. 3–30). Somerville: Cascadilla.

Rankin, T. (2015). Learner corpora and grammar. In S. Granger, G. Gilquin, & F. Meunier (Eds.), *The Cambridge handbook of learner corpus research* (pp. 231–254). Cambridge: Cambridge University Press.

Regan, V. (2004). The relationship between the group and the individual and the acquisition of native speaker variation patterns: A preliminary study. *International Review of Applied Linguistics in Language Teaching, 42*(4), 335–348.

Regan, V., Howard, M., & Lemée, I. (2009). *The acquisition of sociolinguistic competence in a study abroad context*. Clevedon: Multilingual Matters.

Rehner, K. (2002). The development of aspects of linguistic and discourse competence by advanced second language learners of French (Doctoral dissertation, University of Toronto). *Dissertation Abstracts International, 63*, 12.

Rehner, K., & Mougeon, R. (1999). Variation in the spoken French of immersion students: To *ne* or not to *ne*, that is the sociolinguistic question. *Canadian Modern Language Review, 56*(1), 124–154.

Rehner, K., Mougeon, R., & Nadasdi, T. (2003). The learning of sociolinguistic variation by advanced FLS learners: The case of *nous* versus *on* in immersion French. *Studies in Second Language Acquisition, 25*(1), 127–156.

Schmidt, L. B. (2018). L2 development of perceptual categorization of dialectal sounds: A study in Spanish. *Studies in Second Language Acquisition, 4*(4), 857–882.

Solon, M., Linford, B., & Geeslin, K. L. (2018). Acquisition of sociophonetic variation: Intervocalic /d/ reduction in native and nonnative Spanish. *Revista Española de Lingüística Aplicada, 31*(1), 309–344.

Szmrecsany, B. (2017). Variationist sociolinguistics and corpus-based variationist linguistics; overlap and cross-pollination potential. *Canadian Journal of Linguistics, 62*(4), 685–701.

Tagliamonte, S. A. (2012). *Variationist sociolinguistics: Change, observation, and interpretation*. New York: Wiley-Blackwell.

Tarone, E. (2007). Sociolinguistic approaches to second language acquisition research: 1997 to 2007. *Modern Language Journal, 91*, 837–848.

Tarone, E., & Liu, G. Q. (1995). Situational context, variation and second-language acquisition theory. In G. Cook & B. Seidlhofer (Eds.), *Principles and practice in the study of language and learning: A Festschrift for H. G. Widdowson* (pp. 107–124). Oxford: Oxford University Press.

Tracy-Ventura, N., & Myles, F. (2015). The importance of task variability in the design of learner corpora for SLA research. *International Journal of Learner Corpus Research, 1*(1), 58–95.

van Rooy, B. (2015). Annotating learner corpora. In S. Granger, G. Gilquin, & F. Meunier (Eds.), *The Cambridge handbook of learner corpus research* (pp. 79–105). Cambridge: Cambridge University Press.

Walker, J. A. (2010). *Variation in linguistic systems*. New York: Routledge.

Young, R. (1991). *Variation in interlanguage morphology*. New York: Peter Lang Publishing.

18

Pragmatic Approaches

Julieta Fernández and Shelley Staples

Introduction

Corpus methods, whereby principled collections of written or oral texts can be analyzed for patterns, have fueled, and have been fueled by, a renewed and intensified focus on functional approaches to language acquisition. The term "functional approaches" has been used to describe a range of approaches, such as systemic functional linguistics or cognitive linguistics, which are concerned with how learners use language to create meaning. What unifies these approaches is a rejection of the idea that language is an abstract, isolated system that can be separated from the speakers who use language and the social context in which they do so. Instead, these approaches argue that language is shaped not only by human cognition but also by the ways and the contexts in which it is used (McEnery & Hardie, 2012). Language forms develop in order to communicate complex meanings (Mitchell, Myles, & Marsden, 2013). Learners' pragmatic needs drive their additional language (L2) development.

One of the major examples of functional SLA research is the European Science Foundation (ESF) project, which systematically analyzed how immigrant workers in West European countries learned the local language. The ESF research team sought to determine contextual communicative factors which lead to L2 linguistic development or to fossilization (Klein & Perdue, 1992). To that end, they collected audio and video recordings from small groups of uninstructed adult learners of five different European languages (Dutch, English, French, German, and Swedish) over the period of two and half years. Their assumption was that these learners would have a strong desire to integrate into the communities to which they had emigrated, and that they would need to interact in the language daily. Based on their results, the ESF team put forward what they refer to as the L2 'Basic Variety' (BV). The BV is a relatively stable "proto-grammar stage" (Mitchell, Myles, & Marsden, 2013, p. 216) which develops as part of the process of acquiring an additional language in an uninstructed setting and is "versatile and highly efficient for most communicative purposes" (Klein & Perdue, 1997, p. 303). Within this perspective, communicative factors are seen as 'pushing' L2 acquisition as structural factors 'shape" it (Watorek & Perdue, 2005).

In this chapter, we address an area that highlights the importance of meaning making in L2 learning which has been investigated using corpora: L2 pragmatics. Pragmatics studies language use in social interaction. When communicating, (second) language users make choices among different linguistic forms within the constraints of social interaction (or social 'norms'), with tangible effects on other participants in the interaction (Crystal, 1997). Pragmatics is hence an inherently functional approach to language in that it begins by examining the communicative needs of the speakers to then study how they are communicated through linguistic forms in situated social interaction (LoCastro, 2003).

One area that has received much attention in L2 pragmatics is speech acts. They are the "minimal units of linguistic communication" (Searle, 1969, p. 16), or units of language that perform actions. The pragmatic function of a particular speech act varies with the type of activity and interactional context. Different categorizations of speech acts have been put forward based on their function, for example 'directives' (which 'direct' the listener to do something) and 'expressives' (through which the speakers 'express' or convey their psychological state). Speech acts have further been classified as direct and indirect. In direct speech acts, the form of the utterance matches the action being performed, for example, when an imperative is used to give an order (e.g., 'come here!'). In indirect acts, the form and the function do not match, for example when a question about ability is used to get the interlocutor to do something ('can you pass the salt?').

Another area of L2 pragmatics research is pragmatic marker (PM) use. PMs are expressions that have lost much of their propositional meaning and are not completely integrated with other structures in the sentence. They are essential, however, in that they point to the relationship between what is said and the context (textual meaning), and mark a relationship between the speakers, what they are saying, and who they are talking to (intersubjective meaning). Here, we use PMs as an umbrella term that includes discourse markers (e.g., 'first'), general extenders (e.g., 'and stuff'), and stance markers (e.g., 'possibly').

Prosody and formulaic language are two relatively less researched areas of L2 pragmatics that nonetheless play an important role in communicating pragmatic functions, often in combination with PMs. Prosodic patterns such as rising or falling intonation, or stress of particular words within an utterance help guide an interlocutor towards an understanding of indirect speech acts. When prosodic patterns do not match expectations (e.g., a lack of pitch movement where rising or falling intonation is expected), listeners may view the speaker negatively.

There are different ways in which formulaic language has been conceptualized within SLA, primarily within usage-based models (see Chapter 13, this volume). Referred to as 'conversational routines' (Aijmer, 1996), 'conventional expressions', or 'pragmatic routines' (Bardovi-Harlig, 2019) within the pragmatics literature, formulaic language also plays a major role in communicating pragmatic functions given their social and situational meanings. Taking a functional approach, Aijmer (1996) argues that conversational routines "have become specialized or 'entrenched' for a discourse function which predominates over or replaces the literal referential meaning" (p. 11). Bardovi-Harlig (2019), in turn, defines conventional expressions as "(a) multiword expressions; (b) related to context; (c) characteristic of a speech community; and (d) illocutionary transparent" (p. 99).

Core Issues and Topics

The scope of research in L2 pragmatics has broadened widely from an initial focus mainly on speech acts (e.g., Kasper & Dahl, 1991) to many different aspects involved in the development of L2 pragmatic capacities, as well as a revision of some fundamental concepts (for example, what is 'appropriate' or 'authentic' behavior in an interaction). Some of the central questions that L2 pragmatics has tried to answer throughout the years have related to the relationship between L1 and L2 pragmatic capacity and development; the relationship between grammatical knowledge, general language proficiency, and pragmatic abilities; a description of pragmatic competence at advanced levels; an exploration of the extent to which L2 pragmatic features are learnable, and the types of pedagogical interventions that are more effective for L2 pragmatic learning, among many others (see Culpeper, Mackey, & Taguchi, 2018 for a more exhaustive list). Here, we focus on three key questions in L2 pragmatics research that have been investigated using learner corpora through a necessarily brief selection of L2 corpus pragmatic studies.

Differences in L1 and L2 Pragmatic Performance

In the 1980s and 1990s, L2 pragmatics saw an increase in cross-linguistic studies, because it was assumed that languages varied in how they conveyed pragmatic meanings, especially in the areas of speech acts and politeness (Culpeper, Mackey, & Taguchi, 2018). Several L2 corpus pragmatics studies that have compared pragmatic language performance in an L1 and an L2 have a cross-sectional design and compare the use of pragmatic features within two different corpora. As an illustration, Buysse (2017) compared the use of the PM 'you know' in the *Louvain Corpus of Native English Conversation* (LOCNEC) with its use by intermediate to advanced learners of English with multiple L1s (Dutch, German, French, and Spanish) in the *Louvain International Database of Spoken English Interlanguage* (LINDSEI). He found that the L2 English speakers, regardless of L1, used 'you know' with lower frequency than their L1 English counterparts. However, he found no differences in terms of the pragmatic functions for which 'you know' was used.

Another pragmatic feature that has been widely examined in corpus analysis comparing L1 and L2 pragmatic performance are stance markers (e.g., epistemic markers such as 'possibly' and 'definitely' and attitude markers such as 'actually' or 'surprisingly'). Much of the work has emphasized the differences in the use of stance features between L1 and L2 writers, particularly with respect to register awareness. A number of the studies employ Hyland's (2005) model of stance and engagement. This model draws loosely on Systemic Functional Linguistic principles but uses lists of words associated with stance and engagement (hedges, boosters, attitude markers, self-mentions, and engagement markers) to facilitate a corpus-based approach. Lee and Deakin (2016), for example, used Hyland's model to compare L1 writers (from the *Michigan Corpus of Upper Level Student Papers*) and L2 writers in First Year Writing Courses. They found that higher rated L2 writers used stance features at a similar rate to L1 writers, whereas lower rated L2 writers used fewer stance markers, particularly hedges.

Within the study of prosody, Gut (2009) examined differences between L1 German speakers' use of English and L1 English speakers' use of German in the *Learning Prosody in a Foreign Language* (LeaP) corpus. The LeaP corpus is one of the few learner corpora that focuses on differences in the use of phonetic and prosodic features across L1s (L2 speakers of English from 16 different backgrounds; L2 speakers of German from 21 different L1s). One of the key findings of the study is that there was more variation between intonation and speech rhythm across spoken registers (read speech, free speech in an interview situation, retellings of a story, and reading of nonsense word lists) than there were across L1/L2 groups (both English and German). This study has broad implications in that any studies of prosodic features need to take register into account in order to ensure comparable analyses. That said, key differences were found in the types of intonational phrasing, tone choice, pitch range, and use of pitch accent between L1/L2 groups for both English and German. These differences have implications for pragmatics, given that the greater use of level tone by non-native English speakers has been shown to communicate an impression of an uninterested or bored speaker (Kang, 2010).

Proficiency and Learners' Pragmatic Development

Within L2 pragmatics, proficiency has been extensively studied as one of the central sources of individual variation in learners' pragmatic performance (Taguchi & Roever, 2017). L2 corpus pragmatics studies point to a complex relationship between L2 proficiency and the use of different pragmatic features. For example, learners at higher levels of proficiency have been found to use PMs in spoken discourse with more frequency and a wider variety than lower proficiency learners (e.g., Fernández, Gates Tapia, & Lu, 2014). In contrast, in writing, higher proficiency learners were found to use fewer overt stance features (such as 'my opinion is' and more indirect hedging devices such as 'about' and 'maybe') than their lower level counterparts (Lee & Deakin, 2016).

Proficiency also appears to play an important role in learners' comprehension and production of speech acts and politeness strategies, with the great majority of studies addressing production. Higher proficiency learners tend to be less direct, use more semantic formulas and more modification, and give more explanations, reasons, and accounts than lower level learners (Taguchi & Roever, 2017). For example, Gablasova and Brezina (2018) investigated differences in the use of politeness strategies by learners at three proficiency levels when performing 'yes-but' speech acts of disagreement. They found that with increasing proficiency, their participants used more 'yes-but' constructions, a greater variety and complexity of modification of individual expressions, and an increased number and a wider range of downtoners, to express disagreement.

In the area of formulaic language use, L2 pragmatics research has shown that learners' production of pragmatic routines tends to increase at higher proficiency levels (e.g., Bardovi-Harlig & Bastos, 2011), although proficiency does not seem to play a major role in their recognition (e.g., Taguchi, 2013). In written discourse, formulaic language may be used to express stance more frequently at lower levels and to express referential relationships within informational content at higher levels (Chen & Baker, 2016; Yan & Staples, 2020).

Effects of Instruction on Pragmatic Development

Instructed pragmatics research indicates that it is beneficial to increase learners' awareness of pragmatic features, provide ample practice through focused interaction, and engineer opportunities for more agentive uses of language (Culpeper et al., 2018). Within the L2 corpus research, Fung and Carter (2007), for example, argue for the need to give pedagogical attention to pragmatic features, such as interpersonal (e.g., 'basically', 'actually') and cognitive PMs (e.g., 'I mean', 'I think'), which are often neglected in instructional materials. One of the ways to increase learners' awareness of PMs is via corpus-informed instruction, as suggested by L2 corpus research. Drawing on the *Michigan Corpus of Academic Spoken English* (MICASE, Simpson, Briggs, Ovens, & Swales, 2002), Fernández and Yuldashev (2015), for example, show that a corpus-informed teaching of 'smallwords' (e.g., 'I think', 'I mean', and 'you know') functions in an academic context was well received by international teaching assistants (ITAs) in training, and had immediate positive results (with ITAs incorporating the use of smallwords in their subsequent presentations) (see also Bardovi-Harlig & Mossman, 2017).

Another approach is illustrated in Belz and Vyatkina's (2008) semester-long study, in which they successfully developed and implemented a longitudinal pedagogical intervention on the use of four German modal particles (MPs) –'ja', 'denn', 'doch', and 'mal' (stance markers), as well as German pronominal adverbs (da-compounds). Their "developmental pedagogical intervention" (Belz & Vyatkina, 2005, p. 20) drew language learners' attention to their own language production, with a special emphasis given to the study's focal features and had a positive effect on learners' use of these features. Toward the end of the study, the participants approximated the L1 German speakers in terms of frequency of use, demonstrating a trend toward general pragmatic appropriateness. This study suggests that drawing on learner corpora in pedagogical practice with a focus on usage variety and/or frequency of different pragmatic features may facilitate language development. As noted by Vyatkina and Cunningham (2015), the study also "showed the value of developmental corpora as a means of providing ongoing iterative instruction and assessment to language learners" (p. 298).

Main Research Methods

Data in pragmatics are often described as 'authentic,' or 'naturally occurring' if they would have occurred regardless of the study being conducted. On the other hand, if the data are deliberately obtained for the purposes of a study, they are considered 'elicited'. Authentic data can be written (e.g., a collection of newspaper articles), spoken (e.g., a dinner interaction), or hybrid (e.g., a speech which was written to be read). Elicited data can be obtained in multiple ways, most commonly through the use of Discourse Completion Tasks (DCTs), role-plays, interviews, scaled-response questionnaires, and think-aloud protocols, among other instruments. Depending on how they are compiled, corpora can be considered authentic or elicited (see Chapter 11). Another distinction is made between 'attested' data, that is language that speakers have used, and 'intuitive' or 'introspective' data, which is language that the speakers have reflected on (O'Keeffe, Clancy, & Adolphs, 2011). Learner corpus analysis is a relatively newer methodology within L2 pragmatics. While the scope of research within L2 corpus pragmatics is still somewhat limited, as illustrated above, several studies have examined issues in traditional areas of L2 pragmatic research, such as learners' performance of speech acts, PMs, prosody, and formulaic language. Here, we briefly mention the traditional methods used to examine these areas and focus on the ways in which corpus methods have been adapted to study them.

The study of speech acts has adopted multiple methodologies, although in the general pragmatics literature, there has been a preference for the use of DCTs. When identifying speech acts using corpora, researchers encounter some of the similar challenges they would face in identifying speech acts in other types of naturally-occurring learner discourse but often on a much larger scale. Corpus researchers often have to spend considerable time and effort searching and identifying pragmatic phenomena at the discourse level because form and function are not always fixed, as is the case with different speech act realizations (e.g., 'it's cold in here' could be a complaint or a request). As a result, they often have the need to start from "either a discourse particle with a fixed form that can easily be retrieved from a large corpus, or a speech function that is generally realized in a small number of variant patterns" (Jucker et al., 2009, p. 4) and then continue with a bottom-up (usually manual) approach. This can involve searching for language commonly used to perform specific pragmatic meanings, for example, 'like/love your' for compliments (Taavitsainen & Jucker, 2008). With the help of corpus tools, researchers can then calculate frequencies of occurrence, determine contexts of use, and describe their pragmatic functions. For example, Reinhardt (2007) first identified a register in which directives are likely to occur due to its situational characteristics, i.e., instructor-student interactions during office hours. He searched the ITA corpus for representative strings of language with directive intent (such as 'must' or 'have to'). He then used grounded analysis to classify them into three groups drawing on existing pragmatic theory – core lexical devices, syntactic-level devices, and discourse-level devices.

Pragmatic tagging is another possibility for the corpus-based analysis of speech acts, although it is not without its complications. De Felice and Deane (2012) exemplifies how tagging can successfully be used for the identification of speech acts. The results of their study are significant because they suggest that it is possible to develop an automatic tagger that can identify speech acts with relatively high accuracy. Other tools yet to be explored in the automatic identification of speech acts in L2 discourse include Weisser's *Dialogue Annotation and Research Tool* (DART; Weisser, 2014). In the case of requests, for example, DART can be used to code question types (i.e., 'wh-' or 'yes/no') and then to code for pragmatic information based on those structures, such as request for information, request for directive, or suggestion for wh-questions. When necessary, the program also gives the researcher the possibility to manually correct a tag that has been automatically assigned.

An alternative way in which corpora can be used to investigate speech acts is to compile a corpus using tasks that elicit speech acts, for example through role-plays, which often result in data that more closely reflect natural discourse than DCTs. As an illustration, Staples (2015) created a corpus of role-play nurse-patient interactions centered on a patient whose father had just died and was suffering from grief. Given this context, expressions of empathy emerged and were more easily analyzed than they would be in other contexts.

Various methodologies have also been used to study PMs (e.g., discourse analysis or matched-guise technique), with corpus analysis featuring prominently. This is partly due to PMs' uninflected nature, which makes them fairly easy to find through a word search (Vyatkina & Cunningham, 2015). A sizeable portion of this research has drawn comparisons between L1 and L2 use of different PMs. Methodologically, the problem with making these types of comparisons when drawing on naturally occurring data is that it is not easy to establish "comparable conditions with respect to factors which might influence the use of discourse markers" (Müller, 2005, p. 241). As a result, the types of inferences that can be drawn are somewhat limited. Müller (2005) was able to overcome this limitation by having the native speakers (NSs) and non-native speakers (NNSs) in her corpus perform the exact same tasks. The downside of this approach is the relatively constrained nature of the interactions that this type of design is able to elicit (which in Müller's case had a predefined topic and were carried out in a lab setting). What Müller lost in 'naturalness' of the data, she gained in a design that allowed her to make valid comparisons between the groups. Another study that demonstrates ways to overcome this potential limitation of contrastive analysis is Belz and Vyatkina (2005). Their longitudinal corpus includes interactions in L1 German, L2 German, L1 English, and L2 English (*Telekorp*), thus providing a "built-in control corpus" in L1 German and English (p. 20) and circumventing the need to find a separate reference corpus.

Prosody has been a somewhat neglected area of pragmatic research, and this is even more the case in L2 corpus pragmatic research. Due to its more labor-intensive process, there has been less effort to gather spoken corpora, and, even when spoken corpora have been compiled, most of the focus has been on lexico-grammatical analysis. There are some notable exceptions, including the study of discourse-based intonation using the *Hong Kong Corpus of Spoken English* (HKCSE; Cheng, Greaves, & Warren, 2008). This corpus was created specifically for the analysis of intonation, prominence, and pitch in various registers, and provides important findings on variation across registers and speakers (e.g., those in higher positions of power) that is informative for language learning. It is especially suited for investigating pragmatic, cross-cultural differences in such speech acts as disagreement (Cheng & Warren, 2005). It is important to note, however, that this corpus was compiled in a very specific language-learning context (Hong Kong), and the results might not be generalizable to other L2 populations. A recent study from Romero-Trillo (2019) also demonstrates how an analysis of prosody can be applied to learner corpora such as LINDSEI. His examination of the Spanish L1 subcorpus indicates that English L1 speakers used more fall-rise tones than Spanish L1 (English L2) speakers in the same context, which he explains is a more "emphatic" tone. More fine-grained analysis of the pragmatic functions of tones in this context, as well as an account for speaker role (L1 speakers were interviewers in LINDSEI), would add to an already pioneering study.

Conventional expressions have been studied using oral DCTs, role-plays, and elicited conversations. Within corpus linguistics, formulaic language has been a fruitful area of inquiry for investigating SLA, particularly as a bottom-up method that identifies recurrent sequences (often referred to as lexical bundles in the corpus linguistics literature). A subset of these studies has specifically focused on the pragmatic functions of these phraseological sequences in L2 discourse. Functional frameworks have been proposed and followed in a number of studies (e.g., Biber, Conrad, & Cortes, 2004). These frameworks draw on the different types of language functions in spoken and written registers. For example, Biber, Conrad, and Cortes (2004) focused on a three-tiered framework for bundles: stance bundles (e.g., 'you need to know'), which express a writer or speaker's attitudes, opinions, or beliefs about an idea (most commonly found in spoken discourse); discourse organizing bundles (e.g., 'what I want to do is'), which serve to provide a structure for previous and upcoming discourse; and referential bundles (e.g., 'one of the things'), which provide references to surrounding text or concepts/items outside the text, and are more commonly found in writing (see Granger & Paquot, 2008: referential phrasemes, textual phrasemes, communicative phrasemes). Despite the differences in the use of these functional categories across registers, this framework has primarily been used within L2 corpus studies for investigating written discourse (although there are some studies of spoken language, such as Aijmer's 2009 investigation of the use of 'I don't know' in LINDSEI).

Finally, in terms of research design, while there is a handful of SLA studies drawing on longitudinal L2 corpora (e.g., Belz & Vyatkina, 2005), to date, studies of longitudinal L2 corpus pragmatics do not abound. In fact, work in learner corpus pragmatics has largely been cross-sectional in nature. There are calls for more longitudinal work in most areas of SLA (e.g., Ortega & Byrnes, 2008), and the study of L2 pragmatic development is no exception. One study that demonstrates the potential contributions of longitudinal learner corpora to the study of L2 pragmatic development is Polat (2011). Polat examined the frequency of use of three PMs (i.e., 'you know', 'like', and 'well') in the speech of a Turkish untutored L2 speaker compared to their use in the *Santa Barbara Corpus of Spoken American English* (SBCSAE, Du Bois et al., 2000). Her study highlights the non-linear nature of language learning, a crucial factor in SLA that can be lost in cross-sectional studies of L2 pragmatics. More longitudinal work is needed that investigates learners' performance in its own right, or with contextually appropriate comparisons.

Representative Corpora and Research

The European Science Foundation (ESF) Second Language Data Bank comprises spoken data from 40 untutored adult immigrants in five different European countries – England, France, Germany, Sweden, and the Netherlands – over a period of 2.5 years. The L2 speakers had Arabic, Finnish, Italian, Punjabi, Spanish, and Turkish as their L1. The participants were audio and video recorded undertaking a series of tasks, including role-plays, informal interaction, storytelling, and picture description. The corpus that is now available on Talkbank.org (see Chapter 12, this volume) is a "spin-off" that has been utilized for several other projects (Perdue, 2000), including a series of studies to make observations about functional grammar, such as the development of the linguistic means to express temporality (e.g., Klein & Perdue, 1992). The ESF project, and many of the research projects that resulted from it, influenced "our understanding of the semantic and pragmatic universals which characterize human linguistic behavior and play an important part in language acquisition" (Myles, 2000, p. 71).

The *International Corpus of Learner English* (ICLE) is one of the best known and most used learner corpora in the world. ICLE consists of 6,085 argumentative essays of approximately 700 words, totaling 3.7 million words and representing sixteen different L1 backgrounds. The learners are university age (about 20 years old) studying English in an EFL context, categorized as intermediate to advanced learners of English. One notable study is a book-length exploration of academic vocabulary, which includes an examination of language used for rhetorical functions in the ICLE compared with the BNC Academic Humanities (BNC-AC-HUM) subcorpus (Paquot, 2010). As Paquot (2010) shows, writers in the ICLE used different language to perform the function of exemplification than that found in the BNC-AC-HUM corpus. For example, ICLE writers used 'like' for exemplification at a rate similar to that found in speech, fiction, and news writing and much more frequently than in the BNC-AC-HUM. Paquot found similar preferences for language used more frequently in speech when the ICLE writers performed other rhetorical functions such as cause and effect, comparison and contrast, and introductions of topics and ideas. This study provides a rich resource for understanding how learner L2 writing differs lexically and rhetorically from expert writing.

The *Spanish Learner Language Oral Corpora* is a collection of spoken L2 Spanish produced by L1 UK English speakers, from beginners to advanced level (advanced learners spent a year studying abroad in Spain). For comparison purposes, NSs were also recorded undertaking the same tasks. The resulting database of L2 Spanish contains digital sound files of learner speech, in varying genres, accompanied by transcripts in CHAT format (see Chapter 12, this volume). Fernández (2013) investigated the use of general extenders (e.g., '*y eso*', 'and that') by the same L2 learners across registers, finding that GEs were more frequent in dialogic tasks such as pair discussion and interview and less frequent in monologic tasks such as narratives. This study underscores the importance of including contextual factors such as register when examining the use of PMs by L2 learners.

Future Directions

This chapter has demonstrated some of the contributions corpora can make to functional perspectives on L2 learning with a focus on L2 pragmatics. The following section outlines areas we consider crucial for future research in learner corpus research in pragmatics.

Based on performance data alone, it is challenging to tell whether learners do not know or are willingly deviating from the norm(s) of the L2 culture. Having the metapragmatic knowledge to deviate from these norms can actually be interpreted as pragmatic development (Taguchi & Roever, 2017). Thus, the combination of performance data with some type of introspection data would appear beneficial in future research. In addition, performance data has the potential of being "affected by frequency bias, and corpus evidence may simply miss out on critical examples of less frequent structures" (Tracy-Ventura et al., 2016, p. 118). As such, focus on frequency of production "can be at the expense of developing knowledge of what is possible and appropriate" (Cook, 1999, p. 65). Thus, introspective data can also shed light on language use where frequency of language instances can be a useful point of departure as opposed to the end point of exploration (see Chapter 10, this volume).

To build on the important work in the area of prosody and L2 pragmatics within corpus linguistics, researchers need (to develop) better tools for the automatic or semi-automatic identification of suprasegmental features from speech files. Automated methods have only been successful so far for speech rhythm and fluency, and even these studies rely primarily on read speech, which is not helpful for pragmatics research (e.g., Ferrenge, 2013). For naturally occurring data in L1 corpora, a mixture of automated and manual coding seems feasible (see, e.g., the C-ORAL-ROM project, Cresti & Moneglia, 2005), but there is a need for better computational models for L2 data since even existing frameworks like ToBI (Tone and Break Indices; Beckman, Hirschberg, & Shattuck-Hufnagel, 2005) do not take into account L2 learners. In the LeaP corpus, for example, Gut (2009) manually annotated all suprasegmental elements, but this required three years of analysis. Given these current limitations, researchers are also advised to narrow down the areas in which they investigate prosody-pragmatic connections to speech acts or larger pragmatic units such as moves or phases. Pilot work will be important to identify areas of interest for further investigation (see Staples, 2015 for an example of such a process). Importantly, with the inclusion of more longitudinal corpora, the prosody-pragmatic interface can be examined in terms of pragmatic development.

Multi-dimensional analysis (MDA) incorporates situational analysis (e.g., an analysis of communicative purposes, power differentials, etc.) along with linguistic analysis to functionally interpret linguistic patterns within the context of register (for more details, see Biber, 1988). Despite its potential for pragmatics research, MDA remains largely focused on lexico-grammatical analysis. In order to understand pragmatic functions such as expression of stance, features such as intonation and stress can be added to the list of variables that have been established for this function (e.g., modals, epistemic adverbs, complement clauses controlled by stance verbs, nouns, and adjectives, see Biber, 2006). One challenge for researchers to undertake this approach is developing skills in the coding of linguistic phenomena within multiple domains (prosody, lexis, grammar, syntax) and the knowledge of multivariate statistical analysis (Berber-Sardinha & Veirano-Pinto, 2019).

There are also promising models from computational linguistics that use multiple linguistic levels to establish syntactic, discourse level, and prosodic cues to identify 'dialog acts' which can be considered as similar to speech acts (e.g., *Dialogue Act Markup in Several Layers*, DAMSL, Jurafsky, 2006). However, their applications can only be used by researchers who either have programming skills or can collaborate with computational linguists. In addition, the DAMSL system still requires accuracy testing for L2 data. For future research in this area, collaboration between pragmatics scholars and computational linguists appears to be a necessity.

Another method that is frequently used in corpus linguistics that seems promising for pragmatics researchers is the move analysis, in which researchers manually code stretches of discourse for functional elements (e.g., the identification of a research gap in research article introductions, Swales, 1990). As Tardy and Swales (2014) indicate, move analysis, as a part of genre analysis, allows researchers to examine "how things get done, when language is used to accomplish them" (p. 165, quoting Martin, 1985), explicitly connecting this method of discourse analysis to the goals of Austin's (1962) *How to do things with words*. Similar to other pragmatic approaches, move analysis focuses on contextualization of language use and its functions.

This approach has predominantly been applied to L1 writing but can be applied to L2 contexts and to spoken 'moves' as well, often called 'phases' within conversation analytic frameworks (see Have, 1989). Although moves and phases need to be manually identified, like speech acts, they are less time-consuming to code since they represent larger discourse units. They can be seen as a middle ground that allows researchers to identify pragmatic functions but does not necessarily require the coding of individual utterances/sentences. For example, by identifying the opening phase in a dialogue, researchers can then examine distinctive language for that phase (using automated tools such as part-of-speech tagging) which can be further analyzed at the level of the speech act (e.g., greetings) (see, e.g., Staples, 2015). Examining differences in the linguistic attributes of phases either cross-linguistically or developmentally can help researchers understand distinct functional characteristics of L2 speakers' interactions.

Further Reading

Aijmer, K., & Rühlemann, C. (2014). *Corpus pragmatics: A handbook*. Cambridge: Cambridge University Press.

This handbook covers a comprehensive range of important topics in understanding how pragmatics research can benefit from the corpus-based methodology, even if it provides little on learner corpora in L2 pragmatics research. Particularly notable are Garcia's analysis of speech acts, which demonstrates the use of manual coding at the initial stages of coding, and Weisser's discussion of existing tools and the potential of annotation and automated analysis of speech acts.

Romero-Trillo, J. (Series Ed.) (2016). *Yearbook of corpus linguistics and pragmatics. Global implications for society and education in the networked age*. Cham: Springer.

This yearly publication brings together state-of-the-art studies addressing current debates and developments in a wide range of areas at the intersection between corpus and pragmatics. The studies provide useful models and references to L2 pragmatics that can help budding, as well as seasoned researchers, familiarize themselves with using corpora to examine L2 pragmatic development.

Related Topics

Chapters 10, 13, and 30.

References

Aijmer, K. (1996). *Conversational routines in English: Convention and creativity*. Studies in language and linguistics. London: Longman.

Aijmer, K. (2009). "So er I just sort of I dunno I think it's just because...": A corpus study of "I do not know" and "dunno" in learner spoken English. In A. H. Jucker, D. Schreier, & M. Hundt (Eds.), *Corpora: Pragmatics and discourse* (pp. 151–166). Amsterdam: Rodopi.

Aijmer, K., & Rühlemann, C. (2014). *Corpus pragmatics: A handbook*. Cambridge: Cambridge University Press.

Austin, J. L. (1962). *How to do things with words*. Oxford: Clarendon Press.

Bardovi-Harlig, K. (2019). Formulaic language in second language pragmatics research. In A. Siyanova-Chanturia & A. Pellicer-Sanchez (Eds.), *Understanding formulaic language: A second language acquisition perspective* (pp. 97–114). London: Routledge.

Bardovi-Harlig, K., & Bastos, M. T. (2011). Proficiency, length of stay, and intensity of interaction and the acquisition of conventional expressions in L2 pragmatics. *Intercultural Pragmatics, 8*(3), 347–384.

Bardovi-Harlig, K., & Mossman, S. (2017). Corpus-based materials development for teaching and learning pragmatic routines. In B. Tomlinson (Ed.), *SLA research and materials development for language learning* (pp. 250–267). New York: Routledge.

Beckman, M. E., Hirschberg, J., & Shattuck-Hufnagel, S. (2005). The original ToBI system and the evolution of the ToBI framework. In S. A. Jun (Ed.), *Prosodic typology – The phonology of intonation and phrasing* (pp. 9–54). Oxford: Oxford University Press.

Belz, J. A., & Vyatkina, N. (2005). Learner corpus analysis and the development of L2 pragmatic competence in networked intercultural language study: The case of German modal particles. *Canadian Modern Language Review, 62*(1), 17–48.

Belz, J. A., & Vyatkina, N. (2008). The pedagogical mediation of a developmental learner corpus for classroom-based language instruction. *Language Learning and Technology, 12*(3), 33–52.

Berber-Sardinha, T., & Veirano-Pinto, M. (2019). *Multi-dimensional analysis: Research methods and current issues*. London: Bloomsbury Publishing.

Biber, D. (1988). *Variation across speech and writing*. Cambridge: Cambridge University Press.

Biber, D. (2006). Stance in spoken and written university registers. *Journal of English for Academic Purposes, 5*(2), 97–116.

Biber, D., Conrad, S., & Cortes, V. (2004). If you look at …: Lexical bundles in university teaching and textbooks. *Applied Linguistics, 25*(3), 371–405.

Buysse, L. (2017). The pragmatic marker *you know* in learner Englishes. *Journal of Pragmatics, 121*, 40–57.

Chen, Y.-H., & Baker, P. (2016). Investigating criterial discourse features across second language development: Lexical bundles in rated learner essays, CEFR B1, B2 and C1. *Applied Linguistics, 6*(1), 849–880.

Cheng, W., Greaves, D., & Warren, M. (2008). *A corpus-driven study of discourse intonation*. Amsterdam: John Benjamins.

Cheng, W., & Warren, M. (2005). //→ well I have a DIFferent //↘ THINking you know//: Disagreement in Hong Kong business discourse: A corpus-driven approach. In F. Bargiela-Chiappini & M. Gotti (Eds.), *Asian business discourse(s)* (pp. 241–270). Frankfurt: Peter Lang Publishing.

Cook, G. (1999). Communicative competence. In K. Johnson & H. Johnson (Eds.), *Encyclopedic dictionary of applied linguistics* (pp. 62–68). Oxford: Blackwell Publishing.

Cresti, E., & Moneglia, M. (2005). *C-ORAL-ROM: Integrated reference corpora for spoken romance languages*. Amsterdam: John Benjamins.

Crystal, D. (Ed.) (1997). *The Cambridge encyclopedia of language* (2nd ed.). Cambridge: Cambridge University Press.

Culpeper, J., Mackey, A., & Taguchi, N. (2018). *Second language pragmatics: From theory to research*. New York: Routledge.

De Felice, R., & Deane, P. (2012). *Identifying speech acts in e-mails: Toward automated scoring of the TOEIC® E-mail Task*. ETS research report no. RR-12-16. Princeton: Educational Testing Service.

Du Bois, J. W., Chafe, W., Meyer, C., Thompson, S. A., Englebretson, R., & Martey, N. (2000–2005). *Santa Barbara corpus of spoken American English* (1–4). Philadelphia: Linguistic Data Consortium.

Fernández, J. (2013). A corpus-based study of vague language use by learners of Spanish in a study abroad context. In C. Kinginger (Ed.), *Social and cultural aspects of language learning in study abroad* (pp. 299–332). Philadelphia: John Benjamins.

Fernández, J., Gates Tapia, A., & Lu, X. (2014). Oral proficiency and pragmatic marker use in L2 spoken Spanish: The case of *pues* and *bueno*. *Journal of Pragmatics, 74*, 150–164.

Fernández, J., & Yuldashev, A. (2015). Using a corpus-informed pedagogical intervention to develop awareness toward appropriate lexicogrammatical choices. *L2 Journal*, *7*(4), 91–107.

Ferrenge, E. (2013). Automatic suprasegmental parameter extraction in learner corpora. In A. Díaz-Negrillo, N. Ballier, & P. Thompson (Eds.), *Automatic treatment and analysis of learner corpus data* (pp. 151–168). Philadelphia: John Benjamins.

Fung, L., & Carter, R. (2007). Discourse markers and spoken English: Native and learner use in pedagogic settings. *Applied Linguistics*, *28*(3), 410–439.

Gablasova, D., & Brezina, V. (2018). Disagreement in L2 spoken English: From learner corpus research to corpus-based teaching materials. In V. Brezina & L. Flowerdew (Eds.), *Learner corpus research: New perspectives and applications* (pp. 69–89). London: Bloomsbury Publishing Academic.

Granger, S., & Paquot, M. (2008). Disentangling the phraseological web. In S. Granger & F. Meunier (Eds.), *Phraseology: An interdisciplinary perspective* (pp. 27–49). Philadelphia: John Benjamins.

Gut, U. (2009). *Non-native speech: A corpus-based analysis of phonological and phonetic properties of L2 English and German*. Frankfort: Peter Lang Publishing.

Have, P. t. (1989). The consultation as genre. In B. Torode (Ed.), *Text and talk as social practice: Discourse difference and division in speech and writing* (pp. 115–135). Dordrecht: Foris Publications.

Hyland, K. (2005). Stance and engagement: A model of interaction in academic discourse. *Discourse Studies*, *7*(2), 173–192.

Jucker, A., Schreier, D., & Hundt, M. (Eds.) (2009). *Corpora: Pragmatics and discourse*. Amsterdam: Rodopi.

Jurafsky, D. (2006). Pragmatics and computational linguistics. In L. Horn & G. Ward (Eds.), *The handbook of pragmatics* (pp. 578–604). Oxford: Blackwell Publishing.

Kang, O. (2010). Relative salience of suprasegmental features on judgments of L2 comprehensibility and accentedness. *System*, *38*(2), 301–315.

Kasper, G., & Dahl, M. (1991). Research methods in interlanguage pragmatics. *Studies in Second Language Acquisition*, *13*(2), 215–247.

Klein, W., & Perdue, C. (1992). *Utterance structure: Developing grammars again*. Amsterdam: John Benjamins.

Klein, W., & Perdue, C. (1997). The basic variety (or: Couldn't natural languages be much simpler?). *Second Language Research*, *13*(4), 301–347.

Lee, J. J., & Deakin, L. (2016). Interactions in L1 and L2 undergraduate student writing: Interactional metadiscourse in successful and less-successful argumentative essays. *Journal of Second Language Writing*, *33*, 21–34.

LoCastro, V. (2003). *An introduction to pragmatics: Social action for language teachers*. Ann Arbor: University of Michigan Press.

Martin, J. R. (1985). *Factual writing: Exploring and challenging social reality* (republished 1989). Oxford: Oxford University Press.

McEnery, T., & Hardie, A. (2012). *Corpus linguistics: Method, theory and practice*. Cambridge: Cambridge University Press.

Mitchell, R., Myles, F., & Marsden, E. (2013). *Second language learning theories*. London: Routledge.

Müller, S. (2005). *Discourse markers in native and non-native English discourse*. Philadelphia: John Benjamins.

Myles, F. (2000). Change and continuity in second language acquisition research. In H. Trappes-Lomax (Ed.), *Change and continuity in applied linguistics: Selected papers from the annual meeting of the British Association for Applied Linguistics* (pp. 68–81). Clevedon: British Association for Applied Linguistics, with Multilingual Matters.

O'Keeffe, A., Clancy, B., & Adolphs, S. (2011). *Introducing pragmatics in use*. London: Routledge.

Ortega, L., & Byrnes, H. (2008). *The longitudinal study of advanced L2 capacities*. London: Routledge.

Paquot, M. (2010). *Academic vocabulary in learner writing: From extraction to analysis*. London: Bloomsbury Publishing.

Perdue, C. (Ed.) (1993). *Adult language acquisition: Cross-linguistic perspective* (2 vols). Cambridge: Cambridge University Press.

Perdue, C. (2000). Introduction. Organizing principles of learner varieties. *Studies in Second Language Acquisition*, *22*(3), 299–305.

Polat, B. (2011). Investigating acquisition of discourse markers through a developmental learner corpus. *Journal of Pragmatics*, *43*(15), 3745–3756.

Reinhardt, J. (2007). *Directives usage by ITAs: An applied learner corpus analysis*. Doctoral Dissertation. The Pennsylvania State University, University Park.

Romero-Trillo, J. (Series Ed.) (2016). *Yearbook of corpus linguistics and pragmatics. Global implications for society and education in the networked age.* Cham: Springer.

Romero-Trillo, J. (2019). Prosodic pragmatics and feedback in intercultural communication. *Journal of Pragmatics, 151,* 91–102.

Searle, J. (1969). *Speech acts. An essay in the philosophy of language.* New York: Cambridge University Press.

Simpson, R. C., Briggs, S. L., Ovens, J., & Swales, J. M. (2002). *The Michigan corpus of academic spoken English.* Ann Arbor: The Regents of the University of Michigan.

Staples, S. (2015). *The discourse of nurse-patient interactions: Contrasting the communicative styles of U.S. and international nurses.* Philadelphia: John Benjamins.

Swales, J. (1990). *Genre analysis: English in academic and research settings.* Cambridge: Cambridge University Press.

Taavitsainen, I., & Jucker, A. H. (2008). Methinks you seem more beautiful than ever. Compliments and gender in the history of English. In A. H. Jucker & I. Taavitsainen (Eds.), *Speech acts in the history of English* (pp. 195–228). Philadelphia: John Benjamins.

Taguchi, N. (2013). Production of routines in L2 English: Effect of proficiency and study abroad experience. *System, 41*(1), 109–121.

Taguchi, N., & Roever, C. (2017). *Second language pragmatics.* Oxford: Oxford University Press.

Tardy, C. M., & Swales, J. M. (2014). Genre analysis. In A. Barron & K. P. Schneider (Eds.), *Pragmatics of discourse* (pp. 165–187). Berlin: Mouton de Gruyter.

Tracy-Ventura, N., Mitchell, R., & McManus, K. (2016). The LANGSNAP longitudinal learner corpus. Design and use. In M. Alonso-Ramos (Ed.), *Spanish learner corpus research. Current trends and future perspectives* (pp. 117–142). Philadelphia: John Benjamins.

Vyatkina, N., & Cunningham, D. J. (2015). Learner corpora and pragmatics. In S. Granger, G. Gilquin, & F. Meunier (Eds.), *The Cambridge handbook of learner corpus research* (pp. 281–304). Cambridge: Cambridge University Press.

Watorek, M., & Perdue, C. (2005). Psycholinguistic studies on the acquisition of French as a second language: The 'learner variety' approach. In J. M. Dewaele (Ed.), *Focus on French as a foreign language: Multidisciplinary approaches* (pp. 1–16). Tonawanda: Multilingual Matters.

Weisser, M. (2014). Speech act annotation. In K. Aijmer & C. Rühlemann (Eds.), *Corpus pragmatics: A handbook* (pp. 84–113). Cambridge: Cambridge University Press.

Yan, X., & Staples, S. (2020). Fitting MD analysis in an argument-based validity framework for writing assessment: Explanation and generalization inferences for the ECPE. *Language Testing, 37*(2), 189–214.

Corpora and Instructed Second Language Acquisition

Rosamond Mitchell

Introduction

In a recent introductory text, instructed second language acquisition (ISLA) is defined as:

> a theoretically and empirically based field of academic inquiry that aims to understand how the systematic manipulation of the mechanisms of learning and/or the conditions under which they occur enable or facilitate the development and acquisition of a language other than one's first.

(Loewen, 2015, p. 2)

There is also by now a considerable volume of work in applied corpus linguistics that is intended to contribute to the same goal, i.e. to optimize the mechanisms and conditions of language learning. This work first began in the late 1960s (McEnery & Wilson, 1997), but as described in Boulton's timeline (2017), the main impetus can be traced back to Johns' (1990) proposal of the concept of data-driven learning (DDL) and the launch in 1994 of the conference series *Teaching and Language Corpora*. Research and development in this tradition is now substantial; a recent meta-analysis takes into account 64 empirical studies of DDL (Boulton & Cobb, 2017). However, in Loewen's 2015 textbook and in a related handbook (Loewen & Sato, 2017), there is very limited reference to corpus-informed pedagogy and its potential to facilitate ISLA. This chapter sets out to connect the two fields, paying particular attention to their orientation to SLA theory and how far their perspectives are shared or different.

Core Issues and Topics

In this section, we begin by examining the types of L2 learning theory which underpin ISLA on the one hand and corpus-informed pedagogy on the other. We then explore three separate corpus types, their relationship with instruction, and their contribution to the interpretation of instructed learning: native speaker (NS) or "expert" corpora and their use as sources of pedagogic materials and activities (Friginal, 2018); learner corpora and their pedagogic applications (Chambers, 2015; Granger, 2015); and classroom corpora as a source of evidence on instructed SLA (Collins, Trofimovich, White, Cardoso, & Horst, 2009; Reder, Harris, & Kristen, 2003).

Perspectives on L2 Acquisition

As Chapter 4 (this volume) shows, SLA theory is currently quite diverse. Loewen (2015) argues that three theoretical strands are of particular relevance to ISLA: the interaction approach, skill acquisition theory, and input processing (p. 9). The interaction approach is important to ISLA because it provides theoretical support for meaning-oriented classroom activities such as those involved in task-based learning and additionally provides a rationale for different types of feedback on learners' L2 productions. The interaction approach is also compatible with ideas of "focus on form" and "noticing", i.e. that acquisition of L2 form is promoted when learners pay momentary attention to form, in the course of meaning-based communication. ISLA researchers in this tradition have tried various means of promoting noticing, including the "input flood", where input is manipulated to include many examples of a target construction, and "input enhancement", where target forms are highlighted in some way in classroom input, e.g. through bolded text (see commentary by Loewen, 2015, pp. 70–71). Skill acquisition theory, on the other hand, provides a rationale for provision of metalinguistic explanations and development of language awareness ("declarative knowledge"), characteristic of the language classroom, as well as for opportunities to practice and rehearse language forms (so as to proceduralize new knowledge). Finally, input processing theory supports classroom activities which promote learners' attention to the meaning and functions of L2 morphosyntactic features not found in L1 (known as "processing instruction": VanPatten, 2004). Regarding the nature of language itself, i.e. the object to be learned, Loewen and other ISLA adherents typically adopt a fairly traditional view, subdividing language knowledge into grammar, vocabulary, pronunciation, and pragmatics.

Corpus researchers have a somewhat different theoretical orientation on L2 learning, commonly stressing more usage- and input-based perspectives (Ellis, Simpson-Vlach, Römer, O'Donnell, & Wulff, 2015; Leech, 2011); see Chapter 13, this volume, for a full discussion of usage-based approaches. When discussing the application of corpora in L2 instruction, this usage-based perspective may, however, be combined with ideas of "noticing" and development of metalinguistic awareness, as well as more general educational ideas about learner autonomy:

> The underlying rationale is that [exploitation of corpora] provides the massive contextualised exposure needed for language learning, but in a more controlled way than purely haphazard exposure via regular reading or listening, thus promoting or enhancing noticing, language awareness, autonomy, and "better learners".
>
> *(Boulton, 2017, p. 483)*

> Not only does DDL raise learners' awareness of the way language is used in real-life communicative situations, but it also develops their autonomy by encouraging them to take responsibility for their own learning.
>
> *(Szudarski, 2018, p. 104)*

Specifically, proponents of corpus-based DDL commonly refer to constructivist learning theory, according to which learners "build knowledge actively, largely through inductive processes" (Collentine, 2000, p. 48). Applied to SLA, the expectation is that learners can "construct their L2 knowledge independently by exploring the linguistic data compiled from corpora, such as concordances, that provide multiple sentential examples of how a target linguistic item is used" (Lee, Warschauer, & Lee, 2019, p. 722). While concordance data can show resemblances to focus on form tools such as input flood and input enhancement, there is, of course, one major difference; whereas input flood and input enhancement try to promote momentary awareness of a target L2 form within a continuous, meaningful text, concordance lines centering on target L2 items are typically drawn from much larger corpora and presented out of textual context. It seems debatable therefore whether inductive engagement with corpus data promotes noticing/focus on form, as suggested by Lee et al. (2019) or rather promotes focus on formS and the development of metalinguistic awareness; we return to this issue below.

Finally, it needs to be acknowledged that researchers investigating classroom corpora may adopt very different perspectives on SLA, including sociocultural theory (Ohta, 2001), L2 socialization theory (Cekaite, 2017), and learning through participation in a classroom community of practice (Hellermann, 2008), as well as usage-based theory (Eskildsen, Cadierno & Li, 2015).

Corpus researchers' view of the nature of language is also rather different from that prevailing in ISLA research, stressing "its fuzzy, probabilistic nature and the importance of lexical patterns, collocations, chunks, frequencies and distributions" (Boulton, 2017, p. 483). Much greater attention is paid to lexis, relatively speaking, and to formulaic language or "lexical bundles", as building blocks in both language use and L2 acquisition (Ellis et al., 2015).

Instructional Uses of Expert Reference Corpora

It is a longstanding concern of language educators to teach "authentic" language and also to focus the curriculum on domains of language which will be most useful to their students. Corpus linguistics offers new tools potentially supporting both these aims.

Indirect Instructional Uses of Reference Corpora

Since the mid-20th century, educators have been concerned with word frequency, believing that the commonest words in a language should be taught first; this interest led to such publications as the *General Service List for English* (West, 1953) and *Le français fondamental* (Gougenheim, Michea, Rivenc, & Sauvageon, 1956), both based on early, hand-analyzed corpora. Digitally supported corpus linguistics has provided frequency lists grounded in much larger corpora, which can also address specialist interests (such as the *Academic Vocabulary List* of Gardner and Davies, based on a subdomain of the COCA corpus: 2014). They have also allowed for creation of lists of phrases and multiword units, such as work on "lexical bundles" in the English of higher education (Biber & Barbieri, 2007) or the *Academic Keyword List* of Paquot (2010), grounded in the British National Corpus. Pedagogically, corpus-derived wordlists can be used to organize and sequence explicit vocabulary instruction (as in Schmitt & Schmitt, 2011).

Since the first COBUILD dictionary (published in 1987), reference works on English have also increasingly been grounded in reference corpora; for a discussion of the impact of corpus linguistics on lexicography, see Hanks (2012). Well-known grammars in this tradition include the *Longman Grammar of Spoken and Written English* (Biber et al., 1999), and the *Cambridge Grammar of English* (Carter & McCarthy, 2006). A review by Meunier and Reppen (2015) illustrates how such material differs from non-corpus-based manuals in its treatment of a particular grammatical topic (the English passive), whereas Paquot (2018) emphasizes how corpus-informed grammars pay more consistent attention to variation in grammatical usage and to the close interconnections between lexis and grammar.

Reference works such as grammar manuals and dictionaries primarily support the development of metalinguistic understanding and knowledge about language. Coursebooks contribute to these types of understanding as well, but in many settings, they are also learners' main source for both L2 input and L2 practice. However, the impact of corpus linguistics on coursebook production has been much more limited. Granger (2015) comments on a "general lack of uptake of corpus data by coursebook designers" (p. 494), and Paquot (2018) remarks that textbooks "lag behind" (p. 364). Textbooks themselves are becoming a target of analysis with corpus linguistic tools (Meunier & Gouverneur, 2009), and such research offers insights into the kind of L2 input which textbooks make available. Indeed, researchers using corpus methods continue to identify a distinctive pedagogic register in lower level textbooks ("School English") which differs from the "authentic" usage found in wider corpora (Römer, 2004). However, such analyses offer no direct insights into how learners use textbook material to learn.

Direct Instructional Uses of Reference Corpora

So far, we have outlined "indirect" uses of expert corpora, in the development of teaching materials. "Direct" applications of such corpora include their use as reference sources for teachers about current language usage in particular registers or academic fields and also as input for language students. Data-driven learning (DDL) involves exposing students directly to corpus data in some form, so as to provide them with controlled yet "authentic" input, exemplifying language usage in relevant domains. As we have seen, different rationales have been offered for DDL in terms of learning theory: that "massive but controlled exposure to authentic input" (Cobb & Boulton, 2015, p. 481) can lead to unconscious acquisition of underlying patterns of lexis, pragmatics etc., and also that it provides opportunities for conscious "noticing" and the building of metalinguistic awareness through "focus on form" (Chambers, 2015, p. 451), while promoting learner engagement and autonomy. DDL has been tried in varied forms, ranging from providing students with paper-based corpus extracts consisting of pre-selected sets of concordance lines plus accompanying analysis tasks to training them to analyze major corpora for themselves in a more open-ended way. More recently, DDL may also include dynamic web searches using familiar tools such as Google (Boulton, 2015; Luo & Zhou, 2017).

Several reviews and meta-analyses of DDL research have been published (for example, Boulton & Cobb, 2017; Cobb & Boulton, 2015; Flowerdew, 2015a; Luo & Zhou, 2017; Lee et al., 2019). These surveys show that most DDL studies have been concerned with L2 English and have focused on intermediate or advanced students with good access to digital technologies, often in higher education. Boulton and Cobb (2017) also note some preference for the use of DDL in EFL settings, notably in Asia, rather than in ESL settings, where rich L2 input is more generally available. DDL is of special interest in genre-specific pedagogy, especially English for Academic Purposes (Boulton, Carter-Thomas & Rowley-Jolivet, 2012; Flowerdew, 2015b), and with respect to the development of vocabulary (including lexical bundles and collocations) and the skill of writing. While many DDL interventions make use of major NS corpora such as BNC, Brown, or COCA, others make use of locally built corpora, such as collections of research papers from particular disciplines. DDL practitioners may also encourage EAP students to create their own personal corpora of relevant academic materials (Charles, 2012). A good number of studies show positive reactions from students introduced to DDL, but others have reported some negative reactions especially where time must be invested in mastering concordancing tools (e.g. Luo & Liao, 2015, with College English classes in China). However, it seems that rising general computer literacy and increasing access to easy-to-use tools (including general search engines) may be reducing these problems (Daskalovska, 2015). Boulton and Cobb (2017) also note a recent increase in use of DDL with lower level students of general English.

Regarding the foci of DDL, the literature reports projects and activities which set out to teach vocabulary (including collocations and lexical bundles), grammar, and aspects of both spoken and written discourse, using a wide range of corpora and concordancers (AntConc, LexTutor, BNCweb etc: Friginal, 2018, Part C). Projects are also reported which exploit corpora of different types to support feedback and error correction. In a study by Crosthwaite (2017), for example, graduate students were trained to draw upon corpus resources using SKELL or BNCweb to correct errors in their own writing, manipulating part-of-speech queries and information on collocations and frequencies. From an SLA perspective, while some of these initiatives offer rationales deriving from usage-based learning theory (e.g. McNair, 2018), most of them seem to rely primarily on conscious noticing and pattern-finding, so as to build deeper metalinguistic awareness (Flowerdew, 2015b; Lee et al., 2019).

Instructional Uses of Learner Corpora

As described in Chapter 3 (this volume), learner corpora are systematic collections of authentic, uncorrected L2 texts or other types of L2 productions. The instructional uses of learner corpora can also be divided into "indirect" and "direct" uses, reviewed by Chambers (2015), Granger (2015), and Paquot (2018). From an ISLA perspective, a key distinction is how far learner corpora are used as a source of information on learner errors (in comparison with expert usage), and how far they are a source of positive information on developmental routes and sequences.

Regarding "indirect" uses, Granger (2015) reviews the impact of learner corpora and associated error analyses on instructional materials. She identifies a number of Longman lexicographic publications, including the *Longman dictionary of contemporary English* (3rd edition: 1999), as the earliest to be systematically informed by a learner corpus (*Longman Learners' Corpus*: LLC). The LLC was drawn upon to make sure that dictionary entries used vocabulary familiar to learners and to highlight spelling, collocational, and lexicogrammatical errors which were "well attested". Similarly, the *Macmillan English dictionary for advanced learners* (2nd edition: Rundell, 2007) is informed by the *International Corpus of Learner English* (ICLE). This dictionary includes advice on widespread and generic L2 errors (i.e. those produced by learners regardless of L1 background), in the form of "Get it right" notes. The web-based *Louvain EAP dictionary* (Granger & Paquot, 2015) also uses ICLE data systematically, offering both generic and L1-specific error notes.

Granger (2015) finds that the use of learner corpora elsewhere is much more limited. Regarding reference grammars, she notes that the *Cambridge Grammar of English* (Carter & McCarthy, 2006) and associated publications are grounded (as we have seen earlier) in the *Cambridge English Corpus* (CEC). A subcomponent of CEC is the *Cambridge Learner Corpus* (CLC), comprising written scripts from Cambridge English examinations; it now totals 55+ million words, with a significant error-coded component (O'Keeffe & Mark, 2017). However, in Granger's (2015) view, the *Cambridge Grammar* use of CLC data to provide error warnings is unsystematic and still reliant on intuition: "the focus tends to be on errors that grammarians know to be problematic rather than errors emerging from systematic analysis of the learner corpus" (p. 492). We have already noted that writers of published coursebooks pay little attention to reference corpora (Burton, 2012). Granger confirms that this is even less the case with respect to learner corpora.

Nonetheless, some examples of the "indirect" use of learner corpora to inform teaching materials can be found. Some educators have developed in-house materials on the basis of local learner corpora; for example, Rankin and Schiftner (2011) analyzed German students' use of complex and marginal English prepositions (*concerning, regarding* ...), and devised relevant pedagogic materials, including exercises based on NS data drawn from BYU-BNC, alongside learner data drawn from ICLE. Another area of activity is CALL; Granger (2015) quotes examples of CALL programs addressing L1-specific grammar errors identified through learner corpus analysis, such as misuse of English articles among Chinese-speaking learners, or over-use of passivization among Korean speakers.

The second potential "indirect" use of learner corpora is to influence general curriculum design and assessment by providing information on learners' overall progress and development, i.e. what they can do, as opposed to the errors that they may make. The *English Profile Project* is advancing this perspective (McCarthy, 2016; O'Keeffe & Mark, 2017). Originally grounded in the CLC, this project has set out to identify the linguistic capabilities reflecting the functionally described levels of the Common European Framework for Languages (CEFR: Council of Europe,

2001). So far, two profiles have been produced (*English Grammar Profile, English Vocabulary Profile*: www.englishprofile.org). For grammar, for example: "through the EGP, it is aimed to arrive at a corpus-based description of what learners can do with grammar at each level of the CEFR based on what they have written in Cambridge exams" (O'Keeffe & Mark, 2017, p. 464). The challenges of using such descriptions to drive syllabus design are discussed by O'Keeffe and Mark. In line with usage-based learning theory, these authors note that forms do not appear fully-fledged in learner productions in a stepwise manner, but instead appear initially in limited, high frequency, and prototypical uses, followed by long term development in "how and when" a given form is deployed (O'Keeffe & Mark, 2017, p. 469). They recommend that items should be sequenced for instruction in line with criteria which mainly exploit their relative frequency and correctness of usage in the learner corpus; O'Donnell (2013) makes somewhat similar proposals. McCarthy (2016) is especially optimistic that learner corpora can inform advanced level curriculum design: "by looking not only at the less frequent structures but also at new or previously neglected meanings and functions of structures already known, we can deliver genuine increments to the grammatical repertoire of learners" (p. 112). However, the full operationalization of such proposals still seems somewhat distant.

The use of learner corpora in DDL also remains somewhat underdeveloped. Early on, it was described by Granger (2002) as "highly controversial", because of the supposed "danger of exposing learners to erroneous data" (p. 26). Nonetheless, she saw it as potentially productive for both form-focused instruction and "noticing" activities. A pioneering study by Seidlhofer (2002) demonstrated students' high engagement in activities in which they firstly compared lexicogrammar and vocabulary in their own written texts with those in a similar NS text, and later explored similar features in larger expert corpora. Later studies have confirmed the motivational power for students of working with learner corpora. Hardy, Römer, and Roberson (2015) report a study in which students used the *Michigan Corpus of Upper-Level Student Papers* (MICUSP) and appropriate corpus tools to "explore central aspects of academic writing and develop context- and discipline-specific writing skills" (p. 3); participants subsequently reported high satisfaction levels and gains in confidence as writers. Cotos (2014) conducted a classroom quasi-experiment over one semester, in which two groups of international students used DDL to explore the properties of linking adverbials (LAs) in written English (*however, namely, thus* etc.). One group explored a corpus of published research articles, alongside their own written assignments, while a comparison group analyzed the research articles only. Both groups started the semester with similar knowledge of LAs, and both made learning gains, but the articles+assignments corpus group significantly outperformed the articles-only corpus group. The former also reported quite extensive reflections connecting exemplar data to their own writing; the main learning strategy of the articles-only group remained the memorization of concordance lines and phrases.

Classroom Corpora, L2 Interaction, and L2 Learning

The account provided above suggests that from an ISLA perspective, both reference and learner corpora are primarily significant for their direct and indirect contribution to focus-on-form learning activities and the development of learners' metalinguistic knowledge. Here we consider briefly the potential contribution to our understanding of ISLA of L2 classroom corpora, i.e. collections of authentic classroom transcripts which can be analyzed using corpus tools. While typically much smaller than reference and learner corpora, a classroom corpus documents the learning environment itself, as well as instructed learners' engagement with it. In practice, L2 classroom corpora have provided evidence regarding (a) L2 input (in the form of teacher talk), and its impact on learner development and (b) the development of students' L2 interactional competence.

Classroom corpus studies focusing on L2 teacher input include the work of Collins and associates (e.g. Collins et al., 2009), Myles and associates (e.g. Myles, Mitchell & David, 2012), and Mougeon and associates (e.g. Mougeon & Rehner, 2017). Collins et al. (2009) describe a 110,000-word corpus of ESL lessons for 11- and 12-year-old French-speaking learners in Quebec and analyze the teacher input from a usage-based perspective. They explore the evidence available to the students within this corpus for various English forms: the present progressive -*ing* and irregular simple past (typically acquired relatively early), the regular simple past, and the possessive determiners *his* and *her* (typically acquired relatively late). All of these forms were infrequent in the corpus, with the exception of irregular simple past (*was, had,* etc). However, possessive -*ing* was much more phonologically salient in teacher talk than regular simple past forms or the determiners *his* and *her*. In addition, when *his* and *her* were found, they rarely occurred in contexts with unambiguous gender reference (*his daughter, her brother*). Thus Collins et al. explain the relative difficulty of acquisition of these forms, in the classroom setting, in line with the suggestions of Ellis (2006) regarding the importance of input frequency plus psycholinguistic factors likely to mediate frequency effects and inhibit the processing of L2 input. Myles et al. (2012) analyze a corpus of elementary school L2 French lessons, and show that frequency in teacher input is the main driver of L2 vocabulary development; Mougeon and Rehner (2017) analyze a corpus of L2 French high school lessons and show that learners' production of more/less formal features of spoken L2 French is related to their degree of exposure to teacher talk (more formal) and/or to French outside the classroom (less formal).

Other classroom corpora have been created and analyzed to explore a range of sociocultural perspectives on ISLA. Cekaite (2017) presents an empirical study of the L2 socialization of 7-year-old children in a migrant reception class in Sweden, drawing on a 90-hour video corpus and adopting a qualitative approach to the analysis of lesson transcripts, showing how the children are socialized into the role of "good student", and develop appropriate linguistic practices. Ohta (2001) analyses similar transcripts from a corpus of L2 Japanese lessons, with adult students, using concepts from sociocultural theory such as scaffolding, self-regulation, and private speech to interpret students' classroom talk and appropriation of L2 forms.

Perhaps the most ambitious corpus project of this type is the *Portland Multimedia Adult English Learner Corpus* (MAELC: Reder, Harris & Kristen, 2003). Over a period of four years, this project videorecorded 4,000+ hours of adult ESOL classroom interaction. This corpus has been used to study the development of learners' interactional competence, from usage-based and "community of practice" perspectives (Eskildsen, Cadierno & Li, 2015; Hellermann, 2008). An important contribution of these classroom corpus studies is to demonstrate the existence within classrooms of usage-based learning, itself somewhat marginalized in current ISLA theory; a study illustrating this approach (Eskildsen & Wagner, 2015) is discussed below in the section *Representative Corpora and Research*.

Main Research Methods

We have described earlier the use of reference corpora such as BNC or COCA as sources for the design of instructional materials, as well as the use of learner corpora such as ICLE or *Cambridge Learner English* as sources of advice on common errors and on curriculum design. Otherwise, most research on corpora and instructed SLA is classroom based and concerns aspects of DDL.

Most early DDL studies take the form of action research, conducted by a teacher-researcher, and this tradition is still active (Chambers, 2015, p. 450). Such studies commonly report interventions in which students were trained to carry out corpus investigations, with commentaries on the challenges encountered, evaluation surveys to document attitudes of students and teachers, and occasional longer-term follow-up (e.g. Charles, 2012, 2014). In 2017, Crosthwaite could still comment that "the majority of DDL studies have focused on perceptions or favorability towards

DDL as a concept" (p. 448). A study by Chen and Flowerdew (2018) exemplifying this tradition is discussed below in *Representative corpora and research.*

However, recent reviews (e.g. Boulton & Cobb, 2017; Cobb & Boulton, 2015; Lee et al., 2019) report growing research into the language learning outcomes of DDL. Boulton and Cobb (2017) located over 200 empirical DDL studies, of which 64 met criteria for inclusion in a statistical meta-analysis. These studies followed two basic designs: pre-test/post-test (P/P) studies with single groups of participants and quasi-experimental studies with parallel control and experimental groups (C/E). The findings of the meta-analysis were generally favorable to DDL; for both types of study, the mean gains (on a variety of immediate post-tests) had large effect sizes (d=1.5 for P/P studies, d=0.95 for C/E studies). Some more detailed conclusions provide useful pointers for future development of DDL. Boulton and Cobb (2017) claim that the approach has been shown most clearly to be effective in foreign language settings, with both undergraduate and graduate students; the hands-on use of concordancers (see Chapter 6, this volume) led to somewhat higher gains than paper-based activities; intermediate students made gains similar to those of advanced students; and the main learning gains were found in the areas of vocabulary and lexicogrammar (although other skills have attracted much less research). They view the quality of DDL research to be generally acceptable, although capable of improvement in terms of reporting, following Larson-Hall and Plonsky (2015); an important limitation is the scarcity of longitudinal studies. Boulton and Cobb (2017) are also cautious about relating their findings about the effectiveness of DDL to any underlying ISLA theory, beyond the claim related to noticing that "learners seem able to perceive language patterns despite the lines chopped off the concordance output" (p. 386). A DDL experiment by Daskalovska (2015) is introduced in the next section.

Representative Corpora and Research

Chen and Flowerdew (2018) describe in detail a pedagogic innovation, consisting in a workshop for PhD students from varied disciplines, on how to exploit corpus resources to improve and develop their own academic writing. During a 3.5-hour session, participants were introduced to Google Scholar searches, to BNCweb, and to AntConc, and supported in conducting a range of focused searches, e.g. around the use of particular sentence patterns or lexical items for various discourse functions in specialized disciplinary subcorpora of BNC. Sample searches included those appearing in Table 19.1.

Participants were also shown how to create their own specialized corpora of relevant articles. Over several repeat sessions, 341 students experienced the workshop. Responses to an evaluation questionnaire were very positive, and some participants were contacted again after 6–8 months, to document their current use of corpora. These case study students all reported using corpora in some way to support their writing, although relying on existing corpora (including BNCweb)

Table 19.1 Sample Searches from Chen & Flowerdew (2018, p. 103)

Language problem (2)	Writing problem (3)
What are the verbs we can use when we need to report/interpret results of a study?	How do I make claims or present arguments in research writing?
Take *indicate* as an example; how can we use this type of verb in writing?	Focused section: all the sections
Queried word: *indicate* (all forms)	Discourse features: making claims, boosters and hedges
Corpus skills: the use of wildcards, sort results, frequency breakdown	Queried pattern: *it…that, it…to*
	Corpus skills: advanced search function, sort, concordance plot, file view

rather than creating their own; none were using AntConc, and two out of three preferred simple searches with Google Scholar.

Daskalovska (2015) reports an experiment conducted with first-year students of English at a university in Macedonia concerning the learning of English verb-adverb collocations (VACs, e.g. *to forget easily, to be properly advised*). The participants were divided into experimental and comparison groups (n=21, n=25, respectively); a pre-test showed no significant difference in knowledge of VACs. Over a 2-hour period, the experimental group were trained to use BNC-BYU, and then carried out a series of tasks for a given list of verbs:

(1) finding the first 10 most frequent adverb collocates of the given verbs,
(2) noticing the more usual position of the adverbs and writing down the most frequently used adverbs before and after the verbs,
(3) generating and analyzing concordance lines for the collocations, and
(4) summarizing the results and preparing a short presentation on their findings.

(Daskalovska, 2015, p. 133)

Meanwhile, the comparison group undertook textbook-based activities involving matching and/or selecting VACs. Both groups completed a post-test and a delayed post-test 3 weeks later; on both post-tests the experimental group significantly out-performed the comparison group. Daskalovska (2015) interprets the greater success of the experimental group in terms of richer L2 input and greater opportunity for L2 noticing and L2 processing (p. 137).

Eskildsen and his associates have carried out a range of case studies of individual adult ESOL learners documented in the MAELC corpus. They use conversation analysis methods to trace the emergence in classroom discourse of a range of language forms (English negation, question forms, verbs of motion), from usage-based and sociocultural perspectives.

Eskildsen and Wagner (2015) exploit the video nature of the MAELC corpus and present a multimodal analysis of student participation and development. Eskildsen and Wagner trace the emergence in the speech of learner Carlos of the English prepositions *under* and *across*. They identify all occasions when Carlos uses these prepositions and how they relate to occurrences in the speech of the teacher and of other students. An important dimension is the iconic gesturing which accompanies both prepositions, in the speech of all participants. In the case of *under*, the teacher's iconic gesturing supports Carlos' first encounter with, and use of, the word; his own later uses of *under* are accompanied by similar gestures, although modified somewhat when scaffolding another student, and diminishing as his use of the form becomes more fluent. In the case of *across*, his paraphrases and accompanying gestures make it clear that Carlos first of all interprets the word in the sense of "crossing a boundary" and only gradually integrates another meaning of the word, in the expression *across from* ("facing"), with appropriate gestural modifications. The researchers summarize the learning process they have observed in terms of usage-based theory, as a "slow process of taking in affordances from the environment and making them one's own in subsequent uses in similar situations" (p. 291).

Future Directions

We began this chapter by pointing out the theory-related gap which currently exists between ISLA researchers and those who adopt corpus-based practices in the language classroom. The chapter has indeed shown that some learning theories which are central to ISLA have underpinned corpus-related research, notably the strong reliance of DDL practice on claims regarding the noticing hypothesis and the development of learners' metalinguistic knowledge. However, extended discussions of learning theory are rare in the DDL literature, as are detailed investigations of learning processes. How L2 learners process concordance data, for example, and how far the learning which takes place from exploration of reference corpora can be explained, at least in part, by usage-based theory or comprises mainly the development of declarative L2 knowledge, urgently requires investigation, using up to date psycholinguistic techniques such as eye tracking or self-paced reading. It would be especially interesting to investigate more precisely how the psycholinguistic processing of varied corpus data promotes "depth" of acquisition of lexicogrammatical meanings and functions, as suggested e.g. by McCarthy (2016) and by Lee et al. (2019). Turning to more applied issues, the rise of experimental studies of DDL is important and positive, but better developed explanations are required for how students are learning through DDL, if its potential application with wider groups of students is to be better understood. An obvious issue is the need to trial DDL with a wider range of languages (see Colmenares López, 2018, for Spanish DDL), as relevant expert and learner corpora become available. Meanwhile, research on classroom corpora documents the contribution of usage-based learning to classroom development, a theme relatively neglected in current ISLA theory. Overall, this chapter demonstrates the need for stronger connections between ISLA theorists and corpus practitioners, which could benefit all sides, in particular those concerned with theorizing advanced and discipline-specific language learning.

Further Reading

Flowerdew, L. (2015a). Data-driven learning and language learning theories: Whither the twain shall meet. In A. Lenko-Szymanska & A. Boulton (Eds.), *Multiple affordances of language corpora for data-driven learning* (pp. 15–36). Amsterdam: John Benjamins.

This book chapter is an extended critical discussion of the language learning theories underpinning DDL; Flowerdew deals at greatest length with the noticing hypothesis but also discusses constructivist learning, and sociocultural theory and explores their applications in empirical DDL research.

Friginal, E. (2018). *Corpus linguistics for English teachers: Tools, online resources, and classroom activities.* Abingdon: Routledge.

This book provides an overview of corpus applications in English language teaching, including information on current corpora and corpus tools, an introduction to DDL, and an annotated bibliography of research studies. Much of the book presents DDL projects concerned with vocabulary, grammar, and spoken/written discourse, which is particularly useful for teacher-researchers seeking ideas for their own DDL action research projects.

Hellermann, J. (2008). *Social actions for classroom language learning.* Clevedon: Multilingual Matters.

This is a book length account of the MAELC classroom corpus, which provides a rich demonstration of the potential of such corpora for detailed longitudinal studies of the development of L2 interactional competence using conversation analysis methodology.

Related Topics

Chapters 4, 13, and 20.

References

Biber, D., & Barbieri, F. (2007). Lexical bundles in university spoken and written registers. *English for Specific Purposes, 26*(3), 263–286.
Biber, D., Johansson, S., Leech, G., Conrad, S., & Finegan, E. (1999). *Longman grammar of spoken and written English.* Harlow: Pearson Education Ltd.
Boulton, A. (2015). Applying data-driven learning to the web. In A. Lenko-Szymanska & A. Boulton (Eds.), *Multiple affordances of language corpora for data-driven learning* (pp. 267–296). Amsterdam: John Benjamins.
Boulton, A. (2017). Corpora in language teaching and learning. *Language Teaching, 50*(4), 483–506.

Boulton, A., Carter-Thomas, S., & Rowley-Jolivet, E. (Eds.) (2012). *Corpus informed research and learning in ESP: Issues and applications*. Amsterdam: John Benjamins.

Boulton, A., & Cobb, T. (2017). Corpus use in language learning: A meta-analysis. *Language Learning*, *67*(2), 348–393.

Burton, G. (2012). Corpora and coursebooks: Destined to be strangers for ever? *Corpora*, *7*(1), 91–108.

Carter, R., & McCarthy, M. (2006). *Cambridge grammar of English*. Cambridge: Cambridge University Press.

Cekaite, A. (2017). What makes a child a good language learner? interactional competence, identity, and immersion in a Swedish classroom. *Annual Review of Applied Linguistics*, *37*, 45–61.

Chambers, A. (2015). The learner corpus as a pedagogic corpus. In S. Granger, G. Gilquin, & F. Meunier (Eds.), *The Cambridge handbook of learner corpus research* (pp. 445–464). Cambridge: Cambridge University Press.

Charles, M. (2012). 'Proper vocabulary and juicy collocations': EAP students evaluate do-it-yourself corpus building. *English for Specific Purposes*, *31*(2), 93–102.

Charles, M. (2014). Getting the corpus habit: EAP students' long-term use of personal corpora. *English for Specific Purposes*, *35*, 30–40.

Chen, M., & Flowerdew, J. (2018). Introducing data-driven learning to PhD students for research writing purposes: A territory-wide project in Hong Kong. *English for Specific Purposes*, *50*, 97–112.

Cobb, T., & Boulton, A. (2015). Classroom applications of corpus analysis. In D. Biber & R. Reppen (Eds.), *The Cambridge handbook of English corpus linguistics* (pp. 478–497). Cambridge: Cambridge University Press.

Collentine, J. (2000). Insights into the construction of grammatical knowledge provided by user-behavior tracking technologies. *Language Learning and Technology*, *3*(2), 44–57.

Collins, L., Trofimovich, P., White, J., Cardoso, W., & Horst, M. (2009). Some input on the easy/difficult grammar question: An empirical study. *The Modern Language Journal*, *93*(3), 336–353.

Colmenares López, J. J. (2018). *Data-driven learning: Evidence from Spanish as a foreign language*. Doctoral Dissertation. Northern Arizona University, Flagstaff.

Cotos, E. (2014). Enhancing writing pedagogy with learner corpus data. *ReCALL*, *26*(2), 202–224.

Council of Europe. (2001). *Common European framework of reference for languages*. Cambridge: Cambridge University Press.

Crosthwaite, P. (2017). Retesting the limits of data-driven learning: Feedback and error correction. *Computer Assisted Language Learning*, *30*(6), 447–473.

Daskalovska, N. (2015). Corpus-based versus traditional learning of collocations. *Computer Assisted Language Learning*, *28*(2), 130–144.

Ellis, N. C. (2006).). Selective attention and transfer phenomena in L2 acquisition: Contingency, cue competition, salience, interference, overshadowing, blocking, and perceptual learning. *Applied Linguistics*, *27*(2), 164–194.

Ellis, N. C., Simpson-Vlach, R., Römer, U., O'Donnell, M. B., & Wulff, S. (2015). Learner corpora and formulaic language in second language acquisition research. In S. Granger, G. Gilquin, & F. Meunier (Eds.), *The Cambridge handbook of learner corpus research* (pp. 357–378). Cambridge: Cambridge University Press.

Eskildsen, S. W., Cadierno, T., & Li, P. (2015). On the development of motion constructions in four learners of English as L2. In T. Cadierno & S. W. Eskildsen (Eds.), *Usage-based perspectives on second language learning* (pp. 207–232). Berlin: De Gruyter.

Eskildsen, S. W., & Wagner, J. (2015). Embodied L2 construction learning. *Language Learning*, *65*(2), 268–297.

Flowerdew, L. (2015a). Data-driven learning and language learning theories: Whither the twain shall meet. In A. Lenko-Szymanska & A. Boulton (Eds.), *Multiple affordances of language corpora for data-driven learning* (pp. 15–36). Amsterdam: John Benjamins.

Flowerdew, L. (2015b). Corpus-based research and pedagogy in EAP: From lexis to genre. *Language Teaching*, *48*(1), 99–116.

Friginal, E. (2018). *Corpus linguistics for English teachers: Tools, online resources, and classroom activities*. Abingdon: Routledge.

Gardner, D., & Davies, M. (2014). A new academic vocabulary list. *Applied Linguistics*, *35*(3), 305–327.

Gougenheim, G., Michea, R., Rivenc, P., & Sauvageot, A. (1956). *L'élaboration du français élémentaire: Etude sur l'établissement d'un vocabulaire et d'une grammaire de base*. Paris: Didier.

Granger, S. (2002). A bird's eye view of learner corpus research. In S. Granger, J. Hung, & S. Petch-Tyson (Eds.), *Computer learner corpora, second language acquisition and foreign language teaching* (pp. 3–23). Amsterdam: John Benjamins.

Granger, S. (2015). The contribution of learner corpora to reference and instructional materials design. In S. Granger, G. Gilquin, & F. Meunier (Eds.), *The Cambridge handbook of learner corpus research* (pp. 486–510). Cambridge: Cambridge University Press.

Granger, S., & Paquot, M. (2015). Electronic lexicography goes local: Design and structures of a needs-driven online academic writing aid. *Lexicographica*, *31*(1), 118–141.

Hanks, P. (2012). The corpus revolution in lexicography. *International Journal of Lexicography*, *25*(4), 398–436.

Hardy, J. A., Römer, U., & Roberson, A. (2015). The power of relevant models: Using a corpus of student writing to introduce disciplinary practices in a first year composition course. *Across the Disciplines*, *12*(1), 1–20.

Hellermann, J. (2008). *Social actions for classroom language learning*. Clevedon: Multilingual Matters.

Johns, T. (1990). From printout to handout: Grammar and vocabulary teaching in the context of data-driven learning. *CALL Austria*, *10*, 14–34.

Larson-Hall, J., & Plonsky, L. (2015). Reporting and interpreting quantitative research findings: What gets reported and recommendations for the field. *Language Learning*, *65*(S1), 127–159.

Lee, H., Warschauer, M., & Lee, J. H. (2019). The effects of corpus use on second language vocabulary learning: A multilevel meta-analysis. *Applied Linguistics*, *40*(5), 721–753.

Leech, G. (2011). Frequency, corpora and language learning. In F. Meunier, S. De Cock, & G. Gilquin (Eds.), *Taste for corpora: In honour of Sylviane Granger* (pp. 7–31). Amsterdam: John Benjamins.

Loewen, S. (2015). *Introduction to instructed second language acquisition*. New York: Routledge.

Loewen, S., & Sato, M. (Eds.) (2017). *The Routledge handbook of instructed second language acquisition*. Abingdon: Routledge.

Luo, Q., & Liao, Y. (2015). Using corpora for error correction in EFL learners' writing. *Journal of Language Teaching and Research*, *6*(6), 1333–1342.

Luo, Q., & Zhou, J. (2017). Data-driven learning in second language writing class: A survey of empirical studies. *International Journal of Emerging Technologies in Learning (IJET)*, *12*(3), 182–196.

McCarthy, M. (2016). Putting the CEFR to good use: Designing grammars based on learner-corpus evidence. *Language Teaching*, *49*(1), 99–115.

McEnery, T., & Wilson, A. (1997). Teaching and language corpora. *ReCALL*, *9*(1), 5–14.

McNair, J. (2018). Using a concordance for vocabulary learning with pre-intermediate EFL students. In E. Friginal, *Corpus linguistics for English teachers: New tools, online resources, and classroom activities* (pp. 224–232). New York: Routledge.

Meunier, F., & Gouverneur, C. (2009). New types of corpora for new educational challenges: Collecting, annotating and exploiting a corpus of textbook material. In K. Aijmer (Ed.), *Corpora and language teaching* (pp. 179–202). Amsterdam: John Benjamins.

Meunier, F., & Reppen, R. (2015). Corpus versus non-corpus-informed pedagogical materials: Grammar as the focus. In D. Biber & R. Reppen (Eds.), *The Cambridge handbook of English corpus linguistics* (pp. 498–514). Cambridge: Cambridge University Press.

Mougeon, R., & Rehner, K. (2017). The influence of classroom input and community exposure on the learning of variable grammar. *Bilingualism: Language and Cognition*, *20*(1), 21–22.

Myles, F., Mitchell, R., & David, A. (2012). *Learning French from ages 5,7, and 11: An investigation into starting ages, rates and routes of learning amongst early foreign language learners* (RES-062-23-1545), ESRC End of Award Report.

O'Donnell, M. (2013). From learner corpora to curriculum design: An empirical approach to staging the teaching of grammatical concepts. *Procedia - Social and Behavioral Sciences*, *95*, 571–580.

Ohta, A. S. (2001). *Second language acquisition processes in the classroom: Learning Japanese*. Mahwah: Lawrence Erlbaum.

O'Keeffe, A., & Mark, G. (2017). The English grammar profile of learner competence. *International Journal of Corpus Linguistics*, *22*(4), 457–489.

Paquot, M. (2010). *Academic vocabulary in learner writing: From extraction to analysis*. London: Continuum.

Paquot, M. (2018). Corpus research for language teaching and learning. In A. Phakiti, P. De Costa, L. Plonsky, & S. Starfield (Eds.), *The Palgrave handbook of applied linguistics research methodology* (pp. 359–374). London: Palgrave Macmillan.

Rankin, T., & Schiftner, B. (2011). Marginal prepositions in learner English: Applying local corpus data. *International Journal of Corpus Linguistics*, *16*(3), 412–434.

Reder, S., Harris, K., & Kristen, S. (2003). A multimedia adult learner corpus. *TESOL Quarterly*, *37*, 546–557.

Römer, U. (2004). Comparing real and ideal language learner input: The use of an EFL textbook corpus in corpus linguistics and language teaching. In G. Aston, S. Bernardini, & D. Stewart (Eds.), *Corpora and language learners* (pp. 151–168). Amsterdam: Rodopi.

Rundell, M. (Ed.) (2007). *Macmillan English dictionary for advanced learners* (2nd ed.). Oxford: Macmillan.

Schmitt, D., & Schmitt, N. (2011). *Focus on vocabulary 2: Mastering the academic word list.* White Plains: Pearson Education.

Seidlhofer, B. (2002). Pedagogy and local learner corpora: Working with learning-driven data. In S. Granger, J. Hung, & S. Petch-Tyson (Eds.), *Computer learner corpora, second language acquisition and foreign language teaching* (pp. 213–234). Amsterdam: John Benjamins.

Szudarski, P. (2018). *Corpus linguistics for vocabulary: A guide for research.* London: Routledge.

VanPatten, B. (Ed.) (2004). *Processing instruction: Theory, research and commentary.* Mahwah: Lawrence Erlbaum.

West, M. (1953). *A general service list of English words.* London: Longman, Green & Co.

PART IV
SLA CONSTRUCTS AND CORPORA

20

Input

Anita Thomas and Annelie Ädel

Introduction

Input, broadly defined, corresponds to "the language that learners are exposed to" (Gass, 2015, p. 183). Although all researchers in second language acquisition (SLA) would agree with the notion that there is no language learning without input, systematic research on input and its theoretical and empirical characteristics is still at an early stage. A complicating issue is that the definition and role of input in SLA vary according to the theoretical approach taken (see e.g. Gurzynski-Weiss et al., 2018).

Input in SLA was long disregarded given its secondary role compared to innate universal principles in generative approaches (see Chapter 16, this volume). A key concept in this theoretical framework, and especially in first language acquisition, is the *poverty of stimulus*, referring to a "mismatch between the input that [L1] children are exposed to and their ultimate attainment" (White, 2015, p. 34). Thus, input was seen as secondary and insufficient for explaining what a learner can understand and produce. However, Steven Krashen, a generativist interested in SLA, put the focus on input as a way of explaining the difference between language learning in classrooms and informal contexts. Krashen (1981) argued that the input encountered in a classroom could not have the same positive effect on learning because of the presence of metalinguistic and corrective discourse, which is inadequate for a learner's needs. Instead, he argued that only input in a natural setting could contribute to language acquisition, provided that it matched the learner's linguistic level regarding comprehensibility. At the time, Krashen's theoretical positions were poorly received, mostly due to their lack of empirical evidence.

It was around the turn of the millennium that renewed interest in the role of input in SLA was sparked, largely prompted by research following usage-based approaches. In these approaches, experience with the target language is considered to have a direct impact on the learner's representation of the language (Barlow & Kemmer, 2000, pp. viii–ix; Bybee, 2008). Contrary to the top-down learning process advanced by the generative approach, where a set of pre-established universal constraints drive the acquisition process, usage-based approaches claim a close relation between learners' experience with the target language and their development of the linguistic system. Here, SLA is considered a dynamic bottom-up process dependent on the language to which the learner is exposed, or the input. Exploring this claim, research is focused on the description of learner input characteristics, and corpora are considered suitable tools for this purpose. Corpora are seen as representing language in use, with the full gamut of inter- and intraindividual variation, and are not based on guesswork or prescription. In this line of research, linguistic structures are examined in terms of frequency and distribution alongside factors known to influence input processing, such as repetition, saliency, attention, and memory capacity (Ellis et al., 2016). The combined study of input characteristics as found in corpora and influencing processing factors allows usage-based research to make predictions about the relative ease/difficulty of learning specific target language structures (see Ellis, 2002; Chapter 13, this volume).

Corpora are also used for the study of input characteristics in conversation (see Chapter 21, this volume). Research adopting an interactionist approach has found that conversation allows a high degree of joint attention and promotes activities that enhance language development, such as negotiation of meaning, feedback or recasts, and opportunities for the learner to notice the gap between output and input and do hypothesis testing (e.g. Gass, 2015). The study of syntactic priming, presented later in this chapter, is one way of mapping the direct effects of input on learner production in interaction.

In usage-based and interactionist approaches, corpora play a central role by providing primary sources of data to study the influence of language exposure on SLA, the characteristics of specific linguistic structures in the input, the relative richness of the linguistic environment, and the interaction between input and output as enacted in conversation. While it is typically not possible to capture all of the linguistic input a specific learner is exposed to, target language corpora provide insights into how linguistic phenomena are distributed and how they vary depending on contextual variables such as mode, type of text, task, and topic. They help us see what is typical in a target language and how the systematic variation across registers or varieties is patterned. Until more corpora of actual learner input become available, a corpus of L1 speech/writing can be used as a proxy for learner input or to illustrate language features which learners will likely be exposed to.

Finally, corpora of learner language have been used to analyze learners' linguistic development to estimate what type of input learners at a specific linguistic level need, for example, in the case of recurrent misuse, overuse, or underuse of specific linguistic items, or as documentation of what learners have taken up (Granger, 2009). In research where the input is manipulated (Madlener, 2018) or where all the input to the learner is controlled, as in first exposure studies (Dimroth, 2018), the relationship between input and output can be studied unusually directly and possible input effects can be isolated. The link between input and learner production is indeed of importance for improving classroom teaching (see Chapter 19, this volume).

Core Issues and Topics

Input Frequency

Corpora are key sources for learning more about input characteristics in the target language in general and in specific language use. Linguistic items are not evenly distributed in the language as a whole, nor in the input to learners. While intuitively we may be able to name very frequent or infrequent words and expressions in languages we know well, intuition may also be flawed, even misleading. A point often made in corpus-based work is that evidence from a (suitable) corpus is "richer and more reliable than information from alternative sources, including the use of intuition by native speakers" (Barlow, 2002, p. 3, see also Gries, 2005; Tracy-Ventura & Cuesta Medina, 2018).

Psycholinguistic research has shown that the frequency with which different items in the input appear to the learner influences the way they are represented in memory; language learners are sensitive to statistical regularities (Ellis, 2002). More frequent items will be better represented in memory, which in turn will make them more accessible when comprehending or producing language (Bybee, 2008). For example, when a given verb is very frequent in one specific form, this form will be more accessible than the other forms of the same verb. The frequency of occurrence of an item – the number of times it appears in a text – is referred to as *token frequency*, illustrated, for example, through the number of definite articles in this sentence (three). When several items follow the same pattern, such as past tense verbs in English with regular *-ed* as compared to irregular forms, there will be *type frequency* effects (see Nicoladis et al., 2007, for an illustration). Type frequency corresponds to a psycholinguistic process of pattern detection and memorization which results in similar items being placed in the same category. Categorization is not fixed, but dynamic, and can change with experience (Barlow & Kemmer, 2000, p. ix; Bybee, 2008). In SLA, such a change may occur when a learner, after some experience with the target language, is able to perceive differences in form-function mappings among words that are homophones and which had previously been perceived as identical. The number of language items belonging to a specific pattern determines the pattern's productivity, that is, how easily the pattern will be applied to unknown items or used as default (Bybee, 2008, p. 221). In French, for example, regular verbs ending in *-er* (*parler* 'to speak') form such a frequent pattern (90% of all verbs; Riegel et al. 2009, p. 467) that it tends to be used by default. As illustrated in (1), the past participle of the irregular verb *prendre* 'take' is constructed as if it were regular – in regular verbs, the past participle always ends with the sound [e] – but the correct form is *pris*.

(1) et alors *ils ont prenfe]* la voiture mais la voiture était pleine
'and then *they have taked* ('took') the car but the car was full'

Information about the frequency of forms and constructions in the input can be used to form hypotheses about why certain forms are learned more quickly than others and why learners overgeneralize (producing 'teached' instead of 'taught' by analogy with the most common patterns, cf. (1) above) or why certain forms are overused or underused (Nicoladis et al., 2007). For illustration, Thomas (2009, 2010) compared the frequency of regular verbs in different input sources of spoken French and the production of selected forms in an experimental test administered to beginner learners of French (see Figure 20.1). The verbs all belonged to the dominant group of regular verbs ending with *-er* in the infinitive. These verbs occur in two main forms in spoken French: (i) one used for the present tense in the singular and third-person plural, as in [paʁl]) and (ii) one corresponding to several functions such as the second person plural, the infinitive, the past participle, and the French *imparfait*, as in [paʁle]. In a first step, the two verb forms were analyzed in corpora representing different input situations:

- proficient French-speaking interlocutors in recorded conversation with adult learners of French at beginner levels;
- teachers of French in classroom interactions;
- French as spoken in France.

The analysis demonstrated differences in the distribution of the two forms across the above-mentioned interactions and revealed three groups of verbs: (a) those frequent in ([paʁl]), (b) those frequent in the multifunctional ([paʁle]), and (c) those frequent in both. In other words, the verbs did not have the same distribution patterns, as the proportion of the two most common forms was not the same for the verbs in the analyzed input sources.

In a pilot study involving spontaneous data from a corpus of learner production (Thomas, 2009), the results showed that the learners followed the distribution of forms found in the analysis of input data (reported above). However, the pilot did not reveal what form the learners would have produced in the less frequent context of a given verb, because these contexts were simply not produced. This reflects a limitation typical of corpus studies; what learners do with the L2

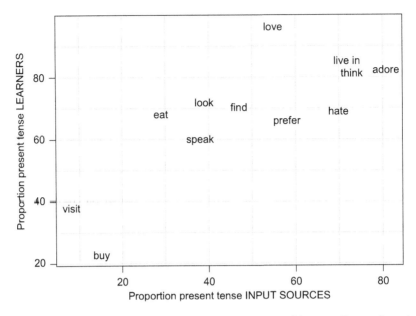

Figure 20.1   Correlation between the Analyzed Input Sources and Learner Output in an Imitation Test (Based on Thomas 2009, 2010).

may be only partially revealed in naturally-occurring data. Thus, and in particular for researchers interested in the influence of input, it may be beneficial to complement corpus-based and experimental methods (see Chapter 10, this volume).

Thomas (2009, 2010) developed an imitation test in order to force the learners to deal with a verb form in two different syntactic contexts, the singular present tense and the infinitive. The test (available on IRIS: https://www.iris-database.org/iris/app/home/detail?id=york%3a805502&ref=search) presented each verb once in a stimulus sentence with a verb in the present tense (3rd person singular) and once in the infinitive. It was administered to 33 beginner learners of French. Figure 20.1 displays the correlation between the proportion of the present tense forms in the analyzed input sources (on the x axis) and the learners' production in the imitation test (on the y axis). A strong correlation was found for most of the verbs, where the learners produced the present tense with most verbs, even when the infinitive was presented in the stimulus, suggesting that the present tense was more readily available, functioning as the default form, for most verbs. This corresponds to the dominance of the present tense in French L2 beginner classrooms. 'Buy' and 'visit' were the only verbs that were preferred in the infinitive; these two verbs were also the most frequent in that form in the input.

Example (2) illustrates the different kinds of production of the present tense form in an infinitive context: one learner (A) changed the syntax of the stimulus, whereas another learner (B) kept the syntactic frame but used the present tense form after the modal verb.

(2) Stimulus: En mars Marie *veut habiter* à Paris
        'In March Marie *wants to live* in Paris'
    Sample learner output A: En mars Marie *habite* ['lives in'] à Paris
    Sample learner output B: En mars Marie *veut habite* ['wants to lives in'] à Paris

Beyond Frequency: Other Input Factors

Despite its significance, frequency cannot be considered in isolation. It is not sufficient for an item to be frequent in order to be noticed by learners. Many highly frequent linguistic units, such as auxiliaries, are redundant and/or unstressed, making them likely to go unnoticed in the input. Results from corpus-based research within usage-based and psycholinguistic approaches have shown that several linguistic factors, in combination with frequency, influence the degree of ease/difficulty of learning a specific construction (see Ellis et al., 2016 for a synthesis; see also Chapter 13, this volume). One of these is *saliency*, which corresponds to the degree to which an element is perceptible among other elements. For instance, in a verb phrase, an auxiliary is often less prominent than the verb conveying the lexical meaning, both phonologically (being unstressed) and semantically (being redundant). Another important factor is the *reliability* (also referred to as *contingency* in the literature) of form-function mappings; a form that is reliably associated with a single function will be more easily learned than a form that corresponds to several functions (Ellis et al. 2016, p. 61ff).

Several corpus studies have challenged traditional hypotheses about the role of linguistic categories in first and second language learning. Wulff et al. (2009), for example, addressed the Aspect Hypothesis (Andersen & Shirai, 1994), which states that learners' development of tense-aspect morphology is sensitive to the inherent semantic aspect of verbs. The hypothesis predicts that the first verbs to be produced in the past tense will be telic, that is, involving an inherent end point, as in *finish* or *explode*. The traditional explanation for this pattern is that telicity is a particularly salient cognitive feature for past tense. Wulff et al. (2009) analyzed two large spoken English corpora, the *Michigan Corpus of Academic Spoken English* and the spoken section of the *British National Corpus* (BNC), to determine the association between verbs and grammatical forms. The corpora were considered an approximation of the type of language input to which learners are commonly exposed – specifically adults who learn the L2 at secondary and university levels.

The results showed that, for each tense-aspect morpheme (past, past perfect, present, and progressive), the most frequent verbs accounted for the majority of all occurrences for a given morpheme. This type of distribution, with few items representing the majority of all occurrences of the category, is called *Zipfian* (Ellis et al. 2016, p. 57). However, it appeared that verbs such as BE were the most frequent for several tense-aspect categories. This implies that frequency alone does not explain learners' developmental pattern. A reanalysis of the data using the method of distinctive collexeme analysis (Gries & Stefanowitsch, 2004), which can "quantify the reliability of form-function mapping and the degree to which a form is distinctive of a particular function" (p. 358), showed that the most distinctive verbs for past and perfect were indeed highly telic verbs (see Tracy-Ventura & Cuesta Medina, 2018, for a conceptual replication study using Spanish data). In other words, given the Zipfian distribution, these verbs can be considered prototypical for their category. This suggests that the association between past tense and telic verbs by learners can be related to frequency in addition to the distribution of the forms and the reliability of the form-function association (categories of tense-aspect) in the input to learners.

A comparison with output data in the form of the first verbs produced by learners suggests that, when distinctiveness and frequency bias coincide, acquisition is facilitated. This hypothesis is supported in several studies comparing input data and learner production (e.g. Ellis et al., 2016).

Comparisons between corpora representing potential input to learners and learners' actual production suggest that language processing and language learning correlate with input properties and experience with the target language, as predicted by usage-based approaches (Bybee, 2008; see also Crossley et al., 2016, for correlations between input and output for vocabulary learning).

Corpus-informed Input in Language Teaching and Learning

Language descriptions based on corpus data have the potential to substantially improve input quality in instructional classroom contexts (see a meta-analysis by Doulton & Cobb, 2017). Only a small proportion of instructed language learning contexts to date involve direct uses of corpora, while indirect uses are more frequent, especially in English L2 teaching and learning (see Chapter 19, this volume). It is above all in reference tools such as dictionaries and grammars that corpora have made an impact, where corpora are used to highlight typical patterns in the language, map register variation, and provide 'authentic' examples (Boulton, 2017).

The question of how effective corpus data is as input in the language classroom concerns not only researchers, but language teachers and learners alike. Data-Driven Learning (DDL: Johns, 1991) has most often been used with relatively advanced learners; studies assessing DDL task or course designs often stress that this is preferred, but there is also evidence that beginners can benefit from such methods. One suggestion for supporting beginners in particular is to present the corpus-based input on paper rather than give direct access to corpora on computer, so as to exert greater control of the learners' focus (e.g. Chujo & Oghigian, 2012).

Chujo and Oghigian (2012) focus on grammar instruction to a population of EFL beginners studying engineering at a Japanese university. Previous work by the authors had shown that DDL work with beginners was perceived as successful by the learners, but this was based on learner feedback, which represents relatively indirect evidence of gains made in the L2. In the 2012 follow-up, they describe a study design involving two experimental DDL groups and a control non-DDL group compared over time, providing clearer evidence of the positive effects of DDL. Through pre-tests and post-tests targeting specific language structures that the course centered on, they could show in what ways the experimental groups made significant gains in ways that the control group did not (and vice versa). Based on such results, the researchers could claim that their DDL method of grammar instruction was validated.

Main Research Methods and Tools

Corpus-based methods for the study of input in SLA aim to test the relationship between input characteristics and learner production and development as hypothesized most often by usage-based approaches. Here, we will present two main research methods: one for the study of input characteristics and degree of difficulty of a grammatical phenomenon and one for the study of the effect of input in interaction, as evidenced through lexical and syntactic priming effects.

Input Characteristics and Learning Trajectory

The attempt to find correlations between learners' developmental paths and characteristics of language use is one of the most exciting challenges in SLA. Results from such studies add to the debate on the contribution of input versus other (internal) principles such as the age of onset of acquisition or universal grammar principles (Ågren et al., 2014).

One of the main methodological challenges when designing a study comparing learner production with learner input is which corpus should represent the input. Ideally, we would like to have a digital record of all the language a learner hears and sees, which we could then compare to the learner's own production. For practical and ethical reasons, this may not be feasible. In the absence of this type of material, we need data that come as close as possible to the input. Typical input data used in previous research include teacher talk in classroom recordings, textbooks, proficient written/spoken target language use represented in large reference corpora, or proficient interlocutors in written/spoken conversation with learners. All these input sources reflect the variation of input in different situations and with different participant roles.

Researchers who are able to use an already existing corpus to examine their research questions will save much time and effort, especially in the case of spoken data. Spoken corpus data is transcribed and sometimes linked to the audio/video source. Most online spoken corpora include tools that make it possible to search for word combinations or words by grammatical function. Many learner and classroom corpora are transcribed with specific programs, such as CLAN (MacWhinney, 2000) or EXMARaLDA (Schmidt & Wörner, 2014).

An important issue when running a corpus search is to ensure that the results include all instances of the target linguistic phenomenon. For example, a researcher investigating the distribution of relative pronoun 'which' compared to 'that' needs to exclude other functions of these word forms to achieve precision in the search. Finding relevant items in a corpus may be greatly helped by part-of-speech (POS) tagging and syntactic parsing, which are done automatically (see Chapters 5 and 6, this volume). Tools such as TreeTagger or MOR in CLAN automatically annotate text files with POS and other information and help to restrict a search to a specific syntactic function, such as 'which' used as a relative pronoun. The accuracy of the annotation varies between languages and is never 100%.

Two very useful tools in CLAN are FREQ and COMBO. FREQ automatically calculates the number of tokens and types for a given search, and COMBO presents the searched word or word combination directly in the transcription. COMBO makes it possible to specify the number of turns before and after each hit, which is especially useful when the interest lies in whether the learner reuses a specific construction within a certain number of turns. These tools were used by Thomas (2009, 2010) in the study presented above.

Collins et al. (2009) addressed the question of the role of input characteristics through a study that aimed to establish *input profiles* for easy versus difficult grammatical constructions, based on the analysis of the speech of three teachers from a corpus of 40 hours of instructional talk to French-speaking learners in an intensive English classroom setting. As they were interested in factors that contribute to making a linguistic structure easy or difficult to learn, they compared the simple past and the possessive determiners *his/her*, which are learned late, and the progressive, which is typically produced early and correctly.

In a first step, finite verbs were coded for tense (present and past) and aspect (progressive), and possessive determiners were annotated. The number of times each linguistic form appeared in the corpus (token frequency) was calculated. The percentage of each form was then calculated, by dividing the number of tokens of a specific form by the total number of tokens of all the forms from the same grammatical category (e.g. the occurrences of *his* compared to all possessive determiners). It was found that all three features were infrequent (10% or less). The regular past tense corresponded to only 2% of all the analyzed verb forms, which means that past tense is more frequent with irregular verbs and that the "regularity" of past tense is rare in the input (low type frequency). By contrast, the progressive appears in the same form for all verbs (with the suffix -*ing*), which makes the pattern easier to notice (high type frequency).

Collins et al. (2009) next wanted to know whether the verbs that were used most often in the teachers' speech belonged to the most frequent verbs in English in general. They used the tool *Range,* which can be found on the *Compleat Lexical Tutor* website (https://www.lextutor. ca). *Range* compares the forms in a given text to a large reference corpus (the BNC for English) in which the words have been ordered into frequency bands, based on the 1,000 most frequent tokens, the 2,000 most frequent, etc. *Range* is also included in the *Vocabprofile* software available at the same website, which displays the frequency band of each word in the uploaded text by color and in separate lists. Collins et al. (2009) found that, while 98% of the irregular verbs appeared in the list of the 1,000 most frequent words (which is expected as irregular verbs are usually highly frequent), only 58% of the regular verbs did.

These and other measures (semantic scope, perceptual salience) were finally assembled in an *input profile* for each of the three grammatical features. The more difficult grammatical constructions (the simple past and possessive *his/her*) scored low on all measures, while the easier construction (the progressive) had high type frequency, moderate semantic scope and high perceptual salience. These measures seem to make the progressive more accessible in the input than the other two, which correlates with observations that the progressive is acquired earlier.

As the study is based on classroom input, the authors raise the issue of manipulating such input to make grammatical categories at the difficult end of the continuum more salient to learners. This area of research has important implications for L2 teaching. However, more studies, such as Collins et al. (2009), are needed to explore further the relation between input characteristics and relative ease/difficulty of acquisition.

Direct Effects of Input in Interaction: Syntactic Priming

Another issue in research on input is how features that typically occur in interaction contribute to L2 learning. One way of examining the effect of input in interaction is to consider syntactic (or structural) priming: "the tendency for speakers to produce a structure that was present in the recent discourse, rather than an alternative structure that can express a similar meaning (Bock, 1986)" (McDonough et al., 2015, p. 77). A priming effect can be said to occur when interlocutor A produces a specific syntactic structure, such as the prepositional dative structure "she gave a present to him", and interlocutor B reuses the same structure, as in "no, he gave a present to her", even though another structure would have been possible (as in the corresponding double object construction "he gave her a present"). Syntactic priming is an effect of mutual adaptation or alignment in L2 interaction due to activation in memory.

The study of syntactic priming in spontaneous spoken or written interaction is of interest because it can tell us how syntactic structures in the input are reused (or not) by learners. Most studies on syntactic priming have used what could be called "pseudo-corpora", in the sense that the interactional processes are modelled on shorter sequences with a high degree of control over the prime. However, there are studies researching syntactic priming through less controlled corpus data, such as Michel and Cappellini (2019), whose data consist of video-recorded conversations between French-Chinese pairs and written chats between learners of German and a language tutor. The overarching research question concerned the frequency and nature of structural (and lexical) alignment in interactions involving an L2 learner. All conversations were transcribed and coded for instances of priming. For the lexical alignment, the free tool *voyant* (https://voyant-tools.org) was used to identify units of three or more words that appeared at least twice in the same conversation. Once these units were identified, the conversations were manually coded for alignment. Syntactic structures that occurred at least five times within a conversation were coded, for example, the number of *have* + complement or passive constructions.

The coding of the alignment was done manually. The first occurrence of a recurring item was coded as the prime and subsequent occurrences as targets. The distance between prime and target(s) had to be no longer than six turns for the spoken and eight turns for the written data (the number of chat turns on the screen). The choice of the number of turns (or the length of time) between a prime and its target(s) is much debated and requires careful consideration (see Michel & Capellini, 2019, p. 210, for a discussion). Finally, the coding also distinguished between alignment to self and to the interlocutor. Figure 20.2 illustrates the coding.

In order to control for text length, the number of primes followed by target(s) (= alignment) was divided by the total number of occurrences in the conversation and the number of potential primes *not* followed by a target (= nonalignment) by the total number of occurrences in the conversation.

The results showed a larger number of *lexical* alignments in the video data and more *structural* alignment in the written chats. The authors attribute the difference to either increased salience in the written format or a task effect. The video data involved free conversations, but the written chat was an argumentative task, which may have triggered the use of specific structures.

FRENCH VIDEO TELETANDEM—Example structural alignment		
Turn	Speaker	Utterance
1	A	tu es dans un café *[PRIME]* euh dans un comment ça s'appelle? tu es pas chez toi *[structural self-alignment 1 to PRIME]* là c'est une salle avec tous les ordinateurs non? tu comprends? [you in a café ehm in a what is the name? You are not at home there it's a room with all the computers, isn't it? Do you understand?]
2	B	*pardon?* [sorry?]
3	A	c'est euh *tu n'es pas chez toi là? [structural self-alignment 2 to PRIME]* [it's ehm you are not at home there?]
4	A	j'ai dit *tu n'es pas chez toi [structural self-alignment 3 to PRIME]* [I said you are not at home]

Figure 20.2 Sample Coding from Michel and Cappellini (2019, p. 198).

The authors stress the importance of developing research methods to better understand how interaction can support SLA.

Representative Corpora and Research

CLAPI (*Corpus de LAngue Parlée en Interaction* 'Corpus of Spoken Language in Interaction') is a multimedia database containing 40 corpora of "social interactions in different contexts: professional, private, institutional, commercial, medical, and educational situations" (http://clapi.is h-lyon.cnrs.fr/V3_Accueil.php?interface_langue=EN). There is a total of 63 hours of searchable interactions, mostly involving native speakers, 140 transcripts, and 46 hours of downloadable data. Transcriptions are available in an orthographic format, corresponding to traditional written French, and in a format with phonological reductions mirroring spoken French (e.g. *bonjour* 'hello' presented as *b'jour* or *'jour*). Informal conversational activities predominate, as the corpora were designed for interaction research. There is an online search interface where it is possible to search for words, lemmas, and series of characters, or interactional features such as pauses, segments, and utterance initial/final position.

CLAPI is a resource for research on the specifics of French spoken interaction, for example, greetings and leave-takings, the organization of turn-taking, and the use of discourse markers, or for the analysis of extended interactional sequences. In terms of authentic input for SLA, as it stands, it may be difficult for French learners and even for teachers to work with CLAPI. To facilitate the use of the material in teaching, pedagogical worksheets are available at http://clapi.ish-lyon.cnrs.fr/ FLE/accueil.php, covering lexical, grammatical, and interactional types of activities.

The application of interactional corpora that were initially collected for research in L2 teaching is not self-evident. One issue is that recordings of authentic interactions between native speakers may be difficult to understand. However, naturally occurring examples can be used as input to practice comprehension at different levels. Thomas et al. (2016) examined whether there is a correlation between the results of a classic comprehension test and the understanding of an interactional sequence. The study was based on an experimental task carried out in L2 French by 22 university students at different proficiency levels (the links to the CLAPI sequences used can be found in the article). The participants watched short video interactions involving a disagreement. The extracts had undergone analysis from a conversational perspective in order to estimate the CEFR level of the sequences. The participants first reported on what they had understood from the sequence and next were asked to pause the video when spotting signs of disagreement. The results showed, first, that the sequences were accessible to all the learners, but that the contextualization of the sequences played a role for *accurate* comprehension. Second, the correlation was strong between the learners' proficiency level, as established through a traditional comprehension test, and their degree of comprehension of the recordings. There were differences in the way the learners approached the content: The beginners took a global approach based on the comprehension of some lexical items that were put together to "make a story", whereas the advanced learners essentially quoted key moments of the interaction verbatim. These results are especially interesting from the perspective of input from corpora. Depending on the learners' proficiency level, contextualization and instructions regarding the focus of attention may vary, but there is no reason not to expose learners to natural and complex interactions even at beginner levels.

The *Michigan Corpus of Academic Spoken English* (MICASE; https://quod.lib.umich.edu/m/micase/) includes almost 2 million words of language spoken in different contexts at a US university, ranging from lectures to student group work. It represents some 200 hours of recordings from different academic disciplines. It was not originally designed for learners as end users, even if the corpus developers definitely had international students – hence advanced language learners – in mind when developing the corpus. Interestingly, international students and faculty are also represented in the corpus, as about 15% of MICASE was produced by non-native speakers of English. This is one of many features that have been marked up, thus allowing comparisons between native and non-native production. The decision not to exclude non-native speakers from the corpus is justified by the fact that the native/non-native speaker distinction has become difficult to maintain in today's globalized and internationalized research world, where English often serves as a common language. Indeed, the use of English as a lingua franca has consequences for how input is characterized and for our views of target language norms.

The rationale for the MICASE project was to gain a better understanding of the nature of academic speech. The overarching research question was whether academic speech was more similar to scholarly writing or everyday conversation. The corpus testifies to a trend in Languages for Specific Purposes, which is to analyze naturally occurring discourse patterns and contextual features in relatively small specialized corpora representing specific genres and different academic disciplines. There is a companion handbook for both teachers and researchers which provides details about the contexts of the included speech events.

An example of a MICASE-based pedagogical project is Bardovi-Harlig, Mossman, and Su (2017), who had ESL students at a US university use the corpus in both direct and indirect ways in order to notice and practice pragmatic routines for (dis)agreement and self-clarification. The corpus has also been used in SLA research (see Wulff et al., 2009, summarized above) as a proxy for input.

Future Directions

There is a long tradition of using corpora to study both L1 and L2 development, whereas the use of corpora to learn more about how language development can be explained and even supported by input properties is more recent. In this chapter, we have presented ways in which the characteristics of linguistic structures in terms of frequency and availability in the input can be examined and compared to learner production and how corpora can be used as input to learners in the language classroom.

One aspect that strikes us when reviewing previous research on the connections between input and learner output is that it is very often the case that only one reference corpus is used to formulate hypotheses about the development of specific linguistic structures in the target language. Very few studies compare different types of input. This commonly adopted approach may obscure the fact that language use is characterized by variation. Research on the role of age of onset of acquisition suggests that the quality and quantity of input could be key factors in explaining differences in the trajectories of learners of different ages (see Lambelet & Berthele, 2015). Corpus studies comparing the characteristics of input to learners of different ages, for example children versus adults, would allow us to test this hypothesis empirically.

Another example of an issue that needs further empirical investigation is the long-standing assumption that classroom input is distorted compared to naturalistic input. Gurzynski-Weiss et al. (2018) collected data from five native-speaking Spanish instructors and compared their production inside versus outside the classroom. They studied the use of subject pronouns, a phenomenon that is subject to variation in the input, especially on the discourse level. The results showed that the "rates of subject forms in learner language are related to the classroom input to which the learners are exposed" (p. 307). However, on the level of pragmatic/discourse constraints, the patterns attested for learners were "only partially reflected in the classroom input" (p. 308). This kind of comparison is a promising research avenue for learning more about possible differences between naturalistic and classroom input. However, before investigating the notion that non-classroom language necessarily provides better input than classroom language, as Krashen (1981) famously argued, we need more research on the extent to which the classroom provides an opportunity to optimize the input for learning, as suggested by the Collins et al. (2009) study presented above. In the same vein, more research is also needed to evaluate the effects of using corpora as input in language classrooms (Boulton, 2017).

The last direction we want to mention is based on the observation that input in SLA is not always easy to control and describe, especially in the case of widespread languages to which learners have easy access outside of the classroom – English is, of course, a case in point. Linguistic affordances of the Internet and digital opportunities for interacting in an L2 most certainly have an impact on learners. This could be seen as presenting a challenge (not to mention interesting opportunities for data collection!) to studies on input and requires innovative thinking regarding phenomena such as learning in the wild (Eskildsen, 2018) and Extramural English, driven for example by gaming and other net-based community interaction.

Further Reading

Boulton, A. (2017). Corpora in language teaching and learning. *Language Teaching, 50*(4), 483–506.

This article summarizes previous work on the use of corpora in language teaching and learning from the pioneering publications to 2017. It mostly covers publications in English and mainly on L1/L2 English, but also offers an overview of different uses of corpora as input in second language acquisition and teaching.

Crossley, S., Kyle, K., & Salsbury, T. (2016). A usage-based investigation of L2 lexical acquisition: The role of input and output. *The Modern Language Journal, 100*(3), 702–715.

This article presents findings based on input data from a longitudinal corpus with naturalistic interaction between interlocutors with L1 or L2 English. The relation between input and output for vocabulary learning is analyzed in terms of saliency, convergence, and longitudinal L2 development.

Dimroth, C. (2018). Beyond statistical learning: Communication principles and language internal factors shape grammar in child and adult beginners learning Polish through controlled exposure. *Language Learning, 68*(4), 863–905.

This article presents results from a *first exposure* study, in which all the input is controlled. The study is an attempt to disentangle predictions based on input in a usage-based approach from those based on the classic 'learner variety', representing learner-internal factors. This critical but fair discussion of the influence of input characteristics as compared to other language learning mechanisms is a promising research avenue.

Related Topics

Chapters 10, 13, 19, and 21.

References

Ågren, M., Granfeldt, J., & Thomas, A. (2014). Combined effects of age of onset and input on the development of different grammatical structures. A study of simultaneous and successive bilingual acquisition of French. *Linguistic Approaches to Bilingualism, 1*(1), 162–193. doi:10.1075/lab.1.1.03agr

Andersen, R. W., & Shirai, Y. (1994). Discourse motivations for some cognitive acquisition principles. *Studies in Second Language Acquisition, 16*(2), 133–156.

Bardovi-Harlig, K., Mossman, S., & Su, Y. (2017). The effect of corpus-based instruction on pragmatic routines. *Language Learning and Technology, 21*(3), 76–103.

Barlow, M. (2002). Corpora, concordancing, and language teaching. In *Proceedings of the 2002 KAMALL international conference*. Daejon, Korea.

Barlow, M., & Kemmer, S. (2000). Introduction: A usage-based conception of language. In M. Barlow & S. Kemmer (Eds.), *Usage based models of language* (pp. vii–xxviii). Stanford: CSLI Publications.

Bock, K. (1986). Syntactic persistence in language production. *Cognitive Psychology, 18*(3), 355–387.

Boulton, A., & Cobb, T. (2017). Corpus use in language learning: A meta-analysis. *Language Learning, 67*(2), 348–393. doi:10.1111/lang.12224

Bybee, J. (2008). Usage-based grammar and second language acquisition. In P. Robinson & N. C. Ellis (Eds.), *Handbook of cognitive linguistics and second language acquisition* (pp. 216–236). New York: Routledge.

Chujo, K., & Oghigian, K. (2012). DDL for EFL beginners: A report on student gains and views on paper-based concordancing and the role of L1. In J. Thomas & A. Boulton (Eds.), *Input, process and product: Developments and teaching and language corpora* (pp. 170–183). Brno: Masaryk University Press.

Collins, L., Trofimovich, P., White, J., Cardoso, W., & Horst, M. (2009). Some input on the easy/difficult grammar question: An empirical study. *The Modern Language Journal, 93*(3), 336–353. doi:10.1111/j.1540-4781.2009.00894.x

Ellis, N. C. (2002). Frequency effects in language processing: A review with implications for theories of implicit and explicit language acquisition. *Studies in Second Language Acquisition, 24*(2), 143–188. doi:10.1017/S0272263102002024

Ellis, N. C., Römer, U., & O'Donnell, M. B. (2016). *Usage-based approaches to language acquisition and processing: Cognitive and corpus investigations of construction grammar*. Chichester: Wiley.

Eskildsen, S. W. (2018). 'We're learning a lot of new words': Encountering new L2 vocabulary outside of class. *The Modern Language Journal, 102*(Suppl. 1), 46–63. doi:10.1111/modl.12451

Gass, S. M. (2015). Comprehensible input and output in classroom interaction. In N. Markee (Ed.), *The handbook of classroom discourse and interaction* (pp. 182–197). Chichester: Wiley.

Granger, S. (2009). The contribution of learner corpora to second language acquisition and foreign language teaching. In K. Aijmer (Ed.), *Corpora and language teaching* (vol. 33, pp. 13–32). Amsterdam: John Benjamins.

Gries, S. Th. (2005). Syntactic priming: A corpus-based approach. *Journal of Psycholinguistic Research, 34*(4), 365–399.

Gries, S. Th., & Stefanowitsch, A. (2004). Extending collostructional analysis: A corpus-based perspectives on 'alternations'. *International Journal of Corpus Linguistics, 9*(1), 97–129.

Gurzynski-Weiss, L., Geeslin, K. L., Daidone, D., Linford, B., Long, A. Y., Michalski, I., & Solon, M. (2018). Examining multifaceted sources of input. In A. E. Tyler, L. Ortega, M. Uno, & H. I. Park (Eds.), *Usage-inspired L2 instruction. Researched pedagogy* (pp. 291–311). Amsterdam: John Benjamins.

Johns, T. (1991). Should you be persuaded: Two samples of data-driven learning materials. *English Language Research Journal, 4*, 1–16.

Krashen, S. (1981). *Second language acquisition and second language learning*. Oxford: Pergamon Press.

Lambelet, A., & Berthele, R. (2015). *Age and foreign language learning in school*. London: Palgrave Macmillan.

MacWhinney, B. (2000). *The CHILDES project: Tools for analyzing talk* (3rd ed.). Mahwah, NJ: Lawrence Erlbaum.

Madlener, K. (2018). Do findings from artificial language learning generalize to second language classrooms? In A. E. Tyler, L. Ortega, M. Uno, & H. I. Park (Eds.), *Usage-inspired L2 instruction. Researched pedagogy* (pp. 211–234). Amsterdam: John Benjamins.

McDonough, K., Neumann, H., & Trofimovich, P. (2015). Eliciting production of L2 target structures through priming activities. *Canadian Modern Language Review, 71*(1), 75–95. doi:10.3138/cmlr.2023

Michel, M., & Cappellini, M. (2019). Alignment during synchronous video versus written chat L2 interactions: A methodological exploration. *Annual Review of Applied Linguistics, 39*, 189–216. doi:10.1017/S0267190519000072

Nicoladis, E., Palmer, A., & Marentette, P. (2007). The role of type and token frequency in using past tense morphemes correctly. *Developmental Science, 10*(2), 237–254. doi:10.1111/j.1467-7687.2007.00582

Riegel, M., Pellat, J. C., & Rioul, R. (2009 [1994]). *Grammaire méthodique du français* (4th ed.). Paris: Presses Universitaires de France.

Schmidt, T., & Wörner, K. (2014). EXMARaLDA. In J. Durand, U. Gut, & G. Kristoffersen (Eds.), *The Oxford handbook of corpus phonology* (pp. 402–419). Oxford: Oxford University Press.

Thomas, A. (2009). *Les apprenants parlent-ils à l'infinitif? Influence de l'input sur la production des verbes par des apprenants adultes du français* (Études romanes de Lund 87). Retrieved from http://lup.lub.lu.se /search/ws/files/5369358/1473802.pdf

Thomas, A. (2010). The influence of lexical aspect and input frequency in the L2 French of adult beginners. *Nordic Journal of Linguistics*, *33*(2), 169–196. doi:10.1017/S0332586510000144

Thomas, A., Granfeldt, J., Jouin-Chardon, E., & Etienne, C. (2016). Conversations authentiques et CECR: Compréhension globale d'interactions naturelles par des apprenants de FLE. *Cahiers AFLS*, *20*(1), 1–43.

Tracy-Ventura, N., & Cuesta Medina, J. A. (2018). Can native-speaker corpora help explain L2 acquisition of tense and aspect? A study of the "input". *International Journal of Learner Corpus Research*, *4*(2), 277–300. doi:10.1075/ijlcr.17001.tra

White, L. (2015). Linguistic theory, universal grammar, and second language acquisition. In B. VanPatten & J. Williams (Eds.), *Theories in second language acquisition: An introduction* (pp. 34–53). New York: Taylor & Francis.

Wulff, S., Ellis, N. C., Römer, U., Bardovi-Harlig, K., & Leblanc, C. J. (2009). The acquisition of tense-aspect: Converging evidence from corpora and telicity ratings. *The Modern Language Journal*, *93*(3), 354–369. doi:10.1111/j.1540-4781.2009.00895

21

Interaction

Nicole Ziegler and Alison Mackey

Introduction

When we talk about interaction within the field of second language acquisition (SLA), we mean the conversations in which learners and their interlocutors take part (Mackey, Abbuhl, & Gass, 2012; Ziegler & Mackey, 2017). Hatch (1978) first advanced the claim that learners' knowledge of form and structure might be acquired through their conversational interactions, highlighting the idea that language learning, including the development of syntactic knowledge, "evolves out of learning how to carry on conversations, out of learning how to communicate" (p. 63). The interaction hypothesis (Hatch, 1978; Long, 1981) came out of this claim that interactions provide learners with important opportunities to acquire information about the accuracy and appropriateness of their utterances through input (the language that a learner is exposed to through listening, reading, writing, speaking, or other mediums; see Chapter 20, this volume), opportunities for output (learners' language production), and positive (a model or reformulation of the correct form) and negative evidence (input or feedback that provides direct or indirect evidence about erroneous production). By drawing learners' attention to their linguistic errors and the gaps between their interlanguage and the target language, feedback creates an environment that can drive L2 learning. Hatch's work was expanded in Long's original interaction hypothesis (1981) where he proposed that conversational interaction, particularly with native speakers, was a necessary and sufficient condition for SLA. He claimed interaction provides learners with opportunities to receive input (made comprehensible by interactional modifications that take place as part of negotiations) that can arise from communication issues. Other recent updates include Mackey and Gass (2012) and Mackey (2012), who focus, in addition to the above tenets, on the role that interaction can play in inducing learners to notice or pay attention to linguistic forms that occur during conversation and which appear to be problematic in some way.

A large and diverse body of empirical evidence demonstrating how interaction facilitates and supports second language (L2) learning and development exists (e.g., Keck et al., 2006; Mackey, 2020; Mackey & Goo, 2007; Mackey & Sachs, 2012; Plonsky & Kim, 2016; Ziegler, 2016), with the benefits of engaging in conversational interaction in second language learning having been recognized across various theoretical frameworks in SLA (e.g., the cognitive-interactionist paradigm, sociocultural theory [SCT], etc.). For example, sociocultural theorists (Lantolf et al., 2015) believe, based on Vygotsky's (1978, 1987) pioneering work, that developmental processes occur as a part and result of participation in cultural, linguistic, family, peer group, school, and other interactions, and language learning is part of this. In other words, interaction within a socio-cultural framework is understood as a direct mediator on learners' cognition and their developing interlanguage system. Studies of interaction, feedback, and tasks conducted in this paradigm use many of the same materials and methods as the ones carried out from the interactionist perspective, which we discuss next, although the emphasis of many of them tends to be on production rather than on development. A number of interesting studies in this line of research have been carried out by Swain and her colleagues investigating how second language learners, often in classrooms, can progress their linguistic development by talking, either in the L1 or L2, about features of the new language (Swain & Lapkin, 2002; Swain et al., 2009). SCT argues that the individual emerges from and is grounded in social interaction (Vygotsky et al., 1994), resulting from not only social relationships but also the cognitive activities associated with mediated social interaction.

In contrast, a cognitive-interactionist approach is grounded in a perspective that allows for the examination of learners' performance and production separate from social factors and relationships. This cognitive-interactionist approach to SLA is distinguished from other approaches to interaction in the field by its essential components, such as focus on form, the noticing hypothesis, and the modified output hypothesis. The approach maintains that conversational adjustments occurring during communication benefit L2 development by providing learners with opportunities to receive modified comprehensible input and interactional feedback, to notice gaps between their interlanguage and the target language features, and to produce output (Gass & Mackey, 2006, 2007; Mackey et al., 2012). Put slightly differently, interaction provides learners with negotiation opportunities and facilitates acquisition through input, output, and internal learner capacities, including attention and noticing (Long, 1996). The cognitive-interactionist approach is grounded in the notion that communication, and more specifically, interaction, is a driving force behind language learning, with the research of the past few decades investigating and illuminating the relationship between communication, learning, and mediating factors such as noticing and attention. Interaction research in this tradition focuses on how language is acquired; in other words, the main concern is how learners best learn languages.

In terms of interaction and corpora, a growing number of recent studies have drawn on learner corpora as a way to investigate instances of authentic interaction for L2 learning and teaching (e.g., Castello, 2013), exploring learners' production, performance, and development from socially-oriented, usage-based, and cognitive perspectives. Interactional corpus data, particularly longitudinal data, may provide opportunities for the exploration of how grammatical, lexical, pragmatic, or interactional features, such as motion construction or negotiation, emerge or change over time, providing insight into how interaction may support learners' development and performance over time. In addition, corpora that include first language data provide opportunities for baseline comparisons, allowing researchers to gain a better understanding of the extent to which learners' production across different stages of development may vary from that of native speakers. Although there are a number of theoretical perspectives regarding the role of interaction for SLA, this chapter will focus primarily on cognitive interactionist and usage-based perspectives, as it is in these approaches that the majority of interactional corpus research is grounded.

Core Issues and Topics

(How) Does Interaction Facilitate Learning?

Interaction has inspired research into a wide range of interactional factors and processes and has moved from a primary emphasis on examining whether or not interaction impacts L2 learning outcomes to exploring *how* interaction can differentially impact specific areas of development and performance. Research has also sought to explore how the mode of interaction, including technology-mediated contexts, may mitigate or support the benefits associated with interaction. For some examples of early non-corpus research in the area of interaction, see Gass and Varonis (1994), Long (1985), Mackey (1999), and Pica (1994). Recently, interaction researchers have begun drawing on corpora to answer these questions. Corpora are seen as providing interaction researchers with new opportunities to enhance understanding of the role interaction can play in L2 learning and further our knowledge of how interaction facilitates L2 development and performance.

Patterns, Developmental Sequences, and Interaction-driven Learning in Learner Corpora

A good example of how learner corpora are being used to explain the interaction-learning connection can be seen in developmental sequence work. A great deal of existing research has sought to examine how interaction can encourage and facilitate the development of specific features of L2 grammar, such as question formation (e.g., Mackey, 1999; McDonough & Mackey, 2008; Oliver & Mackey, 2003). Classroom and laboratory research has provided evidence for the theory that interaction can drive progression through developmental sequences (e.g., McDonough, 2005; McDonough & Mackey, 2006). Recently, though, using learner corpora, Eskildsen (2015) drew on classroom interaction corpus data to provide a different perspective to the one taken in non-corpus research, as his study focused on the acquisition of patterns and schemas that emerge through the corpora of two learners' interaction in the classroom. Eskildsen's study used longitudinal data taken from the *Multimedia Adult English Learner Corpus* (MAELC) to examine how two Spanish-speaking students acquired yes/no and WH interrogatives. In the study, Eskildsen reconceptualized developmental sequences in question formation in terms of the emergence of interrelated multi-word units (e.g., "this is", "are you") and utterance schemas (e.g., "WH COPULA", "AUX DO"). Eskildsen suggested that the corpus data present evidence for pattern-based approaches to L2 learning, with his findings illustrating learners' acquisition of different patterns that they subsequently used for different purposes at different points in time. This highlights how interaction provides opportunities for learners to encounter L2 constructions in meaningful contexts and conversations, without which they would be unlikely to "derive the abstract characteristics that link the examples as utterance schemas and schematic constructions that ultimately allow for the understanding of new examples of the same kind but also for the learner to move beyond the purely formulaic" (Eskildsen, 2015. p. 57). Corpus analysis therefore provided new insights into how previously identified developmental sequences may emerge in classroom interaction.

Technology-mediated Communication, Interaction, and Learner Corpora

In recent years, corpus linguistics methods have increased in use and importance in applied linguistics in general (Biber & Reppen, 2015), which has led to interest from interaction and task researchers. In task-based approaches to language learning (and teaching), tasks are a vehicle for interaction to occur, and elements of tasks are often manipulated to impact elements of interaction and consequently, L2 learning. In technology-mediated interaction in particular, tasks are often designed for interaction to occur. An example of this can be seen in Collentine and Collentine (2013) who explored L2 Spanish learners' structural alignment during task-based interactions in a 3D virtual environment using synchronous-computer mediated communication (SCMC). A corpus of the SCMC text-chat interactions was created in order to examine the relationship between learners' adjacent turns, focusing specifically on the extent to which learners implicitly encouraged one another's use of nominal clauses. Structural alignment, which is thought to reduce the processing demands placed on learners during interaction, takes place when learners are drawing on similar mental L2 representations during interaction, which potentially leads to the production of similar structures and features. By tagging the resulting corpus of text-chat interactions for lexical and part-of-speech information, the authors were able to systematically search for features of interest. This L2 corpus was then also compared with an L1 Spanish interview and conversation sub-corpus created from the *Corpus del Español* (Biber et al., 2006), in order to study alignment and convergence across native and non-native speaker interaction. Results indicated evidence for convergence, with learners more likely to produce nominal clauses in turns immediately following their interlocutors' use of the same structure. Learners also demonstrated more convergence than was found in the native speaker corpus, potentially due to learners' use of alignment as a learning strategy to reduce processing demands. Previous research has suggested that alignment is used by less proficient speakers as an interactional strategy (Branigan et al., 2010; Garrod & Clark, 1993), as it allows interlocutors to use fewer cognitive resources than they would if they were repeatedly using novel structures (Pickering & Garrod, 2004). This study is indicative of an increasing number of studies that rely on corpus methods to better understand the processes of language development.

Corpus-based Research on Interaction and Learning: Current Trends

Seeking to gain insights into the extent to which interactional features thought to be beneficial for L2 development (e.g., negotiation, feedback, modified output, language-related episodes) can and do occur in learner-learner interaction, Crawford, McDonough, and Brun-Mercer (2018) used different techniques from a wide range of existing studies on learner-learner interaction (e.g., Philp et al., 2014), employing corpus techniques to examine how learners collaborate during interactional tasks. Data consisted of paired oral test interactions drawn from the *Corpus of Collaborative Oral Tasks* (McDonough et al., 2014), in which learners completed both an individual opinion task as well as a paired information exchange task. Data were also coded for length and 146 lexico-grammatical features using the Biber Tagger (Biber, 1988). Descriptive analyses revealed similar mean time length for both high- and low-collaboration interactions, although the high-collaborations had greater mean word count, significantly more turns, and fewer words per turn. A key feature analysis (Biber & Egbert, 2018) of lexico-grammatical features associated with high- and low-collaboration interactions was also used to compare and rank relevant features across the two corpora, finding that first and second person pronouns, all pronouns combined, wh-questions, deletion, and subordinate conjunctions were all associated with high-collaboration interactions. As McDonough et al. (2014) highlight, these lexico-grammatical features function in terms of responding to interlocutors' contributions, engaging with each other's ideas, and offering feedback. Although previous research suggested that these features are often used by learners to criticize contributions or state personal opinions (Storch, 2002), these corpus-based findings suggest they might also be used by learners to show agreement and provide expressions of gratitude (Crawford et al., 2018). Results also highlighted features associated with high-mutuality and high-equality (Storch, 2002), previously identified as part of equitable interactions, thereby providing further support for previous research. Such findings demonstrate the valuable contributions to be made by the use of corpus linguistic techniques in interaction research, as they provide important empirical evidence regarding the differences in lexico-grammatical features associated with high- and low-quality interaction.

Expanding Findings in Interaction Research: The Role of Learner Corpora in Gesture

Matsumoto and Dobs (2017) examined the role of gestures and how they may be used to support alignment during interactions in beginning and advanced level L2 classrooms. These interactions were collected and organized as part of a digitized-video corpus supported by the Center for Research on English Language Learning and Teaching at the Pennsylvania State University. Interactions between teachers and students demonstrated that teachers and students used abstract deictic gestures and metaphoric gestures as part of their interactions, emphasizing the importance of these as interactional resources. Results also illustrated how students used recurrent gestures to demonstrate their understanding of temporal concepts and to construct alignment with their teachers. For example, learners imitated their teachers' gestures, a process that may have facilitated internalization (Lantolf & Thorne, 2006) of the abstract temporal concept (Matsumoto & Dobs, 2017). Multimodal data revealed that students and instructors attended to each other's gestures and speech and used repeating gestures to establish intersubjectivity and alignment, potentially reducing their cognitive load and providing subsequent learning opportunities. Furthermore, the results suggest that teachers should raise their awareness of their use of gesture in the classroom, as learners attend to and align with their instructional gestures. Similarly, teachers should attend to learners' use of gesture to explain and demonstrate their developing understanding of grammatical concepts, as learning processes may be revealed through gesture rather than solely through speech.

Previous research suggests that gestures provide learners with important communicative information, with early studies indicating that gestures may be used to supplement gaps in learners' vocabulary knowledge (Bialystok, 1990; Faerch & Kasper, 1983). More recent work reveals that gestures are not restricted to a supplementary role, but instead complement speech and interaction. For example, Gullberg's (1998) results indicated that learners used gesture to inform their interlocutors that they were searching for a word or needed help with an expression, providing information important to the success of the interaction. Research has also shown that gesture directly impacts L2 development, with studies illustrating improved listening comprehension when learners were able to view video showing the speaker's facial expressions in addition to hearing an audio track (Kellerman, 1992; Sueyoshi & Hardison, 2005). Using the multimodal resources of the MAELC corpus, Eskildsen and Wagner (2015) investigated how talk and related embodied activities, namely gestures, reveal L2 learning processes within an interactional context. Taken together, these corpus-based findings provide important information regarding how interaction can support the processes of noticing and internalization, highlighting how learners align their production to their interlocutors in a relatively under-studied area of interaction, that of gesture research.

Main Research Methods and Tools

Methods to Prepare Corpora for Interactional Research

Interaction has been investigated using a diverse range of approaches to elicit, measure, and describe the quantity and quality of learners' production and performance. In general, interaction research involves learners interacting with another language learner and completing a communicative task or activity. Typically, learners' oral interactions are audio or video recorded and are then transcribed in varying levels of detail, depending on the theoretical framing and the focus of the analysis. Sometimes coding can be done "live" (i.e., as the researcher hears or sees interaction occur). Transcribing oral interaction can be a challenging task. Decisions need to be made regarding, for example, whether and how to signal overlapping talk and how to address the difficulties of transcribing or using transcriptions of spoken data produced in learner-learner interactions and/or busy classroom environments where it is often not easy to know who was talking. Additionally, it is uncommon for corpora to pay specific attention to interactional features, meaning that researchers hoping to make use of available spoken corpora may not find them useful for interactional research. Ideally, corpora to be used for interactional research would make use of transcription and coding techniques that would allow interactionist researchers to explore things important for this line of research including, for example, the quantity and quality of learners' interaction in terms of interactional features, such as negotiation, feedback, repair, and language-related episodes ([LREs] when learners discuss various features of the target language).

Researchers working with text-chat data in CALL environments may, for example, transcribe for utterances that were deleted or added before transmission to an interlocutor. This method provides a more holistic transcript of an interaction than relying on only the transmitted information (Smith, 2008), as learners may self-correct utterances or correct based on interaction with another interlocutor. If only the "polished" versions of a text are studied, important examples of self-repair may be lost. Following video-enhanced transcription, which captures what the learner produced rather than only what they transmitted, further conventions may then be applied to the transcript, resulting in a narrower transcription that usually follows previously established norms to support reliability, validity, and comparability.

Transcription (and analyses) in interaction-driven work may also be triangulated with emic perspectives, where, for example, scholars seek to investigate how learners orient to each other's actions and how they orient to the action of learning (Pekarek-Doehler, 2012). Researchers, particularly those using video, may also consider how the field size, camera placement, focus, and whether the shots are static or moving, may affect the ability of the coder to reconstruct or understand the dynamic nature of the situation. Video recordings provide unique affordances in interaction, particularly in terms of gesture and the ability to analyze the embodied practices of the participants (Mondada, 2012). Because technology has progressed such that it is now possible to obtain accurate data of interactions which draw upon multiple meaning making resources, multimodal corpora, such as the MAELC, are able to offer unique opportunities for researchers seeking to apply a finely grained transcription and/or gesture-based coding scheme to the data. The MAELC corpus includes not only the transcriptions of the language produced by learners, but also information about the speaker and addressee, code-switching, and modality of the language produced. Paralinguistic features, such as laughter, miscues and repairs, intraturn pauses, and major phrase-level intonation are also included in the transcriptions to allow researchers to search and account for the multidimensionality of interaction. Transcripts were also flagged with asterisks to note nontarget production, providing researchers with a methodology for tracking emergent features.

Methods of Analysis in Interactional Corpora

A large body of research grounded in the cognitive interactionist perspective has been concerned with how interaction impacts learners' performance in oral and written contexts (Housen, Kuiken, & Vedder, 2012). Results suggest that the complexity, accuracy, and fluency (CAF) of learners' production varies according to a range of factors previously identified as important to interaction, such as task characteristics, interlocutor, and mode of communication. According to Housen et al. (2012), although there is a lack of consensus in terms of how CAF dimensions have been conceptualized, they might broadly be defined as follows: a) complexity is the use of a wide and diverse selection of grammatical structures and lexical items (see Chapter 24, this volume); b) accuracy is represented by error-free and target-like production (see Chapter 23, this volume); and c) fluency refers to learners' ability to produce the target language without non-native pausing, hesitation, or repair (see Chapter 22, this volume). Given the technological advances in the field, there are now tools to measure complexity (e.g., *Coh-Metrix*, McNamara et al., 2013), fluency (e.g., *CLAN*, MacWhinney, 2000; *Praat*, Boersma & Weenink, 2013), and lexical diversity (e.g., *AntWordProfiler*, Anthony, 2015; *LexTutor*, Cobb, 2010) in corpora. Fortunately, quite a few corpora are already, or can be, error-tagged for automatic accuracy measurements (Michel, 2017; see also Chapter 7, this volume). Part of speech tagging can also be useful for analysis of interactional corpora. As demonstrated by Crawford et al. (2018) and Collentine and Collentine (2013), tags can be used to analyze interaction by, for example, characterizing high- versus low-collaborative peer interactions in terms of lexico-grammatical features that have been tagged in a learner corpus.

Because much of the coding in interaction research (e.g., interactional features, uptake, explicit vs. implicit feedback, LREs, modified output) is conducted manually, researchers should be aware of issues in validity, which might be defined within coding as the extent that the coding categories and procedures support accurate interpretations, and reliability, which is concerned with the occurrence of errors in coding and measurement (Révész, 2011). In other words, reliable coding schema should lead to similar coding by different raters. Unfortunately, corpora are not always reliably coded and tagged. Dickinson and Meurers (2003a, 2003b) have proposed standards for detecting errors in the corpus tagging process. With reliable coding and tagging, corpus-based examinations of interaction data may allow for potentially improved generalizability and more systematic examination of various interactional features, thus improving the validity of interaction research.

Overall, interaction research is a highly complex, time-consuming and potentially expensive endeavor, because the majority of transcription and analysis conducted must be done manually. These methodological challenges underscore the need for researchers to have access to annotated interactional corpora to allow for continued exploration into how interaction affects the process and products of SLA and also the need for interaction researchers to be more aware of the sorts of codes and tags that will be helpful in developing corpora.

Representative Corpora and Research

The MAELC corpus (Reder et al., 2003) is a multimedia learner corpus consisting of continuously recorded video and audio data of low-level adult ESL classrooms. Containing approximately 5,000 hours of classroom instruction and involving approximately 1,000 learners, this corpus is a rich resource for examining early stages of adult SLA. Although there are a growing number of learner corpora (e.g., McEnery et al., 2019), the MAELC offers unique affordances with its multimodal data and focus on low-level and early developmental stages of L2 learning, development, and performance. Transcripts and the associated video and audio recordings are available, with six synchronized video cameras and microphones having been used to record each class, thus providing a comprehensive snapshot of each instance of classroom instruction and interaction. In order to facilitate searching of the corpus, a specially developed software (*ClassAction*) was used to tag for activity and content codes and transcriptions within the multimedia corpus. This software also provides researchers with the opportunity to add their own codes, annotations, or transcription details. Initial transcripts include first language production by learners as well as the target language production, thus supporting error analysis, and the corpus may be searched according to language, feature, or classroom code, thereby supporting the connections between pedagogical activities and L2 learning (Reder et al., 2003). These classroom codes are based on the Communicative Orientation of Language Teaching (COLT) observation scheme (Fröhlich et al., 1985) and the Foci for Observing Communications Used in Settings ([FOCUS], Fanselow, 1977) and are applied in overlapping, parallel segments to the recordings of real-time classes. These segments specify cameras, microphones, and the starting and end points within an individual media file. Importantly, indexed codes offer descriptions of the instructional activities used in the classroom and how the classroom is organized, focusing on what is observable rather than making inferences about instructors' possible intentions. Participation pattern codes are also indexed in the corpus and reflect the grouping of the class (e.g., teacher or student fronted; individual, private, or public; pair, group, or free movement).

Activities within the classroom are also tagged and indexed according to the prompt that initiates an activity, the information used in the activity, and the language students used to participate in the activity (Reder et al., 2003).

The MAELC corpus provides researchers with searchable and codable data on traditionally difficult to observe phenomena, such as emerging features within the classroom interaction of low-proficiency learners. A growing body of research has drawn on this corpus to provide insight into L2 development emerging from interaction (see http://www.labschool.pdx.edu/resear ch/current/publications.html for a running list of publications). Much of this work has focused on usage-based or Conversation Analysis (CA) approaches to interaction and learning. For example, Li, Eskildsen, and Cadierno (2014) examined how Carlos, an L1-Spanish learner of English, expressed and developed specific motion constructions and their underlying semantic components over time. Drawing on the multimodal data from MAELC, this study examined Carlos' development of motion construction over three and a half years of classroom interaction, with results indicating expansion from limited linguistic resources to more varied and creative instances of use. Focusing on the same learner, Eskildsen (2014), as alluded to earlier, concluded that early L2 learning was grounded in recurring multi-word expressions and utterance schemas, with development occurring slowly and in a piecemeal fashion. Eskildsen's analysis uses trace-back techniques to track the emergence of Carlos' utterances, providing supporting evidence for the important role that multi-word expressions play in language learning.

This multimodal corpus is freely available, with the Lab School requesting that inquiries be made via email to receive access.

The *Telecollaborative Learner Corpus of English and German* (Telekorp) is a bilingual, longitudinal, 1.5-million-word corpus consisting of computer-mediated communication, including asynchronous (email) and synchronous (text chat) interactions (Belz, 2004). Collected from approximately 200 participants over a period of five years, with each year representing a different group of American fourth-semester German-as-a-second language students and German students enrolled in a teacher education seminar, this corpus is comprised of teacher-guided tasks that were completed via email or text-chat during an eight-week long teleconferencing partnership. Students were required to participate in telecollaboration for a minimum of two hours per week. The resulting discourse was then entered into a searchable, web-based tool and archived according to language, mode of interaction, type of student, year of data collection, and student name.

Belz (2004) and colleagues (Belz & Vyatkina, 2005, 2008) have used these data to examine learners' development of grammatical structures as well as pragmatic competence. For example, Belz (2004) used a subset of this corpus to examine *da*-compound use by learners of German. Results indicated that learners may initially use the target structure as formulaic phrases, with subsequent development revealing the use of *da*-compounds to reference anaphorically nominal or prepositional phrases, with the last stage of use appearing to be cataphoric. Drawing on cross-sectional and longitudinal data to examine the emergence of the target form in learners' interlanguage, findings show that use of *da*-compounds emerged along this pathway for multiple learners, providing evidence for the potential of a developmental sequence. Belz and Vyatkina (2005) used a different subset of Telekorp to examine learners' pragmatic development. Using excerpts from the L2 German corpus as the foundation for the multiple pedagogical interventions to which learners were exposed, their use of modal particles was investigated over time. The L1 German data archived in the corpus was used as the control, providing a baseline comparison that demonstrated the lack of modal particles produced by learners before the intervention. Microgenetic analyses, supported by the comprehensive record of production of each learner through their telecollaborative interactions, revealed incremental changes in learners' use of modal particles and their meta-pragmatic awareness over time.

Future Directions

As learner corpus research expands, interaction researchers are being provided with access to larger amounts of empirical data than was previously possible, allowing for novel approaches to the investigation of the role of interaction in SLA. Corpus-driven approaches offer interaction researchers opportunities to systematically identify and analyze key lexical, grammatical, or discourse features, providing insights into how they emerge in L2 learner production. Interactional corpora may also provide data through which researchers can examine features which may otherwise be difficult to elicit or observe, such as avoidance in SCMC corpora, providing large-scale quantitative support for findings also found with small sample sizes or individual observations.

Although the use of interactional corpora offers researchers exciting new opportunities to deepen our understanding of the process and progression of L2 development, there are nonetheless challenges to consider. For example, current learner corpora that include interactional data are relatively small, especially in relation to L1 corpora, which can limit research designs and statistical tests. Also, due to the complex nature of interaction, the organization and subsequent tagging of key interactional factors in corpora is a critical and difficult step in need of attention. For example, research suggests there are a number of factors, such as type of interlocutor, mode, setting, and task features, that influence and mediate learners' performance. Corpus designers may need to consider how these influencing variables may be used as potential search criteria, thus helping to facilitate future research into these important areas of interest in interaction research. In addition, scholars may need to consider how the complexities of interaction, such as overlapping speech or how learners use gesture, can be systematically and reliably tagged for search and retrieval. Also, because different theoretical approaches may operationalize interaction in different ways, with SCT approaches needing additional information on social relationships, for example, tagging may need to be considered from multiple theoretical perspectives. Previous work (Philp & Mackey, 2010) has highlighted how researchers may benefit from approaching interactional data from both cognitive and social perspectives, thereby providing a more holistic and comprehensive understanding of interaction and its role for SLA. Similarly, SLA and corpus researchers interested in interaction may find that collaboration offers ideal opportunities to better understand how interaction supports and facilitates L2 learning and development. For example, McEnery et al. (2019) highlight the challenges of collaboration between the fields of second language acquisition and learner corpus research. Based on the scarce amount of collaboration published in the last ten years, they argue that Granger's (1998) prediction that corpora "will soon be accepted as a bona fide data type in SLA research" (p. 17) is misguided and indeed, given that it is more than a decade since that prediction, they appear to be correct. Nevertheless, McEnery et al. (2019) believe in the potentialities of collaborative research between the fields. To promote fruitful collaboration, they discuss Bronstein's (2003) model for collaboration in order to encourage future work between learner corpus researchers (LCR) and second language acquisition (SLA) researchers, given that there has been minimal work between the two to date. Suggesting how to constructively collaborate, McEnery et al. suggest: (a) trying to understand the theoretical and methodological practices and limitations of both their own field and that of researchers they plan to collaborate with; (b) creating opportunities for collaboration in the form of symposia, conferences, and journals; (c) compromising productively when disagreements arise; (d) viewing the goals of collaboration from both the perspectives of SLA and LCR; and finally, (e) reflecting on the collaborative experience using the reflection to improve future work between the fields.

Interactional learner corpora provide researchers with access to not only large amounts of data, but also longitudinal data of individual learners over time. Corpora with multiple data points for individual learners offer researchers a unique opportunity to scale up investigations of the effects of interaction. In other words, although results for the immediate effects on interaction are promising, more longitudinal research is needed to enhance our knowledge of the role of interaction on learners' long-term learning. Longitudinal data will provide crucial information regarding the relationship between interaction and development, enhancing our understanding of the durability and delayed impact of interaction on learners' development and performance. Longitudinal investigations will also provide opportunities to potentially observe instances of noticing and how this necessary condition of SLA influences the emergence and internalization of target features, a process that would be unobservable with one-shot designs or short-term individual observations. In addition, corpus-based approaches provide interaction researchers with opportunities to improve issues in validity and reliability that have been highlighted in previous research (e.g., Plonsky, 2011; Plonsky & Gass, 2011; Ziegler, 2016), a welcome area of expansion for contributing methodologically robust research.

Further Reading

Mackey, A. (2020). *Interaction, feedback and task research in L2 learning: Methods and design.* Cambridge: Cambridge University Press.

A user-friendly text for novice to experienced researchers, this work is designed to help situate interaction-based research within the context of SLA research, guide the formation of research questions, and inform study design. Containing real-world research examples, concise and practical application activities, and an introduction to state-of-the-art methodological tools, this volume is designed for researchers interested in conducting research in interaction, corrective feedback, and task-based teaching in an L2 setting.

Smith, B. (2008). Methodological hurdles in capturing CMC data: The case of the missing self-repair. *Language Learning and Technology, 12*(1), 85–103.

This study addresses the importance of methodology in analyzing computer-assisted language learning, highlighting the impact of data collection and evaluation on the interpretation of findings on self-repair in computer-moderated communication. In addition to results showing that self-repair manifests differently in face-to-face and synchronous computer-moderated communication, the study also calls on researchers to align data collection methodology to the medium being studied and abandon outdated practices, like printing out chat logs.

Ziegler, N., & Mackey, A. (2017). Interactional feedback in synchronous computer-mediated communication: A review of the state of the art. In H. Nassaji & E. Kartchava (Eds.), *Corrective feedback in second language teaching and learning* (pp. 80–94). London: Routledge.

This piece synthesizes the benefits learners of all ages, L2s, and instructional contexts reap from interactional feedback as they acquire language. Negotiation for meaning, selective attention, and corrective feedback are all simultaneously driving not only learners' interactions, but also developing learner interlanguage into productive target language use.

Related Topics

Chapters 3, 5, 8, and 11.

References

Anthony, L. (2015). *AntWordProfiler (1.4.1 version) [Computer program].* Tokyo: Waseda University. Retrieved from http://www.laurenceanthony.net/
Belz, J. (2004). Learner corpus analysis and the development of foreign language proficiency. *System, 32*(4), 577–591.
Belz, J., & Vyatkina, N. (2005). Learner corpus analysis and the development of L2 pragmatic competence in networked intercultural language study: The case of German modal particles. *Canadian Modern Language Review, 62*(1), 17–48.
Belz, J., & Vyatkina, N. (2008). The pedagogical mediation of a developmental learner corpus for classroom-based language instruction. *Language Learning and Technology, 12*(3), 33–52.

Bialystok, E. (1990). *Communication strategies: A psychological analysis of second-language use*. Oxford: Blackwell Publishing.

Biber, D. (1988). *Variation across speech and writing*. Cambridge: Cambridge University Press.

Biber, D., Davies, M., Jones, J. K., & Tracy-Ventura, N. (2006). Spoken and written register variation in Spanish: A multi-dimensional analysis. *Corpora*, *1*(1), 1–37.

Biber, D., & Egbert, J. (2018). *Register variation online*. Cambridge: Cambridge University Press.

Biber, D., & Reppen, R. (Eds.) (2015). *The Cambridge handbook of English corpus linguistics*. Cambridge: Cambridge University Press.

Boersma, P., & Weenink, D. (2013). *Praat: Doing phonetics by computer [Computer program]*. Retrieved from http://www.praat.org/

Branigan, H., Pickering, M., Pearson, J., & McLean, J. (2010). Linguistic alignment between people and computers. *Journal of Pragmatics*, *42*(9), 2355–2368.

Bronstein, L. R. (2003). A model for interdisciplinary collaboration. *Social Work*, *48*(3), 297–306.

Castello, E. (2013). Integrating learner corpus data into the assessment of spoken interaction in English in an Italian university context. In S. Granger, G. Gilquin, & F. Meunier (Eds.), *Twenty years of learner corpus research: Looking back, moving forward* (pp. 61–74). Corpora and Language in Use—Proceedings 1, Louvain-la-Neuve: Presses Universitaires de Louvain.

Cobb, T. (2010). Web vocabprofile, an adaptation of heatley, nation & Coxhead's (2002). *Range [Computer Program]*. Retrieved from http://www.lextutor.ca/vp/

Collentine, J., & Collentine, K. (2013). A corpus approach to studying structural convergence in task-based Spanish L2 interactions. In K. McDonough & A. Mackey (Eds.), *Second language interaction in diverse educational contexts* (pp. 167–188). Amsterdam: John Benjamins.

Crawford, W. J., McDonough, K., & Brun-Mercer, N. (2018). Identifying linguistic markers of collaboration in second language peer interaction: A lexico-grammatical approach. *TESOL Quarterly*, *53*(1), 180–207.

Dickinson, M., & Meurers, W. D. (2003a). Detecting errors in part-of-speech annotation. In *10th conference of the European chapter of the association for computational linguistics*. Budapest, Hungary, pp. 107–114.

Dickinson, M., & Meurers, W. D. (2003b). Detecting inconsistencies in treebanks. In *Proceedings of the TLT* (Vol. 3, pp. 45–56). Växjö, Sweden.

Eskildsen, S. W. (2014). What's new? A usage-based classroom study of linguistic routines and creativity in L2 learning. *International Review of Applied Linguistics in Language Teaching*, *52*(1), 1–30.

Eskildsen, S. W. (2015). What counts as a developmental sequence? Exemplar-based L2 learning of English questions. *Language Learning*, *65*(1), 33–62.

Eskildsen, S. W., & Wagner, J. (2015). Embodied L2 construction learning. *Language Learning*, *65*(2), 268–297.

Faerch, C., & Kasper, G. (1983). Plans and strategies in foreign language communication. In C. Faerch & G. Kasper (Eds.), *Strategies in interlanguage communication* (pp. 20–60). New York: Longman.

Fanselow, J. F. (1977). Beyond Rashomon: Conceptualizing and describing the teaching act. *TESOL Quarterly*, *11*(1), 17–39.

Fröhlich, M., Spada, N., Allen, P., & Frohlich, M. (1985). Differences in the communicative orientation of L2 classrooms. *TESOL Quarterly*, *19*(1), 27–57.

Garrod, S., & Clark, A. (1993). The development of dialogue coordination skills in schoolchildren. *Language and Cognitive Processes*, *8*(1), 101–126,

Gass, S. M., & Mackey, A. (2006). Input, interaction and output: An overview. *AILA Review*, *19*(1), 3–17.

Gass, S. M., & Mackey, A. (2007). *Data elicitation for second and foreign language research*. Mahwah: Lawrence Erlbaum Associates.

Gass, S. M., & Varonis, E. M. (1994). Input, interaction, and second language *production. Studies in Second Language Acquisition*, *16*(3), 283–302.

Granger, S. (1998). The computer learner corpus: A versatile new source of data for SLA research. In S. Granger (Ed.), *Learner English on computer* (pp. 3–18). New York: Longman.

Gullberg, M. (1998). *Gesture as a communication strategy in second language discourse: A study of learners of French and Swedish* (vol. 35). Lund: Lunds University Press.

Hatch, E. (1978). Acquisition of syntax in a second language. In J. Richards (Ed.), *Understanding second and foreign language learning: Issues and approaches* (pp. 34–70). Rowley, MA: Newbury House.

Housen, A., Kuiken, F., & Vedder, I. (Eds.) (2012). *Complexity, accuracy and fluency. Dimensions of L2 performance and proficiency: Complexity, accuracy, and fluency in SLA* (pp. 1–20). Amsterdam: John Benjamins.

Keck, C. M., Iberri-Shea, G., Tracy-Ventura, N., & Wa-Mbaleka, S. (2006). Investigating the empirical link between task-based interaction and acquisition: A meta-analysis. In J. M. Norris & L. Ortega (Eds.), *Synthesizing research on language learning and teaching* (pp. 91–131). Amsterdam: John Benjamins.

Kellerman, S. (1992). 'I see what you mean': The role of kinesic behavior in listening and implications for foreign and second language learning. *Applied Linguistics*, *13*(3), 239–258.

Lantolf, J., & Thorne, S. (2006). *Sociocultural theory and the genesis of second language development.* Oxford: Oxford University Press.

Lantolf, J., Thorne, S. L., & Poehler, M. (2015). Sociocultural theory and second language development. In B. VanPatten & J. Williams (Eds.), *Theories in second language acquisition* (pp. 207–226). London: Routledge.

Li, P., Eskildsen, S. W., & Cadierno, T. (2014). Tracing an L2 learner's motion constructions over time: A usage-based classroom investigation. *The Modern Language Journal*, *98*(2), 612–628.

Long, M. H. (1981). Input, interaction, and second language acquisition. *Annals of the New York Academy of Sciences*, *379*, 259–278.

Long, M. H. (1985). Input and second-language acquisition theory. In S. M. Gass & C. Madden (Eds.), *Input in second language acquisition* (pp. 377–393). Rowley, MA: Newbury House.

Long, M. H. (1996). The role of the linguistic environment in second language acquisition. In W. C. Ritchie & T. K. Bhatia (Eds.), *Handbook of language acquisition* (pp. 413–468). Cambridge: Academic Press.

Mackey, A. (1999). Input, interaction, and second language development: An empirical study of question formation in ESL. *Studies in Second Language Acquisition*, *21*(4), 557–587.

Mackey, A. (2012). *Input, interaction, and corrective feedback in L2 learning.* Oxford: Oxford University Press.

Mackey, A. (2020). *Interaction, feedback and task research in L2 learning: Methods and design.* Cambridge: Cambridge University Press.

Mackey, A., Abbuhl, R., & Gass, S. M. (2012). Interactionist approaches. In S. Gass & A. Mackey (Eds.), *The Routledge handbook of second language acquisition* (pp. 7–23). London: Routledge.

Mackey, A., & Gass, S. M. (2012). Introduction. In A. Mackey & S. M. Gass (Eds.). *Research methods in second language acquisition: A practical guide* (pp. 1–4). Oxford: Wiley-Blackwell.

Mackey, A., & Goo, J. (2007). Interaction research in SLA: A meta-analysis and research synthesis. In A. Mackey (Ed.), *Conversational interaction in SLA: A collection of empirical studies* (pp. 408–452). Oxford: Oxford University Press.

Mackey, A., & Sachs, R. (2012). Older learners in SLA research: A first look at working memory, feedback, and L2 development. *Language Learning*, *62*(3), 704–740.

MacWhinney, B. (2000). *The CHILDES project: Tools for analyzing talk. [Computer program].* Retrieved from https://childes.talkbank.org/

Matsumoto, Y., & Dobs, A. M. (2017). Pedagogical gestures as interactional resources for teaching and learning tense and aspect in the ESL grammar classroom. *Language Learning*, *67*(1), 7–42.

McDonough, K. (2005). Identifying the impact of negative feedback and learners' responses on ESL question development. *Studies in Second Language Acquisition*, *27*(1), 79–103.

McDonough, K., Crawford, W. J., & De Vleeschauwer, J. (2014). Summary writing in a Thai EFL university context. *Journal of Second Language Writing*, *24*, 20–32.

McDonough, K., & Mackey, A. (2006). Responses to recasts: Repetitions, primed production, and linguistic development. *Language Learning*, *56*(4), 693–720.

McDonough, K., & Mackey, A. (2008). Syntactic priming and ESL question development. *Studies in Second Language Acquisition*, *30*(1), 31–47.

McEnery, T., Brezina, V., Gablasova, D., & Banerjee, J. (2019). Corpus linguistics, learner corpora, and SLA: Employing technology to analyze language use. *Annual Review of Applied Linguistics*, *39*, 74–92.

McNamara, D. S., Louwerse, M. M., Cai, Z., & Graesser, A. (2013). *Coh-Metrix version 3.0.* Retrieved from http://cohmetrix.com

Michel, M. (2017). Complexity, accuracy and fluency (CAF). In S. Loewen & M. Sato (Eds.), *The Routledge handbook of instructed second language acquisition* (pp. 50–68). London: Routledge.

Mondada, L. (2012). The dynamics of embodied participation and language choice in multilingual meetings. *Language in Society*, *41*(2), 213–235.

Oliver, R., & Mackey, A. (2003). Interactional context and feedback in child ESL classrooms. *The Modern Language Journal*, *87*(4), 519–543.

Pekarek-Doehler, S. (2012). Conversation analysis and second language acquisition: CA-SLA. In C. Chapelle (Ed.), *The encyclopedia of applied linguistics* (pp. 1–8). Oxford: Wiley-Blackwell.

Philp, J., Adams, R., & Iwashita, N. (Eds.) (2014). *Peer interaction and second language learning.* London: Routledge.

Philp, J., & Mackey, A. (2010). Interaction research: What can socially informed approaches offer to cognitivists (and vice versa)? In R. Batstone (Ed.), *Sociocognitive perspectives on language use and language learning* (pp. 210–228). Oxford: Oxford University Press.

Pica, T. (1994). Research on negotiation: What does it reveal about second language learning conditions, processes, and outcomes? *Language Learning, 44*(3), 493–527.

Pickering, M., & Garrod, S. (2004). Toward a mechanistic psychology of dialogue. *Behavioral and Brain Sciences, 27*(2), 169–225.

Plonsky, L. (2011). *Study quality in SLA: A cumulative and developmental assessment of designs, analyses, reporting practices, and outcomes in quantitative L2 research.* (Publication No. 3468535) [Doctoral dissertation, Michigan State University]. ProQuest Dissertations and Theses Global.

Plonsky, L., & Gass, S. (2011). Quantitative research methods, study quality, and outcomes: The case of interaction research. *Language Learning, 61*(2), 325–366.

Plonsky, L., & Kim, Y. (2016). Task-based learner production: A substantive and methodological review. *Annual Review of Applied Linguistics, 36*, 73–97.

Reder, S., Harris, K., & Setzler, K. (2003). The multimedia adult ESL learner corpus. *TESOL Quarterly, 37*(3), 546–557.

Révész, A. (2011). Task complexity, focus on L2 constructions, and individual differences: A classroom-based study. *The Modern Language Journal, 95*, 162–181.

Smith, B. (2008). Methodological hurdles in capturing CMC data: The case of the missing self-repair. *Language Learning and Technology, 12*(1), 85–103.

Storch, N. (2002). Relationships formed in dyadic interaction and opportunity for learning. *International Journal of Educational Research, 37*(3–4), 305–322.

Sueyoshi, A., & Hardison, D. M. (2005). The role of gestures and facial cues in second language listening comprehension. *Language Learning, 55*(4), 661–699.

Swain, M., & Lapkin, S. (2002). Talking it through: Two French immersion learners' response to reformulation. *International Journal of Educational Research, 37*(3–4), 285–304.

Swain, M., Lapkin, S., Knouzi, I., Suzuki, W., & Brooks, L. (2009). Languaging: University students learn the grammatical concept of voice in French. *The Modern Language Journal, 93*(1), 5–29.

Vygotsky, L. S. (1978). *Mind in society: The development of higher psychological processes.* Cambridge, MA: Harvard University Press.

Vygotsky, L. S. (1987). *Thinking and speech: The collected works of L. S. Vygotsky, Problems of general psychology* (vol. 1). New York: Plenum Press.

Vygotsky, L. S., van der Veer, R. E., Valsiner, J. E., & Prout, T. T. (1994). *The Vygotsky reader.* Oxford: Basil Blackwell.

Ziegler, N. (2016). Synchronous computer-mediated communication and interaction: A meta-analysis. *Studies in Second Language Acquisition, 38*(3), 553–586.

Ziegler, N., & Mackey, A. (2017). Interactional feedback in synchronous computer-mediated communication: A review of the state of the art. In H. Nassaji & E. Kartchava (Eds.), *Corrective feedback in second language teaching and learning* (pp. 80 94). London: Routledge.

22

Fluency

Amanda Huensch

Introduction

As has been pointed out on many occasions in work investigating oral fluency, the term fluency has multiple and varied definitions. Thus, it is important to begin by specifying how fluency is conceptualized in second language (L2) research. The first consideration is to differentiate between a "broad" view of fluency, which it is equated with general proficiency, and a "narrow" view of fluency in which fluency refers to the pace, flow, and tempo of a learner's speech (Lennon, 1990, p. 389). It is the narrow definition of fluency that is the topic of inquiry in much second language acquisition (SLA) research. Lennon (1990) also focused on fluency as a perceptual phenomenon in claiming that "fluency is an impression on the listener's part that the psycholinguistic processes of speech planning and speech production are functioning easily and efficiently" (p. 391). Thus, fluency is not merely a concept that can be boiled down to measuring how many words a learner can utter between hesitations, but rather it represents a complex relationship between processes occurring in a learner's planning and production of speech, characteristics of how that speech is uttered, and interpretations of how that speech is perceived by a listener. Segalowitz (2010) labelled these three senses of fluency as (a) cognitive fluency, (b) utterance fluency, and (c) perceived fluency. Cognitive fluency "refers to the fluid operation (speed, efficiency) of the cognitive processes responsible for performing L2 speech acts" (Segalowitz, 2016, p. 82) whereas utterance fluency refers to observable characteristics of the speech signal (e.g., features related to pausing, pace, hesitation), and perceived fluency refers to judgements made by listeners on the basis of utterance fluency features. Derwing (2017) summarized the relationship between these senses of fluency by stating that "cognitive fluency underlies utterance fluency, which affects listeners' perception of fluency" (p. 250).

Identifying cognitive fluency as a learner's ability to efficiently plan and produce speech necessitates considerations of how speech production occurs. One model that has been highly influential in L2 research is Levelt (1999)'s model of speech production, which is made up of the stages of *Conceptualization* (i.e., message planning), *Formulation* (i.e., lexical, grammatical, phonological encoding), and *Articulation* (i.e., conversion into speech), along with self-monitoring. Segalowitz (2010) drew from the work of Levelt (1989, 1999), de Bot (1992), and Kormos (2006) to construct a "blueprint" of an L2 speaker including "fluency vulnerability points" which represent locations in the model where an L2 speaker might encounter different types of processing difficulties and therefore might exhibit disfluency (Segalowitz, 2010, p. 17). Measurements of utterance fluency have been used as a way to draw conclusions about successes/difficulties at different points in the speech production process (e.g., Skehan, Foster, & Shum, 2016; Towell, Hawkins, & Bazergui, 1996). The advent of learner corpus research (LCR) in the 1980s has resulted in an impressive and growing amount and variety of learner language data available to L2 acquisition researchers (Gilquin & Granger, 2015), including those that allow for investigations of L2 fluency. As recently argued in a special issue of the *International Journal of Learner Corpus Research* "the study of fluency and disfluency in L2 versus L1 speech with the help of corpora and tools for visualization allows a better and wider understanding of the phonetic mechanisms of cognitive processes involved in L2 discourse" (Trouvain et al., 2017, p. 111).

With these definitions in mind, we now turn to core issues and topics in L2 fluency research that have been investigated with learner corpora. However, as a final note, it is useful to clarify how 'learner corpora' and 'corpus-based techniques' are conceived of in this chapter, as not all of the studies referenced self-identify as using corpora. A broad definition of these terms is adopted; thus, the work focused on in this chapter is that which in some way has automated analyses of a collection of texts in its investigation of L2 fluency.

Core Issues and Topics

Native Speaker vs. Non-Native Speaker Fluency

One strand of research in which L2 fluency has been investigated with learner corpora explores the extent to which the utterance fluency of learners differs from that of native speakers (NS). While both learners and native speakers are expected to show signs of disfluency when speaking, lack of automaticity and limited linguistic knowledge may differentiate the learner from a native speaker (Kormos, 2006). As a general approach, work in this area compares the fluency characteristics of native and non-native speaker (NNS) speech from talkers who have completed identical or similar tasks (e.g., Belz, Sauer, Lüdeling & Mooshammer, 2017; De Jong, 2016; Foster & Tavakoli, 2009; Götz, 2013; Gut, 2009; Huensch & Tracy-Ventura, 2017a; Kahng, 2014; Skehan et al., 2016; Tavakoli, 2011). Corpus-based comparisons of native speaker and learner speech have provided some evidence that, for example, learners demonstrate greater fluency variability across speaking tasks (e.g., read speech vs. narrative retelling) than native speakers (Gut, 2009).

De Jong (2016) compared the speech of L1 and L2 speakers of Dutch who completed a variety of monologic speaking tasks (e.g., describe a crime you just witnessed to a police officer). Data, transcribed in the Computerized Language Analysis program (CLAN, MacWhinney, 2000; Chapter 12, this volume), were explored with regard to the frequency, location, and duration of silences and filled (e.g., *um*, *uh*) pauses. Based on previous research (e.g., Davies, 2003), De Jong was particularly interested in exploring the extent to which learner and native speaker pause behavior differed within versus between utterances (coded as Analysis of Speech Units [ASU], Foster, Tonkyn, Wigglesworth, 2000). Results indicated that at utterance boundaries, learners and native speakers did not significantly differ in their likelihood to pause nor in the length of their pauses. In contrast, within utterances, learners paused both more often and for longer durations than native speakers. Based on these findings, De Jong argued that the within-utterance pausing behavior of L2 speakers, as opposed to between-utterance, is reflective of trouble with *Formulation*, possibly due to limited L2 knowledge and skills.

L2 Fluency Development

A second focus of L2 fluency research is to better understand how L2 fluency develops over time as proficiency increases. Some corpora designed to answer these questions are structured cross-sectionally, such as the *Parallèle Oral en Langue Etrangère* 'Parallel Oral Foreign Language'

(PAROLE) corpus (Hilton et al., 2008), designed to investigate learner language (L2 English, French, and Italian) at different proficiency levels and the *What is Speaking Proficiency* (WiSP) corpus (De Jong et al., 2012), which includes English and Turkish L1 learners of L2 Dutch. Both corpora gathered further information about learners that would be necessary in understanding their proficiency. For example, in PAROLE, learners completed a variety of other tasks to gain information about their language learning motivation, aptitude, experience, etc. In WiSP, learners completed a productive vocabulary task designed to be a separate measure of proficiency from the speaking tasks. With these data, the researchers were able to test whether learners at different proficiency levels exhibited different oral fluency characteristics.

In addition to cross-sectional corpora, longitudinal corpora have also been used to investigate L2 fluency development (e.g., the *Learning Prosody in a Foreign Language* [LeaP] corpus; Gut, 2009, 2017; the *Languages and Social Networks Abroad Project* [LANGSNAP] corpus, Huensch & Tracy-Ventura, 2017a). Some SLA researchers have argued that longitudinal data like these are critical for investigations of development because they allow explorations of how learning occurs over time (Myles, 2008; Ortega & Byrnes, 2008; Ortega & Iberri-Shea, 2005). Meunier and Littré (2013) reasoned that the use of longitudinal learner corpora "can enable researchers interested in L2 acquisition to test hypotheses on larger and better constructed databases, using the options offered by computer-based annotation and analysis corpus tools" (p. 72). Gut (2017) used a subcorpus of the LeaP corpus to investigate phonological development (including L2 fluency) over time for learners in three different contexts (i.e., study abroad, study abroad with phonology course, at-home phonology course). Of particular relevance to the current discussion is that while the corpus was originally designed to study phonological acquisition, it was not compiled specifically to explore the effects of learning context. Gut discussed the advantages and challenges of using corpora in this way (i.e., not for their originally intended purpose). On the one hand, using the corpus meant having missing data points and heterogeneous and unbalanced groups. Nevertheless, using a previously annotated corpus not only saved time, but perhaps more importantly allowed for the simultaneous investigation of a wide variety of phonological features (in addition to fluency) and both quantitative and qualitative data analyses.

L1-L2 Fluency Relationships

Beyond proficiency level and native speaker status, many other factors are likely to contribute to variation in an individual's L2 utterance fluency and indeed have been the focus of research on L2 fluency. An important consideration in L2 fluency research is to differentiate L2-specific cognitive fluency from more general cognitive processing, including that which regulates the L1 (Segalowitz, 2016). Factors such as speaking task, topic familiarity, planning time, first language, time spent in an immersion context, etc. are all likely to play a role in observed variation. One final area of L2 fluency research that has recently been of interest to scholars is the extent to which one's L1 speaking style relates to fluency characteristics in the same individual's L2 speech (e.g., De Jong et al., 2015; De Jong & Mora, 2017; Derwing et al., 2009; Garcia Lecumberri et al., 2017; Gósy, Gyarmathy, & Beke, 2017; Huensch & Tracy-Ventura, 2017b). In other words, this work attempts to tease apart the potential contribution of L1 speaking style in explaining L2 utterance fluency. In order to do so, studies have compared the speech of the same individuals in both their L1 and L2 on the same or similar tasks.

Gósy et al. (2017), for example, examined the frequency, form, location, and formant structure of filled pauses using the *Hungarian English Database* (HunEng-D), which is comprised of L1 Hungarian and L2 English speech from the same speakers who vary according to age and proficiency level. They found that while filled pauses were shorter in the L1 than L2, their form, location, and articulation were similar, demonstrating transfer of Hungarian filled pausing characteristics into the L2. In De Jong et al. (2015), L1 speakers of English and Turkish who were learning Dutch as an L2 (a subset from the WiSP corpus) completed similar monologic speaking tasks in both languages. Analyses indicated that all seven measures of fluency in their study (including those representing speed, breakdown, and repair fluency, see the *Measurements of Oral Fluency* section) were correlated between L1 and L2 fluency ranging in strength from 0.37 to 0.76. Additionally, they conducted regression analyses to test whether L2 measures of fluency 'corrected' for L1 fluency (i.e., using the saved residuals from models predicting L2 fluency from L1 fluency) would better predict L2 proficiency as measured by a productive vocabulary task. The results indicated that for one of the seven measurements of fluency, mean syllable duration, the corrected measure was a stronger predictor of proficiency.

With these core issues and topics in mind, we next turn to the main research methods and tools that have been used in learner corpus research to investigate L2 fluency, including common types of speech data, utterance fluency measurements, and the software and tools used for data transcription, coding, and analysis.

Main Research Methods

Types of Speech Data

As mentioned previously, an important aspect of corpora designed to investigate SLA topics and issues is that they often include a variety of additional information about the participants' proficiency, motivation, age, gender, language learning history, etc. (see Chapter 5, this volume). Regarding the speech data itself, investigations of L2 fluency have been conducted with a variety of tasks ranging from tightly controlled passage reading to less controlled spontaneous speech tasks such as semi-structured interviews. Decisions made about which speaking tasks to include are often connected to the original purpose of compiling the corpus. For example, given its focus on the acquisition of phonology (and not only the development of L2 fluency), the LeaP corpus (Gut, 2009) included a word-list reading task (in addition to three other tasks: an interview, a reading passage, and a story retelling) to explore the acquisition of stress. In order to investigate disfluency in dialogic speech, Belz et al. (2017) used the *Berlin Map Task Corpus* (BeMaTaC, Sauer & Lüdeling, 2016) in which participants instructed their partners (who could not see them) to recreate a route on a map that contained landmarks. Many oral corpora include multiple types of speech data. For instance, in the PAROLE corpus (Hilton et al., 2008), learners and NSs completed the same three tasks: two narrative retellings based on videos and an autobiographical narrative describing an accident that had occurred in the past. Similarly, the HunEng-D corpus (Gósy et al., 2017) included responses to interview questions (e.g., give your opinion about a topic of current interest), retelling a story, completing a map-task/role-play with another learner, and a word-list reading. The use of a variety of speaking styles allows researchers to additionally explore the extent to which L2 fluency varies across tasks (see also Chapter 27, this volume).

Measurements of Oral Fluency

When conducting a scan of the L2 fluency literature, it becomes quickly apparent that measures of oral fluency are varied and diverse. Some examples of tables listing measures used can be found in Kormos (2006, p. 163) and Derwing, (2017, p. 247). Skehan (2003) and Tavakoli and Skehan (2005) categorized commonly used measures as representing three types of fluency: speed, breakdown, and repair. Speed fluency represents dimensions of pace and includes measures such as speech rate (often words/syllables/characters per minute/second). Breakdown fluency relates to pausing phenomena and includes measures such as the number of silent pauses per minute/X number of words. Breakdown fluency measures can be further categorized into those that provide information about the location, duration, and frequency of pauses. For example, the measure of mean silent pause duration within clauses provides information about both length and location whereas the measure of the number of filled pauses per 100 words provides information about frequency alone. As discussed in the *Core Issues and Topics* section, recent investigations of L1–L2 and NS–NNS fluency provide compelling evidence that pause location is an important consideration when measuring aspects of breakdown fluency (see also Hilton, 2008; Skehan et al., 2016). Thus, when manually coding pauses in corpora,[1] it appears that including information about their location is particularly important. Finally, repair fluency is concerned with self-correction and reformulation and therefore includes measures such as the number of repetitions per minute/X number of words and the number of corrections per minute/X number of words, among others.

It is relevant to acknowledge the somewhat large number of possible measurements that can and have been used to investigate L2 fluency. While not specifically focused on LCR, a recent scoping review of fluency literature from the field of study abroad (SA) concluded "that oral fluency has been investigated with little methodological consistency in SA research" (Tullock & Ortega, 2017, p. 13). Given this, it is relevant to identify the source of some of the inconsistency as well as how researchers justify their choices of utterance fluency measurements. Taking a closer look at the measures of breakdown fluency, which include silent pausing, a typical difference across studies relates to the threshold set for considering what should be coded as a silent pause. Durations in the fluency literature can range from 100ms (Riazantseva, 2001) to 1000ms (Götz, 2013), with many set at 250ms or 400ms. De Jong and Bosker (2013) attempted to provide empirical evidence for an optimal cut-off point for silent pauses. They calculated measures of breakdown fluency with lower bound cut-offs ranging from 20ms to 1000ms and conducted Pearson correlations between those measurements and a measure of L2 proficiency based on vocabulary knowledge. The results indicated "that a lower cut-off point for silent pauses of 250–300ms leads to the highest correlation between the number of silent pauses and a measure of L2 proficiency (vocabulary knowledge)" (p. 20). Segalowitz (2016) argued that De Jong and Bosker's approach of justifying their choice of operationalization of silent pauses based on a "cognitive measure of L2 proficiency" is an important step in "the discussion of how utterance fluency reflects cognition" (p. 82).

One approach used to justify choices of utterance fluency measurements is to consider those measurements which best predict ratings of perceived fluency (e.g., Bosker et al., 2013; Kahng, 2018; Kormos & Dénes, 2004) and/or whether there are intercorrelations among measurements. Bosker et al. (2013) examined the extent to which measures of speed, breakdown, and repair fluency could predict fluency ratings (from 20 untrained raters) and demonstrated via linear regression analyses that measurements of speed and breakdown fluency best predicted the ratings, although measurements of repair fluency also contributed to the models but less so.

A final issue that arises in the measurement of oral fluency relates to potential cross-linguistic differences when comparing fluency across languages. Aspects of a language such as syllable inventories or morphological processes might contribute to differences in measurements of speed fluency such as mean syllable duration and mean length of run (Gut, 2009, p. 96). When comparing languages such as English and Spanish or German and French, the syllable inventories of one language (English and German in these cases) are such that is it possible that the number of phones within a syllable will be greater in those languages as opposed to the comparisons (Spanish and French). Studies have provided some indication that speech rates using these measures show slower rates for languages with greater syllable inventories (e.g., Pellegrino et al. 2011, Huensch & Tracy-Ventura, 2017b, comparing English and Spanish; Trouvain & Möbius, 2014, comparing French and German). Garcia Lecumberri et al. (2017) addressed this issue by normalizing speech rate across speakers by taking into consideration average rates from native speakers. The effects of phonotactics on speed fluency measurements are not the only cross-linguistic differences indicated by the literature. There is also evidence that cross-linguistic differences in pausing characteristics may also be present (see e.g., Riazantseva, 2001).

Software and Tools for Data Coding and Analysis

One advantage of using corpora or corpus-based techniques to investigate L2 fluency is that they allow for (at least partially) automated analysis of a large amount of data. However, it is often necessary to manually transcribe and code the data in order to conduct automated analyses that either output information such as the frequency, duration, and location of phenomena or simply calculate measures of oral fluency. Manually transcribing data and coding for fluency features is likely time-consuming and therefore also quite expensive (Ballier & Martin, 2013; Staples, 2015). This is partly why many scholars have argued for the public sharing of corpora that have been formatted with agreed-upon conventions (e.g., MacWhinney, 2017; Myles, 2008). Hilton (2009) provided a detailed description of the manual transcription and coding of the PAROLE corpus using the CLAN program and following transcription conventions in the format of the Codes for the Human Analysis of Transcripts (CHAT) as well as a description of some of the automated analyses they were able to conduct with such coding. For example, CLAN includes commands that will automatically count the frequency of repetitions coded with the symbol [/] (e.g., in [/] in the summer) as well as commands such as MLU which calculates the mean length of utterances. Transcripts following CHAT conventions in CLAN provide impressive interoperability with other programs (MacWhinney, 2017) commonly used for annotating aspects of fluency such as EUDICO Linguistic Annotator (ELAN, https://tla.mpi.nl/tools/tla-tools/elan/) and Praat (Boersma & Weenink, 2015). While software like ELAN and Praat have advantages for annotating, programs such as CLAN or Annotation of Information Structure (ANNIS, Krause & Zeldes, 2016) are perhaps better suited for analysis, as they are designed for more extensive queries. One of the goals of Hilton (2009) in providing such a detailed description of their manual transcription and coding was to inform and contribute to future automatization. For interested readers, Ballier and Martin (2013, 2015) provide useful summaries and comparisons of software that have been used in the annotation of spoken learner corpora.

Praat is another commonly used program in fluency analyses (see e.g., Gósy et al., 2017; Tracy-Ventura & Huensch, 2018), especially those that include the investigation of additional phonological phenomena such as intonation and vowel quality (e.g., Garcia Lecumberri et al., 2017; Gut, 2012). Praat includes built-in features for automating some of the coding often necessary for fluency analysis. For example, the *Annotate To TextGrid (silences)...* command automatically segments the sound file into silent and sounding segments (one can customize the length of the silences, among other things). Of course, the program cannot differentiate between speech and noise of another form (e.g., laughter, filled pauses, a door slamming), so depending on the recording quality and the amount of background noise in the file, manual checking is necessary. Once the TextGrid is segmented, Praat scripts can be written to quickly and efficiently output data for simple analysis such as the number and duration of the pauses, etc. Additionally, De Jong and Wempe (2009) reported on a Praat script they developed to detect syllable nuclei which can be used to automatically count syllables. In conjunction with the automatic identification of silences, speech rate can be automatically calculated. De Jong and Wempe compared automated and manual coding and demonstrated high correlation (r=0.8) for a subset of the data. The differences found between manual and automatic coding were mainly the result of the script not identifying some of the unstressed syllables that were coded manually. Hilton (2009) additionally pointed out that the script does not differentiate between speech and filled pauses, which for some of the participants in the PAROLE corpus, would lead to an overestimation of speech rate. Thus, researchers using automated scripts for syllable counting are recommended to test the accuracy against manual coding with a subset of data.

Gut (2012) presented a detailed description of the transcription and coding of the LeaP corpus using Praat and additionally discussed the issue of interrater reliability for the different types of annotations completed. Perhaps not surprisingly, she reported that those annotations which were the most complex resulted in the lowest agreement. For example, one process of coding only required annotators to indicate whether something was a consonant, vowel, or pause. At this level, agreement was near perfect (κ=0.99). Another process of coding showed much lower agreement (κ=0.23) when annotators were required to first segment speech into syllables and then provide phonetic transcription (Gut, 2012, p. 11).

Representative Corpora and Research

In this section, three corpora are described along with some of the investigations of fluency that have been conducted using them. The corpora are the *Louvain International Database of Spoken English Interlanguage* (LINDSEI; Gilquin, De Cock, & Granger, 2010), the LANGSNAP corpus (Mitchell, Tracy-Ventura, & McManus, 2017), and the *Diapix Foreign Language Corpus* (DiapixFL, Garcia Lecumberri et al., 2017). These three corpora were chosen because their data are available to researchers (either freely or for a fee), they represent a variety of languages and speaking tasks, and they were compiled to investigate different combinations of the core issues and topics presented earlier in this chapter.

The LINDSEI corpus (Gilquin, De Cock, & Granger 2010) is a collection of speech from advanced EFL learners from 11 different L1s (Bulgarian, Chinese, Dutch, French, German, Greek, Italian, Japanese, Polish, Spanish, Swedish), with additional L1s continuing to be added. LINDSEI was designed to be an oral counterpart to the *International Corpus of Learner English* (ICLE) (Granger, 1998), which is a written corpus of argumentative essays. Each of the LINDSEI subcorpora was constructed following the same guidelines for comparison purposes. For each L1, the participants included approximately 50 university students typically in the third or fourth year of their studies. Speech data were collected from interviews comprised of three parts: a warm-up during which speakers completed a monologic task in which they spoke about a given topic, an informal interview (dialogic) in which they answered questions about their lives at university, hobbies, etc., and a picture description task. The *Louvain Corpus of Native English Conversation* (LOCNEC, De Cock, 2004) is a native speaker corpus of British university students that was compiled to allow for comparison with LINDSEI. The LINDSEI corpus (not including sound files) and handbook are available to the research community and require purchase. One of the main advantages of the LINDSEI corpus and its NS counterpart LOCNEC is that they were designed to be maximally similar to allow for both NS-NNS and cross-linguistic comparison.

LINDSEI has been used for an impressive number of investigations (see https://uclouvain.be/en/research-institutes/ilc/cecl/lindsei-bibliography.html), including those focused on fluency (e.g., Brand & Götz, 2011; Götz, 2013; Quan & Weisser, 2015). Here, I focus on the work that has used the German subcorpus of LINDSEI (LINDSEI-GE) as well as the LOCNEC to investigate L2 fluency (e.g., Brand & Götz, 2011; Götz (2013). Brand and Götz conducted quantitative analyses of accuracy and fluency with the 50 German L1 learners and the NSs from the LOCNEC corpus. This analysis was supplemented by qualitative analysis with a subset of five speakers chosen based on their varying accuracy/fluency profiles (e.g., the least accurate learner, the most fluent learner). Finally, the speech samples from the qualitative analysis were used as stimuli in a perceived fluency experiment in which 50 NSs of English rated how proficient they thought the speakers were. One interesting finding from this study is that across both quantitative and qualitative analyses, much individual variation was found with the fluency variables whereas the same was not true for accuracy. With the same corpora, Götz (2013) provided a thorough comparative analysis of native and non-native fluency characteristics including the less frequently investigated discourse markers (e.g., *like*, *well*) and small words (e.g., *sort of*, *kind of*). Her analysis demonstrated that, in comparison to NSs, learners showed less variation in their use of both discourse markers and small words, and they typically repeated the same ones instead of varying them.

The LANGSNAP corpus (Mitchell, Tracy-Ventura, McManus, 2017) is the result of a 2-year longitudinal project investigating language development before, during, and after study/residence abroad. Participants were L2 learners of French (*n*=29) or Spanish (*n*=27) who were university language majors required to spend the third year of their four-year undergraduate program abroad. Data were collected at six times between May 2011 and February 2013: once before, three times during, and two times after a nine-month stay abroad and included a variety of tasks such as picture-based oral narratives, semi-structured interviews about the participants' experiences, daily lives and future plans, a measure of proficiency (elicited imitation test), etc. NSs of Spanish (*n*=10) and French (*n*=10) also completed the narrative and interview tasks for comparison purposes. The oral production data were transcribed in CLAN following CHAT conventions and are freely available with the audio files at http://langsnap.soton.ac.uk/ and on Talkbank.org (see Chapter 12, this volume).

Data in the LANGSNAP corpus have been used for several investigations of oral fluency including explorations of L1–L2 fluency relationships (Huensch & Tracy-Ventura, 2017b) and tracking development longitudinally (Huensch & Tracy-Ventura, 2017a). Huensch and Tracy-Ventura (2017a) used the Spanish subset of the LANGSNAP corpus to explore the development and retention of nine measures of speed, breakdown, and repair fluency. The results indicated differential trends in the development and maintenance of different measures of fluency which led the authors to argue that measures reflect different sub-dimensions of fluency. In 2016, three years after the final data collection wave in LANGSNAP, participants were invited to take part in a new round of data collection. Approximately 60% (*n*=33) agreed to participate (these data are available on Talkbank.org and at http://scholarcommons.usf.edu/langsnap/). Huensch et al. (2019) investigated the possible outcomes of attrition/development/maintenance of L2 fluency three years after the end of formal instruction and explored the extent to which variables such as proficiency at the end of residence abroad and language exposure could predict changes in fluency. While previous research investigating first language attrition had not indicated reduced language exposure as a strong predictor of attrition (Mehotcheva, 2010), results from Huensch et al. with instructed learners indicated that the maintenance of some aspects of speed and breakdown fluency (e.g., speech rate and silent pauses) were influenced by language exposure and not by proficiency at the end of study abroad. The LANGSNAP studies demonstrate just some of the possibilities for investigating L2 fluency with a longitudinal corpus.

The *DiapixFL* corpus is a bi-directional corpus designed to allow for investigations that consider both individual differences in speaking style as well as potential cross-linguistic differences between the speaker's L1 and L2. Speakers in the corpus (*n*=24) include two groups: Spanish L1 learners of L2 English and English L1 learners of L2 Spanish. Both groups completed tasks in their L1 and L2. The task was a dialogic spot-the-difference task adapted from the DiapixUK materials (Baker & Hazan, 2011). In this task, participants were each presented with a picture which differed from their counterparts, and they worked together to identify the differences. Data were transcribed and annotated in *Mtrans* (Villegas et al., 2011) and are freely available at https://datashare.is.ed.ac.uk/handle/10283/346.

Using this corpus, Garcia Lecumberri et al. (2017) attempted to tease apart cross-linguistic factors from those of native/non-native speech to explore a variety of features of oral speech made possible by a dialogic corpus. Similar to Gut (2017), the corpus analysis presented in Garcia Lecumberri et al. allowed for not only an investigation of L2 fluency, but also phonological features such as pitch and vowel formant analyses. Of particular interest to issues of L2 fluency, the results of the analysis of speech rate (measured as words per minute) indicated effects of both nativeness and language being spoken (i.e., English vs. Spanish). Specifically, while it was the case that speech rate was generally slower for non-native speech, the greater number of monosyllabic words in English vs. Spanish meant that this reduction was less pronounced for the Spanish native speakers when speaking their L2 (English). The findings from Garcia Lecumberri et al. demonstrate how this type of bi-directional corpus design can help further tease apart the effects of nativeness and cross-linguistic influence in the study of L2 fluency.

Future Directions

Investigations of L2 fluency have benefitted from the recent growth in learner corpus research. This section provides several suggestions for future work in this area. Given the fact that, currently, much of the transcription and coding of corpora for fluency analysis are done manually and furthermore that this coding is time-consuming and can result in low reliability for some of the most complex annotations, it appears that a pressing need still exists for principled ways of automatizing coding. This would include new developments in automated processes as well as comparisons with manually coded corpora to allow for a better understanding of what can be reasonably expected when it comes to reliability.

In addition to automating processes, however, there are other ways to alleviate the time-consuming nature of coding and annotating data. The public sharing of annotated corpora using agreed-upon conventions for annotation allows for new investigations as well as potential for replication. While a great deal of data and tasks are available, the continued sharing, especially as pertains to coding decisions, could be another way to help ensure clarity (and perhaps encourage consistency) across studies. For example, Tracy-Ventura and Huensch (2018) in their critical reflection on the processes and decision-making involved in the creation of a publicly-shared, longitudinal corpus discussed the complexities of coding their data into utterances in CLAN (in this case, ASUs) particularly given the fact that they were coding across multiple languages (English, French, and Spanish) but having to base decisions on literature published about the coding of English. The sharing of detailed coding procedures (e.g., Hilton, 2009) would allow for continued open discussion among the community as well as making steps in ensuring the comparability across corpora, not to mention saving time.

Another area of future research that is just in its infancy in L2 fluency is further investigations into individual differences. Most studies exploring L2 fluency report large amounts of individual variation regardless of the aspect of fluency. Some work in LCR providing promising directions is that which combines quantitative analyses with the corpus as a whole with qualitative analyses of individual speakers (e.g., Brand & Götz, 2011; Gut, 2017). As described in the *Representative Corpora and Research* section, Brand and Götz (2011) qualitatively analyzed a subset of speakers who represented different learner profiles based on their quantitative analyses (e.g., those with the most/fewest grammatical errors, most fluent speech, average error and fluency scores). Using this approach, Brand and Götz demonstrated that the speaker with average scores for fluency and accuracy was rated as the most proficient indicating that raters relied on a variety of variables to rate proficiency. Learner corpora appear to be particularly well-suited for investigations of this kind that combine large-scale quantitative analyses with more detailed qualitative analyses with a subset of speakers.

Further Reading

Götz, S. (2013). *Fluency in native and non-native English speech.* Amsterdam: John Benjamins.

This book begins with a thorough introduction to issues in native and non-native fluency before providing an in-depth analysis and comparison of fluency features in the L2 English LINDSEI-GE and the English L1 LOCNEC corpora.

Gut, U. (2009). *Non-native speech: A corpus-based analysis of phonological and phonetic properties of L2 English and German.* Frankfurt: Peter Lang Publishing.

Arguing for the use of a corpus-based approach for investigations of second language acquisition, this book explores L2 phonological acquisition by investigating L2 English and L2 German speech from the LeaP corpus.

Segalowitz, N. (2010). *Cognitive bases of second language fluency.* New York: Routledge.

This book is an in-depth introduction to L2 fluency from a cognitive science perspective that draws upon work from a variety of fields to bring together multiple perspectives.

Related Topics

Chapters 12, 24, and 25.

Note

1 Further information about how this coding is accomplished can be found in the *Software and Tools for Data Coding and Analysis* section.

References

Baker, R., & Hazan, V. (2011). DiapixUK: Task materials for the elicitation of multiple spontaneous speech dialogs. *Behavior Research Methods, 43*(3), 761–770.

Ballier, N., & Martin, P. (2013). Developing corpus interoperability for phonetic investigation of learner corpora. In N. Ballier, A. Diaz-Negrillo, & P. Thompson (Eds.), *Automatic treatment and analysis of learner corpus data* (pp. 33–64). Amsterdam: John Benjamins.

Ballier, N., & Martin, P. (2015). Speech annotation of learner corpora. In A. Granger, G. Gilquin, & F. Meunier (Eds.), *The Cambridge handbook of learner corpus research* (pp. 107–134). Cambridge: Cambridge University Press.

Belz, M., Sauer, S., Lüdeling, A., & Mooshammer, C. (2017). Fluently disfluent? Pauses and repairs of advanced learners and native speakers of German. *International Journal of Learner Corpus Research, 3*(2), 118–148.

Boersma, P., & Weenink, D. (2015). *Praat: Doing phonetics by computer (5.4.18 version) [Computer program].* Retrieved from http://www.praat.org/

Bosker, H. R., Pinget, A. F., Quené, H., Sanders, T., & De Jong, N. H. (2013). What makes speech sound fluent? The contributions of pauses, speed, and repairs. *Language Testing, 30*(2), 159–175.

Brand, C., & Götz, S. (2011). Fluency versus accuracy in advanced spoken learner language: A multi-method approach. *International Journal of Corpus Linguistics, 16*(2), 255–275.

Davies, A. (2003). *Native speaker: Myth and reality.* Clevedon: Multilingual Matters.

de Bot, K. (1992). A bilingual production model: Levelt's "Speaking" model adapted. *Applied Linguistics, 13*, 1–24.

De Cock, S. (2004). Preferred sequences of words in NS and NNS speech. *Belgian Journal of English Language and Literatures, 2*, 225–246.

De Jong, N. H. (2016). Predicting pauses in L1 and L2 speech: The effects of utterance boundaries and word frequency. *International Review of Applied Linguistics in Language Teaching, 54*(2), 113–132.

De Jong, N. H., & Bosker, H. R. (2013). Choosing a threshold for silent pauses to measure second language fluency. In R. Eklund (Ed.). *Proceedings of the 6th workshop on Disfluency in Spontaneous Speech (DiSS)* (pp. 17–20). Stockholm: Royal Institute of Technology.

De Jong, N. H., Groenhout, R., Schoonen, R., & Hulstijn, J. H. (2015). Second language fluency: Speaking style or proficiency? Correcting measures of second language fluency for first language behavior. *Applied Psycholinguistics, 36*(2), 223–243.

De Jong, N. H., & Mora, J. (2017). Does having good articulatory skills lead to more fluent speech in first and second languages? *Studies in Second Language Acquisition, 41*(1), 1–13. doi:10.1017/S0272263117000389

De Jong, N. H., Steinel, M. P., Florijn, A. F., Schoonen, R., & Hulstijn, J. H. (2012). Facets of speaking proficiency. *Studies in Second Language Acquisition, 34*(1), 5–34.

De Jong, N. H., & Wempe, T. (2009). Praat script to detect syllable nuclei and measure speech rate automatically. *Behavior Research Methods, 41*(2), 385–390.

Derwing, T. M. (2017). L2 Fluency development. In S. Loewen & M. Sato (Eds.), *The Routledge handbook of instructed second language acquisition* (pp. 246–259). New York: Routledge.

Derwing, T. M., Munro, M., Thomson, R. I., & Rossiter, M. J. (2009). The relationship between L1 fluency and L2 fluency development. *Studies in Second Language Acquisition, 31*(4), 533–557.

Foster, P., & Tavakoli, P. (2009). Native speakers and task performance: Comparing effects on complexity, fluency, and lexical diversity. *Language Learning, 59*(4), 866–896.

Foster, P., Tonkyn, A., & Wigglesworth, G. (2000). Measuring spoken language: A unit for all reasons. *Applied Linguistics, 21*(3), 354–375.

Garcia Lecumberri, M. L., Cooke, M., Wester, M., Cooke, M., & Wester, M. (2017). A bi-directional task-based corpus of learners' conversational speech. *International Journal of Learner Corpus Research, 3*(2), 175–195.

Gilquin, G., De Cock, S., & Granger, S. (2010). *The Louvain International Database of Spoken English Interlanguage. Handbook and CD-ROM.* Louvain, Belgium: Presses Universitaires de Louvain.

Gilquin, G., & Granger, S. (2015). Learner language. In D. Biber & R. Reppen (Eds.), *The Cambridge handbook of English corpus linguistics* (pp. 418–436). Cambridge: Cambridge University Press.

Gósy, M., Gyarmathy, D., & Beke, A. (2017). Phonetic analysis of filled pauses based on a Hungarian-English learner corpus. *International Journal of Learner Corpus Research, 3*(2), 149–174.

Götz, S. (2013). *Fluency in native and non-native English speech.* Amsterdam: John Benjamins.

Granger, S. (1998). The computerized learner corpus: A versatile new source of data for SLA research. In S. Granger (Ed.), *Learner English on computer* (pp. 3–18). London: Longman.

Gut, U. (2009). *Non-native speech: A corpus-based analysis of phonological and phonetic properties of L2 English and German.* Frankfurt: Peter Lang Publishing.

Gut, U. (2012). The LeaP corpus. A multilingual corpus of spoken learner German and learner English. In T. Schmidt, & K. Wörner (Eds.), *Multilingual corpora and multilingual corpus analysis* (pp. 3–23). Amsterdam: John Benjamins.

Gut, U. (2017). Phonological development in different learning contexts. *International Journal of Learner Corpus Research, 3*(2), 196–222.

Hilton, H. (2008). The link between vocabulary knowledge and spoken L2 fluency. *Language Learning Journal, 36*(2), 153–166.

Hilton, H. (2009). Annotation and analyses of temporal aspects of spoken fluency. *CALICO Journal, 26*(3), 644–661.

Hilton, H., Osborne, N. J., Derive, M.-J., Succo, N., O'Donnell, J., Billard, S., & Rutigliano-Daspet, S. (2008). *Corpus PAROLE (Laboratoire LLS, Université de Savoie). TalkBank: SLA data.* Pittsburgh: Carnegie-Mellon University. Retrieved from https://slabank.talkbank.org/

Huensch, A., & Tracy-Ventura, N. (2017a). L2 utterance fluency development before, during, and after residence abroad: A multidimensional investigation. *The Modern Language Journal, 101*(2), 275–293.

Huensch, A., & Tracy-Ventura, N. (2017b). Understanding second language fluency behavior: The effects of individual differences in first language fluency, cross-linguistic differences, and proficiency over time. *Applied Psycholinguistics, 38*(4), 755–785.

Huensch, A., Tracy-Ventura, N., Bridges, J., & Cuesta-Media, J. (2019). Variables affecting the maintenance of L2 proficiency and fluency four years post-study abroad. *Study Abroad Research in Second Language Acquisition and International Education, 4*(1), 96–125.

Kahng, J. (2014). Exploring utterance and cognitive fluency of L1 and L2 English speakers: Temporal measures and stimulated recall. *Language Learning, 64*(4), 809–854.

Kahng, J. (2018). The effect of pause location on perceived fluency. *Applied Psycholinguistics, 39*(3), 569–591.

Kormos, J. (2006). *Speech production and second language acquisition.* Mahwah: Lawrence Erlbaum Associates.

Kormos, J., & Dénes, M. (2004). Exploring measures and perceptions of fluency in the speech of second language learners. *System, 32*(2), 145–164.

Krause, T., & Zeldes, A. (2016). ANNIS3: A new architecture for generic corpus query and visualization. *Digital Scholarship in the Humanities, 31*(1), 118–139.

Lennon, P. (1990). Investigating fluency in EFL: A quantitative approach. *Language Learning, 40*(3), 387–417.

Levelt, W. (1989). *Speaking: From intention to articulation.* Cambridge: MIT Press.

Levelt, W. (1999). Producing spoken language: A blueprint of the speaker. In C. Brown & P. Hagoort (Eds.), *The neurocognition of language* (pp. 83–122). Oxford: Oxford University Press.

MacWhinney, B. (2000). *The CHILDES project: Tools for analyzing talk* (3rd ed.). Mahwah: Lawrence Erlbaum Associates.

MacWhinney, B. (2017). A shared platform for studying second language acquisition. *Language Learning, 67*(S1), 254–275.

Mehotcheva, T. H. (2010). *After the fiesta is over: Foreign language attrition of Spanish in Dutch and German Erasmus students.* Doctoral Dissertation. University of Groningen, The Netherlands.

Meunier, F., & Littré, D. (2013). Tracking learners' progress: Adopting a dual "corpus cum experimental data" approach. *The Modern Language Journal, 97*(S1), 61–76.

Mitchell, R., Tracy-Ventura, N., & McManus, K. (2017). *The anglophone student abroad: Identity, social relationships and language learning.* New York: Routledge.

Myles, F. (2008). Investigating learner language development with electronic longitudinal corpora: Theoretical and methodological issues. In L. Ortega & H. Byrnes (Eds.), *The longitudinal study of advanced L2 capacities* (pp. 58–72). New York: Routledge.

Ortega, L., & Byrnes, H. (2008). *The longitudinal study of advanced L2 capacities.* New York: Routledge.

Ortega, L., & Iberri-Shea, G. (2005). Longitudinal research in second language acquisition: Recent trends and future directions. *Annual Review of Applied Linguistics, 25,* 26–45.

Pellegrino, F., Coupé, C., & Marsico, E. (2011). A cross-language perspective on speech information rate. *Language, 87*(3), 539–558.

Quan, L., & Weisser, M. (2015). A study of "self-repair" operations in conversation by Chinese English learners. *System, 49,* 39–49.

Riazantseva, A. (2001). Second language proficiency and pausing: A study of Russian speakers of English. *Studies in Second Language Acquisition, 23*(4), 497–526.

Sauer, S., & Lüdeling, A. (2016). Flexible multi-layer spoken dialogue corpora. *International Journal of Corpus Linguistics, 21*(3), 419–438.

Segalowitz, N. (2010). *Cognitive bases of second language fluency.* New York: Routledge.

Segalowitz, N. (2016). Second language fluency and its underlying cognitive and social determinants. *International Review of Applied Linguistics, 54*(2), 79–95.

Skehan, P. (2003). Task-based instruction. *Language Teaching, 36*(1), 1–14.

Skehan, P., Foster, P., & Shum, S. (2016). Ladders and snakes in second language fluency. *International Review of Applied Linguistics in Language Teaching, 54*(2), 97–111.

Staples, S. (2015). Spoken discourse. In D. Biber & R. Reppen (Eds.), *The Cambridge handbook of English corpus linguistics* (pp. 271–291). Cambridge: Cambridge University Press.

Tavakoli, P. (2011). Pausing patterns: Differences between L2 learners and native speakers. *ELT Journal, 65*(1), 71–79.

Tavakoli, P., & Skehan, P. (2005). Strategic planning, task structure, and performance testing. In R. Ellis (Ed.), *Planning and task performance in a second language* (pp. 239–276). Amsterdam: John Benjamins.

Towell, R., Hawkins, R., & Bazergui, N. (1996). The development of fluency in advanced learners of French. *Applied Linguistics, 17*(1), 84–119.

Tracy-Ventura, N., & Huensch, A. (2018). The potential of publicly shared longitudinal learner corpora in SLA research. In A. Gudmestad & A. Edmonds (Eds.), *Critical reflections on data in second language acquisition.* Amsterdam: John Benjamins. doi:10.1075/lllt.51.07tra

Trouvain, J., & Möbius, B. (2014). Sources of variation of articulation rate in native and non-native speech: Comparisons of French and German. *Proceedings of the Speech Prosody, SP7,* 275–279.

Trouvain, J., Zimmerer, F., Möbius, B., Gósy, M., & Bonneau, A. (2017). Segmental, prosodic and fluency features in phonetic learner corpora: Introduction to the special issue. *International Journal of Learner Corpus Research, 3*(2), 105–117.

Tullock, B., & Ortega, L. (2017). Fluency and multilingualism in study abroad: Lessons from a scoping review. *System, 71,* 7–21.

Villegas, J., Cooke, M., Aubanel, V., & Piccolino-Boniforti, M. A. (2011). MTRANS: A multi-channel, multi-tier speech annotation tool. *Proceedings of the 12th annual conference of the international speech communication association: INTERSPEECH, 3237–3240.* Florence, Italy.

23

Accuracy

Jennifer Thewissen

Introduction

As one component of the complexity-accuracy-fluency (CAF) triad, accuracy tends to be defined as the ability to produce "error-free" speech or writing (Housen & Kuiken, 2009, p. 461). Wolfe-Quintero, Inagaki, and Kim (1998) define it as "the conformity of second language knowledge to target language norms" (p. 4). The study of accuracy is operationalized via Error Analysis (EA), i.e. the systematic analysis of learner errors, which are broadly defined as "a linguistic form or combination of forms which, in the same context and under similar conditions of production would, in all likelihood, not be produced by the speakers' native speaker counterparts" (Lennon, 1991, p. 182). Of the three CAF constructs, accuracy has even been presented as the "simplest construct of CAF" (Craven, 2017, p. 25). However, anyone who has actively undertaken error analysis (Chapter 7, this volume) would probably object to it being qualified as the "simplest" construct of the triad. As will become clear from this chapter, accuracy remains a slippery, thorny, and multifaceted concept with its own set of challenging issues such as the usage norm against which errors should be considered, which accuracy measures to apply (Polio & Shea, 2014), or the highly context-dependent nature of what constitutes an error (Wulff & Gries, 2011).

Historically, accuracy has served as a key source of evidence in the elaboration of SLA theories since the beginning of the field in the 1960s. Accuracy was a main construct within the Contrastive Analysis Hypothesis (CAH) which existed in a strong and a weak version (Lado, 1957). The strong version of CAH claimed that errors were predictable: second language (L2) structures which were different from the first language (L1) would create difficulty (errors), whereas those structures which were similar in the L1 and the L2 would lead to accurate use of the L2. The weak version of CAH did not aim to predict errors before they occurred. Rather, the starting point was the analysis of actual learner language and the subsequent explanation of errors exclusively in terms of L1 interference. In the late 1960s, CAH came under criticism mainly for over- and underpredicting errors and for explaining errors in terms of L1 transfer only. This paved the way for the Error Analysis (EA) method (Corder, 1971; Chapter 7, this volume) which considered errors as a window into SLA processes and which lives on to this day in the form of computer-aided error analysis (error analysis carried out on learner corpora).

Another early SLA theory which heavily relied on accuracy-related evidence is the Natural Order Hypothesis (Krashen, 1977), which posited that language learners acquired L2 structures in a pre-determined order. This hypothesis was a reaction to CAH, as it claimed that L2 acquisition was not merely about habit formation but was rather a question of moving through developmental stages. The so-called 'morpheme studies' (e.g. Dulay & Burt, 1974; Hakuta, 1976) were the first to investigate the possibility that English grammatical morphemes (e.g. third person singular -*s*, plural -*s*, irregular past, progressive -*ing*, articles, etc.) followed a natural order of acquisition. Accuracy played a key role here, as the resulting order of acquisition was based on the accuracy score with which each morpheme was used in obligatory contexts (e.g. the irregular past with a 60% accuracy score was considered to be acquired before another morpheme with a lower accuracy percentage). Recent work on morpheme acquisition has since convincingly challenged the natural order claims by empirically showing that there are in fact clear L1 effects on the order in which English morphemes are acquired (Díez-Bedmar & Papp, 2008; Murakami & Alexopoulou, 2016).

The 1980s/1990s constituted somewhat of a turning point for the study of accuracy when Skehan (1989) proposed that accuracy be studied alongside complexity and fluency in what has since become known as the complexity-accuracy-fluency (CAF) triad. Two major SLA hypotheses have emerged from the study of CAF, both of which are still being actively tested in the SLA and learner corpus literature to date: the Limited Attentional Capacity Model or Trade-Off Hypothesis (Skehan, 1989) appeals to L2 cognitive processes and states that, because attentional capacity is limited, learners will tend to prioritize one aspect (e.g. accuracy) over another (e.g. complexity). Skehan explains that this may happen as a function of task characteristics, with cognitively more complex tasks forcing learners to prioritize one construct over another. The second hypothesis, namely, the Cognition Hypothesis (Robinson, 2001), claims that more complex task characteristics will in fact foster both more complex and more accurate L2 output. What both these hypotheses have in common is the idea that the CAF components "exist in an organic relationship with one another" (Larsen-Freeman, 2009, p. 582). A second major event in the 1990s was the advent of the first learner corpora, which gave error analysis a new lease of life in the shape of computer-aided error analysis (Dagneaux, Denness, & Granger, 1998; Chapter 7, this volume). To-date, analyzing errors on the basis of learner corpora has triggered an impressive amount of research activity (see Thewissen, 2015 for an overview of learner corpus research (LCR) accuracy studies).

Accuracy has also had to contend with some disapproving voices over the years. For example, Bley-Vroman (1983) explicitly rejected the notion of error and claimed that studying learner language by relying on target language concepts (obligatory context, error, etc.) was a "comparative fallacy" which impeded the study of interlanguage as a system in its own right. Currently, voices from Global Englishes/English as a Lingua Franca studies (Jenkins, 2006) have also spoken out against errors, preferring the terms *innovations* and *emerging L2 norms*. While these views impact our thinking about the developing norms against which to study accuracy, they have not spelt the death of research into this construct which is still considered an essential L2 component in SLA, LCR, language pedagogy, and language assessment.

Core Issues and Topics

The first core issue assesses the place of accuracy within a number of current SLA theories, mainly Usage-based Theory, Complex Dynamic Systems Theory (see Chapters 13–14, this volume), and Interactionist Theory (see Chapter 21, this volume, about the construct of interaction). The number of SLA theories presented here is necessarily selective, and the reader is referred to Section III of this handbook for further discussion of other theories. The second core issue presents how accuracy has been studied in LCR, while the third discusses some of the challenges involved in studying accuracy in spoken learner corpus data.

Accuracy in Current SLA Theories

Accuracy Within Usage-based Theory

One of the basic tenets of Usage-based (UB) approaches (Ellis & Wulff, 2014; Wulff & Ellis, 2018; Chapter 13, this volume) is that L2 learning is primarily dependent on the linguistic input learners receive. Although this input leads to successful L1 development, it often does not suffice for SLA, which is necessarily limited in its end state (Ellis & Sagarra, 2010). What this concretely means is that SLA often falls short of native-like ability as reflected, among others, by the presence of errors. Among the many constructs included within UB approaches, three can be identified as jointly contributing to some of the limitations in accuracy which characterize SLA, namely (1) salience, (2) redundancy, and (3) learned attention[1]. Salience is linked to the construct of frequency. It refers to the property of a feature to stand out from the rest and thus possibly enter into subsequent cognitive processing and learning (Wulff & Ellis, 2018, p. 43). This concept contributes to explaining why certain aspects of English accuracy such as grammatical function words (e.g. articles, prepositions) and bound morphemes (e.g. third-person singular -s, plural-s, derivational affixes) tend to remain error-prone even beyond the elementary levels of proficiency. Because these constructions are highly frequent, short, and unstressed, they tend to lose their salience for L2 learners who may find it difficult to systematically use them accurately. This means that frequency of use does not necessarily result in accuracy of use. If this were the case, "English articles and prepositions, which are the most frequent words in the English language, should not pose such an obstinate challenge to the average language learner" (Ellis & Wulff, 2014, p. 84).

The effects of low salience are compounded by redundancy, which refers to the fact that certain grammatical morphemes may appear in seemingly redundant contexts. Tense markers, for instance, can be used in clauses which already contain explicit time markers, e.g. *she went swimming yesterday*, where both *went* and *yesterday* express past time. To ease the cognitive burden of using two means of expressing past time, L2 learners may only express tense via explicit time markers, e.g. *she *go swimming yesterday*, which results in inaccurate verb tense use.

Learned attention, or blocking, refers to the "attentional biases" (Wulff & Ellis, 2018, p. 47) which result from the learners' mother tongue. The ubiquitous presence of the L1 may literally 'block' fully successful second language learning for certain learners (see e.g. Ellis & Sagarra, 2010, for a study of the effects of blocking on the acquisition of temporal reference). Transfer errors which can be traced back to L1 use typically result from blocking. According to UB theory, therefore, SLA requires learners to continually *reconfigure* the attentional biases induced by their L1. Accuracy plays a key role in this respect, as certain errors can be considered proof that reconfiguration is indeed taking place and that learners are attempting to discover the systematicities underlying the L2. Ellis and Wulff (2014) illustrate this with the U-shaped pattern of development. U-shaped development refers to language which initially appears to display a high level of accuracy (e.g. accurate use of the simple past form *went*), then deviates from the target norm (e.g. **goed*) before once again conforming to L2 norms. Rather than a sign of regression, such errors encouragingly signal that learners are in fact progressing by reorganising their L2 system to take into account newly acquired knowledge. From a UB perspective, errors can thus be viewed as a cognitive necessity, the driving force behind L2 reconfiguration. The need for reconfiguration consequently implies that UB theorists see language learning as a complex-adaptive system which involves learners continuously fine-tuning their L2 knowledge with, literally, much trial and error along the way.

Accuracy Within Complex Dynamic Systems Theory

Complex Dynamic Systems Theory (DST) (de Bot, Lowie, & Verspoor 2007; Chapter 14, this volume) shares the view expressed by UB theorists that SLA is a complex-adaptive system,

The L2 system includes many interconnected subsystems which are in constant flux and change depending on a complex multitude of interacting variables (e.g. intelligence, aptitude, motivation, L1, L2, to name but a few).

From a DST perspective, accuracy is seen as one component of the L2 system among many others, and thus, it would make little sense to study it in isolation. DST regularly studies accuracy alongside complexity and/or fluency so as to gain insight into their dynamic relationship and identify areas of trade-off (improvement in one construct at the expense of another) as well as areas where the constructs develop in support of each other as 'connected growers' (Norris & Ortega, 2009; Rosmawati, 2014; Verspoor, Schmid, & Xu, 2012). This tends to be done longitudinally by concentrating on a small group of individual learners so as to capture the "messy little details" (de Bot et al., 2007, p. 19) which, according to DST, best represent the complexities of what is really happening in the SLA process.

Verspoor et al. (2012) is an SLA study carried out from a DST perspective. Rather than concentrate on individual learners, however, the authors investigated CAF among a large group of students and adopted a pseudo-longitudinal (different learners at different proficiency levels) rather than a purely longitudinal (the same learners across time) research design. Verspoor et al. (2012) coded 469 learner texts according to 64 variables pertaining to complexity, accuracy, and fluency. The learner texts were produced by Dutch-speaking EFL learners at five proficiency levels, ranging from beginner (A1.1) to intermediate (B1.1). The aim was to find which of the 64 variables discriminate best between the proficiency levels and what the changes in sub-systems across proficiency levels might indicate about L2 development. In terms of accuracy, the authors found that the discriminatory power of accuracy on its own was only moderately useful, as it did not discriminate consistently between all proficiency levels. The results highlight that accuracy is but one aspect of the L2 developmental picture and that it is most meaningfully studied alongside other constructs such as syntactic and lexical complexity which also play a key role in discriminating between proficiency levels.

DST work shows that we have come a long way since the days of the Contrastive Analysis Hypothesis when learner language was almost exclusively analyzed for its erroneous nature. DST sees SLA as developing in many directions simultaneously, accuracy being just one source of evidence among many others.

Accuracy Within Interactionist and Sociocultural Approaches

The Interaction Hypothesis (Long, 1981) states that SLA is promoted by face-to-face interaction during which learners negotiate meaning and receive negative feedback on their output. The aim of negative feedback is to foster cognitive comparisons so that learners will notice the gap (errors) between their own interlanguage and the target language and thereby reconfigure their second language representations. Accuracy occupies pride of place within Interactionist SLA, as it is within this approach that the "feedback studies" (Russel & Spada, 2006; Polio, 2012) are carried out. These studies investigate the relationship between types of feedback (e.g. providing meta-linguistic rules, recasts, teacher clarification requests, etc.) and their impact on L2 accuracy. Much of the research on written error correction has been prompted by Truscott's (1996) 'shocking' claim that this practice was ineffective and should be abandoned altogether. To this day, Sachs and Polio (2007) admit that the effectiveness of written error correction remains an open question, as it is dependent on a number of key factors, including the developmental stages reached by the learners: those learners who are not developmentally ready to acquire an L2 form may not reap the benefits of negative feedback (see also Pienemann's 1998 Processability Theory about the fixed L2 developmental stages of SLA; Chapter 15, this volume).

Interactionist approaches to SLA partly overlap with Sociocultural Theory (Lantolf & Thorne, 2007) which also claims that interaction contributes to SLA. This interaction occurs in different cultural and linguistic settings such as family life, schools, sporting activities, etc. A few studies have zoomed in on accuracy within the sociocultural approach. Wigglesworth and Storch (2009), for instance, compared the impact of individual vs. pair EFL writing on complexity, accuracy and fluency. They found that writing collaboratively positively impacted accuracy but not complexity and fluency. Working together enabled the learners to pool their linguistic knowledge and produce more accurate texts.

Accuracy in Learner Corpus Research

SLA and LCR may have more in common than meets the eye when studying accuracy. SLA views language as a dynamic system which changes over time. In keeping with this, LCR has also been actively attempting to capture the dynamics of L2 accuracy development by relying both on longitudinal (Meunier & Littré, 2013) and pseudo-longitudinal learner corpus data (Díez-Bedmar, 2015; Götz, 2015; Hawkins & Filipović, 2012; O'Donnell et al., 2009; Thewissen, 2015). Rather than focus on the messy little details that are characteristic of individual learners, developmental LCR into accuracy has mainly concentrated on how accuracy develops across groups of learners at different levels of proficiency. This has been made possible by error tagging learner corpus data, a method which involves annotating the errors found in a learner corpus according to a well-defined and documented error taxonomy (see Chapter 7, this volume). The annotation process remains largely manual but is facilitated by a number of existing computer software tools (see the *Main Research Methods* section below). Error tagged learner corpora are valuable to the fields of language pedagogy and language testing in that they enable the elaboration of "accuracy profiles" at various proficiency levels. Considerable attention so far has been paid to specifying the Common European Framework (CEFR) (Council of Europe, 2001) descriptor levels (the A1 to C2 levels) which have been criticized for being overly vague. The English Profile Programme (EPP) (Hawkins & Buttery, 2010; Hawkins & Filipović, 2012), for instance, uses the *Cambridge Learner Corpus* and its error annotations to identify 'criterial features' for each of the CEFR proficiency levels as they apply to English. Criterial features include, but are not limited to, L2 errors. An error type is said to be 'criterial' if it helps distinguish between pairs of adjacent levels and therefore contributes to assessment decisions. The EPP found evidence of errors which steadily decrease as proficiency increases (e.g. derivation of determiner, *Shes name is Anna*) while other error types decrease between certain levels but not others (e.g. noun countability errors, *I don't have any *monies*). Interestingly, the results also indicate the presence of U-shaped patterns of development (errors which increase after B1 then decline again by C2) (e.g. noun agreement errors, *one of my friend*). In a similar vein, Thewissen (2015) used error-tagged data from the *International Corpus of Learner English* (ICLE) (Granger et al., 2009) to feed learner corpus-attested accuracy information into the existing CEFR descriptors for grammatical accuracy, vocabulary control, and orthographic control at proficiency levels B1, B2, C1, and C2. O'Donnell et al. (2009), for their part, report on the TREACLE[2] project which uses two learner corpora, namely WriCLE (Rollinson & Mendikoetxea, 2010) and MiLC (Andreu et al., 2010) and their error codes to capture the grammatical profiles of Spanish-speaking EFL learners at different proficiency levels. This line of LCR has shown that, rather than developing linearly, accuracy is a dynamic construct in its own right, with different error types following various developmental paths across the proficiency range.

In addition to capturing accuracy developmentally, LCR has also been making a conscious effort to include more SLA theory in investigations of accuracy. Wulff and Gries (2011) are a case in point. They adopted a usage-based approach to the study of accuracy and proposed a constructionist definition of this concept: "accuracy in L2 production is the selection of a construction (…) in its preferred context within a particular target variety and genre" (Wulff & Gries, 2011, p. 70). Using data from ICLE, they studied the use of several English constructions by Dutch and

German-speaking EFL learners, including the ditransitive (e.g. *they gave the squirrel the nut*) and prepositional dative (e.g. *they gave the nut to the squirrel*) constructions. Strictly speaking, both these constructions are syntactically 'accurate' in English but, depending on the context of use, native speakers tend to prefer the use of one construction over another, as certain verbs in English are distinctively associated with either one of these constructions. Ditransitive verbs tend to be used to express a transfer between an agent and a recipient (e.g. *they gave the students the answers*), whereas the prepositional dative construction is more typically used when there is a perceived distance between the agent and the recipient (e.g. *they sold the restaurant to the franchise group*). The study revealed that, in spite of some non-idiomatic choices, the learner groups were very much in line with native-speaker use of these two constructions and were generally able to form strong generalisations about the L2. This study is interesting in that it pushes the boundaries of the traditional definition of accuracy as a dichotomous choice between 'right' vs. 'wrong' and rather views it as "a gradual phenomenon that transcends an NS-NNS divide" (Wulff & Gries, 2011, p. 70). The authors argue that accuracy will increase proportionally to the extent that learners succeed in making the right generalizations regarding the use of specific constructions in specific contexts of use.

Accuracy in Spoken Learner Corpora

To date, error analysis in LCR has mainly been carried out on the basis of written language which already constitutes a challenge in itself (see Chapter 7, this volume). Although research which explores accuracy on the basis of spoken learner corpora does exist (e.g. Brand & Götz, 2011; Götz, 2015; Gráf, 2017), it comparatively remains a rather underexplored area, as it is confronted with a number of challenging issues.

One issue is that an error in writing and an error in speech are not necessarily the same thing. Speech is not held up to the same prescriptive pedestal as writing, meaning that the concept of what constitutes an error in speech is frequently a question of gradient acceptability. A number of "non-standard" uses of English which could be tagged as erroneous in written corpus data would perhaps be tolerated in spoken data:

- forms with "there is/are", e.g. *there 's too many people in the room* (where *there are* would be the prescriptive alternative),
- double negatives, e.g. *he didn't see nobody,*
- the use of "less" or "amount" with countable nouns, e.g. *less students, the amount of assignments,*
- non-standard tense and aspect use such as the use of the progressive with typically stative verbs (e.g. *am I understanding this right?*) or the use of the present perfect with explicit past time adverbials (e.g. *I have just finished the book two days ago*),
- the use of the third person singular, e.g. *she don't care whether he comes or not.*

LCR into spoken accuracy has remained very tight-lipped on what to do with regard to such non-standard features in the error detection stage, sweeping these challenges under the carpet. Detecting errors in spoken learner corpus data is further complicated by the presence of disfluencies (false starts, self-corrections, repeats, etc.) which can be difficult to distinguish from errors themselves (Gilquin & De Cock, 2011). The publication of an error tagging manual with recommendations regarding how to operationalize errors in speech vs. writing would greatly benefit LCR. Such work would also contribute to illustrating the relativity of the very notion of error and the fact that "a fool-proof definition of error" (Gráf, 2017, p. 133) does not exist. In fact, erroneousness is best viewed as a context-dependent construct which exists on a continuum between actual deviations and more acceptable forms.

Main Research Methods

Measures of Accuracy in SLA

Traditionally, global accuracy in SLA is measured by gauging whether a syntactic unit, be it the sentence, the T-unit, or the clause is error free. Frequent measures include the ratio of error-free T-units per T-unit (EFT/T), error-free clauses per clause (EFC/C), and error-free sentences per sentence (ES/S) (Polio & Shea, 2014). SLA work has stressed the practicality of such holistic measures which tend to show stronger discriminatory power in the evaluation of accuracy in L2 performance than local measures that track the evolution of specific L2 features (e.g. article errors, agreement errors, etc.). Some SLA work has nevertheless chosen to exclusively rely on local accuracy measures by focussing on detailed error types such as article errors in highly specific contexts (cf. Shintani & Ellis, 2013 who studied the accurate use of the indefinite article in two restricted contexts). Rather than choosing between global or local measures, Evans et al. (2014, p. 34) suggest that accuracy might best be captured by combining the two.

Next to global accuracy measures, SLA has also developed sophisticated error counting measures such as obligatory occasion analysis which was first proposed by Brown (1973) for the study of morpheme acquisition in first language acquisition. It was later used in the context of second language acquisition (Dulay & Burt, 1974; Hakuta, 1976) and was adapted by Pica (1984) to also include suppliance in non-obligatory contexts (viz. over-suppliance such as *they dances every week*). The operationalisation formula is as follows:

$$\frac{\text{Numerator: } n \text{ correct suppliances in contexts}}{\text{Denominator: Total obligatory contexts} \left(+\text{oversuppliance} \right)} \times 100 = \text{percent accuracy}$$

Because this measure depends on the identification of obligatory contexts for a specific L2 feature, its use tends to be limited to discrete items such as grammatical morphemes for which obligatory uses are more easily identifiable than for other L2 features (e.g. lexical errors).

A recently developed accuracy measure in SLA is the weighted clause ratio (WCR) (Evans et al., 2014; Foster & Wigglesworth, 2016) which is more specifically concerned with error gravity. Because it is assumed that errors will affect comprehensibility to varying degrees, WCR proposes "a means of analysis where each clause is assigned a weight based on the ease of retrieving meaning" (Evans et al., 2014, p. 36), as suggested in Table 23.1.

Although the WCR method is worthy in its own right, determining error gravity may raise a number of issues such as the reliability with which errors can be classified on a minor to serious scale. As explained in the *Core Issues and Topics* section, accuracy cannot be defined in absolute terms. It is essentially a matter of degree and notions such as 'error gravity' can become dangerously subjective. Albrechtsen, Henriksen, and Faerch (1980) explain this when they say that

Table 23.1 Weighted Clause Ratio Operationalisation (Foster & Wigglesworth, 2016, p. 106)

Error type	Definition	Weighting
No error	Accurate clause	1
Level 1 error	The clause has minor (e.g. morphosyntactic errors) which do not impede meaning.	0.8
Level 2 error	The clause has more serious errors (e.g. word choice or word order) that make the intended meaning harder to recover.	0.5
Level 3 error	The clause has errors that make the intended meaning difficult to recover.	0.1

deciding on the seriousness of an error "is perhaps not primarily a function of its inherent qualities, but of the context in which it occurs" (p. 393).

Measures of Accuracy in LCR

LCR has less typically relied on the syntactic denominators (clauses, T-units) employed in SLA accuracy measures. Rather, LCR accuracy studies have heavily, although not exclusively, relied on (a) raw or normalized error frequencies (e.g. article errors/total word frequency) and (b) error percentages (e.g. % article errors/total errors in the data) to report their quantitative results (note that SLA researchers have also used these measures).

Besides these broad error counts, LCR has also drawn on other SLA methods to measure accuracy. Obligatory occasion analysis, for example, has been applied to learner corpora to study aspects of L2 accuracy such as article use at different proficiency levels (Díez-Bedmar, 2015) or by different learner populations (Díez-Bedmar & Papp, 2008) as well as morpheme acquisition orders (Murakami & Alexopoulou, 2016).

LCR has additionally developed accuracy measurement methods of its own such as potential occasion analysis (Thewissen, 2015). Rather than searching for *obligatory* contexts of use, potential occasion analysis relies on *potential* contexts for errors. The method combines manually error-tagged and automatically part-of-speech (POS) tagged learner corpus data[3] (see Chapter 5, this volume) in order to calculate errors as ratios of each relevant word class, e.g. the number of subordinator errors out of the total subordinators in the learner data.

$$\frac{\text{Numerator: } n \text{ subordinator errors in error-tagged data}}{\text{Denominator: Total subordinators in POS-tagged data}} \times 100 = \text{percent erroneousness}$$

Potential occasion analysis can be seen as a workable compromise between the highly detailed nature of obligatory occasion analysis and overly broad error frequencies and percentages. Similar to obligatory occasion analysis, it puts findings into perspective by considering the ratio of accurate vs. inaccurate use. It is strongly recommended that accuracy studies carefully consider which denominator is the most suitable when counting errors and that, when possible, they avoid reporting about errors purely as broad frequencies and error percentages as this may lead to gross misinterpretation of results[4].

Corpus Methods and Tools for the Analysis of Accuracy

Another methodological difference between SLA and LCR is that LCR has relied on error tagging to annotate errors in learner corpora (see Chapter 7, this volume). LCR has developed two main error tagging architectures. The first is a flat annotation system where error tags (labels) and corrections are inserted directly into the learner file itself, for example: *Money is the real problem of* <GA corr="0">*the*</GA> *society in this world.* GA denotes the presence of a grammatical article error, namely the redundant use of 'the' where a zero article ("0") should have been used. While flat annotation methods continue to be extremely helpful in learner corpus accuracy studies, one of their main limitations is that they tend to only allow for a single interpretation of errors, as it is often not possible to suggest different error tags or correction possibilities for the same error. The second error tagging architecture used in LCR is the multi-layered stand-off annotation system (Lüdeling & Hirschmann, 2015) where the error tags and corrections are stored separately from the learner text and therefore do not "corrupt" the corpus data. In the example below taken from Lüdeling and Hirschmann (2015, p. 145), the learner used the phrase 'dependance on gambling'. Annotator 1 (target hypothesis 1) only corrected the orthographic error in 'dependance' whereas annotator 2 suggested a more idiomatic phrase altogether ('gambling addiction').

- *Learner utterance: dependance on gambling*
- *Target Hypothesis 1: dependence on gambling*
- *Target Hypothesis 2: gambling addiction*

The multi-level stand-off system is more flexible than its flat annotation counterpart, as it is possible to define as many error annotation layers as possible. Multiple annotator analyses of the same error can be viewed together to subsequently make informed annotation decisions. This method does justice to the fact that accuracy is a relative concept, as it highlights the unavoidable disagreements among annotators, in terms of both error identification and correction. It is thus suggested that, when possible, multi-level stand-off systems be preferred over their flat counterparts in learner corpus accuracy research.

LCR has developed a number of user-friendly tools to systematize the error tagging procedure and assist the subsequent quantitative and qualitative analyses of the data. Two of these, the Université catholique de Louvain Error Editor (UCLEEv2) (Granger & Paquot, forthcoming 2020) and the UAM Corpus Tool (UAMCT) (O'Donnell, 2008; http://www.corpustool.com/) are described here. UCLEEv2 is a flat annotation system which includes particularly useful features for the study of accuracy: (1) it includes a drop-down menu which lists the error tags used so as to help speed up tag insertion, as well as a box for correction insertion; (2) it uses a checking function which allows for intra-coder consistency to be verified by highlighting specific error tags with different colors; (3) errors can be viewed in context (concordances) by searching on the error tag, the error itself or the correction; (4) descriptive statistics are computed, including absolute frequencies of error tags per individual text, error tag percentages, and relative error frequencies per tokens; this statistical information can be exported into external statistical packages; (5) tailor-made exercises based on the error-tagged data can be automatically created in UCLEEv2.

The UAMCT relies on a multi-level stand-off annotation architecture where the error tags are stored separately from the raw learner data. Similarly to UCLEEv2, UAMCT enables the creation of tailor-made error taxonomies which can be fed into the system and can easily be edited along the way. The tool generates general statistics (e.g. word and sentence counts, average word and sentence length, lexical density), contrastive statistics at the group level (comparisons of error numbers in different subcorpora along with chi-square significance results), and, importantly, inter-coder statistics (Polio & Shea, 2014) which are too rarely reported in accuracy research in general.

Representative Corpora and Research

Alexopoulou et al. (2017) use the *EF-Cambridge Open Language Database* (EFCAMDAT) (Geertzen, Alexopoulou, & Korhonen, 2014), an open-access corpus of free writings submitted to the online school of EF Education First by learners of English from A1 to C2. More than 60% of the scripts have been coded for errors by EF teachers[5] using 24 error labels and are publicly available via the online corpus interface. The authors use EFCAMDAT to test the impact of task complexity (task design features) on L2 complexity and accuracy. The authors tested Skehan's Limited Attentional Capacity Hypothesis and Robinson's Cognition Hypothesis. Some preliminary findings suggest that accuracy effects were not very pronounced overall and could not be accounted for by task design features. In other words, error rates did not significantly vary across tasks (descriptive vs. narrative vs. professional writing). Complexity was found to be partly influenced by task type, with the least cognitively demanding tasks (e.g. writing a job application) eliciting low levels of L2 complexity, thereby tentatively pointing towards Robinson's Cognition Hypothesis.

Using data from the ICLE (French-, German-, and Spanish-speaking EFL learners), Thewissen (2013) took a developmental approach to the construct of accuracy and studied its dynamic development across CEFR proficiency levels B1, B2, C1, and C2. The c. 150,000-word corpus sample was exhaustively error tagged following the Louvain error taxonomy (Granger et al., 2008) which distinguishes between 46 different error types pertaining to form, grammar, lexis, lexico-grammar, word order, and punctuation. Errors at each proficiency level were quantified using the potential occasion analysis method and were subsequently submitted to a number of inferential statistical tests. The results indicated that different error types followed different developmental paths. A majority of local error types (e.g. spelling errors, morphological errors, errors on uncountables, verb agreement errors, etc.) were found to decrease mainly between levels B1 and B2, showing signs of stabilisation across the B2-C1-C2 levels. This finding led to the tentative conclusion that changes in accuracy might be most marked between the lower intermediate (B1) and upper-intermediate (B2) levels and that other constructs pertaining to complexity, for instance, would be needed to further characterize the B2 to C2 proficiency range. Such findings are in keeping with claims made in the SLA literature (Norris & Ortega, 2009) according to which different constructs may have different discriminatory power depending on the L2 proficiency level.

Future Directions

Although research on accuracy has evolved substantially since the 1970s, more challenges lie ahead. First, accuracy in LCR has thus far mainly been studied by investigating the impact of one independent factor (mainly the mother tongue background or the proficiency level) on resulting error profiles. It is suggested that adopting multi-factorial research designs (Gries, 2015) in the study of accuracy is a way forward for LCR. The rich metadata provided in learner corpora make them an ideal testbed to study the combined impact of multiple independent variables on accuracy profiles (e.g. the combined effect of both the mother tongue background and the proficiency level on accuracy, as well as the impact of task complexity factors).

The time has also come for LCR to adopt a more integrative approach to the study of accuracy which means studying it alongside complexity and fluency. LCR has, on the whole, tended to treat each of the CAF constructs independently of each other in what Larsen-Freeman (2009) calls a "reductionist approach" (p. 582). While this has been useful to help advance our understanding of each concept separately, we still know very little about the interactions between CAF in LCR. Concretely, this could be done by carrying out detailed qualitative analyses of the contexts in which errors actually occur. For instance, Thewissen and Anishchanka (2019) recently found that verb-agreement errors (e.g. *he say) from B1 to C2 frequently occurred in syntactically complex environments (e.g. in subordinate and relative clauses, following complex noun phrases, etc.), meaning that syntactically complex L2 contexts do indeed trigger certain lapses in accuracy.

Further Reading

Foster, P., & Wigglesworth, G. (2016). Capturing accuracy in second language performance: The case for a weighted clause ratio. *Annual Review of Applied Linguistics, 36*, 98–116.

This article reviews the variety of global and local accuracy measures used in SLA before presenting the weighted clause ratio measure.

Polio, C. (2012). The relevance of second language acquisition theory to the written error correction debate. *Journal of Second Language Writing, 21*(4), 375–389.

This paper discusses written error correction from the perspective of various SLA theories and what they have to say about the written error correction debate.

Polio, C., & Shea, M. (2014). An investigation into current measures of linguistic accuracy in second language writing research. *Journal of Second Language Writing, 26*(1), 10–27.

This is a description of accuracy measures used in recent SLA research. The paper argues that interrater reliability and detailed coding guidelines are still underreported. The authors applied those measures to their own data set to test their reliability.

Related Topics

Chapters 7, 13, 14, 15, and 21.

Notes

1 These concepts were initially proposed by usage-based theorists in reference to the "basic variety" of interlanguage, namely learners in the early stages of acquisition in naturalistic settings. They also go some way towards explaining the errors made by intermediate to advanced learners in instructional settings.
2 Teaching Resource Extraction from an Annotated Corpus of Learner English.
3 See Díez-Bedmar and Pérez-Paredes (2012) for other LCR accuracy measures such as 'effective use' and 'effective selection'.
4 POS taggers may perform rather poorly on lower proficiency learner data. However, they have been found to perform well on upper-intermediate to advanced learner data (Van Rooy & Schäfer, 2003).
5 The fact that many teachers around the world annotated the texts for errors raises the question of the reliability of the annotation.

References

Albrechtsen, D., Henriksen, B., & Faerch, C. (1980). Native speaker reactions to learners' spoken interlanguage. *Language Learning, 30*(2), 365–396.

Alexopoulou, T., Michel, M., Murakami, A., & Meurers, D. (2017). Task effects on linguistic complexity and accuracy: A large-scale learner corpus analysis employing natural language processing techniques. *Language Learning, 67*(1), 180–208.

Andreu, M., Astor, A., Boquera, M., MacDonald, P., Montero, B., & Pérez, C. (2010). Analysing EFL learner output in the MiLC project: An error it's*, but which tag? In M. C. Campoy, B. Belles-Fortuno, & M. L. Gea-Valor (Eds.), *Corpus-based approaches to English language teaching* (pp. 167–179). London: Continuum.

Bley-Vroman, R. (1983). The comparative fallacy in interlanguage studies: The case of systematicity. *Language Learning, 33*(1), 1–17.

Brand, C., & Götz, S. (2011). Fluency versus accuracy in advanced spoken learner language: A multi-method approach. *International Journal of Corpus Linguistics, 16*(2), 255–275.

Brown, R. (1973). *A first language: The early stages*. Cambridge, MA: Harvard University Press.

Corder, S. P. (1971). Idiosyncratic dialects and error analysis. In J. Richards (Ed.), *Error analysis: Perspectives on second language acquisition* (pp. 19–27). London: Longman.

Craven, L. (2017). Measuring language performance: Complexity, accuracy and fluency measures. In *West east institute international academic conference proceedings* (pp. 25–27). Barcelona: WEI.

Dagneaux, E., Denness, S., & Granger, S. (1998). Computer-aided error analysis. *System, 26*(2), 163–174.

de Bot, K., Lowie, W., & Verspoor, M. (2007). A dynamic systems theory approach to second language acquisition. *Bilingualism: Language and Cognition, 10*(1), 7–21.

Díez-Bedmar, M. B. (2015). Article use and criterial features in Spanish EFL writing: A pilot study from CEFR Benjamins. A2 to B2 levels. In M. Callies & S. Götz (Eds.), *Learner corpora in language testing and assessment* (pp. 163–190). Amsterdam: John Benjamins.

Díez-Bedmar, M. B., & Papp, S. (2008). The use of the English article system by Chinese and Spanish learners. In G. Gilquin, S. Papp, & M. B. Díez-Bedmar (Eds.), *Linking up contrastive and learner corpus research* (pp. 147–175). Amsterdam: Rodopi.

Díez-Bedmar, M. B., & Pérez-Paredes, P. (2012). A cross-sectional analysis of the use of the English article system in Spanish learner writing. In Y. Tono, Y. Kawaguchi, & M. Minegishi (Eds.), *Developmental and cross-linguistic perspectives in learner corpus research* (pp. 139–158). Amsterdam: John Benjamins.

Dulay, H., & Burt, M. (1974). Natural sequences in child second language acquisition. *Language Learning*, *24*(1), 37–53.

Ellis, N. C., & Sagarra, N. (2010). The bounds of adult language acquisition: Blocking and learned attention. *Studies in Second Language Acquisition*, *32*(4), 553–580.

Ellis, N. C., & Wulff, S. (2014). Usage-based approaches to. In S. L. A. In, B. VanPatten, & J. Williams (Eds.), *Theories in second language acquisition: An introduction* (pp. 75–93). New York: Routledge.

Evans, N. K., Hartshorn, K. J., Cox, T. L., & de Jel, T. M. (2014). Measuring written linguistic accuracy with weighted clause ratios: A question of validity. *Journal of Second Language Writing*, *24*(1), 33–50.

Foster, P., & Wigglesworth, G. (2016). Capturing accuracy in second language performance: The case for a weighted clause ratio. *Annual Review of Applied Linguistics*, *36*, 98–116.

Geertzen, J., Alexopoulou, T., & Korhonen, A. (2014). Automatic linguistic annotation of large scale L2 databases: The EF-Cambridge Open Language Database (EFCAMDAT). In R. T. Millar et al. (Eds.), *Selected proceedings of the 2012 second language research forum. Building bridges between disciplines* (pp. 240–254). Cascadilla Proceedings Project.

Gilquin, G., & De Cock, S. (2011). Errors and disfluencies in spoken corpora: Setting the scene. *International Journal of Corpus Linguistics*, *16*(2), 141–172.

Götz, S. (2015). Tense and aspect errors in spoken learner language: Implications for language testing and assessment. In M. Callies & S. Götz (Eds.), *Learner corpora in language testing and assessment* (pp. 191–215). Amsterdam: John Benjamins.

Gráf, T. (2017). Verb errors in advanced learner English. *Acta Universitatis Carolinae, Philologica/Prague Studies in English*, *1*, 131–149.

Granger, S., Dagneaux, E., Meunier, F., & Paquot, M. (2009). *The international corpus of learner English. Handbook and CD-ROM. Version 2*. Louvain-la-Neuve: Presses universitaires de Louvain.

Granger, S., Meunier, F., Neff, J., Swallow, H., & Thewissen, J. (2008). *The Louvain error tagging manual. Version 2.0*. Louvain-la-Neuve: Centre for English Corpus Linguistics, Université catholique de Louvain.

Granger, S., & Paquot, M. (in press). *Université catholique de Louvain Error Editor - UCLEE User guide (2.0 version)*. Louvain-la-Neuve: Centre for English Corpus Linguistics, Université catholique de Louvain.

Gries, S. Th. (2015). Statistics for learner corpus research. In S. Granger, G. Gilquin, & F. Meunier (Eds.), *The Cambridge handbook of learner corpus research* (pp. 159–181). Cambridge: Cambridge University Press.

Hakuta, K. (1976). A case study of a Japanese child learning English as a second language. *Language Learning*, *26*(2), 321–351.

Hawkins, J., & Buttery, P. (2010). Criterial features in learner corpora: Theory and illustrations. *English Profile Journal*, *1*(1), 1–23.

Hawkins, J., & Filipović, L. (2012). *Criterial features in the learning of English: Specifying the reference levels of the common European framework*. Cambridge: Cambridge University Press.

Housen, A., & Kuiken, F. (2009). Complexity, accuracy, and fluency in second language acquisition. *Applied Linguistics*, *30*(4), 461–473.

Jenkins, J. (2006). Points of view and blind spots: ELF and SLA. *International Journal of Applied Linguistics*, *16*(2), 137–291.

Krashen, S. (1977). Some issues relating to the monitor model. In H. D. Brown, C. Yorio, & R. Crymes (Eds.), *On TESOL '77: Teaching and learning English as a second language: Trends in research and practice* (pp. 144–158). Washington: TESOL.

Lado, R. (1957). *Linguistics across cultures*. Ann Arbor: University of Michigan Press.

Lantolf, J., & Thorne, S. L. (2007). Sociocultural theory and second language learning. In B. van Patten & J. Williams (Eds.), *Theories in second language acquisition* (pp. 201–224). Mahwah: Lawrence Erlbaum.

Larsen-Freeman, D. (2009). Adjusting expectations: The study of complexity, accuracy, and fluency in second language acquisition. *Applied Linguistics*, *30*(4), 579–589.

Lennon, P. (1991). Error: Some problems of definition, identification, and distinction. *Applied Linguistics*, *12*(2), 180–196.

Long, M. H. (1981). Input, interaction, and second language acquisition. *Annals of the New York Academy of Sciences*, *379*, 259–278.

Lüdeling, A., & Hirschmann, H. (2015). Error annotation systems. In G. Gilquin, S. Granger, & F. Meunier (Eds.), *The Cambridge handbook of learner corpus research* (pp. 135–158). Cambridge: Cambridge University Press.

Meunier, F., & Littré, D. (2013). Tracking learners' progress: Adopting a dual 'corpus cum experimental data' approach. *Modern Language Journal*, *97*(1), 61–76.

Murakami, A., & Alexopoulou, T. (2016). L1 influence on the acquisition order of English grammatical morphemes. A learner corpus study. *Studies in Second Language Acquisition*, *38*(3), 365–401.

Norris, J. M., & Ortega, L. (2009). Towards an organic approach to investigating CAF in instructed SLA: The case of complexity. *Applied Linguistics*, *330*(4), 555–578.

O'Donnell, M. (2008). The UAM CorpusTool: Software for corpus annotation and exploration. In B. Callejas & M. Carmen (Eds.), *Applied linguistics now: Understanding language and mind* (pp. 1433–1447). Almería: Universidad de Almería.

O'Donnell, M., Murcia, S., García, R., Molina, C., Rollinson, P., MacDonald, P., … Boquera, M. (2009). Exploring the proficiency of English learners: The TREACLE project. In M. Mahlberg, V. González-Díaz, & C. Smith (Eds.). *Proceedings of the fifth corpus linguistics* (pp. 20–23). Liverpool: University of Liverpool.

Pica, T. (1984). Methods of morpheme quantification: Their effect on the interpretation of second language data. *Studies in Second Language Acquisition*, *6*(1), 69–78.

Pienemann, M. (1998). *Language processing and second language development: Processability theory*. Amsterdam: John Benjamins.

Polio, C. (2012). The relevance of second language acquisition theory to the written error correction debate. *Journal of Second Language Writing*, *21*(4), 375–389.

Polio, C., & Shea, M. (2014). An investigation into current measures of linguistic accuracy in second language writing research. *Journal of Second Language Writing*, *26*(1), 10–27.

Robinson, P. (2001). Task complexity, cognitive resources, and syllabus design: A triadic framework for examining task influences on. In S. L. A. In & P. Robinson (Ed.), *Cognition and second language instruction* (pp. 287–318). Cambridge: Cambridge University Press.

Rollinson, P., & Mendikoetxea, A. (2010). Learner corpora and second language acquisition: Introducing WriCLE. In J. L. Bueno Alonso et al. (Eds.), *Analizar datos: Describir variación/Analysing data: Describing variation* (pp. 1–12). Vigo: Universidade de Vigo (Servizo de Publicacións).

Rosmawati, R. (2014). Dynamic development of complexity and accuracy: A case study in second language academic writing. *Australian Review of Applied Linguistics*, *37*(2), 75–100.

Russell, J., & Spada, N. (2006). The effectiveness of corrective feedback for the acquisition of L2 grammar: A meta-analysis of the research. In J. M. Norris & L. Ortega (Eds.), *Synthesizing research on language learning and teaching* (pp. 133–164). Amsterdam: John Benjamins Publishing Company.

Sachs, R., & Polio, C. (2007). Learners' uses of two types of corrective feedback on a L2 writing revision task. *Studies in Second Language Acquisition*, *29*(1), 67–100.

Shintani, N., & Ellis, R. (2013). The comparative effect of direct written corrective feedback and metalinguistic explanation on learners' explicit and implicit knowledge of the English indefinite article. *Journal of Second Language Writing*, *22*(3), 286–306.

Skehan, P. (1989). *Individual differences in second language learning*. London: Edward Arnold.

Thewissen, J. (2013). Capturing L2 accuracy developmental patterns: Insights from an error-tagged EFL learner corpus. *Modern Language Journal*, *97*(1), 77–101.

Thewissen, J. (2015). *Accuracy across proficiency levels: A learner corpus approach (Vol. 2. corpora and language in use)*. Louvain-la-Neuve: Presses universitaires de louvain.

Thewissen, J., & Anishchanka, A. (2019, September 13). An integrative approach to L2 accuracy and complexity development. Paper presented at the 5th learner corpus research conference. University of Warsaw, Poland.

Truscott, J. (1996). The case against grammar correction in L2 writing classes. *Language Learning*, *46*(2), 327–369.

Van Rooy, B., & Schäfer, L. (2003). Automatic POS tagging of a learner corpus: The influence of learner error on tagger accuracy. In D. Archer, P. Wilson, & T. McEnery (Eds.). *Proceedings of the corpus linguistics 2003 conference* (pp. 835–844). UCREL, Lancaster University (England).

Verspoor, M., Schmid, M., & Xu, X. (2012). A dynamic usage-based perspective on L2 writing. *Journal of Second Language Writing*, *21*(3), 239–263.

Wigglesworth, G., & Storch, N. (2009). Pair vs. individual writing: Effects on fluency, complexity, and accuracy. *Language Testing*, *26*(3), 445–466.

Wolfe-Quintero, K., Inagaki, S., & Kim, H.-Y. (1998). Second language development in writing: Measures of fluency, accuracy, and complexity. Technical report No. 17. University of Hawai'i, Second Language Teaching and Curriculum Centre, Honolulu.

Wulff, S., & Ellis, N. C. (2018). Usage-based approaches to. In S. L. A. In, D. Miller, F. Bayram, J. Rothman, & L. Serratrice (Eds.), *Bilingual cognition and language: The state of the science across its subfields* (pp. 37–56). Amsterdam: John Benjamins.

Wulff, S., & Gries, S. Th. (2011). Corpus-driven methods for assessing accuracy in learner production. In P. Robinson (Ed.), *Second language task complexity: Researching the cognition hypothesis of language learning and performance* (pp. 61–87). Amsterdam: John Benjamins.

24

Complexity

Nina Vyatkina and Alex Housen

Introduction

In the past few decades, the notion of complexity has raised significant interest in a wide range of disciplines, including Second Language Acquisition (SLA) research. Already in the 1970s and 1980s, the notions of *complexification* and its antonym, *simplification,* figured prominently in the first theoretical models of SLA (e.g., Andersen, 1983). Skehan (1989) was the first to propose a model of SLA that added complexity as one of three basic dimensions (with accuracy and fluency) in terms of which L2 learners' performance, proficiency, and development could be investigated (see also Chapters 22 and 23, this volume). At that time, L2 complexity was also given its working definition, which is still widely used today, as the range of forms (i.e. items, structures, patterns, rules) available to a learner and the degree of elaboration of these forms (Ortega, 2003).

Complexity has been measured by means of (subjective) ratings and, more typically, (objective) quantitative measures, of which there are many (see reviews in Ortega, 2003; Wolfe-Quintero, Inagaki, & Kim, 1998). Early studies of L2 complexity (1970s–early 2000s) typically handled a limited amount of learner language, as most coding of complexity indicators was conducted manually. The measures were limited to a handful of global, broad measures such as average length of syntactic units (sentences, T-units, clauses) in words and amount of embedding (ratio of subordinate clauses to total clauses). Higher values of these measures were found to be associated with higher L2 proficiency. However, the progress in complexity research was slowing down at the turn of the century, due to its narrow focus on a few measures, lack of theoretical motivation for these measures, and other methodological limitations. The seminal article by Norris and Ortega (2009) triggered a new wave of interest with their call for a more 'organic approach' to the study of L2 complexity. In particular, Norris and Ortega invited researchers to supplement global, coarse-grained measures (e.g., mean length of sentence, clauses per T-unit) with finer-grained, more specific measures of phrasal and clausal complexity (e.g., infinitival phrases, passives) and to explore the dynamic relationships among different measures at different stages of L2 development. They also called for building connections to corpus linguistics. This call was echoed by Bulté and Housen (2012), who reviewed 40 studies (1995–2008) and concluded that the majority had used 1–2 complexity measures only, "probably due to the lack of adequate computational tools for automatic complexity measurement and the labour-intensiveness of manual computation" (p. 34).

The situation changed drastically in the 2010s with the development of Natural Language Processing (NLP) tools (especially those with open access) that expanded the repertoire of complexity measures as well as enabled automatic retrieval and analysis of large amounts of language production data from learner corpora. Recently, the field has seen an exponential growth of studies that explored SLA-motivated research questions with Learner Corpus Research (LCR) tools and methods. Rich and nuanced analyses have revealed a more intricate picture of L2 complexity and its development over time, have pointed to significant effects of various learner, register, and task variables, and have prompted researchers to take a more critical look at L2 complexity as a construct.

It is worth noting that it is not always easy to distinguish between LCR and non-LCR L2 complexity studies. Many studies have been conducted on learner production data not characterized by authors as learner corpora. The difference between such data pools (or convenience corpora) and learner corpora seems to be that the former are smaller in size, limited in terms of registers and text types, and collected and utilized only for a specific study (or a few studies), with no declared intent of making them available to a larger research community – which is typical of learner corpora.

Core Issues and Topics

Defining L2 Complexity

Empirical L2 research on complexity has produced many inconsistent and inconclusive results (Bulté & Housen, 2012; Pallotti, 2015). The problematic status of the complexity construct in SLA research is mainly due to its complex (i.e. multidimensional, multi-faceted, and multilayered) nature and its resultant polysemy. Indeed, the term complex(ity) has been equated with a seemingly disparate variety of terms such as (more) advanced, late(r) acquired, (more) developed, (more) proficient, (more) sophisticated, (more) challenging, (more) difficult, (more) problematic, (more) elaborate, (more) embedded, (more) frequent, long(er), rare(r), (more) marked, (more) diverse or varied, rich(er), better, and (more) mature. The question is whether all these terms refer to one and the same underlying construct or to conceptually distinct and analytically separable constructs that may or may not be empirically (cor)related. To overcome this terminological confusion, researchers have recently called for a more parsimonious approach to defining L2 complexity strictly in terms of *absolute complexity*, which refers to quantitative properties of linguistic structures or systems, as reflected by the number and range of phonemic, lexical, syntactic, or morphological items, structures, or rules in a language (Bulté & Housen, 2012). The overwhelming majority of studies have used syntactic or lexical complexity measures, or combinations thereof, whereas interest in other measures (e.g., morphological complexity) started emerging only recently.

L2 Complexity Measures As Indicators of L2 Proficiency and Development

Syntactic Complexity

Syntactic complexity has been the most popular construct, defined as breadth (length, diversity) and depth (embeddedness) of syntactic units: T-units, AS-units, sentences, clauses, and phrases (Bulté & Housen, 2012, p. 27). The overwhelming majority of syntactic complexity studies have based their findings on the material of academic L2 English essays written by university students. Ortega's (2003) meta-analysis of 25 pre-corpus era (1975–1998) SLA studies found that values of four measures linearly increased with increasing proficiency: mean length of sentence (MLS), mean length of T-unit (MLTU), mean length of clause (MLC), and clauses per T-unit (C/TU).

She also found that for these measures to significantly discriminate between proficiency levels, at least one year of instructed study was necessary.

Ortega (2003) has cautioned that her meta-analysis was limited to global syntactic complexity metrics and invited researchers to explore more specific metrics as well as their dynamic relationships in future studies. Norris and Ortega (2009) later hypothesized that the generally attested developmental increase in values of the most global measures – MLS and MLTU – was caused by growth in different lower-level measures at different L2 proficiency levels: coordination at beginning levels, subordination at intermediate levels, and phrasal elaboration at advanced levels.

Subsequent LCR studies have largely confirmed this hypothesis. Byrnes, Maxim, and Norris (2010) analyzed a corpus of learner essays written at the end of four curricular levels of a US university L2 German program both cross-sectionally and longitudinally. In both designs, they found a significant increase in the sentence length over all levels, whereas subordination increased up to level 3 (intermediate proficiency) and then plateaued, and mean length of clause (attributed to noun phrase complexification) started increasing only at the juncture between levels 2 and 3 (thus marking a transition to more advanced proficiency). While Byrnes et al. (2010) coded their data manually for only three global measures, subsequent LCR studies have employed multiple measures of both global and specific syntactic complexity using NLP tools. Lu (2010) introduced his L2 Syntactic Complexity Analyzer (SCA) for 14 such measures and applied them to a corpus of academic essays of Chinese learners of English. He found that higher proficiency learners produced longer clauses and T-units as a result of increased use of complex phrases (coordinate phrases and complex nominals). These findings were further expanded by multidimensional LCR studies (see section *Task Effects / Register Differences*).

Lexical Complexity

Lexical complexity (Bulté & Housen, 2012, p. 28) has been defined as lexical breadth, subdivided into density (ratio of lexical to function words) and diversity (type-token ratio or TTR), and depth, subdivided into compositionality (morphemes or syllables per word) and sophistication (ratio of rare words). TTR was the first automatically calculated lexical measure to be used in L2 complexity research. However, its validity has been questioned because of heavy dependence on text length, and adjusted TTR as well as other diversity measures have been proposed instead, such as the Measure of Textual Lexical Diversity (MTLD, McCarthy & Jarvis, 2010).

Gradually, with the development of NLP tools, researchers started applying a wide range of lexical measures to the study of L2 complexity. The L2 Lexical Complexity Analyzer (LCA; Lu, 2012) automatically computes 25 lexical measures. Lu (2012) applied it to a spoken L2 English (L1 Chinese) corpus and found that several measures of lexical diversity, but not density or sophistication, correlated with holistic measures of text quality. Lexical diversity measures were also stronger proficiency predictors in a cross-sectional learner corpus of L2 French and L2 English (L1 Dutch) oral narratives (De Clercq, 2015) and better short-term development indicators in L2 English written descriptive essays (Bulté & Housen, 2014) than other types of lexical measures. Furthermore, longitudinal LCR studies have shown that lexical diversity develops in a curvilinear rather than a linear fashion; a steep initial increase is followed by a gradual flattening of the curve (Daller, Turlik, & Weir, 2013; Mitchell, Tracy-Ventura, & McManus, 2017).

Combining Syntactic and Lexical Measures

L2 complexity studies that combined both syntactic and lexical complexity measures generally found that "different subcomponents of syntactic and lexical complexity [...] develop at a different pace" (Bulté & Housen, 2014, p. 42). In a cross-sectional study of L2 English (L1 Dutch) written narratives with 64 hand-coded complexity and accuracy measures, Verspoor, Schmid, and Xu (2012) found that significant differences between adjacent proficiency levels alternated between lexical and syntactic measures. Longitudinal studies showed similar results. Verspoor, Lowie, and van Dijk (2008) explored the writing of an advanced L2 English learner over three years from the Complex Dynamic Systems Theory standpoint (see Chapter 14, this volume). They found that, despite an overall increase in global syntactic (MLS) and lexical complexity (TTR), there were considerable peaks and dips in the growth curve. Furthermore, dips in lexical complexity were accompanied by peaks in syntactic complexity and vice versa, and only at the end of the observation period did both types of measures develop in unison.

Morphological Complexity

Investigations of morphological complexity in L2 corpora have been taken up only recently. One such study is De Clercq and Housen (2019),which is presented in the section *Representative Corpora and Research*. Another study is Brezina and Pallotti (2019), who built on the Morphological Complexity Index (MCI): the diversity of morphological exponents (the forms taken by lexemes to express grammatical categories and functions) in a text sample (Pallotti, 2015). Brezina and Pallotti developed an automated, web-based version of the MCI analyzer which they applied to two corpora of argumentative written texts from native and non-native speakers of Italian and English (respectively, a morphologically rich and poor language). They found that MCI varied between native and non-native speakers of Italian and was significantly lower in lower proficiency learner samples. In L2 Italian, MCI was strongly correlated with proficiency and also showed significant correlations with other measures of complexity, such as lexical diversity and sentence length. However, when applied to a corpus of advanced L2 English learners, MCI remained constant across natives and learners and did not correlate with other complexity measures. These results suggest that morphological L2 complexity is a function of speakers' proficiency and the specific language under investigation; for languages with a relatively simple inflectional morphology, such as English, learners will quickly reach a threshold level after which inflectional morphological diversity remains constant.

Lexico-grammatical Complexity

Whereas the studies reviewed above consider complexity measures at different linguistic levels as tapping into distinct constructs, others have assumed an integrated view of complexity as a lexico-grammatical construct. Paquot (2019) has introduced the construct of *phraseological* complexity, operationally defined as the diversity of phraseological units in text samples (type-token ratio of specific words co-occurring in grammatical relations, e.g., adjective + noun, verb + direct object) and the sophistication of those units (the mutual information score of these units). Paquot found that these lexico-grammatical measures reliably discriminated between upper-intermediate to advanced proficiency levels in a written L2 English corpus, unlike separate syntactic and lexical complexity measures.

Researchers working in the usage-based *construction grammar* paradigm (see Chapter 13, this volume) also argue that complexity measures should integrate both grammatical and lexical properties. Kyle (2016) and Kyle, Crossley, and Berger (2017) developed TAASSC and TAALES – automated syntactic and lexical complexity analyzers for English – that offer, in addition to traditional measures (such as ones in Lu's SCA and LCA), an impressive range of usage-based measures. What sets these measures apart from traditional ones is their interface nature; they go beyond length, frequency, and ratios of discrete syntactic and lexical elements and take into account frequency of occurrence of lexical items within specific syntactic constructions as well as strength of association between lexical items and constructions. In a series of recent studies, Kyle and colleagues applied TAASSC and TAALES to the learner corpus of TOEFL exams and found that usage-based measures, especially at the phrasal level, predicted learner writing quality better than traditional measures (Kyle & Crossley, 2018; Kim, Crossley & Kyle, 2018). These usage-based studies were in part informed by functional multi-dimensional approaches to corpus research reviewed in the next section.

Task Effects

The definition of task (not unlike complexity) has been the subject of much SLA debate that is beyond the scope of this chapter (see, e.g., Robinson, 2011; Skehan, 1998). For our purposes here, we consider task effects associated with several design features of learner language data elicitation procedures applied in L2 complexity research: *register* and *cognitive task complexity*.

Register Differences

Register differences have been extensively studied by Biber and colleagues in their L1 corpus research spanning several decades since the 1980s (Biber, 1988). Their approach was termed functional and multidimensional because it showed that multiple heterogeneous linguistic units (e.g., syntactic units, parts-of-speech, semantic word classes, lexical items) co-occur in specific registers to express certain communicative functions (see Chapter 18, this volume). A designated NLP tool, the *Biber Tagger* (Biber, 1988, see also Nini, 2014), was developed for annotating corpora for a wide range of these features. As far as linguistic complexity is concerned, the researchers have argued that its nature depends on the register: e.g., longer phrases and sentences are needed to express arguments, whereas multiple and varied subordinate clauses are needed in narration (e.g., Biber & Gray, 2010). Based on these findings from L1 English corpora, Biber, Gray, and Poonpon (2011) also hypothesized that L2 writing should exhibit spoken complexity features at beginning proficiency levels and written complexity features at later stages (which was in line with SLA studies like Norris & Ortega, 2009, discussed above). This assumption was confirmed by Taguchi, Crawford, and Wetzel (2013) and Parkinson and Musgrave (2014), who found more noun modifiers and fewer dependent clauses in the writing of more proficient L2 English learners. Biber, Gray, and Staples (2016) explored the corpus of spoken and written TOEFL exam productions and found that not only mode and register but also L2 proficiency were robust predictors of two sets of lexico-grammatical features, one characterizing the orate and the other the literate dimension. For example, written texts, informational summaries, and higher-rated texts had more nouns, nominalizations, and noun phrase modifiers, whereas spoken texts, personal accounts, and lower-rated texts had more finite adverbial clauses and adverbs. Yoon and Polio (2017) found similar register-related effects in a written ESL corpus: namely, MLS and phrasal complexity were higher in argumentative than in narrative essays. Furthermore, lexical sophistication and richness was higher in argumentative essays, whereas lexical diversity was higher in narrative essays.

Cognitive Task Complexity

The effects of cognitive task complexity (Robinson, 2011; Skehan, 1998) on the complexity of language production have received considerable attention in Task-Based Language Teaching (TBLT) SLA studies (e.g., Ellis, 2005; Kuiken & Vedder, 2012; Lambert & Kormos, 2014; Révész, Kourtali, & Mazgutova, 2017; Vasylets, Gilabert, & Manchón, 2017). Collectively, this research indicated that cognitively more complex tasks (in terms of reasoning demands made on the learner), written tasks, and tasks that allow for pre-task or online planning tend to result in syntactically and lexically more complex language (e.g., more subordination, longer clauses and sentences, more diverse and sophisticated vocabulary). On the other hand, some results were inconsistent across studies, as shown in Bulté and Housen's (2012) review of 40 TBLT studies on complexity.

Until recently, there has been little overlap between TBLT research and LCR because data elicitation tasks in the available larger learner corpora have not been differentiated by nuanced task complexity conditions (Alexopoulou, Michel, Murakami, & Meurers, 2017). Alexopoulou et al. (2017) classified essay prompts in the EFCAMDAT corpus from three registers *post hoc* according to the level of cognitive load each task imposed on the learner. They found the register effect to be stronger than the cognitive load effect: i.e., complexity values were similar within one register for both the simple and difficult prompt. More specifically, the authors found that narratives were more complex than descriptions based on three global syntactic complexity measures (MLS, MLC, C/TU) and the MTLD (lexical measure).

L1 and L2 Effects

Most L2 complexity studies reviewed above have been conducted on ESL learner productions with only a few representatives from different L1s which has made it impossible to explore L1 and L2 effects. Crossley and McNamara (2012) was one of the first LCR studies that focused on the L1 variable. They found that lexical complexity measures were the strongest predictor for L1 identification, but that syntactic phrasal complexity also distinguished between four L1 groups from the ICLE corpus. Lu and Ai (2015) conducted a comparative study on a larger scale and found that all 14 syntactic measures from Lu's SCA tool reliably discriminated among ICLE essays from seven L1 groups as well as L1 English essays. Research of the L2 effect also shows that complexity develops differently in the acquisition of different languages (see Housen, De Clercq, Kuiken, & Vedder, 2019). Future LCR studies that would tie L1 and L2 effects on complexity to differences in linguistic typology are needed (Miestamo, 2008).

Main Research Methods

Methods

As can be inferred from the review above, learner corpus complexity research has typically been quantitative in nature. Most studies have been cross-sectional, although a recent trend toward more longitudinal research can be observed. Early L2 complexity studies have applied t-tests and ANOVAs to compare cross-sections of L2 data, as was typical of SLA research in general. More recently, there has been a gradual shift in both SLA and LCR to multifactorial methods (see Chapters 8 and 9, this volume, for more information). For example, Biber et al. (2016) used a factor analysis with General Linear Models to group complexity features and to explore which independent variables (mode, register, proficiency) predicted co-occurrence of these features. Kim et al. (2018) used a Principal Component Analysis to cluster complexity measures that were highly correlated with each other into groups and to then reduce the variables to a smaller set of derived variables. In a longitudinal study, Chan, Verspoor, and Vahtrick (2015) applied the Hidden Markov Model to explore the development of complexity in L2 speech and writing of two identical twins. With the help of this non-linear method, the authors found that values for specific complexity measures changed dynamically and that developmental paths of the twins differed drastically (contrary to expectations).

Tools

One distinctive characteristic of LCR is the use of NLP tools (Meurers & Dickinson, 2017) for extracting and computing frequencies of linguistic features. The number and variety of these features has been growing exponentially, as reflected in Table 24.1. The use of some tools requires considerable computational expertise whereas others, especially more recent ones, can be used by a regular "teacher, textbook writer, or second language acquisition researcher" due to their "user-friendly interface and visualization features" (Chen & Meurers, 2016, pp. 113–114). It is important to note that, like other NLP tools, complexity analyzers have originally been developed for and trained on texts produced by native speakers, but many have also been applied to learner texts. The accuracy of NLP tools for learner data (i.e., non-standard language data) has been a subject of debate, and complexity analyzers are no exception. For example, while MLS or MLTU can be fairly reliably calculated in learner written texts, lexical diversity ratios may be inflated due to spelling errors or the number of subordinate clauses miscalculated due to lexical or syntactic errors (Meurers & Dickinson, 2017). In a much-needed study of reliability and validity of complexity analyzers, Polio and Yoon (2018) explored the SCA (Lu, 2010) and Coh-Metrix (McNamara, Graesser, McCarthy, & Cai, 2012) tools. They found that the majority of syntactic complexity measures in both tools served as reliable and valid identifiers of register differences in L2 written data, although some measures were not transparent and consistent. Automatic coding and analysis problems are augmented in the case of spoken learner data, which, depending on the transcription format used, typically need to undergo multiple steps of preliminary data segmentation and 'cleaning'.

Representative Corpora and Research

Most research reviewed above was conducted on written L2 English data. To highlight some other corpora and associated studies, this section presents an L2 German corpus and a spoken corpus of three L2s – English, French, and Dutch – that have been analyzed in terms of linguistic complexity.

Falko (*FehlerAnnotiertes LernerKOrpus*) is an error-annotated learner corpus of German as a Foreign Language available with free and open access on the website maintained by the corpus linguistics team at the Humboldt University Berlin (https://www.linguistik.hu-berlin.de/de/institut/professuren/korpuslinguistik/forschung/falko). Falko consists of several German as a Foreign Language subcorpora, all of them comprising academic essays written by learners of German at different universities around the world. What sets Falko apart from other error-annotated learner corpora (e.g., ICLE) is that its texts are annotated on multiple layers including the so-called "target hypotheses", or explicit corrections of learner errors by annotators (see also Chapter 7, this volume). This unique feature of Falko allows for analyzing learner language complexity separately from accuracy. To illustrate this, we review an L2 complexity study conducted on KANDEL (*Kansas Developmental Learner corpus*; Vyatkina, 2016). KANDEL is a Falko subcorpus that comprises short essays collected at dense time intervals from American learners of German as they progressed from no or minimal L2 proficiency to intermediate proficiency over two years of instructed collegiate study.

Vyatkina, Hirschmann, and Golcher (2015) explored KANDEL for the development of a specific type of syntactic complexity, operationally defined as syntactic modification. Modifiers were defined as optional elements that attach to the heads of noun phrases, verb phrases, or sentences. To find surface proxies for modifiers, the corpus was searched for POS tags for attributively and predicatively used adjectives, ordinal numerals, adverbs, subordinating conjunctions, and relative pronouns. However, automated POS-tagging was not applied to raw texts here because many spelling and grammatical mistakes made by beginning learners were expected to lead to many tagger errors. Instead, the "Target Hypothesis 1" annotation layer and its automatically assigned POS-tags were used (see Chapter 5, this volume). These annotations contain minimal corrections of spelling and morpho-syntactic errors to form a grammatical German sentence, while keeping it as close to the original surface structure as possible and leaving semantic, pragmatic, and discourse errors uncorrected (Lüdeling & Hirschmann, 2015; see also Chapter 7, this volume).

Table 24.1 List of Automated Tools for Text Complexity Analysis in Chronological Order of Publication

Title	Website	Target language(s)	Complexity features	Reference
Computerized Language Analysis (CLAN)	https://talkbank.org	English, French, German	Some basic lexical and syntactic (TTR, VOCD, MLT, MLU)	MacWhinney (2000)
The Compleat Lexical Tutor	http://www.lextutor.ca	English, French	Lexical rarity (a sophistication measure)	Cobb (n. d.)
Text Inspector	http://textinspector.com	English	Lexical diversity	Bax (n. d.)
L2 Syntactic Complexity Analyzer	http://www.personal.psu.edu/xxl13/downloads/l2sca.html	English	14 syntactic	Lu (2010)
Lexical Complexity Analyzer	http://www.personal.psu.edu/xxl13/downloads/lca.html	English	25 lexical	Lu (2012)
Coh-Metrix	http://cohmetrix.com	English	100+ lexico-grammatical	McNamara et al. (2012)
T-Scan	https://github.com/proycon/tscan	Dutch	lexical, syntactic, morphological	Pander Maat et al. (2014)
Multidimensional Analysis Tagger	https://sites.google.com/site/multidimensionaltagger/	English	Multiple lexico-grammatical, based on Biber (1988)	Nini (2014)
Lancaster Vocab Analysis Tool (LancsLex)	http://corpora.lancs.ac.uk/vocab/index.php	English	Lexical diversity and rarity	Brezina and Gablasova (2015)
CorpusExplorer	http://corpusexplorer.de	German	45 lexical	Rüdiger (2016)
Tool for the Automatic Analysis of Syntactic Sophistication and Complexity (TAASSC)	https://www.linguisticanalysistools.org/taassc.html	English	Multiple lexico-grammatical	Kyle (2016)
Common Text Analysis Platform (CTAP)	http://www.ctapweb.com/home.html	English (German in development)	170+ lexical and syntactic	Chen and Meurers (2016)
Tool for the Automatic Analysis of Lexical Sophistication (TAALES)	https://www.linguisticanalysistools.org/taales.html	English	400+ lexical	Kyle et al. (2017)
Morpho complexity tool	http://corpora.lancs.ac.uk/vocab/analyse_morph.php	English and Italian (French, German, Spanish in development)	Morphological (one index)	Brezina and Pallotti (2019)

The study found that learners started using syntactic modification from their very first essay written in German, but the frequencies of different modifiers changed as they progressed in their studies. In particular, the increase in more structurally complex (inflected, clausal) modifiers was accompanied by a decrease in less complex modifiers. Furthermore, the growth trends were not linear but curvilinear, with smoother or abrupt curves for different measures. Finally, the instruction did not appear to cause the onset of development or to change its direction but instead to modulate growth curves.

The *Brussels Instructed Language Learner Corpus* (BILLC) consists of oral and written L2 English, French, and Dutch production data, collected both cross-sectionally and longitudinally, from L2 learners from a range of L1 backgrounds (mainly Dutch, French, English, Italian, and German), age levels (child, adolescent, and adult learners) and learning contexts (traditional foreign-language classrooms, CLIL/immersion, European School). This multilingual corpus contains narrative, descriptive, and argumentative texts. The data have been transcribed in the CHAT format (MacWhinney, 2000), segmented into clausal units, and parts of the corpus were error and/or POS annotated. BILLC will be freely online accessible via a Vrije Universiteit Brussel server in the foreseeable future. Studies that have used this corpus for complexity analyses were carried out on a parallel bilingual subcorpus of 100 L2 French and 100 L2 English oral narratives representing four different proficiency levels and collected cross-sectionally from Dutch-speaking 12–18-year-old students learning these two L2s in the Flemish education system. Data from matched native speakers of French and English served as benchmarks for the complexity analyses. De Clercq (2015) and De Clercq and Housen (2017) focused on lexical complexity and syntactic complexity, respectively (see section *Core Issues and Topics*). De Clercq and Housen (2019) focused on morphological complexity; this study will be reviewed here as an illustration.

De Clercq and Housen (2019) examined how and when cross-linguistic differences in the complexity of morphological systems surface in oral L2 productions and to what extent measures of morphological complexity can function as cross-linguistically reliable indices of linguistic development. Additionally, the study compared three recently proposed measures that operationalize the notion of complexity in different ways: the Morphological Complexity Index (MCI; Pallotti, 2015), the Types per Family index (T/F-I; Horst & Collins, 2006), and the measure of Inflectional Diversity (ID; Malvern, Chipere, Richards, & Durán, 2004). While all three measures operationalize complexity as diversity, they differ considerably in scope and in their mathematical operationalization. The study aimed at verifying whether these measures function more effectively as metrics of development in French, a morphologically richer language, than in English, a morphologically poorer language. All three measures were found to increase more strongly and more significantly across the four proficiency levels in French than in English. Contrary to expectations, learners in both languages eventually reached native speaker levels of morphological diversity, although at lower proficiency levels in English than in French.

When comparing the findings of the three measures, considerable differences in attained levels of morphological complexity were found. The range of scores and developmental trends for the ID and MCI measures were the most similar for both target languages, although MCI scores covered a more comparable range in English and French, while scores for ID were overall higher in the French data than in the English data. The scores obtained by the TF-I differed from the other two measures and indicated few differences across proficiency levels and languages. The authors conclude that MCI seems to be best suited for corpora similar to BILLC, especially because it works for shorter texts with a low ratio of word forms to lemmas.

Future Directions

This chapter has highlighted the need for further conceptual clarification and operational refinement of L2 complexity constructs, reliable and valid corpus annotation, and automated retrieval of non-redundant measures. First, existing measures need to be evaluated for their capacity to validly and reliably assess complexity of relatively small text samples, which are typical of L2 data and L2 corpora. Many learner corpora may now be sufficiently large (in terms of the total number of words they contain) but they are frequently made up of short text samples (e.g. only 50–500 words long or even shorter), which detracts from the reliability and the usability of many of the currently available complexity measures. This specific issue of data 'scarcity' in LCR needs to be addressed. On the other hand, LCR is uniquely positioned to take advantage of big data and associated research methods. An example of how large corpora can be used for comparative LCR purposes is Alexopoulou et al. (2017) described in the section *Core Issues and Topics*. Furthermore, in order to better understand the cross-linguistic manifestations of complexity in the course of L2 development, there is a need for massive parallel (or multilingual) learner corpora and computational tools for their analysis. Such massive parallel corpora are now being compiled in language typology research (Cysouw & Wälchli, 2007).

Next, new conceptualizations of L2 linguistic complexity and new measures are needed, including measures based on information-theoretic definitions of complexity (Ehret & Szmrecsanyi, 2019). There is also need to go beyond syntactic and lexical complexity to investigate its other types (morphological complexity, phonological complexity, complexity at the interfaces). While the recent inclusion of morphological diversity measures (such as the MCI, TF-I, and ID discussed in this chapter), syntactic diversity measures (as in De Clercq & Housen, 2019), and phraseological diversity and sophistication (as in Paquot, 2019) is already an important step toward finding valid and cross-linguistically representative and reliable indicators, future research should consider measures beyond diversity and sophistication. For instance, with respect to morphological complexity, L2 research could implement approaches developed in language typology, where studies have also looked at the degree of deviation from a base form, the number of morphological elements in a word (Dammel & Kürschner, 2008), or morphological productivity (Lüdeling, Hirschmann, & Shadrova, 2017). Such a broadening of perspective and scope could also prove informative for the study of a typologically wider range of L2s. Future research should also reach out beyond linguistic complexity and explore other manifestations such as propositional and interactional complexity (Bulté & Housen, 2012; Vasylets et al., 2017).

Finally, given the multicomponential and multidimensional nature of L2 complexity, the restricted scope of individual complexity measures, the non-linear character of individual developmental paths provided on the basis of individual measures, and the complex relationships between the individual measures and components, it may be worthwhile to combine different complexity measures in order to obtain a perhaps less detailed and fine-grained, but more comprehensive picture of overall L2 complexity and its development. Particularly when the aim is to assess (overall) L2 development or proficiency, combined measures have the potential of outperforming individual measures, since they offer a more global picture of L2 complexity. Such an undertaking necessarily involves the reduction of multiple dimensions into a single one and losing detailed information, but on the other hand, single scores have the advantage of being easier to interpret than multiple scores, especially when many distinct dimensions are involved.

To conclude, corpus-based research on L2 complexity has rich potential. Beyond providing yardsticks for L2 development and descriptors of L2 performance, this research can make significant contributions to theory construction in SLA by capturing relevant properties of interlanguage at each developmental stage. LCR studies can also help identify the developmental mechanisms for how and why L2 learners develop L2 features in a particular order. With larger and more representative corpora, a wider range of L2s, learner and task variables, and the application of longitudinal and multidimensional designs and data analysis methods, both LCR and SLA can be propelled into new, mutually enriching directions.

Further Reading

Connor-Linton, J., & Polio, C. (Eds.) (2014). Comparing perspectives on L2 writing: Multiple analyses of a common corpus [Special Issue]. *Journal of Second Language Writing, 26*, 1–9.

This special issue presents five studies of a common corpus of L2 English writing – the Michigan State University (MSU) corpus. The corpus comprises descriptive essays collected from students in an intensive English program at three time points over an academic semester. What sets this volume apart is that the same language data was analyzed from five different perspectives that focus, respectively, on accuracy, collocational strength, manually and automatically annotated complexity measures, and multidimensional analysis. All five studies also explored learner development over time and correlations of linguistic measures with holistic writing quality ratings.

Housen, A., De Clercq, B., Kuiken, F., & Vedder, I. (Eds.) (2019). Linguistic complexity [Special Issue]. *Second Language Research, 35*(1).

This recently published special issue charts new directions in L2 complexity research. Its editorial provides an overview of current methodological practices, discusses interfaces of L2 complexity research with theoretical and typological linguistics, and problematizes existing definitions and operationalizations of the complexity construct. The volume's five empirical studies focus on previously underexplored aspects of L2 complexity: morphological complexity, phraseological variety and sophistication, L1 effects, and compressibility of texts (an information-theoretical concept).

Vyatkina, N. (Ed.) (2015). New developments in the study of L2 writing complexity [Special Issue]. *Journal of Second Language Writing, 29*, 1–2.

The five empirical contributions to this special issue all focus on L2 writing and address the development in lexical and syntactic complexity in L1 English and L2 German, L1 identification of L2 English essays based on complexity measures, complexity in CMC data from the TBLT perspective, as well as advanced writing complexity from the Systemic-Functional Linguistics perspective. Ortega's (2015) extended commentary synthesizes the accomplishments in the field and proposes future research directions.

Related Topics

Chapters 5, 8, 9, 13, 14, 18, 22, and 23.

References

Alexopoulou, T., Michel, M., Murakami, A., & Meurers, D. (2017). Task effects on linguistic complexity and accuracy: A large-scale learner corpus analysis employing natural language processing techniques. *Language Learning, 67*(S1), 180–208.

Andersen, R. (1983). *Pidginization and creolization as language acquisition.* Rowley: Newbury House Publishers.

Bax, S. (n. d.). *Text inspector. [Computer software].* Retrieved from http://textinspector.com

Biber, D. (1988). *Variation across speech and writing.* Cambridge: Cambridge University Press.

Biber, D., & Gray, B. (2010). Challenging stereotypes about academic writing: Complexity, elaboration, explicitness. *Journal of English for Academic Purposes, 9*(1), 2–20.

Biber, D., Gray, B., & Poonpon, K. (2011). Should we use the characteristics of conversation to measure grammatical complexity in L2 writing development? *TESOL Quarterly, 45*(1), 5–35.

Biber, D., Gray, B., & Staples, S. (2016). Predicting patterns of grammatical complexity across language exam task types and proficiency levels. *Applied Linguistics, 37*(5), 639–668.

Brezina, V., & Gablasova, D. (2015). Is there a core general vocabulary? Introducing the new general service list. *Applied Linguistics, 36*(1), 1–22.

Brezina, V., & Pallotti, G. (2019). Morphological complexity in written L2 texts. *Second Language Research, 35*(1), 99–119.

Bulté, B., & Housen, A. (2012). Defining and operationalising L2 complexity. In A. Housen, F. Kuiken, & I. Vedder (Eds.), *Dimensions of L2 performance and proficiency: Complexity, accuracy and fluency in SLA* (pp. 21–46). Amsterdam: John Benjamins.

Bulté, B., & Housen, A. (2014). Conceptualizing and measuring short-term changes in L2 writing complexity. *Journal of Second Language Writing, 26*, 42–65.

Byrnes, H., Maxim, H., & Norris, J. M. (2010). Realizing advanced foreign language writing development in collegiate education: Curricular design, pedagogy, assessment [Monograph]. *Modern Language Journal, 94*(Suppl.1), i-235.

Chan, H., Verspoor, M., & Vahtrick, L. (2015). Dynamic development in speaking versus writing in identical twins. *Language Learning, 65*(2), 298–325.

Chen, X. B., & Meurers, D. (2016). CTAP: A web-based tool supporting automatic complexity analysis. In *Proceedings of the workshop on computational linguistics for linguistic complexity*. Osaka: The International Committee on Computational Linguistics. Retrieved from https://www.aclweb.org/anthology/W16-4113/

Cobb, T. (n. d.). *Compleat lexical tutor. [Computer software]*. Retrieved from http://www.lextutor.ca

Connor-Linton, J., & Polio, C. (Eds.) (2014). Comparing perspectives on L2 writing: Multiple analyses of a common corpus [Special Issue]. *Journal of Second Language Writing, 26*.

Crossley, S. A., & McNamara, D. S. (2012). Detecting the first language of second language writers using automated indices of cohesion, lexical sophistication, syntactic complexity and conceptual knowledge. In S. Jarvis & S. Crossley (Eds.), *Approaching language transfer through text classification: Explorations in the detection-based approach* (pp. 106–126). Bristol: Multilingual Matters.

Cysouw, M., & Wälchli, B. (2007). Parallel texts: Using translational equivalents in linguistic typology. *Language Typology and Universals, 60*(2), 95–99.

Daller, M., Turlik, J., & Weir, I. (2013). Vocabulary acquisition and the learning curve. In S. Jarvis & M. Daller (Eds.), *Vocabulary knowledge: Human ratings and automated measures* (pp. 185–217). Amsterdam: John Benjamins.

Dammel, A., & Kürschner, S. (2008). Complexity in nominal plural allomorphy: A contrastive survey of ten Germanic languages. In M. Miestamo, K. Sinnemäki, & F. Karlsson (Eds.), *Language complexity: Typology, contact, change* (pp. 243–261). Amsterdam: John Benjamins.

De Clercq, B. (2015). The development of lexical complexity in second language acquisition: A cross-linguistic study of L2 French and English. *EUROSLA Yearbook, 15*, 69–94.

De Clercq, B., & Housen, A. (2017). A cross-linguistic perspective on syntactic complexity in L2 development: Syntactic elaboration and diversity. *Modern Language Journal, 101*(2), 315–334.

De Clercq, B., & Housen, A. (2019). The development of morphological complexity: A cross-linguistic study of L2 French and English. *Second Language Research, 35*(1), 71–97.

Ehret, K., & Szmrecsanyi, B. (2019). Compressing learner language: An information-theoretic measure of complexity in SLA production data. texts. *Second Language Research, 35*(1), 23–45.

Ellis, R. (Ed.) (2005). *Planning and task performance in a second language*. Amsterdam: John Benjamins.

Horst, M., & Collins, L. (2006). From faible to strong: How does their vocabulary grow? *Canadian Modern Language Review/ La Revue Canadienne des Langues Vivantes, 63*(1), 83–106.

Housen, A., De Clercq, B., Kuiken, F., & Vedder, I. (Eds.) (2019). Linguistic complexity [Special Issue]. *Second Language Research, 35*(1).

Kim, M., Crossley, S. A., & Kyle, K. (2018). Lexical sophistication as a multidimensional phenomenon: Relations to second language lexical proficiency, development, and writing quality. *Modern Language Journal, 102*(1), 120–141.

Kuiken, F., & Vedder, I. (2012). Syntactic complexity, lexical variation and accuracy as a function of task complexity and proficiency level in L2 writing and speaking. In A. Housen, F. Kuiken, & I. Vedder (Eds.), *Dimensions of L2 performance and proficiency: Complexity, accuracy and fluency in SLA* (pp. 143–170). Amsterdam: John Benjamins.

Kyle, K. (2016). *Measuring syntactic development in L2 writing: Fine grained indices of syntactic complexity and usage-based indices of syntactic sophistication*. Doctoral dissertation. Retrieved from http://scholarworks.gsu.edu/alesl_diss/35

Kyle, K., & Crossley, S. A. (2018). Measuring syntactic complexity in L2 writing using fine-grained clausal and phrasal indices. *Modern Language Journal, 102*(2), 333–349.

Kyle, K., Crossley, S. A., & Berger, C. (2017). The tool for the analysis of lexical sophistication (TAALES): Version 2.0. *Behavior Research Methods, 50*(3) 1–17.

Lambert, C., & Kormos, J. (2014). Complexity, accuracy, and fluency in task-based L2 research: Toward more developmentally based measures of second language acquisition. *Applied Linguistics, 35*(5), 606–614.

Lu, X. (2010). Automatic analysis of syntactic complexity in second language writing. *International Journal of Corpus Linguistics, 15*(4), 474–496.

Lu, X. (2012). The relationship of lexical richness to the quality of ESL learners' oral narratives. *Modern Language Journal, 96*(2), 190–208.

Lu, X., & Ai, H. (2015). Syntactic complexity in college-level English writing: Differences among writers with diverse L1 backgrounds. *Journal of Second Language Writing, 29*, 16–27.

Lüdeling, A., & Hirschmann, H. (2015). Error annotation systems. In S. Granger, F. Meunier, & G. Gilquin (Eds.), *The Cambridge handbook of learner corpus research* (pp. 135–158). Cambridge: Cambridge University Press.

Lüdeling, A., Hirschmann, H., & Shadrova, A. (2017). Linguistic models, acquisition theories, and learner corpora: Morphological productivity in SLA research exemplified by complex verbs in German. *Language Learning, 67*(S1), 96–129.

MacWhinney, B. (2000). *The CHILDES project: Tools for analyzing talk* (3rd ed.). Mahwah: Lawrence Erlbaum Associates.

Malvern, D., Chipere, N., Richards, B., & Durán, P. (2004). *Lexical diversity and language development: Quantification and assessment.* Houndmills: Palgrave Macmillan.

McCarthy, P. M., & Jarvis, S. (2010). MTLD, vocd-D, and HD-D: A validation study of sophisticated approaches to lexical diversity assessment. *Behavior Research Methods, 42*(2), 381–392.

McNamara, D. S., Graesser, A. C., McCarthy, P. M., & Cai, Z. (2012). *Automated evaluation of text and discourse with coh-metrix.* Cambridge: Cambridge University Press.

Meurers, D., & Dickinson, M. (2017). Evidence and interpretation in language learning research: Opportunities for collaboration with computational linguistics. *Language Learning, 67*(S1), 66–95.

Miestamo, M. (2008). Grammatical complexity in a cross-linguistic perspective. In M. Miestamo, K. Sinnemäki, & F. Karlsson (Eds.), *Language complexity: Typology, contact, change* (pp. 23–42). Amsterdam: John Benjamins.

Mitchell, R., Tracy-Ventura, N., & McManus, K. (2017). *Anglophone students abroad: Identity, social relationships and language learning.* New York: Routledge.

Nini, A. (2014). *Multidimensional analysis tagger 1.2: manual.* Retrieved from http://sites.google.com/site/multidimensionaltagger

Norris, J. M., & Ortega, L. (2009). Towards an organic approach to investigating CAF in instructed SLA: The case of complexity. *Applied Linguistics, 30*(4), 555–578.

Ortega, L. (2003). Syntactic complexity measures and their relationship to L2 proficiency: A research synthesis of college-level L2 writing. *Applied Linguistics, 24*(4), 492–518.

Ortega, L. (2015). Syntactic complexity in L2 writing: Progress and expansion. *Journal of Second Language Writing, 29,* 82–94.

Pallotti, G. (2015). A simple view of linguistic complexity. *Second Language Research, 31*(1), 117–134.

Pander Maat, H., Kraf, R., van den Bosch, A., Dekker, N., van Gompel, M., Kleijn, S., Sanders, T., & van der Sloot, K. (2014). T-scan: A new tool for analyzing Dutch text. *Computational Linguistics in the Netherlands Journal, 4,* 53–74.

Paquot, M. (2019). The phraseological dimension in interlanguage complexity research. *Second Language Research, 35*(1), 121–145.

Parkinson, J., & Musgrave, J. (2014). Development of noun phrase complexity in the writing of English for academic purposes students. *Journal of English for Academic Purposes, 14,* 48–59.

Polio, C., & Yoon, H.-J. (2018). The reliability and validity of automated tools for examining variation in syntactic complexity across genres. *International Journal of Applied Linguistics, 28*(1), 165–188.

Révész, A., Kourtali, N.-E., & Mazgutova, D. (2017). Effects of task complexity on L2 writing behaviors and linguistic complexity. *Language Learning, 67*(1), 208–241.

Robinson, P. (2011). *Second language task complexity: Researching the cognition hypothesis of language learning and performance.* Amsterdam: John Benjamins.

Rüdiger, J. O. (2016). *Corpus explorer V2.0. [Computer software].* Retrieved from http://corpusexplorer.de

Skehan, P. (1989). *Individual differences in second language learning.* London: Edward Arnold.

Skehan, P. (1998). *A cognitive approach to language learning.* Oxford: Oxford University Press.

Taguchi, N., Crawford, W., & Wetzel, D. Z. (2013). What linguistic features are indicative of writing quality? A case of argumentative essays in a college composition program. *TESOL Quarterly, 47*(2), 420–430.

Vasylets, O., Gilabert, R., & Manchón, R. M. (2017). The effects of mode and task complexity on second language production. *Language Learning, 67*(2), 394–430.

Verspoor, M., Lowie, W., & van Dijk, M. (2008). Variability in second language development from a dynamic systems perspective. *The Modern Language Journal, 92*(2), 214–231.

Verspoor, M., Schmid, M. S., & Xu, X. (2012). A dynamic usage-based perspective on L2 writing. *Journal of Second Language Writing, 21*(3), 239–263.

Vyatkina, N. (Ed.) (2015). New developments in the study of L2 writing complexity [Special Issue]. *Journal of Second Language Writing, 29.*

Vyatkina, N. (2016). KANDEL: A developmental corpus of learner German. *International Journal of Learner Corpus Research, 2*(1), 102–120.

Vyatkina, N., Hirschmann, H., & Golcher, F. (2015). Syntactic modification at early stages of L2 German writing development: A longitudinal learner corpus study. *Journal of Second Language Writing, 29,* 28–50.

Wolfe-Quintero, K., Inagaki, S., & Kim, H.-Y. (1998). *Second language development in writing: Measures of fluency, accuracy, and complexity*. Honolulu: National Foreign Language Resource Center.

Yoon, H., & Polio, C. (2017). ESL students' linguistic development in two written genres. *TESOL Quarterly, 51*(2), 275–301.

25

Lexis

Kristopher Kyle

Introduction

Lexical knowledge is an essential aspect of productive and receptive second language use and has therefore been an important issue in second language acquisition (SLA) research. Researchers have investigated how many words must be learned to complete certain tasks (Hu & Nation, 2000) and which words are the most useful to be learned (Nation & Waring, 1997). Research has also focused on the optimal contexts for lexical acquisition including various types of explicit classroom instruction (Hulstijn & Laufer, 2001) and types of incidental learning such as extensive reading (Pigada & Schmitt, 2006) and extensive viewing (Peters & Webb, 2018). Much work on lexical acquisition has focused on receptive lexical knowledge. However, a growing number of studies have also investigated the development of productive lexical knowledge, both in controlled production tasks (Laufer & Nation, 1999; Webb, 2005) and in free production tasks (Bardel, Gudmundson, & Lindqvist, 2012; Crossley, Salsbury, & McNamara, 2010; Laufer & Nation, 1995).

Corpora have been used for two primary purposes in studies of lexical acquisition. First, corpora such as the *British National Corpus* (BNC; BNC Consortium, 2007) and the *Corpus of Contemporary American English* (COCA; Davies, 2010), which are reference corpora, have been used to model vocabulary use in particular contexts (e.g., the United Kingdom or the United States) or particular registers (e.g., academic language). Such information has been used to create tests of receptive vocabulary knowledge such as the Vocabulary Size Test (Nation & Beglar, 2007) and the Vocabulary Levels Test (McLean & Kramer, 2015; Schmitt, Schmitt, & Clapham, 2001). The use of corpora for the development of assessment tools helps avoid biases from particular individual test item creators and allows test developers to control for the frequency of linguistic features across items and tasks. Reference corpora have also been used as a proxy for learner input when actual learner input is unknown (see Chapter 20, this volume) (Crossley et al., 2010; Laufer, 1991) and to model the relative sophistication (e.g., difficulty or rarity) of words (Kyle & Crossley, 2015; Laufer & Nation, 1995).

Learner corpora, texts produced by L2 learners, have been used as focal data in studies of lexical development. Most studies have examined differences in lexical use across proficiency levels (Kyle & Crossley, 2015; Laufer & Nation, 1995). Increasingly, however, longitudinal development has also been investigated using corpora such as the *Languages and Social Networks Abroad Project* corpus (LANGSNAP; Tracy-Ventura, Mitchell, & McManus, 2016) and the

Salsbury corpus (Salsbury, 2000). Longitudinal studies have highlighted actual L2 developmental trajectories and, in some cases, have indicated that these trajectories do not always follow the trends observed across proficiency levels.

There are two main constructs that are used to model productive lexical knowledge (often referred to as lexical richness). These include the diversity of words in a text and the sophistication of the words in text. Lexical diversity refers to the number of unique words a language user produces in a particular language sample. The working hypothesis is that higher proficiency language users will have productive knowledge of (and therefore use) a wider variety of words. Lexical sophistication refers to the relative difficulty of learning/using a word, which is often measured using reference-corpus frequency. The working hypothesis is that words that are more frequent in the input are easier to learn (with some caveats, see discussion below). For the most part, lexical diversity and sophistication have been treated as distinct constructs, although there have been some attempts to combine them (Daller, Van Hout, & Treffers-Daller, 2003). This chapter focuses on the ways that productive lexical knowledge has been investigated using learner corpora.

Core Issues and Topics

Measuring productive lexical knowledge in learner production tasks is an important but complex endeavor. This section introduces a number of different methodological choices that are available and discusses important features (e.g., strengths and weaknesses) of each. It should be stated from the outset that there are not clear cut general recommendations with regard to the choices that researchers investigating lexical development should make. This is because particular research questions (and learner corpora) will shed light on different aspects of lexical development – what is important is that methodological choices fit the purpose of a particular study.

What Counts As a Word?

When measuring lexical diversity and sophistication, an important issue is the way in which a word is defined. Word forms are generally defined as strings of letters separated by white space and/or punctuation. When a word is defined as a word form, each word form is treated as distinct. For example, *speaks*, *spoke*, and *speaker* would all be treated as distinct words. Lemmas include all inflected forms of a particular word. For example, *speaks* and *spoke* would be considered components of the lemma *speak*, but *speaker* would be considered a distinct lemma. A word family (Nation, 2001) includes all inflected forms of a word and most derived forms of a word (up to Level 6 on Bauer & Nation's, 1993, word hierarchy). For example, *speaks*, *spoke*, and *speaker* would be considered members of the same family. While it is possible to use any of the three definitions for words mentioned above, it is important to consider the theoretical and/or practical rationale for this decision (and to clearly report one's choice).

Although many studies analyze all words produced by learners, some studies make a distinction between function words and content words. Function words are closed-class, grammatical words such as articles, prepositions, and conjunctions (among many others). Content words are open-class words such as nouns, adjectives, most verbs, and some adverbs (Lu, 2012; Quirk, Greenbaum, Leech, & Svartik, 1985). Lexical verbs (with the exception of the copular verb *to be*) are generally considered content words, whereas auxiliary verbs and the copular *to be* are generally considered function words. A number of studies have indicated that function word and content word use tend to differ. Kyle and Crossley (2015), for example, found that more lexically proficient writers tend to use less frequent content words but more frequent function words.

Issues in Measuring Lexical Diversity

Lexical diversity indices are used to measure a language user's breadth of vocabulary knowledge. Because it is presumed that more advanced language users will have a larger vocabulary, it is also assumed that they will use a wider variety of words than a less advanced language user to accomplish a particular communicative task. Perhaps the best-known measure of lexical diversity is the simple type-token ratio (TTR), which is calculated as the number of types (unique words) divided by the number of tokens (total words). A higher TTR value represents greater lexical diversity, whereas a lower TTR value represents less lexical diversity. However, TTR has been demonstrated to be intrinsically connected to the length of a text. Longer texts tend to have lower TTR values (i.e., have more repeated words) than shorter texts, which means that a language user that produces more language (which is an indicator of higher proficiency) may receive a lower lexical diversity score (which is an indicator of lower proficiency) than a language user that produces less language. This phenomenon has been demonstrated repeatedly both in L1 texts (McCarthy & Jarvis, 2007) and in L2 texts (Koizumi & In'nami, 2012). A number of solutions to the issue of length have been proposed (and widely used) in the literature, such as root TTR (also referred to as Guiraud's index; Guiraud, 1960), log TTR (Herdan, 1964), VocD/HDD (Malvern & Richards, 1997; McCarthy & Jarvis, 2010), and the measure of textual lexical diversity (MTLD; McCarthy & Jarvis, 2007). Validation research suggests that most TTR corrections are still affected by text length (and in the case of log TTR and root TTR these effects are as strong as TTR). However, it appears that VocD, HDD (which is a simplified and more reliable version of VocD), and MTLD are only minimally affected by text length.

Another issue that has not fully been addressed is that prototypical lexical diversity indices are not sensitive to the kinds of words that occur in a text. A text that includes diverse but simple words such as *this food is very good* would earn the same diversity score as *nominalization is a crucial feature*. There has been some attempt to combine diversity and sophistication such as advanced TTR and advanced Guiraud (Daller et al., 2003). However, because these solutions are based on diversity measures that are strongly correlated with text length, they may not be ideal. Additionally, Jarvis (2013, 2017) has suggested that the construct of diversity is multidimensional and should be measured in a multivariate manner (i.e., using multiple measures; see below).

Issues in Measuring Lexical Sophistication

Although the issues of reliability, construct validity, and length effects cannot be completely ignored when assessing lexical sophistication, the biggest issues deal with how sophistication is conceptualized and measured. A number of approaches for measuring lexical sophistication are outlined below.

Frequency

Reference corpus word frequency is the most common method of estimating the sophistication of a particular word. Two main methods have been used to measure the frequency-based sophistication of words in a learner text. The first method is to divide frequency scores into groups (called "bands") based on the rank (see Nation, 2016). Typically, bands of 1,000 words have been used, although recently smaller bands have also been used (Cobb, 2018). For example, words such as *before, book*, and *give* are among the most frequent 1,000 (1K list) in the BNC. Words such as *bridge*, *discover*, and *promote* fall between the most frequent 1,000 and 2,000 (2K list) in the BNC. Due to the fact that word frequencies follow a Zipfian distribution (i.e., a small number of highly frequent words account for a majority of the items in a corpus), words on the 1k and 2k bands represent particularly useful/common words, whereas words in other bands (e.g., 5k or 6k) represent particularly uncommon words (see Nation, 2016; Zipf, 1935). Bands are primarily created using word families (see *What Counts as a Word*) and are reported for both types and tokens. When used for measuring lexical sophistication, the proportion of words in a text beyond the 2K level is often used (Crossley, Cobb, & McNamara, 2013; Laufer & Nation, 1995), although more statistically sophisticated measures such as P_Lex (Meara & Bell, 2001) and S (Kojima & Yamashita, 2014) have also been developed.

The second main method is to calculate mean reference corpus frequency scores for the words in a text. In this method, which has mainly been used with word forms or lemmas (Guo, Crossley, & McNamara, 2013; Kyle, Crossley, & Berger, 2018), each word form or lemma in a text is given a reference corpus frequency score. An average score for all the words in the text is then calculated (as noted above, this can also be restricted to content word or function words). Mean frequency scores reflect the continuous nature of frequency scores and are arguably more precise than band scores. As Crossley et al. (2013) note, each method has its advantages and disadvantages. What is most important is to understand the ramifications of the choices made (and to clearly report the method used and its rationale).

Features Beyond Frequency

Although frequency has played an important role in the measurement of lexical sophistication, research is increasingly demonstrating that other factors such as contextual distinctiveness, psycholinguistic word information, and collocational knowledge (among many others) are important factors for modeling development and differences between L2 proficiency levels.

Contextual distinctiveness refers to the number of contexts (e.g., texts, paragraphs, or sentences) in which a word tends to occur. One way to measure contextual distinctiveness is to consider a corpus text as a context and count the number of texts in which a particular word occurs in a particular corpus. Research has suggested that this method, which is referred to as range, may be a better predictor of lexical sophistication than mean frequency (Kyle & Crossley, 2015; Kyle, Crossley, et al., 2018) because frequency counts can be skewed by particular items being used frequently in a small number of texts. For example, the lemmas *somewhere* and *physicist* both occur 1,455 times (16.746 times per million) in the academic section of the COCA (and fall within the lemmatized 4k list). The lemma *somewhere*, however, occurs in over twice as many texts (1203, 5.66%) than the lemma *physicist*, which occurs in 494 (2.32%) texts. Because *physicist* is less likely to be encountered than *somewhere* (and therefore less likely to be learned), it would be considered more sophisticated. More computationally sophisticated corpus-derived methods of calculating contextual distinctiveness are also used, including *entropy* (Gries & Ellis, 2015) and *SemD* (Hoffman, Ralph, & Rogers, 2013).

Psycholinguistic word information indices measure lexical characteristics that cannot be obtained through corpus analysis. These indices are based on humans' perceptions of particular lexical features based on behavioral data (e.g., surveys). Concreteness, which refers to the concreteness/abstractness of the meaning denoted by a particular word, has been commonly used to model lexical proficiency (Crossley, Kyle, & Salsbury, 2016). Words such as *ladder*, *nectarine*, and *popcorn* earn high concreteness scores, whereas *variously*, *wisdom*, and *biased* earn low concreteness scores. Research has suggested that more concrete words are easier to learn (Paivio, 1971; Schwanenflugel, Harnishfeger, & Stowe, 1988). Accordingly, L2 users who are more lexically proficient tend to use words that are less concrete (Kyle, Crossley, et al., 2018). Other commonly used psycholinguistic word information norms include age of acquisition, familiarity, imageability, and meaningfulness (Kyle, Crossley, et al., 2018).

Although the characteristics of particular words such as frequency, range, etc. have been useful in measuring lexical proficiency and developmental trajectories, an important aspect of lexical knowledge is collocational knowledge (e.g., Nation, 2001; Sinclair, 1991). Accordingly, recent investigations have examined the relationship between collocation and L2 lexical proficiency and/or development (Bestgen & Granger, 2014). These studies have indicated that more proficient L2 users tend to use more frequent and more strongly associated bigrams and trigrams (contiguous two- and three-word sequences) on average. Further, in many cases, bigram and trigram indices have demonstrated stronger relationships with lexical proficiency scores than commonly used word-level indices (Kyle, Crossley, et al., 2018). Such findings underscore the role of collocational knowledge in perceptions of lexical proficiency and demonstrate the importance of including such measures in related studies.

Main Research Methods

When studying lexical diversity and/or lexical sophistication in learner corpora, a number of methodological issues must be addressed in addition to those raised in the previous section. These are outlined below, followed by a review of a number of freely available automatic text analysis tools.

Cross-sectional and Longitudinal Designs

Cross-sectional studies investigate differences in lexical use in L2 writers and speakers across proficiency levels, which are usually assigned through independent language proficiency test scores (e.g., Laufer & Nation, 1995) or production quality scores (e.g., Kyle & Crossley, 2015). Although cross-sectional studies have varied in the number of participants, the use of learner corpora and automated analysis tools have made it possible to include hundreds or even thousands of participants, which contributes to the generalizability of any identified trends. Cross-sectional studies provide insights into the characteristics of lexical use at particular benchmarks but do not necessarily indicate the developmental path(s) individuals take to reach those benchmarks (Ortega & Byrnes, 2008). Longitudinal studies investigate the changes that occur in individuals' L2 lexical use in writing and/or speaking over a period of time. Due to the time involved in collecting longitudinal data and issues such as participant attrition, longitudinal studies tend to include a small number of participants. Longitudinal studies can highlight productive lexical development trajectories (and the degree to which trajectories are similar/dissimilar across individuals), but do not necessarily indicate differences across proficiency levels (although if the corpus includes proficiency data, this can be explicitly examined).

A majority of lexis-focused learner corpus studies have been cross-sectional in nature, likely due to the relative ease of collecting large amounts of data in a relatively short period of time. Generally, cross-sectional studies have indicated that more proficient L2 learners tend to use a wider variety of words (Lu, 2012) and words that are more sophisticated (Kyle & Crossley, 2015; Laufer & Nation, 1995). There have been fewer lexis-focused longitudinal learner corpus studies. The results with regard to lexical diversity have shown similar trends as cross-sectional studies, wherein learners use more diverse vocabulary over time (Crossley, Salsbury, & McNamara, 2009). Results with regard to lexical sophistication, however, have been mixed. Some studies, such as Laufer (1991), have found that learners tend to use more infrequent words (i.e., more sophisticated words) over time. Other studies, however, have found that learner productions tend not to change with regard to word frequencies, despite demonstrable increases in overall language proficiency (Crossley, Skalicky, Kyle & Monteiro, 2019). Divergent findings highlight the importance of distinguishing between a cross-sectional focus on proficiency benchmarks and a longitudinal focus on developmental trends.

Task and Topic

An important factor when measuring lexical development is the interaction between the characteristics of lexical use and the role of task and topic/prompt. In order to make accurate claims regarding the relationship between productive lexical knowledge and proficiency (e.g., the characteristics of particular developmental benchmarks) or regarding lexical development, differences in use across these features must be accounted for. Research has demonstrated that different types of tasks and different topics/prompts elicit responses that vary with regard to lexical use (e.g., Alexopoulou, Michel, Murakami, & Meurers, 2017).

There are a number of methods that can be used to control for topics and tasks in both cross-sectional and longitudinal studies. While there are a variety of factors that can affect data collection procedures, the following guidelines can be seen as ideal practices, although these may not be practical in every situation. For cross-sectional studies, it is important to ensure that tasks and topics are consistent across proficiency levels. It is also helpful to include multiple topics to determine the degree to which the trends observed across proficiency levels are stable across tasks. This allows researchers to investigate the relationship between lexical use and proficiency and provides the opportunity to determine whether this relationship is stable across writing topics.

For longitudinal studies, it is also important to control for topic effects. One approach is to use a counterbalanced text collection design. A very simple example of counterbalancing is when there are two data collection periods and two writing topics. In this case, half of the participants would respond to topic A during the first period and topic B during the second period. The other half of the participants would do the opposite. However, longitudinal studies should generally include more than two collection points. Table 25.1 comprises a hypothetical data collection plan for a longitudinal study involving 90 participants and three writing collection periods. For another related approach, see Tracy-Ventura (2017).

Univariate and Multivariate Investigations

Many learner corpus studies related to lexical diversity and lexical sophistication have at least implicitly treated lexical development as a unidimensional phenomenon. These studies have either investigated a single independent variable (e.g., word frequency or MTLD) or investigated multiple independent variables in separate analyses (e.g., word frequency and MTLD). While these studies have identified important relationships between particular indices and development/ proficiency, they have often neglected to investigate the degree to which these indices overlap and/or provide complementary information. Increasingly, however, research has indicated that

Table 25.1 Counterbalanced Collection Scheme for Three Collection Points and Topics

Collection group	N	Time 1	Time 2	Time 3
Group 1	15	Topic A	Topic B	Topic C
Group 2	15	Topic A	Topic C	Topic B
Group 3	15	Topic B	Topic A	Topic C
Group 4	15	Topic B	Topic C	Topic A
Group 5	15	Topic C	Topic A	Topic B
Group 6	15	Topic C	Topic B	Topic A

the constructs of lexical diversity and lexical sophistication are indeed multidimensional. Jarvis (2013, 2017), for example, proposed that the construct of lexical diversity is composed of a number of different distinct but complementary sub-constructs including variability, volume, evenness, rarity, dispersion, and disparity. Using these constructs, Jarvis constructed a predictor model that explained 89% of the variance in human judgments in lexical diversity, which is almost twice the variance explained by the strongest single predictor.

Treating the construct of lexical sophistication as multivariate has also contributed to our understanding of development and proficiency differences. Kyle, Crossley, et al. (2018), for example, found that a wide variety of non-collinear indices of lexical sophistication demonstrated small to medium relationships with human judgements of written lexical proficiency. However, a multivariate regression model using these variables demonstrated a large relationship with lexical proficiency scores and explained 58% of the variance. Importantly, frequency only contributed a small amount of the variance explained by the model whereas indices such as bigram association strength, lemma range, and lemma hypernymy accounted for a much larger portion of this variance. Studies such as Jarvis (2013, 2017) and Kyle, Crossley, et al. (2018) among many others highlight the importance of conceptualizing lexical diversity and lexical sophistication as complex, multivariate constructs.

Tools

One important advantage of learner corpus research in the exploration of lexis is that large amounts of data can be analyzed in a relatively short period of time using automatic and semi-automatic analysis tools. Many tools have been cited frequently in the literature, and even more are available online. When deciding which tool(s) to use, it is important to minimally consider a) the indices that are calculated by the tool, b) how transparent index calculation is, c) whether texts must be processed one at a time or can be batch processed (i.e., whether large learner corpora can be efficiently analyzed), and d) whether sensitive texts can be securely processed (i.e., can be processed on one's computer as opposed to over an internet connection). The tools described below represent tools that are freely available for research purposes and have been widely represented in the literature.

CLAN

The computerized language analysis (CLAN) tool (MacWhinney & Snow, 1990) was designed to analyze L1 language acquisition, but has since been used in a variety of second language acquisition studies (e.g., Tracy-Ventura, 2017). CLAN is a freely available desktop tool that calculates a number of features related to the variety of linguistic phenomena and can be used to analyze a variety of languages. In L2 lexical development research, CLAN has been notably used for the calculation of vocD, which is a type-token ratio approximation that is relatively independent of text length (McCarthy & Jarvis, 2007). At the time of writing, CLAN is the only publicly and freely available tool that calculates vocD in batch processing mode. CLAN also calculates a variety of other indices of lexical diversity and can be used to tag files for part of speech (allowing for a wide number of subsequent analyses).

Coh-metrix

Coh-Metrix (McNamara, Graesser, McCarthy & Cai, 2014) is a text analysis tool for English that has been used in a large number of cross-sectional and longitudinal studies over the past decade (Crossley et al., 2009; Guo et al., 2013). Coh-Metrix calculates a number of features related to cohesion, syntactic complexity, lexical diversity, and lexical sophistication. With regard to lexical diversity, the freely available version of the tool calculates type token ratios for content words and all words, vocD, and MTLD. The tool also includes a number of indices related to lexical sophistication such as word frequency, concreteness, and hypernymy, among others. Coh-metrix has undeniably been an important tool for the analysis of lexical development. However, the version of the tool that is publicly available requires users to upload a single text file at a time, which limits the number of texts that can be processed in a reasonable amount of time.

L2 Lexical Complexity Analyzer

The L2 lexical complexity analyzer (Lu, 2012) calculates five indices of lexical sophistication, one index of lexical density, and 19 indices of lexical diversity, including a number of popular variations of TTR such as root TTR. Additionally, part of speech specific diversity indices are also available. The L2 lexical complexity analyzer can be used in batch mode as a Python script on Mac and Linux that is freely available on Lu's website (http://www.personal.psu.edu/xxl13/) and can also batch-process up to 200 files using an online interface (www.aihaiyang.com). The only limitations to the L2 lexical complexity analyzer are that it does not include important length-stable indices such as vocD/HD-D or MTLD, and it can only be used with English.

Range/VocabProfile/Ant Profiler

Range (Heatley & Nation, 1994) was one of the original freely available tools for the analysis of frequency. Various versions of Range calculate word family-based frequency profiles for the 1K and 2K lists derived from the General Service List (West, 1953), the Academic Word List (Coxhead, 2000), and the BNC-COCA 25 (Cobb, 2018). Output is provided both for types and tokens, and all of the files in a particular folder can be processed securely on a user's desktop. While the Range program is only available for computers running a Windows operating system, AntProfiler (Anthony, 2014), is available on both Windows and Mac operating systems. VocabProfile (Cobb, 2018) is an online version of Range that provides excellent visualization tools for analyzing the frequency distributions of word families in a text in both English and French. VocabProfile also allows for up to 25 texts to be processed automatically.

TAALED

The Tool for the Automatic Analysis of Lexical Diversity (TAALED; Kyle, Jarvis, & Crossley, 2018) is a freely available desktop tool that includes a range of classic and newly developed indices of lexical diversity. Included are classic TTR transformation indices such as Guiraud's index and Maas' index. Also included are more complex indices such as moving average TTR, HD-D, and MTLD. TAALED allows for batch processing and works on all major operating systems. TAALED was designed to work with English but can also process other languages as long as they are pre-tokenized and are encoded in UTF-8.

TAALES

The tool for the automatic analysis of lexical sophistication (TAALES; Kyle & Crossley, 2015; Kyle, Crossley, et al., 2018) is a publicly and freely available tool that calculates over 500 indices of lexical sophistication across 12 index categories such as word frequency, contextual diversity, contextual distinctiveness, concreteness, hypernymy, and psycholinguistic decision norms, among many others. TAALES also provides collocation information at the bigram and trigram levels. One benefit of TAALES is that it allows users to choose from a wide variety of reference corpora such as the BNC, SubtLEXus (Brysbaert & New, 2009), and each subcorpus of the COCA. Furthermore, it allows users to distinguish between scores for lemmas and words, content words and function words, types and tokens, and log transformed versus non-transformed versions. The number of choices available may also be considered a limitation, as a certain amount of background knowledge is needed to select appropriate indices. Additionally, TAALES only works with English (although projects are underway to include other languages such as Spanish). TAALES securely processes text files on a users' computer (versions are available for all major operating systems) and is able to process all files in a particular folder, enabling massive amounts of data to be processed automatically. One final notable feature of TAALES is that it provides supplementary item-level scores for each text, which allows users to see exactly how text-level summary scores are computed.

Representative Corpora and Research

A variety of corpora have been used to investigate productive lexical development and the differences in lexical use across proficiency levels. Below are two examples of longitudinal corpora and research studies that have used these corpora. Although not represented below, a number of cross-sectional corpora that may be appropriate for the investigation of lexical use across proficiency levels are freely available such as the *International Corpus Network of Asian Learners of English* (ICNALE; Ishikawa, 2011), which includes both written and monologic spoken data, and the *National Institute of Information and Communications Technology Japanese Learner English Corpus* (Izumi, Uchimoto, & Isahara, 2004), which includes dialogic transcripts from oral proficiency interviews.

LANGSNAP is a freely available longitudinal learner corpus of language learners that participated in a university study abroad program. The corpus includes an L2 French component (29 participants) and an L2 Spanish component (27 participants). Each component of the corpus represents a 21-month period, of which nine-months were a study abroad experience in France, Spain, or Mexico. The language samples in the corpus comprise three task types, including oral interviews, written argumentative essays, and oral picture-based narratives. Participants completed these tasks at the beginning of the study prior to departure, three times during the study abroad experience, and twice after returning. Three sets of tasks prompts were used, and each was repeated so that the first collection point (prior to departure) and the fourth collection point (at the end of the study abroad experience), which were one year apart, included the same task prompts. Proficiency assessments were also administered at multiple points during the study. In addition to the L2 participants, L1 participants also completed the tasks to serve as a baseline (see Tracy-Ventura et al., 2016). Furthermore, additional data were collected from a subset of the population (n = 33) 36 months after the end of the project (Tracy-Ventura, Huensch, & Mitchell, forthcoming).

Tracy-Ventura (2017) used a subset of the Spanish component of the LANGSNAP corpus to investigate changes in lexical knowledge over the first year of the study. Data for the study included scores from a receptive vocabulary knowledge test (X-Lex; Meara & Milton, 2003), oral interviews, oral narratives, and written argumentative essays collected before the participants left for their study abroad trip and near the end of their trip (collection points one and four). For each of the production tasks, participants completed the exact same task at the collection points that were considered. The results indicated that learners' performance on the receptive vocabulary test improved significantly (with a large effect, d = 1.32). With regard to productive vocabulary knowledge, Tracy-Ventura found significant differences (with a small effect) in low-frequency lemma use (3K–5K bands) for all words between the collection periods. The L2 Spanish learners used more low-frequency words at the end of the study-abroad experience than they did prior to departure, which is in line with what would be expected from previous research (e.g., Laufer, 1991).

The *Salsbury corpus* (Salsbury, 2000) is a dense longitudinal corpus that has been used in a number of studies to investigate L2 lexical development (Crossley et al., 2009, 2010; Kim, Crossley, & Kyle, 2018). The corpus comprises oral and written productions collected numerous times over the course of an academic year from six learners of L2 English. All participants that contributed to the study were enrolled in an English for academic purposes program at a large public university in the United States. In addition to the oral and written data, institutional TOEFL exams were administered four times during the collection period, allowing for external verification that the participants were making L2 proficiency gains over time. The oral component of the corpus comprises data from six interview sessions that included a variety of topics and tasks that ranged from picture description tasks to open-ended discussions (see Crossley et al., 2009). The written component of the corpus comprises free writes collected ten times over the course of one year. Participants were instructed to write about anything they wanted to, and their free writes ranged from descriptions of their days to topics that were more argumentative in nature. At the time of writing, the corpus is not publicly available.

Crossley et al. (2010) used the oral portion of the *Salsbury corpus* to investigate lexical development with regard to reference-corpus frequency and the use of polysemous words. The results indicated that during the first semester, lexical development was evident with regard to both average polysemy values and average frequency values. Over time, participants tended to use words that were more polysemous (i.e., had more senses) and also used words that occur more frequently in a reference corpus. In the second semester, however, no significant changes with regard to either polysemy or frequency was observed. A follow-up qualitative analysis, however, indicated that although the learners tended to use similar word forms, they tended to use a wider variety of senses related to those word forms. For example, in the first third of the year, participants used two senses of the word *play*, but in the second two-thirds of the year, they used an additional six senses of the word. Importantly, this study demonstrated that factors beyond frequency such as polysemy provide valuable insights into lexical learning and that word form frequency values do not always adequately capture gains in productive lexical knowledge.

Future Directions

The past decade has seen a large expansion in learner corpus-based work on productive lexical development and proficiency level differences in lexical use. One important vein of this research has worked to address issues in the measurement of lexical diversity (e.g., McCarthy & Jarvis, 2010; Koizumi & In'nami, 2012) and lexical sophistication (e.g., Crossley et al., 2013). Another vein of research has explored the bounds of both lexical diversity (Jarvis, 2013) and lexical sophistication (Crossley et al., 2009; Kyle, Crossley, et al., 2018) by treating these constructs as complex and multivariate and/or by exploring the use of a wide range of previously unexplored lexical features (e.g., concreteness, hypernymy, polysemy, word neighborhoods, etc.). While this literature has been rich, informative, and exciting, a number of issues still need to be addressed.

First, L2 researchers need to have greater awareness of the range of indices of lexical diversity and sophistication and relative strengths and limitations of each. For example, despite a preponderance of evidence that suggests that indices of lexical diversity such as root TTR (i.e., Guiraud's index) are extremely sensitive to text length, they still are often employed in L2 studies in favor of indices that are much less sensitive to text length such as MTLD, vocD, or HDD. With regard to the measurement of lexical sophistication, one important hindrance to the knowledgeable measurement of the construct is the sheer number of indices available and the exploratory nature of much of this work. To move the field forward, work is needed to consolidate our understanding of the construct of lexical sophistication. Additionally, although a wide range of lexical diversity and sophistication analysis tools and indices are available for English, much fewer are available for other languages. Another issue is that many prominent studies of lexical diversity and sophistication have been conducted using a small range of learner corpora. To more fully understand the nature of these constructs, it is important to investigate a wide range of tightly controlled corpora that differ with regard to topic, task, population, and L1. Finally, more work is needed to determine how much data (i.e., how long texts must be) is needed to obtain reliable measurements of productive lexical knowledge in learner corpus data. While a small amount of data on this topic is available (Jarvis, 2002; Koizumi & In'nami, 2012; Kojima & Yamashita, 2014), more is needed, especially with regard to indices of lexical sophistication.

Further Reading

Jarvis, S., & Daller, M. (Eds.) (2013). *Vocabulary knowledge: Human ratings and automated measures* (vol. 47). Amsterdam: John Benjamins.

This edited volume provides an excellent introduction to a variety of methods of measuring lexical diversity and sophistication.

Kyle, K., Crossley, S., & Berger, C. M. (2018). The tool for the automatic analysis of lexical sophistication (TAALES): Version 2.0. *Behavior Research Methods*.

This article serves as an introduction to the wide range of indices available to measure lexical sophistication.

Nation, I. S. P. (2016). *Making and using word lists for language learning and testing*. Amsterdam: John Benjamins Publishing Company.

This book provides an excellent overview of considerations when creating and/or using word lists, both for profiling vocabulary (i.e., measuring sophistication via bands) and more generally.

Related Topics

Chapters 5, 9, and 13.

References

Alexopoulou, T., Michel, M., Murakami, A., & Meurers, D. (2017). Task effects on linguistic complexity and accuracy: A large-scale learner corpus analysis employing natural language processing techniques. *Language Learning*, *67*(S1), 180–208.

Anthony, L. (2014). *AntWordProfiler (Version 1.4. 1)[Computer software]*. Tokyo: Waseda University.

Bardel, C., Gudmundson, A., & Lindqvist, C. (2012). Aspects of lexical sophistication in advanced learners' oral production: Vocabulary acquisition and use in L2 French and Italian. *Studies in Second Language Acquisition*, *34*(2), 269–290.

Bauer, L., & Nation, I. S. P. (1993). Word families. *International Journal of Lexicography*, *6*(4), 253–279.

Bestgen, Y., & Granger, S. (2014). Quantifying the development of phraseological competence in L2 English writing: An automated approach. *Journal of Second Language Writing*, *26*, 28–41. doi:10.1016/j.jslw.2014.09.004

BNC Consortium (2007). *The British national corpus, version 3*. Retrieved from http://www.natcorp.ox.ac.uk/

Brysbaert, M., & New, B. (2009). Moving beyond Kucera and Francis: A critical evaluation of current word frequency norms and the introduction of a new and improved word frequency measure for American English. *Behavior Research Methods*, *41*(4), 977–990. doi 10.3758/BRM.41.4.977

Cobb, T. (2018). *Web VocabProfile*.

Coxhead, A. (2000). A new academic word list. *TESOL Quarterly*, *34*(2), 213–238.

Crossley, S. A., Cobb, T., & McNamara, D. S. (2013). Comparing count-based and band-based indices of word frequency: Implications for active vocabulary research and pedagogical applications. *System*, *41*(4), 965–981. doi:10.1016/j.system.2013.08.002

Crossley, S. A., Kyle, K., & Salsbury, T. (2016). A usage-based investigation of L2 lexical acquisition: The role of input and output. *The Modern Language Journal*, *100*(3), 702–715.

Crossley, S. A., Salsbury, T., & McNamara, D. (2009). Measuring L2 lexical growth using hypernymic relationships. *Language Learning, 59*(2), 307–334.

Crossley, S. A., Salsbury, T., & McNamara, D. (2010). The development of polysemy and frequency use in English second language speakers. *Language Learning, 60*(3), 573–605. doi:10.1111/j.1467-9922.2010.00568.x

Crossley, S. A., Skalicky, S., Kyle, K., & Monteiro, K. (2019). Absolute frequency effects in second language lexical acquisition. *Studies in Second Language Acquisition, 41*(4), 721–744. doi:10.1017/S0272263118000268

Daller, H., Van Hout, R., & Treffers-Daller, J. (2003). Lexical richness in the spontaneous speech of bilinguals. *Applied Linguistics, 24*(2), 197–222.

Davies, M. (2010). The corpus of contemporary American English as the first reliable monitor corpus of English. *Literary and Linguistic Computing, 25*(4), 447–464. doi:10.1093/llc/fqq018

Gries, S. Th., & Ellis, N. C. (2015). Statistical measures for usage-based linguistics. *Language Learning, 65*(S1), 228–255. doi:10.1111/lang.12119

Guiraud, P. (1960). *Problèmes et méthodes de la statistique linguistique*. Dordrecht, The Netherlands: D. Reidel.

Guo, L., Crossley, S. A., & McNamara, D. S. (2013). Predicting human judgments of essay quality in both integrated and independent second language writing samples: A comparison study. *Assessing Writing, 18*(3), 218–238.

Heatley, A., & Nation, I. S. P. (1994). *Range [Computer program]*. Victoria University of Wellington. Retrieved from http://Www.Vuw.Ac.Nz/Lals/

Herdan, G. (1964). *Quantitative linguistics*. London: Butterworths.

Hoffman, P., Ralph, M. A. L., & Rogers, T. T. (2013). Semantic diversity: A measure of semantic ambiguity based on variability in the contextual usage of words. *Behavior Research Methods, 45*(3), 718–730.

Hu, H., & Nation, I. S. P. (2000). What vocabulary size is needed to read unsimplified texts. *Reading in a Foreign Language, 8*, 689–696.

Hulstijn, J. H., & Laufer, B. (2001). Some empirical evidence for the involvement load hypothesis in vocabulary acquisition. *Language Learning, 51*(3), 539–558.

Ishikawa, S. (2011). A new horizon in learner corpus studies: The aim of the ICNALE project. In G. Weir, S. Ishikawa, & K. Poonpol (Eds.), *Corpora and Language Technologies in Teaching, Learning and Research*, (pp. 3–11). Glasgow: University of Strathclyde.

Izumi, E., Uchimoto, K., & Isahara, H. (2004). The NICT JLE corpus: Exploiting the language learners' speech database for research and education. *International Journal of the Computer, the Internet and Management, 12*(2), 119–125.

Jarvis, S. (2002). Short texts, best-fitting curves and new measures of lexical diversity. *Language Testing, 19*(1), 57–84. doi:10.1191/0265532202lt220oa

Jarvis, S. (2013). Capturing the diversity in lexical diversity. *Language Learning, 63*(Suppl.1), 87–106.

Jarvis, S. (2017). Grounding lexical diversity in human judgments. *Language Testing, 34*(4), 537–553.

Jarvis, S., & Daller, M. (Eds.) (2013). *Vocabulary knowledge: Human ratings and automated measures* (vol. 47). Amsterdam: John Benjamins.

Kim, M., Crossley, S. A., & Kyle, K. (2018). Lexical sophistication as a multidimensional phenomenon: Relations to second language lexical proficiency, development, and writing quality. *The Modern Language Journal, 102*(1), 120–141.

Koizumi, R., & In'nami, Y. (2012). Effects of text length on lexical diversity measures: Using short texts with less than 200 tokens. *System, 40*(4), 554–564.

Kojima, M., & Yamashita, J. (2014). Reliability of lexical richness measures based on word lists in short second language productions. *System, 42*, 23–33.

Kyle, K., & Crossley, S. A. (2015). Automatically assessing lexical sophistication: Indices, tools, findings, and application. *TESOL Quarterly, 49*(4), 757–786. doi:10.1002/tesq.194

Kyle, K., Crossley, S. A., & Berger, C. M. (2018). The tool for the automatic analysis of lexical sophistication (TAALES): Version 2.0, *Behavior Research Methods, 50*(3), 1030–1046. doi:10.3758/s13428-017-0924-4

Kyle, K., Jarvis, S., & Crossley, S. A. (2018). *The tool for the automatic analysis of lexical diversity (TAALED)*. Retrieved from http://www.linguisticanalysistools.org/TAALED.html

Laufer, B. (1991). The development of L2 lexis in the expression of the advanced learner. *The Modern Language Journal, 75*(4), 440–448.

Laufer, B., & Nation, I. S. P. (1995). Vocabulary size and use: Lexical richness in L2 written production. *Applied Linguistics, 16*(3), 307–322. doi:10.1093/applin/16.3.307

Laufer, B., & Nation, I. S. P. (1999). A vocabulary-size test of controlled productive ability. *Language Testing, 16*(1), 33–51.

Lu, X. (2012). The relationship of lexical richness to the quality of ESL learners' oral narratives. *The Modern Language Journal*, *96*(2), 190–208.

MacWhinney, B., & Snow, C. (1990). The child language data exchange system: An update. *Journal of Child Language*, *17*(2), 457–472.

Malvern, D. D., & Richards, B. J. (1997). A new measure of lexical diversity. *British Studies in Applied Linguistics*, *12*, 58–71.

McCarthy, P. M., & Jarvis, S. (2007). vocd: A theoretical and empirical evaluation. *Language Testing*, *24*(4), 459–488.

McCarthy, P. M., & Jarvis, S. (2010). MTLD, vocd-D, and HD-D: A validation study of sophisticated approaches to lexical diversity assessment. *Behavior Research Methods*, *42*(2), 381–392. doi:10.3758/BRM.42.2.381

McLean, S., & Kramer, B. (2015). The creation of a new vocabulary levels test. *Shiken*, *19*(2), 1–11.

McNamara, D. S., Graesser, A. C., McCarthy, P. M., & Cai, Z. (2014). *Automated evaluation of text and discourse with Coh-Metrix*. Cambridge: Cambridge University Press.

Meara, P., & Bell, H. (2001). P_Lex: A simple and effective way of describing the lexical characteristics of short L2 texts. *Prospect*, *3*, 5–19.

Meara, P., & Milton, J. (2003). *The Swansea levels test*. Newbury: Express.

Nation, I. S. P. (2001). *Learning vocabulary in another language*. Cambridge: Cambridge University Press.

Nation, I. S. P. (2016). *Making and using word lists for language learning and testing*. Amsterdam: John Benjamins.

Nation, I. S. P., & Beglar, D. (2007). A vocabulary size test. *Language Teacher*, *31*(7), 9–13.

Nation, I. S. P., & Waring, R. (1997). Vocabulary size, text coverage and word lists. *Vocabulary: Description, Acquisition and Pedagogy*, *14*, 6–19.

Ortega, L., & Byrnes, H. (2008). Theorizing advancedness, setting up the longitudinal research agenda. In L. Ortega & H. Byrnes (Eds.), *The longitudinal study of advanced L2 capacities* (pp. 281–300). New York: Routledge.

Paivio, A. (1971). *Imagery and verbal processes*. New York: Holt, Rinehart, and Winston.

Peters, E., & Webb, S. (2018). Incidental vocabulary acquisition through viewing L2 television and factors that affect learning. *Studies in Second Language Acquisition*, 40(3), 551–577.

Pigada, M., & Schmitt, N. (2006). Vocabulary acquisition from extensive reading: A case study. *Reading in a Foreign Language*, *18*(1), 1.

Quirk, R., Greenbaum, S., Leech, G., & Svartik, J. (1985). *A comprehensive grammar of the English language*. London: Longman.

Salsbury, T. (2000). *The acquisitional grammaticalization of unreal conditionals and modality in L2 English: A longitudinal perspective*. Unpublished doctoral dissertation. Bloomington, IN: Indiana University.

Schmitt, N., Schmitt, D., & Clapham, C. (2001). Developing and exploring the behaviour of two new versions of the vocabulary levels test. *Language Testing*, *18*(1), 55–88.

Schwanenflugel, P. J., Harnishfeger, K. K., & Stowe, R. W. (1988). Context availability and lexical decisions for abstract and concrete words. *Journal of Memory and Language*, *27*(5), 499–520.

Sinclair, J. (1991). *Corpus, concordance, collocation*. Oxford: Oxford University Press.

Tracy-Ventura, N. (2017). Combining corpora and experimental data to investigate language learning during residence abroad: A study of lexical sophistication. *System*, *71*, 35–45.

Tracy-Ventura, N., Huensch, A., & Mitchell, R. (in press). Understanding the long-term evolution of L2 lexical diversity: The contribution of a longitudinal learner corpus. In B. LeBruyn & M. Paquot (Eds.), *Learner corpus research meets second language acquisition*. Cambridge: Cambridge University Press.

Tracy-Ventura, N., Mitchell, R., & McManus, K. (2016). The LANGSNAP longitudinal learner corpus. *Spanish Learner Corpus Research: Current Trends and Future Perspectives*, *78*, 117.

Webb, S. (2005). Receptive and productive vocabulary learning: The effects of reading and writing on word knowledge. *Studies in Second Language Acquisition*, *27*(1), 33–52.

West, M. (1953). *A general service list of English words: With semantic frequencies and a supplementary word-list for the writing of popular science and technology*. Reading: Addison-Wesley Longman Limited.

Zipf, G. K. (1935). *The psycho-biology of language: An introduction to dynamic philology*. Cambridge, MA: MIT Press.

26

Crosslinguistic Influence

Ann-Kristin Helland Gujord

Introduction

A distinct feature of L2 learners is the knowledge that they already possess of both their L1 (or L1s) and other previously-acquired languages (either partially or fully). How this prior language knowledge affects the L2 has been investigated as 'transfer' or 'crosslinguistic influence' (CLI). Today, these two terms are used interchangeably (Jarvis, 2017; Jarvis & Pavlenko, 2008; Odlin & Yu, 2016), and refer to "the influence of a person's knowledge of one language on that person's knowledge or use of another language" (Jarvis and Pavlenko, 2008, p. 1). Unlike previous definitions of these concepts, which often included an explicit reference to the L1, this definition does not say anything about the status of the languages involved or the direction of the influence, thus recognizing that (1) languages other than the L1 may affect subsequent language learning, and (2) this influence can work in the opposite direction (i.e., languages learned later in life may affect languages previously acquired). Still, research on CLI – particularly Learner Corpus Research (LCR) – has primarily been concerned with the role of the L1 in the learning of an L2. Therefore, it follows that more is known about how learners' L1s affect language learning later in life than about how an already acquired L2 may affect the L1 or the learning of an additional Lx.

People have always understood through experience that the languages we know can influence one another, and long before Second Language Acquisition (SLA) was established as a research field, scholars recognized the CLI phenomenon (see Jarvis & Pavlenko, 2008 or Jarvis, 2016). In early SLA research, CLI was regarded as the most important factor affecting L2 learning; research on CLI then was closely linked to the Contrastive Analysis Hypothesis, and transfer from the L1 was perceived as an obstacle to second language acquisition (Fries, 1945; Lado, 1957). Starting in the late 1960s, many SLA researchers, particularly in the USA, either turned away from the investigation of transfer completely or regarded it as one factor among many affecting the learning process. At the end of the 1970s and during the 1980s, one of the most important developments in transfer research took place; researchers moved from focusing solely on documenting transfer to investigating the 'transferability' of defined items, seeking to understand why and when something is transferred (Jarvis & Pavlenko, 2008). Today, most current models and frameworks of SLA incorporate CLI to some degree. In several theories, such as MacWhinney's Competition Model (1992), CLI is even assigned a prominent role in the acquisitional process (Odlin & Yu, 2016). In usage-based approaches, transfer is also important as experience with the L1 results in 'attentional biases' (see Chapter 13, this volume or Ellis, 2006).

CLI has always been a prominent research topic in LCR. The majority of corpus-based L2 studies have made use of a comparative design in which one or more learner corpora are compared to an L1 corpus. In fact, for many years, L1 influence was the primary variable investigated in LCR. Corpus-based transfer research has been instrumental in two ways. First, during the last decade there has been growth in empirical descriptive studies that give more insights into when transfer takes place, which language use areas it may affect, and what the consequences of CLI may be. Second, focus on methodological aspects of transfer research has increased, and LCR's contribution is perhaps most evident in how it helps ensure quality and rigor in CLI research and document a broader range of transfer effects.

Core Issues and Topics

Three Perspectives on 'Transfer'

The literature contains three different understandings of what CLI entails (Alonso, 2002; Jarvis, 2000;).[1] First, the traditional view considers CLI to involve a process of transferring knowledge from one language (usually the L1) to another (usually the L2). In this perspective, CLI occurs because learners make interlingual connections between features of two or more languages. These mental associations are formed as learners subjectively (and usually unconsciously) assume structures, words, or concepts in the L1 and L2 to be related (see Ringbom, 2007). For instance, Gujord has shown that the reason Somali L2 learners of Norwegian overuse the preterit in contexts requiring the present perfect in Norwegian is that they assume the general past form in their L1 to be similar to the preterit in the L2 (Gujord, 2017).

Second, transfer is also sometimes described as a communication strategy. This view has often been associated with the ignorance hypothesis, which explains transfer as a temporary tool that learners utilize when they lack knowledge of the target language (Alonso, 2002; Jarvis & Pavlenko, 2008). However, a more positive perspective of transfer as a beneficial strategy for L2 learning can also be found in sociocultural and interactional approaches (see Chapter 21, this volume), where many studies, such as Swain and Lapkin (2000), have shown how L2 learners exploit their knowledge of the L1 effectively in collaborative interactions.

Finally, a third construction of transfer has recently emerged: transfer as "inert outcome" (Jarvis, 2000, p. 250). The term "inert" refers to a non-dynamic condition, which is the conceptual and linguistic knowledge learners have of languages (p. 299). "Outcome," then, comprises the transfer effect arising from the learner's exhibition of a specific knowledge base. Thus, from this perspective, CLI takes place even when the learner has not made any interlingual identification or conscious comparison of the languages in question. This view of transfer is closely connected to a conceptual approach to language similarities and differences (see below for more about conceptual transfer), as well as to the latest theoretical advances in general linguistic and psychological research that explore the relationships between language and cognition. The unifying hypothesis for the various studies conducted within this approach is that a correlation exists within languages between linguistic structure and principles of information organization. In other words, the way we organize and present information when we speak or write is rooted in structural properties of the language. Hence, when we learn languages, we do not only learn specific grammar and vocabulary, we also learn a specific way of conceptualizing and verbalizing events (see below for more information).

All three of these views of CLI are utilized in SLA research, but that is not the case for LCR. Most corpus studies build on just one model: the traditional view of CLI as a process. Based on comparative designs (see *Main Research Methods* section), corpus-based transfer studies have chiefly documented the many ways learners can exploit their existing L1 grammatical and lexical knowledge when using the L2. Particularly, corpus-based studies have helped to broaden the scope of the linguistic phenomena investigated (e.g. lexis, phraseology, morphology) and to describe the range of linguistic effects this process of transferring knowledge may have on a learner's language. In contrast, using transfer as a strategy for communication and learning has not yet been widely studied in LCR. However, that does not mean that such perspectives could not be pursued more systematically, for example, with spoken corpora of social interactions and classroom conversations. Similarly, the exploration of transfer within a conceptual framework (transfer as inert outcome) will require specific types of learner corpora. Thus, corpora that consist of learner language collected under the exact same conditions and with the same stimuli could be instrumental in exploring hypotheses of how conceptual and semantic differences in languages may affect L2 learning and use (Jarvis, 2017), an area that remains underexplored.

Why Does Crosslinguistic Influence Occur?

Since research on CLI began investigating transferability, that is, exploring why and when CLI does or does not take place, various factors that govern its occurrence and affect its likelihood have been identified (Jarvis & Pavlenko, 2008). These factors are often called constraints, which Odlin defines as "anything that prevents the learner from either noticing a similarity in the first place or from deciding that the similarity is a real and helpful one" (Odlin, 2003, p. 454).

The degree of congruence between the L1 and the L2 is recognized as the most central constraint on CLI (Jarvis & Pavlenko, 2008). Therefore, CLI is more likely to take place when objective similarities between the L1 and L2 exist and/or when the languages are typologically related. The prevalence of transfer effects is also believed to be higher when learners assume that the L1 and L2 are similar and perceive their L1 knowledge as relevant for the use of specific L2 features. However, objective and subjective similarities (and differences) do not always coincide. For instance, Spanish learners of English and English learners of Spanish may falsely believe that *asistir* ('to attend' in Spanish) and *assist* ('to help someone' in English) have the same meaning although in reality they are false cognates. Two related constraints are markedness and prototypicality. Jarvis and Pavlenko treat these as one because they are associated with many of the same characteristics. Markedness and prototypicality "relate to the degree which a form, feature, or structure is marked, special, atypical, or language-specific versus being unmarked, basic, prototypical, or universal" (2008, p. 186). The two features are also associated with learners' intuition about how universal (and typical) a form, feature, or structure is (p. 188). Accordingly, learners are more prone to transfer those forms that they perceive as being more universal and accessible than those they see as language specific (e.g., idiomatic expressions; see Kellerman's (1983) 'learner's psychotypology,' which refers to learner's perception of the 'distance' between their L1 and the target language). For example, Scandinavian languages such as Norwegian and Swedish have subject-verb inversion, which is a typologically rare language feature. Learners of English with a Scandinavian language background, however, do not transfer subject-verb inversion from their L1 to the English L2, most probably because they consider subject-verb inversion a marked (i.e. atypical or less frequent) structure.

There are many other types of constraints, including:

- Developmental constraints: In morpho-syntax, for example, learners have been shown to follow the same developmental sequences in the learning process and make the same mistakes regardless of L1 background.
- Experiential constraints: For instance, there is less phonological transfer among young learners; similarly, people who have lived a long time in an L2 environment sometimes experience transfer effects in the opposite direction, i.e. their L2 influences their L1 (e.g., Schmid, 2016).

- • Environmental constraints: Positive transfer seems to be more likely in formal learning settings, and negative transfer in informal settings; some tasks also seem to foster more transfer effects than others.[2]

Most of what we currently know about constraints comes from SLA research. Studies of constraints require methods that enable the study of how various factors affect transfer, both in isolation and interaction. Hence, if future corpus-based transfer research builds on corpora with rich metadata and utilizes appropriate statistical methods (see Chapter 9, this volume), our current knowledge of constraints could be revisited and perhaps expanded.

Where Can We Observe Crosslinguistic Influence?

CLI operates in all linguistic subsystems (syntax, lexis, etc.) and in both perception and production (Jarvis & Pavlenko, 2008; Odlin, 1989). As explained above, types of transfer such as phonological, orthographical, morphological, syntactic, semantic, lexical, discursive, pragmatic, and sociolinguistic have typically been attributed to structural and semantic similarities and differences between languages. However, these linguistic subsystems may be affected by crosslinguistic influence differently. In contrast to phonological and lexical transfer, for example, morphological and syntactic transfer may not appear overtly; for example, learners will usually not transfer inflectional morphemes from one language into another. However, they may manifest themselves more subtly in learners' production and perception, as seen in the studies of von Stutterheim and Nüse (2003) and Bylund and Jarvis (2011), which showed how grammatical aspects (i.e., progressive or imperfective aspect) in learners' L1s may affect how they conceptualize events in the L2.

Crosslinguistic influence has been extensively documented in the area of lexis. In particular, corpus-based transfer studies of recurrent word combinations (lexical bundles, n-grams) have demonstrated that lexical transfer is not only about making mistakes and using false cognates. It is also about selecting preferred word combinations for which there is often a direct equivalent in the L1 (Jarvis & Paquot, 2012; Paquot, 2013). Recently, corpus-based studies have also helped to document the existence of transfer effects in areas thought to be more impervious to transfer, such as temporal morphology (Gujord, 2017; Jarvis & Odlin, 2000).

CLI can also be caused by similarities and differences in the conceptual categories and structures that underlie linguistic encoding (Jarvis & Pavlenko, 2008). For example, language-specific principles of event construal (e.g., the role of grammatical aspect on event construal) are difficult to restructure in a second language. As a result, CLI sometimes occurs because L2 learners fail to acquire the preferred patterns of event construal in the L2 as they draw on patterns from their L1 or other previously-learned languages (Bylund & Jarvis, 2011; von Stutterheim & Nüse, 2003). Studies of conceptual transfer have thus far relied on types of data other than corpora, e.g. experimental data such as eye tracking, speech onset time, and various judgement tasks. An exception is Golden (2017), who argued that conceptual transfer is a plausible explanation for the differences she observed in how different L1 groups express emotions in texts extracted from the ASK Norwegian learner corpus.

As mentioned in the introduction, CLI is observable in both L1 and L2+ learning and use, yet most research to date has focused on forward transfer, i.e. how learners' knowledge and use of prior-learned languages affects their subsequent languages. However, the L2 may also affect the L1 or other languages previously acquired (reverse transfer), and the L2 may affect the L3 (lateral transfer) (Cenoz, Hufeisen, & Jessner, 2001; Rothman, Alonso, & Puig-Mayenco, 2019). To the best of this author's knowledge, there are almost no corpus-based studies of reverse or lateral transfer. An exception is Martins and Pinharandas Nunes' (2013) corpus-based study of Chinese learners of L3 Portuguese. Based on oral recordings of event descriptions, the researchers claimed to find preliminary evidence for instances of lexical, morphological, and semantic transfer from the learners' English L2 to their Portuguese L3.

What Are the Effects of Crosslinguistic Influence?

CLI can have a range of consequences for L2 learning. When knowledge of previously-acquired languages assists and leads to greater accuracy and a faster rate of L2 learning, we say that positive transfer occurs. When the influence of (predominantly) the native language leads to learning difficulties, we speak of negative transfer or interference. The most straightforward manifestations of negative transfer take the form of errors (omission or incorrect distribution of forms). Negative transfer may also cause learners to progress more slowly with specific forms or patterns in the L2. Most state-of-the-art reviews of transfer posit that it affects the rate but not the route or course of development; CLI cannot affect how something is learned, but when it is learned (e.g., Ortega, 2013). However, recent corpus-based studies have challenged this generalization (Luk & Shirai, 2009; Murakami & Alexopoulou, 2016).

Corpus-based transfer studies have also been instrumental in shifting emphasis from L1-induced errors and difficulties to other more subtle effects of CLI. Particularly, the focus has been on detecting L1-specific patterns of overuse and underuse of L2 structures or words (see Chapter 8, this volume). Overuse and underuse do not often result in errors but still make learner language stand out from that of native speakers. In the area of lexis and phraseology, for example, a number of corpus-based studies have shown that learners from different L1s differ from each other, and from native speakers, in the frequencies with which they produce words and word combinations in the target language. This line of research suggests that learners' preferred patterns for lexical sequence production can be traced back to patterns in their L1, including how corresponding word sequences are used and how frequent they are in the L1 (e.g., Paquot, 2017).

Not all effects of CLI are directly observable in learner corpora. For instance, it would be particularly difficult to provide corpus-based evidence of L1-based avoidance, i.e. a phenomenon by which learners sometimes decide not to use a specific form or structure to avoid difficulties (see Schachter, 1974). Written learner corpora are typically made up of final products and do not provide relevant information about the writing process. In addition, unlike the more constrained data types used in SLA, learner texts or spoken productions are often not elicited with a view toward creating specific contexts that encourage learners to use particular linguistic structures. As a result, it will often be impossible in a learner corpus to ascribe lack of use to avoidance. Similarly, conceptual transfer effects cannot easily be detected in corpus data, at least not when a corpus is the only data source (see Golden, 2017; Gujord, 2017; Jarvis, 2017). Therefore, to investigate these manifestations of CLI, adopting a mixed-method approach with corpus data and experimental data is recommended (see Chapter 10, this volume).

Main Research Methods

In recent decades, an important topic in transfer research has been how to best design studies that produce findings which verify the existence or non-existence of CLI. This section focuses on two methodological frameworks that have been widely used in corpus-based transfer research. The first is Granger's (1996) Integrated Contrastive Model (ICM), a framework developed within LCR. The second is Jarvis's framework, which originated from a methodological synthesis in SLA.

Granger's (1996) Integrated Contrastive Model and the Role of Contrastive Analyses in Transfer Research

The study of CLI "depends greatly on the systematic comparisons of languages provided by contrastive analyses" (Odlin, 1989, p. 28). Regardless of whether one understands CLI as a process, a strategy, or an inert outcome, contrastive knowledge of the languages involved is essential. Sylviane Granger's research at UCLouvain, Belgium, has played a leading role here by

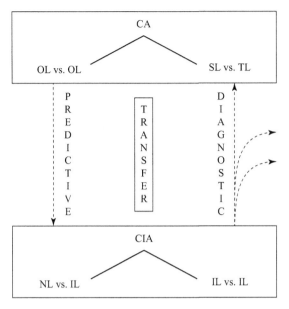

Figure 26.1 Integrated Contrastive Model (From Gilquin, 2000/2001, p. 100, Based on Granger, 1996, p. 47).

demonstrating how transfer studies can benefit from L1 and L2 corpora and by highlighting the importance of using empirically validated contrastive data as a basis for research. Granger put forward the Integrated Contrastive Model (Granger, 1996; Chapter 8, this volume), a model that was later refined and developed by others such as Gilquin (2008). The core of the ICM model (see Figure 26.1) is the combination of traditional contrastive analysis (CA) and contrastive inter-language analysis (CIA). This second component represents an innovative use of contrastive analysis that involves comparing learners' use of the target language to native language use as identified by authentic data from corpora. According to Granger (1996), the researcher can for-mulate predictions about learner language behavior based on CA data, and these can then be tested by CIA data.

ICM comprises two types of contrastive analysis: 1) comparisons of different languages, i.e. the L1 and the L2 (CA), and 2) comparisons of two varieties of the same language (CIA), either of a native language and a non-native language, or of two or more non-native varieties (interlanguages) produced by learners with different L1 backgrounds. Part of the purpose of the Integrated Contrastive Model was to re-evaluate earlier contrastive claims and test them against authentic data extracted from multilingual corpora. This was important because many previous contrastive studies and contrastive statements were "largely intuition-based" and not empirically founded (Granger, 2003, p. 18). The compilation of the *International Corpus of Learner English* (ICLE), initiated by Granger, allowed for large scale comparative studies of learner language based on authentic contrastive data, and many ICLE-studies have demonstrated the usefulness of Granger's contrastive methodology in the study of CLI.

Jarvis's (2000) Framework: Evidence/Arguments for Transfer Effects in Learner Language

In SLA, methods for detecting transfer were brought to the fore by Scott Jarvis. In 2000, he claimed that CLI had largely been treated as a "you-know-it-when-you-see-it phenomenon"

(p. 246), and that the field needed to establish a rigorous methodological framework in order to elaborate more closely on the nature of L1 influence and its interactions with other factors. Jarvis's framework encompasses the following parts:

(1) a theory-neutral definition of the phenomenon,
(2) a list of accepted and sufficient evidence for transfer effects, and
(3) a register of outside variables.

Jarvis' (2000) theory-neutral definition describes CLI as "any instance of learner data where a statistically significant correlation (or probability-based relation) is shown to exist between some feature of learners' IL [interlanguage] performance and their L1 background" (p. 252). This definition does not detail the nature of transfer, but it places emphasis on the empirical evidence needed for claiming transfer effects in interlanguages.

As for evidence for CLI, Jarvis included four types in his framework, which he presented, exemplified, and refined over several publications (e.g., Jarvis, 2010, 2016, 2017). The first two types of evidence aim to detect group-based behavior; the relevant question is whether learners from the same group perform similarly to each other, and differently from learners from other groups:

1. Intragroup homogeneity (comparing the L2 performance of learners from the same group)
2. Intergroup heterogeneity (comparing the L2 performance of learners from different groups)

The latter two aim to detect source-based behavior, i.e. whether the L2 performance can be traced back to the source language (e.g. L1). This can be done by investigating two phenomena:

3. Cross-language congruity, which refers to agreement between the performance of the learner in the L2 and the L1 (comparing the L2 performance and the L1 performance of the same learners)
4. Intralingual contrast, which refers to specific differences between the L1 and the L2 (comparing the learner's L2 performance to linguistic contrasts between the L1 and L2)

To illustrate, to argue for transfer effects, the interlanguage behavior the researcher observes must be similar for learners with shared L1's (intragroup homogeneity). Thus, to claim that learners of L1s without grammatical gender (e.g. English, Vietnamese) will experience more difficulties with gender assignment in L2s with gender marking (e.g. Norwegian, German) due to their L1 background, the researcher must first document that incorrect gender assignment is a pattern that is typically observed among learners with the same genderless L1 background. Next, the researcher also needs to investigate whether these difficulties are specific to learners with this particular language background (intergroup heterogeneity). In other words, it is not enough to document that L1 English and L1 Vietnamese learners tend to assign incorrect gender in German or Norwegian L2. The researcher will also have to compare their gender assignment to that found in learners with an L1 background other than English or Vietnamese, preferably learners who have gender assignment in their L1. However, in order to draw firm conclusions about whether transfer is present in a certain situation, such comparisons of group-based interlanguage behavior alone are insufficient. The next step is to gather evidence that the interlanguage behavior identified as specific to a particular language group can be traced back to the source language. There are two ways of verifying whether the learner performance is motivated by the corresponding features in the source language. Based on evidence 3, cross-language congruity, researchers can investigate whether the interlanguage behavior has a parallel in L1 behavior. In the case of the Vietnamese learners of L2s with grammatical gender, the researcher could empirically validate that Vietnamese learners do not mark gender on nouns in Vietnamese, but instead, make systematic use of classifiers on nouns according to properties such as animacy and geometrical shape. Whether or not the L2 performance can be traced back to the source language can also be detected by evidence 4, intralingual contrast. The researcher then closely inspects whether the linguistic contrasts between the L1 and the L2 re-emerge in the learners' L2 use. Thus, the researcher who is studying transfer in the acquisition of grammatical gender could examine the learners' use of a combination of L2 features that are relevant to grammatical gender marking (e.g. adjective inflection, noun phrase inflection) in order to investigate whether or not the observed difficulties with gender assignment in German or Norwegian L2 reflect a unique combination of influences from the L1. Regarding Vietnamese-speaking learners acquiring a genderless L2, Vietnamese has multiple classifiers (i.e., words that accompany nouns), and languages with gender have multiple grammatical genders. Although these two types of nominal classification systems are different, one hypothesis would be that Vietnamese-speaking learners try to impose their classifier system onto the grammatical gender system in the L2. For instance, Ragnhildstveit (2017) observed that Vietnamese learners of Norwegian rely more on semantic considerations when assigning gender to nouns, as they frequently use the optional Norwegian feminine gender in cases where the noun denotes a feminine entity. Given that the classification in Vietnamese depends on the semantics of the noun referent, it could be argued that the source of this behavior is the Vietnamese-speaking learners' knowledge of the noun classifier system in Vietnamese.

The comparison-based approach described here rests upon comparisons of languages and interlanguage performances. Such studies should ideally build on the four types of evidence illustrated above, although, as underscored by Jarvis, it is not always feasible or even necessary to gather all four; the main goal is to rule out other possible explanations (Jarvis, 2010, 2016).

The comparison-based approach, here presented by Jarvis' model and Grangers' model, is by far the most widely used method for transfer studies in SLA and LCR. However, another approach put forward by Jarvis (2010), the detection-based approach, has also emerged on the basis of advances in LCR and is valuable because these transfer studies are always corpus-based. Detection-based studies approach transfer from a different angle than the comparison-based studies; they do not rely on initial contrastive comparisons of languages and interlanguage performances. Instead, they build on the assumption that if there are effects of CLI in the interlanguage, these source-language specific patterns will be detectable as long as the computer system is fed enough information about the relevant L2 features (Jarvis, 2010). Detection-based studies typically seek to identify L2 writers' L1 backgrounds by applying machine-learning methods to the analysis of linguistic features of L2 texts (see Jarvis & Crossley, 2012).

In addition to types of evidence or identification criteria, Jarvis (2000) also listed variables that transfer studies should take into account. These are age, personality, motivation, language aptitude, social, educational, and cultural background, language background, type and amount of target language exposure, target proficiency level, distance between the L1 and the target language, task type/area of language use, and prototypicality/markedness of linguistic features (Jarvis, 2000). These variables should be included in transfer studies to ensure that potential L1 influence is not obscured by other factors which could also influence L2 acquisition and use. Furthermore, they help to preclude claims of evidence for transfer in cases where the detected pattern has resulted from another type of influence or a combination of influences (Jarvis, 2000). Many studies do not include information about all these variables. The challenge is not so much to gather the information needed and to build corpora with significant background information from the L2 writers or speakers. Rather, the real challenge is to exploit all the information in the analysis of transfer, which calls for multifactorial studies that allow for analysis of the influence of various independent variables, both isolated and in interaction with one another (see Chapter 9, this volume).

Notably, the models presented here share several features, as they both relate to the CLI phenomenon and incorporate two types of contrastive analysis (Gilquin, 2008). Particularly, effects 3 and 4 of Jarvis's framework align with the thinking behind Granger's model. The most important difference between the two models is found in the purpose. Whereas Jarvis aims to provide a rigorous method for determining whether learner performance can be ascribed to CLI, Granger aims at predicting and diagnosing CLI based on corpus data (Gilquin, 2008).

Representative Corpora and Research

The Norwegian learner corpus ASK, developed by Kari Tenfjord at the University of Bergen, Norway, contains 1,700 texts (1.1 million-word tokens) written as responses to two different official tests of Norwegian for adult immigrants (Meurer, 2012; Tenfjord, Meurer, & Hofland, 2006). The corpus includes interlanguage data from learners with 10 different L1s, which represent a typologically diverse group of languages (Albanian, Bosnian-Croatian-Serbian, Dutch, English, German, Polish, Russian, Somali, Spanish, and Vietnamese). ASK was automatically tagged for grammatical information and manually annotated for various types of deviations from the native language norm (Tenfjord, Meurer, & Hofland, 2006; see also Chapter 7 on error analysis). Based on the annotation of the original learner texts, a second version of the same texts, the corrected texts, has also been released. In addition, a control corpus was compiled from responses to the same tests written by native speakers of Norwegian. The test takers provided personal information (sex, age, country of origin, educational background, knowledge of English, length of residence, current status, L2 exposure, etc.), and texts from seven of the L1s were reassessed and linked to the Common European Framework of Reference for Languages (Carlsen, 2012).

Gujord (2017) shows how a corpus-based study enables investigating CLI in areas purportedly less affected by the knowledge of previously-acquired languages. Gujord used Jarvis's (2000) framework to investigate the use of preterit and perfect morphology in L2 Norwegian by 73 Vietnamese-speaking and 88 Somali-speaking learners. The Norwegian perfect construction has no counterpart in Somali, but its prototypical function parallels the use of temporal/aspectual markers in Vietnamese. This analysis revealed transfer effects manifested as statistically significant occurrences of incorrect encoding. For example, Somali learners erroneously exchanged the preterit for the present perfect and vice versa. Accordingly, compared to Vietnamese learners, Somali learners were more likely to produce incorrect sentences in Norwegian such as *Jeg har flyttet mange ganger da jeg bodde i PLACE[3] ("I have moved many times when I lived in PLACE") and *Jeg tenkte meg å bli sykepleier siden jeg var barn" ('I thought of being a nurse since I was a child').

Launched in 1990 by Sylviane Granger of UCLouvain in Belgium, ICLEv3 is one of the largest learner corpora, with its third version containing 5 million words distributed over 3,640 texts (Granger et al., 2020) and argumentative essays written by high-intermediate to advanced learners of English as a foreign language from 25 different L1 backgrounds (Bulgarian, Brazilian Portuguese, Chinese, Czech, Dutch, Finnish, French, German, Greek, Hungarian, Italian, Japanese, Korean, Lithuanian, Macedonian, Norwegian, Pakistani, Persian, Polish, Russian, Serbian, Spanish, Swedish, Turkish, and Tswana). The students provided background information, such as L1, age, sex, and educational background. ICLE is also grammatically annotated.

Paquot's (2017) study of recurrent sequences in texts extracted from a selection of ICLE subcorpora exemplifies the power of corpus-based methods in the investigation of lexical transfer and demonstrates how corpus-based transfer studies can shed light on transfer constraints (in this case, frequency). Paquot investigated 1) whether Spanish and French speakers were influenced by their L1 (Spanish and French) in the frequency with which they used 3-word lexical bundles in English and 2) whether the differences between the L1 groups' use of lexical bundles could be attributed to frequency differences in Spanish and French. The study made use of Jarvis's (2000) framework to analyze these discourse oriented lexical bundles. Paquot concluded that the French and Spanish learners showed a preference in their use of English lexical bundles that reflected their L1 frequency patterns. She also showed that differences in the use of lexical bundles between the L1 groups reflected frequency differences of those same lexical bundles between Spanish and French.

Future Directions

The most obvious contributions of LCR to transfer studies are empirical and methodological. Some of the recent, carefully designed corpus studies have provided generalizable knowledge of CLI based on large samples of data with methodological and argumentative rigor. Corpus-based transfer studies have enabled researchers to discover subtle patterns that are difficult to capture in other types of data, particularly in the area of lexis. However, there are several issues in CLI that remain insufficiently investigated and which future corpus-based transfer research should explore. First, one relationship that is not yet clearly understood is the connection between transfer and L2 proficiency. The compilation of more longitudinal learner corpora could assist, as it would make possible future research tracking the development of individual learners over time, preferably from the initial stage. In addition, the field needs corpus-based transfer studies that build on the combination of an L1 corpus and a learner corpus with text or speech produced by the same group of learners. Such 'same-writer-bilingual designs' (Ortega, 2015, p. 84) would make it possible to compare L1 and L2 performance more directly and possibly at the individual level as well, providing, for instance, important insights into the relationship between L1 and proficiency.

Future corpus-based transfer studies should also build on corpora of learner language produced by beginning learners. Learner corpus data from the earliest stage of acquisition could offer insight into the timing of CLI and bring new empirical findings into the discussion of whether transfer operates in the initial stages (e.g., Pienemann & Håkansson, 2007). In this way, learner corpus research could also help address another bias in SLA research in general, and transfer studies more particularly: the majority of contributors are intermediate or advanced L2 learners.

Another major challenge in CLI research is to disentangle the effects of transfer from those of other sources that influence the learning process (e.g., Jarvis, 2000). According to Wulff and Gries (2015), the majority of LCR-based research has not yet realized its potential to model complex phenomena in SLA. However, advances in this area are important, as the use of more complex statistical procedures to analyze the interplay between multiple independent variables and their effect on the dependent variable could offer important insights into the question of when transfer occurs (see Chapter 9, this volume).

Corpus-based studies have mostly investigated forward transfer; however, in the future, corpus-based transfer research should underscore the importance of studying the full range of learners' multilingual backgrounds instead of focusing exclusively on CLI from the learners' L1s. Corpus-based transfer studies could reveal how transfer works in several directions and specifically explore how the languages of multilinguals affect each other. Our understanding of L1 attrition could also benefit more from corpus-based approaches.

Moreover, the research on L2 English in SLA and LCR is heavily favored, and much of our knowledge of CLI rests upon researching this demographic. However, due to the increasing corpora available for different languages (both L1s and L2s), corpus-based studies of transfer could validate or even challenge earlier assumptions, such as the belief that CLI primarily occurs when the languages involved are similar. Because most participants in SLA studies have a European language background and thus an L1 typologically similar to the L2 (English), such generalized knowledge should be tested against other L1s and L2s.

LCR has sometimes been criticized by SLA researchers for being too descriptive and not sufficiently oriented toward SLA theories (Rankin, 2015). However, learner corpora could contribute to theoretical discussion in a variety of ways. Valuable sources of data in transfer studies could be informed by various emergentist theories of L2 learning, where frequency of input is an important construct (see, for instance, Paquot, 2017). They could also be valuable resources in processing-based accounts of L2 learning, such as MacWhinney's Competition Model (1992), wherein learner corpora would suitably ground the testing of transfer predictions (e.g., Ragnhildstveit, 2017).

Finally, most corpora today are cross-sectional and composed of written data; however, the steady growth in types of learner corpora increases opportunities for researchers to widen their scope and strengthen what we know less about, e.g. how and to what extent transfer operates in areas such as discourse and pragmatics (Gilquin, 2015; Paquot & Plonsky, 2017). The range and size of learner corpora, along with the effective tools used in learner corpus research, is what has made corpus-based studies advantageous for L1 influence research in the first place. In the future, corpus-based transfer studies should expand their scope and strive to unveil the complexity of the relationship between the languages of multilinguals and its consequences for language learning and use.

Further Reading

Cenoz, J., Hufeisen, B., & Jessner, U. (2001). *Cross-linguistic influence in third language acquisition: Psycholinguistic perspectives*. Clevedon: Multilingual Matters.

Although more recent publications on transfer in third language acquisition exist, this monograph is a good starting point because it is still the most comprehensive account of how transfer from one or several L1s and L2s may operate in subsequent language learning.

Jarvis, S., & Crossley, S. A. (2012). *Approaching language transfer through text classification: Explorations in the detection-based approach*. Bristol: Multilingual Matters.

This book introduces the detection-based approach and exemplifies through a number of studies how L2 writers' L1 background can be detected using different procedures and tools, and by investigating specific features of L2 texts.

Jarvis, S., & Pavlenko, A. (2008). *Crosslinguistic influence in language and cognition*. New York: Routledge.

This monograph is still the most comprehensive synthesis of CLI research. It introduces and redefines methodological and theoretical issues in transfer research within a cognitive framework.

Related Topics

Chapters 7, 8, 9, 13, 21, 25, and 30.

Notes

1 Jarvis (2000) and Alonso (2002) also mention a fourth view: transfer as a constraint on learner hypotheses proposed by Schachter (1983) and discussed by Selinker (1992). However, it is not clear how this view differs from the process view of transfer, and furthermore, this view is not fronted in today's literature.
2 See chapter 6 in Jarvis and Pavlenko (2008) for an account of factors influencing the nature and occurrence of CLI.
3 Place is made anonymous.

References

Alonso, R. (2002). Transfer: Constraint, process, strategy or inert outcome? *Revista de Filología y su Didáctica*, *25*, 85–101.
Bylund, E., & Jarvis, S. (2011). L2 effects on L1 event conceptualization. *Bilingualism: Language and Cognition*, *14*(1), 47–59. doi:10.1017/S1366728010000180

Carlsen, C. (2012). Proficiency level - A fuzzy variable in computer learner corpora. *Applied Linguistics*, *33*(1), 1–24. doi:10.1093/applin/amr047

Ellis, N. (2006). Selective attention and transfer phenomena in L2 acquisition: Contingency, cue competition, salience, interference, overshadowing, blocking, and perceptual learning. *Applied Linguistics*, *27*(2), 164–194. doi:10.1093/applin/aml015

Fries, C. C. (1945). *Teaching and learning English as a foreign language*. Ann Arbor: University of Michigan Press.

Gilquin, G. (2000/2001). The integrated contrastive model: Spicing up your data. *Languages in Contrast*, *3*(1), 95–123. doi:10.1075/lic.3.1.05gil

Gilquin, G. (2008). Combining contrastive and interlanguage analysis to apprehend transfer: Detection, explanation, evaluation. In G. Gilquin, S. Papp, & M. Belén Díez-Bedmar (Eds.), *Linking up contrastive and learner corpus research* (pp. 3–33). Amsterdam: Rodopi. doi:10.1163/9789401206204_002.

Gilquin, G. (2015). From design to collection of learner corpora. In S. Granger, G. Gilquin, & F. Meunier (Eds.), *The Cambridge handbook of learner corpus research* (pp. 9–34). Cambridge: Cambridge University Press.

Golden, A. (2017). Emotions negotiated in L2 texts: A corpus study of written production by adult learners on a Norwegian test. In A. Golden, S. Jarvis, & K. Tenfjord (Eds.), *Crosslinguistic influence and distinctive patterns of language learning: Findings and insights from a learner corpus* (pp. 188–230). Bristol: Multilingual Matters.

Granger, S. (1996). From CA to CIA and back: An integrated approach to computerized bilingual and learner corpora. In K. Aijmer, B. Altenberg, & M. Johansson (Eds.), *Languages in contrast: Papers from a symposium on text-based cross-linguistic studies, Lund 4-5 March 1994* (pp. 37–51). Lund: Lund University Press.

Granger, S. (2003). The corpus approach: A common way forward for contrastive linguistics and translation studies. In S. Granger, J. Lerot, & S. Petch-Tyson (Eds.), *Corpus-based approaches to contrastive linguistics and translation studies* (pp. 17–29). Amsterdam: Ropodi.

Granger, S., Dupont, M., Meunier, F., Naets, H., & Paquot, M. (2020). *The international corpus of learner English: Version 3*. Louvain-la-Neuve: Presses universitaires de Louvain.

Gujord, A. K. H. (2017). The "perfect candidate" for transfer: A discussion of L1 influence in L2 acquisition of tense-aspect morphology. In A. Golden, S. Jarvis, & K. Tenfjord (Eds.), *Crosslinguistic influence and distinctive patterns of language learning: Findings and insights from a learner corpus* (pp. 29–63). Bristol: Multilingual Matters.

Jarvis, S. (2000). Methodological rigor in the study of transfer: Identifying L1 influence in the interlanguage lexicon. *Language Learning*, *50*(2), 245–309. doi:10.1111/0023-8333.00118

Jarvis, S. (2010). Comparison-based and detection-based approaches to transfer research. In L. Roberts, M. Howard, M. Ó. Laoire, & D. Singleton (Eds.), *EUROSLA yearbook* (pp. 169–192). Amsterdam: John Benjamins.

Jarvis, S. (2016). The scope of transfer research. In L. Yu & T. Odlin (Eds.), *New perspectives on transfer in second language learning* (pp. 17–47). Bristol: Multilingual Matters.

Jarvis, S. (2017). Transfer: An overview with an expanded scope. In A. Golden, S. Jarvis. & K. Tenfjord (Eds.), *Crosslinguistic influence and distinct patterns of language learning. Findings and insights from a learner corpus* (pp. 12–28). Bristol: Multilingual Matters.

Jarvis, S., & Crossley, S. A. (2012). *Approaching language transfer through text classification: Explorations in the detection-based approach*. Bristol: Multilingual Matters.

Jarvis, S., & Odlin, T. (2000). Morphological type, spatial reference, and language transfer. *Studies in Second Language Acquisition*, *22*(4), 535–556. doi:10.1017/S0272263100004034

Jarvis, S., & Paquot, M. (2012). Exploring the role of n-grams in L1 identification. In S. Jarvis & S. A. Crossley (Eds.), *Approaching language transfer through text classification: Explorations in the detection-based approach* (pp. 71–105). Bristol: Multilingual Matters.

Jarvis, S., & Pavlenko, A. (2008). *Crosslinguistic influence in language and cognition*. New York: Routledge.

Kellerman, E. (1983). Now you see it, now you don't. In S. Gass & L. Selinker (Eds.), *Language transfer in language learning* (pp. 112–134). Rowley: Newbury House.

Lado, R. (1957). *Linguistics across cultures: Applied linguistics for language teachers*. Ann Arbor: The University of Michigan Press.

Luk, Z. P., & Shirai, Y. (2009). Is the acquisition order of grammatical morphemes impervious to L1 knowledge? Evidence from the acquisition of plural −s, articles, and possessives. *Language Learning*, *59*(4), 721–754. doi:10.1111/j.1467-9922.2009.00524.x

MacWhinney, B. (1992). Transfer and competition in second language learning. In R. J. Harris (Ed.), *Cognitive processing in bilinguals* (pp. 371–390). Amsterdam: North-Holland.

Martins, C., & Nunes, Pinharanda (2013). L2 to L3 transfer: Learner corpora analyses. *Learner Corpus Studies in Asia and the World, 1*, 271–281.

Meurer, P. (2012). ASK - norsk *andrespråkskorpus*. Bergen: University Computing. Retrieved from http://clarino.uib.no/ask/ask

Murakami, A., & Alexopoulou, T. (2016). L1 influence on the acquisition order of English grammatical morphemes: A learner corpus study. *Studies in Second Language Acquisition, 38*(3), 365–401. doi:10.1017/S0272263115000352

Odlin, T. (1989). *Language transfer: Cross-linguistic influence in language learning*. Cambridge: Cambridge University Press.

Odlin, T. (2003). Cross-linguistic influence. In C. J. Doughty & M. H. Long (Eds.), *The handbook of second language acquisition* (pp. 436–486). Oxford: Blackwell Publishing.

Odlin, T., & Yu, L. (2016). Introduction. In L. Yu & T. Odlin (Eds.). *New perspectives on transfer in second language acquisition* (pp. 1–16). Bristol: Multilingual Matters.

Ortega, L. (2013). *Understanding second language acquisition*. New York: Routledge.

Ortega, L. (2015). Syntactic complexity in L2 writing: Progress and expansion. *Journal of Second Language Writing, 29*, 82–94. doi:10.1016/j.jslw.2015.06.008

Paquot, M. (2013). Lexical bundles and L1 transfer effects. *International Journal of Corpus Linguistics, 18*(3), 391–417. doi:10.1075/ijcl.18.3.06paq

Paquot, M. (2017). L1 frequency in foreign language acquisition: Recurrent word combinations in French and Spanish EFL learner writing. *Second Language Research, 33*(1), 13–32. doi:10.1177%2F0267658315620265

Paquot, M., & Plonsky, L. (2017). Quantitative research methods and study quality in learner corpus research. *International Journal of Corpus Linguistics, 3*(1), 61–94. doi:10.1075/ijlcr.3.1.03paq

Pienemann, M., & Håkansson, G. (2007). Response article full transfer vs. developmentally moderated transfer: A reply to Bohnacker. *Second Language Research, 23*(4), 485–493. doi:10.1177%2F0267658307080332

Ragnhildstveit, S. (2017). Gender assignment and L1 transfer in Norwegian second language learners' written performance. In A. Golden, S. Jarvis, & K. Tenfjord (Eds.), *Crosslinguistic influence and distinctive patterns of language learning: Findings and insights from a learner corpus* (pp. 110–154). Bristol: Multilingual Matters.

Rankin, T. (2015). Learner corpora and grammar. In S. Granger, G. Gilquin, & F. Meunier (Eds.), *The Cambridge handbook of learner corpus research* (pp. 231–254). Cambridge: Cambridge University Press.

Ringbom, H. (2007). *Cross-linguistic similarity in foreign language learning*. Clevedon: Multilingual Matters.

Rothman, J., Alonso, J. G., & Puig-Mayenco, E. (2019). *Third language acquisition and linguistic transfer*. Cambridge: Cambridge University Press.

Schachter, J. (1974). An error in error analysis. *Language Learning, 24*(2), 205–214.

Schmid, M. S. (2016). First language attrition. *Language Teaching, 49*(2), 186–212. doi:10.1017/S0261444815000476

Swain, M., & Lapkin, S. (2000). Task-based second language learning: The uses of the first language. *Language Teaching Research, 4*(3), 251–274. doi:10.1177%2F136216880000400304

Tenfjord, K., Meurer, P., & Hofland, K. (2006). The ASK Corpus–A language learner corpus of Norwegian as a second language. Paper presented at the proceedings of the 5th international conference on language resources and evaluation (LREC). Genova, Italy.

Von Stutterheim, C., & Nüse, R. (2003). Processes of conceptualization in language production: Language-specific perspectives and event construal. *Linguistics, 41*(5), 851–881. doi:10.1515/ling.2003.028

Wulff, S., & Gries, S. Th. (2015). Prenominal adjective order of preferences in Chinese and German L2 English: A multifactorial corpus study. *Linguistic Approaches to Bilingualism, 5*(1), 122–150. doi:10.1075/lab.5.1.05wul

27
Variability

Dana Gablasova

Introduction

Variability in language learning is a central concept in second language acquisition research (Ellis, 2008; Hulstijn, 2013; Romaine, 2003; Tarone, 1988), with VanPatten and Williams (2014) describing it as one of the major phenomena in L2 learning that needs to be accounted for in second language acquisition (SLA) theories. Variability in language learning is a term used to refer to the fact that both the process of how we learn a second language and the outcomes of language learning tend to differ for individual learners or groups of learners even if the conditions for language learning are fairly similar (e.g., Grüter, Lew-Williams, & Fernald, 2012; Robertson, 2000). This variability can be observed and studied at different stages of language acquisition; it can be also observed with respect to different aspects of the language learning process. For example, learners may show variability in their attainment of different linguistic skills such as speaking or comprehension as well as in their acquisition of different subsystems of language such as syntax or lexicon (e.g., Dyson, 2016; McCarthy, 2008; Murakami, 2016; Trenkic, 2007).

Variability in language learning has been observed both between learners as well as within individual learners. Between learners, the learning process can vary, for example, with respect to the rate of their L2 development, that is, the speed at which learners acquire L2 knowledge, or in terms of the amount of L2 knowledge gained by learners in the same period of time (Mitchell, Myles, & Marsden, 2013; Montrul, De La Fuente, Davidson, & Foote, 2013; Myles, 2014). Within individual learners, variability has been described with respect to situations where a learner's interlanguage manifests variable knowledge of a particular linguistic construction; this can occur either around one point in time (at one stage of learning) or is demonstrated over a period of time (e.g., Romaine, 2003; Tarone, 1998). This variable knowledge becomes apparent when learners produce different versions (forms) of a particular construction to express the same function. For example, Ellis (2008, p. 131) gives an account of a young Portuguese learner of English who, within the same communicative event (a game), used two different forms to express a negative construction, 'no + verb' and 'don't + verb' ('No look at my card' and 'Don't look at my card').

In addition to describing the patterns of variability in L2 production, SLA research on variability aims to explain systematic differences in L2 acquisition by different (groups of) learners, identify factors that contribute to this variation, and understand their role in the learning process (Myles, 2015; Tarone, 1988; VanPatten & Williams, 2013). Three groups of factors – linguistic, social and psychological – have been recognized in this research as the main causes leading to L2 variability (Ellis, 1985, 2008; Romaine, 2003; Tarone, 1998). However, while many cases of variation within and between learners can be explained by these factors, it has been argued that a certain degree of variation is likely to be related to the language learning process itself (Ellis, 2008). This notion is central to the paradigm of Dynamic Systems Theory (DST) which considers variability in language acquisition to be an inherent part of language development; as such, DST postulates that variability between different versions of a particular construction (such as in the example on negation given above) becomes particularly prominent and observable at the time when learners move from one stage of language knowledge to another (De Bot, Lowie, & Verspoor, 2007; Verspoor, Lowie, & Van Dijk, 2008; see also Chapter 14, this volume, to read more about DST).

Understanding systematic variation and regular patterns in language production also lies at the heart of corpus linguistics and corpus-based analyses of language use (McEnery & Hardie, 2011; McEnery, Xiao, & Tono, 2006). The field of corpus linguistics offers quantitative methods for describing patterns of L2 variability across different linguistic subsystems and linking these patterns to underlying factors (variables) (McEnery, et al., 2019; Myles, 2015). In this chapter, we will explore how corpora and corpus methods can contribute to our understanding of the nature of L2 variability and the factors that affect language learning outcomes.

Core Issues and Topics

Factors Affecting L2 Variability

Corpus data and corpus methods can be very valuable for identifying patterns of variability in L2 learning that appear across a range of components of language (such as grammar and pragmatics) and at different levels of granularity (e.g., focusing at individual forms or combining them to study language functions). However, as VanPatten and Williams (2014) stress, in addition to describing patterns in L2 learning, it is equally important for SLA research to strive to find an explanation for the observed phenomena. Without doubt, corpora can prove very useful in this task, serving as an effective resource for examining several of the key variables (predictors) that have been linked to L2 variability and learning outcomes (Myles, 2015).

The factors affecting L2 use investigated in corpus-based studies of learner language variability have covered several major areas of interest to SLA researchers (Ädel, 2015; Romaine, 2003). These include i) linguistic variables related to the linguistic characteristics of the target linguistic feature and its context, ii) learner-related variables (e.g., proficiency, L1 background, and learning experience), iii) social variables, related to the social characteristics of a group of speakers (e.g., age and gender), and iv) situational variables, related to the linguistic setting of the communication (e.g., genre/register and task). Although this list suggests that it is possible to address a large number of factors involved in language learning with corpus-based approaches, so far only some of these variables have featured more systematically in corpus-based studies, whereas other variables, although equally important, enjoyed considerably less attention.

Linguistic Variables

Linguistic variables (related to both the target linguistic variable as well as the context in which it was used) have traditionally been of major interest in corpus-based research focusing on variation in both L1 and L2 use and included, for example, linguistic properties of the target linguistic construction such as its morphological, semantic and syntactic characteristics, collocational properties, lexico-grammatical patterns, and frequency of use. This group of variables has proved to be a major factor in L2 variability, especially in combination with variables from the other three categories discussed below (e.g., Deshors, 2015; Gries & Wulff, 2013; Wulff, Römer, &

Swales, 2012). The type of linguistic variables that can be included in studies on L2 variability are demonstrated in the study by Wulff and Gries (2019) that focused on how intermediate-level learners of English make decisions about where to place particles in phrasal verbs and what factors affect learners' decision to either keep the verb and the particle together or to separate them (the former practice is represented in the example 'Max picked up the book' and the latter illustrated by 'Max picked the book up'). In order to explain the variation in learners' placement of the particle, the study considered the effect of linguistic variables which had been found to play a role in L1 speakers' choices about particle placement such as the complexity of the direct object, the semantic properties of the object (e.g., concreteness), the absence or presence of a prepositional phrase in the clause, whether the particle and the verb were part of a formulaic string of words, and a number of phonological predictors such as rhythmic alternation involved in pronouncing the utterance which included the verb and the particle. To illustrate how these linguistic variables can affect the variation in speakers' choice of particle placement, let us consider one of these features, the complexity of the direct object. As Wulff and Gries (2019) explain, previous studies found a consistent preference of L1 speakers to place the particle before a direct object if this involves a long and (often) complex phrase (such as in the example 'Max picked up the heavy book which belonged to his sister'). This tendency is usually explained by speakers' processing abilities, where producing the particle before the long object would involve placing a lower demand on memory than if the speaker opted to produce the long direct object and still had to place the particle at the end. The study investigated whether the variation in the placement of particle by L2 users can be explained by and follows similar systematic processing preferences related to each of the linguistic variables and their combinations.

Learner-related Variables

In addition to linguistic predictors of L2 variability, another major group of variables explored in corpus-based learner language research so far concerned learner-related factors such as individual characteristics of learners or their language learning history (e.g., Brezina & Bottini, 2019). From among these variables, L2 proficiency and L1 background of learners play an especially prominent role in explaining variability observed in learner language (Granger, 2015) and have been studied in relation to a large number of linguistic features. For example, at the level of lexis, researchers addressed the effect of proficiency and L1 background on the learning of individual words and multiword units, combinations of lexical and grammatical features as well as lexical sophistication and diversity (e.g., Gilquin, 2019; Kyle & Crossley, 2015; Laufer & Waldman, 2011; Römer & Berger 2019). This type of research can be illustrated with a study by Granger and Bestgen (2014) who analyzed collocations (i.e. pairs of words that tend to co-occur together) in written production of L2 learners of English from two proficiency levels (intermediate and advanced). The authors reported, among other things, variability in the use of low-frequency, strongly-associated collocations (such as *tectonic plates* and *immortal souls*) between the two proficiency groups, demonstrating the role played by L2 proficiency in the acquisition of formulaic competence. In another example of research that involved the lexical dimension of language knowledge, Römer and Garner (2019) focused on the use of a lexico-grammatical structure, the verb-argument constructions (VACs), in the speech of English learners from Spanish and Italian L1 backgrounds at three levels of proficiency. VACs include constructions such as 'V *about* noun' as in 'she talked about her favorite music'. The results revealed variation in the knowledge and production of VACs that was linked to the difference in the overall L2 proficiency of these learners.

The two learner-related factors, L2 proficiency and L1 background, have also been very productive in corpus research on trends in L2 acquisition and use of grammatical structures. An example of such research on grammatical features is Collentine and Asención-Delaney (2010), who examined the acquisition of Spanish copula verbs *ser* and *estar* + adjective and the use of this structure in written production by L1 English learners of Spanish from three levels of instruction (and by proxy, proficiency). The results revealed variability in learners' production with respect to clusters of lexico-grammatical features that co-occurred with the two structures produced by Spanish learners at different levels of instruction. This insight contributed to the understanding of *ser/estar* acquisition by L2 learners. In another study that looked at variability in learners' grammatical knowledge in relation to their L1 background and proficiency level, Murakami and Alexopoulou (2016) used a learner corpus to investigate the order of acquisition of different morphological features. Focusing specifically on six English grammatical morphemes (articles, past tense *-ed*, plural *-s*, possessive *'s*, progressive *-ing*, and third person *-s*), the study found that the order of acquisition of these morphemes was influenced by and varied in relation to learners' L1 backgrounds, thus challenging the claim that there exists a universal order of acquisition of these grammatical features.

Researchers have also focused on the role of L2 proficiency and L1 background in the investigation of variability in areas that have so far enjoyed less attention in corpus-based SLA research such as pragmatics and fluency. While pragmatic research has traditionally relied on close textual analysis, it is possible to combine it successfully with quantitative corpus-based analysis of patterns. For example, Gablasova and Brezina (2017) used a large spoken corpus representing interactive L2 English to examine variability in L2 pragmatic knowledge by investigating the effect of proficiency on the politeness strategies in the expression of disagreement by learners of English. The study revealed that as the proficiency increased, more politeness markers were employed by L2 speakers, resulting in increasingly complex pragmatic strategies used to deal with the negative speech act of disagreement. With respect to examining variability in L2 fluency, Götz (2019) used learner and native-speaker corpora to analyze how linguistic features related to fluent spoken production (e.g., filled and unfilled pauses) vary in relation to whether these were produced by L1 or L2 speakers.

While L2 proficiency is a key variable in learner corpus research, major issues have been raised with respect to its definition and operationalization in corpus studies of L2 use (e.g., Carlsen 2012). A key concern in this area is related to the fact that the validity of the proficiency information available about learners in corpora representing L2 use as proficiency is often not evaluated (rated) directly but is instead estimated on the basis of proxy measures such as the number of years spent learning L2 or the level of education achieved by the learners in the corpus. The lack of reliable information about L2 proficiency can thus make it difficult to interpret corpus-based studies that report correlations between this variable and language learning outcomes.

Other learner-related variables traditionally of interest to SLA, such as the age of exposure or the type of exposure to L2, have so far received less systematic treatment (for an overview of research see Mukherjee & Götz, 2015) even though the studies that have considered the influence of these variables on learning outcomes of L2 learners (e.g., Bulon, 2020.; Hendrikx, Van Goethem, & Wulff, 2019) demonstrated that they can act as strong predictors of variability observed in L2 outcomes and thus represent a particularly interesting avenue of corpus-based research on L2 variability. Likewise, cognitive and psychological variables playing a role in the learning process such as working memory, attention, aptitude, and learnings styles have not yet been more fully explored in corpus-based studies. The role of individual differences in language learning is discussed in greater detail in Chapter 30.

Social Variables

With respect to social variables, while several variables such as gender have been given considerable attention in corpus-based studies on native speaker production (e.g., McEnery, Xiao, & Tono, 2006), a similar approach has not yet been adopted in corpus-based SLA-oriented research.

While, understandably, some of the traditional sociolinguistic variables such as social class may not appear to be of direct relevance to SLA concepts and concerns, the investigation of the socio-economic background of learners, their educational level, and age can contribute considerably to our understanding of the variation in learners' language use and their linguistic choices (e.g., Bigelow & Watson, 2011; DeKeyser, 2013). Social variables therefore deserve more systematic attention in corpus research on L2 variability.

Situational Variables

The study of situational variables, related to various aspects of the communicative setting in which the language is produced, has had a long tradition in corpus studies on L1 variation related to the difference in genres, registers, or modes of communication (e.g., Biber, 1988; Biber & Conrad, 2009). This research area is especially relevant to SLA, as in many respects, this set of variables draws on similar principles as task-based research in SLA. It is encouraging to see that corpus-based research studying the effects of different task characteristics on variation in learner production is steadily on the rise (e.g., Ädel, 2008; Alexopoulou et al., 2017; Gablasova & Brezina, 2015; Gablasova, Brezina, McEnery, & Boyd, 2017; Tracy-Ventura & Myles, 2015). In general, these studies, so far, found systematic variation in language use related to the nature of the task and/or setting in which learners produced the language, demonstrating how different aspects of learners' language ability become activated in different communicative conditions.

Main Research Methods

This section focuses on methods and analytical procedures employed in corpus-based research of L2 variability. Three methodological procedures, along with the statistical techniques most commonly associated with them are discussed: i) whole corpus design, ii) individual text/speaker design, and iii) linguistic feature design (for a more detailed discussion of each method see Brezina, 2018). The first two approaches follow a contrastive research design, which most commonly involves a comparison of different groups of language users (e.g., native vs non-native speakers) or a comparison of different levels of one variable (e.g., speakers from different levels of L2 proficiency). The third approach draws on the variationist sociolinguistics tradition used to investigate systematic variation in language use (Labov, 1972) (see Chapter 17, this volume, for a detailed discussion of the approach). It is worth noting that learner language analysis in corpus-based research is undergoing a critical methodological reflection, with the first methodological approach recognized as problematic in certain circumstances and the two remaining approaches becoming more dominant in the field (see also Chapter 8, this volume). Overall, while univariate designs have been common in research so far, multivariate studies of variation in learner language are becoming increasingly frequent (e.g., Gries, 2015; Murakami, 2016; Wulff & Gries, in press), allowing researchers to capture complex interactions among variables and produce more robust models of language production (see Chapter 9, this volume).

Whole Corpus Design

In this research method, data from individual speakers or texts are used in the format of aggregate datasets (corpora), with each corpus compiled to represent a particular independent variable whose effect on L2 variability is to be studied. For example, patterns found in a corpus representing speech of L2 advanced learners can be compared to those from a corpus representing L1 speakers, allowing the investigation of the effect of L2 on the linguistic feature in question. The statistical techniques employed to establish whether the difference in language use in the two (or more) corpora is statistically significant and can thus be attributed to the effect of the independent variable typically include the chi-squared test or log likelihood. For example, Fung and Carter (2007) compared the frequency of discourse markers in spoken academic English of L1 speakers represented by a subsection of the *Cambridge and Nottingham Corpus of Discourse in English* (CANCODE) (Carter, 1998) and in the discourse of Chinese L2 speakers of English from a secondary school in Hong Kong. They reported finding systematic differences between the two groups, which they attributed to the limited exposure to the target language by the Hong Kong learners of English.

This approach has dominated corpus-based research on variability in L1 as well as L2 for a considerable period of time. In more recent research, however, there have been calls for abandoning the methodology due to a number of issues inherent in the analysis, which raise concerns about the validity of findings based on this research design and statistical tests (Bestgen, 2013; Gablasova, Brezina, & McEnery, 2017). One major concern is related to the lack of information about the effect of individual contributions to the overall frequency of the target forms (Brezina & Meyerhoff, 2014); in other words, in this approach, due to the structure of the data (i.e. language production from all speakers is combined together), we do not know whether the instances of the target linguistic feature were produced by a few or many speakers and how typical they may thus be of the whole group of learners represented in the corpus. As a result, the method is gradually being replaced by different methodological approaches (see below).

Individual Text/Speaker Design

This method is similar to the whole-corpus research design in that it involves the comparison of data from two or more corpora that represent an independent variable or its levels and are used to investigate the effect of this variable on variability in learner language. Thus, for example, we can examine the effect of L1 background on the ability of learners to produce appropriate academic collocations using two corpora, each representing learners from a different L1 background. The major difference from the whole-corpus approach lies in the fact that in the individual text/speaker design, the differences in the production of individual language users in each of the corpora are taken into consideration in the statistical techniques used for establishing relationships between patterns in language use and the factors that influence them. Such techniques typically come from the set of generalized linear models of statistical tests (e.g., t-tests, ANOVAs, repeated-measures ANOVA, and correlation) which take into account both the differences between individual contributions in each corpus (within-group differences) as well as the difference between two or more corpora (between-group differences). The approach relies on comparing the frequency with which the target linguistic features occur in each corpus under comparison and is suitable for research of a broad variety of linguistic features, e.g., lexical, lexico-grammatical, morpho-syntactic as well as discourse-related variables. This research design is illustrated in a study by Gablasova, Brezina, McEnery, and Boyd (2017), described in the *Representative Corpora and Research* section.

Linguistic Feature Design

This method focuses on a specific linguistic feature or a set of features and aims to explain their variation in use by L2 learners. The focus of the analysis is on different variants of the same linguistic variable (e.g., different forms expressing negation such as *not, no, none, etc.*) and explaining in what ways their production varies and what influences this variation. When explaining the variation, linguistic, speaker-related, and text-related factors, as well as their interactions (e.g., proficiency of learners, the effect of the task, the type of exposure to L2 experienced by learners) are often taken into consideration (Brezina, 2018, Chapter 6). The statistical techniques involved in this methodology are multivariate statistical tests such as mixed effect modelling and (multiple) logistic regression. The method is very effective in identifying the often complex sources of variability with respect to the use of specific linguistic features in L2 production; however, one of the challenges of this method is related to the relatively limited number of linguistic features that satisfy the conditions for using this approach, such as being able to identify all the obligatory positions in the text (i.e. all the places where the variable should appear). The approach is thus most suitable for investigation of morpho-syntactic features (rather than lexical and discourse features). An example of the application of this research method can be seen in a study by Deshors (2015) reported in the following section.

Representative Corpora and Research

This section provides an overview of two corpora that have been used for studies on variability in L2 spoken production, accompanied by a brief description of an illustrative research study based on each of them.

The *Trinity Lancaster Corpus* (TLC) of spoken L2 English (Gablasova, Brezina, & McEnery, 2019) at present contains more than four million words from over 2,000 L2 speakers in interaction with L1 speakers. The data were collected as part of the *Graded Examinations in Spoken English* (GESE) (Trinity College London, 2016), developed and conducted by Trinity College London, a major international examination board. The corpus contains data from L2 speakers involved in two to four speaking tasks that represent different speaking situations and speaker roles, allowing for analyses of the effect of task on L2 production. The TLC also contains metadata about a number of learner-related variables, including L2 proficiency (B1 to C2 of the CEFR scale), age, and linguistic and cultural background of L2 speakers. A fully comparable corpus of L1 spoken interaction, built along the same principles as the TLC, is currently being developed at Lancaster University.

Applying the individual text/speaker design described above, the TLC was used in a study on second language lexical and pragmatic ability by Gablasova, Brezina, McEnery, and Boyd (2017) to investigate the effect of four different speaking tasks (one monologic and three dialogic tasks) on the expression of epistemic stance in the production of 132 advanced learners of English. The results showed systematic variation in the frequency and type of epistemic markers (e.g., 'maybe', 'I believe') according to the task type, indicating learners' ability to adjust their production of pragmatic markers in relation to the contextual demands of different communicative events. Specifically, the study found that learners' use of epistemic markers varied in relation to the degree of interactiveness of the tasks, speaker role, and topic control.

The *Louvain International Database of Spoken English Interlanguage* (Gilquin, De Cock, & Granger, 2010) consists of over one million words from 554 L2 speakers representing eleven L1 backgrounds, taking part in three speaking tasks with an interviewer (L1 or L2 speaker of English). The corpus also contains information on learner-related variables such as age and gender, as well as information on learning context such as (the length of) stay in an English-speaking country. While the original version of the corpus was compiled and released in 2010, new components of the corpus representing speakers from additional backgrounds (e.g., Turkish, Czech, Brazilian Portuguese, or Finnish) are still being developed, further enhancing the value of the corpus.

The LINDSEI corpus was used by Deshors (2015) in a study on the use of *may* and *can* in spoken and written production of English learners with Chinese and French L1. For the analysis of spoken production, the study used the French (50 interviews) and Chinese (53 interviews) subsections of the LINDSEI corpus. Using logistic regression, Deshors analyzed the relationship between a large variety of morpho-syntactic and semantic features on the variation in the use of the two modals. The results revealed fine-grained differences (e.g., the choice was related to the presence/absence of passive construction) between the use of the two modals by speakers from different L1 backgrounds and further indicated the role of language processing demands and grammatical contexts on the choice of the modals by the two learner groups. The study contributed to the recognition of the need for multivariate research designs in analysis of learner language in order to capture the complex interaction of learner-related and linguistic variables.

Future Directions

Corpus-based research on variability in learner language is a valuable source of information about learner language knowledge and use, complementing SLA studies based on different research traditions and evidence (e.g., experimental and classroom research). This section highlights the areas that can be addressed to further strengthen the significance and relevance of corpus findings to our understanding of why learners vary in their use of language and in their linguistic attainment. Four issues will be discussed here: the role of L1 speakers in the L2-focused corpus-based research, the comparability of corpora, the diversity of the corpus methods used in SLA research, and attention to the so far underrepresented factors affecting L2 variability.

The first issue concerns the role of L1 production in the comparative research framework used by a large number of corpus-based studies on L2 use. In the three research methods described in the *Main Research Methods* section, data from L2 users are frequently compared to data from L1 users, and the L1 production is used as a benchmark against which the L2 production can be evaluated. However, L1 production should not be automatically accepted as a norm in these studies but, rather, should be examined critically (e.g., Granger, 2015; Leech, 1998). It is often the case that if the L2 patterns differ from those found in the L1 corpus, this is commonly seen as problematic on the L2 part and pedagogical interventions are typically suggested based on this difference (e.g., Fung & Carter, 2007). However, to further our understanding of L2 variability, it is equally important to evaluate the quality of L1 production and variation within it (e.g., Dąbrowska, 2012). As demonstrated by psycholinguistic studies of L1 users (e.g., Andringa & Dąbrowska, 2019; Birdsong & Gertken, 2013), L1 linguistic knowledge and practices can differ considerably in relation to variables such as education, age, and socio-economic background. L1 production in corpus-based studies should be therefore examined more systematically (e.g., Gablasova et al., 2017) to enable us to better understand the broader patterns of variation in language in general, helping with the interpretation of corpus findings based on L2 data.

The second issue is related to the representativeness of corpora and their ability to represent the independent variables under investigation. To measure variability meaningfully, we need to ensure that the corpus data collection follows reliable methods and does not introduce additional systematic bias to the data (Gilquin, 2015). For example, if we wish to compare the number of adjectives produced by Chinese and German learners of Italian in order to observe the effect of linguistic background, we have to ensure that the corpora representing the two groups of learners have been collected along the same principles, and thus the language and speakers represented in each corpus differ only with respect to their linguistic background (Gablasova, Brezina, & McEnery, 2017; Gilquin, 2015; Leech, 2007). Without ensuring a high degree of comparability of the corpora, the potential differences discovered between the two groups of speakers could be related to other (confounding) variables such as different education or proficiency levels, or different data collection methods involved in the creation of each of the corpora. While in SLA research, participant information and data collection procedures are typically closely scrutinized (Mackey & Gass, 2005), corpus-based learner studies do not yet routinely follow a similar procedure, which could enhance the validity and generalizability of the findings of this research (Gablasova, Brezina, & McEnery, 2019).

Third, as seen throughout this chapter and, in particular, in *Main research methods*, a variety of corpus-based traditions and methods can be applied to the investigation of variability in learner language. Researchers should thus carefully reflect on the best practice in the field and select the method suitable for the research question(s), corpus structure and design, and linguistic variables involved in their study. It should be stressed that this diversity of approaches is a desirable feature of current and future corpus-based research on learner language, as the methods have a potential to complement each other and non-corpus-based SLA research, allowing for triangulation of different methodological approaches to strengthen our understanding of factors contributing to the variability in L2 use (Egbert & Baker, 2019).

Finally, as highlighted in the discussion in *Factors affecting L2 variability*, some factors related to variability in L2 learning have not yet been explored more fully in corpus-based research although corpus approaches would be well suited for their analysis (e.g., the effect of age on learning outcomes). At present, it may not be possible to investigate these variables systematically, as the relevant corpora of L2 language may not provide sufficient data for exploring the effect of these variables. This challenge needs to be addressed in two ways. First, researchers should be encouraged to consider these variables in their studies, provided the data are available in existing corpora. Second, it is crucial to continue to raise awareness of the importance of these variables among researchers working on the development of learner corpora, so that these variables can be collected during corpus creation and included in the metadata in new corpus projects (for a discussion see Gablasova, Brezina, & McEnery, 2019).

Further Reading

Gilquin, G. (2019). Light verb constructions in spoken L2 English: An exploratory cross-sectional study. *International Journal of Learner Corpus Research, 5*(2), 181–206.

The paper examines the use of light verb constructions (e.g., combinations such as *make a decision*) in L2 spoken English. In addition to examining the effect of L2 proficiency, a relatively frequent variable in research on learner language, the study also explores the effect of a less commonly investigated variable, the type of acquisitional context, and compares the effect of English as a Foreign Language (EFL) and English as a Second Language (ESL).

Gries, S. Th. & Deshors, S. (2014). Using regressions to explore deviations between corpus data and a standard/target: Two suggestions. *Corpora, 9*(1), 109–136.

The paper provides an excellent discussion of the importance of using regression to study variation in L2 learner production in comparative designs with groups of L1 and L2 users. The method and statistical techniques involved in the analysis are demonstrated in a case study on the use of two modals, *can* and *may,* by French and Chinese learners of English.

Murakami, A. (2016). Modelling systematicity and individuality in nonlinear second language development: The case of English grammatical morphemes. *Language Learning, 66*(4), 834–871.

The paper explains and demonstrates the use of mixed-effects models and their potential in analyzing variation in L2 development. In particular, the paper uses a longitudinal learner corpus to analyze variation in the development of accuracy of English grammatical morphemes.

Related Topics

Chapters 14, 17, 26, and 30.

References

Ädel, A. (2008). Involvement features in writing: Do time and interaction trump register awareness? *Language and Computers, 66*(1), 35–53.

Ädel, A. (2015). Variability in learner corpora. In S. Granger, G. Gilquin, & F. Meunier (Eds.), *The Cambridge handbook of learner corpus research* (pp. 379–400). Cambridge: Cambridge University Press.

Alexopoulou, T., Michel, M., Murakami, A., & Meurers, D. (2017). Task effects on linguistic complexity and accuracy: A large-scale learner corpus analysis employing natural language processing techniques. *Language Learning, 67*(s1), 180–208.

Andringa, S., & Dąbrowska, E. (2019). Individual differences in first and second language ultimate attainment and their causes. *Language Learning, 69*(s1), 5–12.

Bestgen, Y. (2013). Inadequacy of the chi-squared test to examine vocabulary differences between corpora. *Literary and Linguistic Computing, 29*(2), 164–170.

Biber, D. (1988). *Variation across speech and writing*. Cambridge: Cambridge University Press.

Biber, D., & Conrad, S. (2009). *Register, genre, and style*. Cambridge: Cambridge University Press.

Bigelow, M., & Watson, J. (2011). The role of educational level, literacy, and orality in L2 learning. In S. M. Gass & A. Mackey (Eds.), *The Routledge handbook of second language acquisition* (pp. 462–475). London: Routledge.

Birdsong, D., & Gertken, L. M. (2013). In faint praise of folly: A critical review of native/non-native speaker comparisons, with examples from native and bilingual processing of French complex syntax. *Language, Interaction and Acquisition/Language, interaction et acquisition, 4*(2), 107–133.

Brezina, V. (2018). *Statistics in corpus linguistics: A practical guide*. Cambridge: Cambridge University Press.

Brezina, V., & Bottini, R. (2019). Review of Castello, Erik, Katherine Ackerley & Francesca Coccetta, Eds. (2015) Studies in learner corpus linguistics research and applications for foreign language teaching and assessment. *International Journal of Learner Corpus Research, 5*(1), 113–117.

Brezina, V., & Meyerhoff, M. (2014). Significant or random? A critical review of sociolinguistic generalisations based on large corpora. *International Journal of Corpus Linguistics, 19*(1), 1–28.

Bulon, A. (2020). Comparing the "phrasicon" of teenagers in immersive and non-immersive settings: Does input quantity impact range and accuracy? *Journal of Immersion and Content-Based Language Education, 8*(1), 107–136.

Carlsen, C. (2012). Proficiency level - A fuzzy variable in computer learner corpora. *Applied Linguistics, 33*(2), 161–183.

Carter, R. (1998). Orders of reality: CANCODE, communication, and culture. *ELT Journal, 52*(1), 43–56.

Collentine, J., & Asención-Delaney, Y. (2010). A corpus-based analysis of the discourse functions of ser/estar+ adjective in three levels of Spanish as FL learners. *Language Learning, 60*(2), 409–445.

Dąbrowska, E. (2012). Different speakers, different grammars: Individual differences in native language attainment. *Linguistic Approaches to Bilingualism, 2*(3), 219–253.

De Bot, K., Lowie, W., & Verspoor, M. (2007). A Dynamic Systems Theory approach to second language acquisition. *Bilingualism: Language and Cognition, 10*(1), 7–21.

DeKeyser, R. M. (2013). Age effects in second language learning: Stepping stones toward better understanding. *Language Learning, 63*(s1), 52–67.

Deshors, S. C. (2015). A multifactorial approach to linguistic structure in L2 spoken and written registers. *Corpus Linguistics and Linguistic Theory, 11*(1), 19–50.

Dyson, B. P. (2016). Variation, individual differences and second language processing: A processability theory study. *Linguistic Approaches to Bilingualism, 6*(4), 341–395.

Egbert, J., & Baker, P. (Eds.) (2019). *Triangulating corpus methodological approaches in linguistic research*. London: Routledge.

Ellis, R. (1985). Sources of variability in interlanguage. *Applied Linguistics, 6*(2), 118–131.

Ellis, R. (2008). *The study of second language acquisition*. Oxford: Oxford University Press.

Fung, L., & Carter, R. (2007). Discourse markers and spoken English: Native and learner use in pedagogic settings. *Applied Linguistics, 28*(3), 410–439.

Gablasova, D., & Brezina, V. (2015). Does speaker role affect the choice of epistemic adverbials in L2 speech? Evidence from the Trinity Lancaster Corpus. In J. Romero-Trillo (Ed.), *Yearbook of corpus linguistics and pragmatics* (pp. 117–136). Dordrecht: Springer.

Gablasova, D., & Brezina, V. (2017). Disagreement in L2 spoken English: From learner corpus research to corpus-based teaching materials. In V. Brezina & L. Flowerdew (Eds.), *Learner corpus research: New perspectives and applications* (pp. 69–89). London: Bloomsbury Publishing.

Gablasova, D., Brezina, V., & McEnery, T. (2017). Exploring learner language through corpora: Comparing and interpreting corpus frequency information. *Language Learning, 67*(s1), 130–154.

Gablasova, D., Brezina, V., & McEnery, T. (2019). The Trinity Lancaster Corpus: Development, description and application. *International Journal of Learner Corpus Research, 5*(2), 119–125.

Gablasova, D., Brezina, V., Mcenery, T., & Boyd, E. (2017). Epistemic stance in spoken L2 English: The effect of task and speaker style. *Applied Linguistics, 38*(5), 613–637.

Gilquin, G. (2015). From design to collection of learner corpora. In S. Granger, G. Gilquin, & F. Meunier (Eds.), *The Cambridge handbook of learner corpus research* (pp. 9–34). Cambridge: Cambridge University Press

Gilquin, G. (2019). Light verb constructions in spoken L2 English: An exploratory cross-sectional study. *International Journal of Learner Corpus Research*, *5*(2), 181–206.

Gilquin, G., De Cock, S., & Granger, S. (2010). *The Louvain International Database of Spoken English Interlanguage. Handbook and CD-ROM*. Louvain-la-Neuve: Presses universitaires de Louvain.

Götz, S. (2019). Filled pauses across proficiency levels, L1s and learning context variables. A multivariate exploration of the Trinity Lancaster Corpus sample. *International Journal of Learner Corpus Research*, *5*(2), 159–180.

Granger, S. (2015). Contrastive interlanguage analysis: A reappraisal. *International Journal of Learner Corpus Research*, *1*(1), 7–24.

Granger, S., & Bestgen, Y. (2014). The use of collocations by intermediate vs. advanced non-native writers: A bigram-based study. *International Review of Applied Linguistics in Language Teaching*, *52*(3), 229–252.

Gries, S. Th. (2015). Statistics for learner corpus research. In S. Granger, G. Gilquin, & F. Meunier (Eds.), *The Cambridge handbook of learner corpus research* (pp. 159–181). Cambridge: Cambridge University Press.

Gries, S. Th., & Wulff, S. (2013). The genitive alternation in Chinese and German ESL learners: Towards a multifactorial notion of context in learner corpus research. *International Journal of Corpus Linguistics*, *18*(3), 327–356.

Grüter, T., Lew-Williams, C., & Fernald, A. (2012). Grammatical gender in L2: A production or a real-time processing problem? *Second Language Research*, *28*(2), 191–215.

Hendrikx, I., Van Goethem, K., & Wulff, S. (2019). Intensifying constructions in French-speaking L2 learners of English and Dutch. *International Journal of Learner Corpus Research*, *5*(1), 63–103.

Hulstijn, J. H. (2013). Is the second language acquisition discipline disintegrating? *Language Teaching*, *46*(4), 511–517.

Kyle, K., & Crossley, S. A. (2015). Automatically assessing lexical sophistication: Indices, tools, findings, and application. *TESOL Quarterly*, *49*(4), 757–786.

Labov, W. (1972). *Sociolinguistic patterns*. Philadelphia: University of Pennsylvania Press.

Laufer, B., & Waldman, T. (2011). Verb-noun collocations in second language writing: A corpus analysis of learners'. *English Language Learning*, *61*(2), 647–672.

Leech, G. (1998). Preface. In S. Granger & G. Leech (Eds.). *Learner English on computer* (pp. xiv-xx). Abingdon: Routledge.

Leech, G. (2007). New resources, or just better old ones? The Holy Grail of representativeness. In M. Hundt, N. Nesselhauf, & C. Biewer (Eds.), *Corpus linguistics and the web* (pp. 134–149). Amsterdam: Rodopi.

Mackey, A., & Gass, S. M. (2005). *Second language research: Methodology and design*. New York: Routledge.

McCarthy, C. (2008). Morphological variability in the comprehension of agreement: An argument for representation over computation. *Second Language Research*, *24*(4), 459–486.

McEnery, T., Brezina, V., Gablasova, D., & Banerjee, J. (2019). Corpus linguistics, learner corpora, and SLA: Employing technology to analyze language use. *Annual Review of Applied Linguistics*, *39*, 74–92.

McEnery, T., & Hardie, A. (2011). *Corpus linguistics: Method, theory and practice*. Cambridge: Cambridge University Press.

McEnery, T., Xiao, R., & Tono, Y. (2006). *Corpus-based language studies: An advanced resource book*. London: Taylor & Francis.

Mitchell, R., Myles, F., & Marsden, E. (2013). *Second language learning theories* (3rd ed.). Oxon: Routledge.

Montrul, S., De La Fuente, I., Davidson, J., & Foote, R. (2013). The role of experience in the acquisition and production of diminutives and gender in Spanish: Evidence from L2 learners and heritage speakers. *Second Language Research*, *29*(1), 87–118.

Mukherjee, J., & Götz, S. (2015). Learner corpora and learning context. In S. Granger, G. Gilquin, & F. Meunier (Eds.), *The Cambridge handbook of learner corpus research* (pp. 423–442). Cambridge: Cambridge University Press.

Murakami, A. (2016). Modelling systematicity and individuality in nonlinear second language development: The case of English grammatical morphemes. *Language Learning*, *66*(4), 834–871.

Murakami, A., & Alexopoulou, T. (2016). L1 influence on the acquisition order of English grammatical morphemes: A learner corpus study. *Studies in Second Language Acquisition*, *38*(3), 365–401.

Myles, F. (2014). Second language acquisition (SLA) research: Its significance for learning and teaching issues. *Subject centre for languages, linguistics and area studies good practice guide*. Retrieved from https://www.llas.ac.uk/resources/gpg/421.html

Myles, F. (2015). Second language acquisition theory and learner corpus research. In S. Granger, G. Gilquin, & F. Meunier (Eds.), *The Cambridge handbook of learner corpus research* (pp. 309–332). Cambridge: Cambridge University Press.

Robertson, D. (2000). Variability in the use of the English article system by Chinese learners of English. *Second Language Research, 16*(2), 135–172.

Romaine, S. (2003). Variation. In C. J. Doughty & M. H. Long (Eds.), *The handbook of second language acquisition* (pp. 410–435). Malden: Blackwell Publishing.

Römer, U., & Berger, C. M. (2019). Observing the emergence of constructional knowledge: Verb patterns in German and Spanish learners of English at different proficiency levels. *Studies in Second Language Acquisition, 41*(5), 1089–1110.

Römer, U., & Garner, J. (2019). The development of verb constructions in spoken learner English. Tracing effects of usage and proficiency. *International Journal of Learner Corpus Research, 5*(2), 207–230.

Tarone, E. (1988). *Variation in interlanguage*. London: Hodder Arnold.

Tracy-Ventura, N., & Myles, F. (2015). The importance of task variability in the design of learner corpora for SLA research. *International Journal of Learner Corpus Research, 1*(1), 58–95.

Trenkic, D. (2007). Variability in second language article production: Beyond the representational deficit vs. processing constraints debate. *Second Language Research, 23*(3), 289–327.

Trinity College London. (2016). *Exam information: Graded Examinations in Spoken English (GESE)*. Retrieved from http://www.trinitycollege.com/site/?id=368

VanPatten, B., & Williams, J. (Eds.) (2014). *Theories in second language acquisition: An introduction* (second edition). New York: Routledge.

Verspoor, M., Lowie, W., & Van Dijk, M. (2008). Variability in second language development from a dynamic systems perspective. *The Modern Language Journal, 92*(2), 214–231.

Wulf, S., & Gries, S. Th. (2019). Particle placement in learner language. *Language Learning, 69*(4), 873–910.

Wulff, S., & Gries, S. Th. (in press). Explaining individual variation in learner corpus research: Some methodological suggestions. In B. Le Bruyn & M. Paquot (Eds.), *Learner corpus research meets second language acquisition*. Cambridge: Cambridge University Press.

Wulff, S., Römer, U., & Swales, J. (2012). Attended/unattended this in academic student writing: Quantitative and qualitative perspectives. *Corpus Linguistics and Linguistic Theory, 8*(1), 129–157.

28

Formulaicity

Fanny Forsberg Lundell

Introduction

One of the major contributions of corpus linguistics has been the discovery that collocations and other types of multi-word combinations are ubiquitous in natural language. Sinclair (1991) introduced the "idiom principle" to refer to the fact that "a language user has available to him or her a large number of semi-preconstructed phrases that constitute single choices, even though they might appear to be analyzable into segments. To some extent, this may reflect the recurrence of similar situations in human affairs; it may illustrate a natural tendency to economy of effort; or it may be motivated in part by the exigencies of real-time conversation" (Sinclair, 1991, p. 110). Erman and Warren (2000) were among the first to quantify proportions of prefabricated language in corpora (both in a spoken and a written corpus of English) and demonstrated that 58.6% of the spoken productions was composed of preconstructed multi-word combinations, compared to 52.3% of the written productions. These figures suggest that prefabricated language is highly present in both spoken and written language. Another important characteristic of prefabricated language is that it is often idiomatic or language specific, a phenomenon also referred to as 'nativelike selection' (cf. Pawley & Syder, 1983; Warren, 2005, for the notion of 'idiomaticity'). For example, English uses the word combination *have a beer*, whereas French uses *prendre une bière* ['take a beer']. This inherent difficulty for the L2 learner is one of the reasons why corpus linguists have become increasingly interested in prefabricated language and often use learner corpora to examine learners' use and development of multi-word combinations, most particularly collocations and lexical bundles (see Paquot & Granger, 2012, and Ellis, Simpson-Vlach, Römer, O'Donnell, & Wulff, 2015 for overviews).

Language learning theories have also increasingly emphasized the role of prefabricated or formulaic language. Both first language and SLA scholars are interested in whether language learning is rule-based or whether language is acquired through chunks. Usage-based models of language acquisition (i.e., models that rely on the principle that language is acquired through use and exposure to natural language) reserve a key role for formulaicity and chunks (see e.g., Ellis, O'Donnell & Römer, 2016; Chapter 13, this volume). Research has also shown that an L2 user's problems with formulaic language have different implications than problems with a grammatical feature or the pronunciation of a phoneme. As Wray (2002) proposed, formulaic language is linked to processing advantages on both a cognitive and a social level. By conveying a message in a conventional manner, the speaker signals familiarity with, and a sense of belonging to, a specific linguistic community. As such, the use of formulaic language is a means of conforming to social norms and expectations and is accordingly of high importance for the L2 learner.

In the field of SLA, work on formulaicity can be divided into two main strands:

1) Research on L2 learners' ability to acquire formulaicity in a target language (i.e., nativelike selection), often with a focus on learners' attempts at using targetlike forms such as *take a beer* instead of *have a beer;*
2) Research on L2-specific formulaicity (i.e., the non-analyzed chunks mostly visible in beginner learner production) and its contribution to the acquisition of grammatical rules (e.g., the use of *je voudrais* ['I would like'] in oral production which is otherwise characterized by present tense only and no other forms in the conditional).

These diverging strands have created an ambiguity with respect to terminology, because what is considered formulaic language in these two strands overlap at times, but this is not always the case.

Importantly, unlike in learner corpus research, in the SLA literature, the focus has often been not so much on recurrent multi-word combinations such as collocations and lexical bundles than on the broader category of formulaic sequences, i.e. "sequence[s], continuous or discontinuous, of words or other elements, which [are], or appear to be, prefabricated: that is, stored and retrieved whole from memory at the time of use, rather than being subject to generation or analysis by the language grammar" (Wray, 2002, p. 9). Accordingly, formulaic language is an umbrella term for a variety of different linguistic structures (including idioms (*grab the bull by its horns*), collocations (*throw a party*), discourse devices (*on the one hand*), routine formulae (*nice to meet you*), but also L2-specific formulaicity (as described above), whose common denominator is recurrence in production and supposed holistic storage in the speaker's mind. However, the issue of whether or not these multi-word combinations are memorized as whole units is still a matter of debate. This is the reason why some researchers, especially corpus linguists, prefer more general, or descriptive terms such as multi-word units, multi-word combinations, multi-word sequences, or multi-word structures. In this chapter, the terms formulaic language and formulaic sequences will however be used, as they cover both targetlike and L2-specific sequences and are also established terms in SLA where they are often used as synonyms for phraseology and multiword sequences, multiword combinations, etc.

Core Issues and Topics

Three major lines of investigation with respect to formulaic language in learner corpora will be discussed in this section: the extent to which L2 learners acquire targetlike formulaicity, the role of cross-linguistic influence, and L2-specific formulaicity.

To What Extent Do Learners Acquire Targetlike Idiomaticity?

One of the most important findings from SLA research using corpora to investigate formulaicity is that formulaic language takes a long time to acquire. There are also differences between the acquisition of formulaic language in spoken and written production. In addition, the time it takes to acquire formulaic language in a target language will depend on the L1/L2 pairings investigated. Many studies have investigated language pairings that are relatively similar, such as L1 French/L2 English. However, English is a language that enjoys special status, given its pervasiveness in media and culture around the world. In the Swedish context, for example, where English has an important presence in society, Wiktorsson (2003) found that the only difference in written production between advanced university students of English (Swedish L1) and native speakers was that the L2 students overused formulaic sequences that were typical of the spoken register, whereas the native speakers used more adjective + noun collocations or verb + noun collocations typical of written language.

Studies that have investigated other language pairs, including more distant language pairs such as English-Hebrew, have reported different types of results. Levitzky-Aviad and Laufer (2013), for example, analyzed L1 Hebrew learners' use of English collocations in both elicited tests and free writing over the course of 8 years. Two of their key findings were that collocations take a particularly long time to develop in free writing and that learners seem to avoid the use of collocations in free production. Forsberg (2010) investigated both a different mode and a different L2: spoken L2 French. Learners ranged from beginner to near-native levels (very advanced L2 users in a second language context). The general finding was that formulaic language in spoken production is a feature that develops late in the learning process: Only the most advanced learners used formulaic language to degrees that approached native speaker use. These still differed, however, from native speakers in the quantity of lexical collocations they used.

Studies have also started to explore the relationship between proficiency as evaluated using the CEFR (*Common European Framework of Reference*) levels and the use of formulaic language. Forsberg and Bartning (2010) and Paquot (2018, 2019) found that formulaic language developed between the B2–C2 levels in L2 French and L2 English, respectively. These results support the view that formulaic language is a good indicator of second language proficiency, especially at advanced and very advanced proficiency levels.

As will become clear in the *Main Research Methods* section, however, the collocation studies discussed above have relied on different definitions of the term 'collocation', with the use of statistical methods for the identification of formulaic language in corpora becoming more frequent over the last decade. Several studies have used association measures (predominantly MI score and t-score), to extract statistically significant word co-occurrences from learner corpora and shed light on how collocations in learner production differ compared to collocations in L1 productions. MI-score usually detects low-frequency, highly cohesive sequences, whereas t-score detects highly frequent collocations. Durrant and Schmitt (2009) examined the use of frequent English collocations by native speakers (NSs) and non-native speakers (NNs) on the basis of written texts. Collocations were measured with MI scores, t-scores, and raw frequency of occurrence. The results showed that the native writers used more low-frequency combinations (MI-defined collocations) than the non-native writers. Granger and Bestgen (2014) also studied MI-defined collocations and t-score defined collocations in the *International Corpus of Learner English* (ICLE; Granger, Dagneaux, Meunier, & Paquot, 2009). Their results pointed in the same direction: learners produced more high-frequency collocations than highly cohesive infrequent ones, and this was particularly characteristic of lower proficiency levels. Finally, O'Donnell, Römer, and Ellis (2013) studied four different corpus-analytic measures in first and second language writing. They found that the infrequent, highly cohesive MI-defined formulas were less frequent in productions by L2 writers and even in those by non-expert native writers. It therefore seems like being able to produce infrequent, cohesive word combinations is a challenge not only for non-native speakers in general, but also for native speakers in specialist genres.

Is L2 Formulaicity Influenced by L1 Patterns?

L1 entrenchment is one of the main obstacles in learning formulaic language in the L2 (Ellis, 2006). L1 entrenchment is a notion from cognitive psychology that refers to the fact that the learners' linguistic system is organized as an emergent network that has been tuned to the cues of the L1 through thousands of hours of L1 processing (Ellis & Wulff, 2015, p. 82). Thus, the preferred word combinations in the L1 will be strongly entrenched in the mental lexicon, and a lot of training will be necessary to modify the already established connections between words if they are not congruent with the L2. Nesselhauf (2005), for example, investigated a subcorpus of the ICLE, the ICLE-GE which contains argumentative essays from learners with German as L1. One of the major findings of her study was that learner collocation errors were often not due to the form of the collocation, for example its degree of restriction (i.e., how many words the component parts can combine with, e.g., in the sequence *dial* a number, *dial* can hardly combine with any other nouns). Rather, the errors were often related to L1 influence (*make homework (should be 'do homework'), possibly from German *Hausaufgaben machen*).

L1 entrenchment will not always lead to errors; it can also be facilitative. For example, some experimental studies have shown that the processing of collocations is facilitated by the congruence phenomenon, i.e., when the collocation is identical in the L1 and the L2 (cf. Wolter & Gyllstad 2011; Peters 2016). L1 entrenchment and the frequency effects associated with it can also be the source of learners' preferences for specific formulaic sequences (e.g., Ellis, O'Donnell, & Römer, 2015; Chapter 13, this volume). A number of studies by Paquot (e.g., 2013, 2014, 2017) have focused on cross-linguistic effects observed through corpora. For example, Paquot (2014) investigated transfer effects in French English as a Foreign Language (EFL) learners' use of recurrent word sequences, in particular two-to four-word lexical bundles overrepresented in the French component of ICLE, compared with nine other ICLE learner sub-corpora. Lexical bundles are "recurrent expressions, regardless of their idiomaticity, and regardless of their structural status" (Biber et al., 1999, p. 990). The learners' idiosyncratic use of lexical bundles was traced back to various properties of French words and word combinations, including their functions in discourse and their frequency of use (see Representative corpora and research below for more details).

Is Formulaicity in First Language Use and Second Language Use the Same Thing?

Myles, Hooper, and Mitchell have explored L2-specific formulaicity in several corpus studies focusing exclusively on sequences that appear to have psycholinguistic status as formulaic sequences in the L2 learner's system. Myles, Mitchell, and Hooper (1998) examined the relationship between formulaic language and rule acquisition in instructed learners who are encouraged by course activities to memorize unanalyzed units (p. 328). In their longitudinal study of English L1 students of French aged 11–14, Myles et al. (1998) quickly identified *j'aime* [I like] and *j'adore* [I love] as possible examples of L2-specific formulaicity. Learners said for example *la Monique j'aime le tennis* [*'Monique I love tennis'] instead of *Monique aime le tennis* [Monique loves tennis], which suggests that the internal structure of *j'aime* is not analyzed and the sequence is produced as a formulaic sequence. At first, learners were very reliant on formulaic sequences, but when their communicative needs increased, they began to break down the sequences and eventually were able to use parts of them productively (e.g., *tu aimes* [you like]). Myles, Mitchell, and Hooper (1999) examined the same phenomenon, among the same group of learners, but this time by studying interrogative formulas in French L2 and their contribution to the development of grammatical rules. In this study, they observed the same relationship. In the 1998 article, the authors reported having seen the formulas as units which, after their decomposition and analysis, often disappeared from the learner's repertoire. In Myles et al. (1999), the authors stressed even more the role of formulas as material serving the acquisition of grammatical rules. They argue that rules and formulas co-exist and that formulas do not necessarily disappear just because they have served the purpose of figuring out grammatical rules.

Drawing on the work of Myles et al. (1998, 1999), Forsberg (2008) examined similar, learner idiosyncratic, non-analytic constructions in the InterFra corpus (https://www.su.se/romklass/

interfra), another corpus of L2 French but with Swedish high school students aged 16 and 17. Results demonstrated very few sequences of the kind described in Myles et al. (1998, 1999), and they completely disappeared after the beginner level. In order to explain this divergence in results, it is important to consider differences related to pedagogical practices and cognitive maturity. It is possible that the students in the studies of Myles and colleagues had been exposed to more drilling of formulaic sequences and very little teaching of grammatical rules. It is also likely that the age difference between the 11–14-year-olds in the studies of Myles and colleagues and the 16–17-year-olds in Forsberg (2008) influenced the capacity to process grammar.

The abovementioned studies show that when speaking of formulaicity or formulaic language, researchers occasionally refer to non-analyzed utterances, which can be particularly frequent in beginner productions (e.g., *j'aime* [I like], *je voudrais* [I would like]). Most of the time, however, researchers mean targetlike combinations of words, such as 'give a speech', which often do not appear until intermediate to advanced levels of L2 acquisition. Thus, it is important to clarify exactly what kind of formulaic language is in focus in a particular study.

Main Research Methods

Two main types of research methods are typically distinguished when it comes to the identification and analysis of (targetlike) formulaic language in corpora: the phraseological approach and the frequency-based approach (see Granger & Paquot, 2008). These methods are discussed in more detail below based on Erman, Forsberg Lundell, and Lewis (2016). See, for example, Wray and Namba (2003), for more information about methods used in studies that focus on L2-specific formulaicity.

Phraseological Approaches to Formulaicity

One key characteristic of phraseological studies is that they usually rely on manual analysis of linguistic characteristics to define and identify different types of formulaic sequences. Proponents of the phraseological approach have adopted the ideas of the Russian phraseologists from the 1940s, 1950s, and 1960s. Russian phraseology was largely oriented towards fixed and semi-fixed expressions, using criteria such as degree of restrictedness of the expression's component parts. Following the Russian approach, scholars such as Cowie (1981) categorized word combinations along a continuum of idiomaticity, beginning with free combinations (e.g., 'blow a trumpet') at one end, spanning over restricted collocations ('blow a fuse'), which are partly compositional, and figurative idioms (e.g., 'blow your own trumpet') which are non-compositional, and ending with pure idioms ('blow the gaff'), which are completely opaque, at the other end. Only the last three expressions can be labeled phraseological, because at least one of the members of the word combination has a specialized or figurative sense.

Nesselhauf (2003) argued that the most common identification criterion for phraseologists is that of "arbitrary restriction on substitutability" (2003, p. 225). In her own work on phraseologically defined verb-noun collocations, she made use of two criteria, of which at least one needs to apply to the word combination for it to be labeled a collocation:

1) The sense of the verb (or the noun) is so specific that it only allows its combination with a small set of nouns (or, if the noun is the most specific, a small set of verbs) (e.g. 'dial' as in 'dial a number');

2) The verb (or the noun) cannot be used in this sense with all nouns (or in the case of specific nouns, verbs) that are syntactically and semantically possible (e.g. 'take a picture/photo', but not '*take a film') (2003, p. 225).

Nesselhauf's definition is similar to the criterion of 'restricted exchangeability', presented by Erman & Warren (2000) as one criterion to identify what they call 'prefabs' (a synonym for formulaic sequences). Restricted exchangeability means that at least one member of the prefab cannot be replaced by a synonymous item without causing a change of meaning or function and/ or idiomaticity.

While most phraseologists have adopted an approach based on, e.g. restricted collocability or degree of compositionality to identify and categorize multiword combinations, scholars such as Mel'cuk (1998) have also proposed categorizations based on the function of phraseological units in context.

Frequency-based Approaches to Formulaicity

Researchers working within the frequency-based approach to the study of word combinations rarely focus on formulaic sequences in general (in fact, they would hardly use the term at all) but rather are interested in recurrent word combinations that can be identified on the basis of frequency only (typically lexical bundles) or association measures (i.e. [statistical] collocations).

As first discussed in the *Core Issues and Topics* section, lexical bundles are multi-word sequences that recur frequently and are distributed widely across different texts (e.g., *as far as, at the end of*) (Biber 2010, p. 170). The lexical bundles framework is largely data-driven and retrieval can be fully automatized and applied to sizeable text corpora. Three parameters need to be set: length of word combinations (many studies have analyzed 4-word lexical bundles), minimum frequency threshold and a dispersion criterion (see Chen & Baker, 2010 for more details about these parameters). Although they do not necessarily represent complete structural units, lexical bundles have been found to serve important functions in L1 and L2, for instance, in corpora of academic discourse (see Chen & Baker, 2010; Ädel & Erman, 2012). Differences found between L1 and L2 use of lexical bundles typically include overuse of speech-like lexical bundles (e.g. 'all over the world'), underuse of academic-like bundles built around nouns (e.g. 'the way in which') as well as a less varied repertoire of types of bundles.

As mentioned above, the use of association measures is another approach to identifying collocations. Researchers working with statistical measures often analyze relational collocations (i.e. collocations in a specific grammatical relation), investigating, for instance, adjective + noun collocations (e.g., *severe cold*) or verb + noun collocations (*throw a party*). Here, the term 'collocation' should not be understood as arbitrarily restricted word combinations as in the phraseological approach to word combinations but as words that co-occur significantly more than by chance. In most recent collocation studies, association measures have been computed on the basis of frequencies extracted from large reference corpora (e.g. the *British National Corpus* [BNC], the *Contemporary Corpus of American English* [COCA]), not from learner corpora. There are certainly a number of technical reasons that support this methodological decision, including reasons related to the minimum size of a corpus to compute association measures or the fact that association measures that rely on corpus size cannot be directly compared across corpora. However, the most important reason why researchers used association measures computed from reference native or expert corpora to measure collocational strength in learner language is that such scores represent native-like idiomaticity on the basis of which they could rank co-occurrences in learner corpora and judge their acceptability (e.g. Siyanova & Schmitt, 2008; Durrant & Schmitt, 2009; Granger & Bestgen, 2014)[11].

In learner corpus research, two association measures – Mutual Information and t-score – have been used extensively. Mutual information (MI) is a measure derived from information theory that quantifies the mutual dependency between two variables. The MI-score uses a logarithmic scale to express the ratio between the frequency of the collocation and the frequency of random co-occurrence of the two words in the combination (Church & Hanks, 1990). An MI score of > 3 is a regular threshold for a word combination to be considered a statistically significant collocation (see Hunston, 2002). The t-score, on the other hand, "is calculated as an adjusted value of collocation frequency based on the raw frequency from which random co-occurrence frequency is subtracted. This is then divided by the square root of the raw frequency" (Gablasova, Brezina, & McEnery, 2017, p.162). It is often suggested that MI tends to give prominence to low-frequency collocations whose component words are not often found apart (e.g. *ultimate arbiter, immortal souls,* and *tectonic plates*), whereas the t-score prioritizes combinations of more frequent words (e.g. *long way,* and *hard work*) (Durrant & Schmitt, 2009, p. 67). For this reason, researchers have advocated using both measures (Durrant & Schmitt, 2009; Granger & Bestgen, 2014) (see *Core Issues and Topics* section). Note that the two measures have also been heavily criticized, and there have been calls in the field to broaden the range of statistical techniques used to establish the degree of association between words (e.g., Gries, 2013; see also Wulff, Gries, & Lester, 2018 for a study that relies on Delta-P as an association measure to quantify directional attraction).

Comparing Phraseological and Frequency-based Approaches

Not all sequences that are automatically extracted are necessarily interesting from the perspective of the acquisition of targetlike formulaicity. This is, for example, the case with lexical bundleanalysis, where manual analysis is required in separating what is actually a sequence of interest (i.e., targetlike formulaicity) and what is not (e.g., *as a matter of fact* vs. *the age of the*). Automatic extraction also fails to take into account semantic and pragmatic aspects, which can be very important when identifying conventional sequences, given that it is not only a question of conventional form but also of conventional function. An example of this are all the 'clausal' sequences, described in Erman et al. (2015): In everyday and professional interactions, there are an important number of sequences where the form would maybe not be detected as formulaic, but where a typical pragmatic function is connected to a particular sequence. Examples are *I do realize that* in English or *Je vous rassure* in French ['I assure you']. If conventional sequences are not frequent enough, techniques such as n-gram (i.e. lexical bundle) extraction will not extract them despite their idiomatic nature, especially in small learner corpora.

By contrast, the more manual methods that are typically used by phraseologists would make it possible to identify such sequences. But manual analysis comes with its limitations too. First, there is a limit in the amount of text that can be analyzed manually; as a result, phraseological studies are often small scale. Second, identification and categorization criteria are open to subjective interpretation, which may lead to issues of internal consistency and lack of replicability.

In conclusion, given the advantages and limitations described above, the phraseological approach and the frequency-based approach to formulaicity should be viewed as complementary. Future research would definitely benefit from more studies such as Erman, Lewis, and Fant (2013) that compared different approaches on the same corpora to investigate what each method could reveal about native and non-native use of formulaic language.

Representative Corpora and Research

A substantial amount of corpus research into EFL learners' use of formulaic sequences is based on the *International Corpus of Learner English* (ICLE), which consists of 3.7 million words of argumentative essays by L2 English university students, organized into sixteen subcorpora according to the learners' L1 (e.g., Spanish, Italian, French, and Russian; cf. Granger, Dagneaux, Meunier, & Paquot, 2009). For example, Paquot (2017) made use of the Integrated Contrastive Model, a combination of Contrastive Analysis (CA) and Contrastive Interlanguage Analysis

(CIA) (see Chapters 8 and 26, this volume), to investigate L1 effects on French and Spanish EFL learners' preferred use of three-word lexical bundles with a discourse or stance-oriented function. Word combinations were extracted from the French and Spanish ICLE sub-corpora and the frequency of their translation equivalent forms in the native language were analyzed on the basis of French and Spanish L1 corpora. By means of studying two Romance languages as L1s, Paquot showed that even if congruent forms exist in French and Spanish (*dans le cas de* (fr.) / *en el caso de* (sp.) [in the case of]), L1 speakers differ in their propensity to use 'in the case of' in L2 English: Spanish EFL learners use the English word combination much more often than the French EFL learners. This difference can be related to different frequencies of the bundle in the L1s, with *en el caso de* being about 5 times as frequent in Spanish as *dans le cas de* in French. Paquot (2017) thus makes a call for more studies investigating L1 (frequency) effects on learners' use of formulaic language.

The *Stockholm Multi-Task corpus* (Erman, Denke, Fant, & Forsberg Lundell, 2015) is a spoken corpus and includes comparable data produced by learners of three different L2s, i.e., English, French, and Spanish (all with Swedish as the L1). The corpus was compiled for the purpose of the research programme High Proficiency in Second Language Use (cf. Hyltenstam, Bartning, & Fant, 2018) and data were collected from participants not often included in mainstream SLA studies, i.e., long-residency L2 users, often highly educated, who have resided at least five years in the target language community. The corpus contains five different oral activities (one interview, two role plays, and two retellings; hence the label 'Multi-Task') with 10 L1 speakers and 10 L2 speakers for each language, totaling 60 speakers. Data were recorded in Paris, 2007, Santiago de Chile, 2007, and London, 2008. One of the studies based on this corpus, which deals with multi-word sequences in all three L2s, is Erman et al. (2015). Two different communicative tasks from the *Multi-Task Corpus* were investigated: (1) a role play over the phone and (2) an online retelling of a film clip. Nativelike expression in L2 speech was investigated by comparing quantity and distribution of different types of multiword structures in the speech of highly advanced L2 speakers with that of native speakers. The study showed that two L2 groups (English and Spanish L2) were nativelike in their use of one category of multiword structures, i.e., social routines (e.g., *do you want to have a think about it?*), in the role play. Collocations, the dominant category in the retelling task, were underrepresented in all three L2 groups compared to the native groups. Furthermore, the English NNSs were nativelike on more measurements of multiword structures than the French and Spanish NNSs. These results confirm the status of collocations as being particularly difficult for L2 learners, even after many years of immersion in the target language.

Future Directions

In my view, the future of research on formulaic language in SLA is dependent on diversity at two levels. The first level deals with the languages investigated. The entire field of SLA suffers from a bias towards English as a second language. Although grammar has been investigated more thoroughly for other L2s than English, research on formulaicity is still strikingly limited to the English language. I would therefore suggest that the most needed step forward is the investigation of L2s other than English. Research has already been conducted to some extent on L2 French (Forsberg, 2010), L2 Spanish (Erman, Denke, Fant, & Forsberg Lundell, 2015; Stengers, Boers, & Housen, 2011), and L2 Polish (Jaworski, 1990), but much remains to be done. The study on Polish, although small-scale, is thought-provoking because Jaworski (1990) suggested that Polish speakers use less formulaic language than American English speakers in everyday small talk. Such claims indeed underline the importance of crosslinguistic investigations of formulaicity. This improvement in diversity of course entails the development of learner corpora in L2s other than English. The French Learner Language Oral Corpora (FLLOC) (Myles & Mitchell, 2016) and Spanish Learner Language Oral Corpora (SPLLOC) (Mitchell, Dominguez, Arche, Myles, & Marsden, 2008) initiatives for French and Spanish L2s, for example, constitute laudable efforts to fill this gap, and these corpora could be further explored when it comes to the use of formulaic language.

It will also be important to diversify the language pairs investigated. As seen in the *Core Issues and Topics* section, work has already been done on several languages, but a larger variety of languages needs to be compared. It is possible that formulaic language is one of the language features where L1 influence plays a particularly strong role, including both positive and negative transfer, even at the more advanced proficiency levels. One related research avenue worth investigating would be L3 influence in the acquisition of formulaic language. Is the acquisition of formulaic language affected more by the L1 than by other L2s, or are all the languages that a learner knows of equal importance? This kind of research would also have important implications for language teaching, given that contrastive teaching, which includes the L1 and possibly other L2s, could be beneficial for teaching formulaic language, as shown by e.g., Laufer and Girsai (2008).

The second level of diversification refers to the discursive genres investigated (see Myles, 2015). Learner corpora are often composed of written productions in the form of argumentative essays or spoken productions in the form of interviews and retellings. As a result, to date, we know rather much about how (EFL) learners use formulaic language in argumentative essays, in academic writing, and in life-story interviews. However, we know little of how learners perform in other tasks and situations. One exception is Erman et al. (2015) who attempted to diversify tasks by also including phone calls and different retellings for spoken language and showed that formulaic language use differed depending on the communicative genre. If we want to further our understanding of L2 learners' acquisition of formulaic language, the issue of variation across genres needs to be addressed.

In recent years, "language learning in the wild" (Wagner, 2015) has become an important concept within interactional approaches to SLA. In spite of the practical difficulties surrounding the collection and analysis of such authentic data, a welcome addition to the study of L2 formulaic language would be learner corpora documenting naturally occurring speech. Indeed, such corpora would be of interest to scholars investigating formulaic language, especially in view of the social importance of formulaic language (see Burdelski & Cook, 2012) An increasing number of people will need to learn a second language in order to function in society. In this societal context, the efficient use of formulaic language in spoken production, especially in professional communication, is an area that requires much more research. Wray (2002, p. 94) described the use of formulaic language as a means to further speakers' "promotion of self". If this is the case, then it is a vital linguistic feature for all speakers around the world who need to start a new life in a new language. Applied linguists need materials that allow the investigation of ecologically valid questions. This suggests that future research into formulaic language in second language learner corpora should be more "wild".

Further Reading

Ellis, N. C., Simpson-Vlach, R., Römer, U., O'Donnell, M. B., & Wulff, S. (2015). Learner corpora and formulaic language in second language acquisition research. In S. Granger, G. Gilquin, & F. Meunier (Eds.), *The Cambridge handbook of learner corpus research* (pp. 357–378). Cambridge: Cambridge University Press.

This is a useful overview which connects research on formulaic language in corpora with second language learning theories. It gives valuable pointers with respect to identification issues and how they relate to corpus design matters.

Gablasova, D., Brezina, V., & McEnery, T. (2017). Collocations in corpus-cased language learning research: Identifying, comparing, and interpreting the evidence. *Language Learning, 67*(51), 155–179.

This paper constitutes a critical evaluation of learner corpus research into collocations, with useful discussions on identification procedures and the impact of different genres.

Paquot, M., & Granger, S. (2012). Formulaic language in learner corpora. *Annual Review of Applied Linguistics, 32*, 130–149.

This is a state-of-the art article, with a focus on statistical methods of investigation.

Related Topics

Chapters 8, 13, and 25.

Note

1 Note that automatic extraction of collocations and lexical bundles from reference corpora has also been used for the purpose of creating collocation tests in applied linguistics research (cf. e.g. Forsberg Lundell, Lindqvist, & Edmonds, 2018; Gyllstad 2007).

References

Ädel, A., & Erman, B. (2012). Recurrent word combinations in academic writing by native and non-native speakers of English: A lexical bundles approach. *English for Specific Purposes, 31*(2), 81–92.

Biber, D. (2010). *Longman student grammar of spoken and written English.* India: Pearson Education.

Biber, D., Johansson, S., Leech, G., Conrad, S., & Finegan, E. (1999). *Longman grammar of spoken and written grammar.* Harlow: Longman.

Burdelski, M., & Cook, M. (2012). Formulaic language in language socialization. *Annual Review of Applied Linguistics, 32*, 173–188.

Chen, Y., & Baker, P. (2010). Lexical bundles in L1 and L2 academic writing. *Language Learning and Technology, 14*(2), 20–49.

Church, K. W., & Hanks, P. (1990). Word association norms, mutual information, and lexicography. *Computational Linguistics, 16*(1), 22–29.

Cowie, A. P. (1981). The treatment of collocations and idioms in learners' dictionaries. *Applied Linguistics, 2*(3), 223–235.

Durrant, P., & Schmitt, N. (2009). To what extent do native and non-native writers make use of collocations? *IRAL (International Review of Applied Linguistics in Language Teaching), 47*(2), 157–177.

Ellis, N. C. (2006). Selective attention and transfer phenomena in L2 acquisition: Contingency, cue competition, salience, interference, overshadowing, blocking and perceptual learning. *Applied Linguistics, 27*(2), 164–194.

Ellis, N. C., O'Donnell, M. B., & Römer, U. (2015). Usage-based language learning. In B. MacWhinney & W. O'Grady (Eds.), *The handbook of language emergence* (pp. 163–180). Malden: Blackwell Publishing.

Ellis, N. C., Simpson-Vlach, R., Römer, U., O'Donnell, M. B., & Wulff, S. (2015). Learner corpora and formulaic language in second language acquisition research. In S. Granger, G. Gilquin, & F. Meunier (Eds.), *The Cambridge handbook of learner corpus research* (pp. 357–378). Cambridge: Cambridge University Press.

Ellis, N. C., & Wulff, S. (2015). Usage-based approaches to SLA. In. B. VanPatten & J. Williams (Eds.), *Theories in second language acquisition* (2nd ed., pp. 75–93). New York: Routledge.

Erman, B., Denke, A., Fant, L., & Forsberg Lundell, F. (2015). Nativelike expression in the speech of long-residency L2 users: A study of multiword structures in the speech of L2 English, French and Spanish. *International Journal of Applied Linguistics, 25*(2), 160–182.

Erman, B., Forsberg Lundell, F., & Lewis, M. (2016). Formulaic language – theories, methodologies and implications for second language acquisition. In K. Hyltenstam (Ed.), *Advanced proficiency and exceptional ability in second languages* (pp. 111–147). Berlin: Mouton de Gruyter.

Erman, B., Lewis, M., & Fant, L. (2013). Multiword structures in different materials, and with different goals and methodologies. In J. Romero-Trillo (Ed.), *Yearbook of corpus linguistics and pragmatics* (vol. 1, pp. 77–103). Dordrecht: Springer.

Erman, B., & Warren, B. (2000). The idiom principle and the open choice principle. *Text*, *20*(1), 29–62.

Forsberg, F. (2008). *Le langage préfabriqué – formes, fonctions et fréquences en français parlé L2 et L1*. Oxford: Peter Lang Publishing.

Forsberg, F. (2010). Using conventional sequences in L2 French. *IRAL* (*International Review of Applied Linguistics in Language Teaching*), *48*(1), 25–50.

Forsberg, F., & Bartning, I. (2010). Can linguistic features discriminate between the CEFR-levels? A pilot study on written L2 French. In I. Bartning, M. Martin, & I. Vedder (Eds.), *Communicative proficiency and linguistic development. Intersections between SLA and language testing research* (pp. 133–158). Eurosla monograph series 1.

Forsberg Lundell, F., Lindqvist, C., & Edmonds, A. (2018). Productive collocation knowledge at advanced CEFR levels. Evidence from the development of a test for advanced L2 French. *Canadian Modern Language Review*, *74*(2), 627–649.

Gablasova, D., Brezina, V., & McEnery, T. (2017). Collocations in corpus-cased language learning research: Identifying, comparing, and interpreting the evidence. *Language Learning*, *67*(51), 155–179

Granger, S., & Bestgen, Y. (2014). The use of collocations by intermediate vs. advanced non-native writers: A bigram-based study. *IRAL*, *52*(3), 229–252.

Granger, S., Daneaux, E., Meunier, F., & Paquot, M. (2009). *ICLE: International corpus of learner English*. Louvain-la-Neuve: Presses universitaires de Louvain.

Granger, S., & Paquot, M. (2008). Disentangling the phraseological web. In S. Granger & F. Meunier (Eds.), *Phraseology. An interdisciplinary perspective* (pp. 27–49). Amsterdam: John Benjamins

Gries, S. Th. (2013). 50-something years of work on collocations: What is or should be next. *International Journal of Corpus Linguistics*, *18*(1), 137 165.

Gyllstad, H. (2007). *Testing English collocations: Developing receptive tests for use with advanced Swedish learners*. Doctoral dissertation. English Department. Lunds Universitet.

Hunston, S. (2002). *Corpora in applied linguistics*. Cambridge: Cambridge University Press.

Hyltenstam, K., Bartning, I., & Fant, L. (Eds.) (2018). *High-level proficiency in second language use and multilingual contexts*. Cambridge: Cambridge University Press.

Jaworski, A. (1990). The acquisition and perception of formulaic language and foreign language teaching. *Multilingua*, *9*(4), 397–411.

Laufer, B., & Girsai, N. (2008). Form-focused instruction in second language vocabulary learning: A case for contrastive analysis and translation. *Applied Linguistics*, *29*(4), 694–716.

Levitzky-Aviad, T., & Laufer, B. (2013). Lexical properties in the writing of foreign language learning over eight years of study: Single words and collocations. In C. Bardel, C. Lindqvist, & B. Laufer (Eds.), *L2 Vocabulary acquisition, knowledge and use* (pp. 127–148). New perspectives on assessment and corpus analysis. Eurosla monograph series 2.

Mel'cuk, I. (1998). Collocations and lexical functions. In A. P. Cowie (Ed.), *Phraseology. theory, analysis, and applications* (pp. 23–53). Oxford: Clarendon Press.

Mitchell, R., Dominguez, L., Arche, M., Myles, F., & Marsden, E. (2008). SPLLOC: A new database for second language acquisition research. *EUROSLA Yearbook*, *2008*, 287–304.

Myles, F. (2015). Second language acquisition theory and learner corpus research. In S. Granger, G. Gilquin, & F. Meunier (Eds.), *The Cambridge handbook of learner corpus research* (pp. 309–332). Cambridge: Cambridge University Press.

Myles, F., & Mitchell, R. (2016). *French language learner oral corpora (FLLOC)*. Retrieved from http://www.flloc.soton.ac.uk/index.htm

Myles, F., Mitchell, R., & Hooper, J. (1998). Rote or rule? Exploring the role of formulaic language in classroom foreign language learning. *Language Learning*, *48*(3), 323–363.

Myles, F., Mitchell, R., & Hooper, J. (1999). Interrogative chunks in French, *L2*. A basis for creative construction? *Studies in Second Language Acquisition*, *21*, 49–80.

Nesselhauf, N. (2003). The use of collocations by advanced learners of English and some implications for teaching. *Applied Linguistics*, *24*(2), 223–242.

Nesselhauf, N. (2005). *Collocations in a learner corpus*. Amsterdam: Johan Benjamins.

O'Donnell, M. B., Römer, U., & Ellis, N. C. (2013). The development of formulaic sequences in first and second language writing. Investigating effects of frequency, association and native norm. *International Journal of Corpus Linguistics*, *18*(1), 83–108.

Paquot, M. (2013). Lexical bundles and L1 transfer effects. *International Journal of Corpus Linguistics*, *18*(3), 391–417.

Paquot, M. (2014). Cross-linguistic influence and formulaic language: Recurrent word sequences in French learner writing. *EUROSLA Yearbook 2014*, 240–261.

Paquot, M. (2017). L1 frequency in foreign language acquisition: Recurrent word combinations in French and Spanish EFL learner writing. *Second Language Research*, *33*(1), 13–32.

Paquot, M. (2018). Phraseological competence: A missing component in university entrance language tests? Insights from a study of EFL learners' use of statistical collocations. *Language Assessment Quarterly*, *15*(1), 29–43.

Paquot, M. (2019). The phraseological dimension in interlanguage complexity research. *Second Language Research*, *35*(1), 121–145.

Paquot, M., & Granger, S. (2012). Formulaic language in learner corpora. *Annual Review of Applied Linguistics*, *32*, 130–149.

Pawley, A., & Syder, F. (1983). Two puzzles for linguistic theory: Nativelike selection and nativelike fluency. In J. C. Richards & R. W. Schmidt (Eds.), *Language and communication* (pp. 191–227). London: Longman

Peters, E. (2016). The learning burden of collocations: The role of interlexical and intralexical factors. *Language Teaching Research*, *20*(1), 113–138.

Sinclair, J. (1991). *Corpus, concordance, collocation*. Oxford: Oxford University Press.

Siyanova, A., & Schmitt, N. (2008). L2 learner production and processing of collocation: A multi-study perspective. *Canadian Modern Language Review*, *64*(3), 429–458.

Stengers, H., Boers, F., & Housen, A. (2011). Formulaic sequences and L2 oral proficiency. *International Review of Applied Linguistics in Language Teaching*, *49*(4), 321–343.

Wagner, J. (2015). Designing for language learning in the wild: Creating social infrastructures for second language learning. In T. Cadierno & S. Eskildsen (Eds.), *Usage-based perspectives on second language learning* (pp. 75–104). Berlin: Mouton de Gruyter.

Warren, B. (2005.). A model of idiomaticity. *Nordic Journal of English Studies*, *4*(1), 35–54.

Wiktorsson, M. (2003). *Learning idiomaticity. Lund studies in English 105*. Doctoral dissertation. English Department. Lunds Universitet.

Wolter, B., & Gyllstad, H. (2011). Collocational links in the L2 mental lexicon and the influence of L1 intralexical knowledge. *Applied Linguistics*, *32*(4), 430–449.

Wray, A. (2002). *Formulaic language and the lexicon*. Cambridge: Cambridge University Press.

Wray, A., & Namba, K. (2003). Formulaic language in a Japanese-English bilingual child: A practical approach to data analysis. *Japanese Journal of Multilingualism and Multiculturalism*, *9*(1), 24–51.

Wulff, S., Gries, S. Th., & Lester, N. A. (2018). Optional that in complementation by German and Spanish learners. In A. Tyler, L. Huan, & H. Jan (Eds.), *What is applied cognitive linguistics? Answers from current SLA research* (pp. 99–120). Berlin: De Gruyter Mouton.

29
Context of Learning

Joseph Collentine

Introduction

Context of learning became an important second language acquisition (SLA) construct around the year 2000, largely in response to concerns that L2 research overwhelmingly focused on understanding the internal changes that occur during development. Interest in context of learning emerged from a concern that the ontology of SLA resulting from research (i.e., descriptions of the physical, cultural, and social entities involved in learning a second language, and how they relate to each other) centered narrowly on the relationship between input, output, and mental processes, such that we knew little about the effects of sociolinguistic and sociocultural factors as well as L2 socialization on development (Firth & Wagner, 1997). Some began to approach research from the presumption that learning is situated (i.e., context dependent), adopting a sociocultural perspective (e.g., Lantolf, 2000). Indeed, recent proposals on preparing L2 learners for an increasingly international world encourage educators to consider not just the educational experience of the target 'community' abroad but also local settings where the L2 is productive, such as cultural events, markets, and workplaces (Miano, Bernhardt, & Brates, 2016).

Batstone (2002) and others (e.g., Berns, 1989, Firth & Wagner, 1997), contended that various internal as well as external factors shape the developmental process. Batstone (2002) also argued that it is important to distinguish between two contexts to understand the interaction of internal and external factors. *Communicative contexts* are those where learners use the language to interpret and produce messages in real-world situations, which are inextricably anchored to social and cultural situations (e.g., making a purchase, relating one's needs to a host family, telling a story). *Learning contexts* are curricular or institutional controls on the input, output, and tasks that affect acquisition (e.g., methods). Benson (2011) as well as Reinders and Benson (2017) update Batstone's (2002) proposal, presenting a framework with which researchers can characterize a learning situation according to where development occurs and the methods (if any) involved. The context of learning is characterized by (i) setting and (ii) mode. Setting is a place, or the learning environment's physical and geographical characteristics. Setting is also a social space which establishes relationships between a learner in the place as well as other individuals occupying that space. Mode of learning constitutes the conditions that govern how the setting features affect learning. This can range from the type of methodology employed to the learner's autonomous efforts. A given setting and mode is defined along four dimensions:

- Location: Out-of-class vs. classroom. Out of class situations may involve interactions with a host family abroad, using the L2 in a workplace environment, and even extracurricular activities that promote proficiency.
- Formality: Informal vs. formal. Formal settings normally entail institutional contexts of learning (e.g., a school, a language academy). Informal settings range widely, from naturalistic contexts to individual learning projects where learners develop proficiency for personal or professional enrichment.
- Pedagogy: Non-instructed vs. instructed. This not only entails the extent to which linguistic information is structured through teaching but also relates to the source of information the learner has about the language, which can range from textbooks to self-help software.
- Locus of control: Self-directed vs other-directed. This dimension concerns how decisions about learning are distributed between learners and other participants (e.g., teachers, peers, cohorts, friends). For example, researchers can also characterize a learning situation according to individual factors (e.g., autonomy, agency, identity) that ultimately mediate between the classroom, out-of-class experiences, personal interests, and development, and these may shape the learning context.[11]

A crucial implication of the research on context of learning is that traditional (administrative) distinctions (e.g., study-abroad, immersion programs, domestic in-class settings) may be more nuanced than we suspect upon consideration of each context's setting and mode. Corpus-based research assuming that SLA is a multivariate phenomenon (see Norris & Ortega, 2009) indicates that any given social context favors the use of particular discourse types (e.g., descriptive, narrative, hypothetical), which are in turn characterized by a unique set of lexical, grammatical and pragmatic features (Biber & Gray, 2010; Charles, 2012). It follows that particular settings/modes will expose learners to L2 input and interactions that other settings/modes do not, and learner production will vary in important ways as a function of setting/mode. SLA researchers can better characterize and predict the effects of learning contexts by studying and comparing corpora representing both learners' input and output in a given setting/mode (e.g., classroom, internships, community service, host-family interactions). Uncovering the relationship between inputs and outputs entails the use of multivariate analytical approaches, such as multiple regression, to examine potential cause-effect relationships while taking into account low-frequency phenomena and learner variability (see Chapter 9, this volume) and multidimensional corpus-based analyses that identify the discourse types that learners produce and that learners receive in input (Biber, Davies, Jones, & Tracy-Ventura, 2006).

Core Issues and Topics

Learning Contexts Favor Certain Cognitive Processes, Communicative Demands, and the Acquisition of Certain Linguistic Features

It is undeniable that the acquisition of any given phenomenon is, in part, a function of the cognitive effort needed to produce or process it (Bulté & Housen, 2014). The development of Spanish's copulas *ser* and *estar* progresses slowly because learners need time to automatize the processing of the structures' complex semantic and morphological properties (see VanPatten, 2010). Complex morphology develops according to the amount of information that learners can process between two clauses, which increases over the course of development as the learner is able to manage a number of competing morphosyntactic considerations in working memory (Pienemann, 2015). Yet, corpus linguistics has shown that learners and native speakers (NS) utilize linguistic phenomena not only in response to cognitive pressures but also in response to communicative demands (Mazgutova & Kormos, 2015). Whereas cognitive pressures limit the amount of attentional and memory resources one can dedicate to processing words, grammar, and phrases, communicative pressures define the limits of negotiated meaning and shared knowledge. For instance, situational communication (e.g., speech, synchronized computer-mediated communication [SCMC]) depends on social relationships, location, speech acts, and channel to signal the interpretation of grammar, lexis, and pragmatics. In situational communication, meaning is regularly negotiated (i.e., through conversational adjustments based on feedback; e.g., clarification requests) when physical (e.g., location, pictures in a story), social, or immediate linguistic context (e.g., a prompt, a question) lead to communication failures (Gass & Mackey, 2007). In contrast, extended written communication depends little on situational factors to provide meaning and to license grammar, lexis, and pragmatics. The writer must be specific and depict for the reader the relevant context, such that negotiation is not an option and one can assume little in terms of the knowledge the reader shares. In response to these distinct communicative pressures, situational and displaced communication differ greatly in terms of their structural properties. Based on a series of extensive corpus analyses of oral and academic English, Biber and Gray (2010) report that oral, conversational interaction is verbal and favors the use of subordination. That is, situational communication employs many verbs accompanied by subject and object pronouns, as well as various types of subordination (e.g., nominal, relative, adverbial clauses). Biber and Gray (2010) also show that extended written communication is nominal in nature, requiring that one specify referents and compress information. This leads to a prevalence of derived nouns (e.g., *the construction of X, the language requirement*) and phrasal modification of nouns (e.g., complex adjectival and prepositional modifications).

The communicative pressures of different sociolinguistic contexts require different language functions, such that a given context of learning will favor one or more discourse types. Support for this hypothesis is found in recent SLA research on language for specific purposes. This research has shown that a given discipline (e.g., medicine, engineering, hospitality) biases the use of particular genres. This is most likely due to the fact that "a context's conventions reflect situated social practices and thus they all share a concern with both the social contexts as well as the linguistic features of genres" (Charles, 2012, pp. 142–143). These findings are noteworthy if we assume that community engagement – whether it be abroad or in an internship requiring the use of the L2 – exposes learners to unique genres and discourse types.

Discourse types can be distinguished by the words, phrases, and structures that they bias (Baker, 2010). For instance, corpus research has shown that Spanish hypothetical/irrealis discourse is characterized by a predominance of verbs in the subjunctive, conditional, and imperfect indicative (Biber et al., 2006). As the L2 socialization research has shown, different contexts of learning impose different communicative demands on learners, which in turn will encourage them to use particular discourse types and sets of linguistic features (Kinginger, 2017). Likewise, such biases are likely to be evident in the input that learners receive.

Setting/Mode of a Learning Context Creates Interactions between Input and Learner Output

With the preceding premises and observations in mind, it is not surprising that there is general SLA evidence that the unique characteristics of a communicative and learning context shape what learners know about and what they can do with the L2. Yang (2016) presents a comprehensive meta-analysis of the effects of study-abroad (SA) research. His assessment of this context's effects indicates that changes in learners' pragmatic abilities (e.g., typical ways of affecting target-language speech acts, such as requests) are reported more frequently than we see in research on typical domestic classroom-based learners (see Taguchi, 2011). Additionally, seemingly distinct learning contexts can yield surprisingly similar results. Some research has shown that study-abroad learners demonstrate only modest gains abroad in comparison to domestic counterparts in their grammatical accuracy with structures such as the past tense (e.g., Spanish's preterite/imperfect distinction), the subjunctive, and gender agreement (e.g., DeKeyser, 2010). Corpus research indicates that the input that learners receive, which the setting/mode features establish, influences the nature of L2 output.

Garnier and Schmitt (2016) studied L2 English learners' use of phrasal verbs (e.g., *put off, take out, get in*). Interestingly, amount of formal instruction and time spent abroad were not predictors of phrasal verb production. The most important predictors of the learners' use of any given phrasal verb was its frequency in the baseline NS corpus. This sort of finding generally indicates that the target structure's acquisition is sensitive to frequency effects in input (see Chapter 9, this volume). To be sure, Garnier and Schmitt (2016) found that the time that learners spent reading and social networking (e.g., writing and reading posts) predicted the structure's use. Yet, this relationship between input and output can be contextualized. It may well be that location, formality, and locus-of-control explain the results. The learners' self-directed initiative to access both formal (i.e., published reading materials) and informal (i.e., social networking platforms) input outside of the classroom had a consequential impact on their L2 development. Additionally, the non-instructed pedagogy of personal reading and social networking influenced development of the target structure much more than formal instruction, according to the analysis.

Mougeon and Rehner (2017) also examined the interplay between context of learning, input, and L2 production with corpora from both learners and their teachers in two learning contexts differing in the institutional emphasis on French as an L2 in Canada. They found that learners with little extracurricular experience were extremely influenced by the characteristics of their teachers' input. Conversely, they found that, regardless of the context of learning, students with substantial community experience with Francophone speakers exhibited a high degree of variation with two target phenomena (see *Representative Corpora and Research* below). That is, community contact had a consequential effect on the learners' L2 development. The extremes of the location and formality dimensions seem to have affected the learners' behavior as well as the nature of the input they received. Mougeon and Rehner (2017) report that classroom speech was more formal, containing more standard variants. As such, the classroom-oriented learners produced language reflective of those pressures. However, the informal nature of the out-of-class community experiences appears to have overridden in-class normative pressures.

Fernández (2013) provides insights into the interaction between the acquisition of pragmatic expressions and the input that learners may receive abroad, focusing on general extenders (GEs) such as *y tal* 'and such' and *o algo así* 'or something like that', which are almost entirely ignored in instructed SLA. Fernández (2013) used a corpus of L2 learners of Spanish who had studied abroad in Spain. She was able to characterize the type of input that learners received from a qualitative analysis of four participants who provided information about their social and cultural experiences. Fernández (2013) argues that learners who establish strong speech-community bonds use a greater variety of GEs than less integrated individuals. Thus, the importance of locus of control comes into view. Some learners are self-directed, choosing to build bonds with individuals in the speech community. Phenomena such as GEs may develop in learning contexts where learners must manage conversational interactions and social relationships.

Corpus Research Should Study the Relationship between Setting/Mode, Input, and Output Under Multivariate Assumptions

A comprehensive understanding of the effects of context of learning on SLA will result from an understanding of the complex effects of setting and mode. Recent corpus-based SLA research has shown that important insights arise out of examinations of not just learners' production in different contexts but also the input that they receive (Fernández, 2013, 2015; Garnier & Schmitt, 2016; Mougeon & Rehner, 2017). Additionally, corpus-based analyses that are multivariate in nature can tease apart the complexity of such relationships.

Depending on logistic considerations in the context(s) being studied, a corpus analysis can examine authentic or simulated data (see *Main Research Methods* below). Authentic data sources have the highest ecological validity, entailing actual transcribed recordings or digitized documents (e.g., journals, letters, workplace correspondences) produced by the learner in a given learning context. Such data can also derive from lectures, interactions with teachers and internship peers, films that learners watch, and even social media that students consume. Simulated data sources can also play an important role in understanding the effects of learning context. Although less ecologically valid, learner input gathered from carefully constructed tasks (e.g., role-plays) can be tightly controlled in a comprehensive study with the goal of producing a corpus that represents a wide range of language functions typical of a setting/mode.

Norris and Ortega (2009) encourage researchers to study causes and effects in SLA by considering the potential effects of multiple features on acquisition. They assert that the development of overall proficiency or of individual phenomena (e.g., past-tense abilities) has multivariate roots, that is, the result of multiple sources such as sociolinguistic pressures, learner autonomy, and how lexical and grammatical features work together within different discourse types. Focusing on linguistic complexity, Norris and Ortega (2009) argue that researchers should avoid characterizing performance and development using individual features. For example, metrics such as the amount of subordination and mean-length-of-utterance are, individually, too blunt to capture complexity at all stages of development. Furthermore, these popular measurements essentially overlook the morphological complexity of inflected languages such as Spanish or German, where learners utilize multiple verb tenses and must make gender/number agreement. By extension, considering that the setting and mode of contexts of learning vary along a complex interaction of (at least) four dimensions in response to situational and sociocultural pressures (Benson, 2011; Reinders & Benson, 2017), it would seem difficult to rationalize the selection of a small set of target features to characterize learners' production and the input they receive comprehensively. Univariate approaches to studying SLA – corpus or otherwise – are likely to yield 'false positives' (see Chapter 9, this volume) and spurious conclusions about causation.

As an example of the insights provided by a multivariate analysis, Huensch, Tracy-Ventura, Bridges, and Cuesta Medina (2019) analyzed the attrition/maintenance of learners' L2 abilities four years after the completion of their SA program. They examined the effects of various personal and linguistic variables on the learners' ability to produce free-flowing, uninterrupted speech. Huensch et al.'s regression and correlation analyses found interesting interactions. Learners who continued to have consistent and intense contact with the L2 after their program were those that maintained fluency gains over the four years. Additionally, learners' proficiency level at the SA program's end predicted their propensity to correct errors (e.g., modification of words/phrases) four years later. Taken together, this multivariate analysis highlights the complex and robust interaction that both internal (e.g., L2 proficiency) and external (e.g., locus-of-control) factors have on L2 acquisition.

Main Research Methods

Sampling Considerations in Studying Learning Context

Designing a corpus to understand the effects of context of learning requires careful consideration of sampling procedures. Conclusions drawn from a corpus attain a high degree of reliability when the data represent a cross-section of the communicative contexts where learners produce, interact with, read, and listen to the L2. For each of the settings/modes being studied, researchers must design the corpus to reflect the key locations and pedagogies, the range of formality, and the locus-of-control.

Reliability is also dependent upon the extent to which the data are ecologically valid, that is, the extent to which the data are drawn from real-world settings or mirror everyday life. On the one hand, data from, say, standardized tests (e.g., assessing writing abilities) has questionable ecological validity, because the tasks motivating production lack overall authenticity and the high stakes involved can lead to reactivity (i.e., performing far beyond one's normal ability); test takers may be focused much more on form and target-language conventions studied under instructed conditions than on communicating meaning. On the other hand, there are many logistics to consider in collecting data from informal locations. In learning contexts encouraging a high degree of agency (e.g., community service, internships), students have unique linguistic experiences, making it difficult to operationalize representativeness (Fernández, 2013).

Additionally, recording data from a representative sample of the locations and formalities of a setting/mode necessitates the permission of various parties. Guichon (2017) reminds us of the ethical considerations in the creation of corpora involving students and teachers. Of key concern are privacy and potential harm. Data collected from participants in highly naturalistic conditions may diminish the Hawthorne effect (i.e., extraordinary performance in response to awareness of being observed). Yet, even when research is conducted with informed consent and audited by institutional review, the researcher's responsibility for ensuring privacy and confidentiality is great when the data are digital because they are 'shareable' (Guichon, 2017).

Constructing a Learner Corpus: Simulated and Authentic Data

A valid learner corpus can be constructed with simulated or authentic data. Simulated data entails learners participating in a range of tasks that reflect how the learner uses the L2 in a given context. Authentic data derives directly from samples of what learners produce, read, and hear in a range of communicative contexts in a given setting/mode. While it is undeniable that authentic data have more ecological validity, it is worthwhile to consider that researchers collecting simulated data can easily control the communicative contexts that the corpus ultimately reflects a learning context. Tasks can readily be designed to impose functional constraints on learner production, such as where and with whom the simulated production takes place. Researchers can create role plays emulating communicative and learning contexts common to the learner's experiences (e.g., home-stay situations, internship interactions, etc.). Interestingly, to the extent that instant messaging is now a mainstream mode of communication, corpus researchers can expedite the data-collection process and analysis by situating simulated tasks within SCMC, especially when the goal is to collect spontaneous (i.e., unplanned) data. For instance, Collentine and Collentine (2015) designed a 3D world where classroom learners shopped in various stores to purchase items necessary to put on an elegant party for a family member, although the merchants in the virtual world were not always helpful. Subsequently, learner dyads interacted in SCMC (i.e., instant-messaging chat rooms) to compare their purchases and discuss their interactions with the merchants. In a study-abroad context, for example, students can emulate interactions with merchants or tour-guides. Where learners are involved in community service related to medical services, a task might simply involve a role-play where students play the parts of patient and medical assistant. Similarly, participants could view a video of interactions between a student abroad and a host-family member that involves some sort of dilemma. Subsequently, dyads in SMSC could come to an agreement on a resolution to the problem. Collaborative tools can also situate learner production within a task when the goal is to obtain readily analyzable data representing (semi) extended discourse. In an immersion setting where community service is a component, a task could require that learners produce in a wiki a rough-draft of available construction services.

A learner corpus containing authentic data is most desirable from a validity standpoint. Here, the researcher must collect a range of samples representing communicative contexts relevant to the learners' setting/mode characteristics. Samples can originate from audio/video recordings and/or written samples from coursework or spontaneous writing (see Hellerman, 2008; e.g., correspondences, social media postings). Data can also represent extended discourse, such as the reports that a student in a medical or lab-based internship must produce as part of a curriculum.

Constructing a Corpus of Learner Input

An input corpus can provide valuable insights into the communicative contexts and the discourse types that learners hear and read in a given context of learning (Mendikoetxea, 2013). Again, data can be simulated or authentic. Regarding simulated data, the researcher can sample texts that are theoretically representative of a given context. This goal can be accomplished by obtaining representative samples of input sources that learners report to receive (e.g., a corpus of articles on British soccer if learners reported reading about sports). Concerning authentic data, the researcher can collect actual reading and listening samples from the learners' curriculum, samples of recorded teacher and caregiver (e.g., host-family) interactions, and samples of what learners read and hear in their day-to-day lives (see Reder, Harris, & Setzler, 2003). Both types of baseline data can also provide a wealth of ethnographic information about the context's sociocultural features.

Analysis

Once the corpus has been collected, transcriptions, SCMC data stored in a database, or written samples must be prepared for analysis. Because context of learning is defined by a number of individual, institutional, and sociocultural features, all samples will need to be cross-referenced with relevant metadata so that subsequent analyses can consider these independent variables. Additionally, multivariate analyses are most effective when data is part-of-speech tagged (see Chapter 5, this volume). This allows the researcher to tabulate the occurrence of lexical, grammatical, pragmatic, and discourse features. Any number of tag-count applications are available to tabulate frequencies. For more refined analyses (e.g., controlling for phrasal features such as counting morphemes in certain clause types), researchers can build scripts in Python (http://python.org) or even utilize a Python extension library such as the Natural Language Tool Kit (http://nltk.org). Additionally, the R language and environment for statistical computing and graphics (http://cran.r-project.org) offers a number of tools for conducting corpus tasks such as lexical analysis and even part-of-speech tagging.

Providing an understanding of the relationship between context of learning, the available input therein, and learner production can be attained with exploratory multivariate analyses. Such approaches are *a posteriori* in terms of their assumptions about how a learning context's general setting/mode characteristics influence the input that learners receive and their output. With a diverse set of features (e.g., syntactic, morphological, lexical), multivariate analyses allow researchers to understand learner interlanguage as its own system (Bley-Vroman, 1983) while reducing the assumptions a researcher makes about a context's distinguishing and important features.

Gries and Deshors (this volume) submit that multivariate analyses such as regression analysis can offset several pitfalls of hypothesis testing with learner or NS corpora. For instance, multivariate analyses can account for the fact that important target phenomena (e.g., subjunctive forms, clitic pronouns) occur infrequently in any corpus. Most importantly, multivariate analyses help the researcher to understand acquisition as the result of multiple variables rather than in terms of simple one-to-one cause-effect relationships (Norris & Ortega, 2009). Multidimensional analyses employing exploratory factor analysis can reduce a large number of features that have been tabulated in a corpus to three to four macro variables (i.e., components or latent variables; see Tabachnick & Fidell, 2001). This procedure has many uses, such as identifying the grammatical and lexical features that characterize learner production in different learning contexts and how learners use sets of features in relevant communicative contexts (e.g., conversational interactions, emails, oral presentations). The multidimensional analysis can also be used to characterize the discourse types prevalent in the input in a given setting/mode, which in turn can be used to study correlations between macro input features and learner production, either from a cross-sectional or a longitudinal perspective. A multidimensional analysis of learners' production in a science internship, where they must produce laboratory reports, might reveal the effects of communicating in such displaced discourse on their conversational and/or writing abilities in terms of the linguistic features (e.g., pragmatic, syntactic, lexical) that the learning context biases. For example, as noted above, displaced discourse biases the use of nominals and prepositions, which may ultimately affect the cluster of features that learners favor in some or all aspects of their own production.

Finally, the analysis can be conducted with proprietary statistical software such as SPSS (IBM Corp., 2018) or an open-source solution such as R (R Core Team, 2018). SPSS provides a controlled workflow of sorts, which can make the analysis process quite convenient. R is useful for researchers with statistical backgrounds and offers a number of packages for conducting exploratory factor analysis or principal components analysis.

Representative Corpora and Research

Mougeon and Rehner (2017) is an important study for researchers because it provides insights into the effects of the input that learners receive in and out of the classroom in two contexts of learning, namely, bilingual and immersion learning contexts. The study focuses on learners of French in Ontario, an English-dominant Canadian province. The French-English learners (N = 114) were adolescents (9th–12th grades) in Ontario schools where French is the medium of instruction. The immersion students (N = 41) were adolescent English speakers taking various subjects in French and English. The cross-sectional corpus comprised face-to-face semi-directed interviews coupled with questions about daily activities, such that the dataset represented informal, conversation language. The investigators also gathered data that were directly representative of the input participants received, utilizing a corpus of the production of the learners' teachers. Both groups of learners varied in terms of the amount of extracurricular French interactions they had in the community. Focusing on a variable grammatical structure (i.e., *je vais/je vas* to express a habitual or future action) and a variable discourse marker (i.e., *donc/alors/ça fait que/so*), both well documented in sociolinguistic studies of Ontario French, the study found a complex interaction between context of learning, teacher input, and effects for community experiences. Mougeon and Rehner (2017) found more variable use by teachers in the French-medium context, when both teachers and students were embedded in the Francophone community. They also found that learners with little extracurricular experience were highly influenced by the characteristics of their teachers' input.

Fernández (2013, 2015) provided researchers with insights into how locus-of-control (i.e., agency leading to strong social bonds in the target community) and L2 location (i.e., Spanish in Spain) affect learners' development of pragmatic competence. The studies showcase corpus techniques for comparing learner output with NS baseline data representing the very location where learning occurs. Fernández's (2013) cross-sectional corpus was derived from the *Spanish Learner Language Oral Corpora* (SPLLOC: Mitchell, Dominguez, Arche, Myles, & Marsden,

2008), which comprises data from UK learners of L2 Spanish (N = 120) in grades 9/10 along with both first-year and fourth-year university-level learners. The learners ranged from 180 to 895 classroom hours, and advanced learners spent time abroad studying the L2. The tasks from which the data were derived entailed (depending on the learners' instructional level) picture/photo descriptions, narratives and paired discussions. Fernández (2013) presents a corpus analysis of SA learners' use of general extenders (GEs; e.g., *y tal* 'and such'), arguing that GEs help learners to construct an individual L2 identity. Fernández (2015) seeks to further contextualize her L2 analysis by examining NS use of GEs, sampling the *Corpus Oral de Referencia del Español Contemporáneo* (COREC), containing Spanish interactions representing conversations, television interviews, and academic lectures. She concludes that GEs help a speaker to create meaning with one's interlocutor by signaling adherence to the quantity maxim (e.g., *y tal* can reference shared knowledge) and by marking when one relinquishes a turn. By comparing the learner and the NS analyses, Fernández (2013, 2015) delineates how GEs can establish solidarity and reduce power differences for learners in interactive discourse.

The *Languages and Social Networks Abroad Project* (LANGSNAP), a publicly available corpus (http://langsnap.soton.ac.uk), is a valuable source for understanding the effects of context of learning. It contains data on French and Spanish L2 learners with experience in the classroom and abroad. The research team provides a longitudinal perspective, collecting data on six occasions, before, during, and after residency abroad. It contains spontaneous and (semi)planned data from an oral interview, an oral narrative, and an argumentative essay, and it is part-of-speech tagged. The participants were enrolled as students abroad or served as a language teaching assistant; a few participated in a workplace internship. Tracy-Ventura (2017) analyzes not only learner production in the corpus but also compares the results to an NS baseline. She provides the first extensive analysis of lexical development abroad, focusing on L2 Spanish learners' acquisition of low-frequency lexical items. Tracy-Ventura (2017) triangulates the learner-corpus analysis with a Spanish NS frequency dictionary to compare learners' progress to likely lexical distribution features in their input. The LANGSNAP 3.0 project collected new data from the original participants to study attrition and maintenance after their return from study/residence abroad (see Tracy-Ventura & Huensch, 2018 for details).

The Barcelona Study Abroad and Language Acquisition (SALA) project demonstrates how a comprehensive longitudinal study can document both linguistic and extralinguistic data on L2 learners in formal and study-abroad settings. This ambitious project focuses on bilingual, trilingual, and multilingual language learning at the secondary and tertiary levels in both formal instruction and study (i.e., residency) abroad. The dataset is extensive, comprising longitudinal data based on a battery of 10 instruments measuring learners' linguistic development (speaking, listening, writing, and reading) over 30 months. Additionally, the dataset tracks changes in learners' motivation, attitudes, and intercultural awareness. SALA documents Catalan-Spanish learners of L2 English (N = 80) from formal classroom instruction through their study-abroad experience in an English-speaking country and upon their return home (upf. edu/en/web/allencam/sala). The project is reported in Pérez-Vidal's (2014) edited volume, in which a total of nine studies present corpus analyses of the learners' development of English phonology, fluency, lexis, grammar, and listening comprehension, as well as their motivations and beliefs. The report also describes in detail the institutional characteristics of the learners' contexts of learning. Overall, the study shows that, when there is a tight integration between curricular design and SA experiences (in and out of the classroom), L2 gains can be robust. The study indicates that learners who studied in the SALA project maintain phonological and listening-comprehension gains from being abroad after their return to the domestic context. The study also provides insights into the effects of locus-of-control, suggesting that learners with integrative orientation toward the target culture experience the most lexical and grammatical gains abroad.

Future Directions

More corpus data is needed to understand the effects of context of learning. There exist important models for researchers to emulate. According to the LANGSNAP website (http://langsnap. soton.ac.uk/project.html), the project directors collected not only linguistic data but also extra-linguistic data on learners' evolving social networks, learning opportunities, and social interactions. Such rich datasets can provide information about learners' experiences abroad which researchers can use to estimate the effects of location, formality, and pedagogy. The SALA project report provides similar details, in addition to shedding light on the role of locus-of-control (i.e., agency, autonomy). An ideal project would couple corpus data with a rich dataset of learners' biographical characteristics, propensity for autonomy, and a profile of their L2 contact (e.g., frequency, mode, sociolinguistic) inside and outside of the classroom. To understand the interactions between pedagogy and the distribution of decisions amongst learners and teachers, a corpus could comprise samples of learner production at various points along the continuum of instructed to non-instructed pedagogy. For example, Mougeon and Rehner's (2017) study is arguably quite innovative, as it controlled for both location and formality in a balanced way. A relevant corpus might orient the sampling process according to agency and autonomy, with data representing learner language where agency and autonomy are presumed to be high (e.g., an online curriculum), where they are presumed to be low (e.g., a teacher-focused face-to-face curriculum), and where agency and autonomy reside somewhere in the middle (e.g., a task-based curriculum).

Additionally, to my knowledge, there are no corpora available allowing an analysis of contexts where learners participate in non-teaching internships (e.g., medical, social services, business) nor where they are enrolled in domestic immersion programs, whether these involve an element of community service/engagement or not. One can imagine, however, that, as researchers become more interested in foreign languages for special purposes (e.g. French, German, or Chinese for Specific Purposes), interest in the language that learners produce resulting from such specialized input sources will lead to corpora that fill this gap in our understanding of context of learning.

Further Reading

Collentine, J., & Collentine, K. (2013). A corpus approach to studying structural convergence in task-based Spanish L2 interactions. In K. McDonough & A. Mackey (Eds.), *Second language interaction in diverse educational contexts* (pp. 167–188). Amsterdam: John Benjamins.

This is an empirical study examining learners' use of epistemic morphosyntax in SCMC, examined from a corpus perspective. It employs corpus analytical techniques (e.g., part-of-speech tagging) as well as corpus-based approaches to studying priming (i.e., whether prior exposure to a linguistic phenomenon increases the likelihood that it will be employed subsequently) amongst learners. And, while the study only focuses on classroom learners and does not compare contexts of learning, it provides a template for designing the task-based SCMC data-collection procedures suggested in this chapter. It also demonstrates how to design a NS baseline that reflects the type of input the learners produced in SCMC, which could serve as a template for creating a simulated corpus to model the input that learners receive.

Hellermann, J. (2008). *Social actions for classroom language learning*. Clevedon: Multilingual Matters.

This is a book-length study of learners of English as an L2. The study does not provide a multivariate analysis to study affective variables. Rather, it employs conversational analysis (CA) to provide data-rich longitudinal and cross-sectional accounts of how learners engage (and disengage) from task interactions. The study is particularly interesting in that it provides researchers with a template for documenting and characterizing location, pedagogy, and locus-of-control. Hellerman (2008) utilizes video recordings to document the learners' experiences, and future research can adapt the techniques he employs. Hellerman (2008) also details challenges learners face in integrating into a community of practice at different stages of the learners' program.

Note

1 Reinders and Benson's (2017) framework focuses on characterizing learning situations beyond the classroom. Yet, in my opinion, it is comprehensive enough to contextualize the mental, physical, and sociocultural spaces where a broad range of SLA experiences occur. Indeed, they assert: "language learning beyond the classroom is not just a matter of learning away from the classroom but is rather, in many cases, an extension of classroom learning" (Reinders & Benson, 2017, p. 574).

References

Baker, P. (2010). *Sociolinguistics and corpus linguistics*. Edinburgh: Edinburgh University Press.

Batstone, R. (2002). Contexts of engagement: A discourse perspective on 'intake' and 'pushed output'. *System, 30*(1), 1–14.

Benson, P. (2011). Language learning and teaching beyond the classroom: An introduction to the field. In P. Benson & H. Reinders (Eds.), *Beyond the language classroom* (pp. 7–16). Basingstoke: Palgrave Macmillan.

Berns, M. (1989). Learning and using English in West Germany: A Firthian perspective. *International Review of Applied Linguistics, 85*, 51–65.

Biber, D., Davies, M., Jones, J., & Tracy-Ventura, N. (2006). Spoken and written register variation in Spanish: A multi-dimensional analysis. *Corpora, 1*(1), 1–37.

Biber, D., & Gray, B. (2010). Challenging stereotypes about academic writing: Complexity, elaboration, explicitness. *Journal of English for Academic Purposes, 9*(1), 2–20.

Bley-Vroman, R. (1983). The comparative fallacy in interlanguage studies: The case of systematicity. *Language Learning, 33*(1), 1–17.

Bulté, B., & Housen, A. (2014). Conceptualizing and measuring short-term changes in L2 writing complexity. *Journal of Second Language Writing, 26*, 42–65.

Charles, M. (2012). English for academic purposes. In P. Brian & S. Starfield (Eds.), *The handbook of English for specific purposes* (pp. 137–144). Chichester: Wiley-Blackwell.

Collentine, J., & Collentine, K. (2013). A corpus approach to studying structural convergence in task-based Spanish L2 interactions. In K. McDonough & A. Mackey (Eds.), *Second language interaction in diverse educational contexts* (pp. 167–188). Amsterdam: John Benjamins.

Collentine, J., & Collentine, K. (2015). Input and output grammar instruction in tutorial CALL with a complex grammatical structure. *CALICO, 32*(2), 273–298.

DeKeyser, R. (2010). Monitoring processes in Spanish as a second language during a study abroad program. *Foreign Language Annals, 43*(1), 80–92.

Fernández, J. (2013). A corpus-based study of vague language use by learners of Spanish in a study abroad context. In C. Kinginger (Ed.), *Social and cultural aspects of language learning in study abroad* (pp. 299–332). Amsterdam: John Benjamins.

Fernández, J. (2015). General extender use in spoken Peninsular Spanish: Metapragmatic awareness and pedagogical implications. *Journal of Spanish Language Teaching, 2*(1), 1–17.

Firth, A., & Wagner, J. (1997). On discourse, communication, and (some) fundamental concepts in SLA research. *Modern Language Journal, 81*, 286–300.

Garnier, M., & Schmitt, N. (2016). Picking up polysemous phrasal verbs: How many do learners know and what facilitates this knowledge? *System, 59*, 29–44.

Gass, S., & Mackey, A. (2007). Input, interaction, and output in second language acquisition. In B. VanPatten & J. Williams (Eds.), *Theories in second language acquisition: An introduction* (pp. 175–199). Mahwah: Lawrence Erlbaum.

Guichon, N. (2017). Sharing a multimodal corpus to study webcam- mediated language teaching. *Language Learning and Technology, 21*(1), 55–74.

Hellermann, J. (2008). *Social actions for classroom language learning*. Clevedon: Multilingual Matters.

Huensch, A., Tracy-Ventura, N., Bridges, J., & Cuesta Medina, J. A. (2019). Variables affecting the maintenance of L2 proficiency and fluency four years post-study abroad. *Study Abroad Research in Second Language Acquisition and International Education, 4*(1), 96–125.

IBM Corp. (2018). *IBM SPSS statistics: Version 25*. Armonk: IBM Corp. Retrieved from www.ibm.com/us-en/marketplace/spss-statistics

Kinginger, C. (2017). Language socialization in study abroad. In P. Duff & S. May (Eds.), *Encyclopedia of language and education: Language socialization* (3rd ed, pp. 227–238). Cham: Springer.

Lantolf, J. P. (2000). *Sociocultural theory and second language learning*. Oxford: Oxford University Press.

Mazgutova, D., & Kormos, J. (2015). Syntactic and lexical development in an intensive English for academic purposes programme. *Journal of Second Language Writing, 29*, 3–15.

Mendikoetxea, A. (2013). Corpus-based research in second language Spanish. In K. Geeslin (Ed.), *Handbook of Spanish second language acquisition* (pp. 11–29). Oxford: Wiley-Blackwell.

Miano, A., Bernhardt, E., & Brates, V. (2016). Exploring the effects of a short-term Spanish immersion program in a postsecondary setting. *Foreign Language Annals, 49*(2), 287–301.

Mitchell, R., Domínguez, L., Arche, M. J., Myles, F., & Marsden, E. (2008). SPLLOC: A new database for Spanish second language acquisition research. *EUROSLA Yearbook, 8*, 287–304.

Mougeon, R., & Rehner, K. (2017). The influence of classroom input and community exposure on the learning of variable grammar. *Bilingualism: Language and Cognition, 20*(1), 21–22.

Norris, J. M., & Ortega, L. (2009). Towards an organic approach to investigating CAF in instructed SLA: The case of complexity. *Applied Linguistics, 30*(4), 555–578.

Pérez-Vidal, C. (2014). *Language acquisition in study abroad and formal instruction contexts.* Amsterdam: John Benjamins.

Pienemann, M. (2015). An outline of processability theory and its relationship to other approaches to SLA. *Language Learning, 65*(1), 123–151.

R Core Team (2018). *R: A language and environment for statistical computing.* Vienna: R Foundation for Statistical Computing. Retrieved from www.R-project.org/

Reder, S., Harris, K., & Setzler, K. (2003). A multimedia adult learner corpus. *TESOL Quarterly, 37*(3), 546–557.

Reinders, H., & Benson, P. (2017). Research agenda: Language learning beyond the classroom. *Language Teaching, 50*(4), 561–578.

Tabachnick, B., & Fidell, L. (2001). *Using multivariate statistics.* Needham Heights: Allyn and Bacon.

Taguchi, N. (2011). The effect of L2 proficiency and study abroad experience on pragmatic comprehension. *Language Learning, 61*(3), 904–939.

Tracy-Ventura, N. (2017). Combining corpora and experimental data to investigate language learning during residence abroad: A study of lexical sophistication. *System, 71*, 35–45.

Tracy-Ventura, N., & Huensch, A. (2018). The potential of publicly shared longitudinal learner corpora in SLA research. In A. Gudmestad & A. Edmonds (Eds.), *Critical reflections on data in second language acquisition* (pp. 149–169). Amsterdam: John Benjamins.

VanPatten, B. (2010). Some verbs are more perfect than others: Why learners have difficulty with ser and estar and what it means for instruction. *Hispania, 93*(1), 29–38.

Yang, J. (2016). The effectiveness of study-abroad on second language learning: A meta-analysis. *The Canadian Modern Language Review, 72*(1), 66.

30

Individual Differences

Elma Kerz and Daniel Wiechmann

Introduction

There is a growing recognition that individual differences (henceforth IDs) are ubiquitous across the lifespan both in first and second language acquisition. These differences are due to a number of experience-related, linguistic, cognitive, and affective factors (cf., Kidd, Donnelly, & Christiansen, 2018; for an overview of IDs in SLA, see R. Ellis, 2004). These differences can be observed across the entire linguistic system, from the acquisition of properties of speech as well as the graphotactic and morphological regularities of written words to complex grammatical structures and discourse. Despite their ubiquitous nature, the importance of IDs for language theory has long been downplayed both in L1 and L2 literature, mainly due to the influential impact of traditional generative/nativist perspectives on the acquisition and processing of language outlined below. While IDs in native language attainment have effectively been ignored and relegated to error variance, IDs in L2 acquisition have long been recognized initially due to Carroll's work dating back to 1959. Carroll and colleagues developed the Modern Language Aptitude Test (MLAT), a test designed to tap different cognitive skills related to L2 learning, i.e. phonemic coding, grammatical sensitivity, inductive language learning ability, and associative memory (see Carroll & Sapon, 1959, 2002). Subsequent research found the MLAT to be predictive of L2 learning and achievement (for recent overviews, see Wen, Skehan, Biedroń, Li, & Sparks, 2019; Doughty, 2019; for a metanalysis, see, Li, 2016). However, the impact of this line of research on L2 acquisition research at large and on the development of second language acquisition theory in particular has been minimal. Throughout much of its relatively short history, second language acquisition (SLA) has been preoccupied with the search for universal characteristics, processes, and developmental stages (however, see de Bot, Lowie, & Verspoor, 2007 for L2 research within the framework of complex dynamic system theory; see also Chapter 14 in the current volume). This is reflected in a number of constructs used in the L2 literature – acquisition orders, sequences and stages, benchmarks, zones of proximal and actual development (see, e.g., Mitchell, Myles & Marsden, 2013). This preoccupation may have inhibited the growth of individual differences (ID) research (Skehan, 1991).

This situation is mainly due to the predominance of the Chomskyan (nativist/generative) perspectives in the language sciences and their direct and indirect effects on language acquisition research (see Chomsky's hidden legacy: Christiansen & Chater, 2016). This theoretical approach has emphasized the (un)learnability of the key principles of language structure from exposure and assumed the existence of a biologically endowed Universal Grammar (UG) which guides language acquisition (Chomsky, 1995). Consequently, it has been widely assumed that all native speakers converge on the same grammar (see Dabrowska, 2018 and references therein). In turn, much L2 acquisition research has focused on differences between L1 and L2 acquisition addressing the learning/acquisition divide (Krashen, 1981), the fundamental difference hypothesis (Bley-Vroman, 1989), UG-accessibility (White, 2003), ultimate attainment/steady state (Birdsong, 1992), interfaces (Sorace, 2011), and morphosyntactic processing (e.g., shallow structure hypothesis, Clahsen & Felser, 2006; see also Chapter 16, this volume). Even L2 researchers who would not subscribe to the generative view have typically tacitly assumed that native speaker competence is a convergent, single benchmark for L2 performance and target for L2 development and have investigated L2 learner performance and attainment levels by comparing them with those of native peers.

The Chomskyan hidden legacy may also have left its mark in Learner Corpus Research (henceforth LCR). Although there has been an increasing recognition of the importance of IDs (see e.g., Granger, Gilquin, & Meunier, 2015), LCR has typically aggregated data sets without considering the inter- and intraindividual variation and variability among L2 learners or controlling for the impact of language experience (L2 input) and/or cognitive, affective, and sociodemographic factors. Furthermore, LCR has failed to recognize the existence of IDs in native language (L1) attainment and that L1 skill is a possible source of variation in L2 learning (see work by Cummins dating back to 1970s, e.g. Cummins, 1979, and more recent studies by Sparks and colleagues, e.g. Sparks, Patton & Ganschow, 2012) and has used it as a homogeneous benchmark against which to assess L2 performance. More recently, there has been an explosion of studies uncovering substantial IDs across multiple components of language across the lifespan in native speakers (see e.g., Montag & MacDonald, 2015; Dabrowska, 2018; see also Kidd et al., 2018 for a recent overview). These IDs may result from prior language experience to which individuals have been exposed to, what they have attended to and perceived during this language exposure, their educational and social background, and interactions and variability in general cognitive abilities. The existence of such IDs calls into question the ontological status of aggregate models of L1 knowledge and what they are supposed to represent.

Recent years have witnessed a growing interest in the role of IDs in native language learning and processing as well as a renewed interest in IDs in SLA research. This interest is largely due to recent developments in the language sciences that have challenged the traditional generative/nativist approaches to language acquisition. These developments are driven by, among other things, the existence of large databases (language corpora), new experimental techniques, and more sophisticated statistical techniques and computational tools to analyze language data as well as by the growing number of collaborative interactions between language scientists, cognitive scientists, and computer scientists. A major advance has been in recognizing that language is abundant in statistical regularities and distributional properties and that infants, children, and adults acquire such regularities and properties to boost their acquisition. These developments have been accompanied by a growing popularity of 'emergentist' approaches to both L1 and L2 acquisition, an umbrella term for a family of models of language, encompassing 'usage-based' (a.k.a experience-driven) (see Chapter 13, this volume), 'constraint-based', and 'connectionist' models (see Beckner et al., 2009; Christiansen & Chater, 2016; see also Kidd et al., 2018 for an overview). These approaches share a number of fundamental assumptions that stand in contrast to those of traditional, generative approaches. One of the central assumptions is that language learning (both L1 and L2) is a continuous process that takes place across the lifespan and does not end at some discrete point of time in ontogenetic development, rendering the notion of 'ultimate attainment' superfluous. Because from an emergentist view language knowledge is a "dynamic set of graded patterns emerging from use" with some "emergent stabilities" that is by definition never fully acquired (Larsen Freeman, 2011, pp. 52–3), it is to be expected that, due to a number of cognitive, affective, and socio-demographic factors, individuals differ substantially in their attainment levels across the lifespan and exhibit individually owned developmental trajectories. Importantly, emergentist accounts provide an adequate theoretical framework to situate IDs in language acquisition and put forward a psychologically plausible model of language knowledge of individuals. Due to the developments sketched above, there is now a growing awareness of the necessity of advancing our understanding of the role of IDs both in L1 and L2 acquisition. In a recent comprehensive review in *Trends in Cognitive Sciences*, Kidd et al. (2018) conclude that an adequate theoretical model of language acquisition and processing should be first and foremost constrained by empirical demonstrations of IDs as well as predict and account for the complex interrelationships between variation in the quantity and quality of language input, linguistic, cognitive, and affective factors, and language attainment.

In general, for researchers working from an emergentist perspective, analyses of learner production data supported by natural language processing techniques are central to understanding language acquisition and development, and an important complement to experimental research (see Rebuschat et al., 2017, for a recent special issue). More importantly, as will become evident below, LCR has the potential to advance our understanding of IDs in SLA in, at least, three important ways: First, it can provide valuable insights into the dynamics of individual trajectories in L2 development. Second, it can deepen our knowledge on the role of quantity and quality of linguistic input in L2 development and attainment. And third, it can reveal interesting new lights into the role of diverse factors across linguistic, cognitive, and affective domains in accounting for individual variability in learner productions.

Core Issues and Topics

This section introduces three core issues in studying individual difference in second language acquisition (SLA) using learner corpora and corpus-based techniques. First, we focus on the quantity and quality of the language input that has emerged as key external (exogenous) determinants of both native and nonnative language attainment in emergentist approaches to language acquisition and processing. Second, rather than providing an overview of all ID factors that have traditionally played a role in SLA (e.g. anxiety, motivation, or learning strategies), we provide an updated overview of ID factors informed by recent research in cognitive science (e.g. working memory or [implicit] statistical learning ability). Third, we address methodological issues related to the study of individual trajectories in L2 development.

How Can Learner Corpus Studies Contribute to Understanding the Role of Linguistic Input on L2 Performance and Development?

Emergentist approaches to the acquisition and processing of language eschew the existence of innately specified linguistic knowledge (UG) and instead seek to account for language acquisition in terms of generative cognitive mechanisms rather than internalized linguistic constraints (e.g., Christiansen & Chater, 2016). These approaches assume a direct and immediate relationship between processing and learning, conceiving of them as inseparable, rather than governed by different mechanisms ('two sides of the same coin'). Language acquisition is conceived of as learning how to process linguistic input efficiently (see, language acquisition as skill learning Chater, McCauley, & Christiansen, 2016, or learning-as-processing assumption, Chang, Dell, & Bock, 2006). In these approaches, the quantity and the quality of language input to which the individual is exposed are the key determinants of language development. Children who are exposed to higher amounts of and more diverse linguistic input demonstrate stronger language growth. This stands in contrast to the poverty of stimulus argument that was the backbone for the innate hypothesis (see e.g., Chomsky, 1980). In children's early language environments, the quantity and quality of child-directed speech (CDS) – i.e. the input provided by their caregivers – is shown to be a strong predictor of their language developments. Children who are exposed to higher amounts of and more diverse linguistic input demonstrate stronger language growth, as they are provided with frequent opportunities to learn about the phonemes that make up their language, the boundaries between words and sentences, the words that correspond to the objects and events in their surroundings, and syntactic patterns of sentences (e.g., Huttenlocher et al., 2010; Kuhl 2010). This line of research has benefited greatly from the use of longitudinal corpora (e.g. the corpora of spontaneous adult-child interactions made available through the Child Language Data Exchange System, CHILDES, MacWhinney, 2000)[1] that represent a good sampling of the adult speech (the input component) and children's language productions at successive developmental levels (the output component) (see, MacWhinney, 2010, for the so-called input-output modeling approach; see, e.g. Jones & Rowland, 2017; McCauley & Christiansen, 2018 for more recent studies based on such an approach).

Prior to school entry and formal literacy instruction, children are mostly exposed to statistical regularities and distributional patterns of spoken language. In later stages of acquisition, as the demand for advanced literacy skills increases, children encounter a large amount of vocabulary and syntactic structures that they have not been exposed to before (see Cummins, 2017, for the distinction between 'Basic Interpersonal Communicative Skills' and 'Cognitive Academic Language Proficiency'). In these stages of acquisition, language knowledge emerges as the result of experience with different types of genres/registers in both modalities (spoken and written). An important finding of recent studies is that written language constitutes a key input type in the development of linguistic knowledge, as it provides a source of substantial change in the statistics of an individual's language experience, and that the statistics encountered in comprehension (reading) affect performance in production (Montag & MacDonald, 2015; Seidenberg & MacDonald, 2018). In recent research on native language attainment, IDs in adult speakers have been linked to different types of linguistic input that individuals were being exposed to throughout their lifetime, differences in reading exposure as well as differences in years of formal education (e.g., Dabrowska, 2018 and references therein). These recent findings have led to a renewed interest in studying relationships between L1 and L2 literacy skills (Pae, 2018; Ströbel, Kerz, & Wiechmann, under revision). For example, Pae (2018) is an excellent example of recent research on the relationship between L1 and L2 in reading and writing (including moderating effects of task type and L2 proficiency) that uses the Structural Equation Modeling (SEM) statistical technique that has a number of advantages over correlational or multiple regression analyses (see section on *Main Research Methods* below).

Although it has long been recognized that the statistical properties of L2 input have a significant impact on L2 acquisition (see, e.g. Ellis, 2002 for a review on frequency effects), compared to the bulk of research in the cognitive sciences reviewed above, SLA still has a long way to go. We are aware of the fact that compiling dense longitudinal corpora needed for input-output type of modeling is a time-consuming and challenging task. Before such corpora become available, the first important step towards advancing our understanding of the role of the quantity and quality of L2 input would be the inclusion of 'proxy measures' of L2 linguistic experience, such as socio-demographic factors (SES or parental education, see e.g., Anderson et al., 2018, for the Language and Social Background Questionnaire, LSBQ), self-reported amount of current exposure to English (see e.g., Marian, Blumenfeld, & Kaushanskaya, 2007, for the Language Experience and Proficiency Questionnaire, LEAP-Q), estimates of print exposures (see, e.g. Author Recognition Task, Acheson, Wells & MacDonald, 2008) and the compilation of corpora that approximate the type of (in particular written) language input individuals are likely to be exposed to. One promising line of LCR is investigating to what extent the type of linguistic patterns L2 learners use resemble distributions of such patterns in general corpora of a given target language (see, e.g., Tracy-Ventura & Cuesta Medina, 2018). Another related line of LCR has started compiling pedagogical corpora (see, the *Textbook Material* (TeMA) corpus, Meunier & Gouverneur, 2009). Such corpus resources can also serve as a valuable source to at least approximate the type of linguistic input L2 learners receive in textbooks (for a representative example, see a recent study by Möller, 2017a, and its use of the *Teaching Material Corpus* (TeaMC) resource). The existing corpus resources capturing the nature of L2 classroom input need to be extended to include other types of input L2 learners are likely to be exposed to, such as popular fiction books read by children and young adults (see, e.g., BasiLex, an 11.5 million word corpus of Dutch texts written for children, Tellings et al., 2014).

How Can the Role of Cognitive and Affective Factors Be Investigated in Learner Corpus Research?

In the area of SLA, it is commonly observed that even learners that share a number of commonalities including native language, educational level, and learning scenario (classroom or immersion setting) and follow a common developmental route may differ greatly in their rate of learning and eventual L2 outcomes. Building upon insights from cognitive psychology, SLA research identified a number of ID factors and has linked the variability in L2 outcomes to a range of factors that an individual brings to the task. These factors traditionally include cognitive and learning style, language learning strategies, foreign language aptitude, and a range of affective variables including motivation and anxiety (for overviews, see e.g., Ellis, 2004; Dewaele, 2013). Here, rather than providing an overview of all ID factors that have traditionally played a role in SLA (see above), we introduce a selection of ID factors that have closer connections to recent research in cognitive science and are gaining more prominence in the SLA literature. One cognitive factor that has received considerable attention over the years is language aptitude – succinctly defined as 'talent' for second language learning. In the 1960s, 1970s, and, to some extent, also in the 1980s, L2 aptitude research was influenced by (specific instructional methods) audiolingualism and communicative language teaching with no direct connection to the actual processing mechanisms underlying L2 acquisition. Further, the aptitude construct initially focused on explicit types of learning abilities as reflected in the types of tasks incorporated in the MLAT (Carroll & Sapon, 1959) or Pimsleur's Language Aptitude Battery (PLAB, Pimsleur, 1966). According to a more recent approach to language aptitude (Skehan, 2002), a number of components of aptitude must be differentiated in accordance with the L2 processing stage they correspond to. Interestingly, many of the aptitude components proposed in this approach are closely related to the type of cognitive ID variables investigated in current cognitive sciences literature on native language processing, namely implicit statistical learning ability (in Skehan's model 'inductive language learning ability', 'automatization', 'chunking') and working memory capacity. There is an accumulating body of evidence indicating a tight coupling between IDs in statistical learning ability and variability in native language learning and processing, in both child and adult populations (e.g., Kidd & Arciuli, 2016; Misyak & Christiansen, 2012) and in adult second-language learner populations (e.g., Ettlinger, Morgan-Short, Faretta-Stutenberg, & Wong, 2016). While initially working memory was argued to be a separate construct from aptitude, recently proposals have been made to treat working memory as a key component of L2 aptitude or even equate working memory to L2 aptitude (see Linck et al., 2013, for the development of recent aptitude measures). Another important ID factor, from the affective domain, that, as pointed out by Dewaele and Furnham (2000), has long been an unjustly neglected area of SLA are personality traits (see three models put forward in SLA research to assess these traits: (1) Eysenck PEN model, (2) Myers-Briggs Personality Type model, and (3) Big Five Model).

Although there is a tradition of studying the role of cognitive and affective IDs in SLA, their role has been a neglected area of research in L2 production studies. The available studies have primarily focused on the impact of such IDs on speech production (see Kormos, 2012, for a review article that addresses the scarcity of ID research in L2 writing literature in comparison to L2 speaking literature). A number of earlier studies have examined the effects of IDs in cognitive abilities and affective factors (including WM capacity, aptitude, intelligence, willingness to communicate, motivation, and personality, among others) on L2 productions (see e.g., Dewaele & Furnham, 2000). These studies uncovered a number of interesting patterns in the cognitive and affective factors underlying L2 oral task performance. A more recent study by Kormos and Trebits (2012) investigated the links between components of aptitude and the fluency, accuracy, syntactic complexity, and lexical variety of performance in two types of written and spoken narrative tasks. This study also determined whether and to what extent L2 performance varies in tasks of different cognitive complexity in the written and spoken modes. The findings reported in this study indicated a complex interaction between aptitude components and task performance under different conditions. Two components of language aptitude – i.e. inductive ability and grammatical sensitivity – turned out to be most strongly associated with the complexity and accuracy of L2 performance.

How Can the Dynamics of Individual Trajectories in L2 Development Be Studied in Learner Corpora

Learner corpora are particularly suitable to capture the complex, dynamic, and nonlinear process of L2 development. With the use of such corpora, the dynamics of individual trajectories in L2 development can be tracked simultaneously across multiple components of language, such as syntax or lexis. Adopting a Complex Dynamic System (CDS) perspective (see de Bot, Lowie, & Verspoor, 2007, for a Dynamic Systems Theory approach to second language acquisition), several learner corpus studies have shown that different aspects of L2 knowledge develop at different rates and that learners develop through individually owned trajectories. These studies emphasize the utility of individual case studies – i.e. longitudinal samples of language productions from a selected set of learners – to study an individual's language as it evolves over time, capturing the fluctuations in intraindividual learner corpus data (for a more comprehensive overview of this approach, see Chapters 14 and 27, this volume). A viable complement to such an approach is to quantify individual variation and examine systematic effects simultaneously by using advanced statistical modeling techniques in a large sample of L2 learners of various L1 backgrounds (for more details on these techniques, see the subsequent section).

Main Research Methods

The treatment of individual differences (IDs) in the cognitive sciences, as pointed out in a recent review (Kidd et al., 2018), has historically been uneven: while correlational research has been based on the assumption that there are meaningful IDs that can be assessed and measured by means of psychometric tests and instruments, experimental research has neglected the role of IDs and has instead focused on group-level differences. In experimental approaches, IDs have typically been treated either as measurement error variance or unexplained/unsystematic variance. More recently, IDs are becoming increasingly integrated in experimental studies on language acquisition and processing (e.g. Misyak & Christiansen, 2012; Dabrowska, 2018). These studies investigate the relationship between a range of ID (socio-demographic, linguistic, and cognitive) factors and language using a within-subject design embedded in an individual-differences framework. In such a design, participants are asked to complete questionnaires that elicit information on their socio-demographic background, and their individual linguistic experience is quantified using a variety of measures that provide proxy estimates of an individual's exposure to print material (see examples below). In addition, participants are administered a battery of psychometric tests designed to assess IDs in a number of relevant cognitive factors, such as (verbal) working memory abilities, fluid intelligence and/or (implicit) statistical learning abilities. Language performance, i.e. typically comprehension ability, is assessed using various offline and online measures.[2] In a first step, the results of correlational analyses are presented indicating the strength of (either positive or negative) relationship between two variables expressed in terms of correlation coefficients. In a second step, multiple (mixed-effect) regression modeling is used to determine how well each ID measure predicts language performance measure when controlling for all other remaining predictors. The effect of each predictor variable on the dependent variable is expressed in terms of (standardized) regression coefficients. Another powerful statistical technique that is increasingly being used in language acquisition literature, including SLA research on IDs (see e.g, Pae, 2018; see also In'nami & Koizumi, 2011, for a review) is structural equation modeling (SEM). There are a number of advantages of SEM over traditional statistical methods such as correlational and multiple regression analysis. With the SEM technique, it is possible to investigate structural relationships between several unobserved – or latent – variables, measured by means of corresponding observed – or indicator – variables, in the presence of multiple measurement error. This provides an efficient way for testing structural or causal relationships between target variables. The SEM technique also permits a simultaneous analysis of multiple dependent variables, whereas a multiple regression analysis of this type would require that separate models are fitted for each dependent variable, not allowing a direct comparison between them. For example, Kaufman et al. (2010) used the SEM technique to conduct an extensive investigation of the relationship between implicit statistical learning ability and a variety of cognitive, affective, and language-related tasks. In general, the findings demonstrated a relatively weak correlation of implicit statistical learning ability with psychometric intelligence and with working memory. Interestingly and importantly, IDs in implicit statistical learning ability were associated with academic performance in two foreign language exams and two language-related components of psychometric intelligence. Further, SL ability was significantly associated with several personality traits.

Another important line of IDs research reviewed above has been concerned with how socio-demographic factors, most notably socio-economic status, are related to children's language development, i.e. understanding inter-individual variability in intra-individual patterns of change over time, often referred to as 'growth curves', 'time paths', or 'latent trajectories' (see e.g., Quinn et al., 2015). Mainly due to the predominance of traditional formal linguistic approaches that have downplayed the possibility of IDs in the area of syntax, the lion's share of this research has focused on vocabulary development (however, for an exception, see work by Huttenlocher and colleagues). Similar to experimental studies using a within-subject design, studies in this area have employed a range of statistical techniques ranging from "simple" multiple regression to "more complex" growth curve modeling capturing the shape of individual growth trajectories (linear or nonlinear). It would go beyond the scope of this chapter to introduce all available questionnaires and psychometric tasks used to assess the ID factors outlined above (see https://www.iris-database.org/iris/ for recent efforts to make such instruments and materials available to second language acquisition researchers through a digital repository). In the remainder of this chapter, we will introduce a selection of those. One commonly used questionnaire to assess the language background in second language learners is The Language Experience and Proficiency Questionnaire (LEAP-Q, Marian et al., 2007), an instrument used to obtain general demographic information and more specific information on self-rated proficiency for three language areas (reading, understanding, and speaking) and self-rated current knowledge of L2 English and exposure to the L2. Another very useful, recently introduced instrument designed to capture a number of linguistic and socio-demographic factors is the Language and Social Background Questionnaire (LSBQ) by Anderson et al. (2018). The LSBQ was developed to assess degrees of bilingualism for young adults who live in diverse communities in which English is the official language.

Research on implicit statistical learning ability has primarily employed the Artificial Grammar Learning or the Serial Reaction Time paradigms (see Perruchet & Pacton, 2006, for overviews) (for recent developments in this field and the role of chunking, see Christiansen, 2018). Working memory (WM), in the Baddeley tradition (e.g., Baddeley, 1986), is conceived of as a multicomponent system responsible for the active maintenance (manipulation and retrieval) of information in the face of concurrent cognitive processing and/or distraction. Due to its central role in higher-order cognitive abilities, including arithmetic calculation, reasoning and problem solving, and language processing, much effort has been paid to developing tasks designed to measure individual WM capacity (see Conway et al., 2005, for a comprehensive methodological review; see also Linck et al., 2014, for a recent comprehensive meta-analysis in an SLA context). All of the experimental tasks designed to gauge statistical learning ability or WM capacity can be either implemented in commercial (Presentation™ https://www.neurobs.com/, or e-Prime™ https://pstnet.com/products/e-prime/) or in open-source experimental software, such as OpenSesame (https://osdoc.cogsci.nl/) or PsychoPy (http://www.psychopy.org/).

Representative Corpora and Research

The *EF-Cambridge Open Language Database* (EFCAMDAT) (Geertzen et al., 2013), a large-scale learner corpus compiled from online language learning platforms, consists of writing submitted to Englishtown, the online school of EF Education First. The Englishtown curriculum covers 16 levels that can be mapped to the reference levels of the Common European Framework of Reference for Languages (CEFR): 1–3 (A1),4–6 (A2), 7–9 (B1), 10–12 (B2), 13–15 (C1), 16 (C2). Each level consists of eight units, each including a free writing task. The corpus comprises 83-million-words compiled from 1 million assignments written by 174,000 learners, across a wide range of nationalities and is annotated with information on learner errors, part of speech categories, and grammatical relationships.

Murakami (2016) is a good example of how systematicity, individual variation, and nonlinearity in L2 development can be analyzed in the EFCAMDAT using two state-of-the-art modeling techniques – generalized linear mixed models (GLMM) and generalized additive mixed models (GAMM) – to quantify individual variation and investigate systematic effects simultaneously (GLMM) and to capture the nonlinear nature of L2 development (GAMM). Focusing on L2 learners' development of accuracy of English grammatical morphemes – article accuracy – the study sets out to determine the extent of individual variation in the developmental pattern of morphemes and to investigate whether and to what extent developmental patterns vary depending on the particular morpheme and on whether learners' native languages have an equivalent morpheme. The results of the GLMM and GAMM modeling revealed considerable individual variation in absolute accuracy and in nonlinear development and indicated systematic L1 influence and proficiency effects on absolute accuracy and on longitudinal developmental patterns.

The *Secondary-Level Corpus of Learner English* (ScooLE) (Möller, 2017a, 2017b) (258,586 word tokens) was compiled from argumentative essays elicited from 426 German 16–17-year-old (grade 11) secondary school students learning English in either a standard English as a Foreign Language (EFL) setting or in an EFL plus Content and Integrated Language Learning (CLIL) setting. The learners who contributed to the corpus were also administered a battery of psychometric tests tapping into several cognitive and affective ID variables, which were specifically designed for use with year 7–13 students at secondary school. Cognitive skills were tested using the PSB-R 6–13 intelligence test, which comprises nine subtests. Aspects of motivation and anxiety were assessed by means of the FLM 7–13, which comprises five scales (orientation towards performance and success, perseverance and effort, fear of success, exam anxiety/activating, and exam anxiety/inhibiting).

Möller (2017b) is a great example of how a highly diversified L2 database that includes learner corpus data as well as experimental data from the same learners can be used in a within-subject design to make an important contribution to research on individual differences in SLA. The corpus-data used in the study were selected essays – produced in response to different prompts – taken from the SCooLE. In this study, multiple linear regression modeling was employed to examine whether and to what extent the frequency of use of passive constructions by year 11 secondary school L2 learners of English is related to their scores on the different scales on the psychometric tests.

Future Directions

Due to the developments sketched above, there is a growing awareness of the need to pay greater attention to individual differences (IDs) in both native and non-native language attainment across multiple components of language and across the lifespan. While group-level comparisons are beneficial for a number of reasons, they tend to obscure IDs by aggregating data over individual learners. IDs have to be adequately captured, described, and understood before any claim about the nature of language acquisition can be made, and homogeneous L2 learner samples can only be drawn if factors underlying the variation in that population are adequately understood. A principled and systematic account of individual variation in learning outcomes is required to determine normative rates of language development and to ensure fairness in the assessment of language performance and proficiency and to allow the identification of atypical forms of language development.

The available IDs research has primarily employed behavioral methods in laboratory settings and has focused on language comprehension. Learner Corpus Research (LCR) is a valuable complement to the growing body of ID research situated within emergentist accounts that view production data as a key data type. As recently emphasized by Dell and Chan (2014), language production is the least studied of the three key areas of psycholinguistics – acquisition, comprehension, and production – in literature both on first and second language acquisition. Despite this imbalance, production research is gaining an increasingly central role in psycholinguistic theory and even linguistic theory (see MacDonald's, 2013, production-distribution-comprehension; see, also Chater, McCauley, & Christiansen, 2016).

Emergentist approaches, as outlined above, emphasize that the nature and extent of individuals' experience with language input are key determinants of language development. Research on early child language acquisition has greatly benefited from the existence of CHILDES corpora that allow an input-output modeling approach (see MacWhinney, 2010). Because language acquisition does not end at some discrete point of time in ontogenetic development but instead takes place across the lifespan, collaborative efforts are required to compile longitudinal corpora that capture (or at least approximate) the nature and extent of individuals' experience with L2 input across the lifespan. To gauge variability in the amount of an individual's exposure to L2 input, 'proxy measures' of linguistic experience should be administered in learner corpus studies. In our methodological section, we introduced within-subject designs embedded in an IDs framework. Such designs in which participants are administered a battery of measures assessing a wide range of cognitive abilities and proxies of L2 experience can be combined with L2 performance measures obtained from analyses of learner corpora of written and spoken productions. We have also emphasized the importance of establishing more bi-directional links with not only second language acquisition research but also being informed by recent developments in the cognitive sciences literature on individual differences in language acquisition and processing (see, e.g, a recent comprehensive review by Kidd et al. 2018). And finally, it is important to recognize that there is considerable heterogeneity in when cognitive abilities peak, with some abilities beginning to decline around high school graduation, whereas others do not peak until subjects reach their 40s or later (see Hartshorne & Germine, 2015).

Further Reading

Kormos, J., & Trebits, A. (2012). The role of task complexity, modality and aptitude in narrative task performance. *Language Learning, 62*(2), 439–472.

This study assessed the relationship of traditional components of language aptitude with the measures of lexical and syntactic complexity, accuracy, and fluency in two types of narrative tasks, which were administered both orally and in writing to 44 upper-intermediate Hungarian learners of English. The study also aimed to reveal how narrative performance varies in tasks of different cognitive complexity in the written and spoken modes. The findings suggest a complex interaction between aptitude components and task performance under different conditions.

Lowie, W. M., & Verspoor, M. H. (2019). Individual differences and the ergodicity problem. *Language Learning, 69*, 184–206.

Taking a CDST perspective, this study investigated the effects of motivation and aptitude on writing proficiency gains in a group study and longitudinal case studies of 22 L1 Dutch L2 English university students. L2 written production data were collected over a period of 23 weeks within an academic year. All texts were scored holistically on English proficiency by ten trained raters and regressed on individuals' scores on three dimensions of motivation and foreign language aptitude. The analysis of the aggregated group level data revealed significant increases in rating scores between the first and last two weeks of testing. While ratings scores were not found to be related to any of the ID variables, the study demonstrated the presence of considerable differences in individual learning trajectories.

Pae, T. (2018). Effects of task type and L2 proficiency on the relationship between L1 and L2 in reading and writing: An SEM approach. *Studies in Second Language Acquisition, 40*(1), 63–90.

Pae (2018) systematically investigated the moderating effects of task type and L2 proficiency on the relationship between L1 and L2 simultaneously across reading and writing tasks with different levels of cognitive complexity. The results from structural equation modeling revealed that L1 ability is a significant predictor of L2 ability in both reading and writing, suggesting the existence of interdependent relations between L1 and L2 operations in receptive and productive skills.

Notes

1 See also the Human Speechome Project, https://www.media.mit.edu/cogmac/projects/hsp.html (last accessed 19 December 2019).
2 Offline measures assess the outcome of mental processing, whereas online measures monitor mental processes as they unfold in real time.

References

Acheson, D. J., Wells, J. B., & MacDonald, M. C. (2008). New and updated tests of print exposure and reading abilities in college students. *Behavior Research Methods, 40*(1), 278–289.
Anderson, J. A., Mak, L., Chahi, A. K., & Bialystok, E. (2018). The language and social background questionnaire: Assessing degree of bilingualism in a diverse population. *Behavior Research Methods, 50*(1), 250–263.
Baddeley, A. (1986). Oxford psychology series No 11. *Working memory*. New York.
Beckner, C., Blythe, R., Bybee, J., Christiansen, M. H., Croft, W., Ellis, N. C., … Schoenemann, T. (2009). Language is a complex adaptive system: Position paper. *Language Learning, 59*(S1), 1–26.
Birdsong, D. (1992). Ultimate attainment in second language acquisition. *Language*, 706–755.

Bley-Vroman, R. (1989). What is the logical problem of foreign language learning. *Linguistic Perspectives on Second Language Acquisition, 4*, 1–68.

Carroll, J. B., & Sapon, S. (2002). *Modern language aptitude test (MLAT) Manual. N.* Bethesda: Second Language Testing, Inc. (Originally published in 1959).

Chang, F., Dell, G. S., & Bock, K. (2006). Becoming syntactic. *Psychological Review, 113*(2), 234.

Chater, N., McCauley, S., & Christiansen, M. H. (2016). Language as skill: Intertwining comprehension and production. *Journal of Memory and Language, 89*, 244–254.

Chomsky, N. (1980). Rules and representations. *Behavioral and Brain Sciences, 3*(1), 1–15.

Chomsky, N. (1995). *The minimalist program.* Cambridge: MIT press.

Christiansen, M. H. (2018). Implicit statistical learning: A tale of two literatures. *Topics in Cognitive Science, 11*(3), 468–481.

Christiansen, M. H., & Chater, N. (2016). *Creating language: Integrating evolution, acquisition, and processing.* Cambridge: MIT Press.

Clahsen, H., & Felser, C. (2006). Grammatical processing in language learners. *Applied Psycholinguistics, 27*(1), 3–42.

Conway, A. R., Kane, M. J., Bunting, M. F., Hambrick, D. Z., Wilhelm, O., & Engle, R. W. (2005). Working memory span tasks: A methodological review and user's guide. *Psychonomic Bulletin and Review, 12*(5), 769–786.

Cummins, J. (1979). Linguistic interdependence and educational development of bilingual children. *Review of Educational Research, 49*(2), 222–251.

Cummins, J. (2017). BICS and CALP: Empirical and theoretical status of the distinction. In B. Street & S. May (Eds.), *Literacies and language education. Encyclopedia of language and education* (3rd ed.), (pp. 59–71) Cham: Springer.

Dąbrowska, E. (2018). Experience, aptitude and individual differences in native language ultimate attainment. *Cognition, 178*, 222–235.

de Bot, K., Lowie, W., & Verspoor, M. (2007). A dynamic systems theory approach to second language acquisition. *Bilingualism: Language and Cognition, 10*(1), 7–21.

Dell, G. S., & Chang, F. (2014). The P-chain: Relating sentence production and its disorders to comprehension and acquisition. *Philosophical Transactions of the Royal Society of London Series B, 369*(1634), 20120394.

Dewaele, J. M. (2013). Learner internal and psychological factors. In J. R. Herschensohn & M. Young-Scholten (Eds.), *The Cambridge handbook of second language acquisition* (pp 159–179). Cambridge: Cambridge University Press.

Dewaele, J. M., & Furnham, A. (2000). Personality and speech production: A pilot study of second language learners. *Personality and Individual Differences, 28*(2), 355–365.

Doughty, C. J. (2019). Cognitive language aptitude. *Language Learning, 69*, 101–126.

Ellis, N. C. (2002). Frequency effects in language processing: A review with implications for theories of implicit and explicit language acquisition. *Studies in Second Language Acquisition, 24*(2), 143–188.

Ellis, R. (2004). Individual differences in second language learning. In A. Davies & C. Elder (Eds.), *The handbook of applied linguistics* (pp. 525–551). Oxford: Blackwell Publishing.

Ettlinger, M., Morgan-Short, K., Faretta-Stutenberg, M., & Wong, P. C. (2016). The relationship between artificial and second language learning. *Cognitive Science, 40*(4), 822–847.

Geertzen, J., Alexopoulou, T., & Korhonen, A. (2013, October). Automatic linguistic annotation of large scale L2 databases: The EF-Cambridge Open Language Database (EFCAMDAT). In *Proceedings of the 31st second language research forum.* Somerville: Cascadilla Proceedings Project.

Granger, S., Gilquin, G., & Meunier, F. (Eds.) (2015). *The Cambridge handbook of learner corpus research.* Cambridge: Cambridge University Press.

Hartshorne, J. K., & Germine, L. T. (2015). When does cognitive functioning peak? The asynchronous rise and fall of different cognitive abilities across the life span. *Psychological Science, 26*(4), 433–443.

Huttenlocher, J., Waterfall, H., Vasilyeva, M., Vevea, J., & Hedges, L. V. (2010). Sources of variability in children's language growth. *Cognitive Psychology, 61*(4), 343–365.

In'nami, Y., & Koizumi, R. (2011). Structural equation modeling in language testing and learning research: A review. *Language Assessment Quarterly, 8*(3), 250–276.

Jones, G., & Rowland, C. F. (2017). Diversity not quantity in caregiver speech: Using computational modeling to isolate the effects of the quantity and the diversity of the input on vocabulary growth. *Cognitive Psychology, 98*, 1–21.

Kaufman, S. B., DeYoung, C. G., Gray, J. R., Jiménez, L., Brown, J., & Mackintosh, N. (2010). Implicit learning as an ability. *Cognition, 116*(3), 321–340.

Kidd, E., & Arciuli, J. (2016). Individual differences in statistical learning predict children's comprehension of syntax. *Child Development*, *87*(1), 184–193.

Kidd, E., Donnelly, S., & Christiansen, M. H. (2018). Individual differences in language acquisition and processing. *Trends in Cognitive Sciences*, *22*(2), 154–169.

Kormos, J. (2012). The role of individual differences in L2 writing. *Journal of Second Language Writing*, *21*(4), 390–403.

Kormos, J., & Trebits, A. (2012). The role of task complexity, modality and aptitude in narrative task performance. *Language Learning*, *62*(2), 439–472.

Krashen, S. D. (1981). *Second language acquisition and second language learning*. Oxford: Oxford University Press.

Kuhl, P. K. (2010). Brain mechanisms underlying the critical period for language: Linking theory and practice. *Human Neuroplasticity and Education*, *27*, 33.

Larsen-Freeman, D. (2011). A complexity theory approach to second language development/acquisition. In D. Atkinson (Ed.), *Alternative approaches to second language acquisition* (pp. 47–72). New York: Routledge.

Li, S. (2016). The construct validity of language aptitude: A meta-analysis. *Studies in Second Language Acquisition*, *38*(4), 801–842.

Linck, J. A., Hughes, M. M., Campbell, S. G., Silbert, N. H., Tare, M., Jackson, S. R., … Doughty, C. J. (2013). Hi-lab: A new measure of aptitude for high-level language proficiency. *Language Learning*, *63*(3), 530–566.

Linck, J. A., Osthus, P., Koeth, J. T., & Bunting, M. F. (2014). Working memory and second language comprehension and production: A meta-analysis. *Psychonomic Bulletin and Review*, *21*(4), 861–883.

MacDonald, M. C. (2013). How language production shapes language form and comprehension. *Frontiers in Psychology*, *4*(226), 1–16.

MacWhinney, B. (2000). *The CHILDES project: Tools for analyzing talk - the database* (vol. 2). New York and London: Psychology Press.

MacWhinney, B. (2010). Computational models of child language learning: An introduction. *Journal of Child Language*, *37*(3), 477–485.

Marian, V., Blumenfeld, H. K., & Kaushanskaya, M. (2007). The Language Experience and Proficiency Questionnaire (LEAP-Q): Assessing language profiles in bilinguals and multilinguals. *Journal of Speech, Language, and Hearing Research*, *50*(4), 940–967.

McCauley, S. M., & Christiansen, M. H. (2018). Language learning as language use: A cross-linguistic model of child language development. *Psychological Review*, *126*(1), 1.

Meunier, F., & Gouverneur, C. (2009). New types of corpora for new educational challenges: Collecting, annotating and exploiting a corpus of textbook material. In K. Aijmer (Ed.), *Corpora and language teaching* (pp.179–201). Amsterdam: John Benjamins.

Misyak, J. B., & Christiansen, M. H. (2012). Statistical learning and language: An individual differences study. *Language Learning*, *62*(1), 302–331.

Mitchell, R., Myles, F., & Marsden, E. (2013). *Second language learning theories*. London: Routledge.

Möller, V. (2017a). *Language acquisition in CLIL and non-CLIL settings: Learner corpus and experimental evidence on passive constructions* (vol. 80). Amsterdam: John Benjamins.

Möller, V. (2017b). A statistical analysis of learner corpus data, experimental data and individual differences: Monofactorial vs. multifactorial approaches. In P. de Haan, S. van Vuuren, & R. de Vries (Eds.), *Language, learners and levels: Progression and cariation. Corpora and language in use*, *proceedings 3* (pp. 409–439), Louvain-la-Neuve: Presses universitaires de Louvain.

Montag, J. L., & MacDonald, M. C. (2015). Text exposure predicts spoken production of complex sentences in 8-and 12-year-old children and adults. *Journal of Experimental Psychology: General*, *144*(2), 447.

Murakami, A. (2016). Modeling systematicity and individuality in nonlinear second language development: The case of English grammatical morphemes. Methodological review article. *Language Learning*, *66*(4), 834–871.

Pae, T. (2018). Effects of task type and L2 proficiency on the relationship between L1 and L2 in reading and writing: An SEM approach. *Studies in Second Language Acquisition*, *40*(1), 63–90.

Perruchet, P., & Pacton, S. (2006). Implicit learning and statistical learning: One phenomenon, two approaches. *Trends in Cognitive Sciences*, *10*(5), 233–238.

Pimsleur, P. (1966). *Pimsleur language aptitude battery (form S)*. Harcourt, Brace and World, Incorporated.

Quinn, J. M., Wagner, R. K., Petscher, Y., & Lopez, D. (2015). Developmental relations between vocabulary knowledge and reading comprehension: A latent change score modeling study. *Child Development*, *86*(1), 159–175.

Rebuschat, P. E., Meurers, D., & McEnery, T. (2017). Language learning research at the intersection of experimental, computational and corpus-based approaches. *Language Learning*, *67*(S1), 6–13.

Seidenberg, M. S., & MacDonald, M. C. (2018). The impact of language experience on language and reading. *Topics in Language Disorders*, *38*(1), 66–83.

Skehan, P. (1991). Individual differences in second language learning. *Studies in Second Language Acquisition*, *13*(2), 275–298.

Skehan, P. (2002). Theorizing and updating aptitude. In P. Robinson (Ed.), *Individual differences and instructed language learning* (pp. 69–94). Amsterdam: John Benjamins.

Sorace, A. (2011). Pinning down the concept of interface in bilingualism. *Linguistic Approaches to Bilingualism*, *1*(1), 1–33.

Sparks, R. L., Patton, J., & Ganschow, L. (2012). Profiles of more and less successful L2 learners: A cluster analysis study. *Learning and Individual Differences*, *22*(4), 463–472.

Ströbel, M., Kerz, E., & Wiechmann, D. (2020). The relationship between first and second language writing: Investigating the effects of L1 complexity on L2 complexity in advanced stages of learning. *Language Learning 70*(3), 732–767.

Tellings, A. E. J. M., Hulsbosch, M. A., Vermeer, A., & van den Bosch, A. P. J. (2014). *BasiLex: An 11.5 million words corpus of Dutch texts written for children*. Computational Linguistics in the Netherlands Journal 4: 191–208.

Tracy-Ventura, N., & Cuesta Medina, J. A. (2018). Can native-speaker corpora help explain L2 acquisition of tense and aspect? *International Journal of Learner Corpus Research*, *4*(2), 277–300.

Wen, Z. E., Skehan, P., Biedroń, A., Li, S., & Sparks, R. L. (Eds.) (2019). *Language aptitude: Advancing theory, testing, research and practice*. London: Routledge.

White, L. (2003). On the nature of interlanguage representation: Universal grammar in the second language. In C. Doughty & M. Long (Eds.), *The handbook of second language acquisition* (pp. 19–42). Oxford: Blackwell Publishing Ltd.

PART V
FUTURE DIRECTIONS

31

The Future of Corpora in SLA

Nicole Tracy-Ventura, Magali Paquot, and Florence Myles

Introduction

As the chapters of this handbook have demonstrated, corpora have much to offer second language acquisition (SLA). By adopting electronic formats, we are increasing the amount of data that can be analyzed efficiently and making valuable data more readily available. Considering the rapid development of computerized tools over the last three decades, we are confident that learner and L1 corpora will continue to play very important roles in SLA research. In what follows, we provide several suggestions of ways that both SLA and learner corpus research (LCR) can make necessary improvements in research utilizing corpora. Every one of the chapters in this handbook has concluded with ideas for future directions. In writing this final chapter, we have paid close attention to the suggestions made by our colleagues in addition to adding our own comments. We have organized the suggestions for future research into three main categories: (1) corpus design and preparation, (2) corpus analysis, and (3) Open Science and methodological expertise.

Corpus Design

As discussed in Chapter 3 (this volume), early LCR research was criticized for being overly descriptive and not informed by SLA theory. In response to such criticism, several discussions about the positive contribution of LCR to the analysis of learner language later ensued (e.g., Granger, 2009). SLA researchers also began to acknowledge the benefits of having large collections of learner language that could be analyzed using corpus tools. In a series of publications, Myles (e.g., 2005, 2008, 2015) argued for the benefits of learner corpora from an SLA perspective and highlighted the types of corpora that would be useful for SLA research. She emphasized the importance of hypothesis-testing studies using learner corpora that are appropriately designed to test such hypotheses (e.g., a sufficient number of tokens, including rare structures, a range of languages and proficiencies, a range of different contexts). Over the years, we have witnessed a notable increase in hypothesis-testing learner corpus studies, as the chapters in this handbook have demonstrated. However, we are still at an early stage, and much work is needed. As explained in Chapter 4, "there is not one unified theory of SLA, but rather various theories that differ in how they account for, and the data they use to measure, acquisition" (p. 37). This lack of a single dominant theory of SLA demonstrates the complexity of second language learning and the need to explain a variety of phenomena (e.g., systematicity and variability in interlanguage, crosslinguistic influences, incomplete success and ultimate attainment, differences between learners, the role of social practice, etc.; see Mitchell, Myles, & Marsden, 2019). For some SLA theories and approaches, corpus data are ideal for testing important hypotheses, and Chapters 13–18 in this handbook provide examples of this work. There is much more we can do, however, to improve the design of learner corpora to better address the complexity of SLA. Some important points we discuss in this section include expanding the languages we focus on, diversifying learner characteristics (proficiency, age, etc.), considering different perspectives on what a "control" corpus is, improving collection of metadata, diversifying the kinds of corpora and experimental data collected, and increasing transparency in transcription and annotation.

Expand Learners/Users We Focus On

L1, L2s, L+s

Most studies utilizing learner corpora have included learners/users of English as an L1 or an L2, with English L2 learners undoubtedly being the most studied group. This strong focus on English learning is not surprising considering that according to the British Council there are estimated to be close to two billion learners of English around the world[1]. However, if we are to better understand the process of L2 learning, it is essential that we expand our focus to include different languages, especially typologically distant languages. The field has been working to address this issue, and there have been some welcome developments as evidenced by the increased variety of L2s listed on the Learner Corpora around the World webpage (https://uclouvain.be/en/research-in stitutes/ilc/cecl/learner-corpora-around-the-world.html) managed at the Université catholique de Louvain, Belgium. The Norwegian learner corpus (Andrespråkskorpus = Second Language Corpus), described in Chapter 26 (this volume), is a worthwhile example in that it includes Norwegian L2 language data from adult immigrants with 10 typologically diverse first languages.

Additionally, as a field, we would benefit from building more multilingual corpora as a way to promote cross-linguistic comparisons. For example, the *Learning Prosody in a Foreign Language* (LeaP) corpus (Gut, 2012) described in Chapter 22 (this volume), includes spoken learner German and learner English (by different learners) based on the same tasks (e.g., interviews, story retellings). Another example is the *PARallèle Oral en Langue Etrangère* (PAROLE) corpus (Hilton, 2009), which includes data from learners of English, French, and Italian. However, to study multilingual development/competence, we would also benefit from the development of corpora that include data from speakers naturally engaging in codeswitching and translanguaging during oral (and online) interactions. Tools are already available to handle codeswitching and translanguaging within the same file such as the CLAN program and related CHAT transcription format (see Chapter 12, this volume). Codes can be inserted during transcription that allow for analysis of different languages within a single transcript. Bilingual corpora could be especially useful for studying heritage language learners (Ortega, 2020) and L1 and L2 attrition (Schmid & Köpke, 2019), which are currently underrepresented in research utilizing learner corpora.

Proficiency

Learner corpora have generally focused on intermediate and advanced learners/users. Corpora of beginners are rare but just as important. The purpose of SLA research is to document and explain development from beginning to end. The steps in the process, as well as the end point, are crucial for answering some of the theoretical questions under investigation in the field. Some corpora have included beginner data, along with intermediate and advanced data, such as the cross-sectional corpora compiled within the framework of the *French and Spanish Learner Language Oral Corpora* (FLLOC and SPLLOC) projects described in Chapter 4. Longitudinal corpora that start with true beginners are exceptionally rare but a notable example is the Progression Project (Mitchell, & Dickson, 1997; described in Chapter 11), a FLLOC longitudinal corpus that includes data collected over a two-year period.

Age

In large part due to convenience, most participants in learner corpora are educated adults over the age of 18. Collecting data from younger participants adds some layers of complexity, such as gaining informed consent from parents, yet age is an important variable in SLA research (see Chapter 4, this volume), and corpora of younger learners are needed. The *Multilingual Traditional Immersion and Native Corpus* (MulTINCo) discussed in Chapter 3 includes longitudinal data of French-speaking primary and secondary school children learning English or Dutch in Belgium. In addition to the young age of the participants and being longitudinal, another unique feature of this corpus is that the participants come from two different instructional settings, Content and Language Integrated Language Learning (CLIL) and traditional language classes.

The *Barcelona English Language Corpus* (BELC), discussed in Chapter 11, is another example of how age can be investigated as a variable in research involving learner corpora. This corpus, available on Talkbank.org, includes data from students who differed by age of onset (8, 11, 14, and 18+ years old) and hours of instruction in Catalonia, Spain. In addition to being longitudinal, the corpus includes multiple data types (written composition, oral narrative, oral interview, and role plays). Although a number of publications are based on this corpus (see Muñoz, 2006), so far, few have involved corpus-based methods.

Corpora consisting of data from middle-aged and older adults are quite rare, although they could provide very interesting data for studies of L1 attrition (Schmid & Köpke, 2019) and the long-term retention of instructed learners' L2 skills (Bahrick, 1984).

Context of Learning

A major question in the field of SLA has centered on the role of context in language learning. Many people around the world are learning languages naturalistically, yet available learner corpora tend to be of instructed learners. This bias is likely due to convenience because instructed learners are the population most accessible to us as researchers. However, there are important exceptions such as the *European Science Foundation Corpus* (ESF: Perdue, 1993) described in Chapter 13 that has been used to investigate aspects of usage-based and functional approaches to SLA. More corpora focusing on the language of naturalistic, uninstructed learners are needed, and ideally should be shared publicly like the ESF corpus, which is available on Talkbank.org.

Although instructed learners are often the focus of our research, we rarely build corpora of them interacting naturalistically, for example, when participating in non-teaching internships or community service (see Chapter 29, this volume). Learner corpora documenting learning as a result of instructed learners spending time abroad are available (see the LANGSNAP corpus; Tracy-Ventura et al., 2016), yet they typically do not include authentic interactions with members of participants' social networks. Such data are needed if we are to better understand the kind of language that learners produce in informal naturalistic contexts. These data could be especially useful for understanding to what extent learners vary their language use in different contexts (see also the section on *Learner Language across Communicative Tasks and Registers* below and Chapters 17 and 27, this volume) and how interaction affects subsequent learning (Chapter 21, this volume).

Related to context of learning is instruction type. The MulTINCo corpus (Meunier et al., 2020) described above is a unique corpus comparing learners in CLIL and non-CLIL classes, which helps to discover potential differences between these two learning contexts. Additionally, synchronous-computer mediated communication (SCMC) is another context which is becoming more prevalent, and studies have only just begun to investigate learning in that context (Collentine & Collentine, 2013; Yuldashev et al., 2013).

Another type of corpus that would be useful, not only to examine the role of context of learning but also to improve our understanding of second language development in general, is the input corpus. Researchers often investigate the input available to learners indirectly by analyzing large L1 reference corpora such as the *British National Corpus* (BNC) or the *Corpus of Contemporary American English* (COCA). L1 reference corpora can provide general information about frequency, but they are still not ideal sources of evidence, as they do not provide direct evidence of the native/expert language that learners are exposed to. Although rare, notable examples of genuine input corpora exist such as the *Portland Classroom Corpus* discussed in Chapter 19 and Myles and Mitchell's (2012) *Young Learners Project*, which includes complete video recordings of a set of French lessons taught to English early learners, representing all the input they were ever exposed to in French (they did not have access to input outside the class). Such corpora are essential for investigating questions about the role of input in language learning (see also Collins et al., 2009; Crossley et al., 2016; Chapters 13 and 20, this volume). The somewhat older field of first language acquisition research could provide models of the kind of corpora L2 researchers might want to develop in order to study interactions between learners and other speakers (see more particularly the child-caretaker interaction corpora on the Child Language Data Exchange System, or CHILDES, on Talkbank.org; also Chapter 12, this volume).

Comparison/Control Data

Typically, in LCR and SLA research involving learner corpora, a control corpus of L1 speakers is used for comparison purposes. Most often, these control corpora consist of data from participants of the same age who speak the target language as their L1 (e.g., the *Louvain Corpus of Native English Essays,* or LOCNESS, that is often used for comparison with the *International Corpus of Learner English,* or ICLE; see Granger, 1998). In models such as the Integrated Contrastive Model (Granger, 1996) or Jarvis' (2000) methodological framework for the study of cross-linguistic influence, two native control corpora are used: one with data from L1 speakers of the target language and the other with L1 speakers from the learners' L1 (see Chapters 8 and 26, this volume). The use of L1/native speakers as the comparison has been controversial in SLA in particular, initially because of the 'comparative fallacy' (Bley-Vroman, 1983), which claimed that comparing learners and native speakers obscured important aspects of interlanguage development, and then more recently in discussions of the prevalent use of monolingual L1 controls (see discussion in Chapter 8, this volume). Many researchers argue that this leads to a "monolingual bias" due to equating the end point of L2 acquisition to that of a monolingual speaker "who is held to be the ultimate yardstick of linguistic success" (Ortega, 2014, p. 140). The use of monolingual norms and the idea of a native speaker endpoint when investigating bi- and multilingualism is an issue that future LCR and SLA research need to address more thoroughly. The bilingual and multilingual turn in SLA (see, for example, the edited volume by May, 2013) has sparked important discussions which also apply to the kinds of control data used in learner corpus-based studies.

Researchers have also recently become interested in L2 learners' performance in their own L1, for comparative purposes. As described in Chapter 22 (this volume), this type of data has been especially useful for studies of oral fluency, investigating whether participants' L1 speaking style (e.g., whether they are fast talkers already) influences their gains in L2 oral fluency (e.g., see Huensch & Tracy-Ventura, 2017). Such data can be beneficial for studies on writing as well (Ströbel, et al., 2020). Having this kind of data makes it possible to investigate whether certain individual characteristics or individual preferences affect development in the L2 (see Chapter 30, this volume).

Collect Metadata More Systematically

Many of the variables described above are potentially confounding factors in SLA, and as a result, it is important to document them accurately in the metadata accompanying corpora. As a field, we often consider variables such as age, gender, native language(s), amount of previous instruction, context of learning, country of origin, country of residence, language(s) spoken at home, and amount of extracurricular language use/study. Additional variables that could perhaps become part of the required metadata to accompany a learner corpus include socio-economic status, parents' highest level of education, attitudes toward one's various languages, motivation to learn, learning disabilities, etc. Depending on the goals of the research project, other potentially useful data on individual differences include measures of aptitude and working memory (see Chapter 30, this volume). Inclusion of rich metadata is especially important when corpora are shared publicly and should be provided in the file headers or in accompanying databases (see Chapter 5, this volume, for more information on metadata).

Furthermore, to increase reliable comparability across studies (and corpora), proficiency information should be included in the metadata, and ideally assessed using a standardized measure. Many older learner corpora assessed proficiency based on institutional status, but recently more attention has been placed on the provision of reliable and valid measures of proficiency (Carlsen, 2012). To study the development of morphosyntax or vocabulary, for example, researchers often rely on the cross-sectional comparison of different groups based on proficiency. However, these comparisons are only as reliable as the methods used to differentiate the groups. Therefore, empirically-based assessments of proficiency are needed.

Related to the collection of metadata is the operationalization of these variables across corpora. Where they are operationalized in heterogeneous ways, datasets (and studies based on them) are difficult to compare. One example is the variable 'amount of previous instruction', which is often measured by years of instruction or hours of instruction. Considering the diversity of instructional contexts, operationalizing 'amount of previous instruction' in this way could be unreliable, especially if used to assess proficiency. Another issue is making sure the variables used are maximally informative for theoretical as well as empirical purposes (see Chapter 9, this volume). For example, participants are often grouped into proficiency categories (e.g. beginner vs. intermediate vs. advanced) in LCR and SLA. However, scholars have argued repeatedly for that variable not to be treated as a categorical one since, conceptually, L2 acquisition is best viewed as a continuous process, and, empirically, treating continuous phenomena as categories comes with undesirable statistical consequences (Ortega, 2012; Leal, 2018).

Additionally, most research has assumed that our participants speak only two languages (their L1 and the target language), yet many speakers of the world are multilingual. Considering that SLA research has become more interested in the influence of L2s on learning L3s (e.g., Jessner, Megens, & Graus, 2016), as argued in Chapter 5 (this volume), it will be important to collect data concerning all the languages that participants use/know, not just the L1(s) and the target language, as this is crucial to fully understand the role of cross-linguistic influence. Again, metadata about this important variable must be collected in a detailed and principled way. For example, information about the other languages learners know was collected in ICLE (Granger et al., 2002) using the wording "first other foreign language", "second foreign language", and so on. The challenge here is knowing exactly what level of proficiency was reached and for how long those languages were routinely used. As mentioned above, ideally, standardized proficiency measures would be used to assess proficiency. However, if that is not feasible for all the languages one knows, at the very minimum having participants self-assess their level of proficiency in their additional languages with the self-assessment grid of the Common European Framework of Reference for Languages (Council of Europe, 2001), for example, and providing details about how often they use or used those languages, and in which context, would be more useful than just listing languages studied/learned previously.

One important future step for the field is therefore to work together towards the development of some kind of shared protocol for collecting metadata that would include a minimal list of required variables and recommendations as to how best operationalize them (see Granger & Paquot, 2017 for a more detailed discussion and a proposed list of core variables in learner language).

Consider Corpus Mode, Tasks, and Time

Learner Language Across Communicative Tasks and Registers

As mentioned various times throughout this handbook, written learner corpora are more common than spoken learner corpora, a pattern found in corpus linguistics as well (see Chapter 2). This imbalance is due to the fact that written corpora are more convenient (and less expensive) to compile. Building spoken corpora is a more time-consuming and resource-intensive endeavor. For example, collecting oral data involves recorders and having a quiet place to record. Next, comes the (at least still) laborious step of transcription. Although speech recognition software has improved tremendously, a human is still needed to check the reliability of the transcript. In other words, it may save some time, but careful checking is still required, especially for beginner and intermediate learner language, which typically include more disfluencies and mispronunciations (for beginners, the first question to ask is whether these tools will work at all). Furthermore, preparing a spoken learner corpus requires such a considerable amount of time that corpus builders are often obliged to make certain decisions in transcription and annotation that are more relevant to their research focus. For example, if their focus is on morphosyntax or lexis, they will likely not annotate for length of pauses or overlapping between participants. However, by making both the audio files and the transcripts available to the research community (see e.g., corpora on SLABank), others can customize the transcripts to suit their research purposes. Despite the extra resources needed for building spoken corpora, it is essential that the field make a concerted effort to increase the number of spoken learner corpora. From a learning perspective, spoken corpora are thought to be a better window into SLA processes because in the real-time pressure of communication, learners have less time to use explicit knowledge (Myles, 2015; see also Chapter 12, this volume).

Because the majority of learner corpora are written and collected in schools or universities, the most popular tasks or registers in learner corpora are those typical of academic language, primarily essays. For the same reason, oral corpora often consist of interviews (primarily between a researcher and the participant), narrative retells based on pictures or silent films, or monologues based on a prompt. Interaction corpora that consist of conversations between learners, or informal conversations between learners and L1/expert target language speakers, are sorely needed (see Chapter 21, this volume).

Because many instructed learners are developing in both spoken and written language, it would also benefit the field to create more bimodal corpora that include multiple sources of data from the same learners. Such corpora would allow investigations into L2 users' ability to control different spoken and written registers, which is especially important as proficiency increases. So far, only a few learner corpora include both written and spoken learner data from the same learners such as the LANGSNAP corpus described in Chapter 25 and BELC described in Chapter 12.

Additionally, it is important to keep in mind that some linguistic features are naturally infrequent, and therefore, difficult to elicit naturally without specifically designed tasks. For SLA purposes, tasks eliciting rich/rare language are crucial, which is why corpora designed for SLA are often compiled on the basis of more controlled tasks. This highlights a major difference between SLA and LCR: learner corpora in LCR are typically prepared for general purposes, not for a specific study or research agenda. Irrespective of whether learner corpora are compiled by LCR or SLA specialists, it is important to keep in mind that the language produced by learners in different tasks may vary (see Gablasova, Brezina, McEnery, & Boyd, 2017; Tracy-Ventura & Myles, 2015; also Chapter 27, this volume). Task variability may be due to a number of different reasons such as the task prompt, the interactional demands of the task, the task not naturally eliciting the features under investigation, etc. Furthermore, as demonstrated in the Task-based Language Learning literature, task design and implementation variables (e.g., task complexity, task planning, task repetition, interlocutor characteristics, etc.) may influence learner production in different ways (Kim, 2015). Future research is needed to better understand the role that various aspects of communicative tasks play in learner productions. In the meantime, and although this has not been common practice in learner corpus design so far, piloting the data collection process should become part of the corpus design phase (see Chapter 5, this volume).

Longitudinal Corpora

One common desideratum found across many of the chapters in this handbook, and the field at large (Meunier, 2015; Myles, 2005, 2015), is the need for more longitudinal corpora. All kinds of longitudinal corpora are needed, including dense collections where data are collected multiple times over a year (see work by Chan et al., 2015; Crossley et al., 2016). Verspoor and Lowie (this volume) emphasize the importance of dense longitudinal data for testing Complex Dynamic Systems Theory: "From the studies published so far, we have learned that about 12 data points per academic year is the minimum needed to discover any dynamic pattern, but weekly or bi-weekly data points are preferred" (p. 194). Much longer-term longitudinal corpora are needed as well, in order to investigate how learner language evolves over time from beginner to advanced levels. The collection of such corpora presents enormous logistical difficulties, as the L2 learning process is so lengthy (Myles, 2008). Thus, building longitudinal corpora takes dedication on the part of the participants as well as the researchers. The additional time commitment may add challenges such as difficulties in securing funding for multiple phases of a project, participation attrition, research staff turnover, etc. (see Tracy-Ventura & Huensch, 2018) but the benefits are clear.

Collect Multiple Sources of L2 Data

We have already mentioned the importance of collecting metadata. Here we refer to combining corpora and experimental methods as discussed primarily in Chapter 10 but echoed in other chapters as well. Particularly for questions related to SLA, it is important to have not only examples of learner production but also other evidence of their knowledge. One of the issues with more near-natural production data is that it can offer an incomplete picture of learners' language abilities due to issues such as avoidance, or the task may not provide contexts for a learner to produce certain structures (see Tracy-Ventura & Myles, 2015). Experimental tasks that have been associated with many SLA frameworks attempt to gather specific and more controlled data. Potential useful sources of data that could complement learner corpus data involve the use of psycholinguistic methodologies such as reaction times and eye tracking, which provide information about the real-time processing of language by learners. In learner corpus research, corpora are most often treated as a product. However, it is possible to switch the focus by, for example, investigating writing as a process (see Gánem-Gutiérrez & Gilmore, 2018; Chapter 3, this volume). The *PROcess Corpus of English in EDucation* (PROCEED), for example, is a new type of learner corpus whose compilation involves capturing the keyboard and screen activity by means of keystroke logging and screencasting so as to keep a record of all the steps involved in the writing process (Gilquin, in press).

Take Advantage of Technology

As a field, we should also reflect more on how technology can help at each step of corpus design. For example, new media such as online learning platforms and social media offer unprecedented opportunities for enriching the options for obtaining spoken and written learner data representing a variety of registers, interactional patterns, etc. Several examples of corpora collected online already exist, such as the *Telecollaborative Learner Corpus of English and German* (Telekorp: see Chapter 21, this volume), which includes synchronous and asynchronous interactions between L2 learners of German and L1 German speakers, and the *Corpus Escrito del Español L2* (CEDEL2 version 2, see Chapter 16, this volume), a corpus of L2 Spanish texts collected from learners all over the world via an online interface. These types of online approaches lend themselves well to international collaboration and use of the same procedures, thereby facilitating the compilation of large datasets of comparable data. Relying on Natural Language Processing (NLP) tools and techniques to compile corpora can also scale up the number of learners and the size of our corpora (Meurers & Dickinson, 2017).

Increase Transparency in Transcription, Coding, and Linguistic Annotation

When we work with learner corpora, we make many decisions at the transcription and annotation stages that are often left unreported in publications. Transcription conventions and annotation of oral and written language can differ substantially between corpora. For example, if the investigators who compile a spoken learner corpus are interested in prosodic development, or fluency, or vocabulary development, the transcription will probably look very different, as will how errors are handled. Corpora may also differ in how they are formatted. For example, in CHAT, speech turns are broken into a series of syntactically-defined utterances. Even if the same speaker produces multiple utterances before another speaker's turn, each utterance appears on a new line. This step is done to allow for later analyses such as mean length of utterance (MLU), because CHAT/CLAN were initially developed by L1 acquisition researchers, for whom MLU is an important measure of development. This type of formatting differs from what is typically done in LCR. For written corpora, issues related to spelling errors need consideration too (e.g., Should spelling errors be corrected?). While it may not be possible to detail all the decisions made when transcribing, coding, and annotating a corpus in the methodology section of an article, it is important to be principled and transparent about such decisions, as they are never neutral and are often closely linked to the research agenda. Ensuring that this information is included somewhere accessible, especially when corpora are shared, is important (see below for more on methodological transparency). Gut (2012) and Hilton (2009) are two good examples of methodological publications that explain the decisions made in transcribing and annotating spoken corpora (see also Chapter 22, this volume). For more detail about transparency in error annotation, see Chapters 7 and 23.

As has become evident, many considerations need to be borne in mind when designing a corpus. These will, to a large extent, depend on the research agenda underpinning the collection of the corpus, but complete documentation of metadata and protocols is crucial to ensure shareability and comparability. We now turn to corpus analysis, and the various practices related to it.

Corpus Analysis

Expand the Measures Used

What this handbook demonstrates very well is that methods and tools from corpus linguistics have been used in very creative ways over the last years not only to examine established SLA research questions, but also to open up new domains of enquiry. Corpus-based SLA research that has adopted a usage-based perspective has made extensive use of Collostructional Analysis, a family of corpus methods that allow researchers to quantify the strength of the relationship between lexical items and the grammatical structures they occur in (Stefanowitsch & Gries, 2003). Corpus-derived indices of frequency, distribution, contingency, and recency are also part and parcel of their methodological apparatus (Chapter 13, this volume). Similarly, Paquot (2019) made use of corpus-derived metrics to operationalize the construct of phraseological complexity with a view to bridging the gap between interlanguage complexity research and L2 phraseological studies (Chapters 24 and 28, this volume). There are also more and more studies that have used Multi-Dimensional Analysis (MDA), a corpus technique first developed to describe and compare registers on the basis of a wide range of linguistic co-occurrence patterns (Biber, 1988), so as to investigate learner language across registers and tasks (Biber et al., 2016, Staples et al., 2018; see also Chapters 18 and 29, this volume).

The field of corpus linguistics offers many other good examples of how to use corpus-based tools to investigate different aspects of language (learning) including vocabulary, grammar, phraseology, pragmatics, discourse, phonology, and prosody. Chapter 18, for example, discusses how corpus annotation tools such as Weisser's Dialogue Annotation and Research Tool (DART; Weisser, 2014) could be used to automatically annotate and analyze speech acts or how speech act models from computational linguistics could also be used to inform SLA research on pragmatic language use. This raises two important issues however, i.e. the need to take stock of recent developments in corpus linguistics and NLP (we need to know what tools and techniques are available and what can be done with them), and the need for more multidisciplinary research and collaboration between SLA specialists, corpus linguists, and computational linguists (Meurers & Dickinson, 2017; McEnery et al., 2019).

Related to this is the need to design more text analysis tools that work with different languages. NLP tools such as part-of-speech (POS) taggers or parsers are available for many languages, but because English is the most studied language, most programs dedicated to the measurement of syntactic complexity, lexical sophistication, etc. are designed specifically to work with English. Some exceptions exist, such as CLAN, which is available from Talkbank (see Chapter 12, this volume). CLAN currently has POS taggers and grammatical dependency taggers for 11 different languages, and some of the analysis commands can work on any of these languages. It remains true, however, that if we want to investigate language-specific phenomena such as syntactic complexity or lexical sophistication in languages other than English, we are often first confronted with the challenge of lack of availability of tools. The field would benefit significantly from the development of tools such as those recently developed for English by Xiaofei Lu, Scott Crossley, and Kristopher Kyle, for other languages. Ideally, these tools would also compute measures that are comparable across L2s when possible.

Estimate and Report Reliability

As in other areas of SLA, reporting reliability should be a given (Plonsky & Derrick, 2016; McKay & Plonsky, in press). Here, we refer primarily to inter-rater reliability and instrument reliability. Inter-rater reliability is essential, especially when coding decisions involving a high level of subjective evaluation and/or interpretation are made, such as identifying and categorizing learner errors (Chapters 7 and 23, this volume). Regardless of the level of subjective evaluation involved, however, it should be a necessary step to estimate the amount of measurement error present in a coded dataset that stems from the manual coding and annotating of all types of linguistic features (Révész, 2012). As illustrated in Larsson et al. (in press), checks on reliability at different stages of a learner corpus study will not only facilitate more transparent reporting, but will also enable researchers to identify inconsistencies in the categorization and revise their coding schemes if needs be.

Natural Language Processing (NLP) and corpus analysis tools are also subject to errors, and their reliability should be estimated and reported too (Chapter 5, this volume). An accuracy of more than 90% is expected for automatic lemmatization, POS tagging, and parsing of general language, but this percentage can drop substantially when the corpora being processed differ from the kind of text that the annotation task has originally been trained on (typically newspaper writing) (Newman & Cox, in press). Key issues include, among other things, what impact different types of learner errors have on accuracy and whether automatic techniques can be used to annotate learner language across different proficiency levels (e.g., Does proficiency have an impact on accuracy? Can NLP tools be used on beginners' language?). Tools such as the Syntactic Complexity Analyzer (Lu, 2010) or the Tool for the Automatic Analysis of Cohesion (TAACO; Crossley, Kyle, & Dascalu, 2019) rely on NLP analyses to calculate indices of syntactic complexity or cohesion respectively and, as such, can only provide reliable indices to the extent that the backend NLP processing is reliable. In addition, the research community needs to get a better idea of what it takes for these tools to provide reliable measures (e.g. How minimally long should a learner text be to produce a reliable measure of syntactic complexity or lexical diversity? see Chapter 25, this volume). There is clearly a need for more research into NLP for learner language as featured in a forthcoming issue of the *International Journal of Learner Corpus Research* (Kyle, forthcoming; see also Meurers & Dickinson, 2017).

Instrument reliability should also be the focus of more attention when developing and/or using questionnaires to collect accompanying metadata such as degree of motivation and attitude towards language (learning), as well as language tests to assess language proficiency (see above).

Focus on Intra-corpus Variation: Individuals Matter in Learner Corpora Too

Learner corpus studies have often adopted a group perspective, analyzing large samples of language from many different speakers without taking individual variation into account. This has given rise to the "commonplace misconception among non-corpus linguists that corpora only contain massive pools of data collapsed over anonymized speakers, with no option to tie data points to the individual speaker who produced them" (Wulff & Gries, in press). Recent studies such as Murakami (2016) or Wulff & Gries (in press), however, have shown that, with the right study design and statistical method, it is possible to explore individual variation within and between the texts that make up a learner corpus (Chapters 17 and 30, this volume). More generally, more LCR studies now rely on statistical techniques, such as mixed-effect modelling, that make it possible to control for individual variation even if individual differences are not the primary focus (e.g. Lester, 2019; Crossley, Skalicky, Kyle, & Monteiro, 2019; Paquot et al., in press).

Corpus tools are primarily used on large samples of language from many different speakers. However, the analyses available when data are in an electronic format can be useful when conducting case studies as well. Tracking individual learners over time is important for testing aspects of several SLA theories and approaches, as perhaps best demonstrated in Complex Dynamic Systems Theory (CDST) studies that need multiple language productions from the same learners collected regularly at many measurement points to investigate how variability can inform the study of L2 development as an emerging process (Chapter 14, this volume).

Adopt a Multifactorial Design

A large majority of the learner corpus studies published so far have explored the influence of one independent variable only on learner language, typically non-nativeness in comparisons of native and non-native speakers, or first language background in comparisons of different L1 groups of non-native speakers. The impact of many other learner-related variables, as well as task-related variables, has remained largely unexplored despite the availability of relevant metadata in several learner corpora (Granger, 2009). Similarly, learner corpus studies have typically approached learners' use of vocabulary items, grammatical structures, etc. without adopting a case-by-variable format or modelling the linguistic context in which these phenomena occur (Gries, 2018).

There are reasons for optimism though, as this handbook has demonstrated; more and more studies have recently adopted multifactorial designs to explore the main effects and interaction effects of a wider range of variables (Chapter 9, this volume). This is essential given the complexity of our object of study, i.e. language use, and the complexity of the phenomenon we are trying to explain, i.e. second language acquisition. As put by Gries (2018),

> monofactorial studies of observational data have nothing to contribute to corpus linguistics because (i) no phenomenon is monofactorial and (ii) even if one had a new *mono*factorial hypothesis of a phenomenon, it would still require *multi*factorial testing to determine either (a) whether it either adds anything to what we already know about the phenomenon (by statistically controlling for what we already know) or (b) whether it replaces (parts of) what we already know about the phenomenon.
>
> *(Gries, 2018: p. 295)*

What the above recommendations clearly show is that we will need to up our game when using corpus techniques, NLP tools, and statistics to analyze learner corpora. As argued in Chapters 8 and 9, this volume, a variety of more sophisticated methods and statistical techniques are available to handle the complexities of L2 use and development. Furthermore, the number of textbooks and handbooks that offer a comprehensive yet accessible introduction to corpus methods and statistics for the study of language use is on the rise (e.g. Gries, 2013; Paquot & Gries, in press).

Open Science and Methodological Expertise

Share Learner Corpora and Related Instruments

Increasingly, the field of applied linguistics is supporting Open Science. In SLA for example, the IRIS Digital Repository (Marsden, Mackey, & Plonsky, 2016) is making it possible for researchers to share research instruments. Several journals, such as *Language Learning*, are also encouraging this move (e.g., see Marsden et al., 2019) and offering Open Science Badges designed by the Center for Open Science (https://cos.io/) to acknowledge open data, open materials, and preregistration (https://cos.io/prereg/). With regards to corpora, this involves making our corpora freely available (a practice that is already present in LCR but should be encouraged more, also when it comes to (error-)annotated corpora which are rarely ever shared but are definitely needed for the development of more robust NLP tools), as well as the instruments used in compiling and annotating the corpora (e.g., prompts, picture-based narratives, error-tagging manuals). The latter would ensure, for example, that comparable corpora could be designed with different language pairings, learner proficiencies, and contexts of learning, to test important hypotheses about the development of learner language. The tasks of corpus design and collection are extremely time-consuming and require a high level of expertise in many different areas. The next step will be for all of us to work collaboratively towards achieving a certain level of standardization in the development of best practices and shared protocols for data collection (from the development of common ethical/legal procedures, transcription guidelines, and documents such as consent forms, to a minimal set of learner and task variables to be documented; see above) and data annotation (agreed-upon standards for the annotation of spoken corpora, error annotation, etc.) (Myles, 2015; MacWhinney, 2016; see also Chapter 12, this volume). This would not only enhance quality and re-usability of learner corpora and facilitate inter-study comparability, but, hopefully, also encourage others to embark on learner corpus collection and contribute data. Marsden and Plonsky (2018) outline how methodological transparency and data sharing are prerequisite for reproducibility and replication studies that are considered by many to be fundamental for the progress of science.

Offer More Training on Corpus Tools and Techniques

Workshops are a great way to provide opportunities for researchers to learn new skills. Pre-conference workshops are becoming a regular feature of academic conferences. Recently, we have also seen an increase in the number of online courses, seminars, and workshops, which are a fantastic way of bringing the international SLA/LCR community together. In addition to organized workshops, it would be useful to encourage more informal online and offline interaction among researchers who are analyzing the same type of data with the help of corpus tools or using the same programs to provide a space to discuss challenges they might be facing, potential improvements to specific programs, etc. Collectively, we can also learn more quickly about what programs would be most useful for our purposes among the plethora of tools that are currently available.

Summer schools also provide a space for learning new skills, and it is promising to see that these learning opportunities are increasing too. International associations could be instrumental here and help to organize more training events, whether face-to-face or online.

Increase the Status of Methodological Publications

Methodological publications (and related conference papers[2]) written by corpus designers are incredibly valuable, especially when the relevant corpora are shared publicly. Sometimes this information can be found on a project website, but websites are not always maintained. Having a publication explaining decisions in corpus design makes it possible for future researchers to re-use the data appropriately or design comparable corpora. Methodological publications written by corpus users are extremely useful too, as they can document and showcase good practices in corpus annotation, corpus analysis, etc. Not all journals are willing to publish such articles, but corpus journals are known for this (e.g., *International Journal of Corpus Linguistics, Corpora*). The *International Journal of Learner Corpus Research*, more particularly, now publishes 'corpus reports', 'materials and methods reports', 'software reports', and 'shared task reports'. It is important to publish methodological papers in SLA-oriented journals too, as a way to share best practice and increase visibility but also to recognize the valuable work and required expertise put into corpus collection, corpus transcription, corpus annotation, etc. Some SLA journals are leading the way, with 'Methods Articles' in the *Journal of EuroSLA* (JESLA) and the new 'Methods Showcase Articles' in *Language Learning* (Crossley et al., 2020), and it is to be expected that more journals will follow suit.

Other types of methodologically oriented publications that are now more widely published in SLA journals, but less so in corpus linguistic journals, are methodological reviews, research syntheses and meta-analyses. See, for example, Mizumoto et al. (in press) for a call for more meta-analyses as a means to synthesize findings systematically in corpus linguistics.

Conclusion

As explained at the beginning, the recommendations made here are based on a close reading of the chapters that make up this handbook as well as the relevant literature. It is our hope that they will be well received by the SLA and LCR communities and will serve to increase the use of learner corpora in SLA research. As put by Loewen & Plonsky (2016), "In the end, the goal of research is to have high validity" (p. 200). We believe that these recommendations will contribute to increasing the validity of learner corpus-based studies. By paying more attention to relevant variables and how they are operationalized at all stages of the research process, from corpus design to corpus analysis, we will work towards better construct validity. By expanding the range of L2+ learners and users, as well as the types of tasks and communicative events we analyze, we will strengthen ecological validity. Internal validity of learner corpus studies can be improved by, among other things, designing adequate data collection, transcription, and annotation guidelines, collecting metadata more systematically, and adopting a multifactorial design to analyze their effect on L2 language use, learning, and development. Methodological transparency will be instrumental in achieving enhanced external validity, by allowing reproducibility and replication studies. As a field, we have been improving in these areas, as the scholarship in this handbook demonstrates. It is our sincere hope that this handbook will play a major role in inspiring new research, and we look forward to seeing how the use of corpora in SLA continues to evolve and support our pursuit of understanding L2 development.

Notes

1 https://www.britishcouncil.org/sites/default/files/english-effect-report-v2.pdf
2 Organizers of conferences and the learned societies they represent should also encourage methodological papers/colloquia/strands more. Very often, even the criteria for selection of abstracts are inappropriate for judging methodological contributions, so there is scope for greater flexibility there too.

References

Bahrick, H. P. (1984). Fifty years of second language attrition: Implications for programmatic research. *The Modern Language Journal, 68*(2), 105–118. doi: 10.2307/327136

Biber, D. (1988). *Variation across speech and writing.* Cambridge: Cambridge University Press.

Biber, D., Gray, B., & Staples, S. (2016). Predicting patterns of grammatical complexity across language exam task types and proficiency levels. *Applied Linguistics, 37*(5), 639–668.

Bley-Vroman, R. (1983). The comparative fallacy in interlanguage studies: the case of systematicity. *Language Learning,* 33(1): 1–17.

Carlsen, C. (2012). Proficiency Level—A Fuzzy Variable in Computer Learner Corpora. *Applied Linguistics,* 33(2), 161–183. https://doi.org/10.1093/applin/amr047

Chan, H., Verspoor, M., & Vahtrick, L. (2015). Dynamic development in speaking versus writing in identical twins. *Language Learning, 65*(2), 298–325. https://doi.org/10.1111/lang.12107

Collentine, J., & Collentine, K. (2013). A corpus approach to studying structural convergence in task-based Spanish L2 interactions. In K. McDonough & A. Mackey (Eds.), *Second language interaction in diverse educational contexts* (pp. 167–187). Amsterdam: John Benjamins Publishing.

Collins, L., Trofimovich, P., White, J., Cardoso, W. & Horst, M. (2009). Some input on the easy/difficult grammar question: an empirical study. *The Modern Language Journal,* 93(3): 336–353.

Council of Europe (2001). *Common European framework of reference for languages: Learning, teaching, assessment.* Cambridge: Cambridge University Press.

Crossley, S., Kyle, K. & Salsbury, T. (2016). A usage-based investigation of L2 lexical acquisition: the role of input and output. *The Modern Language Journal,* 100(3): 702–715.

Crossley, S., Kyle, K., & Dascalu, M. (2019). The tool for automatic analysis of cohesion 2.0: Integrating semantic similarity and text overlap. *Behavior Research Methods, 51*(1), 14–27.

Crossley, S., Marsden, E., Ellis, N., Kormos, J., Morgan-Short, K., & Thierry, G. (2020). Introduction of methods showcase articles in language learning. *Language Learning, 70*(1), 5–10. doi:10.1111/lang.12389

Crossley, S., Skalicky, S., Kyle, K., & Monteiro, K. (2019). Absolute frequency effects in second language lexical acquisition. *Studies in Second Language Acquisition, 41*(4), 721–744.

Gablasova, D., Brezina, V., Mcenery, T., & Boyd, E. (2017). Epistemic stance in spoken L2 English: The effect of task and speaker style. *Applied Linguistics, 38*(5), 613–637.

Gánem-Gutierrez, G.A. & Gilmore, A. (2018). Tracking the real-time evolution of a writing event: Second language writers at different proficiency levels. *Language Learning*, *68*(2), 469–506.

Gilquin, G. (in press). Hic sunt dracones: Exploring some terra incognita in learner corpus research. In A. Čermáková & M. Malá (Eds.), *Variation in time and space: Observing the world through corpora*. Berlin: De Gruyter.

Granger, S. (1996). From CA to CIA and back: An integrated approach to computerized bilingual and learner corpora. In K. Aijmer, B. Altenberg & M. Johansson (Eds.), *Languages in contrast. Text-based cross-linguistic studies* (pp. 37–51). Lund: Lund University Press.

Granger, S. (1998). The computer learner corpus: A versatile new source of data for SLA research. In S. Granger (Ed.), *Learner English on computer* (pp. 3–18). London: Addison Wesley Longman.

Granger, S. (2009). The contribution of learner corpora to second language acquisition and foreign language teaching: A critical evaluation. In K. Aijmer (Ed.), *Corpora and language teaching* (pp. 13–32). Amsterdam: John Benjamins.

Granger, S. & Paquot, M. (2017). Towards standardization of metadata for L2 corpora. Invited talk at the CLARIN workshop on Interoperability of Second Language Resources and Tools, 6–8 December 2017, University of Gothenburg, Sweden. Available from https://sweclarin.se/sites/sweclarin.se/files/event_ata chements/Granger_Paquot_Metadata_G%C3%B6teborg_final.pdf (accessed 27 August 2020).

Granger, S., Dagneaux, E., & Meunier, F. (2002). *The international corpus of learner English*. Louvain-la-Neuve: Presses universitaires de louvain.

Gries, S. Th. (2013). *Statistics for linguistics with R* (2nd rev. and ext. ed). Berlin: De Gruyter Mouton.

Gries, S. Th. (2018). On over- and underuse in learner corpus research and multifactoriality in corpus linguistics more generally. *Journal of Second Language Studies*, *1*(2), 276–308.

Gut, U. (2012). The LeaP corpus. A multilingual corpus of spoken learner German and learner English. In T. Schmidt, & K. Wörner (Eds.), *Multilingual corpora and multilingual corpus analysis* (pp. 3–23). Amsterdam: John Benjamins.

Hilton, H. (2009). Annotation and analyses of temporal aspects of spoken fluency. *CALICO Journal*, *26*(3), 644–661.

Huensch, A., & Tracy-Ventura, N. (2017). Understanding second language fluency behavior: The effects of individual differences in first language fluency, cross-linguistic differences, and proficiency over time. *Applied Psycholinguistics*, *38*(4), 755–785.

Jarvis, S. (2000). Methodological rigor in the study of transfer: Identifying L1 influence in the interlanguage lexicon. *Language Learning*, *50*(2), 245–309. doi:10.1111/0023-8333.00118

Jessner, U., Megens, M., & Graus, S. (2016). Crosslinguistic influence in third language acquisition. In R. A. Alonso (Ed.), *Crosslinguistic influence in second language acquisition* (pp. 193–214). Bristol: Multilingual Matters.

Kim, Y. (2015). The role of tasks as vehicles for language learning in classroom interaction. In N. Markee (Ed.), *The Handbook of Classroom Discourse and Interaction* (pp. 163–181). John Wiley & Sons, Inc. https://doi.org/10.1002/9781118531242.ch10

Kyle, K. (Ed.) (forthcoming). Natural language processing for learner corpus research. Guest special issue of the *International Journal of Learner Corpus Research*.

Larsson, T., Paquot, M., & Plonsky, L. (in press). Inter-rater reliability in learner corpus research: Insights from a collaborative study on adverb placement. *International Journal of Learner Corpus Research*.

Leal, T. (2018). Data analysis and sampling. Methodological issues concerning proficiency in SLA research. In A. Gudmestad & A. Edmonds (Eds.), *Critical reflections on data in second language acquisition* (pp. 63–88). Amsterdam: John Benjamins.

Lester, N. (2019). That's hard: Relativizer use in spontaneous L2 speech. *International Journal of Learner Corpus Research*, *5*(1), 1–32.

Loewen, S., & Plonsky, P. (2016). *An A-Z of applied linguistics research methods*. London: Palgrave Macmillan.

Lu, X. (2010). Automatic analysis of syntactic complexity in second language writing. *International Journal of Corpus Linguistics*, *15*(4), 474–496.

MacWhinney, B. (2016). A shared platform for studying second language acquisition. *Language Learning*, *67*(S1), 254–275. doi:10.1111/lang.12220

Marsden, E., Crossley, S., Ellis, N., Kormos, J., Morgan-Short, K., & Thierry, G. (2019). Inclusion of research materials when submitting an article to language learning. *Language Learning*, *69*(4), 795–801. https://doi.org/10.1111/lang.12378

Marsden, E., Mackey, A., & Plonsky, L. (2016). The IRIS repository: Advancing research practice and methodology. In A. Mackey & E. Marsden (Eds.), *Advancing methodology and practice: The IRIS repository of instruments for research into second languages* (pp. 1– 21). New York: Routledge.

Marsden, E., & Plonsky, L. (2018). Conclusion: Data, open science, and methodological reform in second language acquisition research. In A. Gudmestad & A. Edmonds (Eds.), *Critical reflections on data in second language acquisition* (pp. 219–228). Amsterdam: John Benjamins.

McEnery, T., Brezina, V., Gablasova, D., & Banerjee, J. (2019). Corpus linguistics, learner corpora, and SLA : Employing technology to analyze language sse. *Annual Review of Applied Linguistics*, *39*, 74–92. doi:10.1017/S0267190519000096

McKay, T., & Plonsky, L. (in press). Reliability analyses: Estimating error in L2 research. In P. Winke & T. Brunfaut (Eds.), *The Routledge handbook of second language acquisition and language testing*. New York: Routledge.

Meunier, F., Hendrikx, I., Bulon, A., Van Goethem, K., & Naets, H. (2020). MulTINCo: Multilingual traditional immersion and native corpus: Better-documented multi-literacy practices for more refined SLA studies. *International Journal of Bilingual Education and Bilingualism*, DOI: 10.1080/13670050.2020.1786494

Meunier, F. (2015). Developmental patterns in learner corpora. In S. Granger, G. Gilquin, & F. Meunier (Eds.), *The Cambridge Handbook of Learner Corpus Research* (pp. 379–400). Cambridge University Press. https://doi.org/10.1017/CBO9781139649414.017

Meurers, D., & Dickinson, M. (2017). Evidence and interpretation in language learning research: Opportunities for collaboration with computational linguistics. *Language Learning*, *67*(S1), 66–95. doi:10.1111/lang.12233

Mitchell, Rosamond, Myles, F., & Marsden, E. (2019). *Second language learning theories*. London: Routledge.

Mizumoto, A., Plonsky, L., & Egbert, J. (in press). Meta-analyzing corpus linguistic research. In M. Paquot & S. Th. Gries (Eds.), *The practical handbook of corpus linguistics*. Berlin: Springer.

Murakami, A. (2016). Modeling systematicity and individuality in nonlinear second language development: The case of English grammatical morphemes. Methodological review article. *Language Learning*, *66*(4), 834–871.

Myles, F. (2005). Interlanguage corpora and second language acquisition research. *Second* Language Research, *21*, 373–391. https://doi.org/10.1191/0267658305sr252oa

Myles, F. (2008). Investigating learner language development with electronic longitudinal corpora: Theoretical and methodological issues. In L. Ortega & H. Byrnes (Eds.), *The longitudinal study of advanced L2 capacities* (pp. 58–72). New York: Routledge.

Myles, F. (2015). Second language acquisition theory and learner corpus research. In S. Granger, G. Gilquin & F. Meunier (Eds.), *The Cambridge handbook of learner corpus research* (pp. 309–332). Cambridge: Cambridge University Press.

Myles, F. & Mitchell, R. (2012). *Learning French from ages 5, 7, and 11: An investigation into starting ages, rates, and routes of learning amongst early foreign language learners*. ESRC End of Award Report RES-062-23-1545.

Ortega, L. (2012). Interlanguage complexity: A construct in search of theoretical renewal. In B. Kortmann & B. Szmrecsanyi (Eds.), *Linguistic complexity: Second language acquisition, indigenization, contact* (pp. 127–155). Berlin: Mouton de Gruyter.

Ortega, L. (2020). The study of heritage language development from a bilingualism and social justice perspective. *Language Learning*, *70*(S1), 15–53. https://doi.org/10.1111/lang.12347

Paquot, M. (2019). The phraseological dimension in interlanguage complexity research. *Second Language Research*, *35*(1), 121–145.

Paquot, M., & Gries, S. Th. (in press). *A practical handbook of corpus linguistics*. Berlin: Springer.

Paquot, M., Naets, H., & Gries, S. Th. (in press). Using syntactic co-occurrences to trace phraseological complexity development in learner writing: Verb + object structures in LONGDALE. In B. Le Bruyn & M. Paquot (Eds.), *Learner corpus research meets second language acquisition*. Cambridge: Cambridge University Press.

Perdue, C. (Ed.) (1993). *Adult language acquisition: Field methods* (vol. 1). Cambridge: Cambridge University Press.

Plonsky, L., & Derrick, D. J. (2016). A meta-analysis of reliability coefficients in second language research. *Modern Language Journal*, *100*(2), 538–553.

Révész, A. (2012). Coding second language data validly and reliably. In A. Mackey & S. Gass (Eds.), *Research methods in second language acquisition: A practical guide* (pp. 203–221). Hoboken: Wiley-Blackwell.

Schmid, M. S., & Köpke, B. (2019). *The Oxford handbook of language attrition*. Oxford: Oxford University Press.

Staples, S., Biber, D., & Reppen, R. (2018). Using corpus-based register analysis to explore the authenticity of high-stakes language exams: A register comparison of TOEFL iBT and disciplinary writing tasks. *The Modern Language Journal*, *102*(2), 310–332.

Stefanowitsch, A., & Gries, S. Th. (2003). Collostructions: Investigating the interaction between words and constructions. *International Journal of Corpus Linguistics*, *8*(2), 209–243.

Ströbel, M., Kerz, E., & Wiechmann, D. (2020). The relationship between first and second language writing: Investigating the effects of first language complexity on second language complexity in advanced stages of learning. *Language Learning*, 70(3), 732–767. https://doi.org/10.1111/lang.12394

Tracy-Ventura, N., & Huensch, A. (2018). The potential of publicly shared longitudinal learner corpora in SLA research. In A. Gudmestad & A. Edmonds (Eds.), *Critical reflections on data in second language acquisition* (pp 149–169). Amsterdam: John Benjamins.doi:10.1075/lllt.51.07tra

Tracy-Ventura, N., & Myles, F. (2015). The importance of task variability in the design of learner corpora for SLA research. *International Journal of Learner Corpus Research*, *1*(1), 58–95. doi:10.1075/ijlcr.1.1.03tra

Tracy-Ventura, N., Mitchell, R., & McManus, K. (2016). The LANGSNAP longitudinal learner corpus: Design and use. In M. Alonso Ramos (Ed.), *Spanish learner corpus research: Sate of the art* (pp. 117–142). John Benjamins Publishing.

Weisser, M. (2014). Speech act annotation. In K. Aijmer & C. Rühlemann (Eds.), *Corpus pragmatics: A handbook* (pp. 84–113). Cambridge: Cambridge University Press.

Wulff, S., & Gries, S. Th. (in press). Exploring individual variation in learner corpus research: Some methodological suggestions. In B. Le Bruyn & M. Paquot (Eds.), *Learner corpus research meets second language acquisition*. Cambridge: Cambridge University Press.

Yuldashev, A., Fernandez, J., & Thorne, S. L. (2013). Second language learners' contiguous and discontiguous multi-word unit use over time. *The Modern Language Journal*, *97*(S1), 31–45. https://doi.org/10.1111/j.1540-4781.2012.01420.x

Index

Page numbers in **bold** denote tables, in *italic* denote figures

Academic Keyword List 254
Ädel, A. 25, 30, 359, 362, 375
Ai, H. 323
Aijmer, K. 28, 128, 241, 246
Albanian 353
Albrechtsen, D. 311
Alexopoulou, T. 2, 91, 158, 306, 312–313, 323, 327, 337, 349, 361–362
Analysis of Speech Units (ASU) 294, 301
Andersen, R. 41, 86, 129, 271, 318
Anderson, J. A. 397, 401
Anishchanka, A. 314
Annotation of Information Structure (ANNIS) 61, 98, 152, 153, 298
annotations: computer-aided error (CEA) 24; error 62, 91, 93–98, 100, 148–149, 152, 154, 309, 313, 324, 416, 419; fine-grained 111; flat 149, 312–313; in-text 94, 96–97; linguistic 14, 24, 61–63, 298, 416; manual 24, 62, 219; multi-layered standoff 94, 96–98, *98*; part-of-speech 14
AntConc 17, 69, 71, *71*, *77–80*, 79, 84, *85*, 86, 87, 90n8, 111, 148, 162, 170, 255, 259–260
AphasiaBank 159–160, **160**, 163, 167–168
applied linguistics (AL) 19, 95, 145, 153–154, 189, 196, 282, 378, 379n1, 419
apraxia of speech (AoS) 168
Arabic **17**, 26, 170, 184, *184*, 204, 206, 246
Arabic Learner Corpus (ALC) 147–148
Arche, M. J. 42, 46, 137, 170, 206, 216, 220, 378, 389
Asención–Delaney, Y. 360
Austin, J. L. 199, 248
automatic speech recognition (ASR) 159, 168

Baddeley, A. 401
Baker, P. 13, 19, 243, 300, 366, 375, 384

Baldus, L. 139
Ballier, N. 57, 63, 151, 298
Banerjee, J. 19, 145
Barbieri, F. 4, 254
Barcelona Age Factor (BAF) 152
Barcelona English Language Corpus (BELC) 152–153, 165–166, 170, 411, 414
Bardovi-Harlig, K. 2, 180, 241, 243, 276
Barkhuizen, G. 3–4, 23, 134–135
Bartning, I. 152, 372, 377
basic variety (BV) 45, 240, 315n1
Baten, K. 205, 208
Bates, E. 42
Batstone, R. 382
Bayley, R. 228, 231
Bell, P. 46, 53, 55–57, 335
Belz, J. 29, 32, 243, 245–246, 287, 294, 296
Benson, P. 382, 386, 392n1
Berber Sardinha, T. 15, 248
Berger, C. M. 321, 335, 360
Berlin Map Task Corpus (BeMaTaC) 296
Bestgen, Y. 19, 336, 360, 363, 372, 375–376
Biber, D. 2, 13–15, 26, 81, 110, 179, 245, 247–248, 254, 282–283, 322–323, **325**, 362, 373, 375, 383–384, 417
Bickerton, D. 96
BilingBank 146, 158–160, 163, 166, 169
bilingual 37, 46, 93–94, 148, 158, 163, 166, 169–170, 182, 193, 223, 230, 234–235, 287, 326, 354, 389–390, 401, 410, 412
Bley-Vroman, R. 40, 93, 106, 306, 388, 395, 412
Boardman, T. 206
Bonilla, C. 202, 205–208, 210–211
Bosker, H.R. 297
Bosnian 206, 353
Boulton, A. 252–255, 259, 271–272, 277
Boyd, E. 184, 362–364, 415

Brand, C. 299, 301, 310
Brazilian 353, 364
Brezina, V. 12–13, 15–16, **17**, 19, 109–112,
    139–140, 145, 184, 243, 321, **325**, 360–366,
    376, 415
Bridges, J. 386
British Academic Written English (BAWE) 16, 18
British National Corpus (BNC) 11–12, 14–16,
    18–19, 129, 246, 254–256, 258–260, 271, 273,
    332, 334, 339, 375, 412
Bronstein, L. R. 288
Brown, R. 38, 311
Brun-Mercer, N. 283
Brussels Instructed Language Learner Corpus
    (BILLC) 326
Bulgarian 71, *71*, 299, 353
Bulté, B. 192, 197, 318–320, 323, 327, 383
Bussa, R. 13
Buttery, P. 56, 147, 151, 309
Bylund, E. 348
Byrnes, H. 246, 295, 320, 336

Cadierno, T. 179, 254, 258, 287
Caines, A. 56, 93, 147, 151
CALF (complexity, accuracy, lexis, and fluency)
    158, 165, 169–170
Callies, M. 3, 26, 29, 57, 110–111, 145, 150,
    214–215, 219, 222, 224, 233–234
*Cambridge and Nottingham Corpus of Discourse
    in English* (CANCODE) 363
Cambridge English Corpus (CEC) 256
Cambridge Learner Corpus (CLC) 93, 96–97, 99,
    148, 151, 256, 309
Campillos Llanos, L. 57–58, 63
Cancino, H. 192
Cappellini, M. 274, *275*
Carroll, J. B. 123, 394, 398
Carter, R. 110, 243, 254, 256, 363, 365
Casenhiser, D. M. 178
Caspi, T. 196–197
Cekaite, A. 254, 258
Centre for Corpus Approaches to Social Science
    (CASS) 19
Centre for English Corpus Linguistics 26, 33n3,
    146, 184
Chambers, A. 252, 255–256, 258
Chan, H. 192, 196, 323, 406, 415
Chen, M. 259, **259**
child-directed speech (CDS) 397
Child Language Data Exchange System
    (CHILDES) 1, 46, 61, 158–160, **160**, 167–169,
    180, 210, 397, 402, 412
Chinese 17, 78, *79*, 96, 114, 164, 166, 182–183,
    197, 204, 206, 217, 231, 256, 274, 299, 320,
    348, 353, 363–365, 391; Cantonese 86, 99, 164,
    166, 169; Mandarin 45, 86, 99, 122–123, 165,
    169–170, 206, 229, 231
Chomsky, N. 38–40, 213–215, 394–395, 397
Christiansen, M. H. 180, 394–399, 401–402
Chujo, K. 272

clauses per T-unit (C/TU) 318–319, 323; dependent
    (DC/TU) 194, *194*
Cobb, T. 233, 252, 255, 259, 271, 285, **325**,
    334–335, 339
Codes for the Human Analysis of Transcripts
    (CHAT) 61–62, 153, 161–162, 164–165,
    167–168, 170, 247, 298, 300, 326, 410, 416
Cognitive-Functional Linguistics 175
Cohen, J. 96; Kappa 96
Coh-Metrix 285, 324, **325**, 338–339
Collentine, J. 253, 282, 286, 360, 387, 412
Collentine, K. 282, 286, 387, 412
Collins, L. 46, 53, 252, 258, 273–274, 277,
    326, 412
collocational strength 84, *85*, 375
collocations 5, 11, 13, 16, 68–69, 71, 84, 96,
    128, 134–135, 137–140, 148, 175, 180–181,
    254–256, 260, 335–336, 339, 359–360, 363,
    370–377, 379n1
collostructional analysis (CA) 180–181, 417
Common European Framework of Reference for
    Languages (CEFR) 28, 99, 111, 123, 150, 184, 192,
    256–257, 275, 309, 314, 353, 364, 372, 401, 413
Common Language Resources and Technology
    Infrastructure (CLARIN) 163–164
Communicative Orientation of Language Teaching
    (COLT) 286
Competition Model 42, 345, 355; Unified 42
Complex Dynamic Systems Theory (CDST) 175,
    185, 189–193, 195–199, 306–307, 321, 399,
    415, 418
Computerized Language Analysis (CLAN) 61,
    153, 161–162, 164–170, 273, 285, 294, 298,
    300–301, **325**, 338, 410, 416–417
concordance 5, 13, 16, 24–25, 28, 30, 68–76, *71*,
    73, *75–77*, 78, 79–80, 84–86, 90n2, 96, 111,
    164, 180, 217, 253, 255, 257, 259–261, **259**,
    313; *see also* Keyword in Context
concordancer 5, 24 25, 30, 68–71, *73*, 87, 90n2,
    217, 255, 259
Conrad, S. 179, 245, 362
Content and Language Integrated Learning (CLIL)
    31–32, 58, 141, 326, 401, 411
contrastive analysis (CA) 105, 107, 245, 305,
    349–350, *350*, 352, 376
Contrastive Analysis Hypothesis (CAH) 38,
    305–306, 308, 345
Contrastive Interlanguage Analysis (CIA) 4, 27–28,
    27, 105–110, *107*, 112–114, 350, *350*, 376–377
conversation analysis (CA) 43–44, 159, 161, 165,
    167, 248, 260, 287
Cook, V. 4, 134, 136, 139
Corder, S.P. 38, 53, 90, 94, 305
Corpus de LAngue Parlée en Interaction
    (CLAPI) 275
Corpus Español Multimodal de Actos de Habla
    (COR.E.M.A.H.) 153
Corpus of Contemporary American English
    (COCA) 16, 18, 254–255, 258, 332, 335, 339,
    375, 412

Corpus Parlato di Italiano 151
Cortes, V. 245
Cotos, E. 257
Cowie, A. P. 374
Crawford, W. J. 233, 283, 286, 322
critical period 39–40, 214, 219
Croatian 353
Crossley, S. A. 82, 100, 271, 321–323, 332–333, 335–336, 338–339, 341, 352, 360, 412, 415, 417–418, 420
crosslinguistic influence (CLI) 6, 345, 347–349, 410
cross-sectional: corpora 151–152, 207, 295, 340, 389, 410; designs 30, 59, 242; studies 29, 210, 320, 336–337
Crosthwaite, P. 96, 109, 255, 258
Cuesta Medina, J. A. 268, 271, 386, 398
Cummins, J. 395, 397
Cunningham, D. J. 243, 245
Czech 45, 170, 353, 364

Danish 164, 166, 169, 205
Daskalovska, N. 255, 259–260
data collection 30–31, 55–56, 58–60, 64, 136–137, 145, 168, 191–192, 209, 277, 287, 300, 337, 365, 387, 415, 419, 421; materials 60; oral 60; site 59–60
data-driven learning (DDL) 24, 28, 252–253, 255, 257–261, 272
Deakin, L. 242–243
Deane, P. 244
de Bot, K. 359
Deb Roy 190–191
De Clercq, B. 320–321, 323, 326–327
De Felice, R. 244
Deignan, A. 179
De Jong, N. H. 294–295, 297–298
De Knop, S. 138
Dell, G. S. 396, 402
Derwing, T. M. 293, 295–296
Deshors, S. C. 26, 29, 109–114, 128, 182, 234, 359, 364, 388
Dewaele, J. M. 229, 398–399
Dialogue Act Markup in Several Layers (DAMSL) 248
Dialogue Annotation and Research Tool (DART) 244, 417
Diapix Foreign Language Corpus (DiapixFL) 299–300
Díaz-Campos, M. 231
Di Biase, B. 205, 208
Dickinson, M. 63, 93, 286, 323–324, 416–418
Díez-Bedmar, M. B. 54, 86, 90–91, 93–97, 99, 110–111, 306, 309, 312, 315n3
Discourse Completion Tasks (DCTs) 244–245
Dobs, A. M. 283–284
Domínguez, L. 42, 46, 137–138, 140, 170, 206, 216, 220, 222–223, 378, 389
Donaldson, B. 230–231, 234
Dulay, H. C. 38, 90, 92, 306, 311

Durrant, P. 32, 128, 372, 375–376
Dutch 28, 31, 109, 113, 164, 166, 169, *184*, 193, 197, 205, 210, 240, 242, 294–296, 299, 308–309, 320, 324, **325**, 326, 353, 398, 421
Dynamic Systems Theory (DST) 189, 307–308, 359, 399
Dyson, B. P. 204, 206, 208, 210, 358

Edmonds, A. 45, 229, 232
Edwards, A. 109, 113
Egbert, J. 16, 19, 283, 366
electroencephalography (EEG) 45
Ellis, N. C. 2, 41, 45–46, 106, 111, 120, 133, 138, 175, 177–179, 184, 253–254, 258, 268, 271, 307, 335, 345, 370, 372–373, 397
Ellis, R. 3, 23, 58, 133–135, 137, 179, 311, 322, 358–359, 394, 397–398
English: American 16, 18, 27, 78, 108, 377; British 12, 14, 16, 18, 27, 78, 108, 113–114
English as a Lingua Franca (ELF) 27, 93, 109, 149, 276, 306
Erman, B. 180, 370, 374–378
error analysis (EA) 90, 93, 140, 169, 286, 305–306, 310, 353; computer-aided (CEA) 58, 70, 90–91, *92*, 95, 305–306
error tagging 62, 70, 87, 90–97, 99–100, 217, 233, 285, 309–310, 312–314; False Friends (LSF) 92; Louvain 92–93, 96–97; systems 90–97, 100
Eskildsen, S. W. 43–44, 159, 179–180, 254, 258, 260, 277, 282, 284, 287
EUDICO Linguistic Annotator (ELAN) 162, 165, 170, 298
European Science Foundation Corpus (ESF) 1, 45, 54, 149, 168, 177, 180, 184, *184*, 240, 246, 411
event-related potential (ERP) 1, 44–45
experimental data 4, 25–26, 31, 46, 56, 121, *121*, 133–142, **135**, 142n1, 215–216, 219–220, 222, 224n5, 232, 348–349, 402, 410

Faerch, C. 284, 311
Fafulas, S. 229, 231, 235
False Friend (LSF) 92
false positives 19, 74, 119, 386
Fant, L. 376–377
Feature Reassembly Hypothesis (FRH) 214, 217, 220
FehlerAnnotiertes LernerKOrpus (Falko) 98, 100, 152, 154, 324
Fernández, J. 58, 147, 150, 243, 247, 385–387, 389–390
Ferreira-Junior, F. 106, 177–179, 184
Finegan, E. 179
Finnish 28, 184, *184*, 197, 246, 353, 364
Flowerdew, J. 259, **259**
Flowerdew, L. 255–256
FluCalc 165, 169
FluencyBank 158–159, **160**, 168
Foci for Observing Communications Used in Settings (FOCUS) 286
Foreign Language Teaching (FLT) 41, 46

formulaicity 6, 370–377
formulator 201
Forsberg Lundell, F. 152, 180, 372–374, 377
French 13, 26–28, 31, 45–46, 105, 112–114, 134,
138, 140, 149, 151–152, 164, 166, 169–170,
184, 209–210, 223, 229–236, 240, 242, 258,
269–271, 273–275, 295, 297, 299–301, 314,
320, 324, **325**, 326, 339–340, 353–354, 364,
370–374, 376–378, 385, 389–391, 410–412
French Learner Language Oral Corpora (FLLOC)
46, 61, 151, 168, 170, 209, 378, 410–411
frequency list 16, 25, 29, 180, 254
Fuchs, R. 62, 86, 91, 98
Fung, L. 243, 363, 365
Furnham, A. 398–399

Gablasova, D. 2, 16, **17**, 19, 91, 109–112, 139–140,
145, 184, 243, 250, **325**, 361–366, 376, 415
Garcia Lecumberri, M. L. 295, 297–301
Garner, J. R. 184, 360
Garnier, M. 385–386
Garside, R. 13–14
Geeslin, K. L. 229, 231–235, 237
general additive model (GAM) 194, *195*, 196, 198
General Examinations of Spoken English (GESE)
184, 364
general extenders (GEs) 241, 247, 385, 390
generalized additive mixed models (GAMM) 401
generalized linear mixed models (GLMM)
128, 401
generative approaches to second language
acquisition (GenSLA) 213–217, **216**, 219–220,
222–224
German 24, 26–27, 29, 31, 45, 60–61, 69, 78, *79*,
86, 99, 114, 122–123, 128–129, 138, 141,
151–152, 154, 164–167, 169–170, 181–184,
184, 204–205, 208, 210, 240, 242–243,
245–246, 256, 274, 287, 297, 299, 309, 314,
320, 324, **325**, 326, 351–353, 365, 373, 386,
391, 401, 410, 416
Giessen-Long Beach Chaplin Corpus (GLBCC)
32–33
Gilquin, G. 13, 23, 26, 53–54, 56, 58, 69, 93, 106–
111, *107*, 114, 120, 133, 136–138, 140–142,
146, 150–153, 181, 222–223, 231, 294, 299,
310, 350, *350*, 352–353, 355, 360, 364–365,
395, 415
Girsai, N. 378
Glahn, E. 205
Golcher, F. 324
Goldberg, A. E. 175, 178
Golden, A. 348–349
Gósy, M. 295–296, 298
Götz, S. 76, 81, 82, 111, 294, 297, 299–301,
309–310, 361
grammar 13, 18, 38–40, 42, 45, 58, 63, 94, 140,
176, 204, 214, 219–220, 232, 235, 240, 246,
248, 253–257, 272, 282, 314, 346, 359, 371,
374, 377, 384, 390, 417; construction 139, 175,

321; interlanguage (ILG) 213–214, 216–217,
219, 223; Lexical-functional (LFG) 204–205;
lexico- 257, 259, 314; *see also* universal
Granger, S. 2–4, 19, 23–28, 30, 38, 43–44, 53–56,
61, 69–70, 78, 81, 82, 84, 87, 91–93, 95, 97,
105–113, 115n6, 120, 123, 133–136, 138, 140,
145–149, 169, 231, 234, 246, 252, 254, 256–
257, 268, 288, 294, 299, 306, 309, 313–314,
336, 349–350, 352–353, 360, 364–365, 370,
372, 374–376, 395, 409, 412–414, 419
Gray, B. 81, 322, 383
Gray, W. D. 178
Greek 28, 210, 299, 353, 416
Gries, S. 12, 15, 19, 25–26, 30, 62, 87, 110–115,
119–120, 122–124, 128–129, 133, 142,
149, 177, 181–183, 234, 268, 271, 305,
309–310, 314, 335, 354, 359–360, 362,
376, 388, 417–419
Gudmestad, A. 45, 229–235
Guichon, N. 387
Guiraud, P. 192, 194, 197, 334, 339, 341
Gujord, A. K. H. 346, 348–349, 353
Gullberg, M. 284
Gurzynski-Weiss, L. 267, 276
Gustafson-Smiskova, H. 192
Gut, U. 60–61, 148, 150, 242, 247, 294–301,
410, 416

Håkansson, G. 204–205, 354
Hammarberg, B. 205
Hanks, P. 254, 376
Hansen Edwards, J. G. 231, 233–234
Hardie, A. 13, 19, 240, 359
Hardy, J.A. 257
Hasselgård, H. 82, 105–106, 120, 128
Hatch, E. 179, 192, 204, 208, 280
Hebrew 86, 99, 164, 166, 169, 372
Henriksen, B. 311
Hidden Markov Model 196, 323
Hilpert, M. 137, 179
Hilton, H. 149, 295–298, 301, 410, 416
Hindi **17**
Hirschmann, H. 90, 93, 97–98, 312, 324, 327
Holmen, A. 205
HomeBank 159, **160**
Hong Kong Corpus of Spoken English
(HKCSE) 245
Hooper, J. 373
Hou, J. 192
Housen, A. 192, 197, 210–211, 285, 305, 318–321,
323, 326–327, 377, 383
Housen Corpus of Young Learner Interlanguage
(CYLIL) 209–210
Huat, C. M. 29
Huensch, A. 4, 149, 169, 223, 294–295, 297–298,
300–301, 340, 386, 390, 412, 415
Hungarian 45, 170, 231, 295, 353
Hungarian English Database (HunEng-D)
295–296

Hunston, S. 106, 376
Hvenekilde, A. 205
Hyland, K. 57, 242

Inagaki, S. 90, 305, 318
individual differences (IDs) 4, 6, 39–40, 123,
    300–301, 361, 394–400, 402–403, 413, 418
Inflectional Diversity (ID) 326–327, 394, 396,
    398–402
Instructed Second Language Acquisition (ISLA)
    252–254, 256–261
Integrated Contrastive Model (ICM) 105–106, *107*,
    349–350, *350*, 376, 412
Interface Hypothesis (IH) 215–216, 220, 222
Interlanguage Varieties (ILV) 27–29, *27*, 106, 112,
    114, 229, 236
International Corpus Network of Asian Learners of
    English (ICNALE) 149, 340
International Corpus of Crosslinguistic
    Interlanguage (ICCI) 86, 94, 99
International Corpus of Learner English (ICLE)
    2–3, 30, 54, 69, 71, *71*, 78, *79*, 84, *85*, 97,
    105, 109–110, 112, 115n5, 120, 122–123, 134,
    140, 149, 223, 246, 256, 258, 299, 309, 314,
    323–324, 350, 353, 372–373, 376–377, 412–413
international teaching assistants (ITAs) 243–244
Intraclass Correlation Coefficient 96
Ionin, T. 91, 99, 216
Italian 13, **17**, 28, 149, 164, 166, 169, 184, *184*,
    205, 210, 246, 295, 299, 321, **325**, 326, 353,
    360, 365, 376, 410

Jansen, L. 206, 208
Japanese 86, 99, 114, 138, 164, 166, 169, 179, 182,
    204–205, 258, 272, 299, 340, 353,
Japanese English as a Foreign Language Learner
    corpus (JEFLL) 152
Jarvis, S. 114, 115n2, 320, 334, 338–339, 341–342,
    345–354, 355n1, 412
Jäschke, K. 29
Jaworski, A. 377
Jelinek, F. 13
Johansson, S. 105–106, 120, 128, 179
Johns T. 252, 272
Juilland, A. 13

Kansas Developmental Learner corpus
    (KANDEL) 324
Kanwit, M. 229–230, 232
Kaufman, S. B. 400
Kawaguchi, S. 204–205, 208
Keyword in Context (KWIC)-Concordance 71;
    see also concordance
keywords 2, 16, 24, 28, 63, 76, 78
Kim, H.-Y. 90, 138, 305, 318
Kim, M. 322–323, 341
Kim, Y. 280, 415
Klein, W. 1, 45, 240, 246
Korean 26, 256, 353

Kormos, J. 1, 57–58, 293–294, 296–297, 322,
    383, 399
Kortmann, B. 111–113
Krashen, S. D. 38–39, 179, 267, 277, 305, 395;
    Monitor Model 38
Kuiken, F. 192, 285, 305, 322–323
Kyle, K. 198, 321–322, **325**, 332–333, 335–336,
    338–339, 341, 360, 417–418

Labov, W. 228, 362
Langman, J. 230–231
Language and Social Background Questionnaire
    (LSBQ) 397, 401
Language Experience and Proficiency
    Questionnaire (LEAP-Q) 397, 400
language-related episodes (LREs) 283, 285–286
Languages and Social Networks Abroad Project
    (LANGSNAP) 61, 149, 153, 168, 223, 232, 295,
    299–300, 332, 340, 390–391, 411, 414
language testing and assessment (LTA) 90
Lapkin, S. 44, 281, 346
Laporte, S. 113
Larsen-Freeman, D. 93, 106, 189, 197–198, 306,
    314, 395
Larson-Hall, J. 130, 259
Larsson, T. 18, 417
Laufer, B. 128, 332, 335–336, 340, 360, 372, 378
Learner Corpus of Portuguese as Second/Foreign
    Language (COPLE2) 58, 63–64
Learning Prosody in a Foreign Language (LeaP)
    corpus 60–61, 148, 150, 242, 247, 295–296,
    299, 410
Lee, H. 253–256, 259, 261
Lee, J. J. 242–243
Lee, L.-H. 97
Leech, G. 11, 13–14, 18, 179, 253, 333, 365
Lennon, P. 93, 293, 305
Lesonen, S. 197
Less Commonly Taught Languages (LCTL) 150
Lester, N. A. 128–130, 182, 376, 418
Levelt, W. J. M. 201, 293
Levitzky-Aviad, T. 372
Lewis, M. 180, 374, 376
Lexical Aspect Hypothesis 46, 140
lexical complexity analyzer (LCA) 320–321,
    325, 339
lexical-functional grammar (LFG) 204–205
lexicon/lexis 6, 32, 45, 96, 111, 158, 165–166,
    168–170, 176, 191, 197, 213–214, 248, 254–
    255, 314, 336, 338, 347–349, 354, 358, 360,
    372, 384, 390, 399, 414; *see also* CALF
Li, P. 254, 258, 287
Li, X. 93, 229
Linford, B. 229, 231, 233
Lithuanian 353
Littré, D. 2, 25–26, 54, 136, 138, 295, 309
Liu, D. 18
Loerts, H. 192
Loewen, S. 252–253, 421

Long, M. H. 42, 54, 280–282, 308
longitudinal: design 43, 58, 336; research 29, 289, 323; study 29–30, 58, 180, 191, 197, 204, 206, 259, 321, 323, 333, 336–338, 373, 390; *see also* pseudo-longitudinal
Longitudinal Database of Learner English (LONGDALE) 30–31, 223
Louvain Corpus of Native English Conversations (LOCNEC) 81, *85*, 112, 128, 242, 299
Louvain Corpus of Native English Essays (LOCNESS) 84, *85*, 109, 112, 412
Louvain International Database of Spoken English Interlanguage (LINDSEI) 20n1, 69, *75*, 81, *84*, 109, 112, 120, 122–123, 128, 146, 148, 242, 245–246, 299, 364
Lowie, W. 59, 175, 189, 191–198, 307, 321, 359, 394, 399, 415
Lozano, C. 42, 44, 53, 55, 64, 138, 146–147, 151, 215–217, 219–220, 222, 224
Lu, X. 63, 243, 320, 323–324, **325**, 333, 336, 339, 417–418
Lüdeling, A. 90, 93, 97–98, 149, 294, 296, 312, 324, 327
Lund, K. 205

McCarthy, M. 28, 110, 231, 254, 256–257, 261
McCauley, S. M. 180, 396–397, 402
McDonough, K. 44, 178, 274, 282–283
Macedonian 353
McEnery, T. 3, 12–14, 19, 23, 28, 109–112, 115, 139–140, 145, 184, 240, 252, 286, 288, 359, 361–366, 376, 415, 417
Mackey, A. 42, 44, 46, 55–56, 61, 147, 241–242, 280–282, 288, 365, 384, 419
McNamara, D. 285, 323–324, **325**, 332, 335–336, 338
MacWhinney, B. 1, 6, 42, 45–46, 61, 146, 153, 159, 164–167, 170, 175, 210, 273, 285, 294, 298, **325**, 326, 338, 397, 402, 419; Competition Model 345, 355
Mansouri, F. 204, 206
Mäntylä, K. 32
Marburg Corpus of Intermediate Learner English (MILE) 151
Marsden, E. 2, 5, 39, 42, 44–46, 53, 55, 160, 170, 206, 209, 240, 358, 378, 389, 394, 410, 419–420
Martin, P. 57, 63, 151, 298,
Martins, C. 348
Matsumoto, Y. 283–284
Maxim, H. 320
mean length of clause (MLC) 319–320, 323
mean length of sentence (MLS) 318–324
mean length of T-unit (MLTU) 193–194, *194–195*, 319–320, 324
mean length of words (MLW) 194
measure of textual lexical diversity (MTLD) 320, 323, 334, 337, 339, 341
Méli, A. 31
Mellow, J. D. 179

Mendikoetxea, A. 42, 44, 53, 55, 64, 138, 146–147, 151, 215–217, 219–220, 222–223, 309, 388
metadata 4, 24, 46, 54–55, 60, 63, 109, 111, 115, 120, 123, 130, 136, 141, 149–151, 153, 163, 217, 219, 314, 348, 364, 366, 388, 410, 413, 416, 418–419, 421
Meunier, F. 2, 25–26, 28, 30–31, 54, 56, 134, 138, 140, 223, 231, 254, 295, 309, 372, 376, 395, 398, 411, 415
Meurers, W. D. 63, 286, 323–324, **325**, 337, 416–418
Michel, M. 274, *275*, 285, 323, 337
Michigan Corpus of Academic Spoken English (MICASE) 129, 243, 271, 276
Michigan Corpus of Upper-level Student Papers (MICUSP) 18, 242, 257
Minimalist Program (MP) 213–214
Mitchell, R. 39, 42, 44, 46, 57, 137, 147, 149, 152, 205, 209, 220, 223, 232, 240, 258, 299–300, 320, 332, 340, 358, 373, 378, 389, 394, 410–412
Mizumoto, A. 16, 420
Modern Language Aptitude Test (MLAT) 394, 398
Möller, V. 4, 137, 141, 398, 401–402
Morphological Complexity Index (MCI) 321, 326–327
morphology 38, 58, 96, 129, 140, 153, 168, 201–210, **202**, 220, 271, 321, 347–348, 353, 383
Mossman, S. 243, 276
mother tongue 23, 25, 27–28, 30, 32, 55, 60, 105, 107, 109, 113, 136–137, 307, 314; *see also* native language
Mougeon, R. 229, 231, 234, 258, 385–386, 389, 391
Mukherjee, J. 28, 68, 76, 361
Müller, S. 32, 245
multi-dimensional analysis (MDA) 15, 247, 417
multifactorial prediction and deviation analysis using regression/random forests (MuPDAR(F)) 112–113, 128, 180–183
Multilingual Academic Corpus of Assignments– Writing and Speech (MACAWS) 150–151
Multilingual, Traditional, Immersion, and Native Corpus (MulTINCo) 31, 411
Multimedia Adult ESL Learner Corpus (MAELC) 32–33, 150, 258, 260, 282, 284–287
Munafò, M. R. 160, 163
Muñoz, C. 153, 170, 411
Murakami, A. 2, 91, 192, 306, 312, 323, 337, 349, 358, 361–362, 401, 418
Musgrave, J. 322
Myles, F. 2, 4–5, 32, 39, 42, 44, 46, 53, 56–58, 61, 91, 134, 137–140, 142, 145–148, 151–152, 159, 179, 205–206, 209, 214–217, 219–220, 222–224, 232, 236, 240, 246, 258, 295, 298, 358–359, 362, 373–374, 378, 389, 394, 409–410, 412, 414–415, 419

Namba, K. 374
native language (NL) 4, 26, 105–107, 110, 114, 129, 136, 138, 170, 222, 349–350, 353, 377,

394–395, 397–398, 401, 413; non- 81, 105, 111, 129, 149, 350, 396, 402; *see also* mother tongue
natural language processing (NLP) 2, 13, 90, 94, 100, 396, 417–418; tools 23–24, 319–320, 322–324, 416–419
Nesselhauf, N. 84, 373–375
Norris, J.M. 147, 308, 314, 318, 320, 322, 383, 386, 389
Norwegian 150, 205, 346–348, 351–353, 410
Norwegian Second Language Corpus (ASK) 150, 348, 353, 410
Nunes, P. 348
Nüse, R. 348

O'Donnell, M. B. 138, 219, 223, 257, 309, 313, 370, 372–373
Oghigian, K. 272
Ohta, A. S. 254, 258
Ortega, L. 32, 38, 59, 147, 246, 295, 297, 308, 314, 318–320, 322, 336, 349, 354, 383, 386, 389, 410, 412–413
Oxford Quick Placement Test 54
Ozeki, H. 138

Pae, T. 397, 400
Pakistani 353
Pallotti, G. 206, 208, 319, 321, **325**, 326
Papp, S. 96, 306, 312
Paquot, M. 2–3, 26, 46, 53–54, 81, 82, 106, 110, 114–115, 119, 121, 128, 145, 150, 182, 185, 246, 254, 256, 313, 321, 327, 348–349, 353–355, 370, 372–374, 376–377, 414, 417–419
Parallèle Oral en Langue Etrangère (PAROLE) 149, 294–296, 298, 410
Parkinson, J. 322
part-of-speech (POS) tagging 2, 13, 24–25, 62–63, 70, 86, 87, 148–149, 154, 164, 166, 217, 248, 273, 285, 312, 315n4, 324, 388, 390, 417–418
Pavlenko, A. 345–348
Penris, W. 191–192, 196
Perdue, C. 1, 45, 54, 184, 240, 246, 411
Pérez-Paredes, P. 91
Pérez-Vidal, C. 390
Persian 353
Péry-Woodley, M. P. 113
PhonBank 159–160, **160**
Pica, T. 90, 282, 311
Pienemann, M. 42, 201, 204–211, 308, 354, 383
Plonsky, L. 5, 15–16, 26, 46, 53–55, 119, 121, 128, 150, 160, 182, 185, 259, 280, 289, 355, 417, 419–421
Polio, C. 305, 308, 311, 313, 322, 324,
Polish 86, 99, 285, 299, 353, 377
Poonpon, K. 322
Portuguese **17**, 63, 150, 348, 353, 358, 364
Potter, L. 179
Praat 31, 61, 148, 161–162, 165, 169, 285, 298 299

pragmatic marker (PM) 152, 241–247, 364
Pragmatic Principles Violation Hypothesis (PPVH) 215, 220, 222
Preston, D. R. 228–229, 236
Processability Theory (PT) 41–42, 201–202, **202**, 204–211, 308
Progression Project 152, 411
prosody 150, 241–242, 244–245, 247–248, 417; *see also* Learning Prosody in a Foreign Language
Prototype Theory 178
prototypical 141, 178–179, 184, 257, 271, 334, 347, 352–353
pseudo-longitudinal 26, 29, 58–59, 151–152, 308–309
Punjabi 184, *184*, 246
Python 87, 111, 148, 167, 339, 388

Ragnhildstveit, S. 352, 355
Rah, Y. 138
Rankin, T. 219–220, 231, 256, 354
Rautionaho, P. 113
Rayson, P. 71, 78, 112–113
Reference Language Varieties (RLV) 27, *27*, 29
Regan, V. M. 229, 231, 233–234, 237n4
Rehner, K. 229, 231, 234–235, 237n5, 258, 285–286, 389, 391
Reinders, H. 382, 386, 392n1
Reinhardt, J. 244
Reppen, R. 254, 282
Reznicek, M. 63, 98, 152
Roberson, A. 138, 257
Rojo López, A. M. 138–139
Romanian 13
Römer, U. 2, 18, 28, 41, 45, 138, 184, 253, 255, 257, 359–360, 370, 372–373
Romero-Trillo, J. 245
Rosansky, E. 192
Rule, S. 44–46, 151, 209
Russian 13, 99, 151, 170, 353, 374, 376

Sachs, R. 280, 308
Sakai, H. 204
Santa Barbara Corpus of Spoken American English (SBCSAE) 246
Scarcella, R. C. 179
Schiftner, B. 256
Schmid, M. S. 192, 308, 320, 347, 410–411
Schmidt, R. 42
Schmitt, D. 254, 332
Schmitt, N. 128, 139, 178, 254, 332, 372, 375–376, 385–386
Schnur, E. 19
Schumann, J. H. 179, 192
Secondary-Level Corpus of Learner English (ScooLE) 141, 401–402
Second Language Research Instruments (IRIS) 55, 168, 270, 419
Segalowitz, N. 293, 295, 297
Seidlhofer, B. 257
Self-Paced Reading Task (SPRT) 210, 210

Selinker, L. 38, 53, 106, 147, 355n1
Serbian 353
Sethuraman, N. 178
Shirai, Y. 129, 138, 179, 271, 349
Sinclair, J. 16, 54–56, 59, 61, 78, 97, 146–147,
    336, 370
Siyanova, A. 139, 375
Skehan, P. 169, 294, 296–297, 306, 313, 318, 322,
    394, 398
Skill Acquisition Theory 41, 253
SLABank 45–46, 146, 158–160, **160**, 163,
    167–170, 210, 414
Smit, N. 198
Smith, L.B. 191
Solon, M. 229, 233, 235
Somali 346, 353
Spanish 13, **17**, 26, 45–46, 55, 58, 63, 84, 86, 96,
    99, 128–129, 138, 140, 147, 150, 152–153, 164,
    166, 169–170, 179, 184, *184*, 192, 201–202,
    202, 205–206, 208–210, 213, 215, 220, **221**,
    222–223, 229–236, 242, 245–247, 261, 271,
    277, 282 283, 287, 297, 299–301, 309, 314,
    325, 340, 347, 353–354, 360–361, 376–378,
    383–386, 389–390, 416
Spanish Learner Language Oral Corpora 1/2
    (SPLLOC1/2) 42, 46, 140, 147, 149–150, 168,
    170, 205, 207, 209–210, 220, 222–224, 247,
    378, 389, 410
Spanish Learner Oral Corpus (SLOC) 63
Spanish Multimodal Corpus of Speech Acts see
    Corpus Español Multimodal de Actos de Habla
Spoelman, M. 196
Spoken BNC2014 11–12
Staples, S. 150, 243–245, 247–248, 298, 322, 417
Stefanowitsch, A. 129, 181, 271, 417
Storch, N. 283, 309
structural equation modeling (SEM) 397, 400
Study Abroad and Language Acquisition (SALA)
    390–391
Su, Y. 276
Sugaya, N. 179
Swain, M. 42, 44, 229, 281, 346
Swales, J. M. 243, 248, 360
Swedish 30, *184*, 204–205, 240, 299, 347, 353,
    371, 374, 377
synchronous-computer mediated communication
    (SCMC) 282, 288, 384, 387–388, 412
Syntactic Complexity Analyzer (SCA) 320–321,
    323–324, **325**, 418
syntax 31, 111, 168, 170, 178, 181, 191, 197,
    201–210, **202**, 214–215, 248, 270, 348, 358,
    399–400; discourse 214–215, 217, 220, 222–
    223; morpho- 45, 208–209, 211, 347, 413–414
Systemic Functional Linguistics 43, 240, 242
Szmrecsanyi, B. 111–113, 231, 234, 236n1, 327

Taguchi, N. 241–243, 247, 322, 384
TalkBank 45, 146, 152–153, 158–164, **160**, 167,
    169–170, 246, 300, 411–412, 417

Tardy, C. M. 248
target language 23, 26, 31–32, 38, 44–45, 54–55,
    57–59, 63, 76, 92–93, 97, 99, 106, 112, 114,
    115n3, 136, 146, 151, 162, 167, 170, 184, 203,
    211, 222, 231, 234, 267–269, 271–272, 276,
    280–281, 285–286, 305–306, 308, **325**, 326,
    346–347, 349–350, 352, 363, 371, 377, 384,
    387, 398, 412–414
Tavakoli, P. 294, 296
TBIBank 160, 163, 168
Telecollaborative Learner Corpus of English and
    German (Telekorp) 32, 245, 287, 416
Tenfjord, K. 150, 353
Thelen, E. S. L. B. 191
Thewissen, J. 91, 94, 97, 99, 306, 309, 312, 314
Thomas, A. 269–270, 273, 275
Thorne, S. L. 32, 43, 58, 150, 284, 308
Tilma, C. 197
Timperley, M. 19
Tomasello, M. 153, 178
Tool for the Automatic Analysis of Cohesion
    (TAACO) 418
Tool for the Automatic Analysis of Lexical
    Diversity (TAALED) 339
Tool for the Automatic Analysis of Lexical
    Sophistication (TAALES) 321, **325**, 339–340
Tracy-Ventura, N. 2, 4, 42, 46, 56–58, 61, 91,
    137–140, 142, 146–147, 149, 151, 205, 220,
    222–224, 232, 247, 268, 271, 294–295,
    297–301, 320, 332, 337–338, 340, 362, 383,
    386, 390, 398, 411–412, 415
transcription 2, 5–6, 53, 56–57, 60–61, 64, 69, 145,
    149–151, 153, 159–161, 167–169, 273, 275,
    284–286, 296, 298–299, 301, 324, 388, 410,
    414, 416, 419–421
Trinity Lancaster Corpus (TLC) 2, 111, 184, 364
Truscott, J. 308
Tswana 353
Turkish 184, *184*, 246, 295, 353, 364
type-token ratio (TTR) 81, 111, 169, 178, 192, *195*,
    320–321, 334, 338–339

ultimate attainment 26, 39–40, 42, 46, 176, 180,
    185, 214, 219, 223, 267, 395, 410
Unaccusative Hypothesis (UH) 217
Universal Grammar (UG) 40, 176, 213–215, 219,
    272, 395–396
Université catholique de Louvain Error Editor
    (UCLEE) 97, 313–314, 353
Uppsala Student English Corpus (USE) 30
usage-based linguistics (UBL) 175–178, 181,
    184–185

Vacas Matos, M. 153
Vahtrick, L. 192, 196, 323
Valenzuela Manzanares, J. 138–139
Van de Grift, W. 198
van Dijk, M. 192, 321, 359
Van Geert, P. 191, 197

Van Lier, T. 32
Van Mensel, L. 31
VanPatten, B. 253, 358–359, 383
Varonis, E. M. 282
Vedder, I. 192, 285, 322–323
Veirano Pinto, M. 15, 248
verb-argument constructions (VACs) 138, 177–178, 184, 198, 360
Verspoor, M. H. 59, 175, 189, 191–196, 198, 307–308, 320–321, 323, 359, 394, 399, 415
Vietnamese 351–353
Virtual Linguistic Observatory (VLO) 163
vocabulary: academic 246; knowledge 284, 297, 332, 334, 340; learning 271; levels test 332; productive 295–296, 340; size 191; size test 332; spoken 169
von Stutterheim, C. 348
Vyatkina, N. 29, 32, 94, 96, 98, 192, 243, 245–246, 287, 324
Vygotsky, L. S. 43, 280–281

Wagner, J. 106, 167, 258, 260, 284, 378, 382
Waldman, T. 128, 360
Warren, B. 370, 375
weighted clause ratio (WCR) 311, **311**
Weisser, M. 72, 244, 299, 417
Wempe, T. 298
Werner, V. 62, 86, 91, 98
Wetzel, D. Z. 322

What is Speaking Proficiency (WiSP) corpus 295–296
Whatley, M. 233
Wigglesworth, G. 294, 309, 311, **311**
Wiktorsson, M. 371
Williams, J. 358–359
Wolfe-Quintero, K. 90–91, 305, 318
word list 78–81, *80*, 148, 168, 296
WordSmith **17**, 69, 71–73, *72*, *74–77*, 81, *83–84*, 87, 131, 148
working memory (WM) 1, 44–45, 185, 361, 383, 396, 398–401, 413
Wray, A. 32, 179, 370–371, 374, 378
Wulff, S. 2, 112, 114, 123–124, 129–130, 175, 181–183, 253, 271, 276, 305, 307, 309–310, 354, 359–362, 370, 372, 376, 418

Xu, X. 192, 308, 321

Yang, J. 384
Yoon, H.-J. 322, 324
Yuldashev, A. 58, 150, 243, 412

Zaytseva, E. 110–111
Zhang, Y. 204
Zipf, G. K. 178, 335; Law 178
Zipfian distribution 120, 129, 178, 271, 334
Zweitspracherwerb Italienischer und Spanischer Arbeiter (ZISA) Project 210

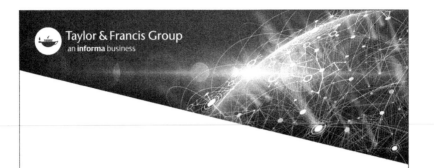

Printed in the United States
By Bookmasters